INDIANA IN THE
WAR OF THE REBELLION

A special printing of twenty-nine hundred copies by the Indiana Historical Society for distribution to its membership in 1960

Issued also as
Indiana Historical Collections
Volume XLI

INDIANA IN THE WAR OF THE REBELLION

REPORT OF THE ADJUTANT GENERAL

A Reprint of Volume 1 of the Eight-Volume Report Prepared by
W. H. H. TERRELL
and Published in 1869

INDIANA HISTORICAL SOCIETY
1960

FOREWORD

In 1869 W. H. H. Terrell issued an eight-volume *Report of the Adjutant General of the State of Indiana* treating of the State's participation in the Civil War. The bulk of this work—volumes 2-8 inclusive—consisted of rosters of Indiana officers and soldiers. The first volume was a 466-page summary—supplemented by 372 pages of statistics and documents—of Indiana's role in the great conflict of the 'sixties.

Adjutant General Terrell in a brief introductory note to Volume I stated that his report did "not aspire to the dignity of a history." Admittedly, the report does not meet present-day standards of good history. In the first place, it is biased. Terrell was a member of Oliver P. Morton's official family. He enjoyed the Governor's confidence and served for a time as his military secretary. In compiling his report he naturally slanted his material in such a way as to present the Chief Executive in the most favorable light. Morton was a patriotic leader, thoroughly devoted to the Union, and he was in large measure responsible for Indiana's enormous contribution to the Northern cause. But he was an ambitious man, impatient of opposition, and he often employed steam-roller tactics against his adversaries. He became a virtual dictator. One has to look between the lines of Terrell's history to obtain glimpses of Morton's unadmirable characteristics.

A second shortcoming of the report is that it deals almost exclusively with military activities. This is because Terrell's responsibility as Adjutant General was restricted largely to military matters. His aim in preparing the report was "to show what was done by *Indiana,* during the war, in raising troops, furnishing arms and supplies, affording relief to the sick and distressed, and . . . contributing to the efficiency of the two hundred and eight thousand men sent to the field, and to the success of the measures of the government in suppressing the rebellion."

Despite its limitations, Terrell's report, and especially the first volume, is an important historical document. It is indispensable to an understanding of Indiana's role in the Civil War, and it throws much valuable light on the war in general. It abounds with information about the mobilization, organization, and equipment of the volunteer forces; it affords revealing insight into the relationships between State and National authorities; it devotes considerable attention to the peace movement and Morton's efforts to combat disloyalty; it tells of the administration of the "Rebel prison" at Camp Morton; and it gives a detailed account of the Indiana and Kentucky raids of John Hunt Morgan.

The authorized edition of Terrell's report was 4,500 copies. The work has long been out of print and hard to obtain. The Indiana Historical Bureau and the Indiana Historical Society are to be commended for re-issuing the first volume of this valuable source. It is especially appropriate that the new edition should be issued as a Civil War Centennial publication, for there is no more suitable way of observing the hundredth anniversary of the conflict than to make readily available sources which will contribute to a better understanding of this tragic but momentous experience.

BELL I. WILEY, *Emory University*
Chairman of Committee on Historical Activities
National Civil War Centennial Commission

EDITORIAL NOTE

In reissuing the text of the first volume of *The Report of the Adjutant General of Indiana,* entitled *Indiana in the War of the Rebellion,* the editors of the Historical Bureau have made very few changes from the original edition. Obvious typographical errors have been corrected, some changes have been made in punctuation, and the material arranged by chapters. All omissions of textual material have been indicated; footnotes have been expanded, and new notes added. Of the statistical and documentary material comprising the 372-page Appendix, only a few pages are included herein: Summary of Troops Furnished by the State of Indiana; Chronological List of Engagements in Which Indiana Troops Participated; and Campaigns in Which Indiana Troops Participated. References to other matters included in the Appendix are given in the footnotes.

The task of assembling the material presented in the eight volumes comprising the *Report* was tremendous, and it is of interest to know something of the man, William H. H. Terrell, who performed it. He was born in Henry County, Kentucky, November 13, 1827, the son of Dr. John Harrison and Sally (Moore) Terrell. The following spring the family moved to Bartholomew County, Indiana. The youth had little formal schooling, but read widely, and by self-guidance and self-instruction he acquired a liberal education. In 1846 he became a clerk of the Madison and Indianapolis Railroad at Edinburg. He then entered the newspaper field, becoming editor and co-publisher of the Columbus *Gazette,* a staunch Whig paper. In the election following the adoption of the new constitution, he was chosen county recorder. Meanwhile, he read law, was admitted to the bar, and when his term as recorder expired, he began to practice this profession. In 1857 he moved to Vincennes.

It is related that when the Civil War began Terrell was recommended to Governor Morton as an able man who could fill any place to which the Governor might assign him. Morton summoned him to Indianapolis and employed him as his military secretary in various tasks including making a list of Indiana companies in service, their location, and information concerning the next probable battles in which they might be involved. Terrell subsequently was made secretary of the Governor's finance department, and ably administered the nearly one million dollars that Morton obtained as a war loan from private sources.

In November, 1864, Terrell was appointed adjutant general of the state, with the rank of colonel. By special legislative enactment, in March, 1865, he was elevated to brigadier general, with the pay and allowance of the rank as allowed in the regular army. In May, 1869, he resigned this office to accept appointment by President Grant of third assistant postmaster general, and in May, 1873, he became United States pension agent at Indianapolis. Upon retirement from this position, in 1877, he returned to private business. On November 19, 1850, Terrell had married Miss Sarah Eliza Church, of Bartholomew County, by whom he had two children, Emma and George Fisher. He died in Indianapolis on May 16, 1884.

When Terrell resigned as adjutant general Governor Morton expressed his appreciation of his service in saying, "I owe to you whatever success I have had in doing my duty to Indiana and my country in assisting to put down the rebellion and establishing peace once more. No person has assisted me as much as you have by your highly appreciated, faithful service. . . ."

CONTENTS

	Page
CONDITION OF THE STATE AT THE COMMENCEMENT OF THE WAR	1
THE CALL TO ARMS	5

The Three Months' Service—Six Regiments, State Troops—Transfer of Six Regiments to United States Service—Raising and Organizing Volunteers—One Hundred Days' Troops

THE DRAFT 49
Draft of 1862—The Enrollment Act of Congress, 1863-4-5

RECRUITING CONTINUED 69
Recruits for the Unexpired Term—Recruiting in Southern States

GOVERNMENT BOUNTIES 75
Rates of Bounties—Bounty to Colored Troops—Local Bounties—Bounty Jumping—Special Premiums for Recruits

RECRUITING FOR THE REGULAR ARMY FROM THE VOLUNTEER FORCES 92
Hancock's First Army Corps—Colored Troops—Veteran Reserve Corps

APPOINTMENTS AND PROMOTIONS 106
Appointments in New Organizations—Appointments to Fill Vacancies—Promotions from Old to New Regiments—Promotions in Medical Staff—Promotions in the Artillery—Honorary Musters

CREDITS FOR TROOPS FURNISHED 119
First Series of Veteran Credits—Second Series of Veteran Credits—Quotas—Third Series of Veteran Credits—Additional Credits—Correction and Summary

INDIANA LEGION 135
State Militia—Organization of the Legion—Reserve Companies

MILITIA LAW OF 1861 172
Defects of the Law—Necessity for Militia Organization

	Page
THE RAID ON NEWBURGH AND EXPEDITION TO KENTUCKY	181

First Invasion of the State, July 18, 1862—Newburgh Captured—The Militia Called Out—Expedition to Kentucky, July, 1862

KIRBY SMITH'S CAMPAIGN—1862 190

Bragg's Invasion of Kentucky—Morgan's Co-operative Raid—Signs of Trouble—Indiana at Work—Battle of Richmond—Results—Siege of Cincinnati—Louisville Threatened—Munfordsville Captured—Resume

THE HINES AND MORGAN RAIDS 204

Invasion of the State, June, 1863—Pursuit and Capture—Invasion of the State, July, 1863—Its Origin and Object—Raid Through Kentucky—Crossing the Ohio—Preparations for Resistance—Response of the People—Disposition of Forces—Advance on Corydon, and the Fight—Going Ahead—At Salem—The Flight and Pursuit—Demonstration at Vernon—Onward—The Pursuit into Ohio—The Accident at Lawrenceburg—Return of the Troops—End of the Raid—Losses and Impressments of Property

MORGAN'S LAST KENTUCKY RAID—JUNE, 1864 255

Indiana Again to the Rescue—The Invasion, Preparations to Meet It—Morgan on the Warpath—Finale of the Raid

ADAM JOHNSON'S THREATENED RAID 262

Expedition into Kentucky, August, 1864

RELATIONS OF INDIANA AND KENTUCKY IN THE WAR 267

Condition of Kentucky; Secession Schemes—Kentucky "Neutrality"—Indiana and Kentucky—Loyal Ascendancy

INTERNAL STATE TROUBLES 288

Political Disturbances—Effect in Protracting the War—Legislative Obstacles to the War—Financial Embarrassments—Review of Legislative Obstructions—Expressions of Popular Feeling Against the War—Encouragement of Desertion—Acts of Violence, Resistance to the Draft, etc.

SECRET TREASONABLE ASSOCIATIONS 368

The Sons of Liberty

CONTENTS

Page

RELIEF OF SOLDIERS AND THEIR FAMILIES 394
Origin of the Indiana Relief System—Organization for Temporary Relief—Establishment of the General Indiana Military Agency—Establishment of the State Sanitary Commission—Collections—Distributions—Opinions of Other States—United States and Indiana Sanitary Commission—Subordinate Military Agencies—Special Agencies—Soldiers' Families

SOLDIERS' HOME AND REST 454
Temporary Provision—Permanent Provision—Ladies' Home—Refugees—Permanent Home for Disabled Soldiers—Conclusion

ALLOTMENT COMMISSIONER—PAY AGENCY 467
Allotment System

THE DEAD HONORED 474
Soldiers' Monuments—Funeral Honors to President Lincoln

MILITARY FINANCES 478
Military Auditing Committee—State Paymaster

RAILROADS, STEAMBOATS AND THE TELEGRAPH IN THE WAR 489
Railroads—Ohio River Packets—The Telegraph

CONTRABAND TRADE 496

MANUFACTURE OF AMMUNITION 499
Indiana State Arsenal—Indianapolis (U. S.) Arsenal

PURCHASE OF ARMS AND WAR MATERIAL FOR THE STATE 516
Want of Arms at the Outbreaking of the War—Purchase of Arms by the State

SUPPLYING THE TROOPS 530
Quartermaster General's Office—Commissary General's Office

CAMP MORTON REBEL PRISON 545

MILITARY ADMINISTRATION 554
Military District of Indiana—Military Departments Which Have Embraced the State of Indiana

APPENDIX

	Page
Troops Furnished by the State of Indiana	561
Table Showing the Organizations of Infantry, Cavalry and Artillery Sent to the Field	564
Indiana's Battle Record	567
INDEX	579

INDIANA IN THE WAR
OF
THE REBELLION

ADJUTANT GENERAL'S REPORT

CONDITION OF THE STATE AT THE COMMENCEMENT OF THE WAR

At an early period, while Indiana was yet a territory, a militia system was devised which gradually grew into one of considerable importance and efficiency. From the formation of the State Government to 1830, the militia was in high repute and afforded the surest channel through which civil positions could be reached. In 1828 there were sixty-five regiments organized into eighteen brigades and seven divisions, with an aggregate of about forty thousand officers and men; and in 1832, the date of the last returns, the aggregate number of officers and men reached fifty [three] thousand nine hundred and thirteen, of which thirty-one were general officers, one hundred and ten general staff officers, five hundred and sixty-six field officers, two thousand one hundred and fifty-four company officers, and fifty-one thousand and fifty-two non-commissioned officers, musicians, artificers and privates. The number of public arms distributed can not now be stated. Gradually the interest, which had been felt in maintaining the militia, weakened and failed to secure that sacrifice of time and means upon which its success had necessarily depended, so that by the year 1834, the organization was entirely abandoned. What became of the arms it is now impossible to tell, but judging from the experience of a later date, it is reasonable to presume that they were scattered and lost, or retained by the disbanded troops.

The military spirit of the people was not again aroused, although efforts were repeatedly made, until the declaration of war against Mexico in 1846, when, under the administration of Governor WHITCOMB, three regiments of volunteers (the First, Second and Third Indiana Infantry) were raised and mustered into the service of the United States. Subsequently, in 1847, two additional regiments (the Fourth and Fifth) were raised for the same service.

On the 14th of June, 1852, an act was passed for the organization of the militia by Congressional Districts; and on the 12th of February, 1855, an "Act concerning the organization of Voluntary Associations" was passed, providing for the formation of military companies by filing articles of association in like manner as provided for organizing building, mining and manufacturing companies. These laws were practically of no value, merely providing, in a general way, for the organization of the militia without regulations sufficient to secure any successful result. Many commissions were issued, in most cases for the mere purpose of conferring honorary military titles upon the recipients; but with the exception of probably a dozen companies (most of which had but a brief existence) formed in various parts of the State in 1859-60, aggregating about five hundred men, no organizations were made.

At the regular session of the Legislature in 1861, Governor LANE in his inaugural message alluded to this subject in the following language:

The importance of a well organized and thoroughly drilled Militia, in the present critical condition of our National affairs, can not be over estimated; and I will most heartily concur with you in any measure which you may devise for the purpose of giving greater efficiency to the present very defective militia laws of our State. A possible (I hope not a probable) contingency may arise during the present session of the Legislature, which will make it necessary and proper for you to appropriate a sum sufficient to equip a portion of the Indiana Militia for the purpose of aiding in the prompt execution of the laws, and in the maintenance of the Government. If this contingency shall occur during your session, I doubt not that you will meet it in a spirit becoming freemen and patriots.

In compliance with the Governor's suggestion, a bill for the organization of the militia on a new and more perfect system was introduced and passed the House of Representatives, but failing to pass the Senate, it did not become a law.

At the outbreaking of the Rebellion, there were perhaps less than five hundred stand of effective first class small arms in the State, besides eight pieces of weather-worn and dismantled cannon and an unknown number of old flint-lock and altered-to-percussion muskets, the most of which were scattered throughout various counties in the hands of private individuals and members of disbanded companies of Militia. Under an act of the Legislature, passed March 5th, 1861, Governor MORTON[1] had taken steps to secure the return of all arms that could be found, and many were thus secured to the State, but upon inspection they were ascertained to be useless except for "guard mounting" and drill practice about the camps.

The report of the Treasurer of State for the year 1861, shows that there was on hand on the 11th day of February of that year, only the sum of $10,368.58 in actual cash, and this sum was made up principally of "trust funds," which could not be touched for general or military purposes.

About the middle of March, 1861, Governor MORTON, in view of the impending rebellion, visited Washington City and endeavored to procure from the general government a supply of arms for State troops. He found that the national

[1] Oliver P. Morton, elected lieutenant governor, became governor on January 16, 1861, following Governor Henry S. Lane's election to the United States Senate.

armories under the treasonable maneuvers of FLOYD, the then late Secretary of War, were almost empty; but after much effort he succeeded in obtaining an *order* for five thousand muskets. Before these were forwarded, however, actual hostilities were begun and Indiana was called upon to bear her part of the burdens of war incident to the defense of the Nation and the suppression of the rebellion. With no militia force or system; almost destitute of arms and munitions; the public treasury depleted to absolute emptiness; the work of preparation for the vigorous performance of her part in the bloody drama was undertaken.

THE CALL TO ARMS

THE THREE MONTHS' SERVICE

The news of the fall of FORT SUMTER was confirmed, after several days and nights of intense suspense, by a dispatch received at Indianapolis on Sunday morning, the 14th of April, 1861. On that day the loyal people of the United States abandoned the field of argument and ceased to discuss measures and plans for the peaceable restoration of the national authority in the revolted States, and with singular unanimity and determination, accepted the issue of war as the only means left to save and perpetuate the national existence and the priceless liberties so long enjoyed.

The unprepared condition of Indiana at this juncture has already been alluded to. She had no money, no arms or munitions, no organized militia! The position of Governor MORTON, who had barely entered upon the duties of his office, was surrounded with responsibilities and embarrassments before unknown and seemingly almost insurmountable; but with a full understanding of the patriotic disposition of the people, and an unfaltering confidence in the justice of the cause in which he was about to engage, not a moment was lost in hesitation or distrust.

The telegraph on the morning of the 15th bore the following message from the Governor to President LINCOLN at Washington:

EXECUTIVE DEPARTMENT OF INDIANA,
INDIANAPOLIS, April 15th, 1861.

To ABRAHAM LINCOLN, *President of the United States:*

On behalf of the State of Indiana, I tender to you, for the defense of the Nation, and to uphold the authority of the Government, *ten thousand men.*

(Signed)   OLIVER P. MORTON, Governor of Indiana

The same day the President issued his proclamation calling forth the militia of the several States of the Union, to the aggregate number of seventy-five thousand, in order to suppress the rebellion and cause the laws to be duly executed. The quota of Indiana was subsequently fixed by the Secretary of War at six regiments of infantry, or riflemen, comprising in officers and men, four thousand six hundred and eighty-three, to serve for the period of three months, unless sooner discharged. On the 16th, the Governor issued a proclamation[1] briefly reciting the acts of rebellion which had brought on the war, and calling upon the loyal and patriotic men of the State to the number of six regiments, to organize themselves into military companies and forthwith report the same to the Adjutant General, in order that they might be speedily mustered into the service of the United States. The Honorable LEWIS WALLACE, of Crawfordsville, who had served in the Mexican war, and had, as a legislator and citizen, taken a deep interest in military affairs, was appointed Adjutant General. Colonel THOMAS A. MORRIS, of Indianapolis, a graduate of the United States Military Academy, and an eminent citizen, was appointed Quartermaster General; and ISAIAH MANSUR, Esq., of Indianapolis, an experienced and prominent merchant, was appointed Commissary General. These appointments were made without solicitation and were in every way unexceptionable, and gave entire satisfaction to the people of the State.

Indianapolis having been designated by the War Department as the place of rendezvous for troops, the commodious Fair Grounds of the Indiana State Board of Agriculture, adjoining the city, were secured for that purpose, and named, in honor of the Governor, "CAMP MORTON." Instructions were issued in general orders by the Adjutant General for the formation of companies; the several military departments

---

[1] *Report of the Adjutant General of the State of Indiana* (8 vols. Indianapolis, 1869), compiled by W. H. H. Terrell, Vol. 1, Appendix, Doc. 120:332. Hereinafter cited as Terrell, *Report.*

were speedily organized for business, and all available measures taken to fill the quota with the least possible delay.

To meet the extraordinary condition of affairs, the Governor issued his call on the 19th of April to the members of the Legislature, requiring them to convene in special session, at the State Capital, on the 24th.

In the meantime, every class of community manifested the wildest enthusiasm and most intense excitement; public meetings to facilitate the formation of companies and to give expression to the sentiments of the people touching their duty in the pending crisis. were held in every city, town and neighborhood, and an ardent and unquenchable military spirit was at once aroused that bid fair to embrace in its sweep every able-bodied man in the State. The day after the call was made five hundred men were in camp, and the Governor, apprehensive (as was the whole country at the time) that an effort would be made by the rebels to take possession of the Federal Capital, proposed to send forward half a regiment, if required, although unable to furnish the necessary arms and equipments. Receiving no reply to this offer from the War Department, it was renewed on the day following and the number increased to one thousand men. By the 19th—three days after the call—there were twenty-four hundred men in camp, and arrivals continued by every train. So rapidly did volunteering proceed, in less than seven days more than twelve thousand men, or nearly three times the quota required, had been tendered. Contests to secure the acceptance of companies were earnest and frequent. The question was not "Who will go?" but, "Who will be allowed to go?" In many cases companies came forward without orders, or rather in defiance of orders, in the hope that they could be received, or that a second call would at once be made, and frequently their enlistment rolls contained twice, and even thrice, the number of names required. Hundreds who were unable to get into companies at home, came singly and in squads to the general rendezvous on their own responsibility, and, by combining with others in like condition, and with fragments from companies having a surplus, formed new companies and joined in the general clamor for acceptance. The response was as gratifying as it was universal and left no doubt as to the entire and lasting devotion of Indiana to the fortunes of the Union. Like the sunlight, the "war fever" permeated every locality. The "Old Flag" at once became sacred and was proudly displayed in every breeze from the highest peaks of churches, school houses and private dwellings. The presentation of a stand of national colors by patriotic ladies to each company was rarely omitted, and, whenever practicable, brass bands were provided to escort them to the general camp.

Throughout the State the people acted in the most liberal and patriotic manner, providing the men with blankets, underclothing, and other necessary supplies which the authorities could not at the moment furnish. Families, suddenly deprived of husbands, fathers and brothers, upon whom they were dependent, were the recipients of all the assistance that abundant hands and free hearts could give. Several railroad companies, operating in the State, announced that they would carry all regularly enlisted volunteers free. Donations of money, in munificent sums, were made by citizens and by the authorities of cities, towns and counties to aid the cause in various ways; and a number of banks and many wealthy capitalists offered to advance large sums to the State until provision should be made by the Legislature, or the General Government, for equipping and providing for the troops. The eminent house of WINSLOW, LANIER & CO., of New York, long and honorably identified with the financial history of the State, tendered a loan of twenty-five thousands dollars, without stipulations as to interest or the time when it should be repaid.

The General Government, being unable to furnish clothing and equipments required by the large force so suddenly brought into service, the State was compelled, through the

Quartermaster General, to become a purchaser of these supplies, in open market, at home. The duties of the Commissary General, in subsisting the troops, were equally as important and responsible. Indeed, every department connected with the service was taxed to the utmost; the duties were novel, and the officers assigned to discharge them inexperienced and unskilled; yet better supplies were not furnished at any subsequent period during the war, or at so cheap a rate.

On the 20th (Saturday), five days after the call, orders were issued for the organization of the regiments. Drs. JOHN S. BOBBS and ALOIS D. GALL were appointed Medical Inspectors, and Major (now Major General) THOMAS J. WOOD, of the regular army, who had been specially detailed by the War Department for the purpose, proceeded to muster the troops into the service of the United States.

On the same day, the Governor, finding it impossible to restrain the tide of volunteers within the narrow limits of the three months' call, and being impressed with the necessity and importance, as well to the General Government as to the State, of immediately placing an overwhelming force in active service, tendered to the Secretary of War six additional regiments, without conditions as to the term of service, with the assurance that they would be organized, if accepted, in six days. Communication with Washington City by telegraph being cut off, no response to this offer was received. On the 23d, in a dispatch forwarded by special messenger, it was renewed, and the Governor at the same time expressed his determination to at once put the six additional regiments in camp and under discipline, and hold them subject, at least for a time, to the demand of the Government. In every quarter, and especially in the counties bordering on the Ohio river, the most serious fears were entertained that the State would be invaded by rebel bands, known to be organizing in Kentucky, the towns on the border plundered, and the country devastated. Every movement of the enemy indicated an early demonstration against the loyal people north of the Potomac and the Ohio. The determination of the Governor to anticipate a second call of the President by organizing and holding in readiness a well disciplined force, was therefore received with much satisfaction, particularly by the volunteers who had tendered their services and were impatiently awaiting at their homes orders to march. Public confidence was further encouraged by the prompt measures set on foot by the Governor to procure, through agents dispatched to the eastern cities and to Canada, a supply of first-class arms for State use, and by the organization in many counties of companies of Home Guards, who were armed for the time being with squirrel rifles and fowling pieces gathered up in their respective neighborhoods.

The Legislature met in extra session on the 24th of April, and in a spirit of entire harmony, proceeded to the important duty of devising such measures as the critical state of the country seemed to demand. The Governor, in his special message,[2] after reviewing the history of the secession movement, and the part already performed by the State in compliance with the President's call, made the following recommendations:

In view of all the facts, it becomes the imperative duty of Indiana to make suitable preparations for the contest by providing ample supplies of men and money to insure the protection of the State and General Government in the prosecution of the war to a speedy and successful termination. I therefore recommend that one million of dollars be appropriated for the purchase of arms and munitions of war, and **for the organization of** such portion of the militia as may be deemed necessary for the emergency; that a militia system be devised and en**acted, looking chiefly** to volunteers, which shall insure the greatest protection to the State and unity and efficiency of the force to be **employed;** that a law be enacted defining and punishing treason against the State; that a law be enacted suspending the collection of debts against those who may be actually employed in the military service of the State, or the United States; that suitable provision be made by the issue of bonds of the State, or otherwise, for raising the money herein recommended to be appropriated; and that all necessary and proper

[2] Terrell, *Report,* 1, Appendix, Doc. 113:308-10. See also Indiana *House Journal,* sp. sess., 1861, p. 24.

legislation be had to protect the business, property and citizens of the State, under the circumstances in which they are placed.

The Legislature, to replenish the treasury, promptly authorized a war loan of two millions of dollars, and made the following appropriations:—For *general military purposes,* one million dollars; for the *purchase of arms,* five hundred thousand dollars; for *contingent military expenses,* one hundred thousand dollars; and for *expenses of organizing and supporting the militia for two years,* one hundred and forty thousand dollars. The following laws were also passed: To organize the Indiana militia; to provide for the employment of six regiments of State troops; to provide for the appointment of a State Paymaster; to authorize counties to appropriate moneys for the protection and maintenance of the families of volunteers, for the purchase of arms and equipments, and for raising and maintaining military companies; and to provide for the punishment of persons guilty of giving material aid and comfort to the enemies of this State, or of the United States, in a time of war.

The three months' regiments were fully organized by the appointment of field and staff officers on the 27th of April, and a thorough course of military training immediately instituted. In the Mexican war the State had five regiments, numbered from the first to the fifth inclusive; to avoid historical confusion, therefore, the new regiments were numbered by beginning with the sixth, as follows:

Sixth Regiment, Colonel THOMAS T. CRITTENDEN.
Seventh Regiment, Colonel EBENEZER DUMONT.
Eighth Regiment, Colonel WILLIAM P. BENTON.
Ninth Regiment, Colonel ROBERT H. MILROY.
Tenth Regiment, Colonel JOSEPH J. REYNOLDS.
Eleventh Regiment, Colonel LEWIS WALLACE.

These regiments constituted the First Brigade, Indiana volunteers, under the following brigade officers, appointed and commissioned by the Governor:

THOMAS A. MORRIS, Brigadier General; JOHN LOVE, Major and Brigade Inspector; MILO S. HASCALL, Captain and Aide-de-Camp. Subsequently CYRUS C. HINES was appointed Captain and Aide-de-Camp, and JOHN A. STEIN, First Lieutenant 10th Indiana Volunteers, was detailed as Acting Assistant Adjutant General, and added to the Brigade staff.

The regiments composing General MORRIS' command, after being well armed and thoroughly equipped by the State, were ordered to Western Virginia. . . .[3]

At the expiration of their term of service, Major General MCCLELLAN addressed Governor MORTON as follows:

HEADQUARTERS ARMY OF OCCUPATION,
WEST VIRGINIA, CAMP NEAR BEVERLY July 21, 1861.
GOVERNOR O. P. MORTON,
Indianapolis, Indiana:
GOVERNOR—I have directed the three months' regiments from Indiana to move to Indianapolis, there to be mustered out and reorganized for three years' service.

I can not permit them to return to you without again expressing my high appreciation of the distinguished valor and endurance of the Indiana troops, and my hope that but a short time will elapse before I have the pleasure of knowing that they are again ready for the field.

I am, very respectfully, your obedient servant,
GEORGE B. MCCLELLAN, Major General U.S.A.

Brigadier General MORRIS also issued the following congratulatory address:

HEADQUARTERS FIRST BRIGADE INDIANA VOLUNTEERS
INDIANAPOLIS, July 29, 1861.
To the Officers and Soldiers of the Brigade:
The term of service for this Brigade, in the army of the United States, having expired, and the relations of officers and soldiers about to be dissolved, the General, in relinquishing his command, deems this a fit occasion to express his entire approbation of the conduct of the Brigade, whether in camp, on the march, or on the field of battle. The

[3] Sketches of the movements and services of the regiments of General Morris' command may be found in Terrell, *Report,* 2:2-32.

General tenders to all, his thanks for the soldierly bearing, the cheerful performance of every duty, and the patient endurance of the privations and fatigues of campaign life, which all have so constantly exhibited. Called suddenly by the National Executive from the ease and luxuries of home life, to the defense of our Government, the officers and soldiers of this Brigade have voluntarily submitted to the privations and restraints of military life; and, with the intelligence of free Americans, have acquired the arts of war as readily as they relinquished their pursuits of peace. They have cheerfully endured the fatigue of long and dreary marches by day and night, through rain and storm; they have borne the exhaustion of hunger for the sake of their country. Their labor and suffering were not in vain. The foe they met and vanquished. They scattered the traitors from their secure entrenchments in the gorges of Laurel Hill, stripped of their munitions of war, to flee before the vengeance of patriots.

Soldiers! you have now returned to the friends whose prayers went with you to the field of strife. They welcome you with pride and exultation. Your State and country acknowledge the value of your labors. May your future career be as your past has been, honorable to yourselves and serviceable to your country.

The General in command, sensible of the great obligation he is under to the members of his Staff, can not refrain from this public acknowledgment of the value of their services.

To Brigade Major Love, he can but feebly express his obligations. To his ripe and practical judgment, his accurate knowledge of the duties of officers and soldiers, his unremitting labors to secure instruction and discipline, to his cheerful and valuable counsel, the General is greatly indebted.

For the valuable services of Captain Benham, of the United States Engineers, not only in the appropriate duties of his station, but in his voluntary and arduous labors in the field, the General desires, in the name of the Brigade, to thank him. He has proved himself not only the skillful engineer, but competent to discharge any and every duty incident to military life.

To Captain Hines, Aide-de-Camp, and to Acting Assistant Adjutant General Stein, the General tenders his acknowledgments for their ready and cheerful performance of the severe duties imposed upon them.

By order of   Brigadier General T. A. MORRIS.
J. A. STEIN, Acting Ass't Adj. Gen.

An account of the re-organization of the regiments composing the First Brigade, for three years' service, will be given under the head of "Raising and Organizing Volunteers" in this volume.[4]

SIX REGIMENTS, STATE TROOPS

Upon the organization of the six regiments of three months' men, under the first call, so anxious and enthusiastic were the people to serve the country, there remained in excess at the general rendezvous, Camp Morton, twenty-nine companies; besides, sixty-eight companies had been raised in different parts of the State and tendered to the Governor for active service; and many more companies would have been raised had the State authorities been able to give any assurance that they would be accepted.

With a view, therefore, of meeting the wishes of the troops already enrolled, as well as to foster and encourage the exuberant spirit of loyalty and patriotism so generally and suddenly manifested by the people, and being fully satisfied that additional forces would soon be required and called for by the General Government, the Governor, on his own responsibility, and under the power vested in him as the Commander-in-Chief of the militia, determined to organize **five regiments of** twelve months' volunteers for the defense of the State, or for general service as the future might require, the regiments to be composed of the first fifty companies already raised and tendered. Instructions were also given to discharge from camp immediately all volunteers enlisted under the first call who were unwilling to enter the service of the State for one year.

On the 6th of May the organization of companies sufficient for five regiments being about completed, the Legislature, then in extra session, passed an act authorizing and requiring the Governor to call into the service of the State six regiments of volunteer militia (five being already raised), to be composed of the companies that had been previously organized and re-

[4] See below, 17-20.

ported to the Adjutant General and which had not been mustered into the service of the United States, the same to be received and mustered into the service of the State in the order in which they were organized and tendered, providing, that if the companies so organized and tendered were not sufficient to complete the regiments, preference in the formation of the remaining companies should be given to counties which were not already represented by companies in the State or United States service. The act also contained the following provisions: The term of service to be twelve months; the regiments to be divided into cavalry, artillery and infantry, as the public service might demand, with the usual officers; the troops to be subject to the order of the Governor with power to transfer them to fill any future requisition made for forces on the State by the President of the United States; the regiments to constitute a brigade, and the Governor to appoint and commission a Brigadier General for the same; the articles of war and the rules and regulations of the United States army to be observed, except that while in the service of the State the commissioned officers should only receive three-fourths the pay of officers of the same grade in the United States army; the Governor to have power, if in his judgment deemed advisable, to temporarily retire the force, or any part thereof, on half pay from active service, after they should have been sufficiently drilled and disciplined, with authority at any time to recall the regiments to active duty, when required for the public safety. The act was approved and put in force on the 7th of May, and orders for the organization of the force were immediately issued. The regiments were designated and camps of rendezvous established as follows:

Twelfth Regiment, Camp Morton, Indianapolis.
Thirteenth Regiment, Camp Sullivan, Indianapolis.
Fourteenth Regiment, Camp Vigo, Terre Haute.
Fifteenth Regiment, Camp Tippecanoe, Lafayette.
Sixteenth Regiment, Camp Wayne, Richmond.
Seventeenth Regiment, Camp Morton, Indianapolis.

Colonel JOSEPH J. REYNOLDS, of the Tenth Regiment (three months' service), then in command of Camp Morton, was appointed Brigadier General by the Governor, and charged with the organization of the regiments. On the 11th of May the Adjutant General reported five regiments as having the full complement of men, to-wit: the Twelfth, Thirteenth, Fourteenth, Fifteenth and Sixteenth, with a surplus of six companies in camp from which, with new enlistments, the Seventeenth Regiment was subsequently formed.

Transfer of Six Regiments to United States Service

The President in the meantime, as was anticipated by the Governor, having called for an additional volunteer force, requisition was made on the State by the Secretary of War, under date May 16th, for four regiments of volunteers to serve for three years or during the war. This call afforded the Governor the opportunity to relieve the State of a portion of the burden incident to maintaining the six regiments already nearly ready for the field, and accordingly, on the 21st of May, orders were issued transferring three of the regiments formed for State service under the Six Regiments bill to the United States service, and authorizing the organization of an additional regiment (the Seventeenth) out of the companies in Camp Morton not mustered into any service, and from such other companies as had been tendered, in their order, leaving two regiments in the State service.

The question of entering the United States service for three years was at once submitted to the State regiments. The Thirteenth, Fourteenth, Fifteenth and Seventeenth regiments promptly accepted the proposition, except a few hundred, who declined to volunteer for three years and who were at once discharged. These regiments were mustered into the United States service and marched for Western Virginia, as follows:

Regiment.	Date of Muster.	Date of Departure.
Fourteenth	June 7, 1861	July 5, 1861
Seventeenth	June 12, 1861	July 1, 1861
Fifteenth	June 14, 1861	July 1, 1861
Thirteenth	June 19, 1861	July 4, 1861

They were brigaded together and placed under command of General REYNOLDS, who was commissioned Brigadier General of Volunteers on the 10th of May, 1861....[5]

The Twelfth and Sixteenth Regiments remained in the State service until the 18th of July, when the Governor procured an order from the President accepting them into the service of the United States for the unexpired portion of their twelve months' enlistment, with the agreement that the General Government should assume all expenses and charges paid by the State on their account. The Twelfth was stationed at Evansville; the Sixteenth at Richmond. They were formally transferred to the United States on the 23d of July, and immediately left for the Potomac, joining the forces under General BANKS, at Pleasant Valley, Maryland....

RAISING AND ORGANIZING VOLUNTEERS

The reader of this Report has already been informed of the recruitment of six regiments of three months' troops and of six regiments of State troops, afterwards transferred to the general service of the United States. It now remains to follow up the plans and efforts made by the Executive of Indiana to further increase the army by the recruitment of additional forces.

Previous to the return of the three months' troops from the Western Virginia campaign, Governor MORTON dispatched messengers to all the regimental commanders with letters urging them to re-enlist, after remaining a reasonable time at their homes, for three years. The regiments returned the latter part

[5] Sketches of the services of General Reynolds' command may be found in Terrell, *Report,* 2:99-130, 145-57.

of July, and after being paid and mustered out, arrangements were made to re-organize them with the least possible delay. This was accomplished in a very short time under the auspices and direction of their former Colonels. Other calls had in the meantime been made, and were in progress of being filled. . . .

Indiana, as will be more fully shown under other heads in this report, never flagged in her efforts to raise men and fill the ranks of her regiments and batteries in the field. If there was any distinguishing characteristic of Governor MORTON's administration, it was a desire, determination and ability to recruit troops. Ever alive to the importance of repairing the waste and ravages of battle and of disease, he regarded it to be his foremost duty to place every able-bodied man, or as many as the wants of the Government demanded, at its disposal. The crowning wish of the Governor, as well as of the people, was that the armies, however large they might be required, should be raised by voluntary enlistments. Not only were the great forces, which the Government put into the field at the beginning of the contest, composed entirely of volunteers, but the ranks were kept full from the same element, and —with the exception of a few men drafted in October, 1862,[6] on the ground of *equalizing* the burthens in localities in arrears—no other resource was resorted to than volunteering in Indiana, until after three years and a half of war. And even then, the number put into the field by conscription was comparatively small, and the war was closed, mainly, as it was begun, by volunteers. This was one of its great peculiarities— it was fought, and brought to a successful termination, by men who chose to defend their country of their own accord.

In these annals *of what Indiana did in the war,* it is but just to future times and to the great history hereafter to be written, that the *facts,* as they occurred, should be permanently recorded. It is not invidious to say that no State was more prompt in furnishing troops than Indiana. Call after call was

[6] See below, 49-55.

made; our men were among the first to respond, and it is a gratifying truth that no demand made upon the State was ever evaded or delayed. Not only were the small contingents in the early part of the war furnished, or anticipated, but the large calls—made after the magnitude of the contest was more clearly seen—were always met with a quick response. No complaints were ever made by the State authorities that the calls were too frequent or too large—though a feeling sprung up that other States were doing less than their share of the work. Being terribly in earnest in the prosecution of the war, Governor MORTON repeatedly urged the necessity of making our forces overwhelming, and no effort was spared to furnish the last man demanded. This earnestness at the head of the State government was contagious, and a large majority of the people were not only united in urging a vigorous prosecution of the war, but their best efforts were exerted to make it vigorous, and the soldiers who went steadily forward carried with them an enthusiastic determination to bring the struggle to a speedy close. The spirit, and valor, and victories of our heroes at the front, in turn, reacted upon the people, and recruiting was greatly stimulated by the fame which the earlier troops acquired by their splendid services in the field.

The manner in which this great work of recruiting was carried on in Indiana must be briefly explained.

Upon receipt of a call from the President, the Governor's plan was to issue a proclamation, stating the requisition made for additional troops, and call upon the citizens to fill it at once. He always endeavored to get the influential men in every neighborhood enlisted in the work. Meetings were held, patriotic and stirring speeches were made, and regularly commissioned recruiting officers were induced to zealously exert themselves everywhere. Under nearly all, if not all, the calls, new regiments were organized. For facilitating organization, camps of rendezvous were established in each Congressional District, and commandants, quartermasters, adjutants, and examining surgeons, were appointed to superintend and press forward rapid organization. These indispensable officers were selected from the men of the district, of influential character, who were especially qualified by energy and capacity for organization, as well as being conspicuous for their local popularity. Commissions were then issued to one man for each company to be raised, with pay for the service; permanent commissions in the organization being conditional upon success in enlisting recruits. Local committees were formed in each township; and, after the first year of the war, local bounties were very generally offered by the counties and townships. A very large proportion of the troops furnished by Indiana, however, originally enlisted without any bounty further than that allowed by the General Government. Recruits were in all cases allowed their choice as to the regiment in which they preferred to serve, though the larger portion of them always selected the new regiments of their own districts.

Recruiting the First Year

In this year were raised the six regiments of three months' troops, six regiments of State troops, afterwards transferred to the United States' service; the three months' regiments were re-organized for the three years' service; the Infantry regiments up to the Fifty-ninth, were recruited, and portions of some others; three regiments of Cavalry and twelve batteries of Artillery were put in the field. These organizations were recruited with the greatest ease. For a long time, more companies were offered than the Governor was authorized to accept, and, as most of the commands were recruited under special authority from the War Department (not being raised to fill a quota under any formal call), the news that another regiment, or two more, or three more, or ten more, was accepted and hailed with delight, and it was only necessary to make selections from the companies tendered, to complete the organizations at once. As the war progressed, and the people learned of the long and toilsome marches the service required, there was a strong preference manifested for Cavalry and Artillery organizations, but in 1861, this was not the case, and if any arm of the service was more in favor than any other, it was the Infantry. General SCOTT positively discouraged the enlistment of Cavalry, and it was thought that the "regular" batteries of "flying" artillery would be sufficient for all emergencies.

It is worthy of remark that most of the organizations which entered the service during this year, re-enlisted, as their terms of service were about to expire, and remained in the field until the close of the war, having a part not only in the first victories which thrilled the Nation, but in the final surrender of the rebel armies which gave it Peace. And there can be no doubt that these early volunteers, by their gallantry, not only greatly stimulated all subsequent recruitment, but, through their long experience as veteran soldiers, excited the zeal and influenced the discipline and efficiency of all later organizations to an almost immeasurable extent.

Subsequent Calls

The winter of 1861-62 was severe, and the unavoidable sufferings of the troops in the field, owing to the want of preparation on the part of the Government to furnish the necessary comforts for a winter campaign—added to the unfavorable nature of the season itself—greatly retarded enlistments, and for a time they almost ceased. The efforts of the Governor and State authorities were not relaxed, however, and several fine regiments were organized and put into the field before spring. The victories of Mill Springs in January, Fort Donelson in February, and Shiloh in April, had a marked effect upon the public mind, and, as the overthrow of the rebellion seemed near at hand, there were indications that as soon as the spring should fairly open, enlistments would again be large; when suddenly an order was received from the War Department to stop recruiting entirely. This was a most unfortunate step, but all efforts to have the order recalled were unavailing, though the dangers that thickly beset us did not allow the entire suspension of recruiting. It was not until the call of July, after the defeats in front of Richmond, that systematic and energetic measures were permitted to raise a large force. This call came at a most unfortunate time. Our armies had, in some degree, lost their prestige. They had not only been defeated but out-generaled, which humiliated and discouraged the troops in the field, and materially detracted from that enthusiasm which was so needful to encourage recruiting at home. Then, the season of the year was unfavorable; the farmers being employed in harvesting, and every body busily engaged. Still the Governor went promptly and energetically to work; camps were formed, commandants appointed, recruiting lieutenants commissioned, and the whole machinery put in motion. The results at first were not encouraging. Recruiting dragged for a time, but the invasion of Kentucky by KIRBY SMITH and the threatened draft under the call of August, were sufficient to bring out the latent resources of the State. How grandly and promptly the response was made will be described hereafter.[7] All quotas were more than filled, and the encouragement the Government gave, by the adoption of a really vigorous policy in the conduct of the war, restored confidence and created the greatest enthusiasm.

The first call in 1863 was in June, for six months' regiments of militia. Four regiments were raised in Indiana, and sent to East Tennessee. Then came the call of October 17, 1863, for three hundred thousand men; followed in February and March, 1864, by calls aggregating four hundred thousand more. The quotas assigned to Indiana under these calls were all filled without resorting to a draft. The "Hundred Days' Movement" followed, and then came the call of July 18, 1864, for five hundred thousand men, followed in December by another call,

[7] See below, 195-201.

the last of the war, for three hundred thousand. These latter calls were filled partially by draft, but mainly by volunteers, as will hereafter be more particularly related.

Conduct of the War

I will not repeat here the facts so often stated in the Report, which show the anxiety and determination of Governor MORTON that Indiana should do her whole duty in the war. He was ever vigilant, energetic, expedient. He could not, and did not, wait the slow and cumbrous movements of the authorities at Washington—even of Mr. LINCOLN himself—to make our armies so strong as to be at once successful, overwhelming. He devised plans of his own, and suggested, urged and pleaded with the Government for the adoption of a more vigorous war policy, and always in favor of enlarging and strengthening, by every possible means, the forces in the field. And often, when it seemed that the Government, by hesitation, inaction and delay, was on the point of sacrificing, or allowing to be sacrificed, the objects of the war by permitting great advantages to be seized by the rebels, the Governor took grave and weighty responsibilities on himself, determined that no fault of his, or of his State, should add to the chances of disaster or defeat. Believing in the correctness of his own views with regard to the perils of the situation, despite the hamperings and objections that continually trammelled him, he often raised troops in advance of any call, and on many occasions made offers, when none were demanded, and though his efforts and offers were sometimes criticized severely, in no single instance did he have to take a backward step. The troops were always needed and were always most acceptable, but the foresight that provided them, and the pressure that attempted to secure their acceptance, did not always receive the appreciation they deserved until the contingencies or misfortunes they were intended to anticipate, or prevent, had actually transpired.

His views on the conduct of the war were frequently and

freely expressed to the President, and carried with them great force. The following letter possesses historical interest:

METROPOLITAN HOTEL, WASHINGTON, October 7, 1862.

His Excellency Abraham Lincoln, President of the United States:

DEAR SIR: I could not leave the city without addressing you this note, and my intense solicitude for the success of our cause must be my apology.

In my opinion, if our arms do not make great progress within the next sixty days, our cause will be almost lost. Our financial system must speedily end. The Government may subsist for a time upon issues of an irredeemable paper currency, which the law has made a legal tender, but the time will come when the people will refuse to sell their commodities and receive this currency in payment, and when this occurs, financial embarrassment and ruin will overwhelm the country. The system may collapse in a single day, and should it occur before the termination of the war, will of itself be sufficient to end it against us. National and individual bankruptcy would be followed by public despair, and the war would be abandoned by common consent. The danger of foreign intervention is daily increasing. The length of time which the rebels have maintained their Government and the success of their arms are rapidly furnishing foreign nations with an excuse to do what they have desired to do from the first— to recognize the Confederacy, and aid it in whatever way they can. You have now immense armies in the field, and all that they require to achieve victory is, that they be led with energy and discretion. The cold professional leader, whose heart is not in the cause, and who regards it as only a professional job, and whose rank and importance would be greatly diminished by the conclusion of the war, will not succeed in a contest like this. I would rely with infinitely more confidence upon the man of strong intellect, whose head is inspired by his heart, who believes that our cause is sacred, and that he is fighting for all that is dear to him and his country, although he be unlearned in military science, than upon the cold and polished professional soldier, whose sympathies, if he have any, are most likely on the other side. It is my solemn conviction that we will never succeed until the leadership of our armies is placed in the hands of men who are greatly in earnest, and who are profoundly convinced of the justice of our cause. Let me beg of you, sir, as I am your friend, a friend of your administration, and the friend of our unfortunate and unhappy country, that you will at once take up the consideration of this subject, and act upon the inspiration of your own heart and the dictates of your own judgment. Another three months like the last six and we are lost—lost. We can not afford to experiment a single day longer with men who have failed continuously for a whole year, who, with the best appointed armies, have done nothing; have thrown away the greatest advantages; evacuated whole States, and retreated for hundreds of miles before an inferior enemy. To try them longer, trusting that they may yet do something, it seems to me, would be imperiling the life of the nation. You have Generals in your armies who have displayed ability, energy and willingness to fight and conquer the enemy. Place them in command, and reject the wicked incapables whom you have patiently tried and found utterly wanting.

I am, with sentiments of great respect, Your obedient servant,

OLIVER P. MORTON.

It will be remembered that in 1862, the country was greatly agitated by the proposition to solve the questions involved in the war by dividing up the States and territories of the Union; and a formidable and mischievous movement was made in favor of the establishment of a new confederacy, to be composed of the Northwestern States. The strong argument urged, and which had great weight with the people, was that those States in their social, commercial and political relations were indivisibly bound to the South, as against New England, and especially that the undisturbed and undisputed right to navigate the Mississippi, was vital to the future prosperity and glory of this section of the country. Of course, to make the project of a Northwestern Confederacy plausible, it was assumed that the States in rebellion could never be conquered, and that the Union to all intents and purposes was broken. Touching these important matters, Governor MORTON expressed his views to the President in the following candid and unequivocal letter:

INDIANAPOLIS, INDIANA, October 27, 1862.

To the President of the United States:

DEAR SIR—The importance of the subject of this letter, and the deep interest I feel in it, must be my excuse for intruding it upon you.

The fate of the North West is trembling in the balance. The result of the late elections admonishes all who understand its import that not an hour is to be lost. The democratic politicians of Ohio, Indiana and Illinois assume that the rebellion will not be crushed, and that the independence of the rebel Confederacy will before many months be practically or expressly acknowledged. Starting upon this hypothesis, they ask the question: What shall be the destiny of Ohio, Indiana and Illinois? Shall they remain attached to the old Government, or shall they secede and form a new one—a Northwestern Confederacy, as a preparatory step to their annexation to the government of the South? This latter project is the programme, and has been for the last twelve months. During the recent campaign it was the staple of every democratic speech, that we had no interests or sympathies in common with the people of the Northern and Eastern States; that New England is fattening at our expense; that the people of New England are cold, selfish, money-making, and, through the medium of tariffs and railroads, are pressing us to the dust; that geographically these States are a part of the Mississippi valley, and, in their political associations and destiny, can not be separated from the other States of that valley; that socially and commercially their sympathies and interests are with those of the people of the Southern States rather than with the people of the North and East; that the Mississippi river is the great artery and outlet of all Western commerce; that the people of the Northwest can never consent to be separated politically from the people who control the mouth of that river; that this war has been forced upon the South for the purpose of abolishing slavery, and that the South had offered reasonable and proper compromises, which, if they had been accepted, would have avoided the war. In some of these arguments there is much truth. Our geographical and social relations are not to be denied; but the most potent appeal is that connected with the free navigation and control of the Mississippi river. The importance of that river to the trade and commerce of the Northwest is so patent as to impress itself with great force upon the most ignorant minds, and requires only to be stated to be at once understood and accepted. And I give it here as my deliberate judgment, that should the misfortune of our arms, or other causes, compel us to the abandonment of this war and the concession of the independence of the rebel States, that Ohio, Indiana and Illinois can only be prevented, if at all, from a new act of secession and annexation to those States, by a bloody and desolating civil war. The South would have the prestige of success, the commerce of the world would be opened to feed and furnish her armies, and she would contend for every foot of land west of the Alleghenies, and in the struggle would be supported by a powerful party in these States.

If the States which have already seceded should succeed in their rebellion, our efforts must then be directed to the preservation of what is left; to maintaining in the Union those States which are termed loyal, and the retention of the territories of the West. May God grant that this contingency shall never happen, but it becomes us as men to look it boldly in the face. Let us take security against it if possible, especially when by so doing we shall be pursuing the surest mode for crushing out the rebellion in every part and restoring the Union to its former limits. The plan which I have to suggest is the complete clearing out of all obstacles to the navigation of the Mississippi river and the thorough conquest of the States upon the western bank. Between the State of Missouri and the Gulf of Mexico on the western bank are the States of Arkansas and Louisiana. Arkansas has a population of about 325,000 white citizens and 111,000 slaves, and a very large per centage of her white population are in the rebel army and serving east of the Mississippi. Of the fighting population of Western Louisiana not less than fifty per cent. are in the rebel army and in service east of the river. The river once in our possession and occupied by our gunboats can never be crossed by a rebel army, and the fighting men now without those States could not get back to their relief. To make the conquest of those States thorough and complete your proclamation should be executed in every county and every township and upon every plantation. All this can be done in less than ninety days with an army of less than 100,000 men. Texas would then be entirely isolated from the rebel Confederacy, and would readily fall into our hands. She has undoubtedly a large Union element in her population, and with her complete separation from the people of the other rebel States, could make but feeble resistance. When this shall have been accomplished, a glance at the map will show what immense advantages will have been obtained. The remaining rebel States, separated by the river, would be cut off effectually from all the territories and from the States of Mexico. The dangers to be apprehended from the French aggressions in Mexico would be avoided. The entire western part of the continent now belonging to the Government would be secured to us, and all communication between the rebel States and the States on the Pacific entirely stopped. The work of conquest in Arkansas and Louisiana would be easy and certain, and the presence of our gunboats in the river would effectually prevent any large force from coming from the east to the relief of these States. The complete emancipation which could and should be made of all the slaves in Arkansas, Louisiana and Texas would place the possession of those States on a very different footing from any other rebel territory which we have heretofore overrun.

But another result, to be gained by the accomplishment of this plan, will be the creation of a guaranty against the further depreciation of the loyalty of the Northwestern States by giving the assurance that, whatever may be the result of the war, the free navigation and control of the Mississippi river will be secured at all events.

With high regard, I have the honor to be,

Very respectfully, Your obedient servant,

OLIVER P. MORTON.

The following letter, selected from a great number on the same subject, forcibly expresses the Governor's views with regard to a vigorous prosecution of the war:

EXECUTIVE DEPARTMENT,

INDIANAPOLIS, January 18, 1864

HIS EXCELLENCY, ABRAHAM LINCOLN,

President of the United States:

SIR—Considerations of the most vital character demand that the war should be substantially ended within the present year.

The truth of this proposition need not be enforced by argument, because it is apparent to every intelligent mind. I therefore respectfully but earnestly urge the necessity of immediately calling for all the men that may be required to bring the war to a safe and speedy termination.

If doubts are entertained that a sufficient number of men will not be procured under the last call, let another be made immediately, and my belief is that the Nation will respond and by a mighty effort promptly raise our armies to the required strength. It is much better to make the estimate too large than too small, and it is much safer to overpower the enemy by numbers than merely to be his equal and rely for success upon the skill of Generals and the chances of battle.

I am also apprehensive that we shall be surprised in the spring by the numbers and strength of the enemy. A terrible conscription is putting almost the entire male population of the rebel States in the army, and we shall find beyond all question that their forces have been greatly increased. If another call for troops should become necessary, and be postponed until next spring or summer, it would take months to get them into the field. The Nation would be greatly disheartened, the continuance of the war be indefinitely prolonged, and our finances deeply and almost fatally depressed.

Men can be more easily raised now than at any future time. It is the winter season when the agricultural population is to a great extent unemployed, and will enter the army far more readily than after farming operations are resumed in the spring. Nothing would so much weaken the administration or repress the ardor of the people as the apprehension that our armies are inadequate to the speedy suppression of the rebellion, and that another call for troops will be necessary at a future time. If the war can be ended sooner, by largely increasing our forces, the sooner our forces will be disbanded, and the immense drain upon the treasury suspended, which is becoming the terror of all intelligent minds. The leaders of the rebellion are making a last and mighty effort to retrieve their desperate fortunes. Let them be met with mightier effort by the Nation, which shall certainly overwhelm them with inevitable ruin.

Very respectfully, Your obedient servant,

OLIVER P. MORTON.

Veteran Re-enlistments

The system of accepting men for short terms of enlistment, at the beginning of the war, proved to be most unfortunate. If the term of service had been uniformly fixed for "during the war," the enthusiastic loyalists of the country would have rushed to the support of the national standard with the same impetuosity as they did when they were called upon to serve only three months. In stating the truth—that the rebellion was not "put down in ninety days"; that the Union forces did not encircle it and crush it, "like an anaconda," within the cycle allotted by the war-worn and battle-scarred chieftain who made the prediction—no reflection is cast upon those who sincerely entertained such views in the early days of the war. War was a new thing to the authorities, as well as to the masses; and it was only after the disaster of "Bull Run" that a realizing sense of the inefficiency and weakness of the North, and the determined spirit of the South, broke in upon the minds of the true adherents of the Government. Bluster, which previously formed so large a part of the war-stock of the North, speedily vanished, and the stern necessity of requiring every man who could "lift a pound," as the Westernism is, or "put a shoulder to the wheel"—either by personal service or influence—became painfully apparent. By seizing indefensible forts, arsenals, mints and posts; by robbing paymasters and confiscating debts due northern merchants; by "lynching" every man and scourging every family that expressed even a lingering affection for the "Old Flag"; by corrupting the old army and winning many accomplished officers to the side of treason; by putting forth bloviating *pronunciamentos,* in which the unity, courage and "high-toned chivalry" of the South were glowingly depicted, and the divisions, cowardice and meanness of the North drawn in free and florid colors—the rebels, for a time, gained largely in confidence, if not in strength. Our "success," so-called, in the West Virginia campaign, in which a few Indiana and Ohio regiments skirmished on several occasions with about an equal force of the enemy, had more than upset the confident assurance of the rebels, and the general feeling prevailed that the war was about over and the Union saved. The disaster of Bull Run, however, dispelled the hallucination. The rebellion proved itself to be a formidable reality, notwithstanding the predictions of leading statesmen and warriors that it would break down of its own weakness before it could fairly straighten itself upon its legs and make a "show of fight."

Then came calls for more troops, though timidly and gingerly made. Six months' men, one year men, and three years' men were accepted; but the War Governors and the people of the West were far in advance of the Government, and so great was the pressure to get their regiments accepted, the authorities at Washington had a warm fight of it to keep back the forces that were tendered. The plea was, that uniforms and the necessary paraphernalia could not be furnished; that quotas were filled already; or that the State had already been permitted to send forward more than its proportion of the men required; and the hint was dropped, more than once, that the conciliating influences of generalship and strategy were sufficient to bring the "insurrection" to an end, with less bloodshed less expense, and in a more congenial way than could be done by the rampageous policy advocated by the sanguinary-minded Governors and people of the West. As the war progressed, or rather lingered, calls for more men came, day by day, and it is hardly necessary to repeat here what Indiana's response always was to the demands made upon her. In the spring of 1862 recruiting was stopped short and square; the regiments then being raised were consolidated, and the opinion seemed to prevail that the strength of the army was entirely adequate to put a sure and sudden end to the war. Soon, however, BANKS, with his army, came whirling out of the Shenandoah Valley, defeated and demoralized; the National Capital was believed to be in danger, and new and nervous calls were again made upon the States.

In the gloomy days of 1863, the Government, and in fact every patriotic supporter of it, began to realize the great want of *more soldiers*. Congress passed the conscription act in March, providing for the enrollment, and draft, if necessary, of all arms-bearing citizens. This was a grand stroke, but it ought to have been done a year and a half before; this, however, nobody knew, until the progress of events demonstrated the necessity. But the conscription act did not fill the measure of the Nation's needs. It was cumbrous, unpopular, and required time to put it in practical execution. Meantime, the discovery was made that [with] the large army of three years' men, and notwithstanding the new volunteers and conscripts that might be obtained, there was still danger that the rebellion would not be suppressed; and the chances were that the war would be indefinitely protracted. The three years' regiments of 1861 were the bulwark and pride of the army. They had fought all over Northern Virginia, in Missouri, Arkansas, Louisiana, Tennessee and Kentucky, and their experience, hardihood and valor won the respect and admiration of all loyal men. But they were only enlisted for three years, and there was no prospect that the war would end within that time. Foreign governments were ogling with the South, and giving fresh encouragement to the rebellion. The confidence in the ability of the North to conquer, weakened as the South strengthened; even our own people became divided among themselves, and the loyal cause lost immensely in that way. Treasonable organizations sprang up in our own midst; deserters flocked home; rebel raids upon our soil became frequent, and doubts entered the minds of the stoutest and bravest as to the final result.

Governor MORTON conferred frequently and freely with the President and Secretary of War, and never failed to advocate the most energetic policy in regard to prosecuting the war. He never lost his self-possession, his confidence in ultimate success, or in the least abated his zeal. His views in reference to incompetent and procrastinating generals, and the importance to the Northwest of opening up the Mississippi, have already been quoted. His leading idea was that the rebellion *could* be put down, but only by an overwhelming force under the leadership of men who were alive to the perils that beset the country, and were earnestly intent upon avoiding them by achieving substantial and crushing victories. On the 7th of May, 1863, he telegraphed President LINCOLN, Secretary STANTON and Secretary CHASE, recommending the enforcement of the conscription act, largely and fully, and that all available force, both land and naval, be at once concentrated to open the Mississippi, that being, in his judgment, the vital point. By personal visits to Washington, and frequent suggestions by letter and telegram, he continually pressed his views upon the Government, and there is abundant evidence that these efforts had important, if not controlling, influence upon the conduct of the war.

The War Department was at length thoroughly awakened to the importance of strengthening the army by the re-enlistment of veterans, and on the 25th of June, 1863, promulgated an order detailing a carefully prepared system, and offering such inducements as it was thought would be sufficient to retain most of the old troops in the field. The following is the order referred to:

WAR DEPARTMENT, ADJUTANT GENERAL'S OFFICE,
WASHINGTON, June 25, 1863.

General Orders, No. 191.

FOR RECRUITING VETERAN VOLUNTEERS

In order to increase the armies now in the field, volunteer infantry, cavalry, and artillery may be enlisted at any time within ninety days from this date, in the respective States, under the regulations hereinafter mentioned. The volunteers so enlisted and such of the three years' troops now in the field as may re-enlist in accordance with the provisions of this order, will constitute a force to be designated "Veteran Volunteers." The regulations for enlisting this force are as follows:

I. The period of service for the enlistments and re-enlistments above mentioned shall be for three years or during the war.

II. All able-bodied men, between the ages of eighteen and forty-five years, who have heretofore been enlisted, and have served for not less than nine months, and can pass the examination required by the mustering regulations, of the United States, may be enlisted under this order as Veteran Volunteers, in accordance with the provisions hereinafter set forth.

III. Every volunteer enlisted and mustered into the service as a Veteran under this order shall be entitled to receive from the United States one month's pay in advance, and a bounty and premium of four hundred and two dollars ($402).

IV. If the Government shall not require these troops for the full period of three years, and they shall be mustered honorably out of the service before the expiration of their term of enlistment, they shall receive, upon being mustered out, the whole amount of bounty remaining unpaid, the same as if the whole term had been served. The legal heirs of volunteers *who die in the service* shall be entitled to receive the whole bounty remaining unpaid at the time of the soldier's death.

V. Veteran volunteers enlisted under this order will be permitted at their option to enter old regiments now in the field; but their service will be continued for the full term of their own enlistment, notwithstanding the expiration of the term for which the regiment was originally enlisted. New organizations will be officered only by persons who have been in the service, and have shown themselves properly qualified for command. As a badge of honorable distinction, "service chevrons" will be furnished by the War Department, to be worn by the Veteran Volunteers.

VI. Officers of regiments whose terms have expired, will be authorized, on proper application, and approval of their respective Governors, to raise companies and regiments within the period of sixty days;

and if the company or regiment authorized to be raised, shall be filled up and mustered into service within the said period of sixty days, the officers may be re-commissioned of the date of their original commissions, and for the time engaged in recruiting they will be entitled to receive the pay belonging to their rank.

VII. Volunteers or militia now in the service, whose term of service will expire in ninety days, and who then shall have been in the service at least nine months, shall be entitled to the aforesaid bounty and premium of $402, provided they re-enlist, before the expiration of their present term, for three years or the war, and said bounty and said premium shall be paid in the manner herein provided for other troops re-entering the service. The new term will commence from the date of re-enlistment.

VIII. *After the expiration of ninety days from this date,* volunteers serving in three years' organizations, who may re-enlist for three years or the war, shall be entitled to the aforesaid bounty and premium of $402, to be paid in the manner herein provided for other troops re-entering the service. The new term will commence from the date of re-enlistment.

IX. Officers in service, whose regiments or companies may re-enlist, in accordance with the provisions of this order, before the expiration of their present term, shall have their commissions continued, so as to preserve their date of rank as fixed by their original muster into the United States service.

X. As soon after the expiration of their original term of enlistment as the exigencies of the service will permit, a furlough of thirty days will be granted to men who may re-enlist in accordance with the provisions of this order.

XI. Volunteers enlisted under this order will be credited as three years' men on the quotas of their respective States. Instructions for the appointment of recruiting officers, and for enlisting Veteran Volunteers, will be immediately issued to the Governors of States.

By order of the Secretary of War:

E. D. TOWNSEND, Assistant Adjutant General.

This order was especially designed to secure the re-enlistment of nine months' men, who entered the service under the call of August 4, 1862, though it included all who had served nine months, as well as such men of the old commands as were at that time out of service. The result did not meet the expectation of the War Department, as but very few men were obtained; and on the 11th of September following, another order was issued, permitting the re-enlistment of three years' volunteers who had less than one year to serve, and granting them the $402 bounty and premium, as provided for in the original order. Still the veterans did not show any strong disposition to avail themselves of this liberal proposition; the re-enlistments were very few, and fell far short of the public necessity. On the 19th of September, Governor MORTON, in a letter to the Secretary of War, stated that quite a number of the first regiments raised in this State were so much reduced as to have each less than one hundred and fifty effective men. He was convinced that the army could be strengthened more speedily by allowing one of these old regiments for each Congressional District to come home and recruit and re-organize, than upon any other plan. The influence of the old veterans upon their friends at home was all important, and the assistance they would receive from leading citizens would enable them to fill their depleted ranks with certainty and of good material.

Again, on the 7th of October, the Governor renewed his proposition in a somewhat more comprehensive form, by a telegram to the Provost Marshal General, as follows:

[By Telegraph]   EXECUTIVE DEPARTMENT,

INDIANAPOLIS, IND., October 7, 1863.

Colonel JAMES B. FRY, *Provost Marshal General, Washington, D. C.:*

I respectfully submit the following plan for filling up the old three (3) years regiments: A certain number of the old regiments, say one from each Congressional District, reduced lowest in point of numbers, or oldest in organization, and three-fourths of which will re-enlist for three years, should be brought home to recruit—officers and men to be furloughed for such time as the Governors of the respective States may determine, for the purpose of recruiting for their respective regiments, the Governor to designate places of rendezvous. At the expiration of the terms of furlough, the regiments to be returned to the field, and a like number of old regiments, upon the same principle, be brought home and recruited, and so on. The men who re-enlist to be mustered out as if their first terms of enlistment had expired for past service, and be paid the four hundred and two dollars ($402.00) bounty awarded to veteran volunteers for future service. This will place the regiments organized in 1861, as regards bounty, on the same footing as those organized in 1862, and it is believed the plan will take so few men from any one corps as not materially to weaken it. [Signed,]

O. P. MORTON, *Governor of Indiana.*

It will be observed the Governor made it a point to require *three-fourths of the old regiments to agree to re-enlist for three years* before being sent home on furlough to recruit. The re-enlistment of veterans under the orders of the War Department "hung fire," and some other plan had to be resorted to. The country could not afford to lose the services of her brave veterans, and it was of the first importance that their ranks should be filled up. After deliberating nearly two weeks, General HALLECK, then Commander-in-Chief of the Army, agreed that Governor MORTON might make requisition upon each General officer commanding a Department in which Indiana troops were serving, for one non-commissioned officer or private from each company, to be selected by the regimental commander, to be sent home on recruiting service, and providing that if vacancies for commissioned offices existed, the non-commissioned officers or privates should be entitled to promotion on recruiting the company to the minimum standard. If there were no vacancies of commissioned officers in any company, the commanding officer of the regiment, in his discretion, could detail one commissioned officer or one enlisted man to recruit for each company. All were to report to the Governor.

These details were promptly made from all the old Indiana regiments; also from the old batteries. The recruiting officers were assigned to duty by the Governor in the neighborhoods where their companies were originally raised. Several thousand recruits were obtained, and while many were thus enabled to secure the promotions which they had so long deserved, the old veterans in the field were greatly encouraged by having their ranks filled up with new men.

The more important work, however, of re-enlisting the old veterans in the field, flagged, and it seemed the whole scheme would prove a failure. The general terms of the re-enlistment and the amount of bounty offered were satisfactory enough, but the provision of granting furloughs of thirty days *"as soon after the expiration of their original term of enlistment as the exigencies of the service will permit,"* was altogether distasteful. They placed but little confidence in such a promise; it was too uncertain and too distant. To obviate this objection the War Department issued an order on the 21st of November, 1863, which authorized "a furlough of at least thirty days *previous* to the expiration of their original enlistment." This stipulation was to be entered upon the re-enlistment rolls, and commanding Generals of armies and departments were required to see that the furloughs were granted and that the men were provided with transportation to their homes at the expense of the Government. These modifications were well received, and soon re-enlistments began to be made in large numbers. To encourage the work, Governor MORTON dispatched special agents to confer with the officers and men in the field, and to bring such influence to bear as would accomplish the desired result. Among the agents who undertook this work, the following deserve honorable mention for their valuable services: General JOHN T. WILDER, Captain HENRY B. HILL, Colonel LAWRENCE S. SHULER, Dr. CALVIN J. WOODS, and SIMON T. POWELL, Esq. All the Indiana military agents, and many of the Indiana general, field and line officers, took special interest in the matter and contributed largely in securing re-enlistments. Liberal local bounties were paid by many localities. Altogether fully three-fourths of the men remaining in the regiments and batteries of 1861 re-enlisted. Many more would have done so but for the opposition of some officers, who were afraid their commands might be broken up, and the inattention and neglect of mustering officers, which caused vexatious delays; and in some cases also, because of a lack of definite instructions and the non-arrival of proper blanks.

These things, trifles though they seem, created disaffection and a feeling of uncertainty in the minds of the men and materially lessened the number of re-enlistments that otherwise might have been obtained.

The troops commenced returning on furlough early in January, 1864, and continued to arrive, as they could be spared from the field, until each organization had been granted this privilege. They were received by the authorities and people with every demonstration of respect and gratitude. An account of the public ovations that were tendered them, will be given hereafter.

The following table shows the veteran organizations and number re-enlisted in each:

Re-Enlisted Veteran Volunteers

Seventh Regiment, Infantry,	47 men.
Eighth Regiment, Infantry,	386 men.
Ninth Regiment, Infantry,	291 men.
Tenth Regiment, Infantry,	72 men.
Eleventh Regiment, Infantry,	296 men.
Thirteenth Regiment, Infantry,	40 men.
Fourteenth Regiment, Infantry,	59 men.
Fifteenth Regiment, Infantry,	74 men.
Seventeenth Regiment, Mounted Infantry,	288 men.
Eighteenth Regiment, Infantry,	334 men.
Nineteenth Regiment, Infantry,	213 men.
Twentieth Regiment, Infantry,	281 men.
Twenty-First Regiment, Heavy Artillery,	503 men.
Twenty-Second Regiment, Infantry,	331 men.
Twenty-Third Regiment, Infantry,	278 men.
Twenty-Fourth Regiment, Infantry,	327 men.
Twenty-Fifth Regiment, Infantry,	284 men.
Twenty-Sixth Regiment, Infantry,	73 men.
Twenty-Seventh Regiment, Infantry,	154 men.
Twenty-Ninth Regiment, Infantry,	372 men.
Thirtieth Regiment, Infantry,	121 men.
Thirty-First Regiment, Infantry,	285 men.
Thirty-Second Regiment, Infantry,	4 men.
Thirty-Third Regiment, Infantry,	460 men.

Thirty-Fourth Regiment, Infantry,...................................... 439 men.
Thirty-Fifth Regiment, Infantry,... 190 men.
Thirty-Sixth Regiment, Infantry,.. 21 men.
Thirty-Seventh Regiment, Infantry,.................................... 193 men.
Thirty-Eighth Regiment, Infantry,...................................... 256 men.
Thirty-Ninth Regiment (Eighth Cavalry), ... 305 men.
Fortieth Regiment, Infantry,... 246 men.
Forty-Second Regiment, Infantry,....................................... 215 men.
Forty-Third Regiment, Infantry,.. 262 men.
Forty-Fourth Regiment, Infantry,.. 220 men.
Forty-Sixth Regiment, Infantry,... 107 men.
Forty-Seventh Regiment, Infantry,...................................... 416 men.
Forty-Eighth Regiment, Infantry,... 284 men.
Forty-Ninth Regiment, Infantry,.. 169 men.
Fiftieth Regiment, Infantry,... 247 men.
Fifty-First Regiment, Infantry,... 295 men.
Fifty-Second Regiment, Infantry,... 370 men.
Fifty-Third Regiment, Infantry,.. 381 men.
Fifty-Seventh Regiment, Infantry,.. 215 men.
Fifty-Eighth Regiment, Infantry,.. 202 men.
Fifty-Ninth Regiment, Infantry,... 241 men.
First Regiment Cavalry,.. 5 men.
Second Regiment Cavalry,... 78 men.
Third Regiment Cavalry,... 15 men.
First Battery, Artillery,.. 5 men.
Second Battery, Artillery,.. 14 men.
Third Battery, Artillery,.. 17 men.
Fifth Battery, Artillery, ... 20 men
Seventh Battery, Artillery,... 33 men.
Eighth Battery, Artillery,... 7 men.
Tenth Battery, Artillery,.. 44 men.
Eleventh Battery, Artillery,.. 8 men.
Twelfth Battery, Artillery,... 48 men.
Thirteenth Battery, Artillery,... 82 men.
Fourteenth Battery, Artillery,.. 68 men.
Sixteenth Battery, Artillery,... 56 men.
Seventeenth Battery, Artillery,... 50 men.
Wilder's (Twenty-Sixth), Battery,.. 56 men.
Total,.. 12,433 [11,453] men.

The furlough allowed was thirty days in the State, and during most of this time each officer and soldier engaged in recruiting, and so successful were their efforts a large number of recruits were added to their ranks.

No just estimate can be made of the importance of thus retaining in the service the hardy and skillful veterans, who had gone through all the trials and triumphs of the war. The Secretary of War, in his report for 1864, truthfully remarks that no other measure, looking to the recruitment of the army, had resulted so advantageously. The great moral effect of these veterans renewing their pledge of service to the Government was everywhere felt. It showed their faith in the cause for which they perilled their lives; it improved and strengthened public opinion, encouraged and stimulated recruiting, and gave assurance to the world that the loyal soldiers of the land were equal to the great work of saving the Nation by the valor of their arms.

Reception of Troops

At the expiration of the term of service of the three months' volunteers, Governor MORTON inaugurated a system of *receptions,* which was continued during the war and which gave much gratification to the "loyal heart" of the people, greatly encouraged the returning soldiers, and to a considerable extent stimulated recruiting. These receptions were announced and the time fixed a day beforehand; a public dinner was prepared, after which the regiment or battery to be received was escorted with appropriate music, amidst the firing of cannon, to the Capitol grounds, or, if the weather was inclement, to a public hall, where addresses of welcome and congratulation were delivered by the Governor and others, on the part of the people of the State, which were usually responded to by the commanding officer of the organization and other officers of the command. The Governor's address included a short military history of the services of the regiment or battery, its campaigns, marches and engagements.

These reception dinners and meetings were always enlivened by the presence of a goodly delegation of the fair ladies of Indianapolis, who were gratified to wait on the gallant soldiers at table, and with them participate in the joyous reunions which followed. At dinner excellent music by a full band gave animation to the repast, as well as on the march to the place of reception and during the exercises at the stand. Frequently the occasion was enlivened by patriotic and humorous songs, by singing clubs and individuals, greatly to the amusement and gratification of all in attendance.

Every regiment and battery, upon its return to the State, was honored with a reception, such as has been described; the hospitalities and thanks of the State were tendered in a lavish and hearty manner by the authorities, aided always by the patriotic citizens, and especially the ladies of Indianapolis; and the happy effect and feeling thus produced and inspired among the soldiers were pleasurable features of the war, and were attended with the best results on the *morale* of the troops. The establishment of the *Soldiers' Home and Rest* enabled the authorities to furnish several regiments at once with a most excellent dinner, while the fair attendants and the soul-stirring music added charms to the occasion that could not fail to be appreciated by the brave men, just from "the front," who had long been deprived of the comforts and graces which abound in the abodes of peace. The influence of these receptions was salutary and cheering, and the weary, war-worn veterans, in the enthusiasm with which they were welcomed, felt that their many toilsome marches and hard-fought battles were amply recompensed by the kind and hearty appreciation of their friends at home.

The re-enlisted Indiana veterans, of whom there were over twelve thousand, were granted furloughs for thirty days upon re-enlisting, or as soon thereafter as their services could be spared. Most of them were in the South, under GRANT and SHERMAN, and returned by way of Jeffersonville, where a large hall was fitted up for their temporary accommodation, well warmed, seated and lighted; and at all hours hot coffee and a substantial luncheon were ready for all who chose to partake. This arrangement was a real relief to the many thousand soldiers, not only from Indiana, but from all the Northern States, who returned on veteran furloughs during the severe winter of 1863-64, and the Governor could not probably have devised anything for their comfort and relief which would have given more satisfaction than the refreshment rooms at Jeffersonville.

At Indianapolis, the returning troops were met at the depot by a messenger, who at once conducted them to the spacious "Home," where comfortable quarters and a "good square meal," smoking hot, was sure to await them. Half an hour was ample time, with the splendid facilities for cooking at the "Home," to prepare an excellent meal—in which pastry, condiments, and vegetables were conspicuous—for a full regiment, and as the time of arrival of troops was usually telegraphed in advance, delays in the preparation of refreshments were of rare occurrence. The perfection to which all these arrangements were brought in the course of the war was attested by thousands of soldiers, and reflected the highest credit on all concerned. In fact, too much can not be said of the munificent liberality which characterized all these efforts, or of the generous disposition of the loyal people of the State, who never, for a moment, withheld the means to administer to the wants, comforts and necessities of our soldiers.

The good feeling created by these receptions was noticeable on all occasions. The men went to their homes, after long absence, in good heart, with animated spirits, and were thus greatly encouraged in the patriotic work in which they were engaged. They had not been forgotten; their Governor and the "brave at home" were not unmindful of their comfort or their interests; their families had been tenderly cared for in their absence, and everything conspired to make them contented and joyous. The result was that our veteran regiments were greatly strengthened by new recruits, who flocked to the old standards by hundreds, encouraged by the honors that were so freely and heartily showered upon those who had pioneered in the glorious duty of saving their Government from the calamity of overthrow and dissolution.

This brief notice would be incomplete without mentioning the very faithful and valuable services of the venerable Colonel JAMES BLAKE, who uniformly acted as Chief Marshal at all the receptions. To him, and likewise to the many ladies who lent the charm of their presence and generously attended the soldiers at the reception dinners, however inclement the weather, the thanks of the State authorities and of the people of the State are due.

ONE HUNDRED DAYS' TROOPS

The spring of 1864 opened with the prospect of much desperate and bloody work before the armies of the East and South. It was urgently stated by Generals GRANT and SHERMAN that every able-bodied soldier was imperatively needed. The grand Atlanta and Richmond campaigns were about to be commenced, and such general measures taken as were believed would result in the overthrow of the rebellion. Indiana was relied upon, with well-grounded confidence, and expected to put into play all her energies to make the army crushingly powerful. The calls of February and March, requiring *over thirty-seven thousand* men had been filled in an almost incredibly short time, and the troops were hurried forward as rapidly as the means of the Government would admit. The twelve thousand re-enlisted veterans, who had been granted a furlough to their homes of thirty days, were promptly returned to their places at the front, and vigorous and successful efforts were made to fill the ranks of all the old organizations. General SHERMAN, at this period, took care to impress upon Governor MORTON the importance of having every man that could be raised, forwarded to his command with the least possible delay. On the 6th of April, he telegraphed:

> The season is advancing and no excuse can be entertained, such as waiting for more recruits. Three hundred men in time, are better than

a thousand too late. Now is the time every soldier should be in his proper place—the front.

Again on the 23d, he telegraphed:

The force of ten thousand I sent up Red River was intended to form a part of my force for the spring campaign, but BANKS can not spare them and I will be short that number. We can not mount half the cavalry already in the service. If the new cavalry regiments will not serve as infantry, I see no prospect of using them except as dismounted cavalry, which is the same thing. I tell you that it is impossible to arm and equip them this season, and even then we could not find horses where we are going. Why not let me use them to guard my roads and relieve other guard troops to that extent? They would be none the worse cavalry for a few months' service with muskets. I can put them in reserve where drill and instruction could go on quite as well as where they now are, and I can arm them as infantry. When horses and equipments come they can be mounted and equipped, and relieved as soon as furloughed regiments arrive, or as soon as A. J. SMITH's command comes out of Red River.

The Governor concurred fully with these views, and several of the new cavalry regiments were at once sent forward as infantry. This unexpected necessity was a great disappointment of course, but the men bore it cheerfully when assurance was given them that their horses and carbines would speedily follow. General SHERMAN was much pleased with the uncomplaining disposition of the troops, and on the 3d of May, sent this telegram to the Governor:

I am well satisfied at the dispatch given to the new cavalry regiments, and will do all in my power to make them an honor to your State. I wish you would use your personal influence to content them with the fact, that all cavalry regiments should undergo preliminary instruction in infantry practice, before being entrusted with horses. The immense waste of fine cavalry horses in the past two years is proof of this.

Yet, notwithstanding the gigantic efforts that were made, it had been for some time clearly apparent to GOVERNOR MORTON that enough men to make a splendid army would be compelled to remain guarding railroads, depots of public stores, and fortifications in the rear of the advancing armies—and it was further evident that if these men, who were trained soldiers, could be relieved of guard duty and placed in the advance, the chances of success would be greatly increased. How this great desideratum could be brought about was then an important and perhaps a vital question. The quotas having been filled, recruiting for the three years' service lapsed into insignificance—it appeared almost impossible to increase the army to the standard required for the mighty operations contemplated in the plans for the campaign.

In this crisis Governors MORTON and BROUGH met at Indianapolis and devised a plan, which afterwards ripened into the "One Hundred Days' movement," whereby it was hoped the troops then engaged as rear guards could be relieved and sent forward for the more important work of fighting the enemy. Accordingly, on the 11th of April, a telegram was sent to the Governors of Illinois, Iowa, Wisconsin and Michigan, inviting them to meet the Governors of Ohio and Indiana at Indianapolis, in consultation on important public business, on the 22d. The meeting was held, Governors YATES of Illinois, STONE of Iowa, BROUGH of Ohio, LEWIS of Wisconsin and MORTON of Indiana being present. (Governor BLAIR of Michigan could not attend but telegraphed his readiness to accede to any measures, which might be adopted for the benefit of the country.) After full discussion, the general features of the plan were agreed to and the Governors immediately proceeded to Washington, to urge its adoption by the President. In this they succeeded. The proposition was in the following form:

To the President of the United States:

I. The Governors of Ohio, Indiana, Illinois, Iowa and Wisconsin offer to the President infantry troops for the approaching campaign, as follows:

    Ohio, ...30,000.
    Indiana, ...20,000.
    Illinois, ...20,000.
    Iowa, ...10,000.
    Wisconsin, ... 5,000.

II. The term of service to be one hundred days, reckoned from the date of muster into the service of the United States, unless sooner discharged.

III. The troops to be mustered into the United States service by regiments, when the regiments are filled up, according to regulations, to the minimum strength—the regiments to be organized according to the regulations of the War Department. The whole number to be furnished within twenty days from the date of notice of the acceptance of this proposition.

IV. The troops to be clothed, armed, equipped, subsisted, transported, and paid as other United States infantry volunteers, and to serve in fortifications, or wherever their services may be required, within or without their respective States.

V. No bounty to be paid the troops, nor the service charged or credited to any draft.

VI. The draft for three years' service to go on in any State or district where the quota is not filled up; but if any officer or soldier in this special service should be drafted, he shall be credited for the service rendered.

JOHN BROUGH, Governor of Ohio.
O. P. MORTON, Governor of Indiana.
RICHARD YATES, Governor of Illinois.
WM. M. STONE, Governor of Iowa.
JAMES T. LEWIS, Governor of Wisconsin.

The foregoing proposition of the Governors is accepted, and the Secretary of War is directed to carry it into execution.

A. LINCOLN.

April 24, 1864.

As soon as the acceptance of the proposition had been decided, the fact was communicated to headquarters at Indianapolis, and preparations made for raising Indiana's quota as soon as possible.[8] That the quota was not raised requires a word of explanation. The attempt was made at the busiest time of the spring season, just after the heavy calls of February and March had been filled, which the people, who had been so largely drawn on before, confidently believed would be the last. No fears of a draft were entertained, and most of the arms-bearing laboring men of the State had entered into en-

[8] Governor Morton's call for "One Hundred Days" troops was issued April 23, 1864. For text see Terrell, *Report*, 1, Appendix, Doc. 126:336.

gagements with farmers for the season. The militia, what there was of it, was organized on the volunteer system for the protection of the border, with the express understanding that it was not to be called into service except for home defense. The militia law gave the Governor no power to compel service, or to send the troops beyond the limits of the State; this force, therefore, as a body, was not available, though many volunteers were obtained from it for the call. In Ohio the case was different, and her quota was entirely and immediately filled by simply transferring the required number from the National Guard to the United States service. Indiana's quota could only be filled by volunteers, and with the most energetic efforts the authorities were able to make only eight regiments, aggregating seven thousand four hundred and fifteen men, could be raised. In Illinois the case was about the same, and for similar reasons her quota was not filled by nearly one-half. Iowa furnished over two thousand and Michigan nearly four thousand.

The Indiana hundred days' men served their term in Tennessee and Alabama, and by relieving older and more experienced troops from the duty of guarding General SHERMAN's communications, supply depots, etc., greatly strengthened his army and assured its success in the arduous and stubbornly contested struggle against Atlanta. The regiments were well officered, were composed of the best material, and by faithful service reflected credit upon themselves and the State. So highly did the Government value their services, the President issued to each man a certificate of thanks.

In concluding this account, I desire to notice a statement made by Mr. WHITELAW REID, in his history of "Ohio in the War." He claims that it was upon the "suggestion" of Governor BROUGH that the meeting of the Governors was held at Washington, and that the proposition which was accepted was "prepared under his direction,"[9] leaving the in-

[9] Whitelaw Reid, *Ohio in the War. Her Statesmen Generals and Soldiers* (2 vols. Cincinnati, 1895), 1:209.

ference very clear that the One Hundred Days' movement originated with the Governor. Such is not the fact. Governor BROUGH did a noble part in that matter, and it is but just to his honored memory that the highest meed of praise be awarded to him. But the idea was first "suggested" by Governor MORTON. It is known to the writer hereof, who was a member of Governor MORTON's military staff and on duty at the executive office at the time, that he conversed freely on the subject of furnishing short-term men to relieve the garrisons and guards in the rear of GRANT and SHERMAN, and indeed matured, substantially, the plan that was afterwards adopted, several weeks before Governor BROUGH came to Indianapolis when the matter was first talked of between them. In fact, Governor BROUGH's visit was on private business relating to railroad affairs, and he called upon Governor MORTON through courtesy and friendship, when the latter explained his plan. The subsequent meeting of the Governors grew out of the first interview. Doubtless all of them had thought about some such movement, but if there is any especial credit due for first suggesting it, Governor MORTON is clearly entitled to it.

THE DRAFT

DRAFT OF 1862

Under the President's instructions, the Secretary of War issued orders on the 4th of August, 1862, calling for three hundred thousand men to serve for nine months, and providing for a draft from the militia, if the quotas of the several loyal States were not filled by the 15th of August. At the time this call was made, the call of July 2d, 1862, also for three hundred thousand men, was still pending. Indiana's quota, under each call, assigned on the basis of population, was twenty-one thousand two hundred and fifty men, making together forty-two thousand five hundred men. By the 20th of September both calls had been filled by volunteers, except six thousand and sixty, and this deficiency was further reduced before the draft was made (October 6th) to three thousand and three men, which number was actually drafted. It is now known that even this small number of men was not due from the State; on the contrary, if the account of troops furnished had been accurately made up at the time, it would have clearly demonstrated that the State had more than filled all her quotas. But the enrollment of the militia and an examination of the best available data of troops previously furnished, showed that of the nine hundred and sixty-nine townships in the State, three hundred and thirty-four were in arrears on their quotas, while the remaining six hundred and thirty-five were in *excess* of theirs, or at least *had filled them*. While the State was not indebted to the Government to the extent of *one man,* it will be seen that three hundred and thirty-four townships were behind on their quotas, as already stated, to the number of six thousand and sixty men. To equalize the burden of furnishing troops between all the townships, which only now became a burden because of the forced drain upon the arms-bearing population of the State, at a time when loyal and disloyal citizens alike had almost "despaired the Republic," it was decidedly proper to require the delinquent townships to make good their delinquencies, and thus place the whole State on an equal footing. This was done—partly by the pressure of the impending draft, which secured volunteers for more than one-half of the delinquency, and by the draft itself for the balance. Governor MORTON, more than any other man, regretted the necessity of resorting to a draft, and, while he was thoroughly satisfied the State was *ahead* on her quota, and really was not justly liable to be conscripted for a single soldier, yet it was apparent that, though many localities had furnished more than their proportion of volunteers, other localities had failed to furnish theirs. A *draft* was looked upon as a disgraceful thing, but the result of this one brought out the plain fact that to make the burden of furnishing troops bear equally upon all localities and communities, all deficiencies should be supplied, and the draft was the only means of doing it. This was equal, just, and right; though it was afterward ascertained that the State was eight thousand and eight men in *excess* of her quota, *on all calls,* at the time the draft was made—October 6, 1862. The true account, upon subsequent adjustment, was as follows: troops called for prior to August 4, 1862, *sixty-four thousand seven hundred and sixty-five;* troops furnished at date of the draft, *ninety-four thousand and twenty-three;* leaving to our credit a *surplus of twenty-nine thousand two hundred and fifty-eight men,* which was enough to fill the call of August 4th, and still leave to the credit of the State, applicable to future calls, *eight thousand and eight men.*

Prior to the issuing of the call of August 14th, recruiting was in a very languid state, and enlistments were made slowly and with great reluctance. Disloyal elements were actively at work throughout the State; desertions were encouraged by rebel sympathizers, and the slow progress made by our armies in the field discouraged and disheartened the friends of the Union cause to a degree that even yet is painful to contemplate. The draft, therefore, became an imperative necessity, and, coupled with the extensive rebel raids of KIRBY SMITH and MORGAN, and the advance of BRAGG'S whole army into Kentucky, which occurred while the calls of July and August were pending, a most wonderful change was wrought, and regiments and batteries were recruited with unexampled rapidity. The facts relating to recruiting during this important period have been so fully given in another part of this report, under the head of "KIRBY SMITH'S CAMPAIGN," it is not necessary to allude to them here. A brief statement of the manner in which the draft of 1862 was conducted may, however, very properly be given, as it was a new and novel feature in our affairs, and deserves a place in the military annals of the State.

The Enrollment

No enrollment of the militia had been made since 1832, when the militia force under the old act of February 10, 1831, appears to have been *fifty-three thousand nine hundred and thirteen men.* Under the call of August 4, 1862, it became necessary to enroll in the militia every able-bodied white male citizen resident within the State over the age of eighteen and under the age of forty-five years. A plan was prepared by the Secretary of War for this purpose, but in many particulars it was impracticable, as applied to this State, because its execution depended upon county officers, some of whom were opposed to any and every means adopted by the Government to fill its armies; Governor MORTON therefore modified the plan somewhat, which modification being approved by the War Department, the enrollment was made accordingly.

The plan contemplated:

1. The appointment of a Commissioner in each county, who was required to appoint a deputy in each township; the

deputies to make the enrollment; the Commissioner to supervise the work.

2. Two lists were to be made in each township; one for those who were in the United States service, and the other for all other residents between the prescribed ages.

3. These lists were to be returned on completion, by a day to be fixed, to the Commissioner for the county, who should then appoint a time when he and his deputies would sit as a Board and hear and determine all excuses. Notice of this day was then to be given, and, when all exemptions were marked off, the lists would be ready for the draft. Upon completion of the lists, the Commissioners of the several counties were required to return them to the General Commissioner at Indianapolis, to enable him to determine the quota of men required from each township preparatory to ordering the draft.

The enrollment was made under many difficulties, and in many cases was unavoidably imperfect, but as its defects could not easily be remedied, it gave tolerable satisfaction. The total militia force of the State (not including ninety-three thousand and forty-one (93,041) volunteers then in service) was two hundred and nine thousand two hundred and sixteen (209,216); of this number thirty-six thousand and thirty-eight (36,038) were exempt from military duty from various causes, leaving one hundred and seventy-three thousand one hundred and seventy-eight (173,178) subject to service.

Passes

While the enrollment was progressing, it became necessary to establish some sort of regulations to prevent citizens liable to be drafted from leaving the State to avoid compulsory military service. A system was therefore devised, with General ASAHEL STONE at its head, by which passes were issued upon proper evidence being shown that the persons who desired to leave the State were on legitimate business and not fleeing from the draft. The commissioners of the several counties were furnished with the necessary blanks and instructions, and issued passes in all proper cases, free of expense. Without a pass of this kind, any citizen liable to draft could be detained by a Marshal until satisfactory evidence was produced that he was not a fugitive from the draft. This arrangement, in itself, amounted to but little, but the moral effect of it was to deter or frighten citizens from cowardly attempting to avoid conscription by leaving the State.

The Draft

The mode of drafting was as follows: The drawing was supervised by the commissioner for the county. The names of all who were liable to draft in each township, respectively, were written on separate ballots, which were carefully folded and placed in a wheel or box, from which a person, blindfolded, drew a number of ballots equal to the quota due from the township being drawn. A notice was then served upon the drafted men, by the Marshal, requiring them to report at the county seat within five days, from which place transportation was furnished to the general rendezvous at Indianapolis.

Upon arrival at the rendezvous, such as wished to furnish substitutes were permitted to do so. The time for presenting substitutes was extended to October 31, 1862, and they were in all respects placed upon the same footing with drafted men. Many of them availed themselves of the privilege granted by the Governor, of volunteering in old regiments for three years, which afterwards caused some misunderstanding, as the principals in many cases claimed exemption on subsequent drafts for the full period of three years. But as they were only drafted for nine months, it was held that the enlistment of substitutes for a longer time was a matter with which principals had nothing to do, and all such claims were rejected.

The draft took place on the sixth of October and passed off very quietly, considering the high state of political feeling which existed at the time; and the perfect fairness with which it was conducted was generally admitted, even by opponents of the war measures of the Government. There was but one disturbance reported, which took place in Blackford county, where a few lawless men destroyed the draft box and by threats and violence prevented the officers from proceeding with the draft on the day appointed; but the third day afterward it was concluded without further disturbance.

Of the three thousand and three (3,003) men drafted, 2,183 reported at the general rendezvous, of which number fourteen hundred and forty-one (1,441) volunteered in old three years' regiments, or in companies for twelve months' service. Seven hundred and forty-two (742) men were assigned, as drafted men, as follows: One company to the Fifty-seventh regiment of infantry, one company to the Eighty-third regiment of infantry, two companies to the First regiment of cavalry, and about thirty men to the Ninety-ninth regiment of infantry. The companies thus organized were permitted to select their own captains; the lieutenants were selected by the Governor from meritorious non-commissioned officers and privates already in the service. Of the balance of the drafted men, three hundred and ninety-six (396) were discharged for disability and other causes, and four hundred and twenty-four (424) failed to report and were classed as deserters.

Commutation

A provision in the Constitution of the State exempts persons, conscientiously opposed to bearing arms, from military duty, but requires that they shall pay an equivalent for such exemption. The enrollment of 1862 shows that there were three thousand one hundred and sixty-nine men of this class. Governor MORTON presented the question of commutation for these exempts to the Secretary of War, who decided that they should be relieved from the draft upon the payment of $200 each. About twelve hundred and fifty "conscientious men" were drafted, and the General Commissioner proceeded to collect from them the commutation money, through his subordinates in the counties. Some twenty-odd thousand dollars was collected, when an appeal from the action of the General

Commissioner was taken. The matter was submitted to the Secretary of War, who, after full investigation, decided that under existing laws the payment of commutation could not be justly required, and thereupon the money was all refunded.

Officers

The draft was conducted by JESSE P. SIDDALL, ESQ., of Richmond, as General Commissioner, assisted by Messrs. JEREMIAH M. WILSON, of Connersville, JOHN F. KIBBEY, of Centreville, and JOHN J. HAYDEN, of Indianapolis, who received the thanks of the Government for the faithful and able manner in which their important and laborious duties were performed.[1] The rendezvous was established at "Camp Sullivan," Indianapolis, and was under command of Colonel JOHN S. WILLIAMS, Sixty-third Indiana Volunteers. In the adjustment of the accounts for the expenses of the draft, Judge HAYDEN acted as General Commissioner *vice* SIDDALL resigned. . . .[2]

THE ENROLLMENT ACT OF CONGRESS, 1863-4-5

In the winter of 1862-63, the impossibility of keeping up our armies by volunteering was so apparent, that the necessity of some more thorough and vigorous system of recruitment was recognized by all loyal adherents of the Government. The attention of Congress being called to the subject early in the session of that winter, after careful and anxious deliberation, the act known as the "Enrollment Act" was passed on the 3d day of March, 1863. The objects of the Act were:

1. To enroll and hold liable to military duty, all citizens capable of bearing arms, not exempt therefrom by its provisions.

---

[1] See *Report of J. P. Siddall, Draft Commissioner* (Indianapolis, 1863). 30 pp.

[2] For a register of officers of this draft, see Terrell, *Report,* 1, Appendix, Doc. 28:185-87.

2. To call forth the national forces by draft when required.

3. To arrest and return deserters.

The great feature of the new law, however, was the establishment of an entire new system of raising recruits for the army. Hitherto the whole matter had been conducted by the States; now, however, it was taken directly in hand by the General Government. For this purpose a new Bureau was established under charge of the Provost Marshal General. To assist him, Provost Marshals were appointed in each Congressional District. For convenience there was also appointed, though not required by the law, an Acting Assistant Provost Marshal General for each State. To these officers and their subordinates, the whole business of enrolling, enlisting, and when quotas were not filled, drafting men to fill the demands of the Government, and arresting deserters, was confided. The authorities of the States of course co-operated and assisted, but the whole machinery of raising men was placed under the immediate charge of the Provost Marshal General. Being thus simplified, and controlled by one Bureau, the great work of recruiting was much more equitably and promptly performed than under the purely volunteer system.

To facilitate the enrollment, the law established in each District a Board of Enrollment, composed of the District Provost Marshal as President, a Commissioner and a Surgeon, appointed by the President of the United States. This Board was directed to divide the District into sub-districts, and appoint every two years an enrolling officer for each sub-district. The enrolling officer was provided with blanks and instructions, and required immediately to proceed to enroll all persons subject to do military duty, noting their age, residence and occupation. These lists were then consolidated and a copy forwarded to the Provost Marshal General.

As soon as the new Bureau was fairly organized, steps were taken to carry out these provisions. The Boards of Enrollment were organized early in May, 1863, and the districts at once sub-divided for the purpose of enrollment; towns, townships, and wards being generally adopted as the most convenient sub-divisions. The enrolling officers were appointed, and sworn to perform their duties and carry out their special instructions, faithfully and impartially, great care being exercised to appoint none but competent and honest men. To find such men willing to undertake the work was a matter of some difficulty, but the list was completed, and the enrollment commenced in earnest about the 25th of May, 1863. This enrollment was to form a complete register of all the national forces not actually in the service; it contained the names of all men liable to draft, and furnished the basis for determining the proportion of troops to be supplied by each sub-district; it exhibited the data for establishing, between the Government and each locality, an account of military service, in which all that was due was to be charged, and all that should be paid was to be credited. A correct enrollment was, therefore, of the utmost importance, not only in justice to those in service, but to those liable to perform military duty under the law, who remained at home. Every step was taken to insure accuracy in making up the enrollment lists; and, on the 17th day of November, 1863, a circular was issued by the Provost Marshal General, directing the Boards of Enrollment to revise and correct their work, to the end that any future call for troops might bear justly and equitably upon all localities alike. Attention to this subject was again called in a circular from the same officer, dated June 25, 1864, and again in a circular issued November 15, 1864. The people of this State were also recommended to lend every exertion to assist in perfecting the enrollment lists, by a circular issued by Brigadier General PITCHER, Acting Assisting Provost Marshal General, dated December 2, 1864, to which was appended a circular issued by the Adjutant General of Indiana, on the same date. The first lists were necessarily very defective, but from continual corrections made in pursuance of the recommendations of the Provost Marshal General and

Adjutant General, it is believed that they at last became as nearly perfect as the system adopted would permit.

After the calls of 1862 were filled, as before detailed, no further call for troops was made until after the first enrollment (under the enrollment act of Congress) had been accomplished. The next call was for four regiments of six months' men, in June, 1863, and these were furnished without delay, by volunteers.

Upon the completion of the enrollment under the "Enrollment Act," the President called for one-fifth of the number enrolled in the first class, in the States and Districts which were in arrears. This call, however, did not affect Indiana, as we had a surplus over all calls of eleven thousand and eleven men.

On the 17th of October, 1863, the President issued another call for three hundred thousand men, increased on the 1st of February, 1864, to five hundred thousand men, and further increased under call of March 14, 1864, to seven hundred thousand. Under these calls, the quota of Indiana was declared to be forty-five thousand five hundred and twenty-nine. To fill this demand, thirty-seven thousand and eleven men enlisted as volunteers, which, added to the eleven thousand and eleven excess over former calls, left still a surplus in favor of the State of two thousand four hundred and ninety-three, without resorting to draft.

On the 23d of April, 1864, a call was made for one hundred days' men, and, in accordance therewith, seven thousand four hundred and fifteen men were furnished by this State.

On the 18th of July, 1864, another call for five hundred thousand men was issued, under which the quota of Indiana was declared to be twenty-five thousand six hundred and sixty-two. This was filled as follows: Drafted men and substitutes, twelve thousand four hundred and seventy-six, of whom six hundred and twenty-three paid commutation; the balance were volunteers, naval recruits, and re-enlisted veterans, not previously credited. The draft under this call was made in the months of September and October, and passed off very quietly.

On the 19th of December, 1864, another call was made, being the last of the war, for three hundred thousand men. The quota of the State was twenty-two thousand five hundred and eighty-two, which was filled principally by volunteers—only two thousand four hundred and twenty-four men having been conscripted by the draft which was made in March, 1865.

The quotas were assigned by districts by the Provost Marshal General, by the following simple proportion—as the total enrollment of the United States is to its quota (the number called for)—so is the enrollment of the district to its quota. The district quotas were in the same manner apportioned among the sub-districts by the District Provost Marshal.

The quotas thus obtained were then reduced by surplus over former calls and excesses in enrollment, and all credits allowed for enlistments previous to the draft. The remainder were drawn by the draft. The call of December 19, 1864, being for 300,000 men, after making deductions for all excesses, the method adopted for distributing quotas was different and somewhat peculiar. The total excess of all the States was added to the number called for, and the quotas determined from this sum, each district having its quota reduced by its own excess. The districts in arrears under former calls were thus required to make up the deficiency under this call, so that a perfect balance between [the States and] the General Government was established.

Before the last call was filled, however, the rebel armies were suddenly and completely overthrown, and recruiting was discontinued. It will be seen that Indiana filled all calls promptly, no deficiencies being left to be filled on subsequent calls, our excess after the calls had been filled varying from 2,000 to 30,000. No fact could more clearly exhibit the splendid patriotism and public spirit of our people, or the vigor and energy of our authorities, than the promptness with which each demand upon the State was met. There was no lagging, no hesitancy; though the quotas were often deemed excessive and unjust, they were always filled with *men*, actual bona-fide soldiers; the demands of the General Government were not cancelled by naval credits, men enlisted in rebellious States or other "dead-head" substitutions; and with but one exception, in no State was there so small a proportion who relieved themselves from service by the payment of a money commutation. These statements are not made in a boastful spirit, nor to reflect upon other States, but justice to our own people demands that their efforts in filling our armies, upon which more than any other cause the suppression of the rebellion depended, should be plainly set forth and clearly recognized.[3]

It is hardly necessary now to describe the minutiae and intricacies of the conscription act and orders made under the same. It is sufficient to say that certain persons, as aliens, disabled citizens, officers of the Government, etc., were exempt from military service and not subject to draft; while all who might be drafted could relieve themselves from service by presenting an acceptable substitute, or the payment of commutation money amounting to $300. No exemptions on account of conscientious scruples were allowed, it being presumed that such persons would relieve themselves by the payment of the $300 commutation. Subsequently, the enrollment act was so amended as to provide that members of religious denominations, who should, by oath or affirmation, declare that they were conscientiously opposed to bearing arms, and who were prohibited from doing so by the rules and articles of faith and practice of said religious denominations, should, when drafted into the military service, be considered non-combatants, and were to be assigned to duty in the hospitals, or to the care of freedmen, or should pay $300 for the benefit of sick and wounded soldiers. No person was entitled to the benefit of this section unless his declaration should be

---

[3] During the war the State got no credit for any of her short-term troops—30, 60, 90 or 100 days' men. [Terrell]

supported by evidence that his deportment has been consistent with such declaration.

Under the law *any* person after draft might still be relieved from service by furnishing a substitute or the payment of $300 commutation. This provision was manifestly unjust; and although it furnished a large "draft and substitute fund," as it was called, with which the Provost Marshal's Bureau was enabled to maintain an extensive establishment and pay large bounties and premiums, the effect of the commutation clause of the law was bad, and it may well be doubted whether its benefits were not overshadowed by its evils. The crowning argument, at the time, among the people was, "a poor man who has not $300 must go to the wars"; "a rich man, who can pay $300, or who can hire a substitute, need not go." Much of the opposition and not a little of the acerbity and bitterness manifested against the war policy of the Government may doubtless be attributed to the unequal bearing upon the people of this commutation clause. The money thus obtained was intended to apply in the procuration of substitutes by the Government, and large bounties were at once offered for volunteers. It was soon demonstrated that the practical effect of this provision was to make an unfair distribution of the burdens of the war. But few substitutes were thus obtained; for, while each call for troops brought a large sum into the treasury, but few men were placed in the army. People who thought the draft was intended to procure men, while other means were provided for raising money, were greatly dissatisfied. Besides, many wealthy communities purchased entire exemption by paying the money value of their quotas in advance of the draft, and made no effort to procure men.

Governor MORTON, after witnessing the baneful effects of the "three hundred dollar" system, and the demoralization wrought by it in the minds of the people, everywhere, protested to the President and Secretary of War against it in the most earnest and emphatic manner. On the 6th of March, 1863, he wrote as follows:

Public feeling has greatly improved in the West within the last six weeks, but I fear the improvement is likely to receive a disastrous check from the construction given to the 13th section of the Conscription Act, which permits a drafted man to relieve himself from the draft by the payment of $300. By this construction every man who can beg or borrow $300, can exempt himself from the draft, and it will fall only upon those who are too poor to raise that sum. I can assure you that this feature in the Bill is creating much excitement and ill-feeling towards the Government among the poorer classes generally, without regard to party, and may, if it is not subdued, lead to a popular storm, under cover of which the execution of the Conscription Act may be greatly hindered, or even defeated, in some portions of the country.

Under this construction, I am satisfied that the draft will not put into the ranks any person who is not working with the Union party; already movements are on foot in the secret societies of Indiana, and among the leaders of the disloyalists, to raise money to purchase the exemption of every anti-war man who may be drafted, who can not raise the money himself; and already the boast is made that the Government shall not have one more of their men for the prosecution of this war.

The matter seems to me of so much importance that I have procured Colonel Rose, the Marshal of the State, who is the bearer of this letter, to visit you, and who can more fully inform you of the views and apprehensions entertained here. From a careful reading of the section, I am of the opinion that a construction can be given to it, without violence, by which it is left discretionary with the Secretary of War to determine whether he will accept of any sum in discharge of the drafted man, and that he may legitimately determine that he will not.

In my judgment, it is of the first importance that this construction, if possible, be immediately given to the act, and published to the world, before a current of feeling shall have set in against the Government. In Indiana, substitutes can not be procured for $300 in any number, if at all, *and the rule should be that every drafted man should be required to serve unless he shall actually produce his substitute.*

I pray you to give this subject your immediate consideration.

But the commutation system was retained for the time being, not withstanding the repeated declarations of General Fry himself, at the head of the Provost Marshal's Bureau, that the measure was impolitic and detrimental to the best interests of the service.

THE DRAFT

On the first of February, 1864, the Governor—who had frequently appealed in person to the authorities at Washington for a repeal or suspension of the $300 clause of the enrollment act—addressed the following characteristic letter to the Provost Marshal General:

STATE OF INDIANA, EXECUTIVE DEPARTMENT,
INDIANAPOLIS, February 1, 1864.

COL. JAMES B. FRY,

Provost Marshal General, Washington City:

DEAR SIR: The call of the President for 200,000 additional troops, appeared in the papers this morning, and meets with my hearty approbation.

I have dispatched Adjutant General NOBLE, the bearer of this letter, to Washington, to settle some questions affecting the quota of Indiana under the last call.

I deem it not improper at this time to call the attention of the Government to a subject which is already receiving much discussion in the Western States (I speak more particularly for Indiana), and which may soon attain a magnitude affecting the popularity of the Administration and the strength of the Government. It is generally thought in the West that the great States of New York and Pennsylvania, comprising more than one-third of the population of all the loyal States, are largely delinquent under the last two calls, to which may perhaps be added one or two other Eastern States, and the feeling is becoming quite strong that before any attempt is made by the Government to draft in States that have regularly furnished their quotas, the Government should first collect from those great States their large and long due arrears of troops. The burdens of the war should be made to fall as nearly as possible equally upon all the States; while this is done the people will bear them cheerfully, but if it shall become apparent that some States are avoiding their share of the burdens, which are thus made to fall more heavily upon others, thereby increasing those to be borne by the others, it will occasion great dissatisfaction, and must result disastrously to the Government.

I have said to my New England friends that it was short-sighted policy for the Eastern States to insist upon a Conscript Law, under which the old and wealthy communities can buy out their conscripts, and under which anti-war communities everywhere can furnish money to exempt the members of their party who may be drafted.

Indiana, and other Western States, are suffering a vast drain upon their population, but they will submit to it patriotically and promptly, if all fare alike. But if some States greatly fail to furnish their men and *buy out* under the draft, or piece out their quotas by colored recruits picked up in rebel States, or elsewhere beyond their own limits, it must occasion great dissatisfaction. In less than a week from this time the anti-war press will howl into the ears of our people that Indiana is threatened with a draft on the 10th of March if she fails to furnish her quota under the new call, while it is believed Pennsylvania and New York are delinquent between one and two hundred thousand, and have been for many months. It is stated, upon the authority of Washington correspondents, that they are yet behind upon the call of 1862, for which the ineffectual draft was made last summer, and the conviction will be fastened upon the public mind, that if those States had done their duty, some of the Western States would be relieved from all responsibility under the last call. There may be too much truth in all this to make it easily answered. The people of Indiana will not be content if their actual and furnished quotas are to be counted against the nominal and unfurnished quotas of other States, and as it is a question of actual flesh and blood, they will not be content that the superior *capital* of the older States can be made to count under the Conscript Law against their *soldiers* which they send to the field.

What I have to say on this subject, I say to the Government, and not to the public. I have labored, and shall labor, to keep down all discontents, and I intend, to the extent of my power, that Indiana shall furnish her quota irrespective of what other States may do.

I know your opinion of the Conscript Law, and that the retention of the commutation clause is against your convictions of justice and sound policy. You understand this subject much better than I do; but you will be able to pardon the suggestions of one who has labored diligently in his sphere, and has but one great purpose, which is, the support of the Government and the Suppression of the Rebellion.

I have not kept pace very accurately with Congressional proceedings, but my impression is that the commutation clause will be retained in some form which will substantially defeat the procurement of new troops within the time when they will be most needed by the Government, and could be most useful for the speedy termination of the war.

I dislike to trouble the Secretary of War in the midst of his great labors with my crude suggestions, but if he has time to hear you read this communication I shall be gratified.

I am, very respectfully and sincerely, yours,

O. P. Morton, Governor of Indiana.

THE DRAFT

So greatly and justly was commutation complained of, it was repealed, except as to conscientious exempts, by Congress on the 4th of July 1864, up to which time no draft under the Conscription Act had taken place in Indiana. The privilege of release upon payment of commutation was continued, until the close of the war, to the class of men known as conscientious exempts. There were, however, during the whole war, but 785 persons of this class who paid commutation from this State. This subject led to many peculiar difficulties, which as they did not affect this State are passed over. Before the draft was applied to Indiana, the principle was clearly recognized that a call for men meant SOLDIERS and not *commutation money*, nor an adjustment of quotas, and the number of men called for from Indiana was always promptly supplied. Of the two hundred and eight thousand three hundred and sixty-seven men furnished for United States' service, only seventeen thousand nine hundred and three were drafted, and of these over three thousand were drafted in 1862, when the State had actually a surplus to her credit, but did not get the benefit of it for reasons explained elsewhere in this Report.

The drafted men of 1864 were assigned to veteran regiments, from 100 to 500 going to each. They performed good service (with the exception of a few hundred bounty-jumpers), many of them being with General SHERMAN in his great campaign through Georgia and the Carolinas, and others materially assisting General THOMAS in the operations which resulted in the destruction of the rebel army under HOOD, in Middle Tennessee. The same remark also applies to the men raised under the last call, with the exception of some six hundred drafted men, who were discharged at Indianapolis, after the surrender of Lee— their services not being needed. Besides the great service thus rendered, the depleted ranks of the heroic regiments which had been thinned by the campaigns of more than three years were filled and many officers, who were denied muster in the grades to which they had been promoted —because of the havoc made in their commands by bullets and disease, whereby they were reduced below the minimum strength—now received their hard-earned and well-deserved advancement.

During the pendency of the drafts recruiting was greatly stimulated. The dread of the draft induced citizens to exert themselves in raising local bounties, the temptation of which was too strong to be resisted, and doubtless many hundreds from pecuniary considerations alone were secured for the army; while others dreaded the draft, owing to the supposed reflection upon the patriotism of any one in not rendering service to the country, until forced into the ranks by the Provost Marshal's inexorable "wheel"; and this dread forced into the army many times the number drawn by the draft itself.

Immediately upon the taking effect of the act, in March 1863, "for enrolling and calling out the National Forces," Colonel JAMES B. FRY, Assistant Adjutant General of the Army, was detailed as Provost Marshal General of the United States, and a separate Bureau was established under his charge through which all business under the act was transacted. Colonel FRY, from long experience and by education, was admirably qualified for the important and multifarious duties of Provost Marshal General. The position was surrounded with many difficulties, growing out of the haste and confusion which had previously attended the recruitment of troops, and the complications that arose in settling former credits and adjusting future quotas in the several States. The intercourse between the Governor and Military Authorities of Indiana and Col. FRY, who was afterwards promoted to the rank of Brigadier General, was extensive and intricate, and, it is but justice to say, he always manifested a disposition to conscientiously and justly facilitate the efforts made by the State Authorities to raise troops in Indiana to the full extent of his power. A more faithful or capable officer could hardly have been called to the performance of this responsible trust.

In organizing the Provost Marshal's Bureau, it was found to be indispensable to have an officer in each State to superintend the operations of the District Provost Marshals and other subordinates of the Bureau, and conduct the intercourse necessary with the State authorities. The law created no such office, but the public demands warranted its establishment in each loyal State. The exigencies of the service limited, as a general rule, the selection of officers to fill these important positions to those incapable of active duty; but notwithstanding this, excellent men for the purpose were secured from the regular and volunteer forces. They were assigned to their posts in April, 1863, under special instructions from the Provost Marshal General, and were designated as acting Assistant Provost Marshals General and Superintendents of the Volunteer Recruiting Service. They established their offices and organized them for business upon the same general plan as that of the Provost Marshal General, but on a scale modified to suit their more limited duties.

Colonel CONRAD BAKER, First Indiana Cavalry Volunteers, was assigned to duty under the above arrangement, upon the recommendation of Governor MORTON, by orders dated April 29, 1863, and immediately established his headquarters at Indianapolis and entered actively upon the work committed to him. His fine ability as a lawyer, superior qualifications as a thorough and methodical business man, with his incorruptible integrity and the experience of eighteen months' active service in the field, made his appointment eminently fit and proper, and entirely acceptable to the people of the State. He co-operated most cordially with the State authorities, and, although no draft was ordered while he was in office, so completely had all the preparations been made, little difficulty was afterwards experienced in carrying out the objects of the conscription law.

Colonel BAKER having been nominated for Lieutenant Governor, and his term of service in the army having expired, he was honorably mustered out on the 17th of August, 1864. He was succeeded by Colonel JAMES G. JONES, Forty-second Indiana Infantry Volunteers, formerly Attorney General of the

State, a gentleman of the highest professional and social standing, a faithful and industrious officer, and for some time previous assistant to Colonel BAKER, as Superintendent of the Recruiting Service. Under his supervision the first draft was made under the enrollment act. His term as Colonel of Volunteers expired on the 10th of October, 1864, and he was honorably discharged from the service at that date.

THOMAS G. PITCHER, a native of Indiana, Major of the Sixteenth United States Regular Infantry and Brigadier General of Volunteers, succeeded Colonel JONES. He had been severely wounded in battle and was incapacitated for active service in the field; but his long experience in the regular army and thorough knowledge of the needs of the service, with the experience he had previously gained as Acting Assistant Provost Marshal General for the State of Vermont, qualified him in an eminent degree for the duties which devolved upon him in Indiana. His first step was to cause the enrollment lists to be carefully corrected and revised, and when the call of December 19th, 1864, appeared he was at once ready to proceed with it, and so actively did he co-operate with the Governor and State military authorities in filling the quota of 22,582, only 2,082 men were required to be drafted to fill the call. General PITCHER remained on duty at Indianapolis, after the business of the Provost Marshal's Bureau had been closed, acting as Chief Mustering Officer and Military Commander of the District of Indiana, from the 25th of September, 1865, to the 17th of August, 1866, when he was relieved and promoted to the Colonelcy of the Forty-fourth Regiment V.R.C., U. S. Infantry. Subsequently he was assigned to duty as Superintendent of the West Point Military Academy, which position he still retains [1869].

RECRUITING CONTINUED

RECRUITS FOR THE UNEXPIRED TERM

From the commencement of the rebellion it was the policy of the Government, in which the authorities of this State heartily concurred, to encourage recruiting to fill the depleted ranks of *old* regiments in the field, rather than the formation of *new* organizations. The increased efficiency of the army and greater economy in its management were among the obvious advantages of such a course. In the summer of 1862 this plan was generally advised and persistently impressed upon the public mind. Letters from the War Department, from General McClellan, and other commanding officers, repeatedly and strongly urged that justice to those regiments which had already achieved a noble fame, as well as justice to the cause, demanded that they should be recruited to their maximum. These high authorities supported their appeal in behalf of old organizations by representing that the comfort and safety of the new recruits, their progress and facility in learning their duties, and the steadiness, ease, and success with which they performed the many difficult tasks of the campaign, were all promoted by association, side by side, in the same ranks, with veteran and experienced soldiers.

But however important it might be to fill up existing organizations, it was a work much more difficult of accomplishment than the formation of new ones. Neither commissions nor warrants could be held out as inducements, the offices being already filled, and the chances of promotion for raw recruits among veteran soldiers were, therefore, slight indeed. The fear of ridicule, and an apprehension that the hardest service would be assigned to commands longest in service, had much influence in determining recruits to prefer new regiments, where they could, in all respects, be the equals of their comrades, and share with them in the hope of promotion.

Recruiting parties had been detailed from most of the old organizations, and were zealously engaged in all parts of the State in filling the ranks of their companies. The general prejudice against enlisting in old regiments proved a great obstacle to the success of their labors. This difficulty was, however, finally obviated to some extent, and a fair proportion of recruits diverted to the desired channel, by the understanding that all such would be mustered out with the regiments in which they should enlist, and not be held for three years from the date of enlistment, as would be the case if they joined the organizations then forming.

This impression, though unauthorized by orders from the War Department, unquestionably emanated from the chief mustering officer and his assistants. It was shared by the recruiting officers and by the State authorities. The Adjutant General of the State, in General Orders No. 96, dated October 7th, 1862, stated that drafted men would be permitted to volunteer in any of the old regiments in the field to serve during their "unexpired term," and that "substitutes for drafted men (of 1862) would be permitted to volunteer in the same manner." The same understanding was had in Iowa, Pennsylvania, and doubtless all other loyal States. The plan of veteranizing had not then been adopted, and there was nothing unreasonable in the supposition that upon a dissolution of an organization, at the expiration of its term of service, all the men composing it would be simultaneously relieved from duty. The fact that recruits were not accepted for the general service, but for particular regiments or batteries, doubtless strengthened the impression. Large numbers of recruits entered the service with this understanding, and though the muster rolls which they signed bound them to serve for "three years unless sooner discharged," yet this was explained by the mustering officers as "a mere technical formality," which would not, in any event, be held to invalidate the verbal agreement.

When, upon the expiration of the term of service of their respective regiments, the original members were mustered out, these recruits demanded their discharge. They had fulfilled their contract with the Government, as they understood it, and had a right to expect that the conditions of that contract, as explained by the officers representing the Government at the time of their enlistment and muster-in, should be observed in good faith. Mustering officers refused compliance with this demand, citing their muster-in rolls as the only admissible evidence in such cases. The men thus retained in the service, in violation of the clearly understood terms on their part of the compact, and by virtue of what the Government officers had assured them was, "a mere technical formality," appealed to the State authorities to interfere in their behalf. Such appeals were frequent and from various departments of the army, this class of recruits having been enlisted in numerous commands. They made no complaint of the severity of the service and expressed no disinclination to its duties, but protested against the manner in which they were held, as a violation alike of the principles of common justice and their rights as men.

With a full knowledge of the circumstances, the authorities could not but feel the force of such a protest. Governor MORTON presented the matter to the Secretary of War, and asked that an order might be issued for the discharge of all Indiana soldiers thus retained in the field. The Secretary declined to take any action in the premises on the ground that their muster rolls bound them to serve for three years, and left him no discretion to interfere in their behalf. Further applications to the War Department proved equally unsuccessful, eliciting only a disclaimer of any responsibility for the alleged misunderstanding, and assurance that the interests of the service would not admit of their being discharged prior to the expiration of their terms of service as shown by their muster rolls.

The Governor subsequently addressed a memorial[1] to Congress on this subject clearly setting forth all the facts, and earnestly requesting that body to grant the relief which the War Department had felt compelled to refuse, and stating that in his opinion, such action was alike "demanded by justice, good faith and sound policy." This memorial failed to secure the required action. The subject was, at various times, under discussion in Congress. It was represented that thousands of troops from a number of States were in the same condition, and that whatever relief was extended to any one of them must be extended to all. So large a portion of our effective force could not be spared without serious detriment to the interests of the service, and notwithstanding the persistent efforts of the State authorities, the men in question were retained until the expirations of their terms, or until their services were no longer required.

RECRUITING IN SOUTHERN STATES

The Governors of States, under an act of Congress, approved July 4th, 1864, were authorized to send recruiting agents into any of the States declared to be in rebellion, except Arkansas, Tennessee and Louisiana, to recruit volunteers who were entitled to be credited upon State quotas, as other volunteers were credited.

Indiana derived no benefit whatever from this provision. Governor MORTON was of opinion that the competition which would spring up between the agents of the Northern States, substitute brokers, bounty agents and quota-fillers, would practically render the law a nuisance, rather than a public benefit, and at the same time he believed that the army would

---

[1] Terrell, *Report*, 1, Appendix, Doc. 127, pp. 336-37. This includes a statement from the Indianapolis *Journal*, June 27, 1864, as well as the Governor's memorial.

be much more efficient if each State would fill its quota with actual and bona fide citizens, who owed service to their country and were interested in its honor and preservation. General SHERMAN took the same view of the matter and would not allow any enlistments in his department; nor would he furnish transportation to agents or recruits, or in any way lend his assent to the scheme. In other departments of the army, however—wherever agents could receive countenance and find protection—many of the States (not including Indiana) made vigorous efforts to enlist men, white and colored, for their quotas and offered large bounties, ranging from $100 to $1,000 per man. The most disgraceful means were resorted to by substitute brokers to obtain these credits, and some of the State agents in their zeal to relieve their citizens from the rigor of the draft, are reported to have acted in a manner highly discreditable. The effect of this competition and strife was seriously felt in the army and was altogether detrimental to the best interests of the service. Many of the military commanders in the field saw this, and believed that the legislation that authorized this mode of recruiting was impolitic and unwise, and they gave it that favor only which the law obliged them to. The old veterans, who had gone into the war at the outbreak, without bounties, even felt less sympathy with the movement than did the military commanders; for they were not blind to the fact that it was not patriotism alone that prompted these extraordinary efforts and liberal offers of money; on the contrary, they felt that a most unjust discrimination was made between old and new recruits—the first class being the real heroes of the war, and the latter drawn in almost at the last hour by the talismanic power of money. They felt, too, that if States did not fill their quotas by volunteering, the draft should be promptly resorted to and vigorously enforced. Doubtless many, who received large bounties, entered the service from entirely patriotic motives, but the fact still remains the same, that the old soldiers, from their standpoint, failed to see or appreciate any patriotism in recruits who joined the army at so late a day and were so lavishly paid for it.

Without calling into question the patriotic efforts and motives of the authorities or people of any other State, it is a gratification to be able to say that Indiana relied solely and only upon her own citizens to fill all her quotas, and that through the influence and energy of Governor MORTON, she more than fulfilled all her obligations to the Government.

GOVERNMENT BOUNTIES

RATES OF BOUNTIES

The bounties paid by the United States during the war[1] commenced with the act of Congress approved July 22d, 1861, which authorized the payment of one hundred dollars to volunteers enlisting for three years.

No other bounty was offered until June 25th, 1863, at which date General Orders No. 191, from the Adjutant General's office, War Department, authorized the payment of four hundred dollars in installments to all veterans re-enlisting for three years or the war. General Orders No. 305, of September 11th, and No. 324, of September 28th, 1863, continued the payment of this bounty of four hundred dollars until April 1st, 1864.

On the 24th of October, 1863, a circular letter from the office of the Provost Marshal General, authorized the payment of a bounty of three hundred dollars to new recruits enlisting in old organizations, to be paid in installments in accordance with conditions named in the circular. This bounty was continued until April 1st, 1864.

By an order from the Adjutant General's office, War Department, dated December 24th, 1863, the payment of three hundred dollars bounty to new recruits enlisting in any three years' organization in service or in process of formation, was authorized, which bounty continued to be paid until April 1st, 1864.

---

[1] A table showing the bounties paid by the United States government—the amount, the authority under which they were paid, to whom paid, and periods of payments—is given in Terrell, *Report,* 1, Appendix, Doc. 13:109-10.

Between March 31st, 1864, and July 19th, of the same year, the only bounty paid by Government was the one hundred dollars authorized by the act of July 22d, 1861.

On the 19th of July, 1864, the Provost Marshal General issued Circular No. 27, which authorized the payment of bounty as follows, based upon the act approved July 4th, 1864:

To recruits enlisting for one year $100
To recruits enlisting for two years 200
To recruits enlisting for three years 300

General Order No. 287, of November 28th, 1864, authorized the payment of a special bounty of three hundred dollars from the draft and substitute fund, to men enlisting in the First Army Corps, in addition to the bounty authorized by Circular No. 27 of July 19th, 1864, from the Provost Marshal General's office, with this exception—the bounty authorized by Circular No. 27, of July 19th, 1864, was the only bounty paid by the United States from the date of that circular to the end of the war.

The one hundred dollars bounty was paid to drafted men or their substitutes, until the passage of the act approved July 4th, 1864, rescinded all authority for the payment of such bounty.

On the 15th of June, 1865, General Orders No. 115 from the Adjutant General's office, War Department, discontinued the payment of bounty to recruits for the military service of the United States, from and after July 1st, 1865.

It will be seen by the foregoing that new recruits, enlisted prior to October 24th, 1863, for three years, received but one hundred dollars, while those enlisted for the same period subsequent to that date received three hundred dollars. This great disparity, though necessitated by the exigencies and demands of the service, was regarded as an act of injustice, justifiable only as a temporary expedient to be rectified by Congress at the earliest practicable day.

GOVERNMENT BOUNTIES

Immediately upon the close of the war, efforts were made in all parts of the country to secure the passage of an act for the equalization of bounties. At the special session of the Legislature, in 1865, a joint resolution was adopted instructing our Senators and requesting our Representatives in Congress to do all in their power to secure the passage of such a law.[2]

The act of Congress approved July 28th, 1866, though leaving much to be desired, was an effort in the right direction. By this act all who enlisted after the 19th day of April, 1861, and have received or are entitled to receive, a bounty of one hundred dollars, and no more, are entitled, if discharged by reason of the expiration of their term of enlistment, or on account of wounds received in the line of duty, to one hundred dollars additional bounty. If they have been discharged for other causes they are entitled to an additional bounty of fifty dollars only, provided they served not less than two of their three years' enlistment.

Men who enlisted after the 19th day of April, 1861, for two years, and have received or are entitled to receive, a bounty of one hundred dollars and no more, if discharged by reason of the causes above named, are entitled to fifty dollars additional bounty.

BOUNTY TO COLORED TROOPS

A letter from the War Department to Major General B. F. BUTLER, dated November 29th, 1863, and a similar letter to Major General Q. A. GILMORE, under date of December 22d, 1863, authorized the payment of a bounty not exceeding ten dollars per man for colored troops.

By an act of Congress approved June 15th, 1864, and supplemental acts approved June 15th, 1866, and July 26th, 1866, respectively, persons of color who have been enlisted and

---

[2] This resolution is given in *ibid.*, 1, Appendix, Doc. 68:267, and in *Laws of Indiana*, sp. sess., 1865, p. 207.

mustered into the military service of the United States, have received or are entitled to receive, bounty as follows:

Those enlisted prior to October 24th, 1863 ....$100
Those enlisted into new regiments between
    October 24th and Dec. 24th, 1863 100
Those enlisted from Oct. 25th, 1863, to March 31st, 1864,
    into old regiments 300
Those enlisted from Dec. 25th, 1863, to March 31st, 1864,
    into new regiments 300
Those enlisted from April 1st, 1864, to June 14th, 1864 100

All colored soldiers who enlisted under the call of October 17th, 1863, and who were enrolled and liable to draft in the State where they enlisted, were granted bounty as follows:

Those enlisted into colored regiments between October 17th,
    1863, and October 24th, 1863 ....$100
Those enlisted into old colored regiments between October 24th,
    1863, and April 1st, 1864 300
Those enlisted into new colored regiments between December 24th,
    1863, and April 1st, 1864 300

All colored soldiers who enlisted after July 18th, 1864, for one, two or three years, were allowed a bounty of one hundred, two hundred or three hundred dollars, respectively, whether free men or slaves.

All enlisted between July 4th and July 18th, 1864, have received or are entitled to receive, one hundred dollars bounty.

The act of Congress approved July 28th, 1866, granting additional bounty to certain classes of volunteers, makes no discrimination as to color.

LOCAL BOUNTIES

But little difficulty was experienced during the first two years of the war in promptly filling all calls made upon this State for troops. Local bounties were not then required to stimulate volunteering, and although in some localities such bounties were paid, the main purpose was to benefit the families of volunteers. This liberality was regarded as a "duty offering" from those who remained at home, to their neighbors who sacrificed peaceful pursuits and pecuniary interests in obedience to the call of their country, rather than as a necessary means of filling up the army.

At the beginning of the year 1863 the State had furnished volunteers largely in excess of her quotas under all calls, but the continuous drain upon her industrial resources soon began to be perceptibly felt, and from the calls of that year the pressure upon the people in many districts having large quotas to fill became so great as to demand that the local authorities should devise some means of relief. Many of the treasuries of counties, cities and towns were empty, or had funds sufficient only for ordinary expenditures and the means of paying bounties could therefore only be obtained by loans. The necessity of procuring money for this purpose was most imperative from the fact that no provision of law required volunteers to be credited to the townships and counties in which they held their legal residence. Each could credit himself in accordance with his interest or preference, and would naturally prefer the township paying the highest bounty, so that a locality offering no pecuniary inducement would be likely to be stripped of its able-bodied men without making any progress in the work of filling its quota and thus become every day less prepared for future calls. To overcome these difficulties the local authorities issued bonds, which were either sold in large sums or paid out as cash to volunteers. In this way districts were enabled to fill their quotas and to avert the dreaded conscription.

The validity of these bonds was doubted by many and the belief very generally prevailed that there was no legal authority for their issue. Bankers and brokers regarded them with suspicion and if prevailed upon to cash them at all, did so at a heavy discount. Every one felt or feared that the courts, if the matter were brought before them would render a decision averse to their validity. But as the issue of the bonds was clearly a duty and necessity, the people of the various localities interested relied upon the Legislature to pass an act legalizing the action of the local authorities, making the bonds binding according to their terms and effect. They were therefore issued and disposed of to a large amount, and upon the meeting of the Legislature in regular session in January, 1865, the subject was brought before it and an act passed legalizing all such bonds and providing for the levy and assessment of taxes for their redemption. The act also prohibited the payment of local bounty under any call that might subsequently be made.[3]

Shortly after the passage of this act citizens in various parts of the State instituted legal proceedings to test the question of its constitutionality. Several decisions of circuit courts affirmed the validity of the law, and the subject finally received a quietus in a decision of the Supreme Court at the November term of 1865, which declared that the act is not in conflict with the law or authority of the United States and is valid.

The aggregate amount expended for local bounties in this State during the war reached the enormous sum of $15,492,876.04, varying in the several counties from $2,719.63, the smallest paid by Starke, to $1,377,199.14, the largest paid by Marion County.[4]

The experience of the country during the late war has elicited much discussion as to the comparative advantages of the different means resorted to for raising troops and many of the best authorities have expressed opinions condemnatory of any plan of recruitment based upon the local bounty system. The exorbitant bounty paid in *advance* by local authorities proved a fruitful source of evil in the inducement thus offered for desertion or "bounty jumping." The Government bounty on the contrary being paid in installments at the expiration of specified periods from the date of enlistment, had a tendency

[3] The text of the act is in Terrell, *Report,* 1, Appendix, Doc. 63:262-63. See also *Laws of Indiana,* 1865, pp. 126-28.

[4] See table showing amounts expended for local bounties by township and county in Terrell, *Report,* 1, Appendix, Doc. 8:75-88.

not only to obtain recruits, but to keep them in the service. Local bounty being paid on enlistment, served to *fill quotas* much more effectually than it filled the depleted ranks of our armies. Local authorities seemed to be aiming at the accomplishment of but one subject—to avoid the draft. They soon learned that a given sum thus paid in advance would fill their quotas much more rapidly than a larger amount to be paid in installments, conditioned upon the length of time the recruit should continue in the service. They did not make it their business to inquire into the probable results of such a course, nor stop to consider that they were, virtually, offering a premium for desertion. The people, with whose money they were operating, relied upon them to relieve their districts from the draft. If they could secure the recruits, and have them accepted and credited on their quotas, their interest ceased. It was not their business to keep their recruits in the service. That duty devolved on the Government.

The local bounty system was no sooner fairly inaugurated than an active competition commenced between different localities. The offer of large bounties in some districts induced the enrolled men of other districts, which were unable to offer corresponding inducements, to enlist on the quotas of their more wealthy competitors, who would thus escape the draft, while districts that had, in this manner, been stripped of their able-bodied men to such an extent perhaps that not more than enough were left to take care of the farms and carry on the most necessary business, would be obliged to submit to the still further exhaustion of the draft. The peculiar hardship and injustice resulting from such competition will be apparent when it is remembered that quotas were based on enrollment. If one township secured to its credit the enrolled men of another township, the latter was deprived of the means of filling its quota, while the Government was defrauded of the men called for from the former to the extent that it had drawn upon the legitimate resources of other districts.

The people of the localities where the largest bounties were paid regarded their munificent expenditure of money as a highly commendable exhibition of patriotism. Some of its practical effects were, however, directly the reverse of what a patriot would have desired. It relieved many of their own men from the performance of their just share of military duty, and created deficits in the quotas of less fortunate localities.

Inequality in bounties was another evil growing out of the system, and was productive of much discontent and ill-feeling among the troops in the field. The amount of money required to procure a given number of recruits increased with each succeeding call until, in some sections of the State, the local authorities paid a local bounty of five hundred dollars per man.[5] And this was low compared with rates prevailing in the middle and eastern States, in some of which one thousand dollars was not considered exorbitant. The great disparity of benefits received was often strikingly illustrated by different portions of the same command. Men who enlisted at the first call, influenced only by patriotic impulses, and with no expectation of bounty, were serving side by side with those who had joined them late in the war, enriched by their tardiness in responding to the call of a common duty. There was some excuse for murmuring when the veterans saw these men coming to the field at the eleventh hour, and reflected that these late recruits had enjoyed years of unprecedented opportunities for the successful prosecution of business, from which they had only been tempted at last, when the war was apparently over, by the influence of money. Veterans felt little inclination to fraternize with their new associates, and were often disposed to indulge in bitter reflections and sarcastic comments.

The impression prevalent throughout the North, as each successive call for troops was issued, that *that* call would be the last, tended greatly to increase the lavish expenditure of

[5] The rate in 1863 ranged from $10 to $100; in 1864 and 1865 from $100 to $500. [Terrell]

money in the shape of local bounties. Thus, in 1864, when the President issued his call of July 18th for five hundred thousand men, few, if any, supposed there would be occasion for another levy. "Let us promptly fill our quotas at whatever cost," was the general sentiment, "for our armies re-enforced by five hundred thousand men, will be able to give the finishing blow to the rebellion." Enormous amounts were raised and the most energetic means employed to secure recruits. But the terms of the call provided for the reduction of the number of men specified by giving *credits* to States for men previously furnished in excess of quotas, and for all men, not previously credited, who had enlisted in the naval service between April 19, 1861, and February 24th, 1864, and when the requirements of the call had been literally complied with, it was found to have produced but 240,000 men. A deficiency of 40,000 men was occasioned by the operations of the enemy in certain States, rendering it impracticable for them to furnish their full quotas. But the main portion of this astounding deficiency, amounting to 220,000 men, was occasioned by *credits* secured for naval recruits, re-enlisted veterans and men previously furnished in excess of quotas.[6] While it is true that in most districts the people were honestly endeavoring to reinforce the army, and that the grand success which was attained was mainly due to the efforts of the State officials, zealous citizens and efficient committees, it is equally certain that many were engaged in "filling quotas" without any scruples as to the means employed. Brokers drove a thriving business in the procurement and sale of "credits," which were as valuable to townships, whose only object was to fill their quotas, as an equal number of *bona fide* enlistments. It is believed that most of the credits obtained in this State for men not actually furnished at the time the credits were made, were obtained by legitimate means in accordance with existing laws

[6] See Seventh Call for Troops, December 19, 1864, in Terrell, *Report*, 1, Appendix, Doc. 4:52.

and orders, and for men who had entered the service as re-enlisted veterans or naval recruits.

This vast discrepancy between the credits secured by the States and the men obtained by the Government necessitated the issue of a supplementary call for three hundred thousand men, on the 19th of December, 1864. Under this call the most extravagant rates of bounty prevailed. The desire to escape the draft was so great that in many localities all other considerations were forgotten. The necessity for able-bodied men to reinforce the army was overlooked by the masses, and every device was employed to get men enlisted and credited, many of whom were entirely unfit for the service, and who, if accepted, had to be discharged without performing any duty, thus entailing enormous local taxation and a heavy expense upon the Government without contributing to the strength of the army.

But however great the objections to the local bounty system, however numerous the avenues it opened to the practice of frauds, it was unquestionably the only means of stimulating recruiting and the only possible way of avoiding a draft, which in communities most firm in their support of the Government was regarded as a reproach upon their patriotism; and although many of our leading military men, those whose positions are calculated to give great weight to their expressed opinions, prefer conscription to any other means of raising armies, it is certain that their views will never become the established opinion of the people at large. If the country should again become involved in war, the same prejudice against involuntary service would be found to exist, and the different States would prefer to raise their quotas of troops by volunteering, keeping conscription in reserve as a last resort.

The opinion of our best men from experience and observation is that to avoid the ruinous effects of competition between different localities, the bounty should be uniform throughout the State, and should, therefore, be regulated by State legislation. This uniform system should be put in operation at the commencement of the war, or upon the first call for troops, before any section shall have furnished any portion of its quota. All parts of the State would then have an equal interest in and derive equal benefit from it, and there would be no injustice in levying a State tax for the payment of the bounty or the redemption of State bonds issued to raise funds for that purpose. In this view of the matter I most earnestly concur.

The bounty should be paid to the volunteer in person by the proper State officers, without the interference of middlemen or brokers, and any agreement by a volunteer with any broker or agent for the payment to him of any part of the money so received should be declared void. The most stringent provisions should be devised to protect recruits from the rapacity of this class of men, whose operations constitute one of the most disgraceful chapters in the history of the late war. Thus regulated by general legislation, the burdens equally divided and the benefits shared alike by the people of all parts of the State, it is believed that the local bounty system would be the best possible incentive to volunteer enlistments.

BOUNTY JUMPING

In the summer and autumn of 1864, many townships in this State escaped the impending draft by offering large local bounties for volunteers to fill their respective quotas. Other townships, where the draft had been made, offered still larger bounties for substitutes to take the places of those whose names had been drawn, but who had not yet been required to report at the designated rendezvous for duty. Liberal bounties were also offered by the Government, a considerable installment of which, together with one month's pay, was paid on the muster of a recruit.

This unprecedented liberality of the Government and local authorities, while it served its intended purpose by promoting *bona fide enlistments,* also opened the way for a vast amount of swindling on the part of individual operators, as well as for more extensive and systematized fraud of organized conspirators.

Hordes of the worst class of men from every country in Europe and the British American provinces, deserters from the rebel army, thieves, pickpockets, and "roughs," mainly from our large cities, thronged our recruiting stations, with a well assumed appearance of patriotic ardor. They were regularly enlisted and mustered in, received their bounties, advance pay and clothing. In a few hours their uniforms would be laid aside, and, donning citizen's dress, they would present themselves to another recruiting officer, and again go through the process of enlistment, muster, and pay, under other names. Thus they would go from city to city, in many instances enlisting several times in the same locality, till their ingenuity in devising disguises would become exhausted, and motives of personal safety, or the hope of a more profitable field of operation elsewhere, would induce them to leave the State.

Organized gangs of these men, employing various agencies to avoid detection, and perhaps occasionally aided by the complicity of recruiting officers, would, in the eye of the law, "fill the quotas" of townships, while the muster rolls of Provost Marshals exhibited only a lot of fictitious and assumed names, which, when called at the rendezvous, met with no response. One officer reported three hundred and eighty-nine enlistments, of which number more than two hundred had deserted almost immediately on receiving their bounties. This was an exceptional case, but it was too nearly paralleled by the returns and muster rolls of many of our Congressional Districts.

It is not supposed that Indiana afforded special facilities for the successful prosecution of this infamous business, nor is it believed that our State was visited by so great a number of this class of "recruits" as other States where bounty money was more lavishly disbursed. But that they came here in immense numbers is an established fact, and it is not less certain that several thousand names on our muster rolls were but the various *aliases* of these scoundrels, some of whom succeeded in enlisting as many as twenty times, and, of course, secured that number of bounties, which would amount to about eight thousand dollars net gain.

Thieves of every class found in the bounty-jumping business agreeable employment. The danger of detection and punishment was less than in their usual criminal pursuits, while the proceeds of their operations required no after process to convert them into available funds.

The business of substitute brokerage and filling the quotas of delinquent districts on contracts was extensively and successfully prosecuted. Many of the parties who engaged in this business amassed considerable fortunes in a few weeks. Some of them, doubtless, owed their astonishing success to complicity with the bounty-jumpers. Gross neglect of duty on the part of some recruiting officers, if not collusion and division of spoils between them and their absconding recruits, greatly facilitated the business and enhanced the difficulties attending its suppression.

The most stringent measures were adopted to arrest an evil which not only involved the squandering of vast sums of money on the worst species of criminals, and the consequent encouragement of a most heinous crime, but threatened the indefinite protraction of the war and jeopardized the ultimate success of the Union cause by filling regimental rolls with a formidable array of names which represented no corresponding force and were as useless for all practical purposes as if they had been copied from obsolete directories.

Colonel A. J. WARNER, Seventeenth Regiment V. R. C., commanding the Post of Indianapolis, and the officers and men of his command, applied themselves in the most energetic and determined manner to the work of detecting and arresting this class of deserters.[7] A large prison was prepared for their reception and a strong guard placed about it. Numerous

---

[7] See General Warner's report to Adjutant General Terrell, October 25, 1866, in Terrell, *Report,* 1, Appendix, Doc. 84:286-87.

squads were collected, manacled together and sent to different commands in the field where they generally embraced the first opportunity of deserting again, often joining rebel guerrilla bands, thus affording another illustration of the well known fact that the effective force of our army was little increased by the unpenitentiaried convicts and scoundrels who were so freely enlisted. Men, who had characters and self-respect to maintain, did the fighting and won the victories.

A number of the worst bounty-jumpers were tried by court martial, and three who were convicted of repeated desertions were publicly shot on the parade grounds near Camp Morton. The severe measures adopted ultimately suppressed the evil in this State by convincing those engaged in the business that the prospective gains were not commensurate with the inevitable risks.

SPECIAL PREMIUMS FOR RECRUITS

To stimulate the recruitment of volunteers, and to enable recruiting officers to defray their extraordinary and necessary expenses while engaged upon recruiting duty, the General Government, through the Provost Marshal General (circular of October 24th, 1863) authorized the payment of premiums from the draft and substitute fund for the presentation of accepted recruits for organizations whose terms would expire in 1864 and 1865, as follows:

For a "veteran" recruit $25.00
For a "raw" recruit 15.00

Colonel CONRAD BAKER, Act. Assistant Provost Marshal General for this State, in the exercise of the discretion allowed by instructions from the Provost Marshal General, did not offer or pay any premiums under the above mentioned authority up to the 16th of November, 1863, when it was agreed between Colonel BAKER and Governor MORTON, that the best and most equitable policy would be for the Governor to offer a premium of $6 for each accepted recruit for either new or old organizations, payable to the recruiting officer, the understanding being that the premiums authorized by the Provost Marshal General should be appropriated to the payment of said $6 premiums. In this way, it was thought a sum could be derived from the premiums authorized to be paid for recruits for old organizations, sufficient to pay the reduced premiums for all organizations. The premium being a *reward* to the recruiting officer and not to the soldier, it was apparent that the object in view, *to raise men,* would be more certainly accomplished if no distinctions were made. It must be borne in mind that the regulations of the Provost Marshal General did not authorize anything to be paid for enlisting men for the new regiments. The plan of the Governor and Acting Assistant Provost Marshal General was, therefore, intended to equalize the premiums so that all who were engaged in recruiting would share alike. While it was of the highest importance that the ranks of the *old* organizations should be filled, it was soon demonstrated that this end could not be fully accomplished by offering a special premium to recruiting officers. The men who were willing to volunteer generally preferred new regiments to old ones, and the Government was in no situation to refuse to accept them; in fact, while every effort was being made to fill up the old organizations, calls were made for new ones, and recruiting officers were as much in need of funds to pay their expenses and as compensation for their trouble in the one case as in the other.

The plan to reduce the premiums to the uniform sum of $6, and *apply it to all* was accordingly proposed to the Provost Marshal General and assented to by that officer. On the 16th of November, 1863, the Governor issued a circular to the following purport: All duly appointed recruiting officers for the new Indiana regiments (including colored troops) and all noncommissioned officers and privates duly detailed to recruit for old Indiana regiments and batteries—and none others—were entitled to a special premium of $6, for each man enlisted by them and duly accepted and mustered into the military service of the United States. The money was paid by the Governor from State funds in his hands, upon duplicate rolls carefully made up, properly receipted by the parties entitled to the premiums, and certified by the mustering and other officers having charge of the recruiting service.

The payment of the premiums was at first limited to the 20th of December, 1863, but the quota not being filled by that time, payment was extended and made applicable to the same class of recruits up to the 5th of February, 1864, when Colonel BAKER, Acting Assistant Provost Marshal General, received positive orders to offer to citizens and enlisted men a reward or premium of $25 for each veteran recruit, and $15 for each new recruit presented and accepted for *old* organizations only.

At this time there had been enlisted for *old* regiments and batteries under the first arrangement, 3,241 "raw" recruits and 45 "veteran" recruits, the premiums for the same at $15 and $25 each, amounting to the sum of $49,740. The Governor had also, through recruiting officers and agents appointed by him, recruited a much larger number of men for *new* organizations, and had paid for all alike the premium of $6. The plan worked well and proved to be a most effective means of recruiting.

After the 5th of February, the Governor continued to pay $6 for each recruit presented, accepted and mustered into new regiments; between that date and the 1st of May, 1864, premiums for recruits for old organizations were paid through the Provost Marshal General's Department at the advanced rate, as aforesaid. The wisdom of the Governor's course in continuing the payment of the $6 premium was manifested in the number of recruits raised for the new regiments—no less than 8,505 recruits having been obtained for them under this plan. Upon final adjustment of the matter, it was ascertained that 11,791 recruits had been raised—the premiums paid by the Governor for the same amounting to $79,746 [$70,746]. Of this amount, the United States through the disbursing officer at Indianapolis, refunded on the 8th of September, 1864, the

GOVERNMENT BOUNTIES

sum of $49,704 [$49,740].[8] Leaving still due the State $20,006 [$21,006], for which reimbursement is claimed from the United States.

With the above exception, no premiums or bounties were offered or paid by the State. Local bounties (paid by counties, townships and cities) were an important inducement in recruiting volunteers, as has been fully described in a separate article on that subject in another part of this volume.

[8] See Terrell's *Communication . . . to the General Assembly, Extra Session, 1865,* p. 13, for the corrected figures.

RECRUITING FOR THE REGULAR ARMY FROM THE VOLUNTEER FORCES.

Notwithstanding the very large number of recruits raised for the regular army in this State, during the years 1861-62, and the encouragement given by the State authorities to this branch of the recruiting service, the War Department, on the 9th of October, 1862, undertook to complete all regular army organizations by enlisting the required number from the volunteers. There was no law for this remarkable proceeding, and no reason for it except that it was a short and easy way of accomplishing the end for which a host of regular officers had for months and months been detached at recruiting stations in all the principal cities and towns in the northern States. The regular army not being able to fill its own ranks, was to be allowed to deplete or break down the ranks of the volunteers. Such a plan was outrageous and unjust to the States, to the volunteer officers, and to the men whose transfer it was thus sought to obtain. Its tendency was to undo all that had been done; to destroy the efforts and influence of the Governors; humble the pride of the States in their troops, and render necessary the muster-out or consolidation of all the skeleton organizations that might be left after the depleting process had performed its work. While the order only authorized the enlistment of volunteers, with their own consent—for either three years or for the remaining portion of the period of three years which they might have to serve, at their option—no leave to recruit was asked or required of regimental or company commanders, but the regular army recruiting officers were permitted, no matter where the volunteers were serving, or however important their duties might be—even when in face

RECRUITING FOR THE REGULAR ARMY   93

of the enemy—to enlist all who were dissatisfied with their officers or with the volunteer service, without regard to consequences. As an inducement, promotion to commissions in the regular army was held out by the order. The recruiting officers, however, were not at all particular about the kind of promises they made, or whether they were covered by the order or not; furloughs were promised for thirty days, and it was given out in many cases that infantry volunteers would be allowed to enter the regular cavalry or artillery; that they would remain in northern cities, or at posts on recruiting or guard duty, free from the deprivations and dangers incident to the field; that increased pay and allowance would be given, and especially that the pay would be more regular and certain, the clothing and subsistence of better quality and issued in larger quantities than to volunteers.

The demoralizing effect of these attempts upon the gallant troops then in service may be easily imagined. Complaints came pouring in from all the officers whose commands were endangered by these "attacks from the regulars," and the Governor was earnestly entreated to use all his influence to cause the obnoxious order to be rescinded. Fully impressed with the danger, discontent and demoralization, as well as the outrageous injustice that would grow out of this ill-advised and distasteful system of recruiting, he sent the following protest to the Secretary of War:

EXECUTIVE DEPARTMENT OF INDIANA,
INDIANAPOLIS, October 29, 1862.

Hon. E. M. STANTON, *Secretary of War, Washington City:*

SIR: The late order of the War Department, allowing officers of the regular army to recruit from volunteer regiments, is becoming a serious inconvenience, and is a great embarrassment to officers of the volunteer corps who have spent considerable time and money in raising their regiments, and have labored hard to enforce discipline and make them efficient.

I feel a deep interest in the prosperity, welfare and success of Indiana regiments, and do not desire to see them unnecessarily embarrassed and deprived of men to whose services they are justly entitled by every right of justice and law.

Many men are dissatisfied with the service, and if you attempt to compel them to do their duty, they threaten to re-enlist in the regular army, and my officers are constantly appealing to me to call your attention to these facts, and request that the order be rescinded. No other one thing is creating so pernicious an influence on the army as this, and I do trust that you will find it consistent to set the order aside.

By order of the Governor: W. R. HOLLOWAY, *Private Secretary*.

Attempts to recruit from the volunteers were not confined alone to regiments in the field. Recruiting officers swarmed around post hospitals, and by brilliant promises and false representations procured many convalescents and hospital attendants, of the volunteers, to enlist as regulars. In November, 1862, when the camps of rendezvous at Indianapolis contained a large number of volunteers who were rapidly being organized for the field, a heavy onslaught was made by the regulars to obtain recruits. The order of the War Department being in full force, its execution could not be resisted, but the Governor determined it should not be enforced in his camps by means of a wilful misrepresentation of facts. He therefore addressed the following communication to the Superintendent of the United States Recruiting Service for Indiana:

EXECUTIVE DEPARTMENT OF INDIANA,

INDIANAPOLIS, November 25th, 1862.

Colonel H. B. CARRINGTON, *Superintendent United States Recruiting Service for Indiana:*

SIR—The practice of allowing United States recruiting officers to recruit from volunteer regiments, now about ready to take the field, is demoralizing and detrimental to the public service in the highest degree. I most earnestly protest against it. It is the invariable rule of these officers, I am informed, to hold out false inducements and misrepresent facts to secure recruits. In some instances volunteers who have left their regiments and joined regular companies have, after discovering the frauds practiced upon them, returned and desired to be reinstated in their original places with the volunteers.

RECRUITING FOR THE REGULAR ARMY

I regard the whole matter as a great outrage, and if continued it will, I fear, greatly retard the movement of troops now under marching orders. Your immediate consideration will greatly oblige,

Very respectfully, your obedient servant,

O. P. MORTON, Governor of Indiana.

The false impressions which had been, or were attempted to be, made were removed from the minds of those upon whom they were intended to operate by the prompt publication of the following announcement:

HEADQUARTERS GENERAL RECRUITING SERVICE,

INDIANAPOLIS, IND., November 25th, 1862.

Being assured that improper representations have been made to induce enlisted volunteers to change to the regular service, and that much dissatisfaction prevails in regiments on the eve of their departure for the field, on account thereof the following statement will correct such misrepresentations as have been reported:

1st. The *bounties* are the *same*. The twenty-five dollar bounty and advance pay is only paid in the regular service to new recruits, or volunteers, who have not already drawn it. The premium is for enlisting new recruits only.

2d. The *pay* is the *same,* and the Government designs to pay each with equal promptness.

3d. The regular soldier need expect no *winter of ease* in northern cities, but to share the exposure of the field with the volunteer.

4th. The promise of "thirty day furloughs" is illegal, and could not have been made by any person with the approval of any army officer.

Regulars and volunteers are in one common cause. The order of the War Department offers ambitious and efficient soldiers in the volunteer service the opportunity to strive for the promotions of the regular service, and was not designed to furnish insubordinate soldiers an outlet of escape from penalties incurred, or as a vent to ill-will against officers who but did their duty.

It is especially important, just now, that the ranks of the battalions about to march should be full; and if the volunteers desire to change their regiment, it is their duty to their officers, and the service, that they declare their wishes forthwith, or be content to remain with their old comrades and the officers who have recruited their companies.

HENRY B. CARRINGTON,

Colonel 18th Infantry, U. S. A., Chief Mustering Officer, Indiana.

Finally, on the 10th of February, 1863, the War Department itself became satisfied that the regular army ought not to be sustained by this plan of recruiting, the progress of the war having made the fact plain that if the rebellion was ever put down it must be done by the gallantry and overwhelming numbers of the volunteer soldiery of the country. All orders authorizing the enlistment of volunteers in the regular army were, therefore, rescinded.

HANCOCK'S FIRST ARMY CORPS

On the 28th of November, 1864, an order was issued by the War Department for raising and organizing twenty thousand infantry under command of Major General WINFIELD S. HANCOCK, U. S. A., to be enlisted for not less than one year, to be designated the First Army Corps, and to be completed in the District of Columbia within one month from the 1st day of December. The privates were to consist only of able-bodied veterans who had served honorably, not less than two years, and therefore not subject to the draft; the officers to be commissioned by the President from such as had honorably served not less than two years. The details accompanying the order required each recruit to be first examined by the Surgeon of the Board of Enrollment, then to present himself to any United States District Provost Marshal, who, if the applicant appeared to be qualified, would furnish a free transportation pass to Washington, where the recruit would be duly enlisted and mustered into service. Each recruit was entitled to a special bounty of $300 at the time of muster in; also the regular government bounty payable in installments, as allowed to other troops, and was required to be credited to the district in which he resided, which of course would entitle him to such local bounty as the locality to which he was credited was paying at the time.

These orders were forwarded to Governor MORTON on the 5th of December, and his co-operation and influence requested in recruiting veterans for the Corps.

RECRUITING FOR THE REGULAR ARMY

It seems a little strange, with all the experience gained by the War Department in raising enormous armies during the three first years of the war, such an embarrassing requirement should have been made, in the order already described, as compelled the recruit to take all the trouble upon himself of being examined by a medical officer and the Provost Marshal, and then to go all the way to Washington at his own expense, except transportation, before he could be enlisted and mustered —with the possible chance, after all, that he might be finally rejected. The veterans, whom it was desired to recruit, did not all live at the same places where the Provost Marshals' offices were located. This involved travel, and perhaps detention at headquarters, for a day or two, to be examined, and all this at the soldier's own expense. Then should he be accepted upon arrival at Washington, his local bounty would remain unadjusted, and he would be in danger of being cheated out of it, or at least charged heavily to get it, besides (it is a supposable case), should the cars fly the track and maim him while *en route* to the "District of Columbia," it is not likely that he would then be received into the service at all, or that the Government would pay him a pension, or that he could even get a "free transportation pass" back to his home. Soldiers of two years' service were not, as a general rule, either lacking in shrewdness or indifferent to their own interests. At the time the effort was made to raise the Corps, it will be remembered that there was no difficulty anywhere in finding opportunities to enlist in new or old regiments. The only difference was in the special bounty offered by the Corps and this in most cases was doubtless overbalanced by the extra trouble involved, and the preference most recruits had for new regiments, where the chances of promotion, especially to veterans, were better, and where they would be associated with friends and acquaintances of their old neighborhoods. It will thus be seen that the proposed plan was about as objectionable and embarrassing as it could well have been made.

The objections above mentioned were apparent to the Governor as soon as he read the order, but he very cheerfully consented to do what he could to encourage recruiting under the proposed plan. At the same time he suggested his doubts to the Secretary of War, of the success of the movement, and offered to raise two regiments of veterans for the Corps, if permitted to recruit and organize them in the same way other regiments were recruited in this State. This offer was rejected. The time for enlisting the Corps was extended, and about the middle of February, 1865, the order was so modified as to permit recruits to be mustered at Indianapolis before being forwarded to Washington. Recruiting continued in an unsuccessful way until the surrender of LEE. The reports on file in this [the Adjutant General's] office show that only one hundred and sixty-eight men were raised for the Corps in this State.

COLORED TROOPS

When the determination was first announced by the Government to organize colored troops (May, 1863), the state of public feeling in the West was not altogether favorable to the employment of that class of persons as soldiers. A number of officers in Indiana regiments had already resigned on account of their hostility to the President's Proclamation of Freedom to the enslaved, and the prejudices of years against the colored man were revived and inflamed whenever they could be aroused by the influence and arguments of those citizens whose political importance had always been subservient to the slave power. The Indiana troops, however, stood fast and evinced in the strongest form their desire to put down the rebellion with the assistance of any means consistent with civilized warfare; though many, no doubt, who deserted in 1862-63 were induced to do so by their pretended friends at home on the ill-founded pretext that the war was a "nigger war"—"to free the niggers"—"to elevate the nigger and make him equal to the white man," etc. But the excitement in regard to the proclamation and the order for enlisting colored troops raged mostly among those who were not in the army and took no part in the war except by endeavoring to weaken the power of the Government and by giving their sympathy to the rebellion. Public opinion, however, rapidly strengthened on the negro question, and it was not long until all material opposition to the employment of colored troops was narrowed down to those who, no matter what was done to carry on the war, doggedly and determinedly maintained their hostility to the full extent their personal safety would admit.

Referring to the Emancipation Proclamation, Governor MORTON, in his annual message, January, 1863, used the following language:

> The President has issued his proclamation, offering freedom to slaves held in certain of the rebellious States. It remains to be seen what effect this proclamation will have in suppressing the rebellion; but whether it be effectual or not, for the purpose for which it was intended, the authority upon which it was issued is beyond question.
>
> If the rebels do not desire the Government of the United States to interfere with their slaves, let them cease to employ them in the prosecution of the war. They should not use them to build fortifications, manage their baggage trains, perform all the labor of the camp and the march, and above all, to raise provisions upon which to subsist their armies. If they employ the institution of slavery as an instrument of war, like other instruments of war, it is subject to destruction. Deprive them of slave labor, and three-fourths of the men composing their armies would be compelled to return home to raise food upon which to subsist themselves and families. If they are permitted to retain slave labor, they are enabled to maintain their armies in great force, and to destroy that force we are compelled to shed much of our best blood. Let us not be more tender of their property than we are of our blood.

These sentiments were generally re-echoed by the people of the State who favored a vigorous prosecution of the war, but no effort was made to raise colored troops to be credited upon our quotas until the 30th of November, 1863, when, in reply to an application, the War Department authorized the Governor to raise a battalion or regiment under the regulations governing the colored branch of the service. He had requested this authority, not so much because our colored citizens were anxious to enter the service, as for the reason that the State had been and was overrun with recruiting agents representing other States, and he had found it necessary, to prevent the men from being enticed away and credited elsewhere, to issue an order (November 5th, 1863) warning all persons so engaged to desist from procuring substitutes or further enlistments, under penalty of being arrested and summarily punished. Orders for recruiting the colored regiment or battalion were promulgated on the 3d of December, and a camp of rendezvous established at Indianapolis, with WILLIAM P. FISHBACK, Esq., as commandant. Six companies were raised aggregating five hundred and eighteen enlisted men. The battalion was afterwards recruited up to a full regiment in Maryland, and was known as the Twenty-eighth United States Colored.[1]

Under the calls of July and December, 1864, a number of colored substitutes were furnished by drafted men in this State, and forwarded to colored regiments in the field. The total number of colored men raised in the State is reported by the Provost Marshal General at one thousand five hundred and thirty-seven, though probably not over eight hundred were credited upon our quotas—the balance having been recruited by other States as before explained.

VETERAN RESERVE CORPS

One of the peculiar features of the war was the organization known as the Invalid Corps, afterwards the Veteran Reserve Corps. No similar organization is to be met with in history. The idea contemplated in the formation of this Corps was to give employment in military duty to all soldiers who

---

[1] For a more extended account of the organization and services of this gallant regiment, see Terrell, *Report,* 3:382-83.

had been by the casualties of the service rendered physically unable to endure the fatigues and hardships of active campaigning in the field.

During the early months of the war, indeed, during nearly the whole of the first two years, the percentage of soldiers disabled and discharged on account of sickness was unusually large. Both officers and men were destitute of the knowledge, gained only by experience, as to the means necessary to preserve health under the novel and arduous duties of military life. The Medical Officers, too, were compelled to work under great embarrassment in this new field, and the hospital accommodations of the army were fearfully limited. Then there was an impression abroad, in both public and official circles, that there were more men in the field than were needed to bring the war to a close, and that the interests of the country demanded the discharge of all men who were disabled from severe and active duty. Thus a very lax system of discharges was adopted, which resulted in thinning the ranks of early regiments to an alarming extent. To form some idea of the extreme to which this depleting process was carried, reference may be had to an order issued in July, 1862, by General BUELL, commanding the Army of the Ohio, concerning the absentees from his command, in which he stated that one fourth of his army was absent from the field, the greater portion of the absentees being in hospitals or at home on sick furloughs, and he directed that there should be a muster in every regiment on the 18th of August and all men absent at that time were to be discharged.

Similar orders were issued by other commanders and were so far carried into effect that, by the end of the year 1862 more than one third of the men of the regiments of 1861 were out of the service. The number of officers discharged was also very large, as but few of the resignations tendered were disapproved.

The evils of these wholesale discharges soon became manifest, but though the whole system of discharge was afterward radically changed, so that not a single private soldier was released from service except after the most thorough examination had shown his utter unfitness for military duty, yet great mischief had already been done, and thoughtful minds were busy in trying to devise expedients for repairing it as far as possible. The men and officers thus discharged at the beginning of the struggle were those who had enlisted without bounties when the first blow was struck, and were generally conspicuous in their respective communities for their patriotism and public spirit. For the most part they were not content to remain idle spectators of the conflict, but were anxious to do whatever their strength would allow towards bringing the war to a close. In addition to these men, there were thousands of others in the hospitals and convalescent camps of the army who were unfitted for active duty and awaiting discharges, who could not be employed to any considerable extent on account of lack of organization and the possibility of being returned to their commands when their strength should be in some degree restored, even if it were only to be returned to the hospital again after a short time.

It was to make available the services of the classes of men above mentioned, that the War Department determined upon the organization of an Invalid Corps. The order for this purpose was issued April 28th, 1863. The Corps was to be organized under the direction of the Provost Marshal General and subject to his orders. Two battalions were to be formed; the first, of men able to carry muskets and perform guard, garrison and general provost duties; the second, of those capable of only the lightest duties, such as clerks, hospital attendants, etc. The first battalion was afterwards organized into regiments, but the second battalion never had any other than company organizations.

Applicants for commissions in the new corps were required to be honorably discharged officers of the volunteer or regular forces, and were compelled to pass a rigid examination before a board of intelligent and experienced officers; and they, as well as the enlisted men, were also carefully examined by competent surgeons as to their physical fitness. Though the disabled men were wanted, those who were incompetent for work were uniformly rejected. Recruiting officers were appointed to re-enlist men for the Corps from those who had been discharged from the service, and orders were sent to Medical Directors, directing the transfer of partially disabled men who were still carried on the rolls of their respective regiments. It is proper to state here that the officers of the Corps were nearly all drawn from those who had been discharged from the service, while very few enlisted men were obtained from that source. The reason for this is probably found in the fact that credits for local bounties were not given for this class of recruits until a late day, and the men preferred—those who could be accepted—enlisting in organizations where they could receive the benefit of the bounties. Enlisted men were, however, transferred from the troops in the field in large numbers. They were examined as to their peculiar fitness for the duties required of the Corps, and lists forwarded of such as were approved to the War Department, and the transfers were made by General Orders from the Secretary of War, giving the name, rank and regiment of each man transferred. They were then dropped from the rolls of their regiments, and were subject only to the orders issued for their new commands. In some instances, when their strength became fully restored, they were re-transferred to their original regiments, though such instances were rare. The men transferred were entitled to discharge at the expiration of the time of their original enlistment, and generally, when a regiment was mustered out of the service, the men who had been transferred from its ranks to the Veteran Reserve Corps were also entitled to discharge. After the close of the war, when regiments were discharged before their terms had expired, the transferred men were for a time held to the expiration of their original terms; but this being manifestly unjust, brought forth innumerable complaints, and after repeated and urgent remonstrances from the State authorities the rule was relaxed, and the men were relieved from service whenever their original regiments were discharged, if they so desired.

The magnitude of this Corps and its importance to the country may be inferred from the fact that just before the surrender of LEE, it comprised twenty-four complete regiments, and one hundred and fifty-three independent companies, numbering 764 commissioned officers and 28,738 enlisted men. These were nearly all men whose services would not have been available in any other way, and they did full duty; if not in the field, they relieved other troops from service in the rear, and enabled our commanders to use all their able-bodied soldiers at the front. The general duties of the Corps consisted principally in guarding rebel prisoners, assisting the Provost Marshals in enforcing the enrollment and draft, arresting deserters, escorting recruits, drafted men and substitutes to the front, keeping order at home, and crushing conspiracies of rebel sympathizers in the North, performing provost duties in northern cities, and guarding all kinds of Government stores and property.

The regiments stationed at Indianapolis were the Fifth, Colonel, afterwards Brevet Brigadier General, A. A. STEVENS, commanding; and the Seventeenth, Colonel, afterwards Brevet Brigadier General, A. J. WARNER, commanding. They attained great perfection in drill, and in zeal and faithfulness were not probably surpassed by any troops engaged in similar duties. The Fifth had charge of Camp Morton rebel prison, and the Seventeenth was assigned to general, provost and miscellaneous duty . . . .[2]

The Corps continued in service until very nearly all the troops of the volunteer army were discharged, the regiments on duty here being relieved December 1st, 1865. Many of the officers were, however, retained for duty in the border and Southern States under the Freedmen's Bureau. So successful

---

[2] See General Warner's report in Terrell, *Report,* 1, Appendix, Doc. 84:286-87.

was the Corps in the discharge of its peculiar duties, that the system has been incorporated into our regular army, and four of the regular regiments are now formed from men partially disabled, upon the same plan as the old organization, so that the Government is able to give honorable and useful employment to many of its maimed and disabled heroes, and the VETERAN RESERVE CORPS has not become a thing of history merely, but will probably be a valuable and vital element in the armies of the nation for years to come.

APPOINTMENTS AND PROMOTIONS

APPOINTMENTS IN NEW ORGANIZATIONS

The duty of appointing field, staff and line officers for the volunteer force, under the three months' call, and under the calls which resulted in the formation of a number of regiments for one and three years, prior to July 22d, 1861, devolved upon the Governor, under orders of the President and the laws of the United States regulating the militia.[1]

On the 22d of July an Act was passed by Congress, "to authorize the employment of Volunteers to aid in enforcing the laws and protecting public property," which expressly conferred upon the Governors of States power to commission all regimental and company officers required for the volunteers raised in their respective States, which power was continued until the close of the war.

When the vast interests at stake in the organization of the volunteer army are considered, involving the life and honor of the nation, the welfare and good fame of the State furnishing the troops, and the individual well being of the volunteers themselves, the importance and responsibility connected with the exercise of the appointing power will be seen to have been very great.

In Indiana, at the commencement of the war, there were but few men of any military skill or experience. The Mexican war, in which we were represented by only five regiments, whose term of service was one year, furnished a number of officers and men whose previous service in the field, though

---

[1] Under the same authority, the Governor appointed Thomas A. Morris and Joseph J. Reynolds brigadier generals, and appointed also their staff officers. [Terrell]

limited, was of much value, and whose example, in promptly responding to the call of the Government, gave great encouragement to the loyal cause.

Aside from this element, and, perhaps half a dozen graduates of the West Point Military Academy, the *material* for officers was wholly raw and inexperienced. For twenty-five years preceding the war, there had been no regularly organized militia, and consequently no benefits could be derived from that source, in the experience of either officers or men. Military instruction on the parade ground, and in our schools and colleges, had received no attention. At any time, and under the most favorable circumstances, the selection and appointment of military officers is responsible and difficult; but especially so when the force to be officered is composed of volunteers, rapidly raised, and intended for immediate service. Time can not be taken to educate and qualify, by thorough drill and discipline, the persons who may be designated to command, and the only course that can be pursued in such a contingency is to select clear-headed, honorable men, whose patriotism may prompt them to become soldiers, trusting to the future to develop, by active service, the qualities that go to make up the successful commander. The judgment of the appointing power is taxed heavily; but as the judgment of every one, when compelled to estimate the untried abilities and fitness of others, is greatly dependent upon and influenced by recommendations, importunities, and surrounding circumstances, the liability to make mistakes is enhanced immensely. Touching this matter, Governor MORTON, in his annual message of 1865, made the following remarks:

> The duty of appointing officers to command our regiments is full of responsibility and embarrassment. I have commissioned many whom I did not know, and for whose fitness I was compelled to rely entirely upon the opinion of others. But it affords me gratification to state that the Indiana officers, as a body, have been found equal to those of any other State; that they have, upon every battle field, sustained the great cause, and shed lustre upon the flag under which they fought. Many have been appointed to high commands, in which they have acquitted themselves

with the greatest honor and ability, and very many have nobly laid down their lives in battle for their country.

Under the liberal ideas which prevail in this country, and the independent spirit which animates all classes of citizens from which the armies of the republic are drawn, the views and wishes of the volunteers regarding their own officers, must to a certain degree, and very properly, be consulted. The elective principle, always popular and in harmony with the spirit of our laws and institutions, is, in this country, when applied to selections for official station, most in favor; and, under circumstances like those existing in Indiana at the outbreaking of the rebellion, the application of this principle, in the selection of company officers at least, is perhaps the safest that could be adopted. At a time when all stand upon the same level as to military experience, elections give assurance of fairness and impartiality which can alone satisfy the expectation and demands of such a people as ours.

In the organization of our forces, the Governor, from the commencement, recognized the justice of giving due consideration to the preferences of the *men* when expressed either by election or petition, yet he never yielded his right and duty to make different selections if, in his own judgment, the public interests would be benefitted thereby. In 1861, the general plan above described was mainly pursued, though in a number of cases gentlemen were authorized to raise companies and regiments with the understanding that they would be commissioned to command them.

The most successful and satisfactory plan, and one that was adopted after a few regiments had been raised, was to call for a regiment from a particular locality, generally a Congressional District, and appoint a commandant to supervise the recruitment of the same, expressly stipulating, however, that such appointment did not confer the right to a commission to command the force when completed, but leaving the selection of officers open until the time for organization arrived. In this way all the material of companies and regiments was developed and opportunity was thus afforded to select the most worthy, the rule being to officer each regiment from its own members, or from those engaged in recruiting it, if qualified and fit persons could be found therein. The claims of those who performed the labor and incurred the expense of raising the troops, were never intentionally overlooked, their standing and qualifications being taken into consideration. Their efforts and influence, and the outlay of time and money necessarily incurred, entitled them to this consideration at the hands of the Executive.

The following statistics in this connection will be interesting:

The whole number of commissions issued during the war by Governor MORTON was 18,884. Of these 6,243 were original appointments made upon the organization of regiments and batteries for the volunteer service; 9,187 were promotions to fill vacancies in the same service; 3,159 were appointments in the Indiana Legion; and 295 were appointments of officers of the draft of 1862.[2]

APPOINTMENTS TO FILL VACANCIES

But few vacancies occurred in commissioned officers until the cold weather of 1861 set in, which brought in its train much exposure and hardship and induced disease to an extent not hitherto known in our army. These causes and a somewhat rigid enforcement of the law of Congress,[3] authorizing department and army commanders to appoint examining boards "to investigate the capacity, qualifications, propriety of conduct and efficiency of commissioned officers," created many vacancies, and it became necessary, therefore, for the Governor to adopt rules for filling the same. As in cases of

[2] See tables showing commissions issued by the Governor in Terrell, *Report,* 1, Appendix, Doc. 5:53-56.
[3] Act of July 22, 1861, Sec. 10. U. S. *Statutes at Large,* 12(1859-63):270.

original appointment, there was no law or authoritative regulation applicable to volunteers on this subject, and the limited experience gained in the war up to that time afforded but little light in devising rules of promotion which would in a just and satisfactory way meet the variety of cases constantly occurring.

In filling vacancies the *good of the service* was, of course, the first paramount object to be attained. The *rights* of officers, non-commissioned officers and privates still serving with the command in which a vacancy existed and the *harmony* so essential to efficient service, were also important points. But there were difficulties in always getting an exact and fair understanding of the situation of affairs in the command so as to enable the Governor to know how the public interest could be best advanced, or the rights of officers and men most surely protected, which made his duty in these respects extremely delicate and often awkwardly embarrassing. The arbitrary rule of promotion observed in the regular army—seniority in rank without reference to companies—can not, for various and obvious reasons, be made applicable to our volunteers. Our companies are raised usually from separate counties, and regiments are formed as nearly as practicable from the troops of neighboring counties. The men generally know each other and are acquainted with their officers, either personally or by reputation. Their organizations are homogeneous and they expect to stand or fall together. To change this *status* when vacancies occur in the field by appointing or promoting outsiders, or strangers, with whom they have no acquaintance or affiliation, ignoring entirely the claims of all who belong to the particular company or command in which the vacancy exists; or by "jumping," as it was called, one not in the line of promotion over one "in the line" entitled to be advanced, would be productive of the greatest injury and demoralization. The true rule of promotion then, it is assumed, is that each company and regimental organization is by right entitled to have all vacancies filled from its own members, provided they possess the proper qualifications. In other words, vacancies should be filled by the promotion of the next officer in "the regular line" in each company, unless objections on account of incompetency, immoral habits, or unfitness be presented by the regimental officers; and vacancies in the field and staff should be subject to the same rule.[4]

From the outset Governor MORTON acted upon this rule, and its manifest justice and the general satisfaction it gave, warrants this explicit detail. Objections to it were frequently made and promotions insisted upon by officers, entirely at variance with its provisions. A general order was therefore issued on the 1st of January, 1862, and forwarded to all officers in the field clearly setting forth the regulations which would govern promotions in the future. An additional order on the same subject, but somewhat more explicit, was issued January 20th, 1865.[5]

A few days after the battle of Pittsburg Landing the attention of the Governor was called by a letter from Major General HALLECK[6] to the importance of promoting non-commissioned officers and privates to the vacancies created by recent battles. The General expressed regret that the Generals commanding had not the power to reward merit and bravery on the field, and appealed to the justice of the Governor, urging that "to reward service in the field by prompt promotion is one of the greatest incentives to individual action, as it is a special mark of personal merit." The Governor had visited the army in person frequently, and fully

---

[4] The Adjutant, Quartermaster, and Commissary were not considered as being in any line of promotion and were not allowed to "jump" to positions in the field or line over others entitled to promotion, unless upon recommendation of a majority of the officers of the command and special fitness being shown. The Sergeant Major was in line of promotion for Adjutant, the Quartermaster Sergeant for Commissary, and First Sergeant for Second Lieutenant. [Terrell]

[5] For the text of these orders, see Terrell, *Report,* 1, Appendix, Docs. 94 and 95:298.

[6] Halleck's letter is given in *ibid.,* 1, Appendix, Doc. 92:297.

appreciated and concurred in General HALLECK'S suggestions. He therefore issued a circular under date of April 26th, 1862, requesting general and field officers commanding Indiana regiments to report and recommend for promotion all commissioned officers, non-commissioned officers and privates who merited it by reason of gallant and distinguished conduct in any engagement with the enemy.[7] Such recommendations were made frequently, and always met with favorable attention.

In the month of September, 1863, it was shown by reports to this Department that a number of the first regiments raised were so much reduced as to have less than one hundred and fifty effective men each. Numerous vacancies existed, but promotions could not be made, however meritorious and deserving the men who were "in line of promotion" might be; for the regulations would permit only a certain number of officers to be mustered when a command became reduced below its minimum. The Governor, therefore, proposed a plan to the War Department for recruiting for these regiments, which, if successfully carried out, would enable all vacancies to be filled, and at the same time add material strength to the army which was then so much needed. The proposition was favorably entertained by the General-in-Chief, and on the 7th [27th] of October, 1863, an order was issued through the War Department,[8] addressed to the Generals commanding the several military departments in which Indiana troops were serving, directing that there be detailed for recruiting from each company of the regiments designated by Governor MORTON, one non-commissioned officer or private, and that said non-commissioned officer or private, if there be a vacancy for a commissioned officer in his company, should be entitled to promotion on recruiting his company to the minimum standard. Requisitions for these details were promptly responded to by most of the old and

---

[7] See Terrell, *Report,* 1, Appendix, Doc. 96:298: "Promotions for Gallantry."
[8] See *ibid.,* 1, Appendix, Doc. 98, p. 299: "Recruiting for Old Regiments—Promotions."

worn-down regiments. The men were stationed in different parts of the State, where their companies were originally formed, and succeeded in raising a large number of recruits. The plan was carried on through the winter of 1863-64 with much success, and enabled many energetic and worthy non-commissioned officers and privates to secure the promotion which they had so long desired.

PROMOTIONS FROM OLD TO NEW REGIMENTS

During the entire continuance of the war, the authorities of this State were engaged in recruiting troops, and new organizations were always in process of formation. The difficulty in making selections of officers for new regiments, from inexperienced and untried citizens, has already been alluded to. With the view of avoiding this difficulty, the Governor determined to avail himself of the ability and experience which the steady progress of the war had developed in officers and men belonging to the "old" regiments. Numerous promotions were thus made with good effect, and the new regiments thus officered were put in condition, through the efforts and knowledge of these experienced officers, to take the field in a comparatively short time. In furtherance of this plan, details from old regiments were often requested by the Governor of commissioned and non-commissioned officers and privates, who had shown ability to assume higher positions, for the purpose of assisting in recruiting under new calls, with the intention of giving them increased rank. To such an extent were these promotions made, the Secretary of War, by direction of the President, on the 14th of August, 1862, felt it to be necessary to issue an order, of which the following is an extract:

The exigencies of the service require that officers now in the field should remain with their commands, and no officer now in the field, in the regular or volunteer service, will, under any circumstances, be detailed to accept a new command.

This order completely checked the promotion of old officers, which had proved so advantageous in insuring early discipline and thorough drill to the new troops. The Governor made an earnest effort to have the order rescinded, but, as the following telegram from the Secretary of War will show, without success:

> Our armies being in the face of the enemy, officers in the field can not be spared for any purpose. The same reason applies to absent officers; if fit for any duty, they should be with their commands, and not leave their men exposed to danger without officers. If on detached duty, it must be performed. The principle on which the order stands, is that soldiers in the field require their officers' presence.

Thus matters rested until October following, when the present Adjutant General, then acting as Military Secretary, was dispatched to Washington, to urge upon the Government such a modification of the foregoing order as the demands of the service seemed to require. Through this effort it was finally agreed by the War Department, that, in cases where the fact was known to the Governor, that the condition of regiments would admit of officers being spared to accept new commissions, promotions might be made. This modification was all that was required, and promotions were made as before, at every convenient opportunity.

PROMOTIONS IN MEDICAL STAFF

In the early stages of the rebellion, but little difficulty was experienced in officering our regiments with Surgeons and Assistant Surgeons of the first class in the profession. But after the lapse of about a year very considerable trouble was experienced in securing medical officers of established reputation and ability. The pressure for appointments from students, newly diploma-ized M.D.'s, and others whose opportunities for practice had been limited, was at all times very great. To Surgeons of standing, whose patriotic impulses led them to offer their services, or who thought of doing so, it

APPOINTMENTS AND PROMOTIONS

became very plain, after the winter campaign of 1861-62, that the duties of a faithful Surgeon in the army were much more laborious than those devolving upon private practice at home; and it was also thought that the pay allowed by the Government was, for the professional services of accomplished and experienced medical men, niggardly and inadequate. It is but fair to presume that the members of this profession are as patriotic and self-sacrificing as men of any other calling in life, but it is nevertheless true that a large majority of those who entered the service in the regiments of 1861-62 (much greater indeed than of any other military position in proportion to the number appointed) did not remain until the close of their terms. The general reason for this I think may be found in the fact that, however faithful and devoted a Surgeon might be, there was no provision for promotion, and no hope for any.[9] In other branches of the service promotion was generally sure and rapid, and it would be strange indeed if medical officers did not feel the same ambition for advancement in rank and pay as was universally felt by others. Another reason of perhaps nearly equal weight, with these officers, was the dangers that beset their own personal health. A Surgeon actively engaged with volunteers— his friends and neighbors—in the field, if disposed to perform his part, can never be idle; day and night in bivouac, or on the march, and especially in battle, he must be very constantly at his post. The nature of his duties interdicts the granting of leave of absence to visit home, or recruit impaired health, to a much greater extent than [with] the other officers; but doubtless the principal cause of the many resignations and the prevailing repugnance on the part of medical men of ability to entering the service, was the ungenerous policy of denying them promotion with increase of pay and emoluments equal to that of other positions of like responsibility and importance.

[9] Assistant Surgeons might be, and frequently were, promoted to Surgeons, but that was the extent. [Terrell]

PROMOTIONS IN THE ARTILLERY

The officers of *Batteries of Light Artillery* furnish another striking instance of injustice in denying promotion. The War Department refused our State the privilege of regimental organizations for her light artillery, although the subject was often pressed and urged by the authorities upon the Government with great pertinacity and earnestness. So our twenty-six batteries, comprising originally about four thousand men, were sent to the field without the hope or prospect of a single promotion, except such as might be given in filling company vacancies occasioned by the casualties of the service. These batteries bore a conspicuous and distinguished part in putting down the rebellion; many of them performed deeds of valor equal to any regiment that ever fought, but their officers were forced to content themselves with the modest rank of Captains and Lieutenants. The Governor did what he could to remedy this by promoting, when opportunity offered, artillery officers to higher places in new cavalry regiments, but the well-being of the batteries only allowed him to take this course in a few instances.

Reference has been made to these inequalities in the hope that should another war unfortunately afflict our country, the great injustice hinted at will not be repeated.

HONORARY MUSTERS

Notwithstanding the efforts of the Government, always heartily seconded by the Military Authorities of this State, to recruit old regiments and batteries to their maximum strength in preference to the formation of new organizations, many of the older commands during the last years of the war were reduced below their minimum strength.

By the regulations of the War Department, framed with more regard to the economy of the service than the merits of individuals, such commands were not entitled to a full roster of officers. It was, however, the practice in this State

APPOINTMENTS AND PROMOTIONS 117

to promote and commission meritorious officers to such rank as they were entitled to in the regular line of promotion, without reference to the strength of their regiments or companies. Such commissions, though they might be of no practical advantage in securing increase of pay and emoluments, were regarded as a proper evidence of appreciation, a deserved mark of distinction and respect.

At the close of the war while preparations were being made for the mustering out of large numbers of volunteer officers with their commands, Governor MORTON addressed a communication to the Secretary of War[10] earnestly requesting that all field and staff officers then in the service, who had been promoted and commissioned to higher grades, but had not been mustered into such grades by reason of their regiments or companies being reduced below the minimum, should be so mustered in upon their said commissions at the date of their muster out. This would give them simply the *rank* to which, had their commands not been reduced below the minimum, they would have been entitled.

It was urged, that while such a muster could furnish no claim for increase of pay or in any other manner affect the pecuniary relations between the Government and the officers interested, it would be regarded by them as a grateful tribute of respect, an appropriate recognition of their faithful services in the suppression of the rebellion and the restoration of the Government. And it seemed no more than an act of simple justice, that officers, who had assumed the responsibilities and performed the duties of the offices to which they had been promoted, should have the titles conferred by their commissions confirmed by authority of the Government in an honorary muster.

The executive authorities of Illinois, Pennsylvania, Wisconsin and other States, whose co-operation was solicited, cordially approved the suggestion of Governor MORTON, and

[10] Governor Morton's letter is given in Terrell, *Report*, 1, Appendix, Doc. 129:340.

wrote to the Secretary of War recommending its favorable consideration. As it was confidently expected that the War Department would take favorable action in the matter, commanding officers of regiments and batteries were informed of the action of the Executive and requested to forward the usual recommendations; and upon receiving these, all vacancies in field, staff and company offices were promptly filled by promotion.

With the issue of these commissions, however, the movement ended. The Secretary of War declined to order the honorary musters on the ground that such action might be held to justify the presentation of claims for extra pay and allowances and lead to troublesome complications.

While this decision is to be regretted as having deprived many gallant officers of a proper record in the national archives of the rank to which they had really attained, it cannot deprive them of what is more valuable, the consciousness of having earned that record, nor can it lessen the esteem in which they are held by their late companions in arms, and they will have the further satisfaction of knowing that their rank and services are faithfully recorded in the military archives of their own State.

CREDITS FOR TROOPS FURNISHED

The War Department (even after the war) did not give the State credit for the number of troops actually furnished, and the most troublesome difficulties grew out of this failure at different times during the war. No adjustment at all was attempted until the first draft was ordered in August, 1862, and then, the settlement was arbitrary and incorrect, for it was afterwards shown that up to that time Indiana had an excess of 25,544 three years' men. The call was for nine months' men, and the quota 21,250, which being reduced to the three years' standard, only required 5,312 men, leaving the State still in excess 20,232 three years' men, applicable to future calls. The Governor was fully satisfied that a correct accounting would show that the State was largely in excess, but as a large number of townships were behind in furnishing their just proportion of men, the draft was submitted to as the easiest way to put on an equal footing all the sub-districts in the State.[1]

After the passage of the Conscription Act by Congress, in March, 1863, the War Department made an exhibit, from the rolls on file, which purported to show all the troops furnished by the State to the 26th of May, 1863, crediting an excess of 24,978 three years' men, and charging 21,250 nine months' men (equal to 5,312 three years' men). Afterwards the Department admitted additional credits up to the 26th of May to the number of 5,279, making the total excess of credits at that date 24,945 three years' men. Prior to the 2nd of September, 1862, no credits were given for enlistments in the regular army, and although no reports are accessible show-

---

[1] See "Draft of 1862," above, 49-55.

ing the number of regulars enlisted in this State up to that time, a fair estimate would fix it at not less than 3,000. This would give us an excess on the 26th of May, 1863, of 27,945 three years' men—not including a large number enlisted in Kentucky, Illinois, New York and other States, for which no credit was allowed.

The Conscription Act was doubtless a very important war measure, but the above exhibit makes it clear that its passage was not necessary to *compel* INDIANA to furnish her quota of troops for the war; nevertheless it did a good work for us— it settled all former credits and deficiencies, and gave us a starting point for the future.

Until the 20th of October, 1863, all credits were given to the State at large; on and after that date they were assigned to townships or other sub-districts, according to the place of credit or residence, as shown by the muster-in rolls. Then commenced the system of local bounties, which has already been explained in preceding pages.

FIRST SERIES OF VETERAN CREDITS

No further difficulty was met with in the settlement of credits between the State and General Government until the re-enlistment of veterans in the field in the winter of 1863-64 gave rise to fresh complications. The following document so fully explains these matters, it is inserted entire:[2]

EXECUTIVE DEPARTMENT OF INDIANA,
ADJUTANT GENERAL'S OFFICE,
INDIANAPOLIS, March 4th, 1861 [1865].

HON. JOHN U. PETTIT, *Speaker of the House of Representatives:*

SIR: In compliance with a resolution of the House of Representatives, passed March 1st, 1865, I have the honor to report, as follows:

The whole number of re-enlisted Veterans of Indiana volunteers authorized up to this date, to be passed to the credit of the State on any of the calls of the President for volunteers or drafted men, is 11,490.

[2] It is also printed in the Indiana *House Journal,* 1865, pp. 864-72.

On the 8th of December, 1863, the War Department issued a circular instructing the Commissaries of Musters, as follows:

"Commissaries of Musters will cause to be entered upon the descriptive roll of Veteran Volunteers, the residence of each man—giving the town, county and State. The same data must also appear on the copy of the roll sent to the Adjutant General of the State in which the men reside. The information must be promptly furnished, as upon it credits of men to the respective States will be made. It is necessary to know the number for the respective towns and counties, so that the credits may be properly distributed through the State. The residences of men re-mustered will, of course, determine the town and county to which they belong."

The rolls of remuster of re-enlisted Veterans were received at the Adjutant General's Office of this State, between the first day of January and thirty-first day of August, 1864, except in the cases of the Veterans of the Eleventh, Thirteenth, Twenty-Fourth, Twenty-Sixth, Thirty-Fourth, Forty-Sixth, Forty-Seventh and Sixtieth Regiments, and Third Cavalry, which were not received until after the draft had actually taken place under the call of July 18, 1864, and then they were furnished by the Adjutant General U. S. A., War Department. Some of these rolls showed the residences of the men, and some contained no information on the subject.

On the 5th of February, 1864, the Adjutant General of the State received the following telegram:

"WASHINGTON, 5th February, 1864.

"Adjutant General Indiana:

"From reports thus far received, I fear that mustering officers in the field have not fully complied with their instructions of December 8th, 1863, in reference to localities to which re-mustered veterans should be credited. Therefore, with the view of comparing records, and to insure prompt and correct crediting of men, I respectfully request that you will consult your records of re-mustered veteran troops, and those of the organizations returned to and arriving in the State, on furlough, and make therefrom a report of the numbers to be credited to the respective localities. Please forward the report to me March 1st, and let it embrace all re-musters reported to you prior to that date.

[Signed,] "THOMAS M. VINCENT, Assistant Adjutant General."

The report required was not completed by March 1st, but further time being given, it was transmitted April 16th, 1864, and embraced all re-musters reported to the Adjutant General prior to that date. The report showed the following credits to the Congressional Districts in this State:[3]

First District	1060	Seventh District	469
Second District	752	Eighth District	457
Third District	663	Ninth District	599
Fourth District	461	Tenth District	398
Fifth District	469	Eleventh District	508
Sixth District	893	State at large	1538

Total credited to Indiana .... 8257 [8267]
Credited to Other States 148

Whole number reported 8405

A similar report was made for the period from April 17th to May 31st, 1864, showing an aggregate of 650, of which 2 were to the State at large and 34 to other States, leaving 614 credited to the State, apportioned as follows:

First District	12	Seventh District	51
Second District	41	Eighth District	55
Third District	14	Ninth District	223
Fourth District	6	Tenth District	96
Fifth District	39	Eleventh District	23
Sixth District	54	State at large	2

Total credited to Indiana 616
Credited to other States 34
Whole number reported 650

[3] The Congressional districts were composed of the following counties at this time: *first district,* Daviess, Dubois, Gibson, Knox, Martin, Pike, Posey, Spencer, Vanderburgh, and Warrick; *second district,* Clark, Crawford, Floyd, Harrison, Orange, Perry, Scott, Washington; *third district,* Bartholomew, Brown, Jackson, Jefferson, Jennings, Lawrence, Monroe, Switzerland; *fourth district,* Dearborn, Decatur, Franklin, Ohio, Ripley, Rush; *fifth district,* Delaware, Fayette, Henry, Randolph, Union, Wayne; *sixth district,* Hancock, Hendricks, Johnson, Marion, Morgan, Shelby; *seventh district,* Clay, Greene, Owen, Parke, Putnam, Sullivan, Vermillion, Vigo; *eighth district,* Boone, Carroll, Clinton, Fountain, Montgomery, Tippecanoe, Warren; *ninth district,* Benton, Cass, Fulton, Jasper, Lake, LaPorte, Marshall, Miami, Newton, Porter, Pulaski, St. Joseph, Starke, White; *tenth district,* Allen, DeKalb, Elkhart, Kosciusko, LaGrange, Noble, Steuben, Whitley; *eleventh district,* Adams, Blackford, Grant, Hamilton, Howard, Huntington, Jay, Madison, Tipton, Wabash, Wells.

Similar reports were made for the months ending June 30th, July 31st and August 31st, 1864, showing an aggregate of 344, of which five were credited to other States, and the remainder distributed as follows:

First District	16	Seventh District	47
Second District	49	Eighth District	20
Third District	190	Ninth District	3
Fourth District	12	Tenth District	2
Fifth District	0	Eleventh District	0
Sixth District	0		

Total credited to Indiana 339
Credited to other States 5
Whole number reported 344

All these reports were made up from the rolls of the re-mustered veterans, and showed in the aggregate 9,193 entitled to be credited to the State, and 187 to other States. Of the former, 7,672 were credited to localities within the State, and 1,540 being reported as having no residence on the rolls, were considered as credited to the State at large. These did not, however, embrace all of the veterans to which the State was entitled to a credit, but only such as this office had rolls for. On the 13th of August, 1864, Assistant Adjutant General, SAMUEL BRECK, in charge of rolls, War Department, reported that he had on file the rolls of veterans (of which this office had no copies) as follows: Eleventh Regiment, 287; Thirteenth Regiment, 189; Twenty-fourth Regiment, 226; Twenty-sixth Regiment, 240; Thirty-fourth Regiment, 447; Forty-sixth Regiment, 285; Forty-seventh, Regiment, 437, Sixtieth Regiment, 115, and Third Cavalry Regiment, 36: total, 2,262. Application was at once made for copies of these rolls, but it was refused, on the ground that the Department could not allow its clerical force to be taken away from the current work to make the copies. They were afterwards, in the latter part of September and first weeks of October, furnished, after the numbers corresponding had been assigned to localities and reported for credit, by the Adjutant General of the State, in pursuance of telegraphic instructions, as follows:

"WASHINGTON, August 26, 1864.

"LAZ. NOBLE, *Adjutant General:*

"Exhibits forwarded by you, dated April 15, May 31, June 30, July 31, give the localities for 9,173 veterans. Forward an exhibit giving the localities to which the additional number claimed by Indiana is to be assigned with a view to credit being passed to the State.

[Signed.]   "THOMAS M. VINCENT, A. A. G."

This exhibit was made up by Adjutant General NOBLE, by apportioning the numbers, *pro rata* throughout the State, of such as had no residences upon the rolls, and by including, in addition, those shown upon supplementary rolls, received after the date of former reports. The whole number embraced in this exhibit was 2,280, apportioned as follows:

First District	159	Seventh District	381
Second District	269	Eighth District	115
Third District	280	Ninth District	113
Fourth District	149	Tenth District	104
Fifth District	219	Eleventh District	365
Sixth District	126		
Total			2280

The veterans thus assigned were 451 of the Twenty-First Regiment, 282 of the Thirty-First Regiment (all from Seventh District); 142 of the Thirty-Fifth Regiment; 213 of the Thirty-Eighth Regiment (mostly from Second District); 287 of the Eleventh Regiment; 215 of the Twenty-Fourth Regiment (from First and Second Districts); 240 of the Twenty-Sixth Regiment; 251 of the Forty-Seventh Regiment (all from Eleventh District); and 199 of detachments of different regiments and batteries. This exhibit was transmitted to Assistant Adjutant General THOMAS M. VINCENT, September 2d, 1864, that officer having signified, by telegraph, that, "as the draft is ordered immediately after September 5th, that date is the latest at which the exhibit of veterans" could "be received so as to be passed to credit."

There was some prospect, at this time, that the draft would be postponed, and Major VINCENT was requested (in case it was) to return the last-named exhibit for revision, as it was not claimed to be perfect. In a report on this subject, made to Governor MORTON by General NOBLE, dated September 10th, 1864, it was urged that "time should be allowed to fairly adjust these credits, and especially to apportion those whose residences are not given on rolls among the townships as near where the veterans actually reside as possible, and this can not be done without a return of the exhibit furnished Major VINCENT, September 2d, for revision. That revision, to give any kind of satisfaction, will take at least four weeks."

Although the Assistant Adjutant General U. S. A., in charge of the adjustment of veteran credits, acknowledged that the State was entitled to a total credit of 11,490, for some unexplained reason the Provost Marshal General failed to direct his Assistant on duty in Indiana to credit the whole number thus acknowledged. Up to September 17th, 1864, only 6,576 had been actually credited, and on that day an order was received, by telegraph, from the Provost Marshal General's Bureau, to give an additional credit of 3,233, leaving still a deficit of 1,681 men.

The attention of the Provost Marshal General being called to the fact that the full number authorized by the Adjutant General U. S. A. had not yet been credited, the following instructions were given:

"WAR DEPARTMENT, PROVOST MARSHAL GENERAL'S OFFICE,
WASHINGTON, September 19th, 1864.

"*Colonel* JAMES G. JONES,

"*Acting Assistant Provost Marshal General, Indianapolis, Indiana.*

"COLONEL: The State of Indiana by report of the Adjutant General of that State, was entitled to be credited in the aggregate with 8,257 re-enlisted Veteran Volunteers to the 15th of April last. Colonel BAKER (your predecessor) states that of this number but 6576 have heretofore been credited; should you upon examination ascertain this to be the case, you will then assign the following number to the credit of the State in accordance with the accompanying statement.

[Signed,] "T .A. DODGE,
"Major V. R. C. in charge of Enrollment Bureau."

First District	162	Seventh District	149
Second District	124	Eighth District	156
Third District	136	Ninth District	191
Fourth District	113	Tenth District	578
Fifth District	128	Eleventh District	171
Sixth District	171		
Total			1681
[*True footing,*			2079]

Adjutant General NOBLE, in pursuance of instructions from Colonel JONES, issued certificates for local credits to cover in part, the 1681 referred to. The certificates issued were for the number stated below:

First District		Seventh District	137
Second District	12	Eighth District	181
Third District	49	Ninth District	173
Fourth District	131	Tenth District	5
Fifth District	163	Eleventh District	197
Sixth District	171		
Total,			1219
Unaccounted for			462
Number authorized to be credited			1681

Of the foregoing facts, all of which appear of record in this office, I have no personal knowledge, the different reports for credit having been made and action taken thereon prior to my entering upon the duties of this office.

The records show the following facts as to the aggregate credits authorized and actually given, prior to my administration:

DISTRICTS.	NO. AUTHORIZED.	NO. ACTUALLY CREDITED.
First	1,409	1,009
Second	1,235	1,219
Third	1,281	1,275
Fourth	741	631
Fifth	855	723
Sixth	1,244	1,343
Seventh	1,085	1,231
Eighth	803	869
Ninth	1,129	1,283
Tenth	1,173	636
Eleventh	1,067	1,044
Total	12,022	11,253 [11,263]

The discrepancy between the numbers reported to Adjutant General United States Army, and approved—11,490—and the number ordered to be credited by the Provost Marshal General, was occasioned by the latter officer committing an error in the number to be given the Tenth District, in his order of September 17th, 1864, for a credit of 1,681, and in the footing of the statement accompanying that order, of 398, and by including the veterans in Indiana organizations, who had upon rolls credited themselves to other States.

In justice to myself, it is proper to state that all of the business relating to the credits hereinbefore mentioned, was transacted during the time the office of Adjutant General was held by my predecessor, General NOBLE, *and that the foregoing statement of facts has been prepared, at my request, by the principal clerk of the late Adjutant General from the books, rolls, and memoranda remaining in this office.*

SECOND SERIES OF VETERAN CREDITS

The following adjustment of veteran credits has been made since my appointment:

On the 4th of February, 1865, Brigadier General T. G. PITCHER, Acting Assistant Provost Marshal General, furnished this office with a "statement of credits given to the State of Indiana on the books" of his office, "for re-enlisted veteran volunteers of that State," showing that but 11,253 of the 11,490 allowed had been actually credited, leaving 237 still unaccredited. Application being made to the Provost Marshal General for authority to credit these omitted veterans, the following telegram was received:

"WAR DEPARTMENT, PROVOST MARSHAL GENERAL'S BUREAU,
WASHINGTON, D. C., February 6th, 1865.
"General W. H. H. Terrell, Adjutant General, Indianapolis, Indiana:

"The credit of re-enlisted veterans to the State of Indiana appears upon our books as 11,490, and agrees with the figures in your office. General PITCHER has been directed to make the distribution of the 237 certified by him as not credited.

[Signed:] "JAMES B. FRY, Provost Marshal General."

It was claimed by me that each of the 237 should be credited as three men on the pending call for one year men, and not as a unit, and the question being referred to the Provost Marshal General's Bureau, it was decided adversely, as will be seen from the following letter, received by General PITCHER:

"WAR DEPARTMENT, PROVOST MARSHAL GENERAL'S BUREAU,
"WASHINGTON, D. C., February 11th, 1865.
"BRIG. GEN. T. G. PITCHER, *Act. Ass't. Provost Marshal General, Indianapolis, Ind.:*

"GENERAL: The Provost Marshal General directs, that, in distributing the credits to which the localities in the State of Indiana are entitled, on account of the 237 veterans authorized by his telegram of the 6th instant, that as these credits have not been applied on the July call, they are each a credit for three years of service, and you will reduce the quotas for the localities entitled to the credit by deducting the number of men to which they are entitled, amounting in the aggregate to 237.

"I am, General, very respectfully, Your Obedient Servant,
[Signed:] "N. L. JEFFRIES, Colonel Veteran Reserve Corps."

The duty of assigning said unassigned re-enlisted veterans for credit, having devolved upon the undersigned, I thought it my duty to assign them to such localities as would pay, for their benefit, a fair local bounty for the credits thus given, and the distribution of the same was accordingly made.[3] . . .

---

[3] The distribution is shown in Terrell's report to the House of Representatives in 1865. *House Journal,* 1865, p. 872. For the complete list of re-enlisted veterans, where credited, and disposition made of their bounties, see Terrell, *Report,* 1, Appendix, Doc. 21:151-55.

Said bounties, being the highest which could be obtained for said credits, were duly paid, and the money deposited by the local authorities in the First National Bank of Indianapolis, to the credit of each Veteran by name, and a certificate of deposit issued for the amount in each case, payable to the order of the proper party, or, in the event of his death, to the order of his widow, or if he have no widow, to his father or widowed mother; otherwise, to his legal heirs. And, in case said bounty shall remain unclaimed for the period of two years, it is provided in the certificate of deposit, that the money shall be paid into the State Treasury to the credit of the fund arising from "Estates without heirs."

All which is respectfully submitted. W. H. H. TERRELL,
Adjutant General of Indiana.

QUOTAS

The quotas, under the several calls, were assigned to the States and Congressional Districts by the Provost Marshal General, and to townships and other sub-districts by the Acting Assistant Provost Marshal, on the basis of the enrollment, taking into consideration the number of troops previously furnished. It was a rare thing for the people of any township or sub-district to be entirely satisfied with their quotas. They were either too large for the number of men enrolled and liable to do military duty, or else proper credit had not been given for all the men previously enlisted. The State authorities also frequently found just reason to object to the general quotas assigned as being excessive and incorrect. Thus, when a draft was ordered to be made on the 10th of March, 1864, it was clearly evident to the mind of the Governor that the quotas assigned to Indiana for the years 1861 and 1862 were largely excessive, and that under any construction or calculation, the then pending quota, as well as all previous ones, had more than been filled. He did not guess at this conclusion, but reached it by a thorough examination of the whole matter from the beginning of the war; and yet a draft was actually insisted on, and Colonel BAKER, Acting Assistant Provost Marshal General for the State, under the orders of his Chief, had fully made all his preparations to commence it at the time designated. This appeared to the Governor flagrantly unjust. The nation was entitled to all the forces it needed, but could rightfully only draw upon a State for its equitable proportion of the general whole; Indiana had furnished more than her share already; it was not right, therefore, to force a draft upon us merely because a few sub-districts were in arrears, which, if allowed time, would wipe out their deficiencies by furnishing volunteers. If all the other States called on had furnished their proportion, there would certainly have been no occasion to require us to furnish more than ours. The Governor very properly protested against such inequality and unfairness, and so plainly did he make the facts appear, the threatened draft was promptly stopped. The following telegrams will fully explain the stand he took:

INDIANAPOLIS, INDIANA, February 29th, 1864.

COLONEL JAMES B. FRY, *Provost Marshal General, Washington, D. C.*

On the basis of *population* shown by the census of 1860, including one-half of the white population of Kentucky, Missouri, Delaware, Maryland, West Virginia, and the District of Columbia, and omitting California, Oregon and all the rebel States and Territories, the calls made on Indiana in 1861 and 1862 were excessive 6,199. On the basis of the *enrollment* the calls during the same year were excessive to the number of 9986. Upon any basis of calculation, with the number of men known to be recruited in the State and re-enlisted in the field, it is certain that the State has more than filled her quota under all the calls. Many localities are paying heavy bounties, and it will occasion great complaint if they are allowed to do this after the quota is filled. Statement mailed to-day.

O. P. MORTON.

INDIANAPOLIS, INDIANA, March 1st, 1864.

COLONEL JAMES B. FRY,

Provost Marshal General, Washington, D. C.

Colonel BAKER has just shown me a dispatch, in which he is required to commence the draft on the 10th of March, in all sub-districts that have not furnished their quotas. Are we to infer from this that sub-districts are to be drafted when the State in the aggregate has filled her quota? O. P. MORTON.

INDIANAPOLIS, INDIANA, March 3d, 1864.

COLONEL JAMES B. FRY,

Provost Marshal General, Washington City:

Let me earnestly invite the Government to pause, before adopting a construction requiring a draft in a State that has filled her quota in the aggregate.

O. P. MORTON.

THIRD SERIES OF VETERAN CREDITS

The Muster-in Rolls of the re-enlisted Veterans of the Eleventh, Thirteenth, Twenty-Fourth, Twenty-Sixth, Thirty-Fourth, Forty-Sixth, Forty-Seventh and Sixtieth Regiments, and Third Cavalry Regiment, were received at this office in September and October, 1864. These rolls showed the residence of most of the men, and the residence thus given settled the question as to local credit, according to the mustering regulations. Prior to their receipt, however, these Veterans had been credited, by Adjutant General NOBLE, by numbers, as part of the State's aggregate credit, and it was decided by the Acting Assistant Provost General, that the credits shown on the rolls could not be given to the localities without a withdrawal of an equal number from other localities, and knowing that the application of such a rule would result in confusion and dissatisfaction, the claim for credits, under it, was not pressed. Applications were, however, made direct to the War Department by parties interested, in behalf of Cass and Marion counties, and this office furnished all the information in its possession to enable the parties to prosecute their claims. The War Department, however, did not arrange the matter satisfactorily. In March, 1865, Governor MORTON gave the subject his personal attention, and obtained from Brigadier General J. B. FRY, Provost Marshal General, an order to credit Cass county with 82 men, Indianapolis and Marion county 172, and Huntington county 56 men, veterans of some of the regiments referred to; and, also, a promise that credits should be given to other counties entitled to them upon the same principle. The localities named were the only ones where the exact numbers were known without a careful examination of the rolls—hence the reason for the order in their case, prior to the orders subsequently given.

On the 18th of March, 1865, General PITCHER received a telegram from General FRY, directing the credits to be made as stated, and copies of the Muster-in- Rolls of such Veterans of the Eleventh, Thirteenth, Twenty-Sixth, Forty-Sixth and Forty-Seventh Regiments, as had credited themselves to localities in Marion, Cass and Huntington counties, were furnished General PITCHER, that he might give the credits to the precise localities named on the rolls. The number thus credited was 310.

On the 28th of March, 1865, the rolls of the Eleventh, Thirteenth, Twenty-Fourth, Twenty-Sixth, Thirty-Fourth, Forty-Sixth and Forty-Seventh Regiments, and Third Cavalry Regiment, were copied with a view of giving General PITCHER information upon which to give the proper credits when General FRY should direct him to do so. These copies did not embrace any of the names shown upon the copies furnished March 18th, 1865, relating to credits in Cass, Marion and Huntington counties. A report, by telegraph, of the numbers shown to the counties entitled to credit, was made to General FRY, March 28th, with the request that he would order the credits to be given accordingly. A report was also prepared to accompany the copies of rolls for General PITCHER, showing the distribution of these credits by townships, counties and Congressional Districts. The whole number shown to be entitled to be credited by this report is 1,381, which is additional to the 310 credited March 18th, 1865, making the whole number 1,691.

On the 29th March, 1865, the Provost Marshal General made the following order, a copy of which was furnished this office by Brigadier General T. G. PITCHER, Acting Assistant Provost Marshal General, April 1st, 1865:

ADJUTANT GENERAL'S REPORT

WAR DEPARTMENT, PROVOST MARSHAL GENERAL'S OFFICE

WASHINGTON, D. C., March 29th, 1865.

BRIG. GEN. T. G. PITCHER, *Act. Asst. Provost Marshal General, Indianapolis, Ind.:*

GENERAL: The Provost Marshal General directs that the following credits for veteran volunteers be given to the localities named below:

Co.	No.	Co.	No.	Co.	No.
Knox	17	Ohio	2	Carroll	52
Daviess	1	Henry	5	Tippecanoe	11
Perry	20	Randolph	4	LaPorte	3
Floyd	1	Johnson	3	Marshall	5
Bartholomew	3	Morgan	17	Allen	26
Jennings	28	Hancock	5	Adams	65
Ripley	4	Vigo	36	Howard	55
Dearborn	45	Vermillion	4	Grant	78
Wayne	7	Clay	5	Madison	90
Union	1	Fountain	1	Parke	2
Fayette	4	Warren	1	Montgomery	38
Hendricks	8	Miami	11	Boone	23
Shelby	5	Pulaski	35	Clinton	9
Marion	11	White	57	Fulton	48
Vanderburgh	8	Kosciusko	9	Jasper	2
Scott	1	Huntington	104	DeKalb	2
Orange	1	Hamilton	6	Wells	102
Jefferson	24	Jay	37	Tipton	43
Switzerland	8	Sullivan	5	Wabash	134
Franklin	1	Putnam	3	Blackford	39
Decatur	7				

I am, General, very respectfully, Your obedient servant.

[Signed:]   G. W. ELCOTT, Capt. Veteran Reserve Corps.

Accordingly, on the 3d of April, 1865, I transmitted to Brigadier General T. G. PITCHER, Acting Assistant Provost Marshal General, the copies of rolls and report referred to, who directed the Provost Marshals of the different Districts to give the credits to the townships indicated in said report, and the same were credited accordingly. This closed all controversies connected with the credits of re-enlisted veterans.

CREDITS FOR TROOPS FURNISHED 133

ADDITIONAL CREDITS

Near the close of the war an act of Congress was passed[4] requiring credit to be given for all troops mustered into the service of the United States for a less period than six months (including three months' men) since the commencement of the rebellion. Indiana was accordingly credited on the last call with 6,409 three months' men, and 7,197 one hundred days' men, making altogether 13,606 men, or 3,574 years of service aggregating 1,191 three years' men. Seventy-one naval enlistments and twenty-one representative recruits were also credited.

CORRECTION AND SUMMARY

The Adjutant General of the Army, at the close of the War reported the grand total of troops, furnished by the State for all terms of service, at 194,363 men. . . . it will be seen that the number reached 208,367, as shown by the rolls and records of this office, for the following terms of service:[5]

Three years' men	165,717
One year men	21,642
Nine months' men	742
Six months' men	4,082
One hundred days' men	7,415
Three months' men	6,308
Sixty days' men	587
Thirty days' men	1,874
Grand Total	208,367

These forces were organized into one hundred and twenty-nine regiments of infantry, thirteen regiments of cavalry, one regiment of heavy artillery and twenty-six batteries of light

[4] Act approved March 3, 1865, Sec. 15. U. S. *Statutes at Large,* 13(1863-65):489.

[5] See table summarizing troops furnished by the State of Indiana, in Terrell, *Report,* 1, Appendix, Doc. 1:5-6, and detailed statement of troops furnished, pp. 6 ff.

artillery, besides independent companies, recruits for HANCOCK's Corps, U.S. Veteran Volunteeer Engineers, etc.; the aggregate number for the several arms of the service being as follows:

Infantry .... 175,776 men.
Cavalry .... 21,605 men.
Artillery .... 10,986 men.

Grand Total.. 208,367 men.

INDIANA LEGION

STATE MILITIA

The act of May 11th, 1861, under which the Legion was organized and all its operations conducted, is discussed elsewhere in this volume. The most important features of the service rendered by this organization are fully detailed under the titles of "Kirby Smith's Campaign," "The Hines and Morgan Raids," and "Morgan's Last Kentucky Raid."[1]

The scarcity of arms prevented the Governor from attempting to place the militia on a war footing until September, 1861. Companies had been organized under the law in almost every county; and on the Ohio river border and in some of the interior counties a number of regiments and battalions were enrolled. Failing to receive arms promptly, many of these organizations were broken up and abandoned—a large proportion of their members enlisting in the volunteer service.

On the 10th of September, 1861, Major JOHN LOVE, of Marion, and Colonel JOHN L. MANSFIELD, of Jefferson, were commissioned to organize the Legion upon a systematic plan for active service, the former with the rank of Major General and the latter with the rank of Brigadier. These gentlemen were by education and experience well qualified to discharge the important trust committed to them; they entered upon their duties with zeal and spirit and by laborious effort, in the face of many difficulties and discouragements, succeeded in effecting a partial organization of the militia in all the southern or border counties of the State. They were greatly aided in their labors by Brigadier Generals JAMES E. BLYTHE, of

[1] See below, 190-261.

Vanderburgh, and ALEXANDER C. DOWNEY, of Ohio, and their subordinate officers, among whom may be worthily mentioned Colonels ENOCH R. JAMES and JOHN A. MANN, of Posey; WILLIAM E. HOLLINGSWORTH, of Vanderburgh; DANIEL F. BATES, of Warrick; JOHN W. CROOKS, of Spencer; CHARLES H. MASON and CHARLES FOURNIER, of Perry; HORATIO WOODBURY and JOHN T. MORGAN, of Crawford; LEWIS JORDAN, Senior, of Harrison; BENJAMIN F. SCRIBNER and WILLIAM W. TULEY, of Floyd; JOHN N. INGRAM and JOHN F. WILLEY, of Clark; SAMUEL B. SERING, of Jefferson; GEORGE W. MALICK and KENNEDY BROWN, of Jennings; OLIVER ORMSBY, of Switzerland; HUGH T. WILLIAMS, of Ohio, and JOHN H. BURKAM, of Dearborn. The Honorable RICHARD W. THOMPSON, of Vigo, and MORTON C. HUNTER, ESQ., of Monroe, were also commissioned Brigadier Generals, and succeeded in organizing several very fine regiments.

For the purpose of producing greater uniformity in drill and discipline, and to infuse a higher degree of military spirit into the minds of the officers and men of the Legion, the Governor ordered an Encampment of Instruction to be held at Indianapolis, commencing on the 16th of October, 1862. A new and complete cantonment, called Burnside Barracks, was erected near the city for this purpose, under the direction of Quartermaster-General STONE. Between three and four hundred officers assembled and were placed under regimental organization. Six companies were formed with the usual company and subordinate officers, and placed under the instruction of Colonel (afterwards Brigadier General) HENRY B. CARRINGTON, of the United States Army, and a suitable corps of assistants, aided by Major General LOVE, as commandant. The organization of companies was maintained during the Encampment, which continued for two weeks; hours of duty were published in general orders prescribing the routine of the camp, and everything was conducted in strict accordance with military regulations and usage. The first week was employed in theoretical and practical instruction in the manual of arms and squad drill; during the second week, company and battalion drill were added, and the members of the Encampment were as thoroughly instructed as the short duration of the school would permit. The officers were highly gratified with the progress made, and upon the breaking up of the Encampment returned to their homes with renewed zeal and determination to make their commands more efficient and reliable for active service.

Major General LOVE having resigned on the 1st of January, 1863, the command devolved upon Brigadier General MANSFIELD, under whom the Legion continued to increase in strength and efficiency. He was promoted Major General July 30, 1864, and was relieved from duty on the 1st of November, 1865, his services being no longer necessary. In addition to the regular military duties which devolved upon General MANSFIELD, he was frequently called upon by the Governor to investigate and settle matters of much public importance in various parts of the State, and through his energetic efforts and sound judgment many internal strifes and troubles were quieted and order maintained. His fine abilities were on many occasions strikingly displayed in allaying public excitement and reconciling the people of disturbed localities to the peculiar and complicated circumstances created by the war.

The Honorable JAMES HUGHES, of Monroe, was appointed Brigadier General on the 1st of July, 1863, and was promoted Major General on the 1st of August, 1864. He took an important part in the MORGAN raid of 1863,[2] and in all subsequent defensive operations within the limits of his division. The expedition to Kentucky in August, 1864,[3] was planned by him, but as the troops were to be sent out of the State, Major General HOVEY, United States Volunteers, was invited to take command—General HUGHES co-operating.

[2] See below, 209-54.
[3] See "Adam Johnson's Threatened Raid," below, 262-66.

Colonel HENRY JORDAN, of Harrison, formerly of the 17th Indiana Mounted Infantry, a brave and accomplished officer, was appointed Brigadier General on the 9th of August, 1864, and was actively employed for several months under General HUGHES in guarding the border between New Albany and Troy, and in quelling disloyal combinations and threatened outbreaks in the counties embraced in his command. His prudence and good management was shown in suppressing the "Orange and Crawford Conspiracy" in October, 1864.[4] This was a formidable combination, organized ostensibly to resist the draft, but, as it turned out, the dishonest appropriation of property appeared to be one of its main objects. It was composed of more than three hundred disloyal citizens, including a number of conscript deserters, and was headed by a number of guerrillas from Kentucky, whose connection with the scheme was induced solely by the hope of plunder. Some fifty flagrant robberies were committed. The Legion very promptly suppressed the movement, and upwards of ninety arrests were made. Further violent proceedings were prevented by calling into active service Captain AYDELOTTE's company of the Sixth Regiment, which was posted at Hartford, Crawford county, by General JORDAN, for about six weeks. This ended the trouble, and the services of an active force being no longer required, General JORDAN was relieved about the close of the year 1864. His brief administration of military affairs, in one of the most disaffected districts of the State, was highly creditable and productive of the best results.

In the early part of July, 1863, upon the request of Governor MORTON, Brigadier General HENRY B. CARRINGTON, United States Volunteers, previously Chief Mustering Officer and Commander of the District of Indiana, then in Ohio, was ordered to report at Indianapolis, for such duty as the Gov-

[4] See below, 363-66, and report of Brig. Gen. Henry Jordan, October 7, 1864, in "Operations of the Indiana Legion and Minute Men, 1863, 1864," in Indiana *Documentary Journal,* 1864, vol. 2, no. 11:448-52.

ernor might assign to him. The MORGAN Raid followed, and General CARRINGTON's fine abilities as a mustering officer and organizer of troops in an emergency were a most valuable acquisition. After the raid was over, he was directed to more thoroughly organize the Legion, and for the ten months succeeding he was industriously and actively engaged in this important work, giving much attention also to the recruitment of volunteers. He visited some thirty-five counties, and spent considerable time in instructing the militia in drill and discipline. About eighteen thousand stand of small arms were issued to the organized Legion, besides a number of pieces of artillery, during the time he was acting under the Governor's orders.[5] Not the least important service rendered by him to the State and Nation was the discovery and exposure of the treasonable organization known as the "Sons of Liberty," which, but for his efforts, would probably have caused much trouble and bloodshed.[6] His great energy and industry, his willingness to assume responsibilities, when required by the demands of the hour, his admirable way of working through or around obstacles, and "stirring up things generally," at times when haste was essential to success, told on many occasions with wonderful effect, and very materially aided in securing for Indiana the proud name she won for the rapidity with which her troops were thrown into the field, and the efficiency of her militia at home. . . .

ORGANIZATION OF THE LEGION[7]

GENERAL-IN-CHIEF.

Major General JOHN LOVE, from September 10th, 1861, to January 1st, 1863.

[5] See Carrington's report on his military administration while on duty in Indiana, in Terrell, *Report,* 1, Appendix, Doc. 77:271-74.

[6] See below, 376, and "Exposure of the Sons of Liberty—a Secret Treasonable Organization, General Carrington's Report" in *ibid.,* 1, Appendix, Doc. 79:274-76.

[7] A complete roster of officers of the Indiana Legion is given in *ibid.,* 3:456-604.

FIRST MILITARY DIVISION.

Major General JOHN L. MANSFIELD, from July 30th, 1864, to November 1st, 1865.

This Division was composed of the Third, Fourth, Fifth, Sixth and Ninth Brigades.

SECOND MILITARY DIVISION.

Major General JAMES HUGHES, commissioned August 1st, 1864.

This Division was composed of the First, Second, Seventh and Eighth Brigades.

FIRST BRIGADE—SECOND DIVISION.

Brigadier General ANDREW LEWIS, commissioned June 7th, 1861; resigned.

Brigadier General JAMES E. BLYTHE, commissioned November 1st, 1861; deceased.

This Brigade was composed of the organized militia in the counties of Posey, Vanderburgh, Warrick, Gibson, Spencer, Dubois, Pike, Knox, Daviess, Martin, Greene and Sullivan.

SECOND BRIGADE—SECOND DIVISION.

Brigadier General JAMES HUGHES, commissioned July 1st, 1863; promoted.

Brigadier General HENRY JORDAN, commissioned August 9th, 1864.

This Brigade was composed of the organized militia in the counties of Perry, Crawford, Harrison, Floyd, Clark, Scott, Washington, Jackson, Brown, Lawrence, Orange, Monroe and Owen.

THIRD BRIGADE—FIRST DIVISION.

Brigadier General JOHN L. MANSFIELD, from September 10th, 1861, to July 30th, 1864.

This Brigade was composed of the organized militia in the counties of Jefferson, Switzerland, Jennings, Batholomew, Morgan, Hendricks, Marion, Johnson, Hamilton and Boone.

FOURTH BRIGADE—FIRST DIVISION.

Brigadier General ALEXANDER C. DOWNEY, commissioned November 1st, 1861.

This Brigade was composed of the organized militia in the counties of Ohio, Dearborn, Ripley, Decatur, Franklin, Union, Fayette, Rush and Shelby.

FIFTH BRIGADE—FIRST DIVISION.

No General Officer commissioned for this Brigade.

It was composed of the organized militia in the counties of Wayne, Hancock, Delaware, Randolph, Henry, Madison, Jay, Blackford and Grant.

SIXTH BRIGADE—FIRST DIVISION.

No General Officer commissioned for this Brigade.

It was composed of the organized militia in the counties of Howard, Wabash, Miami, Cass, Clinton, Carroll, Fulton and Tipton.

SEVENTH BRIGADE—SECOND DIVISION.

No General Officer commissioned for this Brigade.

It was composed of the organized militia in the counties of Vigo, Clay, Putnam, Parke, Vermillion, Fountain, Warren, Benton, Tippecanoe and Montgomery.

EIGHTH BRIGADE—SECOND DIVISION.

No General Officer commissioned for this Brigade.

It was composed of the organized militia in the counties of White, Jasper, Pulaski, Marshall, Newton, St. Joseph, LaPorte, Starke, Porter and Lake.

NINTH BRIGADE—FIRST DIVISION.

No General Officer commissioned for this Brigade.

It was composed of the organized militia in the counties of Allen, DeKalb, Huntington, Kosciusko, LaGrange, Noble, Steuben, Wells, Whitley, Adams and Elkhart.

Brigadier General MORTON C. HUNTER, commissioned November 1st, 1861; assigned to command the *Fifth Brigade,* then composed of the organized militia of the counties of Monroe, Brown, Jackson and Lawrence, which were attached to the Second Brigade, March 27th, 1863. General HUNTER entered the United States service, August 27th, 1862, as Colonel of the Eighty-Second Regiment Indiana Volunteers.

Brigadier General RICHARD W. THOMPSON, commissioned November 1st, 1861; assigned to command the *Sixth Brigade,* then composed of the organized militia in counties of Vigo, Clay, Owen, Greene and Sullivan. The two first named counties were attached to the Seventh Brigade, Owen to the Second Brigade, and Greene and Sullivan to the First Brigade, March 27th, 1863. General THOMPSON entered the U.S. service May 1st, 1863, as Captain and Provost Marshal of the Seventh Congressional District.

THE FIRST REGIMENT, FIRST BRIGADE (*Posey County Regiment*) was partially organized by Colonel ALVIN P. HOVEY, early in the summer of 1861, as soon after the passage of the Act of May 11th, as the necessary orders could be promulgated, appointments made and arms supplied. Colonel HOVEY evinced the utmost zeal, energy and tact, to which the loyal people of his county responded with cordial alacrity, and his command was making rapid progress towards military efficiency, when, about three months from the date of his appointment, he resigned his commission to accept the Colonelcy of the Twenty-fourth Indiana Volunteers. His successor, Colonel ENOCH R. JAMES, continued the work so successfully begun, and soon had nine companies of infantry and one company of artillery fully armed, partially uniformed and well drilled. Company and battalion drills were well attended for several months, and the regiment, on frequent dress parades, received the commendations of military men for their proficiency in the manual of arms and soldierly bearing.

On several occasions, during Colonel JAMES's incumbency, the people of Mount Vernon were alarmed by threats of guerrilla incursions, but the promptness with which the Legion rallied for the defense of the town, allayed public apprehension and restored a sense of security. Detachments from the "Independent Guards" and the "Union Rifles" rendered important service in assisting to make arrests of dangerous characters in Kentucky. In the spring of 1862, a detail of about ten men from each company was called out to guard prisoners at Camp Morton. The men promptly reported at rendezvous, but the order being countermanded, they returned to their homes. Upon the resignation of Colonel JAMES, a little more than one year from the date of his appointment, Colonel JOHN A. MANN was appointed to fill the vacancy, and, entering at once upon his duty, he proceeded to organize two new companies—one of infantry and one of cavalry— to take the places of two of the original companies which had been disbanded on account of most of their members having entered the active volunteer service.

And here it is proper to state that the Legion was the portal through which thousands of the best of our soldiers entered the army. The martial enthusiasm which it awakened and nurtured, could not be satisfied with home service, however important that duty might be regarded, and the Legion soon came to be viewed as the nursery from which the old regiments and batteries of volunteers were to be recruited and new ones organized. While this result was unfavorable to the maintenance of permanency and efficiency in the organization relied upon for home defense, it was of immeasurable importance in securing a ready response to calls for volunteers, and thus enabled the State to promptly fill her quota under each successive call.

The cavalry company, well officered, thoroughly drilled and effectively armed, was often called upon for scouting and picket duty, when the presence of guerrillas on the Kentucky side of the river admonished the military authorities of the necessity of vigilance and preparation.

Immediately after the issue of Governor MORTON's order[8] of September 5th, 1862, for the organization of the reserve militia, Colonel MANN proceeded to organize and drill that portion of the citizens of his county, and in a few days, had twenty-one companies formed. They met regularly and were rapidly advancing in drill and discipline when the Governor's order, relieving them from further attendance, was issued. Unfortunately the order to discontinue drills was understood as applying to the Legion as well as to the newly organized companies, from which misconstruction the *morale* of all the companies of the First Regiment suffered severely, and for a long time much difficulty was experienced by the regimental commander in his efforts to induce them to turn out for company or battalion exercises.

Guerrilla parties, roaming through Henderson, Union and adjacent counties of Kentucky, plundering the inhabitants and committing almost every species of outrage, were a constant source of alarm to the citizens of our southwestern counties, and they were rarely free from apprehensions of raids. During the winter and spring of 1863, alarms occurred with unusual frequency, and the First Regiment was often called

[8] Governor Morton's order placing the militia under arms is given in Terrell, *Report,* 1, Appendix, Doc. 124:334-35.

upon to do guard duty along the river for a distance of thirty miles.

Late at night, on the 9th of July, 1863, Colonel MANN received orders from Governor MORTON to hold his command in readiness for immediate service in preventing rebel reinforcements, the raid of JOHN MORGAN being then in progress through another section of the State. Messengers were dispatched to rally the companies, and although many of the men resided at a distance, some of them as far as fourteen miles from headquarters, such promptitude was displayed that every company, and nearly every man belonging to the regiment, had reported at Mount Vernon before noon of the 10th. At nine P. M., seven companies of infantry embarked on board transports and proceeded up the river, while the cavalry marched in the same direction. Arriving at Evansville, the regiment went into camp with other troops rendezvoused at that point. Rumors of a threatened guerrilla raid, as a countermovement to help MORGAN, into Posey county, induced Colonel MANN to return to Mount Vernon the next day with the cavalry. The infantry remained at Evansville several days, when, it being evident that they could not be used against MORGAN, they were ordered to report to Colonel MANN at Mount Vernon, by whom they were dismissed to their homes.

During the remainder of 1863 unusual quiet reigned along the border, and this command was not called upon for further service.

The year 1864 was characterized by frequent alarms and the services of the First Regiment were varied and arduous. FORREST's raid through Western Kentucky, and his attack on Paducah in March of that year, created an apprehension that he intended moving northward, striking the Ohio at Uniontown or Henderson, and thence raiding upon the border towns of Indiana. The battalion was again called out, and performed guard duty for several days, or until the rebels were reported as moving rapidly to the southward.

A few weeks later, formidable bands of guerrillas appeared along the Kentucky shore, and, with more than their usual boldness, attempted to steal a number of horses from citizens of Mount Vernon and vicinity, but succeeded in securing only a single horse. The Legion was called to arms, and a permanent guard established along the entire border of the county. The services of this regiment in the expedition against JOHNSON's and SEIPERT's forces are detailed in the chapter devoted to "ADAM JOHNSON's Threatened Raid," in this volume.

After that expedition, Western Kentucky was comparatively free from guerrillas, and, although the regiment maintained its organization until the close of the war, it was not again called upon, except for occasional details for brief and unimportant service. There can be no doubt that the efficiency and constant vigilance of the officers and men of the First Regiment prevented frequent guerrilla incursions, and even more formidable invasions, by which incalculable loss and damage would have been inflicted upon the inhabitants of that section of the State. The same remark is applicable to the several regiments in all the border counties.

THE SECOND REGIMENT, FIRST BRIGADE (*Vanderburgh County Regiment*) was organized under Colonel JAMES E. BLYTHE, during the summer of 1861. The regiment proper consisted of nine companies of infantry, and one of artillery; but twenty-five other companies, artillery, cavalry, and infantry, were, at various periods, organized in the county under the Legion law (besides, five other companies were formed, but did not fully comply with the provisions of that act), all of which were regarded as constituting one command, under the Colonel of the Second Regiment, and when formed in battalions, for drill or active duty, were commanded by officers detailed by him. Companies, as fast as organized, were supplied with arms and accoutrements, and several of them procured uniforms. Drills were frequent, and attended, for some time, with such promptness and regularity that the command, in a few months, attained a highly creditable proficiency in company and battalion movements. Colonel BLYTHE having been promoted to the command of the First Brigade, Lieutenant Colonel WILLIAM E. HOLLINGSWORTH was promoted to the Colonelcy, and assumed command of the regiment and independent companies of the county, on the 30th of November, 1861.

During the occupation of Bowling Green and Russellville, Kentucky, by BUCKNER'S command, frequent demonstrations were made in the direction of the Ohio river, threatening the destruction of the locks on Green river, and the capture of the city of Henderson. At one time a force was detailed, by order of General BUCKNER, to destroy the first lock. A regiment of volunteers marched for the protection of the lock, accompanied by a detail of artillery from Colonel HOLLINGSWORTH's command. They succeeded in protecting the threatened point, and held possession of the place for several days.

Other demonstrations were constantly threatening the security of Evansville, and the various companies were kept on the alert. Scouting parties were sent into Kentucky, and up and down the Ohio river, to ascertain the position, numbers and purposes, so far as possible, of rebel forces in that vicinity. Guards were posted at various approaches to the city, and the command was held in readiness to repel an attack at any moment.

The success of the Union forces, in the spring of 1862, compelled the rebels to evacuate Bowling Green and Russellville, and alarms gradually subsided; the pressure of imminent danger was removed, and the command became less vigilant. But upon the receipt of Governor MORTON's order, requiring the organization of the reserve militia, Colonel HOLLINGSWORTH promptly recruited all his companies to about ninety men each, and drilled them two hours daily, until the order discontinuing such special exercises was issued.

The disastrous termination of MCCLELLAN's and POPE's Virginia campaigns encouraged the rebels to renew their operations in Kentucky, and guerrillas again made their appearance on the border. Henderson was threatened, and in several cases details were sent from Colonel HOLLINGSWORTH'S command to support a small force of Union troops stationed there.

ADAM JOHNSON'S raid on Newburgh was the occasion of fresh alarm, and for several nights every company furnished details for guard duty. On the 21st of September, 1862, five companies, under the immediate command of Colonel HOLLINGSWORTH, proceeded to Owensboro, Kentucky, to aid in repelling an attack, but returned without having an opportunity to meet the enemy. On the return trip a Sergeant of Company "A" accidently shot himself through the head, producing instant death.

Threatened raids of Kentucky guerrillas necessitated a great deal of guard duty throughout the ensuing winter and spring, and the efficiency of the command was well maintained.

The Morgan raid in July created in Vanderburgh, as throughout the State, the most intense excitement. Every company in the county rallied, with full ranks, at the first note of alarm, and, going into camp with other troops, awaited orders until the enemy's plans were so far developed that it became evident the First Brigade could not be employed against him.

During the early part of 1864, the duties of the Second Regiment were exceedingly onerous, on account of the necessity of frequent and heavy details for guard duty to protect the border from invasion. In May, one company and parts of several others volunteered for the "Hundred days' service." Colonel HOLLINGSWORTH accepted a captaincy in one of the companies, leaving Lieutenant Colonel VICTOR BISCH —subsequently appointed Colonel—in command. The most important feature of the services rendered by the command during the summer, or at any time thereafter, was its participation in the expedition into Kentucky, under Generals HOVEY and HUGHES, to rout JOHNSON and SEIPERT.[9]

The commanding officers of the Second Regiment have furnished very meager reports of the operations of the Legion in Vanderburgh county, and it is not impossible that important services may have been rendered, of which no mention is here made. It is not too high commendation to say, that in keeping alive the martial spirit, promoting genuine loyalty, and preventing invasions or raids, the officers and men of this command displayed such patriotic zeal as to entitle them to the lasting gratitude of their fellow citizens. The city of Evansville owes its immunity from guerrilla incursions to the fact, well known on the opposite side of the river, that one thousand of her citizens, armed, equipped and organized, could have been called from their beds and formed in line of battle in thirty minutes from the first sound of alarm.

THE THIRD REGIMENT, FIRST BRIGADE (*Warrick County Regiment*), Colonel DANIEL F. BATES, commanding, was organized to the extent of six very efficient companies, in the summer and autumn of 1861. All these companies were armed and equipped, and drilled to a fair degree of proficiency in the manual of arms and in company and battalion evolutions. Two companies located at Newburgh were called out for guard duty during the fall and winter, and maintained the utmost vigilance for several months. In the spring of 1862, the ranks of the battalion had become so thinned by the men volunteering for active field service, that three companies were disbanded. Nine other companies were subsequently, and at different dates, organized and attached to this command. Company drills were maintained throughout the spring months of this year, but the constant drain upon the ranks by volunteering, induced the Colonel commanding (with the consent of General BLYTHE), to call in the arms of two companies, an act which opened the way for the Newburgh

---

[9] See "Adam Johnson's Threatened Raid," below, 262-66.

raid.[10] This event threw the country into intense excitement, and in connection with the presence of large bodies of guerrillas in the vicinity of Green river, Kentucky, caused the regiment to be called out and kept in camp for several days. Many of the men were farmers, and while they were on duty at camp their crops were wasting. As the excitement began to subside, the men were permitted to stay at their homes during the day time, but details of one third of each company were placed on guard every night until the danger was over.

About the 20th of September, Colonel BATES, with four hundred men hastily called together, went to Owensboro, Kentucky, to aid in repelling an attack upon the United States forces stationed there. They arrived too late to participate in the engagement, and after remaining one day returned to Newburgh. During their absence the town had been threatened again and two companies had been called out, who were dismissed to their homes on the return of the Colonel commanding. Details were, however, kept on guard until the 1st of November following. Drills were kept up without regard to weather and to the neglect of all other interests. Eleven militia companies were organized under the Governor's proclamation of September 5th, 1862, and when they were disbanded, the *morale* of the regiment did not suffer as was the case in some other counties. On several occasions battalion dress parades were held, and the command received the commendations of officers of high rank, for their soldierly bearing and marked proficiency in discipline and tactics.

Nothing of greater importance than details for guard duty and scouting was required of the regiment during the winter and spring of 1863, or until the month of July. On the 8th of that month Colonel BATES, in obedience to an order from the Governor called out his entire command to repel an expected attack from rebels acting in concert with JOHN MORGAN. Eight companies of infantry and one company of artil-

[10] See below, 181-84.

lery were stationed at Scuffletown Bar, on the Ohio; one company of cavalry at Newburgh, to be used as scouts; two companies of infantry were mounted and sent out as scouts into Dubois, Orange and Perry counties, to ascertain if MORGAN was moving westward, as was currently reported. The command remained on duty eight days, when all but two companies were permitted to return to their homes, with orders to hold themselves in readiness for instant service if required. The two companies retained were placed on guard at several points on the river, where, on account of the low stage of the water, it was easily fordable. This duty was continued for two weeks.

This regiment was not called upon for further service until the 10th of June, 1864, when General HUGHES ordered the Colonel commanding to go into camp near Newburgh with two companies and be prepared to repel a raid which seemed imminent from threatening demonstrations on the Kentucky border. The cavalry company attached to the regiment was at the same time ordered to report to General HUGHES and, in addition to other service, participated in the expedition into Kentucky. Colonel BATES picketed the river the entire breadth of his county and patroled the bank every night until the 15th of June, when he was ordered to break up his camp and dismiss the men to their homes. The regiment was not subsequently called out.

This regiment was particularly fortunate in continuing throughout the war under the command of the same Colonel, than whom no officer of the Legion exhibited more earnest zeal or more unflinching loyalty. He succeeded in infusing his spirit and energy into his officers and men, and no portion of the command ever hesitated to respond to any call, at whatever sacrifice of personal interests.

FOURTH REGIMENT, FIRST BRIGADE (*Spencer County Regiment*)—JOHN W. CROOKS was commissioned Colonel of the Fourth, or Spencer County Regiment, on the 12th of June, 1861, and continued in command of all the companies organized in that county until March 1st, 1864, when the acceptance of his resignation created a vacancy, which was filled by the appointment of WILLIAM N. WALKER, who retained the command until the last of November, 1864. The entire force organized at various periods in the county and constituting Colonel CROOKS's command, consisted of twenty-five companies, fourteen of which belonged to the Fourth Regiment proper, and eleven of which were organized under the name of the "Grand View Battalion," Lieutenant Colonel L. C. PARKER, commanding.

In arms, equipments and drill this command did not differ materially from those of the lower border counties already described. Its services were also of a similar character. During the months of July, August and September, 1862, not less than twenty alarms of threatened inroads from guerrilla parties called out the companies and kept the people generally in a state of intensive excitement. The citizens of Owensboro made frequent and earnest appeals to Colonel CROOKS for assistance in repelling raids, and seemed to rely upon the Fourth Regiment for the protection of their town. These appeals were cheerfully responded to, the entire command, with many citizen volunteers, having marched to their relief as many as six times, and on one occasion defended the town and the small force stationed there for ninety days. The few loyal men residing in Daviess county, Kentucky, having the assurance that the entire arms-bearing population of Spencer county would fly to their relief if needed, took high Union grounds and succeeded in establishing a tolerably healthy public sentiment.

The most important feature of the operations of Colonel CROOKS's forces was the battle of "Panther Creek," Kentucky, which was fought on the 20th of September, 1862.[11] On the

[11] See General Crooks's report on the Battle of Panther Creek, in Terrell, *Report,* 1, Appendix, Doc. 88:292-93.

morning of that day the town of Owensboro was attacked and captured by the rebels; Colonel NETTER, commanding the post, was killed and his small force driven into such a position that they could offer no effective resistance. Colonel CROOKS received immediate notice of this disaster, and an urgent call for assistance. Rallying a portion of his command, he crossed the river under protection of his artillery, with six hundred men, driving the rebels from and taking possession of the town. Learning that night that the rebels had gone into camp on Panther creek, eight miles from Owensboro, Colonel CROOKS organized a force for the purpose of attacking them. Although the men were much fatigued, many of them having marched more than twenty miles, three hundred and fifty of Colonel CROOKS's men promptly fell into line, and, reinforced by sixty of NETTER's mounted men and a half a dozen citizens of Daviess county, marched with alacrity towards the rebel camp. The Fourth Regiment had one six-pounder cannon. The rebel force consisted of a battalion five hundred strong commanded by Lieutenant Colonel MARTIN. They had one small piece of artillery.

NETTER's mounted men, the advance of Colonel CROOKS's small force, came upon the enemy's camp about daylight, and, having incautiously approached too near, met with so warm a reception that they were speedily dispersed and did not render further assistance. Hearing the discharge of musketry with which the cavalry were greeted, the Fourth Regiment hastened forward and placed their cannon in position, but at the third discharge it became unserviceable and was sent to the rear. The cavalry being dispersed and artillery disabled, our infantry were advanced to within easy musket range of the enemy, and both sides opened a spirited fire, the enemy using his cannon, charged with sacks of Minie balls, with considerable effect. At the end of an hour and a half the enemy's lines began to waiver, seeing which, Colonel CROOKS ordered his men to charge. The movement was effected in gallant style, scattering the rebels in the wildest confusion.

The casualties in the Fourth Regiment were three killed and thirty-five wounded. The mounted men lost two wounded and eight captured. The rebel loss was thirty-six killed, more than seventy wounded and sixteen prisoners. Our forces captured twelve horses, one hundred and forty small arms, and a small amount of camp and garrison equippage.

The result of this little but brilliant affair was in the highest degree creditable to the command engaged, and sufficiently corroborates the statement of the Colonel commanding, that "all did well; both officers and men seemed to vie with each other in deeds of daring."

A few weeks after the engagement at Panther creek, the Fourth Regiment was again most earnestly requested to return to Owensboro, the rebels having threatened to visit the town, and wreak summary vengeance on the small force, constituting its garrison, for their late humiliating defeat.

On the morning of the 6th of October, Colonel CROOKS arrived opposite the town with nearly five hundred men, but there was murmuring in his ranks: "The citizens would not defend themselves; more than half of them were rebel sympathizers; neighbors and friends had been slain in defense of a people who would not fight for themselves; the tobacco crop, the chief reliance of Spencer county as a remunerative product, was suffering for care." Doubtless every man would have crossed the river had the order been given, but their commanding officer thought there was reason in their complaints; he therefore put two pieces of artillery in position to command the town, and notified the officer in command of the garrison that he would not cross, but "proposed to defend the camp and town from this (the Indiana) side of the river." The citizens of Owensboro were notified that as soon as the women and children could be removed after the attack was made upon the garrison, or the town occupied by the rebels, it would be shelled by Colonel CROOKS's artillery. No attack was made at that time, and trouble on the border of Daviess county, Kentucky, ceased.

The efficiency of this organization was maintained throughout the war, but no reports have been made of its operations during the years 1863 and 1864.

FIFTH REGIMENT, SECOND BRIGADE (*Perry County*)— Early in the summer of 1861, Colonel CHARLES H. MASON organized eight companies in Perry county, which, after some unavoidable delay, were armed and equipped by the Quartermaster General. In August, serious troubles began in the counties of Kentucky opposite this county. Several bands of guerrillas were formed, who, not content with the field of operations presented in their own State, constantly made threats against the citizens of Perry county. The Fifth Regiment had, however, made such rapid progress in drill and discipline as to be able not only to defend their own border, but to extend protection, to some extent, to the persecuted unionists on the other side of the Ohio.

On the 25th of August, the guerrillas made a night attack upon the union residents of the town of Hawesville, Kentucky, and aided by many armed inhabitants of secession proclivities, succeeded in driving them out of the town. They crossed the river and appealed to the Legion for protection. Several companies were called out with the view of attacking the guerrillas, but they prudently evacuated the town before daylight, and fell back to a position in a remote part of Hancock county, Kentucky. Such, however, was the aspect of affairs that it was deemed necessary to guard the border of the entire county, to which duty nearly all the companies were assigned for several successive weeks, and until the rebel bands had been consolidated and left that region to join the Confederate army.

In the following October, Hawesville was again visited by guerrillas at night and several members of a Home Guard company which had been organized among the union men of the town and adjacent country, were captured and taken away. A small detachment of the Fifth Regiment immediately crossed the river but could not move with sufficient rapidity to strike an enemy whose chief concern was personal safety. Captain (afterwards Colonel) FOURNIER, under instructions from General BOYLE, authorizing him to act upon his own discretion in any emergency, notified the principal citizens of Hawesville, that they would be held responsible for all outrages committed upon the persons or property of the union men of that town. The salutary effect of this notice was perceptible in unwonted quiet throughout that neighborhood for more than six months.

In June, 1862, the rebels appeared in considerable force in several counties of Kentucky, adjacent to Perry county. In response to an appeal from the Provost Marshal of Hancock county, Colonel FOURNIER with a detachment of the Fifth, again crossed the river and assisted in an attack upon a company of rebels, a part of whom were captured and sent to Louisville. These vigorous measures checked the rebels for a time, but in the following September other guerrilla bands were organized, and the work of plundering the property and maltreating the persons of Kentucky unionists was begun afresh. The rebel battalion, which was so severely chastised by Colonel CROOKS, at Panther creek, fell back into Hancock and Breckinridge counties, and being reinforced by guerrillas, prepared to attack Colonel SHANKS, at Cloverport. Two companies of the Fifth, under command of Colonel FOURNIER, promptly marched to his assistance, but the rebels learning of the arrival of reinforcements, declined to attack, and, a few days later, moved southward across Green river.

During the remainder of 1862, the regiment was not called out, except for drill. It had been augmented by new organizations, until at the close of the year it consisted of sixteen companies, numbering, all told, eight hundred and fifty well drilled and reliable men, all armed and equipped, and ready for service whenever they might be needed.

On the 3d day of February, 1863, the rebels having taken possession of Lewisport, Kentucky, a few miles below Troy (in Spencer county, Indiana), one company of the Fifth was called out for guard duty, at exposed points on the river, but the excitement subsided, and after remaining on duty for three days the company was called in and the men dismissed to their homes. Later in the same month four companies were ordered to march for the protection of Hawesville. The officer in command stationed his force opposite the town, ready to cross if necessary, but no attack was made and the companies were dismissed.

A company of rebel mounted infantry visited Hawesville on the 3d of March, and Colonel FOURNIER prepared to attack them at midnight, an entertainment for which the rebels did not wait.

On the 8th of June a rebel detachment entered Cloverport, Kentucky, and commenced the seizure of horses. Their movements indicated an intention of crossing the river, but the judicious disposal of a detachment of the Fifth frustrated that design.

The gallant part borne by a part of this command in the Hines Raid will be referred to in another part of this report. During the Morgan Raid the entire force was in camp along the river, which was thoroughly guarded, as long as MORGAN was in the State.

About the middle of September, Colonel FOURNIER, with a small force, crossed the river to assist the Provost Marshal of Hancock County in dispersing a company of rebels, but the sudden retreat of the enemy prevented a collision, and the detachment returned the next day.

In January, 1864, the military authorities at Hawesville, again called upon the Fifth, for aid, but Colonel FOURNIER declined further efforts in that direction, on account of the open hostility of the principal citizens of the town to the National Government.

In May the rebels again made their appearance on the border in such numbers that heavy details of the Legion were required for guard and patrol duty, during that and the following month. United States transports passing up and down the Ohio were fired upon from Hawesville, Lewisport, Owensboro and other points.

On the 15th of June, five companies under Captain ESSARY were ordered out to repel an expected attack from a rebel force then stationed at Concordia, Kentucky. The men were posted along the Ohio, on the Indiana shore, from Rono to the mouth of Oil creek. A few shots were exchanged, but the river being too high to cross with horses, and having no other means of transportation, Captain ESSARY was unable to gratify the wishes of his men to attack the enemy on their own ground. Several of the rebels were reported wounded by some of the more expert riflemen of the Legion. The rebels withdrew on the 19th, and the companies on duty were soon after dismissed, but strong details were made for night guard until the 23d.

The United States gunboat "Springfield" was about this time detailed for patrol duty, between Cannelton and New Albany, which had the effect to keep the guerrillas quiet for some weeks, but, on the 24th of July, a strong squad, sorely pressed for clothing and other supplies, attempted to make a descent upon Hawesville. They were dispersed by the guns of the "Springfield," without the aid of the Legion. During August and September, the gunboat having been removed, detachments of four or five companies were constantly required for guard and patrol duty.

On the 3d of October, the entire command was ordered out, and camps were established along the river, from Rono to Troy, a distance of forty miles. This precaution was made necessary by the appearance of rebels, in force, on the border, with the supposed purpose of crossing the Ohio, to aid malcontents in resisting the draft. The Fifth Regiment continued on duty for ten days, or until the rebels had apparently abandoned their purpose of invading this State.

In December, rebel forces, under command of Major W. TAYLOR, of the Confederate army, took possession of Hawesville, and notified the Fifth Regiment that, if left in undisturbed occupancy of the town, they would not molest any of the citizens on the Indiana side of the river. Colonel FOURNIER met the rebel Major on the ferry boat, to discuss the proposition, but no terms were agreed upon, and all communication stopped. On the 23d of the same month, a band of marauders, under one "Captain DAVIDSON," seized the packet "Morning Star" at Lewisport (ten miles below Cannelton) and, after murdering, in cold blood, four Union soldiers, drowning the steward of the boat, and robbing the passengers of all their money and other valuables, compelled the Captain to take them to Hawesville, omitting all intermediate landings. Learning of this affair, Colonel FOURNIER called out the river companies of his command and put his artillery in position opposite Hawesville. A sufficient force could not be rallied during the night to cross the river, with fair prospects of success, against the very considerable force of rebels then collected there; but in the morning the enemy was effectually routed, by a few well-aimed shells, thrown from Colonel FOURNIER's guns, through the streets of the town. This process proved an effectual remedy, as the citizens of Hawesville, assured that their town would be again shelled if occupied by rebels, discontinued the extension of hospitalities to friends whose presence would bring such a calamity upon them.

No further report has been furnished of the operations of this vigilant and determined regiment, but the facts already stated sufficiently attest its zeal and loyalty, and prove that to Colonel FOURNIER (now deceased) and his patriotic officers and men, the citizens of Perry, and interior counties, are indebted for exemption from rebel raids, with the probable loss of life and certain loss of property that would have resulted therefrom. The regiment was an insurmountable barrier between hungry hordes of lawless marauders and outcasts, and the tempting prizes presented on the fertile farms, and in the flourishing towns of Perry county and the contiguous country.

CRAWFORD COUNTY REGIMENT, SECOND BRIGADE (*Not Numbered*)—This command consisted of nine companies, organized at various dates, between June, 1861, and August, 1863. From October 4th, 1861, to September 8th, 1862, the regiment was commanded by Colonel HORATIO WOODBURY, who resigned September 8th, 1862, to accept a commission in the volunteer service, leaving a vacancy which was filled by the appointment of JOHN T. MORGAN, who remained in command, with credit to himself and the service, until his decease in the summer of 1863. The vacancy was filled by the appointment of SAMUEL M. JOHNSTON, under a commission dated August 1st, 1863.

Of the services performed by this regiment, during the incumbency of its first and last commanding officers, no reports have ever been made to this office. From a brief report of Colonel MORGAN, it appears that his command, in the fall of 1862, consisted of five companies, all effectively armed as infantry. A small rifled cannon was manned by a detail from one of the infantry companies.

The intense excitement that pervaded the border in September, 1862, was largely participated in by the citizens of Crawford county. The people of Leavenworth and vicinity, apprehensive of an attack upon the town, requested Colonel MORGAN to take precautionary measures to avert the threatened danger. Accordingly, two companies were deployed as pickets along the river for some distance, above and below the town. This service was discontinued at the expiration of three days. About the same time, a three-inch rifled cannon was issued to Captain G. W. LYON's company for the protection of Leavenworth. This gun was of great use to the citizens of that town, but it was finally captured by the rebels under MORGAN, in 1863, as will be more fully stated in the chapter relating to the Morgan raid, in this volume. The Legion turned out on that occasion to the number of about five hundred—two hundred being mounted, and under command of Captain CHARLES L. LAMB, of Leavenworth. This force promptly marched to the relief of Colonel JORDAN, at Corydon, but did not reach that point until after the enemy had left for Salem. When General HOBSON arrived, in pursuit of the rebels, Captain LAMB'S cavalry was ordered in the advance, and continued with HOBSON'S command until it reached Harrison, Ohio, where it was ordered home. The infantry was sent to New Albany, for the protection of the hospitals and public stores at that post, and remained until the raid was over. The only casualty resulting from this service was the death of Lieutenant CALVIN MARTIN, of the "Fredonia Guards," who died shortly after from disease contracted during the march.

Captain LAMB subsequently organized an "Independent Company of Cavalry," and tendered its services, through the Governor, to the General Government, and was accepted, for special service, for twelve months, unless sooner discharged. The company was mustered into service at Leavenworth, on the 13th of August, 1863, and was engaged during the fall and winter following in arresting deserters, enforcing the conscription law, and in guarding the river border against invasions from rebel cavalry and guerrillas. Permission being granted by the War Department, a large proportion of the men re-enlisted for three years, in the Thirteenth Indiana Cavalry, and the remainder were finally discharged on the 23d day of April, 1864, their services being no longer needed.

As has already been stated, but little information as to the services of the Crawford County Legion can be gleaned from the meager reports that have been received. It is believed, however, that all the companies responded to every call that was made upon them and that they performed their duties as zealously and faithfully as any of the similar organizations on the border.

SIXTH REGIMENT, SECOND BRIGADE *(Harrison County)*— Prior to November 1st, 1861, ten companies had been organized in Harrison county, which at that date numbered in the aggregate 535 men. Four companies were subsequently organized, one of which was cavalry. The command also included an artillery company. One of the largest and most efficient company organizations was disbanded in the summer of 1862, nearly all its members having volunteered in the service of the United States. The same cause greatly reduced the strength of all the remaining companies, not less than six hundred members of the regiment having left its ranks to go to the field during the first two years of the war. For eighteen months after the first companies were organized they were drilled regularly two or three times a week, and subsequently to that period once a week till near the close of the second year, when monthly or semimonthly drills were deemed sufficient. Four regimental drills were holden during 1862, on which occasions the fine appearance of the command elicited much commendation.

The appearance of rebels and other indications of danger on the border in September, 1862, induced the commanding officer, Colonel LEWIS JORDAN, Senior, to call out the regiment and go into camp for seven days, at Mauckport, on the Ohio. Thirty or forty Union refugees, driven by the rebel soldiery and disloyal citizens from Brandenburg, Kentucky, had taken refuge on the Indiana side of the river. Desiring to return to their homes, Colonel JORDAN detailed two hundred and fifty men, under command of Lieutenant Colonel IRVIN, to escort them to Brandenburg and take possession of the town. The order was promptly executed, and on the morning of the 25th of September, Lieutenant Colonel IRVIN entered the place and planted the United States flag on the courthouse. The command captured twelve prisoners, who were released on taking the oath of allegiance. A company of United States cavalry arriving the same day to occupy the town, the detachment returned to Harrison county. At another time two companies marched to the assistance of the Union force at the fort on Salt river, Kentucky, and remained there for several days. Subsequently four companies were ordered to Mauckport, to repel a threatened raid, but returned after two days without opposition. The companies residing on and near the river were constantly on the alert and devoted much time to guard and patrol duty.

Nothing further of material importance appears in the record of this command, until the month of July, 1863, when Colonel JORDAN and a part of the Sixth Regiment, and a number of citizens, were captured at Corydon, by JOHN MORGAN'S force, after the most heroic efforts to prevent the enemy from landing on the soil of our State, and a determined and gallant defense of the town. A full account of this affair is given in another chapter.

SEVENTH REGIMENT, SECOND BRIGADE (*Floyd County*)— From the report of Colonel E. A. MAGINNISS, it appears that this regiment was organized (under command of Colonel B. F. SCRIBNER), during the spring of 1861, and consisted at that time of eighteen companies, numbering in the aggregate 900 men, most of whom were uniformed, but not more than 300 armed.

During the first four months the most satisfactory progress was made in company and battalion drill, but protracted delay in procuring arms and accoutrements created general dissatisfaction, while the organization of two regiments of volunteers in this county and vicinity for the United States service, absorbed many of the officers and men who had been the most active members of the Legion. Every company contributed much of its best material to these two regiments, and several of them were thus entirely deprived of commissioned officers. From these causes most of the companies were disorganized, and the efficiency of those who retained their organization was seriously impaired. Here, as elsewhere, the Legion served the noble purpose of educating young men for active service, and in infusing martial enthusiasm into the public mind.

Colonel SCRIBNER, entering the United States service as Colonel of the Thirty-Eighth Indiana Volunteers, the command of the Seventh passed to Colonel WILLIAM W. TULEY, in September, 1861. During the incumbency of Colonel TULEY, he was requested by General ANDERSON, then on duty in Kentucky, to send KNAPP's artillery company of his command to a point opposite the mouth of Salt river, and to keep it supported by at least one company of infantry. The request was complied with, the artillery remaining on duty at the point designated about three months, during which time three infantry companies participated in the duty of supporting it, relieving each other from time to time. One company was subsequently sent to Indianapolis to assist in guarding prisoners at Camp Morton, in which service it continued several months.

Upon the resignation of Colonel TULEY, in September, 1862, Colonel MAGINNISS was placed in command. He found the regiment, with the exception of four companies, "utterly broken up," and "even these four companies very much shattered"; a condition which was not much improved at the date of his report, in December following. Colonel MAGINNISS attributes the early dissolution of the organization to the "utterly and fatally defective law that gave it birth," a law "which discovers no inducements to allure, nor penalties to compel, men to join the organization."

EIGHTH REGIMENT, SECOND BRIGADE (*Clark and Scott counties*)—No detailed report of the inception and progress of the organization in Clark and Scott counties has been made by any of the officers commanding, nor has this office been furnished with reliable data relative to the services performed by the regiment, or any of the companies attached thereto. JAMES KEIGWIN, of Jeffersonville, was first appointed to the Colonelcy, under commission bearing date August 30th, 1861, but almost immediately vacated the office to accept the Lieutenant Colonelcy of the Forty-Ninth Indiana Volunteers. Colonel JOHN N. INGRAM held the command from September 6th, 1861, to October 13th, 1862, when his resignation created a vacancy which was filled by the appointment of JOHN F. WILLEY. This officer reports twelve companies in Clark and five companies in Scott county at the close of 1862.

Portions of the command were frequently called out to repel threatened incursions of Kentucky guerrillas, and the regiment rendered good service in guarding the shoals on the Ohio, when the water was low and the danger of invasion imminent. With resident rebel sympathizers, of whom there were a considerable number in these counties, the Legion unquestionably exerted a restraining influence. It was a prolific nursery for the volunteer service, a quickener of patriotic impulses, and a conservator of genuine loyalty.

Colonel WILLEY reports the services of his command for 1863-64, as follows:

We had five battalions, and were called into service by order of the Governor, June 20th, to meet the raid under Captain HINES. June 21st, relieved from duty; June 22d, a false alarm; was sent to guard White River bridge; June 24th, dismissed the command; July 6th, 1863, called into service by LAZ. NOBLE, Adjutant General; rendezvoused at Jeffersonville; July 7th, dismissed the command; July 8th, met at Jeffersonville to repel Morgan raid; were in line of battle, but no enemy came; July 15th, relieved from duty and command dismissed; June 9th, 1864, called into service, by order of the Governor, to meet a raid in Kentucky by MORGAN; dismissed June 25th; August 10th, called companies "A" and "H" to picket the Ohio river, in the vicinity of the "Grassy Flats," to stop guerrillas from crossing under rebel JESSE; pickets fired on by guerrillas; returned the fire, but no one hurt; dismissed August 20th, 1864. We had two battalion drills in April, 1864, one regimental drill in May, and one in October. The regiment is well drilled for militia, and are ready and willing to turn out whenever called on.

NINTH REGIMENT, THIRD BRIGADE *(Jefferson County)*— This efficient command was partially organized in the spring and early summer of 1861, under command of Colonel JOHN A. HENDRICKS, who was actively engaged in the prosecution of this work, when he was called to the Lieutenant Colonelcy of the Twenty-Second Indiana Volunteers, and was succeeded by Colonel SAMUEL B. SERING, on the 29th of August, 1861. Ten companies of infantry and one of artillery had been organized up to this date. The artillery had been supplied with three guns, but were destitute of necessary accoutrements. Only one infantry company was armed, and it was not until some months later that arms could be procured for other portions of the command, although about five hundred muskets had previously been issued to independent companies in the county.

On the 19th of September, 1861, General ANDERSON called for aid in defending Louisville from a threatened attack by BUCKNER'S forces. The artillery company and one company of infantry—the only one then armed—together with details from several independent companies, immediately proceeded to Louisville, but the danger having passed, their services were not required, and they returned home. Soon after, a considerable force of rebels encamped in Owen county, Kentucky, about twenty miles from Madison, Indiana, and under their auspices recruiting for the rebel service actively progressed throughout that portion of Kentucky. It was deemed necessary to guard closely against an invasion of the border, and six companies of the Ninth having been supplied with arms, rendered valuable assistance in furnishing guards, and were held in readiness to march to any point where their services might be more imperatively required. From this period, for several succeeding months, the border was comparatively quiet, and the regiment was not called upon for much service beyond regular drills and parades; but on the 26th of May, 1862, the Colonel commanding was ordered to furnish three companies for guard duty at Camp Morton, Indianapolis, where several thousand rebel prisoners were confined. The "Madison Zouaves," "Washington Greys" and "Shelby Greys" volunteered in response to this call, and, proceeding to Indianapolis, were mustered into the United States service for three months, as a part of the Fifty-Fourth Regiment, Indiana Volunteers. Two weeks after their arrival at Camp Morton they were ordered, with other troops, into Kentucky. The "Washington Greys" were detailed for duty on the line of the Louisville and Nashville

Railroad, where they rendered valuable service till the expiration of their term of enlistment. The other two companies acquitted themselves creditably in the battle of Richmond, Kentucky.

In June, 1862, this regiment was again called upon to furnish three companies of infantry for guard duty at Camp Morton rebel prison. The call was immediately responded to by the requisite force, which continued on duty for about sixty days, and until their services were no longer required.

In September, 1862, the border was threatened by the advance of rebel troops under KIRBY SMITH, and three companies, besides several companies of minute-men, were called out and remained on duty for several weeks.

On the 1st of January, 1863, the Ninth Regiment consisted of seven companies—four of infantry, two of cavalry and one of artillery, several of the original companies having been disbanded. There were also eight independent companies in the county, which tendered their services to repel any attempted invasion of the State. During the winter and spring of 1863, there was no occasion to call upon the Ninth for any duty, and, except at the time of the Morgan Raid, in which it rendered important service, the command was not called out during the year. Drills were attended with considerable regularity, and a good degree of discipline was constantly maintained. During the fall of this year, the command was augmented by the organization of another cavalry company, making the entire force on the 1st of January, 1864, four companies of infantry, three of cavalry and one of artillery, all well armed, proficient in drill and thoroughly imbued with martial spirit.

On the 9th of June, 1864, the regiment was called out by order of Governor MORTON and placed on transports ready to proceed to Jeffersonville, for defense against threatened invasion, but the emergency not proving so serious as was apprehended, the men were dismissed after awaiting further orders for several days.

Rebels in large numbers in Trimble and Henry counties, Kentucky, necessitated the guarding of the border during the month of June, to which duty the men were always prompt to respond, although their absence from their farms and other places of business resulted in serious loss. The companies of this regiment were provided with uniforms at their own expense, drilled regularly and never hesitated when called upon for any duty, whatever personal sacrifice its performance might require.

NINTH REGIMENT (*improperly numbered*), THIRD BRIGADE (Jennings County)—From the 27th of May to the 19th of July, 1861, thirteen companies were organized in Jennings county under the command of Colonel GEORGE W. MALICK. In August, 1863, two companies were added. Colonel MALICK has furnished no report of the operations of his command. It appears, however, from other sources that the companies were pretty well armed and occasionally drilled. The county not being situate upon the immediate border, alarms were less frequent than in the border counties, and guard duty was much less arduous. Upon the resignation of Colonel MALICK, in June, 1862, Major KENNEDY BROWN assumed the command and was soon after promoted to the Colonelcy.

On the 13th of July, 1862, the Major commanding was ordered to report with his command at Indianapolis, to guard prisoners at Camp Morton. Six hundred and fifty men promptly responded to the order and immediately reported for duty. Though called out for thirty days their services were required for a longer period, and they were retained for six weeks, giving entire satisfaction by their soldierly deportment and faithful performance of duty. Being mustered out on the 31st of August, the regiment returned to Jennings county, where it continued to drill with regularity and to turn out occasionally on false alarms. One company volunteered to go down the Mississippi river with exchanged prisoners, on which service they were absent nearly a month, losing several men by disease and one by accident.

Of the subsequent services of this regiment nothing is reported except that it was engaged in June, 1864, at Madison, four days, in anticipation of a second raid from Morgan, who was then in Kentucky with a considerable force. The regiment was a very good one, and on all occasions exhibited a commendable readiness to obey any call that might be made.

TENTH REGIMENT, THIRD BRIGADE (*Switzerland County*) —Fifteen companies were organized in Switzerland county between June 17th, 1861, and August 29th, 1863. During the first two years of the war, while martial enthusiasm was at its greatest height, drills and parades were regularly and frequently held.

A portion of this command rendered valuable service in guarding rebel prisoners at Camp Morton, in the summer of 1862, and was always ready when called upon by the proper authorities, to do duty at any point.

At the time of KIRBY SMITH'S and BRAGG'S invasion of Kentucky, eight hundred officers and men of the Tenth, under command of Lieutenant Colonel STEPLETON, volunteered their services, and, under the order of the Governor, guarded the border thoroughly, and held themselves in readiness to march to Louisville to aid in the defense of that city. At one time the Tenth marched to Warsaw, Kentucky, for the protection of that place, and on several occasions was called out to repel threatened invasions. Three companies, at another time, laid upon their arms along the Ohio every night for three weeks, watching and guarding against guerrilla bands, which were swarming in the border counties on the opposite shore.

Meager and imperfect reports from the officers of this command preclude the possibility of enumerating the varied and important services which it rendered, and which secured for it a high rank among the most efficient regiments of the Legion.

ELEVENTH REGIMENT, FOURTH BRIGADE (*Ohio County*) —HUGH T. WILLIAMS was appointed to the Colonelcy of the Eleventh Regiment, on the 25th of September, 1861, and immediately assumed command of the three companies, then organized, which he found in a good state of discipline. Aside from company and battalion drill, no service was required until the following summer.

On the 24th of July, 1862, two companies were called out, one of which was sent to Burlington, Kentucky, to assist in making arrests, and to repel an expected attack upon that place; the other company was held in readiness to move in the same direction, should its support be required. The former company returned, after an absence of two days, having made a number of arrests without serious opposition.

On the 28th of July, 1862, two other companies were organized at Rising Sun, and attached to this command, both of which performed a considerable amount of guard duty, in which other companies to some extent participated.

The threatened raid of KIRBY SMITH, and the dangers of predatory incursions of guerrillas from the neighboring counties in Kentucky, made it necessary to call out the regiment about the 9th of September, 1862. The closest vigilance was required; guard and patrol duty, the collection of all the watercraft, and retention of the same on the Indiana shore of the river, and many other important duties were performed in a highly creditable manner, the command being retained in active service for several weeks. During this time two additional companies were organized and ordered into camp. The command was further increased by four companies of the Eighty-Third Indiana Volunteers, then organizing, and a company of artillery, which were temporarily placed under Colonel WILLIAMS.

On the 18th of September, Colonel WILLIAMS with an adequate force embarked on two gunboats, the "Cottage" and the "Heely," and made a reconnaissance of the country in the vicinity of Hamilton, Kentucky, some eight miles below Rising Sun, for the purpose of discovering a battery supposed to be located there, but did not succeed in finding either the rebels or their guns.

Nothing further of special interest appears in the history of this command except their very gallant conduct at Vernon, at the time of the Morgan Raid, of which a full account is given in another place.

TWELFTH REGIMENT, FOURTH BRIGADE (*Dearborn County*)—Twelve companies were at various times organized in Dearborn county and attached to the Twelfth Regiment. The first commanding officer, Colonel ZEPHANIAH HEUSTIS, held the command from September, 1861, to September, 1862, but made no report of the organization of companies, or of the services performed during that period. Upon the resignation of Colonel HEUSTIS, J. H. BURKAM was appointed to the vacancy. At this time (September 6th, 1862) the regiment consisted of seven companies, five of infantry and two of artillery, numbering in the aggregate five hundred and fifty, rank and file. On the 8th of September, 1862, the regiment was called out and placed on duty along the Ohio to protect the border. This duty was continued for several weeks, the men furnishing their own subsistence. The immediate danger having passed, much difficulty was experienced in keeping up sufficient interest in the organization to insure the continuance of company drills. Entire dependence upon their own resources to defray the expenses of their armories, music, etc., seriously checked military enthusiasm.

Of the subsequent services of this command no report has been rendered, except of their highly creditable participancy in the various movements and operations during the Morgan Raid.

In June, 1864, Colonel BURKAM tendered his resignation and the vacancy in the command was filled by the appointment thereto by Colonel JOHN A. PLATTER. The command was not afterwards called out for duty.

RESERVE COMPANIES OF THE LEGION

A large number of companies of the Legion were organized in various counties north of those bordering on the Ohio river, but only a few of them could be supplied with arms, and consequently but little attention was paid to drill or discipline. Some of these companies turned out in the Morgan Raid, but with this exception they performed but little or no duty during the war. The interior counties were comparatively free from the dangers of raids and their militia therefore did not feel the same interest in maintaining efficient organizations for home defense as was felt in the more exposed counties along our southern border.[12]

[12] For additional details on the services of the Indiana Legion see *Report of Major-General Love, of the Indiana Legion* (Indianapolis, 1863). 72 pp. Included here are also reports of brigade and regimental officers. See also "Operations of the Indiana Legion and Minute Men, 1863, 1864," in Indiana *Documentary Journal,* 1864, vol. 2, no. 11:369-472. This latter item also appeared as a separate imprint, Indianapolis, 1865.

MILITIA LAW OF 1861

The enactment by the Legislature at the Special Session, 1861, of an Act entitled, "AN ACT for the organization and regulation of the Indiana Militia, prescribing penalties for violations of said regulations, providing for the election and appointment of officers, defining the duties of military and civil officers, and penalties for the neglect or violation thereof, providing for Courts Martial, Councils of Adminstration and Military Encampments, making appropriations for the support of said Militia, repealing all laws heretofore enacted on that subject, saving certain acts therein named, and declaring an emergency for the immediate taking effect thereof,"[1] was one of the important measures adopted to meet the emergencies of the war. The militia had not been organized for thirty years, and the fragmentary laws, passed at various times, and remaining unrepealed, were of no force or effect whatever. The act of 1861 aimed to provide for the defense of the State, from external and internal enemies, without drawing upon troops raised for general service under the calls of the President. But our Legislators had little conception and no practical experience of the necessities created by a state of actual war at the threshold of our own homes, and it was reserved for subsequent events to reveal the real nature of the rebellion and the magnitude of the means required to suppress it. The fact that war clothes the lawmakers with extraordinary powers, and that a determined and defiant enemy cannot be subdued by a policy of conciliation and compromise, unless that policy is fortified and backed up by a

[1] The complete militia law is given in Terrell, *Report,* 1, Appendix, Doc. 47:247-55. See also *Laws of Indiana,* sp. sess., 1861, pp. 52-72.

well-appointed military force, was evidently not fully understood by even the most experienced and far-seeing soldiers and statesmen in the land. The Legislature could not, then, have reasonably been expected to frame a militia system, equal to exigencies that few, if any, anticipated, or to provide against dangers of which our own past history gave no intimation. The militia laws of other States had not, in any instance, afforded such evidence of their efficiency as to command general approval, or warrant their adoption. The militia systems of European nations, long accustomed to war and to the maintenance of large armies, were searched in vain for a model, adapted to our condition and circumstances, and the emergencies for which we were required to provide.

A long period of uninterrupted peace and unexampled prosperity in this country had created an independent spirit of self-reliance, which led our people to distrust all protective measures and to discountenance everything tending to interfere with the largest liberty of the citizens. Accustomed to unlimited freedom of action and opinion, the idea that any event, except the commission and conviction of crime, could justify compulsory service, seems scarcely to have been entertained. The *coercive principle,* demanding partial abandonment of business pursuits, and sacrifice of time in learning the act of war, was so at variance with the habits of communities, entirely undisciplined in the school of national adversity, so repugnant to popular notions of personal immunity from restraint—obliging every man, not legally exempt, to qualify for active service and to perform military duty, at stated periods, the necessity for which was based upon remote or apprehended dangers—would not have met with general approval, and, consequently, could not have been enforced; for, under our system of government, popular approval is a prerequisite to the enforcement of statutory enactments. The *voluntary principle* had in its favor the important element of popularity. It accorded with American ideas, and was in harmony with views of republican freedom, universally accepted and cherished. All our wars, from the Revolution down, had been fought and won principally by volunteers, and the traditional renown of our soldiers, serving from motives of patriotism and not *per force,* had grown brighter and brighter, year by year; while conscription, as practiced by foreign nations, was regarded as a despotic exercise of power, a tyrannical invasion of natural rights peculiar to monarchical governments. Thus endeared to the whole people, the system of voluntary service presented the strongest claims as a foundation for the new militia law of 1861, and it was adopted by the Legislature with entire unanimity. While this system of service must ever remain the hope and strength of Free America, it is not, of itself—bare and alone, as presented in the militia law under consideration—equal to the necessities of any State, situated as Indiana was, during the late war.

DEFECTS OF THE LAW

The Indiana Militia Law contained little that was objectionable or impolitic—it simply did not contain enough. It needed more power and less circumlocution. It embodied the voluntary principle, which, in itself, is right, but, in case the militia of the State did not volunteer, there was no remedy. The law went no further, and the Governor and Commander-in-Chief could not go beyond the law. There was no enrollment, as there should have been; and no regulation for organizing any stated quota or proportion of the arms-bearing population liable to do military service; no inducement to voluntary enlistment; no penalty or tax assessed against those who preferred to stand aloof from the organized militia. An appropriation was made for the expenses of the active force, for the years 1861 and 1862, but no practicable provision was made for its disbursement, or distribution, among the active forces, and it was not until after much service had been rendered that a plan could be devised to use the funds, and then only in paying for time actually employed, under the Governor's calls to guard the border and repel raids. All expenses connected with parades, procuring uniforms, and for time spent in organizing and drilling, had to be borne by individuals, the law making no provision for these heavy and necessary outlays. The law granted but little, and compelled nothing. The few regulations it contained, intended to be constraining and stringent, lost their force from the fact that there were few penalties, so insignificant and so seldom exacted they were utterly unheeded by the derelict and delinquent.

When practically tested, therefore, it soon became apparent that the law was radically weak and insufficient; that the essential principle of all effective militia enactments, which *compels* the performance of military duty, in peace as well as in war, was lacking, and that without it but little could be done toward organizing the citizens of the State into permanent and well-disciplined companies and regiments. The little that it did accomplish can not be attributed to any provision intended to enforce military duty, but was rather, and in fact, the result of the dangers that threatened us, and not, strictly speaking, from motives of patriotism, or overweening loyalty. True, there was no deficiency in the loyalty or patriotism of any considerable number in this state, as our grand army of more than two hundred thousand volunteers fully attests, though party spirit during the rebellion ran high, and views were freely entertained by many inimical to the war policy of the Government.

The great drawback was, that the law did not *compel,* but only *invited* service. In the central and northern parts of the State, where there was little or no danger of raids, the Indiana Legion (as the militia was called) was either not organized at all, or, if organized, was not maintained, and therefore amounted to nothing. In the southern counties, and almost exclusively in those bordering on the Ohio river, the case was entirely different. The rebels made free use of Kentucky, and during the whole war, that State was a favorite recruiting rendezvous for the Southern army, and was infested with guerrilla parties, and bands of marauders, always intent, and ready to pounce upon and plunder unprotected communities of Unionists, north or south. There was, therefore, a standing need of a defensive force along the whole river border, from Lawrenceburg to the mouth of the Wabash, and from this cause, almost entirely, emanated those active and efficient organizations of the Legion, whose services are elsewhere recorded in these pages.[2] The people on the border were thus compelled to arm and associate themselves together for their own protection and safety, and in doing this, they ensured the safety and protection of their more favorably located fellow-citizens in the interior of the State, who, from their comparative immunity from danger, did not feel it to be their interest to make any defensive preparations. This appeared unequal, if not unjust. Even on the border, in some of the counties most exposed and liable to invasion, the Legion was organized and maintained with the greatest difficulty, by a comparatively small portion of the inhabitants, giving spasmodic evidence of vitality only when danger appeared, and lapsing into indifference when there was no reason to apprehend immediate trouble.

At the close of the war, or as soon as events indicated that the strength of the rebellion was nearly exhausted, the law suddenly became as inoperative as if it had never been placed on the statute book, and every militia company was disbanded, as if by spontaneous and general consent; thus clearly proving that even the imperfect organization of the home forces had resulted, not from any law requiring the performance of military duty, or from any principle of cohesion that would operate in time of peace, but from the external pressure and impending dangers already mentioned.

In view of these facts, it can not be doubted that a law relying alone upon the generous impulses of the more patriotic members of community to maintain a militia force for the

[2] See above, 135-71.

common good—to voluntarily lay aside their private business for the performance of duties, as much for the benefit of their indifferent neighbors as for themselves—must inevitably fall into disfavor and prove a failure. The burden ought to be distributed equally and justly, for all who are subject to bear arms, under the Constitution of Indiana, undeniably owe so much of service as the public good may require. To fairly accomplish this, the following provisions are essential and vital:

1st. "All able-bodied white male persons, between the ages of eighteen and forty-five years, except such as are exempted by the laws of the United States, or of this State,"[3] should be *enrolled* annually.

2d. The *quota of active militia,* apportioned to the several Congressional Districts, should then be assigned on the basis of the enrollment.

3d. The residue enrolled, or *reserve* militia, should be assessed *an annual tax,* as commutation for exemption from service, which tax should be sufficiently large to support the active militia without any additional assistance from the public treasury.

The law should be free from complications and incongruous details. Means should be provided for enforcing all its provisions promptly; but all minor rules and regulations should be left to the Commander-in-Chief, who, from his intimate connection with the militia and knowledge of its ever-varying wants, could settle these matters understandingly and satisfactorily by issuing general orders, as the necessities of the service might require.

NECESSITY FOR MILITIA ORGANIZATION

The policy of maintaining at all times a well-organized militia force, has been so completely vindicated by past events in our national history, and is so generally admitted by intelli-

---

[3] Constitution of Indiana, Article XII.

gent men of all classes and parties, there is scarcely any occasion for presenting an argument in its favor; yet attempts have been made to accomplish this great end so frequently by legislation in this State, and as often resulted in failure, a few words in elucidation of its importance, and by way of warning, may not be inappropriate.

Remote as is this country from the great military powers of Europe; separated by the broad Atlantic from countries that might, if in close proximity, be troublesome neighbors; having no prospect of rivalry for national supremacy on this continent, and cherishing our "ancient policy" of non-intervention in the affairs of foreign governments, we can never require, and the people will never consent to support a large standing army. The necessity of a constant preparation for war, however, is universally acknowledged. Such a condition is the best conservator and surest guarantor of peace. To dispense with the burden of a large regular force, and at the same time maintain an attitude sufficiently formidable to overawe domestic malcontents and deter foreign aggression, we must rely mainly upon the militia.

But no man, in these enlightened days, is a "natural born soldier," nor do any number of men, however brave, without the benefits conferred by organization, discipline, and "the school of the soldier," constitute an army, when superiority in military science assures success in the field and is of far more importance than untrained numerical strength. It will be remembered that on the day after President LINCOLN issued his first call for troops, several Massachusetts and New York regiments were *en route* for the National Capital. These regiments were armed, uniformed and well trained—the result of the militia system of those States. A moment's reflection will show how vital it might have been to the fortunes of the Government to have been deprived of even this small force. Suppose, in the conspiracy concocted by the statesmen of the rebellion, preparations had been made, as might easily and quietly have been done under discreet leadership, simultaneous with the firing of the first gun on Sumter, to have thrown a force of a few thousand men into Washington. The treasury, archives and all the *ensemble* of the Government could have been captured and utterly destroyed, or carried off, before armed and organized troops could have been sent in sufficient numbers to have prevented the disaster. The prestige of such a bold stroke would have been most crushing to the loyal people of this country, and in the highest degree encouraging to the rebels and to their sympathizers in the old world. While it would have enlightened the officers of our Government as to the earnest determination of the men of the South to make, what at first was looked upon as a petty "insurrection," a formidable and bloody rebellion, unparalled in history, and incited the people of the North to a greater patriotism (if such a thing were possible), it would also have given additional strength and drawn out a corresponding feeling of devotion to the rebel cause. The first grand blunder of the war—"Bull Run," and its effect upon the South—is the best evidence that can be adduced as to the encouragement the rebels would have derived from the capture of Washington. The fall of Richmond crushed the rebellion—the fall of Washington would have "crippled," for a time at least, the Union. The moral effect of such a triumph in their behalf would have told the tremendous power against us, and though the final termination of the struggle must inevitably have been adverse to the enemy, the end would probably have been delayed much longer and the waste of life and treasure much greater than is now recorded in history. Of course "it might have been when IT WAS NOT, is a poor argument as the case turned out, but it is nevertheless an admonition which it will surely not be unwise to heed. Had the loyal States been prepared for war, their militia organized on a sound basis to the extent that even ordinary prudence would dictate, the rebellion would not have lasted through its four long years of desolation and blood.

That the militia was not so organized may be attributed to the same inertia and indifference that now so completely clouds the public mind on this subject.

We live in stirring times. The rebellion may not yet be suppressed. Its fires may only be smouldering. The safest policy for State and Nation is to *act* upon the old motto: "Eternal vigilance is the price of Liberty."

THE RAID ON NEWBURGH AND EXPEDITION TO KENTUCKY

FIRST INVASION OF THE STATE—JULY 18, 1862

The first invasion of this State, or indeed of any of the free States, by an armed and organized force of rebels, occurred on the 18th day of July, 1862, at Newburgh, the principal town of Warrick county, situate on the Ohio river fifteen miles above Evansville. The movement was hardly of a sufficiently formidable character to entitle it to the dignity of an "invasion," as the force consisted of but thirty-two officers and men, whose object was plunder and whose conduct was that of thieves rather than soldiers.

The leader of these marauders was one ADAM R. JOHNSON, a citizen of Henderson, Kentucky, who had previously served in the rebel army, and who was at this time in command of a small force of mounted men, some of whom were deserters from the Federal army—raiding through the southwestern counties of Kentucky, committing outrages upon the persons and depredations upon the property of such citizens as were suspected of sympathy with the Government of the United States. Whether JOHNSON held a commission in the Confederate service at the time of this occurrence, or was acting as an independent guerrilla chief, is not definitely known, but it is known that the rank of Colonel was subsequently conferred upon him with authority to recruit or conscript for BRAGG'S army, and that he made his name infamous by acts of demoniac cruelty. His band became a terror throughout the region they infested, and when, in the summer of 1864, his career of active crime was terminated by a wound that deprived him of sight, there were few, even among the ardent friends of the Southern cause, who felt that his fate was undeserved.

Although Newburgh was not a military post, a hospital had been established there which contained eighty or ninety sick and wounded Union soldiers, with a considerable amount of commissary and hospital stores. The muskets, accoutrements and ammunition of the two Newburgh companies of the Legion, which had been collected in some months previously, were also deposited in the hospital building; while in a warehouse, not far distant, seventy-five sabres and one hundred and thirty holsters and pistols were stored in the boxes in which they had been shipped. There being no indications of danger, no guard was stationed for the protection of the patients in the hospital or the public property.

In nearly every community throughout the North there was a disloyal element—men whose sympathies were with the enemies of the Government and who were dangerous in proportion to their courage and to the opportunities which circumstances presented for mischief. Newburgh was no exception to the general rule, while its particularly exposed position, and the near proximity of a rebel force, presented a most favorable opportunity for secession residents to covertly aid in striking a blow for the cause they so earnestly desired to serve, and for which they were willing to do anything that might be required, except perhaps to fight. Several men of this class had clandestinely crossed the river and had sought interviews with JOHNSON. They had explained to him the situation of affairs, and shown that once in possession of the hospital and the arms of the Legion deposited there, the town and its inhabitants would be at his mercy. Early in the morning, on the day of the raid, one of these domestic traitors visited the camp of JOHNSON's gang, and in concert with the leading spirits of the band, finally consummated arrangements for the proposed surprise.

NEWBURGH CAPTURED

Accordingly, at noon, when most of the citizens were at dinner, JOHNSON appeared on the bank of the river opposite Newburgh, placed his men on a large ferry boat, concealed them as well as possible, and rowed rapidly to the Indiana shore. As soon as the boat touched the landing a dash was made for the hospital, and the warehouse and the arms stored therein were at once secured. Pickets were thrown out in all directions, and the inhabitants were assured that their lives depended on remaining perfectly quiet. JOHNSON informed the citizens that he had a battery planted on the opposite side of the river so as to completely command the town, and that on the first appearance of resistance to any of his demands he would shell and destroy the place. There is reason to believe that this was a fiction, designed to promote quiet on the part of the people, while the work of plunder was going on. The soldiers in the hospital, to the number of eighty-five, were required to sign paroles of honor, in which the leader of the marauders was styled "A. R. JOHNSON, C.S.A." These paroles were never claimed as valid by the Confederate authorities and were held as null and void by those who signed them. While JOHNSON was personally engaged in paroling the sick and wounded soldiers, his men, guided by some of the citizens, commenced the genial business of pillage. Houses were broken open and ransacked; horses were taken from the stables, and coffee, sugar and other articles, that could readily be transported, were stolen in large quantities. In some instances property was spared on the assurance being given that its owners were "all right." Several citizens mingled freely with the invaders, drank with them and appeared delighted with their society. After remaining four or five hours, during which time the boat was kept busy in transporting their plunder, the commander ordered his men to embark and they were speedily transferred to the other shore. After their departure, two men, H. H. CARNEY and ELLIOTT

MEFFORD, who had been suspected of holding communication with the rebels, and who, on this occasion, had been particularly officious in pointing out property for seizure, were attacked and killed by some of the citizens.

THE MILITIA CALLED OUT

Meantime, Colonel DANIEL F. BATES, commanding the Third Regiment, Indiana Legion, was engaged in rallying the county companies of his command. In a short time five companies were ready with arms for duty, but not before the rebels had accomplished their purpose and effected their escape. The wildest rumors were circulated in every direction, and not only Warrick and adjacent counties were alarmed, but the entire State was thoroughly aroused. A courier arrived at Evansville early in the afternoon with intelligence that the Newburgh hospital was being sacked by a large band of Kentucky guerrillas. The signal of danger was given and in less than an hour one thousand men were under arms. Two steamers, the "Eugene" and "Courier," were fired up, and with infantry and artillery on board, proceeded up the river. Colonel WILLIAM E. HOLLINGSWORTH, commanding the Second Regiment, Indiana Legion, also proceeded by the nearest land route to the scene of the disturbance with a small force of mounted men, but neither the water nor land expedition effected anything beyond the destruction, by the former, of the boat in which the rebels had crossed and recrossed the Ohio.

EXPEDITION TO KENTUCKY, JULY, 1862

The situation in Western Kentucky at the time of the raid on Newburgh (July 18th, 1862) was critical. Union men were plundered, and not infrequently murdered in cold blood; many of them were compelled to flee from their homes and abandon their property to merciless thieves, who, in the name of the so-called "Confederacy of America," either appropriated and carried away or destroyed, when they felt they dared do so, all that was useful to them, or destructible. The citizens of South Western Indiana, were subjected to constant alarms and dangers, and were scarcely less secure than their Union neighbors residing on the other side of the Ohio. Henderson city, twelve miles below Evansville, was occupied by the rebels under ADAM JOHNSON; JOHN MORGAN was on his first raid through Central Kentucky, preliminary to the grand invasion of that section of the State by KIRBY SMITH and BRAGG; and everywhere, from the "Blue Grass region" to Paducah, the most energetic efforts were being made to raise recruits for the rebel army. Recruiting stations were opened at all points not occupied by our forces, and independent bands of guerrillas and desperadoes infested every neighborhood, and rendered the lives and property of Union citizens, on both sides of the river, so insecure as to call for immediate and vigorous action.

Governor MORTON had already sent off all effective forces that could be spared to repel the raid then in progress through Central Kentucky,[1] and to enable him to do so had called out a large number of militia to guard the rebel prisoners at Indianapolis. The border counties were thus unavoidably left to protect themselves. The organizations of the Legion, as a general thing, were in poor condition, from lack of arms and experience, to interpose any formidable barrier to the progress of the enemy should he have undertaken to invade the State in any considerable force. Evansville was considered, and really was, in great peril, and the other towns on the lower Ohio river border of the State were exposed to invasion at any moment, and liable to be sacked and destroyed, almost without "let or hindrance." The Governor, therefore, immediately, in receipt of news of the Newburgh outrage, determined to assume the offensive, organize an expedition sufficiently strong to penetrate the heart of the infected territory, and drive the rebels out, whereby he hoped to break up

[1] See "Kirby Smith's Campaign," below, 190-203.

their recruiting stations, restore order in Kentucky, and secure our own border from the dangers that threatened and alarmed it. He accordingly advised with General BOYLE, commanding the District of Kentucky, and asked from him authority to organize an expedition against the rebels in that State, which was readily and gladly granted.

In pursuance of the plans laid for this campaign, Major General LOVE, commanding the Indiana Legion, was dispatched on the 18th of July, at midnight, to Evansville, by special train, with one company of troops, and one thousand stand of arms, a section of field artillery, and a large supply of ammunition. Brigadier General BLYTHE, of the Legion, whose headquarters were at Evansville, was enjoined to exercise the utmost vigilance in watching and guarding exposed points on the Ohio river, pending the arrival of General LOVE; and on the morning of the 19th, a call was made by the Governor for volunteers, and the Legion on the border was ordered on duty.

Among the first to respond were six hundred citizens of Decatur county, recruited in a few hours by Colonels JAMES GAVIN, Seventh Indiana Volunteers, and JOHN T. WILDER, Seventeenth Indiana Volunteers, who happened at the time to be at their homes on short leaves of absence from their regiments. In announcing the readiness of the Decatur volunteers to receive orders for immediate service, Colonel GAVIN telegraphed on the same day the call was issued, as follows:

"These men want to fight. I want to take them where there is danger. They are fighting men. Please arm them and send them off at once where they can do active duty. They are better men than you can get."

The Newburgh raid had aroused the indignation of the people of the whole State, and the disposition to inflict immediate punishment upon the rebels was manifest in every locality and is forcibly indicated in the above dispatch. The Governor replied:

"Bring your men here. I will send them to Evansville immediately, armed for a fight."

On receiving this order, Colonels GAVIN and WILDER started at once for the scene of operations with their enthusiastic volunteers stopping only long enough at Indianapolis to be mustered into the United States service for thirty days, arriving at Evansville on the evening of the 20th. The men were organized into six companies. Two fine companies from Terre Haute (one of them the "Union Rifles," Captain MELVILLE D. TOPPING,[2] splendidly armed and equipped and neatly uniformed) tendered their services, were accepted and reached Evansville also on the 20th. From Lafayette, two companies were accepted under Captains GODLOVE S. ORTH and SAMUEL A. HUFF, and were dispatched to Evansville on the 21st. Governor MORTON also proceeded thither and arrived the same evening. The ten companies thus thrown together were organized as the Seventy-Sixth Regiment Indiana Volunteers.[3] A German company of Terre Haute, one hundred strong, was also sent forward, and numerous tenders of independent companies from many counties were made, but being in excess of the number required were not accepted.

General LOVE arrived at Evansville early on the 19th, and found everything in confusion; but by judicious management, order was soon evoked from chaos, public confidence restored, and preparations speedily completed for the proposed expedition. A steam ram, belonging to the United States, lying at the landing, by direction of the Governor was pressed into service until a gunboat could be procured from the fleet below. Captain TOPPING's company was placed on board and ordered to proceed up Green river to relieve two steamboats, which it was believed the rebels were aiming to capture, and also to protect the locks on that stream.

[2] Afterwards lieutenant colonel of the Seventy-first Regiment, killed at Richmond, Kentucky, August 30, 1862. [Terrell]

[3] For an account of this regiment see Terrell, *Report*, 3:9-11.

The day following (the 20th) General LOVE telegraphed the return of the ram, with Captain TOPPING's company, the safety of the locks, and that the rebels were reported by reliable Union men as having abandoned that line of operations and returned toward Henderson. In addition to the authority given by General BOYLE to the Governor to carry on the war in the Green river country of Kentucky, he ordered Colonel GAVIN to mount his regiment and enjoined upon him to "Drive out the rebel bands in Henderson, Daviess, Webster and Union counties, shooting down all guerrillas in arms and all making armed resistance."

Adding—"They must be shot—nothing else will do; I do not want such prisoners."

In response to the application of the Governor for a gunboat, Captain PENNOCK, of the United States Navy, responded in person, and reported to General LOVE with two armed steamers, the "Clara Dolson" and "Rob Roy," on which were a detachment of Illinois troops, under Colonel MOORE, and a battery, under Major STARRING, detailed by General STRONG, commanding at Cairo. These boats were directed to cruise up and down the river, with the view of protecting the towns from pillage, and affording such assistance to General LOVE as might be required. Captain UNION BETHEL, of Warrick county, reported with a company of the Legion, mounted, and, after unceasing labor, all things were in readiness for a forward movement by midnight of the 21st.

The following dispatch, from the Governor to his Military Secretary, forwarded immediately on his arrival at Evansville, on the 22d, will show the position of affairs at that time, and convey some idea of the rapidity with which the troops— most of them suddenly drawn from their farms and shops, and from widely distant points—had been concentrated, organized, armed, equipped, many of them mounted, and transported to the field of active operations.

About one o'clock this morning, near one thousand infantry, cavalry and artillery, crossed the river to Henderson, and took possession without opposition. At daylight, Colonel GAVIN advanced into the interior, with five hundred men. The ram "Hornet" has gone up the river, with one company (ORTH'S) on board, to visit all the towns. There is much excitement in the country, on both sides of the river. Another company went to Henderson this afternoon.

General LOVE remained a week at Henderson and in that vicinity, sending out detachments into the surrounding country after the rebels, who, as soon as it was ascertained that vigorous means had been resorted to, to hunt them down, suddenly left that part of the State. Several skirmishes occurred, and a few of the enemy, with their horses and arms, were captured. The influence exerted by the presence of our troops was at once marked and salutary; Unionists, who had been compelled to seek safety in Indiana, soon returned, confident of protection; while the disloyal were made to understand that treasonable practices could no longer be indulged in with impunity. Lieutenant Colonel JOHN W. FOSTER, of the Twenty-Fifth Indiana, afterward Colonel of the Sixty-Fifth, was left in command of Henderson. The thirty days' troops continued in service until the expiration of their term, when they were relieved by the Sixty-Fifth Indiana, and returned to their homes.

The course pursued by Governor MORTON for the defense of Kentucky, and for the security of our southern border, was warmly approved by the President and Secretary of War, and was gratefully acknowledged by General BOYLE. It was only occasionally, afterward, that the rebels dared venture back, and then only in small numbers, on hurried forays—plunder and the murder of Union men being their principal objects.

KIRBY SMITH'S CAMPAIGN—1862

BRAGG'S INVASION OF KENTUCKY

In the month of August, 1862, the right wing of General BRAXTON BRAGG's rebel army, consisting of some twenty thousand men, under command of General E. KIRBY SMITH, was concentrated at Knoxville, Tennessee, and other points in that vicinity preparatory to the fulfillment of the part assigned it in the Confederate plan of a general advance upon the North, and a transfer of the seat of war beyond the limits of the Confederacy.

Leaving a force of eight thousand, under command of General STEPHENSON, in front of Cumberland Gap—then occupied by General G. W. MORGAN, with a small division of the Army of the Ohio—General SMITH, with twelve thousand men, the veterans of his command, pressed through Big Creek and Rogers' Gaps of the Cumberland Mountains, and moved towards the "Blue Grass Region" of Kentucky; his obvious intention being to menace, and, if possible, capture and sack Cincinnati, and other cities and towns, north of the Ohio river; destroy important railroads, and break up other means of communication; detain reinforcements from General BUELL, and force the withdrawal, from the front, of a large part of the Union army required for the protection of such exposed and defenseless points, on the Ohio and Indiana border as his advance would threaten. BUELL's army, being thus weakened by demands for home defense, and the new levies, under the second call for three hundred thousand men, not having been raised and sent to the field, the rebel authorities confidently expected the main portion of BRAGG's army, under his immediate command, would be able to enter Kentucky, with comparatively little opposition, and, after capturing Louisville and reinforcing his army by recruits from the disloyal element of Kentucky, form a junction with SMITH, for an extensive line of operations, in any direction circumstances might appear to justify. The hope of securing recruits, in large numbers, was by no means visionary, as it was well known that thousands in Kentucky were only waiting a favorable opportunity to array themselves under the rebel standard, while even at that time, recruiting for JOHN MORGAN's cavalry was being prosecuted with marked success in the southwestern section of the State, and scores of young men were added to SMITH's force in every county along his line of march. A few weeks later, several entire regiments of cavalry were raised in the "Blue Grass Region," which finally left the State with the invaders, splendidly mounted at their own expense.

MORGAN'S CO-OPERATIVE RAID

As a prelude to the grand invasion, General SMITH had dispatched the cavalry force of JOHN MORGAN on an extensive raid through parts of Tennessee and Kentucky. Leaving Knoxville on the 4th of July, MORGAN moved by way of Sparta, Tompkinsville, Lebanon, Cynthiana, Paris, Crab Orchard and Somerset, capturing and paroling small garrisons at many points, securing large accessions of recruits and supplying his men with arms, accoutrements, clothing and horses.

On the 10th, General JEREMIAH T. BOYLE, commanding the District of Kentucky, telegraphed from Frankfort to Governor MORTON for troops:

"Rebels invading Kentucky. Send your battery tonight and any forces you can possibly spare. Put the Legion in order for motion and direct as many as possible to report to my headquarters tomorrow."

The Governor promptly replied:

"Our batteries sent to Washington last week. The only organized United States troops we have are guarding prisoners and can not be spared. I have telegraphed about the Legion, but fear no companies are in shape to move."

At this time Major General LOVE, of the Legion, was on the border endeavoring to organize the militia in Vanderburgh and Posey. He was at once telegraphed to, but replied that there were no companies organized and in condition to answer General BOYLE's call. Generals BLYTHE, MANSFIELD and DOWNEY, of the Legion, were ordered to call out their forces—the last two officers being required, in addition to guarding the border to furnish enough men to guard Camp Morton rebel prison, so as to allow a part of the three months' troops (also of the Legion) then guarding prisoners to be sent to General BOYLE. The result of this order was all that could have been expected; the response was so prompt the Governor was able, on the 11th, to send seven companies —six hundred men—of the Fifty-Fifth Indiana Volunteers, under Lieutenant Colonel MAHAN, fully armed and equipped and well disciplined, to the capital of Kentucky *via* Louisville. The same day General LOVE was ordered from Evansville to Louisville, by the Governor, to confer with General BOYLE in relation to affording him additional relief, if possible, with the Legion.

LOVE reached Louisville on the 14th, and telegraphed the following report:

"I apprehend no danger to Louisville. MORGAN has a force said to be fifteen hundred—not half that in my judgement—with which he doubtless proposes to stop our communications with Nashville, creating confusion and plundering as he goes. One good regiment of cavalry would drive him from the State. Henderson and vicinity are most in danger."

On the same day, in compliance with General BOYLE's requisition, Governor MORTON sent from the Indiana Arsenal two carloads of ammunition by special train for the use of the troops at Frankfort; and on the 17th four hundred men of the Fifty-Fourth Indiana Volunteers, under Lieutenant Colonel KNOX, were sent from Camp Morton to General BOYLE. High excitement prevailed on the border, as the Legion, imperfectly organized as it was, was compelled to take the place of the disciplined forces in charge of Camp Morton, containing four thousand rebel prisoners, and guard the border besides. The Jennings county regiment—ten full companies—responded to the call under Major, afterwards Colonel, KENNEDY BROWN in a body; besides seven other companies from various counties promptly reported, all being mustered into the United States' service for thirty days. The border was thus left to its own resources for defense, and the danger of invasion, for aught the people knew, was immediate and very great.

New difficulties sprang up hourly. On the 12th, while the Governor was trying to help General BOYLE in Kentucky and put the reserve forces of Indiana in a fit condition for home defense, General GREEN CLAY SMITH, commanding at Henderson, Kentucky, telegraphed the commanding officer of the Legion at Evansville, as follows:

"On account of the raid at Tompkinsville, Kentucky, nearly all my troops have been withdrawn from this post, and I feel myself in no condition to resist an attack, which I am informed by reliable citizens will be made upon us within a day or two. Therefore, I wish you would send down, by the first boat, two hundred of your Indiana Legion, with at least five days' rations, so that in case it be necessary I can send them into the country prepared for any emergency."

At this time, it should be remembered, the Legion was scarcely a "skeleton organization"; besides, Evansville was, from its size and importance as a northern city and the vast amount of "plunder" it contained, in quite as much danger of being attacked as Henderson. There was no artillery on the border, and but few of the companies of the Legion enrolled were armed. So, of course, it was impossible to comply with General SMITH's request.

General LOVE, after conferring with the military authorities at Louisville, hastened back to the lower counties on the Ohio river, for the purpose of completing the organization of the Legion, and the Governor succeeded in securing a few thousand muskets for use in that quarter. The raid on Newburgh followed on the 18th of July, and was the means of stirring up the people to a sense of their situation, which they had never known before. Newburgh was captured; GREEN CLAY SMITH was driven out of Henderson; the whole "Green River country" overrun with rebel bands, and the Indiana border threatened with invasion at many points.

MORGAN finished his first raid through Kentucky on the 27th of July, at which date he recrossed the Cumberland into Tennessee, having marched more than a thousand miles in twenty-four days. The command moved to Sparta, where it remained until near the last of August, when it again took the field and moved on Gallatin, capturing the small garrison stationed there. Pushing forward to the Louisville and Nashville Railroad, MORGAN destroyed the track for some distance, and cut the telegraph wires, thus breaking up BUELL's line of supplies and severing his communication with the North. Returning to Gallatin, MORGAN encountered a Federal force of six hundred men, under General JOHNSON, and, after a brief engagement, succeeded in capturing a part and dispersing the remainder. A small detachment of the Fiftieth Indiana Volunteers, under Captain ATKISSON, garrisoning a stockade at Edgefield Junction, repulsed MORGAN's force three times, with heavy loss and successfully held the position.

At Hartsville, Tennessee, on the 28th of August, MORGAN received an order from his commanding officer, General SMITH, to join him at Lexington, Kentucky, on the 2d of September, and the next day marched by way of Scottsville, Glasgow, Columbia, Liberty, Houstonville, Danville and

Nicholasville, cautiously picking his way between Federal forces, as if anxious to avoid a collision, and arriving at Lexington on the 4th of September.

SIGNS OF TROUBLE

The earliest indications of the contemplated invasion by KIRBY SMITH were closely watched by Generals BUELL and G. W. MORGAN, and promptly reported to the War Department and the military authorities of Kentucky, Indiana and Ohio. Impelled by a necessity that admitted of no delay, the Government bent every energy to the work of placing the new levies, under the call of July, in the field. The Secretary of War urgently appealed to this State to use the utmost dispatch in filling its quota, 21,250 men. To this appeal Governor MORTON replied, on the 9th of August, with the assurance that the men would be raised in twenty days.

On the 8th, the Governor received a telegram from General BUELL, then at Huntsville, Alabama, stating that a formidable raid threatened Kentucky, and earnestly recommending that troops should be sent to General BOYLE, with the utmost dispatch. Two days later General BOYLE forwarded a dispatch from General MORGAN, dated at Cumberland Gap, giving the numbers and position of the enemy, as nearly as could be ascertained, and expressing the opinion that SMITH would invade Kentucky by way of Jamestown and Big Creek Gap. This opinion was reiterated on the 12th, with additional details relative to the accumulation of transportation at Knoxville, and other preparatory steps, leaving no doubt of the speedy realization of BUELL'S apprehensions and MORGAN'S predictions.

INDIANA AT WORK

So prompt had been the response of the State to the call of the Government, by the evening of the 11th, not less than 20,000 men were gathered at various rendezvous, waiting to be mustered and armed, and on that day two regiments were forwarded to Kentucky.

The Secretary of War, having authorized General BUELL, to dispose of all troops raised in this State, until further orders, that officer telegraphed from Huntsville, on the 12th, that MORGAN had again crossed the Cumberland, and earnestly urged the forwarding of troops to General BOYLE.

On the morning of the 13th, the Seventieth Regiment left Indianapolis for Louisville, and reported to the commanding officer at Bowling Green on the 15th, being the first of the new levies raised and the first sent to Kentucky from any State, under the then pending call. Another regiment was sent on the 16th, and another on the following day. At the same date the Governor was informed that SMITH's forces were marching through Big Creek Gap; that the rebels, under MORGAN, had again invaded Kentucky, had captured Somerset, and were marching on Glasgow, Bowling Green and other points. In transmitting this speedy information General BOYLE added, " I hope the patriotic soldiers of Indiana will not wait for bounties. Our State will be overrun if they do and your own borders desolated." At this date (as has been noticed) JOHN MORGAN cut off all communication with Nashville, and General BUELL. The intentions of the enemy were now clearly apparent; the formidable invasion of Kentucky was an actual fact, and the danger to our own border imminent.

The people in all parts of the State were thoroughly aroused, and different sections vied with each other as to which should be first to fill its quota. Camps were full of troops impatiently waiting for mustering officers. Arms were not provided by the Government, and could not be procured by the Governor at the moment in sufficient quantity to supply the forces impatiently waiting to be off to the field. Colonel HENRY B. CARRINGTON, of the regular army, one of the most active and efficient mustering officers and organizers in the service, was detailed by the Secretary of War, with orders to relieve Colonel SIMONSON as Chief Mustering and Disbursing officer for the State.¹ Colonel CARRINGTON reported to Governor MORTON on the 18th, and entered upon his duties with a zeal and energy productive of the happiest results. During that day the Seventy-First was mustered and drew their arms.

At this point a difficulty arose, from the fact that funds to pay the advance bounty, to which the men of the Seventy-First were entitled, had not been forwarded from Washington. Many had left their homes suddenly, without providing for the maintenance of their families, expecting to receive the stipulated bounty money in time to remit it before going to the field. They felt a natural reluctance to leaving the State, with the chances of battle in the immediate future, unless the wants of their families could be at least temporarily provided for. Governor MORTON addressed the troops, explaining the urgent necessity of their instant departure, and proposed to send the money to them as soon as it could be obtained. Every murmur was hushed, and the men, with cheerful alacrity, shouldered their guns and started for the front. On the morning of the 19th, the Governor effected an arrangement with citizens and bankers of Indianapolis and Cincinnati for an advance of nearly half a million dollars, and during that day and the succeeding night, the Twelfth and Sixteenth (reorganized), Sixty-Eighth, and Sixty-Ninth regiments were mustered, paid, and started for Kentucky. By the evening of the 20th, the Sixty-Fifth, Sixty-Sixth, and Sixty-Seventh regiments had also been placed under the orders of General BOYLE. The money due the Seventy-First was promptly forwarded and paid on the Richmond battlefield, half an hour before the action opened.

Still the work went on. All the camps of rendezvous were crowded. Mustering Officers, Paymasters, Quartermasters, and Commissaries, worked by day and night. The Governor

¹ See Carrington's report of his services in Indiana in Terrell, *Report,* 1, Appendix, Doc. 77:271-74.

and his military staff labored with little cessation for needful rest. The Seventy-Fourth and Seventy-Fifth Regiments were mustered, and moved forward on the 21st. On the 27th and 28th two regiments were sent forward, and were followed by from one to three regiments daily, for several successive days. The Eighteenth, Nineteenth, and Twenty-First Batteries, Light Artillery, were also filled to the maximum, armed and equipped, and sent to the field. Others were in process of organization, but were delayed for the want of horses, arms, and equipments. The Fifth Cavalry Volunteers was mustered, and assigned to duty on our southern border, and a battalion of the Fourth Cavalry organized and sent to Kentucky.

The Ohio river, at this period, was fordable at many points, and as all available United States troops had been sent out of the State (except the Fifth Cavalry), the duty of defending the border, as before stated, devolved mainly upon the Legion, aided by such minute-men as could be hastily organized and armed.

On the 5th of September, Governor MORTON issued an order,[2] declaring martial law, and closing all places of business in the several cities and towns in the counties bordering on the Ohio river at three o'clock, P. M., each day; requiring all able-bodied white male citizens, between the ages of eighteen and forty-five, residing in said border counties, to organize themselves into companies, elect officers, and report for orders to the commanding officer of the Legion in their respective counties, arming themselves with such arms as could be procured, and paying strict attention to drill and discipline.

This order was obeyed with great spirit and cheerfulness, and so thoroughly was the river guarded and all weak points garrisoned, the peace of the State was securely preserved,

[2] The text of this order is given in Terrell, *Report*, 1, Appendix, Doc. 124:334-35. It was issued as a separate: *Proclamation Calling Out the Militia* (Indianapolis, 1863). 4 pp.

although the Kentucky counties adjacent were swarming with desperate and venturesome bands of guerrillas and marauders.

At the Indiana Arsenal about seven hundred hands were employed in the fabrication of ammunition, turning out an average of 300,000 rounds daily.

BATTLE OF RICHMOND

Events soon proved that the anxiety of General BOYLE to have Indiana's quota hurried into Kentucky, was well founded and the unprecedented efforts made by the State authorities were fully justified. Six regiments, the Twelfth, Sixteenth, Fifty-Fifth, Sixty-Sixth, Sixty-Ninth and Seventy-First, with the Ninety-Fifth Ohio, Eighteenth Kentucky, a detachment of Kentucky cavalry and two batteries manned principally by teamsters and train guards cut off from Cumberland Gap, had been moved beyond Lexington towards the advancing army of General SMITH, and on the 29th and 30th of August, fought the well-contested and sanguinary engagement known as the Battle of Richmond. The eight regiments of infantry were divided into two brigades, the First consisting of the Sixteenth, Fifty-Fifth, Sixty-Ninth and Seventy-First Indiana, under command of Brigadier General MAHLON D. MANSON; and the Second consisting of the Twelfth and Sixty-Sixth Indiana, Eighteenth Kentucky, Ninety-Fifth Ohio, a Battalion of the Third Tennessee, and LANPHEAR's Michigan Battery, under command of Brigadier General CHARLES CRUFT, both experienced and brave officers from this State.

The Indiana regiments had been in the service only from ten to twenty days, during which time they had made such frequent changes of encampments, and had been so heavily drawn upon for guard duty that but little time had been devoted to drill. They were brave and patriotic armed and uniformed men—rather than trained and disciplined soldiers.

The disastrous result of the battle is well known. Two thousand officers and men, including General MANSON, were captured and paroled. The loss in killed and wounded in the Indiana regiments was nearly one thousand. Colonel LINK, of the Twelfth, Lieutenant Colonel WOLFE, of the Sixteenth, and Lieutenant Colonel TOPPING, of the Seventy-First, were among the killed. Nine pieces of artillery fell into the hands of the enemy.

The enemy's forces, by the admission of rebel officers, numbered twelve thousand infantry, four thousand cavalry and sixteen pieces of artillery. General MANSON states that not more than twenty-five hundred men on the Union side were engaged at any one time.

General BOYLE manifested his high appreciation of the gallantry of our troops and the efforts of our authorities in the following dispatch to the President:

LOUISVILLE, September 1st, 1862.

PRESIDENT LINCOLN, *Washington:*

The battle near Richmond was disastrous to us. Six Indiana, one Kentucky, and one Ohio regiment, besides some Kentucky cavalry, were in the engagement. Our troops, especially the Indianians, fought with the courage and gallantry of veterans. If Ohio and Illinois had supported Indiana, and had sent their troops on, the issue of the battle would have been different. Governor MORTON has sent to this State since I have been in command here, over twenty thousand men. If other States had done so well, we could have overwhelmed the enemy. I deplore the loss that noble Indiana has sustained under the circumstances. It was important to meet the enemy before he reached the center of the State, or crossed it, and Indiana appreciating the importance of it, sent her gallant soldiers to meet the insolent foe, no doubt feeling that they would be supported by Ohio, Illinois and Kentucky.

Lexington is reported in possession of the enemy.

[Signed,]   J. T. BOYLE, Brigadier General.

RESULTS

But however disastrous in their immediate results, the more remote effects of this engagement were incalculably advantageous to the Union cause. The hitherto uninterrupted progress of the invading army was checked; time was gained to put Cincinnati in such a state of defense that SMITH, having marched to Lexington, Paris and Cynthiana, and reconnoitered in front of Covington, decided that the time was gone by for an attempt to accomplish the first object of his campaign, and accordingly marched on Frankfort, which place had been evacuated by the Union troops.

SIEGE OF CINCINNATI

On the 6th of September, while SMITH was advancing toward Covington, Major General WRIGHT, commanding the Department, appealed to Governor MORTON for troops to aid in the defense of Cincinnati, which was believed to be in imminent danger. The Eighty-Fifth and Eighty-Sixth regiments were sent forward. Twenty-four pieces of artillery, 3,000 stand of arms, 31,136 rounds of artillery ammunition and 3,365,000 musket cartridges were forwarded from the State Arsenal by special train, and were delivered at Cincinnati and Covington within fifteen hours from the receipt of the requisition. Governor MORTON and his military staff, with a number of officers, among whom were Major General LEW WALLACE, Generals THOMAS A. MORRIS, EBENEZER DUMONT and JOHN LOVE and Major W. W. FRYBARGER, proceeded to Cincinnati to assist in organizing the troops and in other defensive arrangements. General WALLACE was assigned to the command of the defenses, and the experience of the other officers rendered their services peculiarly valuable at so critical a period.

LOUISVILLE THREATENED

No sooner had the withdrawal of SMITH's forces from the vicinity of Covington and their concentration at Frankfort relieved the authorities at Cincinnati from the apprehension of an immediate attack, than the danger which had for some time threatened Louisville, from BRAGG's column, became alarmingly imminent. BRAGG, who had crossed the Tennessee River soon after SMITH had crossed the Cumberland mountains, was steadily moving towards the Ohio, slowly followed by BUELL and his army. The garrison at Bowling Green had been withdrawn at the suggestion of Governor MORTON, and was thereby saved from capture. On the 17th of September he telegraphed General BOYLE recommending that immediate steps be taken to relieve the garrison at Munfordsville, and urging the General commanding to fortify Louisville, suspend business and put the citizens under drill. He also adopted measures to secure light draft boats and have them supplied with artillery to serve as gunboats in patroling the Ohio. Works were planned and batteries placed on the heights of New Albany, under the direction of Colonel CARRINGTON and Major FRYBARGER, to cover the fords and the lowlands west of Louisville.

MUNFORDSVILLE CAPTURED

Meantime the enemy had advanced on Munfordsville, which after a gallant defense of three days under Colonels WILDER and DUNHAM was surrendered to BRAGG's whole army on the morning of the 17th, and the garrison, consisting of the Sixty-Seventh, Sixty-Eighth and Eighty-Ninth, seven companies of the Sixtieth, two companies of the Seventy-Fourth and two hundred and four recruits for the Seventeenth Indiana Regiment, with a few other troops, were paroled, and on the 18th marched to Bowling Green, where BUELL had been resting for some time within sound of the guns of Munfordsville.[3]

This battle, like that of Richmond, though resulting in defeat, served the important purpose of retarding the enemy. Time was gained to perfect the defenses at Louisville, which were so well improved that General BRAGG, having received a negative reply to his demand for the surrender of the city,

[3] The rebels attacked on the 14th and were repulsed with very heavy loss. The surrender was refused until Colonel Wilder personally inspected the enemy's position and satisfied himself that Bragg's whole army was besieging him. [Terrell]

declined to attack and moved towards Bardstown, while BUELL's column entered Louisville, the advance arriving on the 27th.

Governor MORTON and staff had proceeded there on the 22d instant to complete the outfit of newly raised Indiana troops, many of whom had been hurried forward without being suitably equipped for field service. All the old Indiana troops were also visited and such assistance and encouragement rendered as was possible. General BUELL's army was speedily reorganized and re-equipped, and on the 1st of October moved from Louisville to drive the rebel army from Kentucky. The battle of Perryville ("Chaplin Hills") was fought on the 8th, and BRAGG and SMITH at once beat a hasty retreat from the State.

RESUME

While the events already noticed were transpiring in Kentucky and Ohio, the work of raising, organizing and forwarding troops (as has been shown) was vigorously pressed forward in our own State. The first to furnish a regiment under the call of July, 1862, and the first to fill her quota, in a little over one month she had organized more than thirty thousand three years' troops. Her regiments had, with little assistance, fought the battles of Richmond and Munfordsville—checking the enemy in his advance on Cincinnati and Louisville, and participating in every movement made for the expulsion of the invaders from Kentucky. During this period the security of our border was menaced by formidable bands of rebels who were held in check by the untiring vigilance of the Indiana Legion and minute-men, by whom the Ohio river was patroled for a distance of nearly four hundred miles, and about four thousand rebel prisoners securely guarded. Every demand of the General Government, and of neighboring States, was fully and promptly responded to, with a zealous energy that was as acceptable and animating to the loyal cause, as it was unwelcome and disheartening to the rebels.

THE HINES AND MORGAN RAIDS

INVASION OF THE STATE, JUNE, 1863

Some time in May, 1863, a company of Kentucky cavalry, under Captain THOMAS H. HINES, belonging to General JOHN H. MORGAN's division, was sent from the rebel army in Tennessee to Kentucky, to take charge of a camp for recruiting disabled horses, with permission "to operate against the enemy north of the Cumberland river." Improving on the probable scope of this authority, Captain HINES, after "operating" a short time in the line of his "convalescent horse" duties, and against the Union men of Kentucky, on the 17th of June, with the assistance of some wood boats obtained of his friends, crossed into Indiana, eighteen miles above Cannelton, with sixty-two men, his particular object being to pick up as many fresh horses as might conveniently be found. After making arrangements with his ferrymen to meet him in about three days, at a convenient point, he pressed into the interior, in the direction of Paoli, Orange county, taking the precaution to protect his flanks, as completely as the limited extent of his force would allow, by scouts judiciously thrown out. Under the assumed character that he and his gang belonged to the Union army, and were acting under proper orders from General BOYLE, commanding the District of Kentucky, in search of deserters, he at first found but little difficulty in securing a number of excellent horses, leaving his own jaded and broken-down animals in their stead, and coolly and "in due form" giving vouchers upon the Federal Quartermaster at Indianapolis for the difference in value, which he accommodatingly fixed at a satisfactory and liberal rate. But his impudent disguise was soon suspected, and before his arrival on the second day of the raid at Valeene, Orange county, the whole secret of his mission became known, and the alarm, with many exaggerations as to the strength of his force and the damage he had done, spread with astonishing rapidity throughout the counties of Perry, Orange, Crawford, Washington and Harrison and the adjacent country.

It is unofficially reported that at Valeene the rebels demanded cooked rations of the citizens, and, not being supplied to their satisfaction, they attempted to fire the place, with partial success.

Before they reached Paoli, preparations had been made to receive them, learning which they made a sudden detour to the west, and passed round the place, taking horses as they went, to a point about seven miles northeast, where they encountered a force of fifteen armed citizens, whom they captured and plundered. Two more citizens arriving a few moments after, they were ordered to surrender, and, upon refusing, one was knocked off his horse and disabled, and the other shot and mortally wounded while trying to escape. His name was JAMES LISK. At this point they succeeded in procuring a guide, Mr. BRYANT BREEDEN, whom they supposed to be "reliable," and pressed on in their march, though very late at night, to Hardinsburg, Washington county, where they arrived about daylight.

PURSUIT AND CAPTURE

While these events were transpiring, the men of the Legion and such of the citizens as could immediately be armed, made rapid preparations for pursuit. Sixty armed minute-men from Paoli, joined by a number from Valeene and the neighboring settlements, and a mounted battalion of the Legion from Leavenworth, under Majors HORATIO WOODBURY and ROBERT E. CLENDENIN, moved promptly on the rebel trail.

Colonel CHARLES FOURNIER, of Perry county, commanding the Fifth Regiment of the Legion, took active measures to defend the line of the river in the rebel rear. As soon as he was informed of their entrance into the State, he called out as many mounted men as possible, and started for Flint Island Bar, to protect the Government ram "Monarch," then lying at that point entirely exposed, and the destruction of which was supposed to be the object of the raid. He arrived at ten o'clock at night, and finding that HINES had gone northward, and that there was no probable danger of interference with the ram, Captain ESSARY, commanding the second battalion of the Fifth Regiment of the Legion was dispatched with a sufficient force to intercept the enemy at Blue River Island, it having been reported that he would attempt to recross the river at that point. Colonel FOURNIER, as a precaution, so placed the remainder of his command as to certainly protect the ram, should a detachment of the rebels be sent to destroy her.

There were thus two forces closing in upon the marauder—the one under Majors WOODBURY and CLENDENIN, pushing him back to the river, and the other under Captain ESSARY, moving in between him and the expected outlet. The former followed the rebel track through Hardinsburg to near Fredericksburg, in the southwestern part of Washington county, where, learning that the enemy was hastening toward the Ohio, they pressed forward with all possible speed. Arriving within a short distance of Leavenworth, the force was divided, Major WOODBURY taking the upper road leading toward Corydon, and Major CLENDENIN taking the road along the river, so as to reach the anticipated rebel crossing in time to head them off, while the other force, closing in above, would lock them in, and thus compel a fight or surrender.

The combined movement was pressed with vigor. Captain ESSARY promptly reached his destination, and the other portion of our force soon chased the enemy to the expected crossing place, to which he had been compelled to fly nearly a day sooner than he had counted upon; consequently, when he reached the Ohio, at two o'clock P. M., on the 19th, there were no boats ready for his use; a sufficient force to badly whip him was posted in his front and rear, and it was useless to think of getting any relief, under such circumstances, from boats—even should an attempt be made to send them. In this dilemma, the rebel commander maneuvered to avoid a collision with the militia and citizens, and turned to his guide to help him to another crossing place. The guide, being a true Union man, unwillingly impressed into the enemy's service, determined to make the most of his position, and the delay which he bewilderingly(?) caused in finding what he reported to be a practicable ford, enabled the river guard on duty at and near Leavenworth, below, to arm the steamer "Izetta," and start her up stream to aid the land forces in preventing the rebel exodus. In due time, HINES was easily lured by his guide to the Blue River Island, about three miles above Leavenworth, where the channel on the Indiana side is shallow and easily fordable in low water (as it was at the time), with deep and swift water between the island and the southern shore. Major CLENDENIN'S command, including Captain ESSARY'S company, soon came up, and the rebels, thinking their only safety was in crossing the "ford" which lay before them, plunged in with triumphant yells, bearing their booty with them, and soon reached the island. Here, while huddled together, viewing the rather unfavorable prospect beyond, Major CLENDENIN opened fire, and they ineffectually discharged some shots in return, and then, as a last resort, attempted to swim to the Kentucky bank; but the "Izetta," at this opportune moment, opened upon them with a piece of artillery and some small arms, and forced them back—Captain HINES and two men only escaping. Three men were killed, three wounded, and two drowned, according to one report; according to another, four men were killed outright, and four more wounded and drowned. One Captain, one Lieutenant (an Adjutant), and fifty men surrendered as prisoners of war, and were sent to Louisville upon the order of General BOYLE. Five horses were lost in the attempt to cross the river, but the remainder were captured, and those which were stolen from our citizens were returned, while the arms and other property were duly turned over to the Government authorities. Considerable property was stolen by the rebels at Valeene, Hardinsburg, King's Mills, and at farmhouses along their route, but the amount in value has not been reported.

As Major CLENDENIN was receiving the prisoners and taking an account of the captured property, Major WOODBURY, with his mounted force, appeared. They were much disappointed in not arriving in time to participate in the capture, to which their energetic pursuit had largely contributed. The honor of the affair may be fairly divided between Major CLENDENIN, Major WOODBURY and the Legion of Crawford, Perry and Harrison counties. JOHN R. SIMPSON, formerly Adjutant of the Fiftieth Indiana Volunteers, also took part in the capture, organizing and commanding several squads of minute-men hastily banded together from the counties of Washington, Orange, Crawford and Harrison. Mr. BRYANT BREEDEN deserves especial credit for his tact in misguiding the rebels. Private FINDLEY MCNAUGHTON, of the First Indiana Cavalry, who was "gobbled up" as a prisoner, managed, while in the custody of the rebels, to send one of Mr. BREEDEN's little boys, who was following his father "to see the fun," to Leavenworth, with information of the intent of the rebels to re-cross the Ohio above that point, thus enabling the citizens to patrol the channel with the steamer and check their retreat, as has been already stated.

Captain HINES, single-handed and alone, a few days afterwards, joined MORGAN at Brandenburg, and took part in the celebrated raid through Indiana and Ohio in July, 1863. He was a dashing and daring officer; was captured with his chief and with him made his escape from the Ohio penitentiary, and clung to his bold riders with a zeal worthy of a better cause until the final collapse of the rebellion.

INVASION OF THE STATE—JULY, 1863

The invasion of Indiana in the summer of 1863 by a division of rebel troops, under command of General JOHN H. MORGAN, when considered in the light of events then pending, must always be regarded as a prominent feature in our history. No hostile military movement of any consequence, except that resulting in the battle of Tippecanoe, had ever before been made in our territory. The invasion, or "raid," as it was called, was intended, as will be hereafter shown, to distract and disarrange the plans and movements of the Federal forces then threatening the rebel army of the West with annihilation, but in its results proved to be only a wild and reckless adventure, failing almost entirely of its object, and ending in sad discomfiture to the rebel cause. Its projectors sought to make it the means of escape from a *trap* in which the superior generalship and overwhelming strength of ROSECRANS and his co-operators had involved them; it was a desperate makeshift, a kind of "forlorn hope" maneuver, to extricate the army of BRAGG from apparent destruction. While the "raid" was a failure and mistake, it occasioned our people much inconvenience, and created an intense excitement; and the plunderings, burnings and damages, which fell upon our citizens living within its track, were by no means inconsiderable. It is proper, therefore, as a matter of local history, connected with the rebellion, that an account of it should be given in this report.

ITS ORIGIN AND OBJECT

The circumstances which gave rise to the raid may be briefly stated: First—the necessities, in a military sense, of the rebel army in the West; and, second—the condition of feeling on the part of a considerable portion of the people of this and adjoining States, which seemed to promise encouragement to so desperate an enterprise.

As to *the necessities* of the rebels, we have a full, and perhaps fair, account in General BASIL DUKE's "History of Morgan's Cavalry."[1] DUKE was MORGAN's factotum—first serving as his Lieutenant; and afterwards, when the great marauder was made a Brigadier, he was promoted to succeed him as Colonel of the original regiment of "Morgan's Cavalry." He was his confidential adviser and friend, and was with him in all his campaigns, except one. DUKE had, therefore, every opportunity of informing himself of MORGAN's plans and movements, and his admitted ability and sprightliness guarantee his statements as worthy of consideration in the preparation of this narrative. General DUKE substantially says, that just before the raid was undertaken, the position of the rebel army in Tennessee, under BRAGG and BUCKNER, was perilous; that ROSECRANS was strong enough to press BRAGG hard at Tullahoma—BUCKNER, in East Tennessee, being too weak to help him, or even to protect himself against the imminent attack of BURNSIDE—while, in addition, there was a large National force scattered along a convenient line to the east, under General JUDAH, which could keep open communications for ROSECRANS, and resist rebel raids in that quarter so long as the hostile armies remained in their positions, or could be concentrated, when an advance was ordered, and thus make the force on BRAGG still more formidable. The problem, as viewed by the rebels—who well understood the important fact that General JUDAH, in BURNSIDE's department, as DUKE states, was in command of "about 5000 excellent cavalry"—was to avert the immediate danger of a blow upon BRAGG's flank from this cavalry force. General MORGAN advised a raid through Indiana and Ohio, with the double object of preventing BURNSIDE from moving on BUCKNER, in East Tennessee, and preventing JUDAH's cavalry from making a junction with ROSECRANS. His experience in raiding through Kentucky enabled him to argue, with plausibility,

[1] Basil W. Duke, *History of Morgan's Cavalry* (Miami, Ohio, 1867), reprinted by Indiana University Press in 1960.

that a new raid upon that State, alone, would be disastrous and crushed out so quickly that its effects would not justify the risks and dangers of the venture; while, he contended, a *grand foray* through Indiana and Ohio would keep a large force of Union troops employed upon its track for weeks.[2] BRAGG, as he was apt to do, took a "conservative view" of the situation, and would only allow MORGAN to make a raid through Kentucky, expressly stipulating in his order that it should not extend beyond the Ohio river. The *Morgan Raid* was, therefore, made in disobedience of orders, so DUKE positively states. This fact is only important as showing MORGAN'S disposition to have his own way, and, as he generally did, to conduct his campaigns in a peculiarly independent manner, which, by the way, was the great secret of his fame, and the magnet which attracted to his standard so many bright and adventurous young Kentuckians, of whom his command was principally composed. General BRAGG knew the peril of MORGAN'S proposed movement, and evidently feared the effect the isolation, and perhaps loss, of so important and valuable a force of cavalry would have upon his army; but he probably did not appreciate the advantages of its brilliant success, should it be successful, to the same extent that MORGAN hoped.

The "vim" and "dash" of MORGAN impelled him to override the orders of his superior, and like a reckless and desperate bravado as he was, he determined to meet and if possible overcome the dangers which encompassed the rebel army in the West by a *tour de force* that would carry consternation and dismay to the hitherto peaceful regions north of the Ohio.

It is unnecessary here to enter upon details as to *the condition of feeling* entertained by many persons in the North on the subject of the war; the sympathy exhibited in behalf of the rebel cause, not only in legitimate opposition to the policy and

---

[2] The "Raid" lasted five days in Indiana, and twelve and a half days in Ohio. [Terrell]

measures of the Federal Government, but in the commission of illegal acts; the organization of treasonable societies and movements, and the declaration of treasonable sentiments by speeches, newspaper articles, and resolutions; and the effect all the sympathetic evidences may have had in determining MORGAN's extraordinary, bold, and unauthorized course; but the candid historian, in after days, may find in the facts themselves ample material for investigation as to the inducements which detached, at such a perilous crisis, so important a command from BRAGG's army.

BRAGG's situation undoubtedly required a raid, or some similar distracting movement, but if the diversity of sentiment and treasonable evidences, to which allusion has been made, had not reached MORGAN's ears, does it seem probable that the "territory North of the Ohio" would have been deemed good ground upon which to make such a hazardous experiment? His orders were not to come here. Would he have disobeyed his orders and jeopardized the safety of his army, in which he and the whole "Confederacy" felt so much pride, if he had not thought that these friendly indications were founded upon a reality that would "crop out" in substantial form upon his appearance in a country where rebel plunderings and the marauder's torch had not before been known? He was ordered to make a raid through Kentucky, and the temptation to go beyond, for the purpose of recruiting his "mount," and procuring supplies, which his command so much needed, was very great; but is it likely that even these inducements would have caused him to extend his march beyond the prescribed bounds, if treasonable indications of sympathy and assistance had not been shown by means of the press and by other channels through which they sought expression and became known to the rebels in the South?

RAID THROUGH KENTUCKY

MORGAN's division of rebel cavalry—consisting, according to General DUKE, of two brigades, the first numbering 1,460 men, the second 1,000 men, in all 2,460, with four pieces of artillery—started from Alexandria, Tennessee, on the 11th of June, 1863, on the hazardous expedition which was to end in the death or capture of nearly every man connected with it. Its march through the northern edge of Tennessee and through Kentucky, it does not comport with the purpose of this account to relate at any length. It had several pretty hard skirmishes on the way, particularly at the crossing of Green river on the 4th of July, in which it was badly beaten; and on the 5th at Lebanon, where it was successful, but with considerable loss, including General MORGAN'S youngest brother, THOMAS, First Lieutenant, Second Kentucky, who was killed at the last moment of the engagement. The 4th of July, 1863, was remarkably unfortunate for rebels everywhere. MORGAN found it no more auspicious than did PEMBERTON, or LEE, or any other of the dozen commanders who fought on that day, not only against the arms and gallantry of the National troops, but against every sentiment and memory that stirs the blood of the true American!

On the 6th, at dark, about thirty miles from Louisville, a train on the Louisville and Nashville Railroad was captured, and by "tapping" the telegraph wire it was ascertained by MORGAN that he was expected at Louisville. "Tapping the telegraph" was a frequent and sometimes very important operation for MORGAN, as he thereby learned the position of our forces and either avoided them, or prepared to attack them, as he deemed best.

On the morning of the 7th, after crossing Salt river, Captains TAYLOR and MERRIWETHER, of the Tenth Kentucky, were sent forward with a detachment to the Ohio river to capture steamers to carry the division over to this State. At the same time, Captain DAVIS, with two companies, was dispatched to cross the Ohio at Twelve-Mile Island, to give employment to the militia of lower Indiana, and leave the main body free from attack from that quarter, with orders to rejoin the division at Salem. The result of this last enterprise is thus stated by General DUKE: "Captain DAVIS crossed into Indiana with the two companies assigned him, but failed to rejoin the division, and was surrounded by overwhelming numbers, and himself and the greater part of his command captured."[3] This detachment was thus permanently lost to the expedition, as well as three other companies left at various points in Kentucky, leaving the effective force for the invasion, according to DUKE, about 2,200 men.[4]

After sending out these detachments, the division proceeded to Garnettsville, where it remained till midnight, then advanced to Brandenburg, where it arrived about nine o'clock on the morning of the 8th. At Brandenburg it was joined by Captain HINES, who had been "raiding" in a small way a short time before in Crawford, Orange and Harrison counties in this State, but so unprofitably that he left pretty nearly all his command behind him in the hands of our militia.[5]

CROSSING THE OHIO

Brandenburg is a small town situated on a high bluff about fifty miles below Louisville, on the Kentucky shore, and two miles above Mauckport, a small Indiana town. The two officers charged with the duty of providing ferriage for the division, arrived shortly after leaving the main column, and directly captured the steamer "J. T. McCoombs," in the Louisville and Henderson trade. She ran up to the wharf

[3] Duke, *History of Morgan's Cavalry* (1960 edition), 460.
This possibly may be an error, as no report of the affair was ever made by our officers. [Terrell]
[4] The strength of Morgan's army was variously stated. The captain of one of the steamers which carried it over the river reported that it consisted of 5,000 men, 5,100 horses, and 6 guns. General Boyle had information that it was 4,000 strong, and Governor Morton was repeatedly assured that it was 6,000 strong. Duke's account, however, is probably correct, the other estimates being based upon rumors and excited statements received from every direction. Morgan may have received accessions to his force at or about the time he crossed the river, but it was doubtful if they would more than make up his losses in detachments and by straggling and casualties. [Terrell]
[5] See above, 204-8.

about 2 o'clock in the afternoon of the 7th, and the moment she touched, a rebel squad boarded her and took possession. As if fortune were resolved to favor them to the utmost, a second steamer, the "Alice Dean," came in sight 'round the bend below, a short time after, and they prepared to capture her also. As her course made it apparent that she did not intend to land, they ran the "McCoombs" out to her, signaling her to stop. When the two boats touched, a party boarded the "Dean" and secured her, and thus ample means of ferriage were obtained in a very few hours, and all were ready for the arrival of the main column.

Information of these proceedings having reached Lieutenant Colonel WILLIAM J. IRVIN, at Mauckport, he dispatched messengers to Colonel LEWIS JORDAN, at Corydon, requesting troops to assist in preventing the rebels from crossing. The steamer "Lady Pike" coming up the river about the same time was stopped and sent back to Leavenworth for a piece of artillery and its gunners, of the Indiana Legion, then stationed at that point. The boat returned at midnight with a six pounder and thirty men under command of Captain G. W. LYON, of the Crawford county Artillery. To avoid the observation of the rebels at Brandenburg, the boat landed two miles below Mauckport, and the gun was hauled by hand to that place, where Colonel JOHN TIMBERLAKE, with one hundred of the Harrison county Legion, took command and proceeded with the united forces to a point opposite Brandenburg. He crossed Buck creek by means of an old boat, and his men dragged the gun through the fields and placed it in position at 7 o'clock on the morning of the 8th in front of an old house opposite the landing.

For an hour or two the Kentucky bank was concealed by a dense fog. MORGAN arrived before it lifted, and at once began his preparations for crossing. As soon as the fog allowed the opposite bank to be seen, Captain LYON trained his gun on the "McCoombs" and sent a shot through her, frightening off the rebels, who had just commenced embarking, and wounding one of their brigade quartermasters. Several shots were fired after those who were in retreat from the boats, and some were seen to fall as they hurried up the road out of range. Then, being informed that the rebel force was very small, less than 200 men, and hoping to save the steamers, Captain LYON changed the direction of his fire to the groups of cavalry on the bank, driving them out of sight to the rear of the town. Supposing that the rebels had been, by this demonstration, induced to abandon their project of invasion, Colonel TIMBERLAKE ordered the "McCoombs" to cross to the Indiana side and take his command over to Brandenburg, but the order was of course unheeded. In a few minutes some pieces of artillery were put into position by the rebels on Brandenburg heights and opened an accurate and fatal fire on LYON's gun, Lieutenant JAMES H. CURRENT, of the Mauckport Rifles, and citizen GEORGE NANCE, of Harrison county, being killed while working it. Our artillerymen having no covering but the old house, which the rebel guns made untenable, fell back about half a mile out of range, hauling their gun with them. At the same time a portion of the rebel force opened a fusillade upon the remainder of our men who were posted along the bank to resist the passage of the boats, and the fire was sharply returned. Soon, however, the rebel artillery was brought into play, which compelled the little Union force to fall back. The Second Kentucky and Ninth Tennessee Regiments of the rebels were immediately sent across the river, leaving their horses behind them. Colonel TIMBERLAKE, with a small force, rallied to the gun and fired several unavailing shots at the boat while it was crossing.

As soon as a landing was effected, the rebels formed under the bank and advanced, capturing the gun and several prisoners. Colonel TIMBERLAKE seeing he was greatly overmatched, fell back in good order toward Corydon. Major JACOB S. PFRIMMER, of the Sixth Regiment of the Legion, in command of a small body of mounted men, kept up a brisk skirmish with the rebel advance guard, on the different roads leading to

Corydon, till late in the evening, when our retreating force reached the line of battle formed by two hundred men, under Colonel JORDAN, six miles from Corydon, on the Mauckport road. A small squad of the "Mounted Hoosiers," belonging to the Sixth Legion, under Captain WILLIAM FARQUAR, acting as scouts, came into collision with the enemy while they were advancing, but sustained no injury, except the Captain, whose horse under the fire dashed him against a tree, but without disabling him. The scouts skirmished and were on the alert during the night, the rebels having halted near our line, and both parties throwing out pickets.

While this retreat and pursuit were in progress, an interesting state of affairs for MORGAN had been created by a little gunboat. General DUKE relates that directly after the return of the two steamers from their first trip to the Indiana side, a small boat, "tightly boarded up with tiers of heavy oak planking," ran rapidly down the river and opened fire, first on Brandenburg, and then on the rebel force pressing after the Legion. Two of MORGAN's guns in battery on the heights replied, and for an hour a duel was maintained between the boat and the battery, with no particular injury to either, but to the fearful discomfiture of the rebel General and the peril of his enterprise. He could not put a steamer across while the gunboat kept in easy range; a single shot might send the whole to the bottom; consequently he could neither join the two regiments already landed, nor get them back, and he could not tell what force or fate they might meet when fairly out upon Indiana soil. He was cut in two, and the gunboat kept the fragments apart. She held his expedition completely at the command of her guns; but, unaccountably, after an hour's firing, she ran back up the river, and MORGAN at once began sending his force across in the utmost haste.

About five o'clock P. M., the same gunboat came back with two transports (ordinary steamers), with a battalion of the Seventy-First Indiana, under Colonel BIDDLE, and a section of the Twenty-Third Indiana Battery, under Lieutenant Ross.

The gunboat was in advance, under an officer of the Western Flotilla, who commanded the expedition. MORGAN stopped crossing and held his boats around a bend of the river out of range, his battery on the heights firing with rapidity, but without damage, at the little fleet. The officer in command of the gunboat claimed that his craft was only bullet-proof, and that MORGAN'S guns would sink him, and therefore withdrew and proceeded up the river. The two transports remained for some time, and kept up the artillery engagement with the battery on shore until one of Lieutenant Ross's guns became disabled by the breaking of the boat's deck from the recoil, when it being plainly seen that the rebels had decidedly the advantage, the transports also withdrew.

The remainder of MORGAN'S division at once crossed, and advanced and encamped a few miles from the river. They plundered freely. Their historian says they "found the larders unlocked, fires on the hearths, bread half made up, and the chickens parading about the doors with a confidence that was touching, but misplaced." In other words, the rebels helped themselves to whatever they wanted and could find in the houses of the poor people they had scared into the woods. They burned the mill of Mr. PETER LOPP, on Buck creek, three miles from the river, their first exploit in that line in the State.

Four miles south of Corydon one of their soldiers was shot near the house of Rev. PETER GLENN, whom they induced by a flag of truce to come out unarmed to meet them, when they killed him and burned his house and outbuildings.

PREPARATIONS FOR RESISTANCE

The first information of MORGAN'S movements which indicated the probability of his approach to our border, was conveyed to Brigadier General O. B. WILLCOX, commanding the District of Indiana and Michigan, by Major General BURNSIDE, who had received it from Brigadier General J. T. BOYLE, commanding the District of Kentucky, on the 4th of

July, the same day that MORGAN was defeated at Green river bridge. General BOYLE stated that a cavalry force, supposed to be about 4,000 strong, with artillery, commanded by JOHN H. MORGAN, had crossed the Cumberland river, and was advancing upon the Louisville and Nashville Railroad. He also stated that he had no available United States troops in Kentucky, and earnestly requested the assistance of an adequate force to check the invasion. General BURNSIDE ordered the Seventy-First Indiana, and any available cavalry and artillery in the State, to be sent at once to Kentucky. General WILLCOX promptly dispatched the Seventy-First Indiana Regiment, two companies of the Third Indiana Cavalry, and MYERS' Twenty-Third Indiana Battery to Louisville, where they reported to General BOYLE on the following morning. This movement left Indianapolis, of United States troops, only two companies of the Sixty-Third Indiana, doing guard duty at the Soldiers' Home, some hundreds of recently exchanged prisoners of the Fifty-First and Seventy-Third Indiana, and a small number of recruits.

This stripping the State of National troops, though necessitated by the aspect of affairs in Kentucky at the time, was unfortunate, and the more so because our home defenses were in a far less efficient condition than they should have been. Governor MORTON, to whom an invasion of our Southern border was an ever present peril, had used every means in his power to provide adequate defenses, but with far less than satisfactory success. The Legion, though generally organized with more or less completeness throughout the border counties, was too often a mere skeleton, or loose aggregation of citizens, with little military discipline or knowledge. And where better organized and more sedulously drilled, it was too feeble in numbers to present an effectual resistance to veteran enemies. A sufficiency of arms had not been supplied, and as late as the 29th of June, the Governor had telegraphed to the Secretary of War for 2,500 stand of arms and 12 pieces of artillery for State use. But the most serious deficiency was in mounted troops, of which we had not more than two hundred, besides a few squads of armed citizens using their own horses, who were called out by the emergency. Against veteran cavalry, recruiting, as horses became exhausted, by stealing in all directions, raw levies of infantry could not, even with the greatest facilities for transportation, be made very effective. General WILLCOX, General WALLACE and General DOWNEY, all speak particularly of this deficiency and its unfortunate consequences.[6] With one-tenth of the forces we had in arms during the raid, well mounted, MORGAN never could have escaped from the State.

On the reception of information that MORGAN was marching northward through Kentucky, Governor MORTON telegraphed Colonel E. A. MAGINNISS, at New Albany, to order out all the forces at his command, and send a messenger to Colonel JORDAN, of Harrison county, with instructions that he should also order out his command immediately; also to put KNAPP's battery, the German artillery of Floyd county, on a steamer and send it to the mouth of Salt river to prevent guerrillas from crossing the Ohio. He also notified General BOYLE of his purpose to co-operate heartily in any movement to resist MORGAN, and asked information as to the rebel force and its whereabouts. General BOYLE's reply the next day was that he did not know where MORGAN was, but that he had captured the Twentieth Kentucky at Lebanon. Before night General BOYLE's want of information was rather alarmingly supplied, as he telegraphed to Governor MORTON that the companies of our Legion in Clark county, if there were any, should be sent to him at Louisville, as MORGAN was then between Lebanon and Louisville. The next day, the 6th of July, he again telegraphed the Governor that he had learned nothing further of MORGAN's movements, except that the tele-

[6] See Willcox's report on "Military Operations in Indiana," in Terrell, *Report,* 1, Appendix, Doc. 81:280; Wallace's and Downey's reports on Morgan's Raid in "Operations of the Indiana Legion and Minute Men, 1863, 1864," in Indiana *Documentary Journal,* 1864, vol. 2, no. 11: 378-80, 420-22.

graph operator at the Junction reported cannonading as having been heard in the direction of Bardstown. But the General did not believe that MORGAN would come to Louisville, and he did believe that the forces of Generals HOBSON and SHACKLEFORD, then in pursuit, would overtake and beat him. Governor MORTON, as little influenced by General BOYLE's sudden confidence as by his premature alarm, ordered the Legion to retain their organization and arms, and be in readiness for prompt service. Part of the force called out, at the request of General WILLCOX, was ordered to Louisville, and Colonel DELAND's First Michigan Sharpshooters and the Twelfth Michigan Battery were ordered from Michigan to this State.

On the morning of the 8th of July unofficial information was received that the apprehensions which had impelled these precautionary steps were realized, and that MORGAN was on the bank of the Ohio preparing to cross. BURNSIDE, at Cincinnati, was immediately informed of the movement, and a request to the Chief of Ordnance at Washington for a number of batteries of smooth-bored six-pounder and twelve-pounder howitzers was promptly answered that the guns were on the way from St. Louis. To General BOYLE, whose solicitations had deprived us of all our available Government troops, an earnest request was sent that he should dispatch a force to the threatened points to prevent the rebels from crossing, or to drive them out if they had crossed. "You have all our regular troops," said Governor MORTON; "please state what steps have been taken to arrest the progress of the rebels." General BOYLE made no reply. In the evening of the same day news was received that the rebels had crossed. The next day, the 9th, a second dispatch was sent to General BOYLE asking information of MORGAN's movements. No reply was made. To a third dispatch, he answered from New Albany that "MORGAN is near Corydon, and will move either upon New Albany or into the interior of the State. He has no less than 4,000 men and six pieces of artillery. General HOBSON in pursuit of him is at Brandenburg, and has sent for transports to cross his forces. Your cities and towns will be sacked and pillaged if you do not bring out your State forces." This was the first *official* information Governor MORTON had received in regard to the invasion. The sagacity that warned us to bring out our State forces if we would save our towns from pillage, could only be paralleled by the generosity that accompanied the warning with no offer to assist us even with our own troops!

Before the receipt of General BOYLE's belated news, General WILLCOX, co-operating with Governor MORTON, had made such preparations as he could to meet the rebels. He ordered all the railroad cars and locomotives to be secured for the transportation of the militia, their arms and supplies; the Government Quartermaster, Commissary and Ordnance Officers were directed to furnish everything that might be required for properly equipping and supplying the troops, and the Superintendent of the State Arsenal at once put a large force at work in preparing ammunition, of which there was not a sufficient supply.

The receipt of the first official information of the invasion was immediately made the occasion for the publication of a General Order,[7] dated at the Executive Department, July 9th, announcing the presence of a considerable rebel force in the State, and ordering that all able-bodied white male citizens in the several counties south of the National Road should forthwith form themselves into companies of at least sixty persons, elect officers, and arm themselves with such arms as they could procure. The companies thus formed were required to perfect themselves in military drill as rapidly as possible, and hold themselves subject to further orders from the Executive. They were requested to be mounted, in all cases, if possible. Citizens in other parts of the State were earnestly requested to form military companies, and be ready for service

[7] The order is printed in Terrell, *Report,* 1, Appendix, Doc. 99:300.

when called for. Prompt reports by telegraph of the formation of companies were desired. Officers of the Indiana Legion were charged with the execution of the order, and the United States officers were requested to render such assistance as they were able.

At the same time a dispatch was sent to Captain PENNOCK, commanding the river fleet at Cairo, informing him of the invasion, and requesting the assistance of all his available gunboats to prevent the rebels from recrossing the Ohio. The Captain replied that there were six gunboats up the river, and he would at once send more. A request was telegraphed to General BURNSIDE to send back the troops and artillery sent to Kentucky a few days before; and it was suggested to him by the Governor that MORGAN would probably attempt to get back into Kentucky at some point between Madison and Louisville. He therefore urged the propriety of placing a lot of spare artillery, collected at Louisville, upon boats and patroling the river between Louisville and Lawrenceburg. General BURNSIDE promptly replied that he had directed passenger boats not to run between Cincinnati and Louisville without guards, and had requested that a proper disposition be made of the gunboats, both above and below Louisville, to prevent the enemy from recrossing. He ordered General BOYLE to patrol the river, as suggested by the Governor, and assured the latter of sufficient National troops to repel any attack, and of his desire to do whatever he could to protect the State in the emergency. In order to apply the Governor's suggestion of arming ordinary steamers as river patrols, General WILLCOX at once sent Lieutenant Commander GEO. BROWN, of the Navy, then in Indianapolis on leave, to the Ohio to organize and command a number of these extemporary gunboats, which he proceeded to do in a thorough and satisfactory manner. The idea proved to be a good one, and MORGAN'S escape across the river at one of the many fords between Louisville and Cincinnati was probably prevented, and his final capture assured by this means.

Having no arms suitable for cavalry, the Governor purchased of Messrs. B. KITTREDGE & Co., Cincinnati, eight hundred WESSON carbines; and arrangements were made whereby 17,000 muskets, 25,000 sets of accoutrements and 2 batteries of artillery were procured from the St. Louis Arsenal in time to be issued to the rapidly organized militia.

To give the injunctions of the general order issued on the 9th more direct and immediate effect, the Governor, on the day following, addressed a dispatch to prominent and leading citizens in all easily accessible counties in the central and northern portions of the State, requesting that all available men of their neighborhoods be brought to the capital at the earliest moment, organized by companies, with their blankets; and that runners be sent out in their counties to give information and call out all who were willing to volunteer.

RESPONSE OF THE PEOPLE

While the authorities were busy with these preparations, the people were gathering in such numbers as never could have been anticipated, not only along the track of the rebel march, but all over the State. The call of the Governor, the conflicting and exaggerated rumors that were afloat, and the anxious disposition felt in every locality to assist in catching and chastising the invaders, created the greatest excitement and enthusiasm. In less than twenty-four hours after the dispatch was sent out soliciting individual co-operation in bringing out troops, the gentlemen addressed reported an aggregate of 5,000 men for service, and outside of their efforts 10,000 more had been gathered and were on the way to the capital. On the same day, the 10th, the Governor informed General BURNSIDE that he would have 15,000 militia in Indianapolis on that day. Within two days 20,000 men had been actually mustered at Indianapolis, and the authorities had notice of the organization and readiness for service of 45,000 more.

The gathering of 65,000 men in forty-eight hours is such a display of patriotic energy and devotion as may safely challenge a comparison with any similar exhibition in history. And the circumstances under which it was made enhance its magnitude and merit greatly. Farmers were in the midst of harvest; they were weak-handed from the absence of scores of thousands of sons and brothers in the army, and the impossibility of replacing them with other laborers; at the best, the ripening crops could be but indifferently secured, and to desert them to resist the rebels, for they knew not how long, was equivalent, so far as they could tell, to losing them utterly. Manufactories, mills, mechanics' shops, were equally in want of laborers, and would suffer greatly if work were suspended for even a day. Yet farmers left their grain to rot in the fields, mechanics dropped their tools, merchants abandoned their stores, professional men their desks, clerks forgot their ledgers, and students their textbooks, and young and old alike all swarmed in constantly thickening throngs to the capital, or the nearest place of rendezvous, as if there were no duty or interest of that hour but the safety of the State. Indianapolis, which was the great central mustering place, was converted into a huge barrack. There were soldiers in every open lot and square, in every vacant building, in halls, in lofts, in the streets. Railway trains were rushing in every hour, crowded inside and outside with shouting masses. The country roads were cloudy with dust raised by the tread of companies hurrying from every school district and neighborhood.

The labor of organizing and equipping so great a force in so short a time was immense, but the authorities were as zealous as the people, and the work was done. General WILLCOX[8] and his staff officers were vigilant, energetic, sleepless. Major General LEWIS WALLACE, at the request of the Governor, was detailed by the War Department to assist in the defense of the State. Brigadier General HENRY B. CARRINGTON came from Ohio and gave his best efforts to the organization and mustering of the forces, a work in which his experience and energy made him unrivaled. Brigadier General MILO S.

[8] See Willcox's report in Terrell, *Report,* 1, Appendix, Doc. 81:279-80.

HASCALL, on his way to the field, was sent back by General BURNSIDE and ordered to report to the District Commander for any duty he might deem proper, and was assigned to the command of the defenses of Indianapolis.[9] Captain JOHN H. FARQUHAR, of the regulars, was appointed a Brigadier General of the State Militia, and ordered to Evansville to organize a brigade for the protection of the border on the lower Ohio against any counter or co-operative movement that might be made by the rebels in aid of MORGAN. Major General JOHN L. MANSFIELD, of the Legion, was sent to New Albany to bring out the militia on the way, and organize the temporary forces. Colonel W. W. FRYBARGER, of the artillery, was dispatched to the border to organize a force in that branch of the service; and the services of other officers, as will be more particularly stated hereafter, were brought into requisition and disposed to the best advantage.

Offers of assistance from other States were made and accepted. A company of sharpshooters from Mattoon, Illinois, under Captain DAVID H. LANE, splendidly armed with Henry rifles, was assigned to the One-Hundred-and-Third Regiment of Minute-Men. Two other Illinois companies, Captain ASHMORE'S, of Charleston, and Captain FERRIS', of Ashmore, were assigned to the One-Hundred-and-Ninth Regiment of Minute-Men. General SCHOFIELD, commanding at St. Louis, Missouri, sent the Tenth Regiment Kansas Volunteers and the Twelfth Kansas Battery, which were stationed at Mitchell, to intercept rebel reinforcements.

DISPOSITION OF FORCES

In the position of MORGAN after crossing into this State any one of four movements could be attempted, all involving injuries to the loyal people and causing distress of enormous extent. He could move on New Albany and Jeffersonville where there was deposited about $4,000,000 worth of public

[9] See Hascall's report in *ibid.*, 1, Appendix, Doc. 80:276-77.

stores; he could by a judicious distribution of his command burn the bridges and disable the tracks of the Ohio and Mississippi and the Jeffersonville railroads by which the Government was sending troops and supplies to ROSECRANS; he could advance to Indianapolis, as he once avowed it his purpose to do, release the rebel prisoners, and burn the Capitol, the Arsenal and the immense military stores; or, he could push along on a plundering foray, parallel with the Ohio river, if the uprising of the people left no other movement open to him, till he had a chance to recross to Kentucky.

Jeffersonville and New Albany were attached to the District of Kentucky and properly belonged to General BOYLE's command, but Major General JAMES HUGHES, of the Legion, organized and disposed of such forces of the Legion and minutemen as could be raised, for the protection of both places, and the rebels left them unharmed.

As our troops were mostly raw, undisciplined infantry, it was impossible to employ them with any good result, in such strength as they presented during the first days of the raid, against veteran cavalry. General WILLCOX concurred with the State authorities in the plan of obstructing MORGAN's march—scouring the country, felling trees in the roads, tearing up bridges, and creating obstacles wherever it was possible, to delay him till adequate forces could be collected and properly disposed. Our militia, besides that at Indianapolis, was concentrated chiefly at two points on the Ohio and Mississippi Railroad—the Western Division at Mitchell, the Eastern at Seymour, and the cars were collected at these points to carry them wherever they might be needed. Major General HUGHES, after ascertaining that MORGAN would not move against New Albany, went up to Mitchell, where he organized about 2,000 men and held them in readiness to resist an attack upon that point, or move elsewhere as circumstances might require. General JOHN LOVE, acting Brigadier General under appointment and orders from General WILLCOX, took command at Seymour. He reports that there were two regiments of United States volunteers there, and, in addition to these, he organized about 300 minute-men, and a small force of citizens, who, using their own horses, acted as scouts and patrols, and rendered valuable service in that capacity. Colonel SAMUEL B. SERING, of the Legion, had at Madison a force of about 2,000 men, with four pieces of artillery. This force was disposed, with the assistance of Colonel BERNARD F. MULLEN, Thirty-Fifth Indiana Volunteers, so as to guard the river, which was easily fordable at several places in the vicinity of Madison and Hanover, and the roads leading to those places. Trees were felled by the citizens under the direction of the Hon. DAVID C. BRANHAM, and the positions of the troops thus greatly strengthened. General ALEXANDER C. DOWNEY, of Ohio county, ordered two regiments of the Legion, that of Colonel H. T. WILLIAMS, of Ohio county, and that of Colonel J. H. BURKAM, of Dearborn county, to Seymour; and Colonel HARRIS KEENEY, of Switzerland county, with his command, was ordered to Madison.

Colonel SERING had orders, if MORGAN attempted to cross the Ohio at or near Madison, to destroy all the boats if necessary, and defeat the attempt if possible, and similar orders were sent to other commanders at various points on the river. Such disposition of our forces at Indianapolis had been made as to render it impossible for MORGAN to advance upon that place, as he doubtless would have been glad to have done, without incurring certain destruction. His flanks were menaced; reinforcements were cut off; the line of retreat across the Ohio was defended by our best militia and watched by vigilant gunboats and patrol steamers; while before him lay the enormous mass of troops concentrated at the Capital; and behind, close upon his heels, followed General HOBSON with 4,000 mounted men. A single day sufficed to show him how rapidly and fatally the strength of the State was pressing down upon him, and, abandoning all other schemes, he took to flight. It was his only resource. His raid was converted into a stupendous stampede, and his departure from the State was marked by but little of the deliberation and confidence which he exhibited when he entered it.

ADVANCE ON CORYDON, AND THE FIGHT

In our account of Morgan's movements, on the 8th of July, we left him near Corydon, in front of our little force of militia and minute-men, under Colonel LEWIS JORDAN, of the Sixth Legion, consisting, when concentrated, of about 400 men. Colonel JORDAN was assisted by Colonel JOHN TIMBERLAKE, Major LEONIDAS STOUT, Captain GEORGE L. KEY, and Captain JAMES D. IRVIN, as volunteer aides. On the morning of Wednesday, the 8th, as soon as Colonel JORDAN was informed of the invasion, he dispatched a messenger with the information to Surgeon THOMAS W. FRY, who was in command under General BOYLE, of the post of New Albany, and requested reinforcements. Major FRY received the request at 12 o'clock the same day, and promptly communicated it to his superior commander at Louisville, some sixteen hours before the whole rebel force had got up in front of Colonel JORDAN's lines. Three or four messages to the same effect were sent subsequently. Reinforcements of both men and artillery were promised, and there was ample time to have forwarded them before the attack on Thursday afternoon, the 9th, but for some unexplained reason none were sent, and our handful of raw men were left to make the best fight they could.

On the morning of the 9th, our scouts reported the rebel advance moving forward. Falling back slowly, and constantly skirmishing, Colonel JORDAN reached a point on the Mauckport and Laconia roads, about a mile from Corydon, where he formed a line of battle, and constructed such hasty defenses as he could. At ten o'clock the rebels appeared in force along the whole line, and commenced an attack upon our left, which was held by the "Spencer Guards," under Captain GEORGE W. LAHUE. The Guards repelled it vigorously; it was repeated twice, but with the same result, and the loss of quite a number of the assailants, killed and wounded. This determined resistance made it necessary for the enemy to reinforce that portion of their line, and the left was consequently compelled to fall back. An advance was then made upon our entire front, but our men held their ground bravely, and maintained the fight with spirit, and considerable loss to the enemy, for half an hour. Then the rebel reserve being brought up and a regiment thrown in on our flank and rear, cutting off reinforcements, their artillery opening upon our slender defenses at the same moment, Colonel JORDAN was forced to fall back to Corydon. But here further resistance was seen to be worse than useless. The rebels planted artillery, of which we had none, on a hill south of the town and opened fire, and the little band of defenders soon found itself nearly surrounded by a force of veterans numbering eight to one, with retreat cut off. In this position, Colonel JORDAN prudently surrendered his command, then consisting of 345 men, who were shortly afterwards paroled by General MORGAN. Our loss was three killed— HARRY STEPLETON, NATHAN MCKINZIE and WILLIAM HETH; JACOB FERRACE, one of the Commissioners of Harrison county, was mortally, and CALEB GLENN severely, wounded. ISAAC LANG died of heat and exhaustion in the fight. The rebel loss was eight killed and thirty-three wounded. General DUKE says our men "defended their rail piles resolutely," a sufficient proof that they did their duty, and an indication that if the reinforcements and artillery promised from New Albany had been sent to them, the enemy would have met so serious a resistance his march would have been delayed till the fast-gathering forces of the State could have intercepted him, or until General HOBSON's pursuing force could have come up. As it was, the delay was important and the loss inflicted considerable.

Upon the surrender, the rebels marched into and occupied Corydon. MORGAN and his principal officers made their headquarters at KINTNER's hotel, while his men swarmed through the town, plundering without check or discrimination. They took from Messrs. DOUGLASS, DENBO & Co. clothing, hats, caps and boots to the amount of $3,500; Mr. SAMUEL J. WRIGHT'S store was laid under contribution for a large amount of goods; the drug store of Dr. REEDER was plundered, and a number of private houses were entered and robbed of whatever clothing or other desirable articles could be found. The ladies were compelled to cook meals for the robbers, if none or not enough were ready when they "called." The County Treasurer, Mr. WILLISON HISEY, was robbed of $750.00; and upon each of three flouring mills of the town a contribution of $1,000.00 was levied, but remitted upon payment of $2,100.00, which General MORGAN was considerate enough to accept from the three, as a ransom from burning. When asked "by what right he made such a demand," he pointed to his troops, then busily robbing the town, and said, "there is my authority." It was sufficient—if *not* satisfactory. While marching into town, they took prisoners Hon. S. K. WOLFE, State Senator, and SAM'L W. DOUGLASS, Esq., County Auditor, who were engaged with the Legion in the fight, and placing them at the head of the column, compelled them to lead the advance, threatening to shoot them on the spot if the column was fired upon. Our prisoners were robbed of their money, hats, boots, and clothing. Five hundred horses were gathered up and taken from the citizens of Harrison county. Among the plundering crowd was recognized a spy, who had recently been, for a short time, a resident of Corydon, and was well acquainted with the place and people.

GOING AHEAD

Having secured as much plunder and as many fresh horses as possible, and given his command a few hours' rest, late on the afternoon of the 9th, MORGAN marched out of Corydon, leaving behind to the care of the citizens eleven of his wounded, two of whom soon afterwards died. A few miles out of the town, Mr. SPEER H. HURST was wounded while endeavoring to avoid capture, and two boys were shot at and wounded, in the north part of the county. Throwing out detachments on his flanks, MORGAN advanced with the main body northward to Palmyra, where he halted two hours to recuperate and rob; the detachment on the right taking Greenville, in Floyd county, and that on the left entering Paoli, in Orange county. These movements were well calculated to distract the attention of our authorities, and confuse their arrangements to protect important points, as they left it uncertain where he intended to strike. From Paoli, he threatened the Ohio and Mississippi Railroad at Mitchell. From Palmyra, he could strike the New Albany and Salem Railroad at Salem; and from Greenville, he had within easy reach both the New Albany Railroad at New Providence, and the Jeffersonville Railroad at Vienna. MORGAN, however, either deemed it unsafe to scatter his forces in so many directions, or accomplished all he aimed at in simply thus showing himself, for the detachments, after taking all the horses and plundering all the farmhouses within reach in Harrison, Crawford, Orange, Floyd and Washington counties, through portions of each of which they passed, converged towards Salem, in Washington county, where the entire force arrived at nine o'clock on the morning of the 10th.

AT SALEM

They easily dispersed the squads of badly armed minutemen that came out to meet them, entered the town without difficulty, and captured a company of the Washington county Legion, commanded by Captain JOHN DAVIS, which unknowingly came in just after they had entered, for the purpose of receiving their arms and ammunition to resist the raid.[10] A

---

[10] Duke relates this anecdote: "A small swivel, used by the younger population of Salem to celebrate Christmas and the Fourth of July, had been planted to receive us: about eighteen inches long, it was loaded to the muzzle, and mounted in the Public Square by being propped against a stick of firewood. It was not fired, however, for the man deputed to perform that important duty, somewhat astounded by the sudden dash into town, dropped the coal of fire with which he should have touched it off, and before he could get another, the rebels captured the piece. The shuddering imagination refuses to

small force under Hon. JAMES A. CRAVENS, was forced hastily to retreat, and another company, which was on its way to the town upon a train of the New Albany and Salem Railroad, narrowly escaped capture. But for the prudent caution of the engineer, who suspected danger from the number of mounted men he saw near the track, the last mentioned company would have been caught inevitably, and the whole train lost. At Salem, MORGAN burned the large railroad bridge, destroyed several small bridges and culverts, tore up the track for a considerable distance, and burned the depot, with its contents. He also levied $1,000.00 upon each of the mills of the vicinity, and plundered all the stores, and most of the dwellings. In fact, such a scene of pillage was enacted as was certainly never before witnessed in this State, and probably nowhere else. General DUKE'S description of it is too graphic to be omitted. He says:

> This disposition to wholesale plunder exceeded anything that any of us had ever seen before. The great cause for apprehension which our situation might have inspired seemed only to make the men reckless. Calico was the staple article of appropriation. Each man who could get one, tied a bolt of it to his saddle, only to throw it away and get a fresh one at the first opportunity. They did not pillage with any sort of method or reason. It seemed to be a mania, senseless and purposeless. One man carried a bird-cage, with three canaries in it, two days. Another rode with a chafing-dish, which looked like a small metallic coffin, on the pommel of his saddle, until an officer forced him to throw it away. Although the weather was intensely warm, another, still, slung seven pair of skates around his neck, and chuckled over his acquisition! They pillaged like boys robbing an orchard. I would not have believed that such a passion could have been developed so ludicrously among any body of civilized men.

The rebels did not stay long in Salem. Detachments were sent out towards Brownstown, Jackson county, on the direct road to Indianapolis, which was picketed and scouted by two companies of mounted minute-men, under Captain MEEDY W.

contemplate the consequences had that swivel been touched off. *History of Morgan's Cavalry* (1960 edition), 436.

SHIELDS, and towards Orleans. MORGAN soon discovered that his road northward was too hazardous to attempt, and hearing that General HOBSON with a large cavalry force was following hard upon his track, and that the forces of the State were rapidly gathering to intercept him and protect the most important points, he left Salem about two o'clock P. M., and hurried towards the Ohio with the apparent single object of putting that stream between himself and the hornet's nest he had roused, as speedily as possible.

THE FLIGHT AND PURSUIT

General HOBSON with about 4,000 mounted men and some pieces of artillery, of General JUDAH's command, had been following MORGAN through Kentucky for several days. On the morning of the 9th he arrived at Brandenburg, about the time that the rebel advance was skirmishing with our forces on the road to Corydon. A portion of their rear guard was still in sight on this side of the river, and the "Alice Dean," which had been set on fire after serving their purpose, was still burning near the Indiana bank. A number of steamers, in response to General HOBSON's application for means of ferriage, arrived from Louisville about noon, and the command commenced crossing. The advance, instead of pressing on, encamped on a convenient hill and awaited the passage of the main body. They and their horses, however, needed rest; and the advance, alone, was too weak to have rendered any very effective assistance to our force at Corydon. By three o'clock on the morning of the 10th, the entire command had crossed, and the pursuit was resumed. At ten o'clock it reached Corydon, when it was twenty-five miles behind MORGAN, who was then at Salem. After a brief halt, it pushed on and at night encamped within a few miles of Salem.

In the meanwhile MORGAN, by a rapid march to the east, passed through the villages of Canton and New Philadelphia, and reached Vienna, on the Jeffersonville railroad, at six o'clock in the evening. He made no halt there, but pressed on, though his troops were so much wearied they consumed nearly the whole night in passing. The citizens were not molested. At a little grocery near the depot they obtained some provisions and paid for them in "greenbacks." The depot and bridge were burned by a small detachment, while the main body continued its march; but the bridge was repaired a few hours afterward. At this place, General DUKE says, MORGAN "tapped the telegraph," having captured the operator before he could give the alarm, and learned "that orders had been given to the militia to fell timber and blockade all the roads we [the rebels] would be likely to travel—our rapid marching having, hitherto, saved us this annoyance." That night he reached Lexington, the county seat of Scott county, eight miles east of Vienna, and encamped. He, with a small escort, slept in the town. During the night a small party of Colonel SERING'S troops, from Madison, who were out scouting, entered the place, made a few observations and dashed away without molestation.

A movement was commenced to intercept MORGAN at Vienna, on the afternoon of the 10th, by sending a brigade of infantry and a battery of artillery from Jeffersonville by rail, under Brigadier General M. D. MANSON, and the troops were already embarked on the cars in high spirits, when an order from General BOYLE, to whose command the post at Jeffersonville belonged, stopped them.

It is probable that the revelation, made by the appearance of our scouts at Lexington, of the preparations in progress to prevent his reaching the Ohio in the direction of Madison, induced MORGAN to again change his course. From Corydon he had moved northward to Salem, with the probable design of attacking or threatening Indianapolis, but he soon discovered that that route was impracticable, and so changed his course eastward, doubtless in the hope of finding an outlet at some not very distant point across the river, which had now become a serious obstacle and vexation to him. Baffled on almost every hand, he moved out of Lexington on the morning of the 11th, in a northerly direction towards Vernon, throwing out a detachment to make a feint against Madison, and thereby to prevent our troops there from moving up the Madison and Indianapolis Railroad to give him trouble on that line. At Vernon there were two large bridges on the Madison railroad, which he might destroy; and at North Vernon, four miles further north, the Madison railroad crossed the Ohio and Mississippi Railroad, and presented a most inviting field for destruction, and the surest means of preventing pursuit by our troops South and West. But our authorities were as well aware of the importance of these lines of road as he was, and as soon as it was known that he had turned eastward from Salem, General WILLCOX took measures to protect his communications by ordering a part of General LOVE's force, then at Seymour, to Vernon. Colonel WILLIAMS' and Colonel BURKAM's regiments of the Legion were accordingly sent forward, with four pieces of artillery, by the Ohio and Mississippi Railroad, and they were instructed to hold the place at all hazards. General LOVE was also ordered to move to the same point as soon as practicable with the remainder of his force. Leaving Colonel BURKAM at North Vernon, Colonel WILLIAMS took his own regiment and one company of Colonel BURKAM's, with two pieces of artillery, to Vernon, and posted them so as to defend the bridges and the town. With some armed citizens of Jennings county, his whole force was about 400 men.

DEMONSTRATION AT VERNON

MORGAN came in sight of Vernon in the afternoon. "A strong force was posted there," General DUKE states, "which MORGAN did not care to attack," but desiring to get past without betraying his purpose, he sent in a flag of truce and demanded a surrender. At the same he threw out skirmishes along the roads and apparently prepared for an attack, and, under cover of these demonstrations, moved off his main column toward Dupont. Colonel WILLIAMS met the summons to surrender with the reply that he "was abundantly able to hold the place, and if General MORGAN got it, he must take it by hard fighting." It is possible that, notwithstanding the movement of his main column towards Dupont and the feint by which he attempted to cover it, MORGAN expected a surrender, for in a short time he sent a second flag with a similar summons, and he must have felt a little unwilling to give it up, without any effort to secure them, the important objects for which he had come so much farther north than he needed to if he only wanted, as Colonel DUKE intimates, to cross the Madison railroad and keep on his way. If that had been his only purpose, he could have gone directly to Dupont and thus have saved some ten or twelve miles. Colonel WILLIAMS refused to receive the second message, but detained the bearer of the flag until the arrival of General LOVE, which occurred soon after. The General at once sent back, as his answer, a summons to MORGAN himself to surrender. By this time our force had been increased to 1,000 men; and small and illy prepared as it was, General LOVE at once began his preparations for a fight. He sent a flag of truce to MORGAN asking two hours to remove the women and children, and the reply came granting thirty minutes. The non-combatants were at once removed to a wood near by where they would be protected, the guns were placed in position, and the troops disposed so as to make the best defense possible. But no further demonstration was made, except a movement as if the rebels aimed to get in between Vernon and North Vernon, which brought on a slight skirmish and ended "the seige."

It is evident, notwithstanding General DUKE's indifferent allusion to it, that the check at Vernon was something more than an impediment in a convenient road. MORGAN was defeated in an important object; and the fast-thickening dangers caused him to abandon his plans almost as soon as he had undertaken to put them into execution.

While these operations were in progress, Major General WALLACE was started with a brigade of troops just collected and organized at Indianapolis, and Major General HUGHES was ordered with his command from Mitchell, and both proceeded by rail to Vernon with such promptitude that they would have attacked MORGAN early the next morning, had he not in the meantime prudently resumed his flight.

ONWARD

General LOVE, having learned from Mr. Thomas REILEY, Recorder of Jennings county, who had been taken prisoner, that the rebels were at Dupont about one o'clock in the night, sent all his mounted force, consisting of twenty men, under Captain BOYD, to reconnoiter. They picked up some twenty or thirty stragglers, with whom they returned in the morning and confirmed the news as to MORGAN's position. He had halted and camped about midnight near Dupont, on the Madison railroad, some eight miles southeast of Vernon. Detachments, sent out for the purpose, destroyed a portion of the track of the railroad, and burned two large and costly bridges, one on Big creek, a mile south of town, and the other over Graham's Fork. A water tank, twelve freight cars and a warehouse were burned; the telegraph wires were cut; F. F. MAYFIELD's pork house was plundered of 2000 hams, and his store of $1,700 worth of goods. General DUKE says of this operation, that "it was a new feature in the practice of appropriation; every man had a ham slung to his saddle." The other stores in town were robbed of small amounts; horses were taken in all directions, barns plundered and wheat fields destroyed.

At four o'clock on the morning of Sunday, the 12th of July, the rebel advance moved out of Dupont, taking the road to Versailles, in Ripley county. Here was another change of direction to the northward. The object of it was probably to strike the Ohio and Mississippi Railroad at a point eastward from North Vernon, and accomplish there what was so signally defeated at Vernon. One regiment, sent in advance to destroy bridges and capture horses, dashed into Versailles about half past one o'clock, captured Colonel JAMES H. CRAVENS, with 300 militia and minute-men, and the Treasurer of Ripley county, with $5,000 of public funds. The stores and dwellings were pillaged of course.

There was now force enough on MORGAN's track, and ready to be concentrated in his front, to have crushed him in almost a moment if they could have been placed where they were needed. But there were serious obstacles in the way. First, there was the inherent difficulty of pursuing or encountering cavalry with infantry transported by railway. Infantry, it is true, can travel faster in such a case, but must travel on fixed lines, and if cavalry are not accommodating enough to travel on the same lines, the infantry must seek other means of moving. We needed cavalry to supplement the service of our railways, and without it MORGAN could not be "cornered," attacked or held at bay so as to give the infantry time to reach him. Besides he did not want or intend to fight—only to "throw dust" in the eyes of those who were trying to catch him. General HOBSON's force was following as rapidly as possible, certainly, but it labored under the serious disadvantage of pursuing, with jaded and almost broken-down horses, a column which was constantly recruiting itself with fresh ones, and, of course, stripping the country, and leaving scarcely any for the pursuers.

But another difficulty added greatly to the embarrassment of our authorities—the want of correct and consistent information. It was impossible for any merely human intelligence to divine the truth in the flood of conflicting and befogging reports that poured into the Capital. MORGAN marched constantly, with strong detachments thrown well out on his flanks, and thus secured the double advantage of covering a greater extent of horse-producing territory to recruit from, and of bewildering the people along the line as to where he was really going, and to this, no doubt, much of the unreliable and confusing information may be attributed. A few specimens of these reports are here given to show more clearly by what uncertain light our authorities were compelled to act.

On July 10th, the day that Morgan was at Salem, there came reports to the Governor that our forces had retreated through Fredericksburg, Orange county, at daylight, pursued by MORGAN's whole command, 6,000 strong; that 3,000 rebels had taken Paoli, and were advancing upon the Ohio and Mississippi Railroad at Mitchell; that 3,000 rebels had encamped the night before (the 9th, while MORGAN was on the march to Salem) at Palmyra, and were moving towards Vienna; that the rebels were north of Salem—and that Salem had been captured and burned. These were confusing enough, but those on the next day were worse. On the 11th, in the morning, the news came that MORGAN was at Vienna, and thought to be trying to get to the Ohio river, to cross, at Madison Flats; at two o'clock it was reported that our gunboats were engaging the rebels near Madison; and at half-past five, that MORGAN was at Vernon, demanding its surrender. On the 12th it was reported that MORGAN was at Versailles at half-past one in the afternoon; at three, that he had suddenly turned, and, with his whole force, was marching on Indianapolis; shortly after, that he was skirmishing at Sunman's Station, on the Indianapolis and Cincinnati Railroad; at eleven o'clock at night, that he was marching on Aurora and Lawrenceburg, and endeavoring to cross the Ohio at one of those places. A dispatch from Mitchell thickened the confusion by reporting that General BUCKNER had crossed the Ohio at Brandenburg with 16,000 men, had burned Palmyra, and was advancing toward Indianapolis. On the 13th, the day that MORGAN crossed into Ohio, it was reported, first, that he was fighting at Mitchell; then, that he was fighting at Sunman's; again, that he had captured Dillsboro, Dearborn county, and was threatening Lawrenceburg; then, that he had escaped into Ohio at Harrison; and directly afterwards, that he had turned back, and was marching upon Lawrenceburg!

A third difficulty was one in some degree inseparable from

the use of raw troops suddenly called into service. When ordered to move, they were not ready promptly, or their supplies of subsistence or ammunition were not brought up, and the railway trains were behind time. Delays of many hours occurred, which could have been avoided if the managers had acted with sufficient energy, or if officers had not been so much confused by conflicting reports and orders.

With these embarrassments surrounding them and clogging every movement, the authorities began, as soon as it was known that MORGAN had reached Versailles, to prepare to protect the line of the Indianapolis and Cincinnati Railroad, and by concentrating troops upon it, intercept him if possible. General HUGHES, with the troops from Mitchell, started for Osgood, on the Ohio and Mississippi Railroad, as soon as it was known that MORGAN was moving northward from Dupont. General WALLACE, with his own troops and LOVE'S brigade, also moved up from Vernon, having previously pursued the enemy to Dupont, and then having to return to North Vernon to get transportation on the Ohio and Mississippi Railroad. Neither of these forces, however, arrived at Osgood until the rebels had passed. In the meantime, while at Vernon, General WALLACE ordered the collection, by impressment, of all the horses in the neighborhood, to form a cavalry force for pursuit, and entrusted its execution and command to Colonel LAWRENCE S. SHULER, of the One Hundred and Third Regiment minute-men, who worked so vigorously that by four o'clock of the afternoon of the 11th he had mounted one hundred and forty-six men, and started rapidly on the track of the rebels. General WALLACE also, while yet at Vernon, anticipating (as did most of our citizens) that MORGAN would endeavor to escape at or near Lawrenceburg, requested the people of that vicinity, by telegraph, to collect wagons and meet him at a designated point near Osgood. MORGAN was then but twenty-five miles ahead, and General WALLACE was quite confident that a prompt compliance with his request would have enabled him to have made a forced march, and compelled a collision with the enemy. The transportation asked for, however, was not furnished, and the command moved on as rapidly as possible, reaching Sunman's Station on the 14th, General HUGHES being there also. The combined force was about fifty-five hundred strong—amply sufficient to have defeated the rebels, General WALLACE says "in an open field fight"; but the delays of transportation, and the distance to be marched, prevented them from arriving in time.

MORGAN left Versailles at four o'clock on the afternoon of Sunday, the 12th. He destroyed two bridges, tore up the railroad track and captured the telegraph operator at Osgood, and, following along the line of the Ohio and Mississippi Railroad through Pierceville to Milan, destroyed all the bridges as he went. The main body, according to General DUKE, after marching far into the night, reached Sunman's Station, and halted to rest. Here were some 2,500 militia, Colonel JAMES GAVIN's One Hundred and Fourth Regiment of minute-men being among them. His pickets were encountered by the rebel advance about two miles from the railroad, and a slight skirmish ensued. The rebels turned off, not daring to attack our infantry, and not giving them an opportunity to bring on an action. At five o'clock the next morning, the 13th, MORGAN moved eastwardly from his bivouac a few miles from Sunman's, in the direction of the Ohio line, crossing the railroad at three stations—Harmon's, Van Weddon's, and Weisburg. The bridges and track at all these places were destroyed, and a water tank at Van Weddon's burned. Passing rapidly on by Hubbell's corner, New Alsace, Dover and Logan, the rebel advance reached Harrison, Ohio, a little after twelve o'clock noon.

At Sunman's Station, Colonel KLINE G. SHRYOCK, One Hundred and Fifth Regiment of minute-men, finding that MORGAN had crossed the railroad and disabled it, commenced the march with his regiment on foot to Lawrenceburg, the point to which he was originally destined. About a mile out he met Colonel SHULER's cavalry command, which had joined General HOBSON's force on the evening of the 11th, and which was now in the advance. SHULER had followed so strenuously, by five o'clock in the afternoon of the 12th he had come up with the rebel rear guard, and had been pressing close after them ever since. Learning that they were but four or five miles ahead, Colonel SHRYOCK determined to follow Colonel SHULER, so as to support him in case of an encounter. Colonel SHULER came in sight of the rear of the main rebel column at Harrison, Ohio, in the afternoon of the 13th, and, expecting to be able to make an attack, he ordered up Colonel SHYROCK's regiment, which came rapidly forward. The bridge over Whitewater, at Harrison, had been burned, but, after exchanging a few shots across the river, a convenient ford for our cavalry was found, and it entered the town, only to find it pillaged and the enemy flying, as usual. Here Colonel SHULER rested for a few hours, and then continued the pursuit, going as far as Batavia, Ohio, where, as he says, finding the citizens able and ready to protect themselves, he halted and returned home. He speaks in his report very warmly of the enthusiastic welcome given to his command by the people of Ohio.[11] Colonel SHRYOCK marched to Lawrenceburg, whither Colonel GAVIN's regiment had preceded him.

There can be but little doubt that MORGAN's original intention was to "go through" Indiana and Ohio, and his historian intimates that all his attempts and maneuvers to cross the river while in this State, were mere feints. From the dangers that fast gathered on his track after he left Vernon, it can hardly be doubted, had an opportunity offered, he would gladly have escaped across the river long before he crossed the Ohio line. His men were literally worn out for want of sleep and rest. The evening after he left Harrison, it was with the greatest difficulty his first brigade was prevented from going to pieces. "Strong men fell out of their saddles,

[11] See Shuler's report in "Operations of the Indiana Legion and Minute Men, 1863, 1864," in Indiana *Documentary Journal*, 1864, vol. 2, no. 11:431.

and at every halt the officers were compelled to move continually about their respective commands and pull and haul the men who would drop asleep in the road—it was the only way to keep them awake." After leaving Sunman's Station, on the morning of the 13th, in a period of thirty-five hours, he marched more than ninety miles, the greatest march, DUKE says, he ever made. During his brief pilgrimage of five days through the State, he certainly did not feel that he was "master of the situation," by a very great deal.

THE PURSUIT INTO OHIO

As soon as Governor MORTON was informed of the escape of MORGAN into Ohio, he notified Governor TOD of that State, of the fact, and tendered him the services of 5,000 of our State troops; and steps were at once taken to forward as large a force as possible, in pursuance of this proffer. Our authorities hoped that if a vigorous and prompt movement was made, MORGAN might be intercepted at or near Hamilton, Ohio. A brigade of three regiments of minute-men, the One Hundred and Eighth, Colonel WILLIAM C. WILSON; the One Hundred and Sixth, Colonel ISAAC P. GRAY, and the One Hundred and Ninth, Colonel JOHN R. MAHAN, with the Twelfth Michigan Battery of Light Artillery, was ordered to rendezvous at the Indiana Central Railway in Indianapolis, the first two regiments at 3 o'clock P. M., the third at 5 o'clock P. M. of the 13th of July, to take the cars for Hamilton. The regiments reported promptly. The Michigan Battery, while hastening to the rendezvous about dusk, in obedience to the order, met with a fearful accident. The caisson of one of the guns exploded in the middle of the street in the northwestern part of the city, hurling two of the men who were riding upon it many yards through the air, mutilating them frightfully, and of course killing them instantly, and wounding another, and a lad who was passing by at the moment, so badly that they both died a few hours afterward. The remainder of the battery joined the brigade at the railway. Here a most unfortunate and inexcusable detention occurred. The regiments were compelled to wait from five to seven hours before they could get away, delaying their arrival at Hamilton until daybreak, and as late as 10 o'clock on the morning of the 14th. The brigade was at first placed under command of Brigadier General CARRINGTON, with orders to use all dispatch and move with as many troops as could then be transported at 3 o'clock. Learning, at 9 o'clock at night, that he had not started, and that there was no sufficient excuse for his delay, General WILLCOX removed him from the command and gave it to General HASCALL, who at once hastened the movement of the two regiments yet remaining, and reached Hamilton, as he states, "just in time to be too late." The detention was quite mortifying to every one concerned in the expedition, and the opinion prevailed that if the original orders had been carried out, MORGAN would have been overtaken.[12] In the afternoon of the 14th, General HASCALL ordered the whole brigade to Cincinnati; whence, in a day or two, all returned to Indianapolis and were discharged.

THE ACCIDENT AT LAWRENCEBURG

The resistance and pursuit of the rebels was as nearly bloodless as any hostile movement on so large a scale could be, but it was destined to cause more bloodshed after its departure than it did by its presence. On the evening of the 13th, Colonel GAVIN, in command at Lawrenceburg, having been informed that MORGAN had taken Harrison and had turned back and was advancing upon Lawrenceburg, took prompt measures to meet him. He sent out his own regiment, the One Hundred and Fourth, half a mile beyond Hardinsburg on the turnpike where a strong barricade was constructed, and a line of battle was formed along the tow path of the canal so as to use the canal bank as a defense.

[12] See Hascall's report in Terrell, *Report,* 1, Appendix, Doc. 80:277.

Colonel SHRYOCK's regiment, the One Hundred and Fifth, was ordered to take position half a mile in the rear. About nine o'clock at night, while marching to the assigned position through a very short curve in the road at Hardinsburg, the rear of the column seeing the head indistinctly in the darkness, and unaware of the curve which threw the men in front on a line parallel with those in the rear, mistook it for a portion of the expected enemy's force, and a shot accidentally fired at the moment made the impression so strong that they fired into the advance. The advance, of course, mistook the fire for that of the enemy and returned it. Colonel SHRYOCK instantly rode down the line to stop the firing, telling the men that they were killing their comrades, but though promptly obeyed he was too late to prevent a serious catastrophe. Five men were killed, one mortally and eighteen more or less severely wounded. The following is a list of the casualties caused by this sad mistake:

Killed.—Sergeant JOHN GORDON, privates OLIVER P. JONES, WILLIAM FAULKNER, FERDINAND HEFNER and JOHN PORTER.

Wounded.—Captains A. K. BRANHAM and WILLIAM NICHOLSON; Lieutenants WILLIAM E. HART (mortally), SAMUEL BEWSEY and JOEL NEWMAN; Sergeants RICHARD M. BAKER, JOHN PILE and JAMES E. BATES; Privates SAMUEL E. DUNCAN, EDMOND BLOOMFIELD, MARTIN HOOVER, WILLIAM FLINT, DAVID S. GOODING, W. G. JOHNSON, D. W. PARRISH, R. T. RAINES, JABEZ WILSON, ALLEN R. BATES and —— HART.

RETURN OF THE TROOPS

The regiments at all points were discharged and sent home as soon as possible, and measures were taken whereby they were paid for their services by the State in due time at the same rates allowed the soldiers of the United States. On the 15th Governor MORTON issued an address "To the officers and soldiers of the Legion and Minute-men of Indiana,"[13] in which, after reciting the occurrences of the preceding week—the invasion by the rebels, the prompt gathering of sixty-five thousand men to resist them, and the movement to the field within three days of thirty thousand men fully armed and organized—he spoke with just pride of so wonderful an exhibition of the spirit of the people, and of its effect in turning the raid into a desperate flight, and tendered to the troops on behalf of the State his hearty thanks for their alacrity and self-sacrifice in responding to his call. He took occasion also to urge the importance of a thorough organization of the Legion, and his anxiety to see the temporary organizations of the minute-men converted into permanent ones under the law.

END OF THE RAID

Though not within the prescribed limits of this Report, it may still not be out of place to follow as briefly as possible MORGAN's daring movement to its catastrophe.

After leaving Harrison he maneuvered to confuse General BURNSIDE at Cincinnati as to the point at which he would cross the Cincinnati, Hamilton and Dayton Railroad, thinking that once past that line no concentration of troops strong enough to take him could be made in his front. Detachments were sent out in direction of Hamilton, to create the impression that he would advance upon that place, while the main body started directly toward Cincinnati, hoping thus to send the forces that might get in his way, part up to Hamilton and part back to Cincinnati. At this time he had less than 2,000 effective men. His plans for eluding our forces and getting past Cincinnati succeeded, but on the 19th he was overtaken near Buffington Island, in the Ohio river, where he was, much against his will, forced into a sharp fight, which ended in the capture of 700 of his men. A portion of his Ninth Tennessee regiment managed to cross the river in a

---

[13] This address is given in Terrell, *Report,* 1, Appendix, Doc. 102:301.

small flatboat before the fight began, and escaped. With near 1,200 men, he resumed his flight up the river, pursued by HOBSON. About twenty miles above Buffington Island 300 more made their escape by crossing the river, and with them some of the best officers of the command. The weakened and worn-down force was here reorganized, each of the two brigades having only about 400 men. During the night, near Blennerhassett's Island, where he had previously tried to cross, he was almost surrounded, but escaped by leading his men in single file along the side of a steep hill to another road. He escaped capture again at the Muskingum river by passing along a path upon which it was barely possible for a horse to travel, guided, it is presumed, by some of the sympathizing citizens of the vicinity. But he was still pressed upon all sides, more and more closely. His troops were killed or captured in squads at every point. On the 26th, near Salineville, Columbiana county, Ohio, within nine miles of the western boundary of Pennsylvania, his force being reduced to 250 men, and seeing himself hemmed in upon all sides, he surrendered to a militia Captain, dictating almost as he pleased his own terms. This ingenious arrangement, however, was unceremoniously set aside by General SHACKLEFORD, of General HOBSON's command, who soon came up and took charge of MORGAN and his remnant of men as prisoners of war.

Thus ended the Morgan raid. Only four organized companies escaped. Besides these some 300 stragglers got safely away, but as General DUKE mournfully states, "The raid destroyed MORGAN's division, and left but a remnant of the Morgan cavalry."

LOSSES AND IMPRESSMENTS OF PROPERTY

Immediately after the escape of MORGAN, measures were taken by the State and United States' authorities to ascertain the extent and amount of losses and damages caused by the rebels, and the amount of property taken or impressed by the Union forces. Claimants were notified by the Governor that every possible effort would be promptly made to secure a speedy adjustment and payment of all just demands, and they were advised not to sacrifice their claims. General CARRINGTON, then acting under the Governor's orders, was dispatched to and along the route taken by MORGAN, with instructions to adopt such immediate means as would relieve the farmers, then in the midst of their busiest season, from the embarrassments occasioned by the loss of their stock, and to obtain all the information he could as to losses, of all kinds, with the view of perpetuating the testimony necessary to establish all valid claims. It was arranged, for the purpose of affording the farming community temporary relief, in cases where their horses had been lost in the raid or impressed by the Federal forces, that they might retain such animals as were abandoned by either force for present use, and to enable them to gather their harvests, upon giving sufficient security for their good keeping and proper return on proof of ownership, or other direction of the duly constituted authorities. And it was further provided that all horses found by citizens who had lost none, should be turned over to the proper Provost Marshals, subject to such disposition as might thereafter be determined upon. The orders issued in pursuance of this plan,[14] and the energetic efforts made by General CARRINGTON and the officers of the United States Quartermaster's Department (Captain—now General EKIN —and his efficient assistants) resulted in great relief, for the time being, to many farmers who otherwise would have been unable, from the lack of teams, to carry on their work and secure their crops. The claims were duly reported to the proper Departments at Washington for adjustment; but after the authorities had accomplished all this, it was found that there were many insuperable difficulties in the way of effecting fair and satisfactory settlements. The regulations of the U.S. Quartermaster's Department required that all animals

[14] The order is given in Terrell, *Report,* 1, Appendix, Doc. 103:301-2.

abandoned by either Federals or rebels, whether branded "U.S." or "C.S.," or impressed into the United States service, should be collected together, and, if serviceable, turned into the Quartermaster's Department for issue; or, if not serviceable, they should be inspected, condemned, and sold for the benefit of the United States, in accordance with the Army Regulations. No animals were allowed to be returned to claimants even on proof of ownership; nor could payment be made, in the opinion of the Government officials, for any property impressed by the officers of the Federal troops, unless it was clearly shown that the officers who impressed the same were regularly mustered into the United States service. All claims for *damages* by our own troops, and for horses and other property stolen, destroyed or damaged by the rebels, were entirely ignored. There were many cases where farmers lost horses, by the rebels, which were subsequently abandoned or recaptured, and, upon being turned over to the United States authorities, were put up and sold and their former possessors, the *real owners*, to supply themselves with teams, were compelled to purchase and pay for their own property. These hardships were augmented by the fact that large numbers of the horses not stolen by MORGAN on his route were subsequently impressed by officers of the Legion and minute-men, whose vouchers were repudiated at Washington. Thus it will be seen that between the thefts of the enemy and the impressments of our own forces, those who suffered stood but a poor chance of being compensated for their losses from any source.

Governor MORTON very promptly conferred with the authorities at Washington on the subject, but it was assumed by them that there was no law that would authorize any liberal plan of adjustment than the one above indicated and already adopted.[15] So far as the State was concerned, relief

[15] See Morton to Capt. James A. Ekin, Assistant Quartermaster, U. S. A., and M. C. Meigs, Quartermaster General, to Ekin, in Terrell, *Report*, 1, Appendix, Docs. 106-7:303.

from her Treasury, in any shape, was impossible, unless the Legislature, at some future time should prescribe the mode and provide the means to that end. But the Governor, assuming that "the true theory of our government is that it shall protect the people, in their persons and property, against invasion and loss from the public enemy, or injury by domestic insurrection," did not cease his endeavors to procure a settlement through the departments of the General Government. After much correspondence, he finally, on the 19th of December, 1863, forwarded, through the Quartermaster General, a memorial setting forth the facts in regard to the losses, in consequence of the raid, and combating the specious arguments and technical objections, that had been made against the settlement and payment of the claims. This memorial[16] was laid before Congress, and a bill was introduced (March 4th, 1864) for the relief of those citizens of Indiana and Ohio, whose horses and other property were taken by the forces of the United States during the pursuit of Morgan; but it failed to pass.

Nothing further was done, or could be done, until the meeting of the Legislature in January, 1865, when the Governor, in his message, laid the subject before that body, with a recommendation that a commission be appointed to investigate the claims, and that they be paid out of the Treasury, under such regulations as would prevent imposition upon the State. Two bills were introduced, but owing to a want of concert among the friends of the measure, neither of them became a law.

In November, 1865, the Legislature convened in extra session, and the Governor again invoked attention to the claims, and repeated his former recommendations on that subject.[17] A bill was brought forward, providing for the appointment of Commissioners, to adjust the losses, but the

[16] This memorial is in *ibid.,* 1, Appendix, Doc. 109:304.

[17] For extracts from the Governor's messages, see *ibid.,* 1, Appendix, Doc. 110:305.

two Houses failing to agree upon some proposed amendments, it shared the fate of the other bills.

Thus the matter rested until the next regular session of the Legislature, January, 1867, when the subject was again brought to their attention by a communication from the Adjutant General. The result, this time, was favorable; concurrent resolutions were passed on the 11th of March, providing for the appointment, by the Governor, of three Commissioners, whose duties are set forth as follows:[18]

> To hear, determine and adjust all claims for losses which have heretofore accrued by reason of the injury, destruction, loss, or impressment of property, had or held by any inhabitants of this State, by rebel forces under the command of JOHN MORGAN in the year 1863, or caused by the State or National forces engaged in repelling said invasion; or caused by organizing and equipping troops to repel the threatened invasion of the State by the rebel forces under the command of ADAM JOHNSON, in the year 1864.

An attorney to protect the interests of the State, and a Clerk to keep a record of the proceedings of the Commissioners were also provided for. The Commissioners were required to visit the various counties affected by the raids above mentioned, "and examine all claims duly presented and, ascertain the amount of loss thereon, and whether the claim be meritorious, as upon evidence before them they may deem just and equitable." The claims were required to be separated into the following classes:

1. Claims for property taken, or destroyed, or injured by the Union forces, under command of United States officers.
2. Claims for property taken, or destroyed, or injured by the Union forces, under State officers.
3. Property taken, or destroyed, or injured by the rebels.
4. Property taken, or destroyed, or injured, where claimant is unable to identify by which (force) the loss occurred.

The resolutions required the Commissioners to make report of their findings, with a comprehensive abstract of the testi-

[18] Terrell, *Report,* 1, Appendix, Docs. 111-12:305-7.

mony taken, to the Governor on or before the 17th of January, 1868, who will report the same to the next General Assembly, with his recommendations thereon.

In pursuance of said resolutions, Governor BAKER made the following appointments: Hon. SMITH VAWTER, of Jennings; Hon. JOHN I. MORRISON, of Marion; and Colonel JOHN MCCREA, of Monroe, Commissioners; and Colonel CHARLES W. CHAPMAN, of Kosciusko, Attorney. Colonel CHAPMAN declining, General THOS. M. BROWNE, of Randolph, was appointed in his stead. WILLIAM R. BROWNING, Esq., of Bloomington, was selected by the Commissioners as their Clerk.

The Commissioners duly entered upon a vigorous discharge of their important duties, and, up to the time of the present writing (October 15th, 1867) have made good progress. From their high standing and character as citizens and excellent qualifications as businessmen, it may confidently be expected that their labors will be faithfully and ably performed, and that while full justice will be rendered to claimants, the interests of the State will be jealously guarded and protected.

The labors of the Commission were faithfully performed; they visited all the counties interested, and, by patient investigation and research, became fully informed as to the merits of the many claims presented.

Since the foregoing was written, the report of the transactions of the Commission has been filed with the Governor, from which the following facts have been extracted:

COUNTIES			
Harrison	477	$ 86,551.72	$ 81,710.90
Floyd	65	30,291.61	11,188.71
Washington	375	100,668.93	85,613.33
Scott	254	45,479.63	42,031.43
Jefferson	180	53,438.17	47,388.31
Jennings	350	63,270.61	59,187.66
Jackson	7	792.50	792.50
Ripley	324	46,638.28	40,609.25

Dearborn 205   70,217.76   43,415.42
Marion 1   50.00   1,661.97

Totals $497,399.21 $413,599.48

The claims allowed are classified as follows:

Class One (under orders of United States officers)............ $ 58,017.51
Class Two (under orders of State officers)....................... 24,268.80
Class Three (under order of Rebels)................................ 331,288.17
Class Four (under orders of unknown)............................. 35.00

Total amount allowed.. $413,599.48

The whole matter now goes over for the consideration and action of the next Legislature, and will doubtless receive due consideration.[19]

[19] The report of the commissioners, dated December 31, 1867, was printed (8 pp.), and is bound with other pamphlets as No. 3 in Vol. 3 of Civil War pamphlets, Indiana State Library. Governor Baker recommended payment of the claims in his message to the legislature in January, 1869, and a bill was introduced and referred to the Ways and Means Committee. At the special session that same year the bill was taken up and considered and passed both the House and Senate, but the two bodies failed to agree on amendments. Succeeding legislatures likewise failed to provide for payment of the claims. By 1879 the total amount had been pared down to $82,286, and a resolution was passed asking the Federal government to pay that amount. The Quartermaster General's Office sent out investigators to interview claimants, after which the Treasury Department passed on the validity of the claims and the amount to be allowed. During the years 1884 to 1887, Morgan Raid claims amounting to at least $19,018 were paid, along with other claims arising out of the war. See U. S. *Statutes,* 23 (1883-85):577-80; 24 (1885-87):676-77, 778-79, 966. These are not designated as Morgan Raid claims in the acts, but the names and counties indicate that is what they were. Others may have been paid, provision for which have not been found.

MORGAN'S LAST KENTUCKY RAID—JUNE, 1864

INDIANA AGAIN TO THE RESCUE

After the rebel General JOHN H. MORGAN escaped from the Ohio Penitentiary, where he had been confined after his Indiana and Ohio raid of 1863, he was placed in command of the Department of Southwestern Virginia. His recollection of former hearty welcomes by a large and sympathizing portion of the people of the "Blue Grass Region" in Kentucky, and of the luxuries and above all the "spoils" always abundant in that famed locality, and which had so long been denied his followers, made him extremely anxious to visit it again in his "official capacity." He had, therefore, not been long in command before he projected another raid, planned upon an extensive scale, for the purpose, as he represented to the rebel War Department, of preventing the Federals from throwing a formidable force into Southwestern Virginia and destroying the salt works and lead mines which were of vast importance to the Confederate cause. It was afterwards ascertained that it was a part of MORGAN's plan to capture Munfordsville and destroy the great railroad bridge over Green river at that point, a bridge which could not be rebuilt in less than three months, and the destruction of which would have been a great disaster to General SHERMAN's army.

THE INVASION—PREPARATIONS TO MEET IT

The raid was accordingly commenced in the latter part of May, 1864, by MORGAN's division, consisting, according to

Duke's history, of three brigades twenty-four hundred strong, all well mounted except the third brigade of eight hundred men, who, from the success which had previously attended their leader's adventures in the acquisition of "stock," confidently expected to bestride the best horseflesh in Kentucky within a short time.

General BURBRIDGE, commanding the Union forces in Central Kentucky, was then at Lexington, and on the 23d of May telegraphed Governor MORTON as follows:

> Dispatches from Generals HALLECK and CROOK give the best possible assurance that JOHN MORGAN, with a force of about four thousand mounted men, is now entering Kentucky by way of Pound Gap with the intention of marching by way of Richmond, Lexington and Bardstown, and destroying the bridges on the Louisville and Nashville railroad where he can, and then joining JOHNSON by forced marches through Tennessee. I start today with all my available force to meet him. The railroad and Louisville are very defenseless. Can not you send, or have on the border ready to move at any moment to Louisville and on the road, four regiments? Lieutenant Colonel FAIRLEIGH is in command at Louisville and will afford you any information possible.

The Governor's response, on the same day, was characteristic: "One regiment leaves tonight, one tomorrow and two others on Wednesday. If necessary I will call out the militia. Please give me any new information of the invasion, as I do not wish to call out the militia on mistake." The season was a busy one with our farmers; the Legion on the border had performed a great deal of guard duty and other service, and the Governor was, therefore, indisposed to make any additional demand upon them until something more certain could be known as to the strength and movements of the enemy.

The next advices received were from the commanding officer at Louisville, under date of June 8th, as follows; "We are in pressing need of troops. This city and the Louisville and Nashville Railroad are almost defenseless. We hope for four or five thousand men from you for a few days. How many can you give us, and how soon will they be here?" The next morning the Governor forwarded the One Hundred and Thirty-Ninth Regiment, Indiana Volunteers, to Louisville, and it was placed at Muldraugh's Hill to guard the railroad. The same day General HOBSON, commanding the District of Kentucky, telegraphed from Covington to this effect: "I am directed by General BURBRIDGE to call on you for any troops you can send me to Louisville or Frankfort. General BURBRIDGE has nearly all the troops with him near Pound Gap, and the rebels have come into Kentucky in force. They have taken Mount Sterling and burned two bridges on the Lexington and Covington Railroad." In a second dispatch, dated also at Covington on the same day (the 9th), General HOBSON, in reply to an inquiry from Governor MORTON as to the whereabouts of the enemy, said: "The rebels have taken Mount Sterling, Paris and Cynthiana, and are now reported to be 800 strong between here and Paris on the railroad. They have taken Maysville. Nearly all the troops in this part of Kentucky are with General BURBRIDGE in the mountains."

There were no organized volunteer troops in the State at this time subject to the control of the Governor. In view of the danger that appeared to threaten Louisville and other towns on the border, and the possibility that either MORGAN, or guerrilla bands emboldened by his presence in Kentucky, might attempt another foray upon Indiana, the Governor called out the Legion in the counties of Harrison, Floyd, Clark, Jefferson, Jennings and Switzerland. The Jennings regiment was sent to Madison, and with the Jefferson Legion held in readiness to proceed instantly to Louisville by steamers, should the Governor so order. The Harrison and Floyd regiments and the New Albany batteries went into camp at New Albany, and the Clark regiment at Jeffersonville, ready to proceed to Louisville at a moment's notice. The south side of the Ohio river, in the counties of Oldham, Trimble, Carroll and Gallatin, in Kentucky, was filled with roving squads of rebels, recruiting officers and guerrillas. Our home forces were, therefore, compelled to guard all exposed points, which added greatly to the other heavy demands made upon them by their private affairs, and the withdrawal of so many men, awaiting orders to be sent into Kentucky if required.

On the 10th the Forty-Third Regiment, Indiana Volunteers, arrived at Indianapolis from Arkansas on veteran furlough. This gallant body of troops had been at the front for nearly three years, and had re-enlisted for three years longer. The demands of the service would not admit of their being furloughed home to enjoy their thirty days of rest until now. Notwithstanding all this, as soon as they reached the Capital and were informed of the situation of affairs in Kentucky, they volunteered to a man, and placed themselves under the orders of the Governor for immediate service. They were sent to Louisville the following morning, whence they were sent to Frankfort to the relief of Governor BRAMLETTE and a small force who were besieged at that place.

Brigadier General CARRINGTON was also ordered by the Governor to Louisville to observe the situation, and to aid in disposing of the Legion regiments along the Nashville railroad for its protection, should their services be required. Adjutant General NOBLE was sent to New Albany to see that the Legion was in proper condition, and to get the two batteries in shape for moving in case of need. Commissary General STONE was dispatched to New Albany, and then to Madison, to provide quarters and subsistence for the assembled troops. Colonel FRYBARGER fitted out a battery at Indianapolis, and, with a company of well-drilled artillerists, reported at Louisville on the night of the 11th.

At Louisville, nothing scarcely was done by the authorities for defense of the place, until the morning of the 11th, when business was suspended and the citizens organized into military companies. Generals CARRINGTON and NOBLE, and Colonel FRYBARGER, by their presence and advice, contributed largely in placing the city in a condition to resist an attack.

MORGAN ON THE WARPATH

While these preparations were being made, MORGAN was hurrying forward and doing immense mischief. A brief retrospect of his operations is necessary to a just comprehension of the magnitude of his raid, and of the energetic efforts that were made to defeat it.

The rebel column reached Mount Sterling on the morning of the 8th of June, and attacked the garrison stationed there, and soon forced its surrender, with a large quantity of stores, wagons and horses. Leaving two brigades to appropriate the captured horses, and such other property as could be made available, and to destroy the remainder, MORGAN, with his best brigade, immediately pressed forward for Lexington. General BURBRIDGE was at this time hastening to Mount Sterling, though not expected by the rebels for two or three days. By a forced march of ninety miles in thirty hours, he reached Mount Sterling at daybreak on the 9th, surprised and completely routed the rebels, killing large numbers, capturing many prisoners, and scattering a still larger number to the mountains. The brigade of dismounted men was entirely broken up. This was a great disaster to MORGAN'S plans, and seriously interfered with the success of his expedition. On the 10th he entered Lexington, after a slight skirmish, and proceeded to his favorite work of plunder and destruction. The Government depot and stables were burned, and a sufficient number of horses captured to mount all his dismounted men who afterwards straggled in. A detachment had previously been sent to destroy the bridges of the Frankfort and Lexington Railroad, "to prevent," as General DUKE says, "troops arriving from Indiana for the defense of Lexington and Central Kentucky." At the same time another detachment was sent to operate in like manner upon the Kentucky Central Railroad, "to prevent the importation of troops from Cincinnati"; and a force of one hundred men was dispatched to capture Maysville and draw off attention to that quarter. MORGAN instructed the officers commanding these detachments "to accomplish their work thoroughly, but promptly; to create as much excitement as possible; occasion the concentration of (opposing) forces already in the State at points widely apart; to magnify his strength and circulate reports which would bewilder and baffle any attempt to calculate his movements."[1] They were to rejoin him in three or four days. After plundering Lexington, and destroying all the Government property he could find and did not use, MORGAN moved to Georgetown, where he had scores of fraternizing friends—sending one company to demonstrate against Frankfort, where they caused much alarm, and confined to the fortifications around the town a considerable force, including Governor BRAMLETTE and his staff, for several days.

Leaving Georgetown, MORGAN proceeded to Cynthiana, arriving on the morning of the 11th. Here his success was complete. He captured the garrison, four hundred strong, after sharp resistance, plundered freely, burned a portion of the town, and destroyed large quantities of stores.

While the enemy was thus occupied, General HOBSON arrived with some twelve hundred men, and at once engaged a brigade of the enemy, of about the same strength, which was posted on one of the approaches to the village. Word was quickly sent to MORGAN for reinforcements, and he soon succeeded in gaining HOBSON's rear with the balance of his command. Being thus surrounded by a superior force, after a short struggle, HOBSON was forced to surrender.

Thus far, barring the Mount Sterling disaster, everything had gone on swimmingly with the invaders. But General BURBRIDGE had been steadily pursuing, and MORGAN, finding himself likely to be hotly pressed, concentrated his force as well as he was able by calling in his detachments, and on the morning of the 12th prepared to withdraw. BURBRIDGE came

[1] Duke, *History of Morgan's Cavalry* (1960 edition), 523.

up, however, unexpectedly, and made a spirited and vigorous attack, from which the rebels in vain tried to escape. They were compelled to fight, and were defeated with frightful loss.

FINALE OF THE RAID

MORGAN precipitately gathered his scattered fragments together, and made his way back to Virginia with all possible speed. His division was almost destroyed, and many of the scattered survivors deserted their commands altogether, and skulked about the country, or became guerrillas. This was MORGAN's last raid, and the disasters which befell it caused him to lose the confidence of his "government," which he never recovered.

The Legion was relieved and sent to their homes on the 15th, and were commended by the Governor in the warmest terms for their prompt response to his call and the readiness they evinced to rally to the relief of their sister State. Governor BRAMLETTE also, in a letter addressed to Governor MORTON, highly complimented the troops that were sent to Kentucky, and expressed his grateful thanks for the promptness with which the assistance was rendered.

ADAM JOHNSON'S THREATENED RAID

EXPEDITION INTO KENTUCKY—AUGUST, 1864

About the first of July, 1864, several rebel officers, the most prominent of whom were Colonels ADAM R. JOHNSON and ———— SEIPERT, and Majors CHENOWETH and TAYLOR, made their appearance in the counties of Union and Henderson, Kentucky, with a force variously estimated at from seven hundred to twelve hundred men. Colonel JOHNSON had previously achieved much notoriety as the leader of the raid on Newburgh, in this State,[1] and by the cruel and relentless persecution of such citizens of southwestern Kentucky as were suspected of entertaining a lingering sentiment of attachment to the Union cause, or who failed to exhibit either a real or simulated enthusiasm for the cause of the Confederacy. As if fully to sustain his reputation, immediately upon his arrival he began to enforce a rigid conscription, scouring the country with squads of mounted men and pressing into his ranks every man not disqualified by extreme youth, feeble old age, or palpable disability for the performance of military duty. By this means his force was rapidly increased to about two thousand men, the greater portion of whom were well mounted on stolen, "confiscated" or "pressed" horses and mules, and provided with tolerably effective arms of various patterns.

By the services of volunteer scouts, from the Indiana side of the Ohio river, and the friendly offices of a few Union men residing in the rebel-infested district, the operations of JOHNSON and his subordinates became known to Colonel JOHN A. MANN, of Mount Vernon, commanding the First Regi-

---

[1] See above, 181-84.

ment of the Legion, who wisely concluded that the presence of such a force, augmented daily by a merciless conscription, on the immediate border, at a time when the river was so low as to be fordable, without difficulty, at many points, threatened the peace and security of his own and adjacent counties. He caused the fords to be guarded by details of his command, and forwarded full reports of the situation to General CARRINGTON, commanding the District of Indiana. That officer, while fully appreciating the dangers of a raid, was unable to render much assistance. He recommended the utmost vigilance on the part of the Legion, in the most exposed localities, and dispatched Lieutenant FORGEY with thirty men of the Forty-Sixth Regiment to relieve Colonel MANN's command of a portion of the duty of guarding fords. Details of the Legion in Vanderburgh and Warrick counties were also called into service, and disposed along the bank at the most exposed points.

Early in August, Major General JAMES HUGHES, commanding the Legion, established his headquarters temporarily at Evansville, as the most convenient point from which to superintend the defense of the Southwestern border. Major General ALVIN P. HOVEY was at that time at his home, in Mount Vernon, awaiting orders from the War Department. Reliable information reached General HOVEY, to the effect, that Colonels JOHNSON and SEIPERT, were actively preparing to cross the river with their entire forces, and that their programme included not only the seizure and removal of a vast amount of portable property, but the surprise, capture and destruction of several cities and towns, and the burning of White River bridge, and others on the Evansville and Crawfordsville Railroad. This information induced General HOVEY to address a communication to General HUGHES, on the 14th of August, in which he proposed, "if sufficient force could be raised" and placed at his disposal, "to cross the river and attack the camps reported, at and near Morganfield, Kentucky." He expressed the hope that by such a movement, he might be able "to surprise and capture a large number of the force there engaged in conscription and plunder." The plan suggested met the cordial approval of General HUGHES, and was enthusiastically endorsed by the officers and men of the Legion, who responded with cheerful alacrity to the call for volunteers. With characteristic energy, both the general officers, above named, immediately applied themselves to the work of raising and organizing a force, sufficiently formidable for the proposed expedition, and so effective were their efforts, that on the morning of the 17th, three days after the inception of the movement—seven hundred and fifty men, infantry and cavalry, fully equipped, were in rendezvous at Mount Vernon, awaiting marching orders. This force consisted of the Forty-Sixth Regiment, Indiana Infantry Volunteers, Colonel BRINGHURST, commanding, 200 men; the non-veterans of the Thirty-Second Regiment, Indiana Infantry Volunteers, Colonel ERDELMEYER, commanding, 200 men; parts of several companies of infantry and three companies of cavalry of the Legion, from Vanderburgh, Warrick and Posey counties—about 350 men. Five pieces of artillery, belonging to the Legion, were added, and as there were no horses for the guns, it became necessary to press them, which was done by General HOVEY, in Posey, and by General HUGHES, in Vanderburgh, to the infinite disgust of the various owners of fine stock. Five steamers, the "Dunleith," "Cottage," "General Halleck," "Jennie Hopkins" and "Jeannette Rogers," were detained for the purpose of transporting the infantry and to ferry the cavalry and artillery across the river.

On the morning above named, General HOVEY embarked with the infantry on transports, and proceeded down the river, ordering the cavalry and artillery to march along the Indiana shore, till they arrived at a point opposite Uniontown, Kentucky, where they were to effect a crossing on transports, which had been ordered there for that purpose. The entire force arrived at Uniontown, about two o'clock P. M. The movement, its object and destination, had been kept entirely from the knowledge of any one in Kentucky, up to this time, and the General commanding, desired to move with such celerity, as to strike the rebels before they should be apprised even of the inception of the expedition. Accordingly the troops were landed with the utmost dispatch, and forming in column, moved rapidly out upon the Morganfield road. The enemy's pickets were soon encountered by the advance cavalry, and slight skirmishing ensued, but the rebels were too well drilled in retrograde movements to permit the infliction of any serious loss upon them. Continuing the march, our forces at about 5 o'clock, came upon a rebel camp at White Oak Swamp, two miles south of Morganfield. A few prisoners were captured, but the greater portion of JOHNSON's forces broke in wild confusion and fled. It was now too late at night for further operations, and the troops were ordered to camp. Early on the morning of the 18th, General HOVEY, with the Thirty-Second Indiana Volunteers, a part of the Legion infantry, all the cavalry and two pieces of artillery, started on a rapid march to Geiger's Lake, nine miles west of Morganfield, to attack a considerable body of rebels, who were reported to be camped in that vicinity. A body of cavalry was sent in the direction of Shawneetown, Illinois, with orders to form a junction with and support the infantry. The camp was found deserted, the rebels having learned on the previous night of the advance of the Union forces, and consulted their safety by a hasty flight. The cavalry skirmished slightly with straggling squads of the rebels, taking a few prisoners, but failed to find the enemy in anything like formidable numbers. The troops, having accomplished all that could be done, in that direction, returned to Morganfield, where they were met by General HUGHES, who had remained at Evansville, for some time longer than he had intended, being detained by the details of business, imperatively necessary to the success of the expedition. General HUGHES brought the information that

General PAINE, who had been assigned to the command of that part of Kentucky, had landed at Uniontown with several thousand troops, and that General PRENTISS had arrived at Shawneetown, with another detachment of United States volunteers. These arrivals rendered further operations in that vicinity, on the part of General HOVEY's command, unnecessary, and accordingly on the 19th, he moved in the direction of Henderson, by way of Smith's Mills, at which place they captured five or six prisoners, among whom was Captain BATES, Acting Assistant Adjutant General, on the Staff of Colonel SEIPERT, who was severely wounded in attempting to escape.

In searching the baggage and pockets of these prisoners, Colonel MANN found a number of blank paroles for the Indiana Legion— a further and convincing proof that they had intended to cross the river had not their plans been summarily thwarted. Camping for the night near Smith's Mills and continuing the march on the morning of the 20th, the troops arrived at Henderson about noon where they found transports in waiting to ferry the cavalry across the river, and convey the infantry and artillery to Mount Vernon and Evansville.

During the expedition the command was partially subsisted upon the country. Fifty negroes joined our forces and were soon after mustered into the United States service at Evansville. Three commissiond officers and thirty enlisted men of the rebels were captured. The spoils consisted of a small number of horses and mules. All the officers and men of the several commands conducted themselves in a soldierly manner and received the thanks of General HOVEY "for their cheerful co-operation and prompt execution of orders."[2]

[2] See Hovey's report in Terrell, *Report,* 1, Appendix, Doc. 82:282.

RELATIONS OF INDIANA AND KENTUCKY IN THE WAR

For two generations before the outbreak of the rebellion, the relations between Indiana and Kentucky had been peculiarly close and intimate. Probably no other two States were bound together by so many ties. Kentuckians under the lead of GEORGE ROGERS CLARK had conquered our territory from the English. Kentuckians under SCOTT and HARDIN had penetrated our frightful wildernesses to punish Indians and protect the scattered trading posts in which our population was then collected. Kentuckians settled our lands and founded our towns. When TECUMSEH's gigantic schemes of war threatened our destruction, Kentuckians poured across the Ohio to join in that decisive battle at Tippecanoe which forever terminated Indian hostilities within our borders. JOSEPH HAMILTON DAVEISS was a name as dear to Indianians as to Kentuckians. As years passed away, business connections became closer, trade more constant and valuable, and intermarriages strengthened all with the happier ties of family relationship. Under a sense of the duty created by these connections, Governor WRIGHT of this State, soon after his first election, invited Governor CRITTENDEN of Kentucky to visit him, and, by an intercourse of a purely friendly character, by the interchange of hospitalities and kindly feelings, crowned the relations which the history of the States made memorable, with an official recognition. The visit was a striking event, and was soon followed by a return in which Kentucky cordiality and liberality completed what the gratitude and respect of Indiana had happily commenced. A few years afterwards, Governor POWELL paid a visit to Governor

WRIGHT and renewed the interchange of hospitalities. There was everything to hold the States together, nothing to force them apart, when the rebellion came, not to destroy, but to reverse, the past relations of dependence and protection. Kentucky was full of rebel zeal and audacity. Her Governor was little less than an avowed traitor. Rebel military organizations had secured the State's arms. Loyal men, though not out-numbered, were, by the connivance of the authorities, placed at disadvantage. Their border counties were turbulent and dangerous with rebel bands that menaced them and alarmed our own border. No official agents could be trusted to obtain or distribute arms. It seemed for a time as if the State would be dragged out of the Union, protesting and helplessly struggling against the efforts that threatened it. In this crisis her loyal citizens turned to Indiana for help. Governor MORTON had early warned the Federal Government of the danger to be apprehended from Kentucky rebels, and urged the importance of providing promptly and amply for the defense of the State. If Kentucky should be made the refuge of rebels, Indiana could never be safe. It was, therefore, the part of wisdom, in his judgment, to protect all the free States on the Ohio by protecting Kentucky. The Northwest should be defended south of the Ohio. Pursuing this sagacious policy he gave his time and labor freely to the help of the Kentucky Union men, and it is hardly too much to say, that during the time BERIAH MAGOFFIN remained in office, Governor MORTON was, more directly and effectively than any other man, the Guardian of Kentucky. Through him she received, for a time, most of the arms that enabled her loyal men to protect themselves. If help was desired from the National Government, the expectation of it was built mainly upon his efforts. He was informed of every movement as promptly, and his assistance requested as confidently as if he had been their own Governor. If dangerous points needed to be guarded, they were pointed out to him. If invasions were to be met, he was appealed to. His secret agents penetrated all parts of the State, and aided the efforts of her loyal citizens to keep him full informed of her condition. From him the General Government obtained its earliest and best information, and once his advices were so far in advance of ordinary official intelligence that Mr. LINCOLN was inclined to treat his alarm as an idle "skeer," till the first invasion of the State proved too fully how closely he watched his charge. For more than a year Indiana in no small degree maintained to her Mother State that guardianship which had so long and so generously cherished her own feeble childhood. The debt may not have been paid, but nothing that traditional regard and gratitude, and present duty, could do to acknowledge its obligations was left undone.

CONDITION OF KENTUCKY—SECESSION SCHEMES

When Governor MAGOFFIN replied to the President's call for Kentucky's quota of 75,000 volunteers by an insolent refusal, it was by no means certain that he and his associates would not force the State into the rebellion. That this was their purpose, and that plans to effect it had been matured, is very certain. Within a little more than a week after the President's proclamation, on the 24th of April, 1861, Dr. BLACKBURN, of yellow-fever infamy, an agent of MAGOFFIN'S, appeared at a public meeting in New Orleans, held in honor of the Kentucky volunteers for the rebel army, and in a speech, published in the "Picayune" newspaper of that city, said that "he had been authorized by Governor MAGOFFIN to apply to the Governors of Mississippi and Louisiana for arms for his State," that "he had asked for one hundred arms from Mississippi, and Governor PETTUS had generously responded by giving him two hundred muskets. In a few days two more companies from Kentucky might be expected, one to be called the Mississippi Guards, the other the Pelter Rifles." He also stated, that "the centre and west of the State were ready to leave the Union the moment they get arms." This was said on the 24th, nine days after the issuing of the

President's Proclamation. Dr. BLACKBURN had already been in Mississippi, and procured two hundred muskets. He must, therefore, have received his appointment as agent to solicit arms and aid from the rebels to force Kentucky out of the Union, but a day or two after, if not before, the attack was made on Fort Sumter. Carrying out the same scheme, General SIMON BOLIVAR BUCKNER, the chief officer of the State Guard, had, as far as possible, prepared that body for co-operation with the rebels, and had obtained the control of the greater part, if not all, of the State arms.

On the 12th of September, 1861, precisely five months after the attack on Fort Sumter, he published a proclamation to "The People of Kentucky" full of puerile rhetoric and silly metaphor, setting forth, among other specimens of the florid eloquence so peculiar to the slave States, that they "had seen a portion of their own people drawing from beneath the cloak of neutrality the assassin's dagger, which is aimed to pierce our hearts," and, that "with the poignard at our breasts, they expect us to caress the hand of the assassin, and to lick the dust from the iron heel of tyranny which is raised to crush us," and declaring that he will not submit, but on the contrary that he "will fling to the breeze the proud standard of Kentucky, and in every valley and on every hill top let its folds be kissed by the breezes of Heaven," and expecting Kentuckians to join him, and "let our lone star shine an emblem of hope from the deep sky blue of our banner over the brothers who join in the grasp of friendship." Of course a great many of them helped him to "let it shine." Through MAGOFFIN's prostituted power and BUCKNER's sophomorical solicitations, the rebels counted, for many months, a great many more Kentuckians in their ranks than could be found in the armies of the Nation. The lower end of the State was more entirely and bitterly rebel than many sections of the seceded States. Union men were abused, driven away, murdered or plundered, with no more scruple, and no more peril, than if they had been wild beasts. Marauding bands roamed through it at will, and kept our own border in constant terror. There was no law, and no safety for any but rebels. And to the very end of the war this section was the seat of turbulence, disorder and treason. In the more central portions, the celebrated "Blue Grass" region, the wealthiest, oldest and most refined community of the State, though less turbulent, was not less thoroughly treasonable, and furnished from its abundance the means by which the more active rebellion of its accomplices was maintained. In nearly every quarter rebel organizations of more or less strength existed, and secession was confidently anticipated. The position of the Union men was peculiarly perilous. Their Governor was a traitor, their domestic military force had been partly debauched, their arms had been turned against them, and they could not feel at all sure that by official aid and organized intimidation, the secessionists might not carry the State into rebellion. The arms they received through Governor MORTON often had to be secretly distributed and secretly kept. General BUCKNER makes the "clandestine introduction of arms and munitions" one of the counts in his timid indictment against the President; as if his own treason and that of MAGOFFIN, fermenting in the State Guard, had not made an open distribution of arms dangerous.

Besides the difficulty of arming against armed treason, and of resisting lawlessness with powerless laws, the Unionists found themselves, by the cunning of MAGOFFIN and the weakness of McCLELLAN, placed in a position of neutrality, in which the advantage was given to the rebel armies below them, as completely as it was given, by the official encouragement of treason to the rebel conspirators among them. From the beginning, MAGOFFIN seems to have had in view the possibility, by threats or artifice, of excluding the National forces from Kentucky, and giving the rebels, as nearly as practicable, an unobstructed field for their operations. At the very time Dr. BLACKBURN was assuring the people of New Orleans, that Kentucky was arming to go out of the Union, and was begging arms for her, MAGOFFIN was soliciting Governor MORTON and Governor DENNISON, of Ohio, to join him in the abandonment of the National Government and the formation of a neutral combination "to preserve peace between the border States," and act as "mediators between the contending parties." On the 25th of April, 1861, and the day that Dr. BLACKBURN'S speech was published in New Orleans, he sent to Governor MORTON this dispatch: "Will you co-operate with me in a proposition to the government at Washington for peace by the border States as mediators between the contending parties?" Governor MORTON replied at once: "I will unite in any effort for the restoration of the Union and peace, which shall be constitutional and honorable to Indiana and the Federal Government." The next day MAGOFFIN sent another dispatch, stating that he had informed Governor DENNISON that "he would meet that gentleman at Cincinnati the following Tuesday evening," and requesting Governor MORTON to meet them there. Governor MORTON replied at once that he would, and that he expected Governor MAGOFFIN to be there "in person." He went to Cincinnati at the appointed time, but MAGOFFIN, though expressly notified to be present "in person," did not appear. He probably never intended to place his treacherous soul so close to the searching examination of honest men, but if he did he abandoned the intention. An interview, such as Governor MORTON desired, would have been quite sure to expose his duplicity plainly enough to have ruined his power for evil, and he knew it, consequently he sent Colonel THOMAS L. CRITTENDEN in his place, who gave Governor MORTON the following letter on the 30th: "Dear Sir: I have been instructed by the Hon. B. MAGOFFIN, Governor of the State of Kentucky, to solicit the co-operation of yourself and the Hon. WILLIAM DENNISON, Governor of the State of Ohio, in an effort to bring about a *truce* between the General Government and the seceded States until the meeting of Congress in extraordinary session, in the hope that the action of that body may point out the way to a peaceful solution of our national troubles." The similarity, or rather identity, of this proposition of a secret, and soon after an avowed traitor, who abandoned his office and his State to throw himself into the arms of the rebels, with a number of propositions, which were received with marked favor by the majority of the Indiana Legislature of 1863, will strike the reader very forcibly. Governor MORTON replied next day, May 1st:

> I hold that Indiana and Kentucky are but integral parts of the Nation, and as such, are subject to the Government of the United States, and bound to obey the requisitions of the President, issued in pursuance of his constitutional authority; that it is the duty of every State government to prohibit, by all means in its power, the transportation, within its own limits, of arms, military stores and provisions, to any State in open rebellion and hostility to the Government of the United States, and to restrain its citizens from all acts giving aid and comfort to the enemy; that there is no ground in the Constitution midway between the Federal Government and a rebellious State, upon which another State can stand, holding both in check; and that a State must take its stand upon one side or the other; and I invoke the State of Kentucky, by all the sacred ties that bind us together, to take her stand with Indiana, promptly and efficiently, on the side of the Union. The action of the Federal Government in the present contest being strictly in accordance with the constitution and laws of the land; and, entertaining the views above indicated, I am compelled to decline the co-operation solicited by you. I take this occasion to renew the expression of my earnest desire that Kentucky may remain in the Union, and that the intimate political, social and commercial relations which exist between her and Indiana may never be disturbed, but be cemented and strengthened through all coming years.

Two days after the appointed time, MAGOFFIN went to Cincinnati, knowing of course that he would not meet either of the loyal Governors, who, seeing that he had failed, and having no reason to expect him, were unlikely to wait two days to see if he might not change his notion. He had been expressly notified to be there "in person," but made his excuse, when he came, that "he did not know that he was expected," which was a downright falsehood.

His conduct in the whole affair of this Cincinnati convocation showed that he had no purpose to meet the loyal Governors. When notified by Colonel CRITTENDEN, after the meeting in which the latter represented him, that the Governors demanded his presence, and he could plead ignorance no longer, he resorted to another artifice. He waited two days, notified nobody of his purpose, and then, knowing that the Governors were gone, he went to Cincinnati to find, "very much to his" anticipated "disappointment," that he had come too late. He said in excuse of his neglect to give notice of his coming, that he "had started off without taking time to reply." A day or two certainly afforded time for at least an intimation of his coming, which would have detained the Governors till he came. But that was just what he did not want, and so he sent no intimation.

He feared to expose himself to the peril of detection in his duplicity; so he promised to attend, failed to attend, and did attend when he had taken abundant care that nobody else should. He knew his proposition would be rejected, and that nothing would be lost except his own character (which could hardly be better disposed of) by not attending the conference to urge it, while the making the proposition would cover his treasonable schemes a little more deeply or decently, and possibly induce the Union men, driven to extremity as they were, to support it for the sake of peace. If this was his object, he attained it. The Union men, or a portion of them, alarmed at their own peril, and doubtful of the strength of the Government, in some degree, too, misled by the artful management of public journals, which, controlled by rebel sympathizers, pretended to support the Government to make their hostility more effective, made a sort of compromise between MAGOFFIN'S truce and a straight-forward loyalty, which they called neutrality.

KENTUCKY "NEUTRALITY"

For a month or two, Kentucky "neutrality" was debated throughout the country, uniformly denounced or disapproved by loyal men and journals, and as uniformly supported by such papers and people as had before, or have since, shown themselves friends of the rebellion. What it was, or what it meant, nobody knew. Its advocates explained it several times every day from the 1st of May to the 20th of June, or thereabout, but explanations explained nothing, except that Kentucky would not fight for the rebellion, and could not fight for the Government, and did not want either party to cross her borders, so that she might not have to fight for herself. She would be an oasis of peace in a desert of war. The Government was to spare her because she had not seceded, and the rebels were to be kind because she would not help the Government. In this position, Kentucky was decidedly a more mischievous obstruction than she would have been in open rebellion. Her neutrality barricaded all the rebel States of any importance east of the Mississippi river, except Virginia, against any hostile movement from the north, and thus shut up what subsequently proved, under GRANT and SHERMAN to be the direct road to final victory. The rebels might well be content with it, for they would not, and did not, hesitate to disregard it whenever they saw an advantage to be gained. The Government only, as MAGOFFIN and its proposers desired, was placed at a disadvantage by it, for the Government would respect its promise and the sanctity of Kentucky's soil. If that promise should be violated, in order to carry forward some vital military operation, MAGOFFIN and the secessionist "neutrals" would be furnished another pretext for secession, if not an excuse for actual resistance and open collision with the Government. If it should not be violated, the rebels who were no party to it, and would not regard it if they were, would have the advantage of operating in Kentucky without opposition. BASIL DUKE's history of MORGAN's cavalry states the interpretation that the rebels put upon it, and the effect it was intended to have. In the opening of his third chapter, he says:

The position assumed by Kentucky at the inception of the late struggle, and her conduct throughout, excited the surprise, and in no small degree, incurred for her the dislike of both the contending sections. But while both North and South, at some time, doubted her good faith, and complained of her action, *all such sentiments have been entirely forgotten by the latter,* and have become intensified into bitter and undisguised animosity on the part of a large share of the population of the former. The reason is patent. It is the same which, during the war, influenced the Confederates to hope confidently for large assistance from Kentucky, if once enabled to obtain a foothold upon her territory, and caused the Federals, on the other hand, to regard even the loudest and most zealous professors of loyalty as secessionists in disguise, or, at best, Unionists only to save their property. It is the instinctive feeling that the people of Kentucky, on account of kindred blood, common interests, and identity of ideas in all that relates to political rights and the objects of political institutions, may be supposed likely to sympathize and to act with the South.[1]

After exhibiting the causes that produced the devotion to slavery and antagonism to liberal ideas, which was, and is, so predominant in Kentucky, General DUKE alludes to the JOHN BROWN affair, and says: "Because of the strong belief that similar attempts would be repeated, and upon a larger scale, and that quite likely Kentucky would be selected as a field of operations, it is not surprising that the State Guard should have expected an enemy *only from the North,* and that it should have conceived a feeling of *antagonism for the Northern,* and an *instinctive sympathy with the Southern people.*" Neutrality was rightly understood by General DUKE. It was devised by rebel sympathizers, and its object was the benefit of the rebellion, by excluding National forces from Kentucky, and allowing rebel forces to enter at will. There were doubtless many true Union men who gave their adhesion to the project, partly because they thought they saw in it a chance to avoid having their homes made the Nation's battlefield, and partly because they did not know precisely what they did see in it, and took it on speculation. But the true exponents of Kentucky loyalty, HOLT, ROUSSEAU, and their associates, resisted and denounced it throughout.

[1] Duke, *History of Morgan's Cavalry* (1960 edition), 31. The italics are Terrell's.

On the 28th of April, the Legislature met in extraordinary session, upon the proclamation of the Governor. His message was saturated with disloyalty. Its recommendations were little regarded, though a position of "neutrality" was favored by many as a security against the perils of a war raging at their own doors. Two or three days afterward MAGOFFIN issued a proclamation reciting the occurrences which induced it, and concluding as follows: "Now, therefore, I hereby notify and warn all other States, separate or united, especially the United and Confederate States, that I solemnly forbid any movement upon Kentucky soil, or occupation of any post or place therein, for any purpose whatever, until authorized by invitation or permission of the Legislative or Executive authorities." He also forbade "all citizens of Kentucky, whether incorporated in the State Guard, or otherwise, to make any hostile demonstrations against any of the aforesaid sovereignties," to obey orders, and avoid provoking collisions. On the 22d of May, the Legislature disavowed the Governor's "neutrality" proclamation as a "true exponent of the views of the people." Steps had already been taken to raise the State's quota under the President's call, and place it under the command of Major ANDERSON. Two days afterward, the Senate voted that Kentucky would not sever her connection with the Union, but assumed a position of modified neutrality, which held her from joining the forces of either belligerent, but armed her to preserve peace within her own border.

About the middle of June, General McCLELLAN, then in command of the Western Department, made a treaty with the Kentucky authorities, virtually accepting the terms of MAGOFFIN's proclamation, binding the Government to allow no troops to enter on Kentucky soil, "unless *invited* to do so by the State authorities"; and binding Kentucky to remain neutral toward the Southern States "as long as the United States shall respect her position." A reservation was made on the part of the Government that if rebel forces entered the State, the national forces might do so, too, after the lapse of a "*reasonable* time." But hostile combinations formed in the State to attack the Union men, or the States north of the Ohio, could not be suppressed by the national arms without "the invitation of the State authorities," that is Governor MAGOFFIN, whose invitation under such circumstances would be much slower in coming than was his presence at the Cincinnati conference. The treaty, in effect, opened Kentucky to the rebels and shut it to the government, at least during a "reasonable time," which might easily be time enough to work irreparable ruin. Threatened, and in a degree overawed by the furious rebel elements all around them, and embarrassed by a "neutrality" that forbade them to assist the government, or allow the government to relieve them, the Union men came to Governor MORTON for counsel and aid, and they got both.

INDIANA AND KENTUCKY

Within a few days after the attack on Fort Sumter, Governor MORTON issued a proclamation convening the Legislature in extraordinary session, to provide means to enable the State to protect herself and discharge her duty to the Nation. In his message, delivered April 25th, 1861, the very day that MAGOFFIN first set his "neutrality" trap, he said:

To our sister State of Kentucky we turn with hope and affection. She has grown rich and prosperous in the Republic; could she do more if she were out of it? It would be a sad day that would sever the bond which binds these States together, and places us in separate and hostile nations. I appeal to her by the ties of our common kindred and history, by our community of interest, by the sacred obligations that bind us to maintain the Constitution inviolate, to adhere to the Union, and stand fast by the flag in defense of which she has so often shed her best blood. I pray to her to examine her past history, and see how the tide of her prosperity has flowed on unbroken and ever increasing, until her limits are filled with material wealth, and her people are respected, elevated and happy; and then inquire if all this is not the result of that Union she is called upon to break, and of that Government she is invited to dishonor and overthrow. To ask Kentucky to secede is to ask her to commit foul dishonor and suicide. I trust that the good sense and patriotism of her people will not suffer her to be dragged by the current of events, which has been cunningly directed for that purpose, into the vortex of disunion; nor permit her to be artfully inveigled into armed neutrality between the rebellious States and the Federal Government. Such a position would be anomalous and fatal to the peace and perpetuity of the Union. There is no ground in the Constitution midway between a rebellious State and the Federal Government upon which she can stand holding both in check, and restraining the Government from the enforcement of the laws and the exercise of its constituted authority. Such an attitude is at once unconstitutional and hostile. At a time like this, if she is not for the Government, aiding and maintaining it by the observance of all her constitutional obligations, she is against it. If the voice of her people can be heard, I fear not the result. Secession can only triumph, as it has triumphed in other States, by stifling the voice of the people, and by the bold usurpation of demagogues and traitors of the powers which rightfully belong to them alone.[2]

On the 9th of May he wrote to General McCLELLAN at Cincinnati, describing the virulence of the disloyal feeling in Kentucky, especially along the lower portions of the Ohio river, representing the defenseless state of our many flourishing towns exposed to rebel attack, and urging preparations for protecting them, so that if Kentucky should be dragged out of the Union by the threatening elements then so wildly turbulent within her borders, we might at least be safe from invasion and the better able to assist her loyal citizens. On the 24th of May, he, in conjunction with Governor YATES of Illinois, Governor DENNISON of Ohio, Senator TRUMBULL of Illinois, and General McCLELLAN, addressed a memorial to the Government stating, that in their opinion,

The United States should, at an early day, take possession, in force, of prominent points in Kentucky, such as Louisville, Covington, Newport, Columbus, etc., and the railroads leading from them to the South. If Colonel ANDERSON, or others who are loyal to the Government, can raise regiments of loyal men in Kentucky to occupy these points in the first instance, and the Government has the means of arming them, it would be advisable to have them thus occupied. If Kentuckians cannot be found, United States regulars would be the next best for the

[2] The message is in Terrell, *Report,* 1, Appendix, Doc. 113:308-10, and in *House Journal,* sp. sess., 1861, pp. 20-24.

purpose; but in our judgment they should be occupied at an early day, if it has to be done by the volunteer forces from adjoining States. We believe this course will save Kentucky to the Union, otherwise that in the end the secessionists will control her.[3]

This earnest representation of men so distinguished for zeal and fidelity to the Government, shows how alarming the condition of Kentucky was a month after the war broke out. The proclamation of her Governor made her virtually an ally of the rebellion. Many of her influential men — BRECKINRIDGE, MARSHALL, BURNETT, BUCKNER and others—were openly advocating secession. In the lower branch of the Legislature, parties stood 49 for the Union, to 43 for secession. The State Guard, as General DUKE says, strongly sympathized with the rebellion, and its commander was indefatigable in urging sympathy into action. The State arms were in its hands. The rallying of troops to fill the President's call proceeded languidly and promised little. A common interest with the rebel States in the institution which caused the war, naturally created a predisposition to look leniently at their conduct, and previous events had deepened and widened this feeling. In spite of the loyal action of the Legislature a few days later, it is by no means certain that, without the support of the loyal Governors of the adjoining free States, and more directly of Governor MORTON, in arming and encouraging the organization of forces, and watching constantly every movement that might so easily imperil the peace of all, the Unionists might not have had a terrible struggle to save their State, after the rebel forces had overrun the southern and western portions and established themselves at Bowling Green and Columbus.

LOYAL ASCENDANCY

But the rebel element was not left to the enjoyment of "neutrality," unopposed. The "Border State" convention, in-

[3] The memorial is in Governor Morton's Correspondence, Private, Book 1, pp. 39-40.

vited by Virginia, in the interests of the rebellion, to be held at Frankfort, on the 20th of May, failed. The proclamation of neutrality was disavowed. Judge HOLT, irrefutably crushed it, in a masterly argument, and Colonel PRENTISS, of Illinois, shortly afterwards entered the State to disperse a force of rebels forming near Cairo. The election for members of Congress, on the 1st of July, resulted in a popular Union majority, in the State, of fifty-five thousand three hundred and seventy. Before this, about the 1st of June, the gallant and loyal ROUSSEAU had resolved to raise a force of Kentuckians, for the Union. He went to Washington and urged his views. He was authorized, by the President, to carry out his purpose, and he proceeded with characteristic promptness and energy to do it. But still the secession element was so strong, and the Union men so fearful of strengthening it, and giving it pretexts, to excite popular odium, against the government, that, at a meeting held in Louisville, especially to consider what should be done in regard to organizing the proposed force, there were but two or three who advocated its encampment within the State. Some doubted whether any force at all should be raised. ROUSSEAU would not allow any interference with his purpose to raise it, but did submit to the judgment of the meeting, as to its encampment within, or rather out of the State. The result was that he was compelled to establish his camp and rendezvous at Jeffersonville, in this State, where Governor MORTON made him as heartily welcome, as his patriotism and firmness deserved. He named his camp after the loyal JOE HOLT, and soon rallied a gallant force, which he called the "Louisville Legion." Subsequently he organized the Second Kentucky Cavalry, and a battery of Artillery. The solicitude of Governor MORTON to have Kentucky made safe against the secessionists showed itself in his interest in ROUSSEAU's enterprise. He gave permission to our citizens to enlist in the Kentucky regiments at Camp "Joe Holt," and allowed a company of cavalry (Captain WHITE's) to be organized, in Knox county, for the Third Kentucky Cavalry, and a company from Dearborn county was given a like permission. He was, at the same time, in constant consultation with the Union men, exerting himself to secure and distribute arms, to protect our border, to overawe the rebel bands across the river, and to urge energetic action in favor of Kentucky, by the Government. To his efforts, in no small degree, must be attributed the final determination of the President to establish military camps and recruiting posts within the State, as was done at several important points about this time.

MAGOFFIN, fully aware of the encouraging effect, which the organization of Kentucky troops for the Union, in or out of the State, would have, probably fully informed of the intended invasion of the rebel force, which occurred a few days later, and utterly defiant, of the Legislative disavowal of his "neutrality" proclamation, on the 19th of August, wrote to the President, remonstrating against the formation of loyal military camps, and organization of loyal forces in Kentucky, and urging their removal. The President replied on the 24th, stating that what he had done had been done on the solicitation of many Kentuckians, regretting that he could see no wish for the preservation of the Union in the Governor's letter, and declining to comply with the request. The rebel forces entered Kentucky and occupied Bowling Green on the — day of August. On the 3d of September the Legislature met again, and again the Governor's message was foul with feebly suppressed treason. The Legislature was more decidedly and largely opposed to him than it was before. On the 11th of September, it passed, by a vote of seventy-one to twenty-six, a resolution directing the Governor to issue a proclamation ordering the rebel troops to leave the State. Resolutions, reciting the fact of the rebel invasion, directing the State troops to be called out to repel it, inviting "the United States to give that aid and assistance, that protection against invasion, which is granted to each one of the States by the Constitution," and requesting General ANDERSON to enter at once upon the active duties of his command in that District, were also passed by a vote of sixty-eight to twenty-six. Kentucky was now fully enlisted on the side of the Government. "Neutrality" was an obsolete as well as a mischievous doctrine. On the 12th, BUCKNER issued his school-boy declamation, announcing the treason that nobody had ever doubted, and joined the rebels. The Legislature proceeded by a series of acts (which MAGOFFIN approved, finding himself unable to resist the now aroused loyal strength) to prepare the State for her full and faithful duty to the Government. But the rebel invasion, inciting the most violent outrages and open hostility, on the part of the secessionists, created widespread alarm, and the peril increased with the stay of the rebel forces.

Governor MORTON, on the 2d of October, 1861, issued a proclamation, describing the disordered and dangerous condition of Kentucky, and the necessity of an immediate increase of the National army, and appealing to all classes of citizens, capable of bearing arms and able to leave their homes, "to leave their ordinary pursuits, and enroll themselves in the ranks of the army."[4] He also had all the arms, in the arsenal at the Capital, sent to Jeffersonville, and distributed among the Home Guards in both States. A portion of our troops were dispatched to Paducah. Others were speedily thrown forward, under BUELL'S command, to confront BRAGG on Green river. Others still were sent towards the southeast and the defeat of ZOLLICOFFER, at Wild Cat, by the Thirty-Third Indiana Regiment, Colonel JOHN COBURN, and detachments of Ohio and Kentucky troops, followed by the decisive victory of Mill Springs, largely shared by Indiana men, was the first reverse of the series that soon after broke through the line of rebel posts, from the Chesapeake to the Mississippi. A most gallant and successful action was fought by the Thirty-Second Indiana Regiment (German), Colonel WILLICH, in December, with a Texas cavalry regiment, on Green river. In every conflict and movement in Kentucky, Indiana forces were among the foremost. Their blood was among the first to stain

[4] The proclamation is given in Terrell, *Report*, 1, Appendix, Doc. 121:332-33.

the soil, which had sent so many gallant defenders to protect the infancy of their State. The relations of Indiana and Kentucky, from the full assumption of a loyal attitude by the latter till the close of the war, were but little different from those of other States. An extract from the speech of Dr. ROBERT J. BRECKINRIDGE, delivered in Cincinnati, in May, 1862, may fitly conclude this portion of this narrative:

> It was the proximity of Ohio, Indiana and Illinois, the fidelity of the people of the latter States, upon which these men depended—of your people and the other two States, that saved Kentucky. The question was flatly asked by General BOYLE of the army, then a private citizen of Kentucky: "Will you have twelve thousand men ready the moment we ask for them?" It was flatly asked of the governors of Ohio, Indiana and Illinois, and the reply was that they would sustain them; and I suppose I may add that Mr. LINCOLN was telegraphed, asking whether he would assist them, and he said "with my whole power." Mr. BOYLE telegraphed to Governor DENNISON for ten thousand men at call. He replied "you can have them." He also asked for ten thousand men from Indiana and Illinois, and the reply was the same. *This was the salvation of Kentucky.*

The subsequent events of the war which made Indiana, at times, conspicuous as a guardian and ally of Kentucky, need nothing more than an allusion here, as they have elsewhere been related at length. The invasion of General KIRBY SMITH in August, 1862, besides bringing our State most prominently forward in defense of her almost helpless sister State, was the occasion of MAGOFFIN's resignation. Disgusted with the duty of seeing the loyal action of Kentucky, while he could oppose no resistance to it officially, he surrendered his office and went to his friends. The battle of Richmond on the 30th of August—in which six raw Indiana regiments, with an Ohio and one Kentucky regiment, and detachments of cavalry and artillery, under Generals CRUFT and MANSON, of Indiana, opposed nearly three times their force of rebel veterans with such courage and persistence as to defeat, in the end, the main object of the invasion—was an event of especial interest to Indiana. Nearly one thousand of her sons were killed or wounded, and two thousand captured and paroled. The regiments which were composed of men who but little more than a week before had been farmers and mechanics at home, lost every other man of their entire number. Such a record of heroic resistance by recruits is as rare as it is honorable. The delay of the rebel march to the Ohio river, which this battle produced, combined with the amazing rapidity with which freshly organized regiments from Indiana and Ohio, and armies of hardy backwoodsmen, with their "squirrel rifles," poured into Cincinnati, saved that city from the pillage which was one of the objects of the raid.

Previous to this invasion, but doubtless a portion of the same general movement, the guerrilla bands along the Ohio began to assume a bold front, and to threaten our river towns. On the 18th of July they made a raid into the town of Newburgh, Warrick county, committed robberies, excited great alarm, and brought upon themselves a swift visitation of Hoosier wrath. Governor MORTON called for troops for thirty days, and was so promptly supplied that in a little more than two days, with the cordial approval of General BOYLE, he threw an overwhelming force into Henderson, Kentucky, and swept that terribly infested region clean.

MORGAN's raid in July, 1863, with the preliminary adventure of HINES's band of horse thieves, was the next event that illustrated the spirit of Indiana in her relation to Kentucky. The news of MORGAN's advance brought, as did every alarm, an appeal from General BOYLE to Governor MORTON for help, and of course, help was sent. All the Indiana troops in the government service were dispatched to Kentucky at once, and kept there, while MORGAN was riding a race with the wrath of his enemies in our own borders. Governor MORTON had no force to oppose him, and was compelled to supply the place of the men who were defending Kentucky with Home Guards and the sudden levies brought by patriotic indignation, in two days, from every quarter of the State. They did their work, however. MORGAN began retreating almost as soon as he landed, and never halted till his force was annihilated in Ohio.

In May, 1864, MORGAN again invaded Kentucky with a force of three or four thousand men, through Pound Gap. General BURBRIDGE immediately telegraphed to Governor MORTON for four regiments. "One regiment leaves to-night, another to-morrow, and two more next day," was the response. Two weeks afterwards there came an urgent appeal from Louisville: "The city is in danger. We want four or five thousand men." A regiment was sent immediately. The same day General HOBSON telegraphed from Covington for "any troops you can send me to Louisville or Frankfort." Kentucky had then taken every man of Indiana's troops that the Governor had. He called out the militia of several counties, and placed it in the best position for service either at home or across the Ohio. The Forty-Third, re-enlisted veterans, arriving at Indianapolis on the short furlough given to re-enlisted men, at once volunteered to go to Kentucky, and were promptly sent to the relief of Governor BRAMLETTE, besieged in Frankfort. A portion of the Legion was sent to guard the Louisville and Nashville Railroad. By every effort and at every point, Indiana threw herself forward to protect Kentucky. The result of the raid, and the terrible defeat of MORGAN, are familiar to all.

Within two weeks after MORGAN's last raid, Colonel ADAM R. JOHNSON and Colonel SEIPERT, with a force of seven to twelve hundred men, appeared in the vicinity of Henderson, Kentucky, and menaced the lower portion of our border. Revelations made during the "Treason Trials," at Indianapolis, by men concerned in the conspiracy, indicated that JOHNSON's movement, as well as that of MORGAN, was in co-operation with an insurrection intended to be general throughout the Northwest. His plundering steamboats, conscriptions, and other outrages, with his expulsion by Indiana troops under Generals HOVEY and HUGHES, have been already fully **related.**

These events, in which Indiana was, more prominently than any other State, brought forward as the dependence of Kentucky against invasion and domestic dangers, will suffice to make good the declaration at the commencement of this sketch, that though the debt created by the courageous and bloody defense of our infancy may not have been paid, its obligations have at least been acknowledged by the effort to pay it.

INTERNAL STATE TROUBLES

POLITICAL DISTURBANCES

That a feeling of disloyalty rankled in the hearts of many for years previous to the war the history of the times well attests. This gradually ripened and finally culminated in attempted secession, and resulted in actual civil war. If the secession movement had ended with a mere declaration of independence—in a proclamation of a separate nationality, thus leaving the Government of the United States no alternative but to submit to a division of its territory and power or make war upon the recusant States to avert that calamity—it would be difficult to conjecture what aspect the secession movement would have assumed, or what its result would have been. Although the great mass of loyal men were agreed that the Union should be preserved, at all hazards—even the hazard of making war—there was no inconsiderable number of able adherents of the Government who doubted if that result could be secured by a war in which the Government must assume the offensive, strike the first blow, and prosecute it throughout as the military, though not political, aggressor. A very much larger number of opponents of the Government not only doubted the practicability of coercion, but the constitutionality of any interference with secession whatever. And, underlying the more demonstrative feelings of all classes, was the strong, though almost unconscious indisposition—the growth of nearly half a century of peace at home—to unsettle all business, and break up all old habits, by undertaking so unaccustomed and costly an enterprise as war. Before an attack, which should make war a necessity of self-defense, the inert resistance of such a feeling as this would naturally disappear at once, but it could not have been otherwise than a serious obstacle to taking the initiative in a war where fighting was but one of several alternatives. Thus there were three elements of opposition to the policy of making war upon the seceded States to compel their adhesion, or punish their treason: 1st. Loyal feeling which doubted the result. 2d. Disloyal feeling which denounced this, as it had always done every other form of resistance to whatever the South chose to do. 3d. A universal feeling of dislike to deranging all established relations and objects by beginning a new and dangerous work. With three such elements, and the almost certain union of all the slave States against it, the problem of a war of coercion was intricate and perilous.

Happily for the cause of humanity and liberal government, the rebels themselves solved this dangerous problem for us by beginning the war, and thus forcing the Government to fight in defense of its own life, less to compel the obedience of those who repudiated it than to preserve itself for those who adhered to it. Two of the three elements of danger in the great problem of war were thus swept away at a blow. "Loyal distrust" of a coercive war could not hesitate to fight in a defensive war. "Dislike of beginning a war" had no excuse for inaction when war was forced upon it. No element was left to affect the new relations created by the attack upon Fort Sumter but that of "disloyal feeling," which, in the future, as in the past, was ready to follow the South from Fort Sumter to "Armageddon," from the first battle against the Union, to the last battle against the Almighty. The effect of this disloyal feeling was twofold. It contributed greatly to produce the war, and it contributed still more to protract it.

The influence of disloyal Northern feeling in producing the war—In the examination of this point, we are met at the outset by this significant question: If the rebels desired only independence and Union among themselves, why should they have abandoned all the advantages which the condition of public sentiment in the North, as just set forth, gave them to effect it, and begin a war upon the Government? If, as they afterwards so unanimously and persistently asserted, "they wanted only to be alone," why did they not let the Government alone? If they had been content to rest quietly upon the act of separation, and wait for the Government to take the first step in meeting the difficulty which they thus presented, they would have had, as already indicated, some great advantages, which, by any other course, they must inevitably lose. Justice to their intelligence forbids us to doubt that they saw these advantages. They could not but see that, with a large minority of the North, openly favoring their pretensions, with a smaller minority opposing, yet hesitating as to the means of resisting them, and with the natural dislike which existed against proceeding to hostilities when no hostile demonstrations were made by the malcontents of the South, they could pursue no wiser policy than that of "masterly inactivity." Why did they not pursue it? Why did they give up all the advantages of a defensive attitude to take an offensive one? Why did their Secretary of War telegraph from Charleston to Montgomery after the capture of Fort Sumter, that "in thirty days their flag should float over Washington?" Washington was no part of their territory, and it was not only a part of the territory of the Government they had abandoned, but its capital and the seat of its power. Its capture would indicate, and go far toward achieving, the overthrow of that power. It would place in their hands at least the "husk" of the old Government which their new one could fill, and thus claim to be the Government of the Nation. To assume an offensive attitude when a defensive one was so much safer; to begin war when peace offered so many more advantages to the purpose they professed; to declare that they meant to follow up the first hostile blow by the conquest of territory to which they had no claim, and by forcing the old Government from its capital, leaves no conclusion possible, to any candid mind, but that they aimed to overthrow our Government and establish their own upon its ruins. Whatever, therefore, may have been the first purpose of secession, its purpose in making war was unquestionably to drive out the old Government and take its place over all, or as many as it desired, of the adhering States.

To the conception of such a purpose something more was necessary than the knowledge of its own power. It is incredible that one third, and that the poorest in resources, intelligence and vital strength, of a nation, should entertain a purpose to conquer the other two thirds by force. The rebels, therefore, relied upon a greater power than their own in their attempt to displace the old Government by a new confederacy having only for its distinctive cornerstone the institution of human slavery. That power was the spirit of dissension, of faction, of treason in the North. There could have been no other. Foreign aid in a war of conquest they could not have expected. For, however willing foreign nations may have been, and afterwards showed themselves to be, to aid in dividing the nation, they could have no more reason to desire an Union under a slave than a free government. It was Union they dreaded—not a free Union. Foreign aid in effecting a division might have been looked for, but not foreign aid in displacing one Union by another. The rebel hope of help must therefore have looked to this side of the Atlantic. And look where we may, we can see on this side but one field, though an ample one, in which it could find either root or nutriment. That was the *disloyal feeling* at the North. It was extensive enough, and malignant enough, to furnish all the encouragement that men, so long accustomed to political domination, and so likely to magnify their own power, as the rebel leaders were, would need. It controlled all the so-called "loyal slave States" to the degree of rendering their adhesion to the Government a qualified preference over its rebel rival rather than an earnest and absolute devotion. In Maryland it was strong enough to have dragged her out of the Union, if she had not been held back by military grasp. In Missouri its machinations were supported by a fatal strength only paralyzed by the promptitude and energy of LYON and the fidelity of her German citizens. In Kentucky it was not strong enough to overcome her adhesion to the Government, but it was strong enough to force her for a while into the position of a "neutral." In Delaware its strength was ineffective only because it was isolated. Throughout the free States the same feeling prevailed, less determined and less dangerous it may be, but hardly less encouraging to rebel hopes. Of its extent we may judge from the exhibition made of it when the futile conduct and disastrous result of MCCLELLAN'S campaign relieved it of the grasp with which the popular outburst of 1861 had strangled it. It showed itself strong enough to take Indiana out of loyal hands in 1862, and leave her nothing but the iron will and unfailing sagacity of her Governor to prevent her own soil being made the scene of endless and ruinous local wars. It was strong enough to endanger the loyal control of Congress. It was widespread enough to cripple the army by encouragement of desertion, and to provide protection for deserters in every township. It organized secret societies in the interest of the rebellion, of which the members were sworn to resist the just demands of the Government, and obstruct the prosecution of the war. It murdered draft officers, and destroyed enrollment papers. It distributed arms for treasonable uses, and plotted the destruction of Government arsenals and storehouses. It conspired to release rebel prisoners and arm them for a raid upon our own soil. It created riots in nearly every county of the Northwest, and in the East it excited the most inhuman and dastardly mob ever known in this country. This spirit, so general and so dangerous, was not engendered by the war. It showed itself by a hearty and encouraging approval of the Montgomery Constitution on its first publication. It showed itself again in fierce denunciations of the Government on the announcement of the attack on Fort Sumter. That fatal event was made the text for a bitter and general assault upon "abolitionism," not upon secessionism. The righteous wrath of loyal men for a while awed it into silence, if not into inactivity. But the disasters of the Government, and the failures of men whom its own influence had weakened or depraved, encouraged it to show itself again within a year, and what the exhibition was has been stated.

The rebels were as well aware of the existence of this disloyal element in the North as were our own people. Probably they knew even better its character, if not its extent. And with this knowledge it ceases to be a matter of astonishment that they should have begun the war, and begun it for the conquest of the Government. They had reason enough to believe that if once in possession of the capital and the "shell" of the Government, the disloyal feeling would be strong enough to enable them to remain. That, without the encouragement offered by this feeling, the rebels would have remained quiet, improving all the advantages of their defensive attitude, and, if war must come, have left the odium and the injury of beginning it to the Government, can hardly be doubted now. In the history that future times will write, it will not be doubted at all. As the war was inevitable, as it has swept slavery out of existence and decided the great national controversy by the final arbitrament of the sword, it may have been well for the cause of freedom and good government that the rebels were encouraged by any means to begin it. In spite of itself disloyalty did a good work. An overruling Providence, as it has so often done before, brought good out of evil. Let disloyalty then be credited with being a blind and unconscious instrument of God for the success of just those ends it desired to defeat.

EFFECT IN PROTRACTING THE WAR

The disloyal spirit that in a greater or less degree caused the war, contributed even more directly and effectually to protract it. In the pursuit of this purpose it produced or aggravated those internal disturbances which form so prominent a feature of the history of our State during the war, and the exhibition of the character and effects of which forms the object of this portion of the Report. One who judges the efforts of the nation to put down the rebellion, and the difficulties it encountered in the work, only from the strength it displayed in the field, and from the array of rebellious force and enthusiasm opposed to it, can have but an inadequate idea of the real nature of the conflict. Our peril lay less in the armies of the rebels than in the machinations of their Northern friends. If there had been nothing to encounter but the forces of LEE, JOHNSON, BRAGG and BEAUREGARD, the war would have been speedily and well ended. It may well be doubted if hostilities in any formidable shape could have extended beyond the glorious circle of victories that girdled the land in the first days of July, 1863, and crowned "THE FOURTH" with later memories as sacred as those that had gathered about it for eighty-seven years. To an enemy who had no hope of help in his own strength and resources, the prospect of the rebellion, after the surrender of Vicksburg and the defeat at Gettysburg, was desperate. With its territory cut in two; with large armies of well-tried troops and faithful officers menacing all assailable points, and penetrating into the vital regions of the "Confederacy"; with its entire coast blockaded, and all trade cut off, or carried on fitfully and at the imminent peril of destruction; with credit utterly ruined and a currency to which the severest penalties could give only a compulsory circulation; with its largest Western army cut to pieces in successive disastrous battles and its fragments surrendered to the conqueror; with its Eastern army irretrievably defeated; with its scattered posts and forces crushed in a score of battles, as if some fatality had selected *the day* the rebellion had so dishonored as the day of fearful recompense, and with nothing to hope for outside of its own territory and its own strength, the rebellion would have died before the year was out. But the rebels had a better hope than their armies or Generals could give them.

In the very moment of their freshest humiliation their friends in the largest cities of the Union were arming to resist the laws, and encouraged, or at least not rebuked or controlled, by sympathizing State authorities, they for days set all the power of good government at defiance. At the same time friends of the rebellion in this State, and through all the Northwest, were rapidly organizing and arming secret associations to defeat the effort of the Government to obtain recruits, to overthrow State governments, to create local conflicts, and to release rebel prisoners and convert them into rebel armies in our midst. The rebel leaders knew this, and they knew what was even more certain to encourage them to continue the war—that a large portion of the people in this State and some others—an apparent popular majority—denounced the war as "cruel," "inhuman" and "unnecessary," and the Government as "tyrannical" and "usurping," for exercising the powers required to prosecute it, and that they demanded the cessation of hostilities and peace on any terms. It would be difficult to imagine a people so pusillanimous as to be willing to abandon a conflict when so large, apparently almost a controlling, portion of some of the victorious States were eager to give them all they asked. Whatever else they may have been, the rebels were neither cowardly nor pusillanimous. They saw hope, not in the war, but in the political ascendancy of their friends, and they fought on, not to win the fight, but to aid the efforts of those who made bold to assure them of success, let the fight go as it might. Therefore, they fought hopefully till the final campaigns of GRANT and SHERMAN buried their political and military encouragements together. Then the rebellion fell as it would have fallen long before, but for the hopes held out by the disloyal spirit of the North. The war was made perilous by traitors, and not by enemies. It was protracted by efforts at home, not by disasters in the field. Half of our enormous debt, half of our fearful bloodshed and misery, are chargeable directly and solely to the disloyal spirit in the North. The obstructions created by it to effective action, its persistent embarrassments, its systematic discouragements, its malignant slanders, its sleepless, tireless, and unscrupulous baseness, seeking evil everywhere and by every means, must be taken into the account whenever a just judgment is to be formed of the efforts required to suppress the rebellion.

The main object sought by the disloyal element of the North, and especially of Indiana, was the weakening of our armies by encouraging desertion, discouraging, or forcibly resisting recruiting, and by crippling the efforts of the State authorities to send reinforcements to our victorious generals in the field. This object was pursued in several ways, each of which will properly embrace a class of the disturbances and difficulties to which this Report relates.

1. *By legislative action:* which was most formidable—for, being most direct, and operating under the forms of law, it presented the semblance of a claim upon law-abiding citizens, and thereby more surely tended to secure their acquiescence. Happily for the State, such action, though attempted, was never consummated.

2. *By expressions of popular feeling* in the resolutions of local meetings and general conventions, and in the utterances of speakers and newspapers, adverse to the war and denunciatory of the Government.

3. *By the dissemination of disloyal feeling* among the soldiers, through the letters of relatives and friends misrepresenting and condemning the war, urging desertion, and promising protection to deserters.

4. *By organizations,* formed in one or more townships of every county, for the purpose of protecting deserters, resisting the conscription laws of the Government, and obstructing the enlistment or enrollment of recruits.

5. *By a secret and sworn Order,* best known as the "Sons of Liberty," organized with the expressed purpose of assisting the rebellion by resisting the necessary demands of the Government, and prepared, by the arming and drilling of its

members, to resort to active hostilities in the prosecution of its infamous designs.

The malignity and determination of the spirit which sought by such means the overthrow of our armies and our Government, can be appreciated only by keeping in mind the condition of popular feeling against which it had to work, and through which it had to penetrate to become publicly active and visible. The commencement of the war against the Government, proclaimed by the attack on Fort Sumter, raised throughout the whole North a blaze of indignation so intense and universal that it consumed all party animosities, and for a time seemed to fuse all parties into one common mass of patriotic zeal and resolution. It exhibited itself in conspicuous demonstrations of contempt or detestation for all who refused or hesitated to declare their adhesion to the Government. It forced the conductors of obnoxious newspapers to hoist the national flag upon their offices, and to take the oath of allegiance. It pursued those who had made themselves odious by disparaging the Government, or were suspected of disaffection, even to their houses, to force them to declare their support of the cause of the country. It threatened violence in many cases. In some, it actually resorted to violence. And, more clearly exhibiting its strength than all other indications, it poured out tens of thousands of volunteers to fill the President's demand for an army to defend the Government. The struggle in every neighborhood was, not to avoid going into the ranks, but to avoid staying at home. There was no rivalry of parties, but an universal emulation, which seemed to impel every man, whatever his party, to enlist before his neighbor. Old men, excluded by law from service, made false declarations of their ages. Boys, too young, both by law and development, managed, by artifice, to enroll themselves. Recruiting quarters swarmed with eager crowds. The recruiting drum was followed by long processions of men and boys, and even women. No one seemed to think of his party, or only to think of it to strengthen his military zeal. No one paraded his Republicanism as his motive for enlistment. No one spoke of his Democracy except to give emphasis to his determination to fight. No one can tell now, for no one took note then, of the proportion of different parties in the ranks. This grand display of patriotism, unsurpassed, probably unequalled, in the history of the world, only needed official recognition and sympathy to be complete. And this it received fully and promptly. A mere partisan would have used it only to make capital or converts for his party. A selfish man would have perverted it to his own profit. A feeble man would have sunk under the weight of the duty it laid upon him, and done nothing. Even an honest and patriotic man, without the sagacity and breadth of comprehension to see the force and promise of so great a movement, might have checked it by hesitating action, by inadequate measures or injudicious exhibitions of party feeling which would have sooner or later recalled forgotten party divisions. But the Governor of Indiana was neither a feeble man, nor a selfish man, nor a bigoted partisan, nor a man of narrow intellect or irresolute character. With the promptitude and energy that marked his whole administration, he made his own action the embodiment of the spontaneous patriotism of the people. He selected his military advisers indifferently from either party, or, if there was a difference, it was in favor of his past political opponents. He appointed his agents for the purchase of arms with a like disregard of the political chances of the future. He commissioned field officers as his own knowledge, or the recommendations of candid friends, directed him—in many cases not knowing, in all cases not caring, what their party connections had been. In several instances, he selected men who had made themselves conspicuous by their hostility to him for important commands, not to secure valuable services or to conciliate formidable opposition—for the *men* were nothing, or worse—but solely to give the most unequivocal proof possible of his determination to forget party, and all its sympathies, that he might consummate the great work of the people. He deemed it more important that the people should see that he gave himself up wholly to their unselfish movement, and thus establish confidence in his disinterestedness, than that he should refuse commissions to a few trifling men whose incompetence or disaffection would speedily vacate their commands for better men. His complete disregard of party provoked no little censure from some of his friends, who either could not see or could not appreciate a purpose that rose higher than party advantages. He thus gave official form and effective strength to popular feeling. And it was against this feeling, so wonderfully exhibited, so completely consolidated in the military policy of the State, that the disloyal element had to work. Another influence co-operated with the policy of the Governor to strengthen loyal feeling in Indiana. The first campaign in Western Virginia—the only one which either produced or promised a result during the first three months of the war—was carried on largely by Indiana troops, and planned and conducted by an Indiana General, and its progress to complete victory was impeded by no defeat or disaster. Though General MCCLELLAN was in command of the Department, he was not present in the field, and had little or nothing to do with the campaign till General MORRIS had brought it too near a successful close to be defeated. The credit of the first success of the war was thus felt to be largely shared by Indiana, and State pride came to the help of patriotism to crush disloyalty out of sight.

But against all these influences the disloyal element maintained a secret strength that soon showed itself in formidable activity. The success in Western Virginia was soon forgotten in the disaster at Bull Run, in the blockade of Washington, in the aimless skirmishes and frequent defeats, and in the long and unaccountable idleness of the Army of the Potomac. Disloyalty grew in courage during this period of feebleness and inaction. The Government Departments, for a generation filled or controlled by the South, were infested with rebel sympathizers who furnished the enemy information of every movement or purpose of our forces. We planned nothing that was not revealed within the day, and attempted nothing that was not fully prepared for and thwarted. Our Generals were in many cases recent companions or schoolfellows of rebels, and when they were not seduced by social memories and influences into betraying their trust, were too often easily softened into forgetting the duties it imposed. The President was new to his place and to the agencies he must use in the Nation's exigency. He could not know, and consequently could not remove, the spies that swarmed about him. Constant rebel successes, produced by such causes, inspired confidence in final success. When so much had been done, could not the rebels reasonably look for more? Disloyalty began to speak out in sneers and doubts and disparaging suggestions. Growing bolder, it condemned the war and arraigned the constitutionality of the military measures of the Government. It abused Mr. LINCOLN. It charged corruption wherever it could create distrust or disaffection. It began to hold meetings and declare resolutions. It sent private assurances to relatives and friends in the army that the war was a failure, and that desertion was a duty. It was already active and widespread, when the disastrous result of MCCLELLAN's Richmond campaign, following a year of inaction and imbecility, made it open, vehement and dangerous. The arrests of notorious traitors and spies were denounced as "illegal" and "tyrannical." County and local meetings were held in many parts of the State, which declared the war an "abolition crusade," a "cruel" and "unnecessary war against the rights of the South"; the President as a "tyrant" and "usurper" for prosecuting it, and the soldiers "minions," "hirelings" and "LINCOLN dogs" for fighting it. Associations to resist obnoxious laws were formed. Deserters were protected from arrest. Secret treasonable societies were organized, and had, before the beginning of the year 1863, acquired strength enough to make a formidable party and threaten the adhesion of the State to the National Government. They possessed power sufficient to control the Legislature in that year. Dissatisfaction, even among the most loyal, with the feeble conduct of the war, its growing burthens, and the seemingly growing distance of a favorable termination, had added to the disloyal element, in opposition to the National and State administrations, a large amount of strength which had not the least sympathy with it. And thus it was that Disloyalty, deeming itself the impelling motive of all dissatisfaction and opposition, took the foremost place in the Legislature, and dictated the policy of the session.

LEGISLATIVE OBSTACLES TO THE WAR

The anti-war resolutions of local meetings, the declarations of the more indiscreet members of disloyal societies, "that they meant to take the military power out of the hands of the Governor," and the constant denunciation by disloyal newspapers, of every act by which the National Government had sought to protect itself against treason in its own house, indicated very plainly what the course of the disloyal element of the Legislature would be. It is but just to say, that though the course attempted, failed of its object, it vehemently struggled to fulfill its promise.

Rejection of Governor Morton's Message—The first exhibition of the spirit of this element, was made in connection with the communication of the Governor's Message [January 9, 1863]. That document[1] was as important a one as was ever prepared by any state executive for a Legislature. It contained an account of the action of the State authorities, from the commencement of the war, a period of nearly two years; it suggested necessary measures for the better care of our soldiers' families; it recommended important steps, the value of which was fully demonstrated the following summer, for improving the efficiency of the State Militia; it exhibited the civil, as well as military condition of the State, as need-

[1] Given in Terrell, *Report,* 1, Appendix, Doc. 114:310-17.

ing prompt and judicious legislation. It was just what the Legislature needed, and should have been anxious to obtain. On the first day of the session (January 8th, 1863) both branches were organized, and the "General Assembly" fully and formally established. Committees were appointed by both branches to notify the Governor of the fact and to learn when he would deliver his message. He replied that he would deliver it on Friday afternoon (the day following the organization of both Houses, as had been the custom) at any hour the Legislature might designate. At two o'clock the Senate was invited to repair to the hall of the House to hear it. A reply from the President was returned soon after, stating that there was no quorum in the Senate, and that body could not attend. A committee of two was directly appointed by the House to notify the Governor of the condition of the Senate, the resolution adding quite cavalierly, that "the House was unable to say when it could hear the message." Thus warned of the probability that the delivery of his message, in the usual way, might be delayed for days, or deferred altogether, the Governor followed the example of the President of the United States, and of the Governors of very many of the States, and sent it in printed form, by the proper officer, at the usual time, to each body separately. This action filled every requirement both of law and courtesy. The accidental absence of a quorum in the Senate no more affected the existence of the General Assembly than a temporary adjournment. It could be lawfully and formally communicated with by the Governor, in any mode, that any other officer or citizen could communicate with it. The requirement of the Constitution, that the Governor should "give information touching the condition of the State to the General Assembly," no more compelled the personal attendance of the Governor, or the presence of both branches at the same time, at the delivery of the message, than the provision that the people may apply "to the General Assembly for redress of grievances" requires that every petition shall be presented and read by its authors in joint convention. Yet controlled by the disloyal spirit which had grown so strong and defiant, and anxious to signalize its hostility to the Governor and its contempt for the policy he had pursued with distinguished success, the House of Representatives determined, by a vote of 61 to 32, that the message should "not be received," and should be "returned to await the further action of the General Assembly." The pretexts (for there were no reasons) for this action were, that the absence of a quorum from the Senate made the attendance of that body and a joint convention impossible; and that the Constitution required the message to be delivered to the "General Assembly," and there was no General Assembly in session at the time; in other words, unless both houses are in session at the same time, there is no General Assembly, and neither body can act. This construction was simply nonsensical, because the Governor can and does send special messages to either house, or to both houses, frequently during a session, and no thought is entertained of a joint convention to receive them. There is no law or reason demanding a joint convention, or simultaneous session of both houses, to receive a message at the beginning of a session, more than to receive one at the middle or end of it. The Constitution does not require both houses to be in session at the same time, to constitute the General Assembly, or to make its branches capable of action. If it did, the General Assembly would die, or its branches become powerless, with every adjournment of either branch that did not exactly correspond with the adjournment of the other. So unwarranted a rejection of a document, so important as a Governor's Message, and in this case of such peculiar importance, is sufficient to show the spirit that animated the opponents of the war. Committees were subsequently appointed by both Houses, to learn when the Governor would deliver the message, in the usual way. He refused to stultify himself by admitting, by a personal delivery in joint convention, that the first was illegal. He notified the House Committee that he had done his duty, and should do nothing further in the matter. As there was no quorum in the Senate on the first delivery, he sent a second copy to that body, by the Committee, on the 21st of January. But it was never read in either house. The House paid no attention to it, except to treat its author with as much contumely as the rules of deliberative bodies would allow. On the 14th of January, a resolution was introduced into the House, declaring that Governor MORTON "had neglected to deliver his annual Message to the General Assembly"—a deliberate falsehood—and, "therefore, that the House adopt the exalted and patriotic sentiments contained in the message, lately delivered to the Legislature of New York, by his excellency HORATIO SEYMOUR." Against this scandalous proceeding, a number of members, belonging to the majority, not entirely corrupted or controlled by the disloyal element, joined with the friends of the Governor, and defeated it. But the next day a joint resolution was adopted in the House, by a vote of 52 to 35, tendering to Governor SEYMOUR the thanks of the General Assembly of Indiana for his message, and this insult to Governor MORTON, for it was no less and intended to be nothing else, was concurred in by the Senate. In effect the opposition to the war, having rejected Governor MORTON'S message, recognized that of another man in its stead, but in a less offensive manner than that proposed by the resolution of the day before. The Governor had distinguished himself by his energy and success in supporting the war, and the sympathizers with the rebellion saw no more satisfactory way to express their hostility to the war than to contemn its most ardent and efficient advocate.

Arrests of Rebel Sympathizers.—The disloyal spirit which on the second day of the session kicked the Governor's message out of the House, showed itself on the first day in the Senate by refusing to accept a resolution declaring that "the suppression of the rebellion, and the restoration and preservation of the Union of all the States, is the great and paramount object of loyal citizens, and that the members of this Legislature will vote for no man for office who is not in favor of a vigorous prosecution of the war, and is not unalterably opposed to the severance of any State or States from the Union." The vote against this simple declaration of loyalty was 27 to 22. In the House on the same day a similar declaration was refused and buried hopelessly by being referred to the Committee on Federal Relations, by a vote of 58 to 38. Yet immediately afterwards a resolution, laying the basis for an attack upon the Government for arresting traitors and spies, was adopted. On the day following, a preamble and resolution were introduced declaring that "many citizens of this State had been arrested by the authority of the General Government, and confined in military prisons and camps without public charges being preferred against them, and without any opportunity being allowed them to learn or disprove the charges made or alleged against them, and refused a trial, there being no obstruction to the constitutional authority of the Government in this State," and that "the General Assembly denounce all such arrests as acts of tyranny, as flagrant violations of the rights of the people, and demand that such arrests shall hereafter cease." The arrests in all cases were of men who had either been detected in treasonable correspondence with the rebels, or whose sympathy with the rebellion and defiance of the Government were notorious. Yet these denunciations of efforts which were as purely for self-preservation, and as palpably forced upon the Government, as any act ever was, were adopted, under the previous question, by a vote of 58 to 40 [30].

Not content with two exhibitions of sympathy with spies and traitors on two successive days, the adoption of this resolution was immediately followed by the introduction of a series, referring to the same matter, and made still more false and offensive. It stated that certain rights were guaranteed by the Constitution; that "we have witnessed within the past twenty months the violation of all these provisions, by means alike arbitrary, violent, insulting and degrading to a degree unknown to any government on earth, except those avowedly and notoriously wicked, cruel and despotic"; that "the representatives of the people in their legislative capacity deem it their first duty to ascertain the facts connected with the criminal usurpations and wrongs which have been practiced by political arrests, in order to give those who have unlawfully made them, or caused them to be made, the prominence to a position of lasting infamy their conduct merits," and concluded with the appointment of a committee of seven to examine into the alleged arrests, and to report a bill "adequate to protect the people" from them. This was adopted by a vote of 60 to 26. The committee thus appointed spent a large amount of money, examined such witnesses as suited their purpose to create hostility to the Government and to the war, and made a report, of which five thousand copies were published, which, for the credit of their intelligence and self-respect, the signers, who did not assist in writing it, should labor assiduously to destroy. Two or three specimens of its style will suffice to show its character. On page 11—"The United States Marshal, when appealed to, *folds himself more warmly in the flowing cloak of his own luxury,* and with a view to shift the responsibility, he wags his head ominously, and points these outraged citizens to the modern CALIGULA and his willing satraps, who now inhabit the *ancient metropolis of republican liberty."* The officers making arrests are denounced (page 8) as "ambitious adventurers, strutting their brief hour on the stage, *without identity* and without responsibility." The efforts of Congress against the rebellion are thus described (page 21):

> When the nation was bleeding at every pore, when one million of our brothers were engaged in mortal strife, when hoof of fire and sword of flame were scourging the land and making our rivers run red and thick with blood, these remorseless *plunderers* and *robbers* were engaged in schemes of *self-aggrandizement,* and in devising measures to increase our distractions in the States not in rebellion.

INTERNAL STATE TROUBLES 307

Rhetoric like this is worthy of the cause of disloyalty in which it was employed.

On the same day that the two denunciations of the arrests of mischievous rebel-helpers were adopted, a resolution was offered in the Senate, declaring that

> Loyal men do not endorse manifestly despotic acts of the Government, but hold it to be the duty of every citizen of the United States to support the constituted authorities, and in this period of rebellion we will *cheerfully submit to any acts of the General and State Governments, the object of which is the maintenance of the integrity of the Union,* and the *supremacy of the law,* though the act should work detriment to the individual, and that as citizens we should be *as ready to perform our duty to our country,* as we are to assert our rights and privileges.

This was sent away to die in the Committee on Federal Relations. The denunciatory resolutions were adopted at once.

On Friday, the 16th, a resolution was offered in the House setting forth the declaration of JEFFERSON DAVIS that "the West was preparing to secede from the East"; and stating that the Grand Jury of the United States Court[2] had discovered "the existence of a secret political organization held together by horrible and wicked oaths, and having for its purpose the assistance and encouragement of the Southern Confederacy, and the formation of a Northwestern Confederacy with its ultimate annexation to the Southern Confederacy"; and appointing a Committee of five to investigate the matter, and to report what measures should be taken "to protect the Government from the unlawful acts of these treasonable associations." The same House had a few days before voted to investigate and provide against the repetition of the arrests of rebel sympathizers and open enemies of the Government, but *it refused to investigate* the existence and

---

[2] The report of the Grand Jury of the U. S. District Court, District of Indiana, May, 1862, on "Secret Treasonable Organizations in Indiana," is given in Terrell, *Report*, 1, Appendix, Doc. 90: 295-96.

character of secret societies sworn to assist the rebels, by a vote of 57 to 35. On the 20th, another resolution to investigate these societies was offered and after a debate, extending over two days, was killed by a vote of 53 to 36. This was final. The House never disturbed the treasonable societies by a word.

On the 10th of February, a joint resolution was introduced in the House "protesting against the passage of any bill by Congress indemnifying the President or those acting under him from liability to answer for arbitrary arrests," and directing our Congressmen to oppose such bills. This protest had, and could have, no possible effect in holding the President or his officers to liability for arrests in this State, but it could in two ways show the rebels the disposition of their friends: First. As a public declaration that the President should be made to pay damages to every rebel and sympathizer whom he should arrest. Second. By encouraging juries, composed of members of treasonable Orders, to give verdicts for such damages, so that it might be published to the world that, in Indiana, the President or his officers had been punished in damages for arresting notorious supporters and friends of the rebellion. The knowledge of the existence of such a spirit in the North, in strength enough to control the Legislatures of the several States was far more precious to the rebels than any mere military assistance could have been.

Peace Propositions.—After rejecting the Governor's message, denouncing the arrests of rebel sympathizers and spies, and preparing the way for the State laws to obstruct such action in future and thus bring the State into collision with the General Government, the disloyal element proceeded to exhibit its spirit and designs still more unequivocally. On Tuesday, the 13th day of January (the session began on the 8th) an elaborate political essay, in the form of a preamble and series of resolutions, was introduced in the Senate, which with many counterbalancing declarations, and many suggestions of unconstitutional and indefensible action on the part of the Government in prosecuting the war, declared it the duty of the Legislature to sustain the Union and the State and National Governments, but concluded with the unequivocal avowal, which was the animating spirit and aim of all that preceded it, that the Senate was in favor of "compromise and concession," and that "the party in possession of the Government had adopted the war policy, though the experiment had been attended with but little advantage." The astounding falsehood that the Government "had adopted the war policy," as if it had been left to choose, and was the assailant instead of the assailed, coupled with the declaration that "concessions" should be made to those who had, without provocation, made war upon it, shows conclusively the feelings of the disloyal element of the Legislature.

On the following day, the 14th, a long preamble and series of resolutions were offered in the House, stating that the Government "had falsified its pledges," and "under the tyrant's plea of military necessity had usurped powers unwarranted by the Constitution and unsanctioned by the law, destroying all safeguards of freedom and independence"; that the President's Emancipation Proclamation was not permitted to be discussed, as the suspension of the writ of *habeas corpus* was proclaimed purposely to prevent such discussion, "thereby crippling free speech and discussion upon his abolition policy while he might wield the largest army the world ever saw for the purpose of accomplishing his *hellish* scheme of emancipation without regard to State laws, constitutions or reserved rights"; and that "the late elections in Illinois, Indiana, Ohio, New Jersey, Pennsylvania and New York, by the triumph of conservatism over fanaticism, have demonstrated that the people utterly repudiate and condemn the abolition policy of the Administration, and regard his (the President's) unprecedented usurpations of power as a giant stride towards military despotism," and concluding with the resolution, that "while the President persists in his abolition policy in the conduct of the war," etc., "Indiana *will not voluntarily con-*

tribute another man or another dollar, to be used for such wicked, inhuman and unholy purposes." Only perspicacity sharpened by rebel sympathies, could see that setting free the slaves of men warring against the Government—thus making persons, as God made them, of what had before been property—was an "unholy or inhuman" act; and as the emancipation measure was a deadly blow at the rebellion, and operated only in rebel States, not in loyal slave States, opposition to it could have had no motive but that of sympathy with the rebellion. An effort to "table" this proclamation of hope to the rebels was defeated.

On the next day, the 15th, resolutions were offered declaring that "the creation of the State of West Virginia was a breach of the Constitution of Virginia" (as if any obligation rested upon the Government to regard the Constitution of a State in active and implacable hostility to it, after the State itself had repudiated that Constitution and adopted another) —"and of the Nation, and betrays the deliberate purpose of the Administration and the majority in Congress"—both supporting the war—"to set aside the Constitution and establish upon the common ruins of the Union and the sovereignty of the States a revolutionary government, monarchical and military in its character, and in which all the great guarantees of civil liberty will be known no more forever"; that a national convention of all the States should be held at Louisville, Kentucky, to adjust our national difficulties; and that there should be "a cessation of hostilities" to allow such a convention to be held. Of course, the supporters of these resolutions knew, just as well as did the rebels themselves, that "a cessation of hostilities" would be used, and could be offered, for no other purpose than to renew strength for the war against the Government. A motion to lay them on the table was *defeated* by a vote of 61 to 30.

On the same day, in the same body, another resolution was offered instructing our Senators and requesting our Representatives in Congress, to take measures to suspend hostilities, and to call a National Convention.

On the same day, in the same House, as stated in the "Brevier Reports," a joint resolution was introduced "condemning the war, *but not the rebellion,*" which, instead of being peremptorily and indignantly rejected, was sent to the Committee on Federal Relations.

On the day following, the 16th, a petition of sundry citizens of Sullivan county was presented in the same body, and *referred*—not spurned, as any loyal body would have spurned it—urging that *"not one man nor one dollar, be voted to prosecute this infernal abolition war."*

On the same day, in the same House, a series of resolutions was offered, declaring that "he who is not for his country, and his whole country, under all circumstances, is against his country"; that "any word, act, or deed, which is calculated to create divisions and dissensions in the North, and please the rebels, should be condemned and discouraged by every patriot in the land"; and that "the House heartily sanctions and indorses the patriotic sentiments of the last speech made by Hon. STEPHEN A. DOUGLAS, at Chicago, Illinois." The House, instead of adopting so plain a declaration of fidelity to the Government as this, referred it to the Committee on Federal Relations, and *refused* to indorse the sentiments of Mr. DOUGLAS.

On the same day a joint resolution was introduced declaring that "the State of Massachusetts, with a population only about 120,000 smaller than that of Indiana, had been required to furnish only 60,000 soldiers, while Indiana had furnished 102,700"; that "the draft had been rigidly and mercilessly enforced in Indiana, while it was not yet completed in Massachusetts"; and demanding of Congress an inquiry into the causes of "this discrimination in favor of Massachusetts." There could be no other motive for this declaration and demand than a purpose to excite hostility to Massachusetts, as a State favored at our expense, and to the General Government, as willing to show such favoritism—for the statements were monstrous and notorious falsehoods. The draft had not been "mercilessly" enforced here, as everybody knew, for there were only 17,899 men drafted in the State during the whole war, and up to January, 1863, only 3,001 had been drafted—the State's quota having been made up of volunteers almost entirely.[3] Massachusetts, as shown by a detailed statement, made by Governor ANDREW, had furnished, in proportion, as many men as Indiana, allowing for the large number of her citizens who were engaged in the Navy, serving the country quite as efficiently as they could in the army. On the second reading, attempts were made to inquire into the truth of the statements as to the action of Massachusetts, and to strike out the false declaration as to the "merciless enforcement of the draft" here, but all were instantly voted down. A more conspicuous exhibition of mean spite and malignant disloyalty could not have been made, and can not be found in the records of any nation on the globe. On the 7th of February, the resolution failed for want of a constitutional majority, the vote standing forty-two for to eighteen against it.

On the same day, a joint resolution, with a preamble, was introduced in the same body, declaring that "those invested with authority were unable to compose the differences and avert the disasters of the country," and, therefore, a National Convention should be called, to be held in Louisville, on the 4th of July following, "to take into consideration such meas-

---

[3] Indiana's draftees and volunteers were as follows [Terrell]:

Drafted men and substitutes, call of August 4, 1862	3,001
Drafted men and substitutes, call of July 18, 1864	12,474
Drafted men and substitutes, call of December 19, 1864	2,424
Total drafted men and substitutes during the war	17,899
Total volunteers furnished by the state during the war	190,438
GRAND TOTAL	208,367

ures as may best promote peace among the people and union among the States"; that the President "should cause hostilities to cease from and after the first Monday of April until the first Monday in August next, if compatible with public safety"; that the voters of each legislative district should, on the first Monday of April, elect delegates to meet at Indianapolis on the first Tuesday of May; and that such convention of State delegates should elect delegates to the National Convention.

On Monday, the 19th, a preamble and resolutions were offered in the House, declaring it to be "manifest that peace could never be restored by the sword, and that a continuance of the war, under the present policy of the Administration, must eventuate in the utter ruin and decay of our free, renowned and mighty Nation," and that "the seceded States should be received back into the Union on a *liberal compromise*, granting them ungrudgingly all their constitutional rights and guarantees as equal, independent and sovereign States, with such *additional safeguards* as may be necessary to protect them in those rights." Giving "additional guarantees" to States which had thrown away what they already had, and were fighting to destroy all that the loyal States had, will strike most men of average brains as being about as "liberal" as the most cowardly or treacherous men anywhere could ask.

On the same day, in the same body, a resolution was introduced against the policy pursued "in this *unnatural* civil war," that is, "unnatural" on the part of the Government, as "*repugnant* to the Constitution, and in *open violation* of the rights of the several States," and declaring that the House was "opposed to the prosecution of any war, the objects of which are to interfere with domestic relations," that is, with slavery.

On the 27th a series of preambles and resolutions was introduced in the Senate declaring that "the present civil war" was forced upon the country "by the wicked and fanatical factions of the *North* and South"—thus laying no more blame upon those who began the war than upon those who did not;—that "it was filling the land with widows and orphans"—"bankrupting the Government and oppressing the people with taxation beyond their ability to bear"—"destroying the productive industry of the laboring man"—"filling the Northern section with a vagabond and servile race to compete with, or prey upon, the industry of the white man"—"imposing unequal burdens and commercial restrictions upon different portions of the North, sapping the foundations of religion, morality and public virtue; corrupting rulers; destroying personal liberty under the tyrant's plea of necessity; and obliterating from the hearts of the people the spirit of nationality and brotherhood"; that "war is no remedy for disunion"; and that "under the present and recent policy of the Cabinet at Washington arms can never restore the Union." Therefore, in view of these declarations, it was resolved that "we are opposed to a war for the liberation of slaves, and, while that policy is maintained by the Administration, the highest dictates of patriotism impel us to withhold from it our support." ("Patriotism" that would leave the Government unsupported, that rebellion might destroy it, rather than see four millions of slaves set free, and given the right to their own bodies, families and labor, is a product unknown to any age or country but this.) It was also resolved, that "no Union can be maintained until fanaticism on the negro question, North and South, is eradicated"; that "the people of the North must yield up the heresy of Abolitionism or the blessings of the Union"; "Abolitionism and the Union are incompatible"; "Abolitionism is moral treason"; "No patriot can be an Abolitionist." The North is told what it must yield to preserve the Union, but *nothing* is said of *what the South must yield*. "Abolitionism is moral treason," but nothing is said of the treason of capturing mints, arsenals and forts, confiscating Northern debts, or demanding the extension of slavery into territory made forever free by solemn compact. The Union, we are left to infer, is incompatible with Northern fanaticism, but entirely compatible with Southern fanaticism. Northern extremes of sentiment are "moral treason," but Southern extremes are merely injudicious outbursts of patriotic feeling. It was also resolved "that the interests of the white race, as well as the black, demand that the condition and locality of the latter should not be interfered with, and a war, or legislation, or Presidential proclamation, to free the negroes are acts of flagrant violation of the Constitution, and a wicked disregard of the people's voice, and of the best interests of the country, and should be constitutionally resisted by an outraged people." It was also resolved that "the accursed system of arrests"—for aiding the rebellion—"shall cease in the State," and the Legislature declares the "unalterable determination" to maintain the rights invaded by the suspension of the writ of *habeas corpus,* and by the consequent interference with rebel spies and sympathizers, "at every hazard of blood and treasure." It was finally resolved, that our Congressmen be urged and instructed, *"First,* To procure an armistice of at least six months for the purpose of testing the probability of a permanent peace on the basis of the Union; *Second,* To pass a law calling a convention of all the States to consider the state of the country and to devise some plan of settlement by which the Union shall be restored." The "six months' armistice" would enable the rebels to recover from their losses, and prepare for a more vigorous war, while it would keep up the expenses without result and depress the spirit of the North. It was just the thing the rebels wanted.

On the 29th, in the Senate, a fresh encouragement of the rebels was introduced, which declared, "that it was the *imperative duty* of the Chief Executive of the Nation to *proclaim,* and, we therefore, for and in the name of the people of Indiana *demand,* the establishment as soon as practicable of an *armistice,* to the end that a convention of all the States may be held for the adjustment of our national difficulties"; also, "that Congress should labor to provide for such a convention," and in the event that Congress fails to provide for such a convention, "we hereby, in the name of the people of Indiana, invite each and every State in the Federal Union, including the so-called Confederate States, to meet delegates from the State of Indiana in convention at Nashville, Tennessee, on the first Monday, being the first day of June, 1863, each State to send as many delegates as shall equal the number of Senators and Representatives in Congress"; that, for the purpose of carrying out these objects, there should be elected on the first Monday of April, thirteen delegates from the State at large to represent Indiana in that convention, unless Congress should provide for such a convention, in which case the delegates should represent the State in the latter convention; and that if Congress should not provide for a convention the delegates should be paid five dollars per day, and five cents per mile of travel, from the State Treasury. The only feature that distinguishes this from the other propositions for a National Convention is, that it provides for the inauguration of a government, in derogation and defiance of the Constitutional Government; takes the affairs of the nation out of the hands of Congress and the President and puts them into the hands of a body unknown to any law, and thus overturns the Constitution and the Government.

The spirit in which the more determined adherents of the rebel cause acted may be judged from some of the declarations made in the debate on February 10 upon a proposition of the loyal members to create a committee to adjust differences and secure harmonious action on two points: First. The powers and duties of the Governor. Second. The prosecution of the war, and the status of INDIANA as connected therewith. One member said: "This proposition came from the wrong quarter. It reminded him of the fable of the rooster and the horses. The rooster said, 'Gentlemen, don't let us tread on each other's toes.' *If the minority* don't want the majority to tread on their toes, *let them get out of the way.*" Another said, the proposition was idle, *"because it was very well understood by the majority what they would do and the time when it would be done.* The Committee would tend to delay action." Another said, "The resolution was the height of tomfoolery. *The views of both parties were known.* They could never agree on any important question."⁴ That is, the disloyal element would never agree as to the loyal *status* of Indiana in the war, as to the prosecution of the war, or as to the powers of the Governor, whose office as Military Commander-in-Chief it had already been repeatedly declared should be taken from him, for these were the only questions the Committee were to consider. But the resolute rebel sympathizers could not carry all their associates with them and the proposition was adopted.

On the 27th of February resolutions were offered in the House of Representatives declaring that the session was nearly over and that prompt action must be taken to meet the demand for a cessation of hostilities, and, therefore, the Committee on Federal Relations were instructed to report, on the 4th of March following, a bill or joint resolution for a National Convention; for prompt action on the part of Congress in behalf of such a convention; "against the prosecution of the war for another day, or another hour, while the President adheres to his abolition policy"; and that "Indiana will not willingly furnish another man or another dollar for the further prosecution of this wicked and unnatural war (if the Administration is determined to further wage it in spite of the wishes of the people), unless it be explicitly understood that it shall be waged *solely* for the preservation of the Union, with all the rights, dignity and equality of the States unimpaired."

⁴ *Brevier Legislative Reports,* compiled by Ariel and William H. Drapier, 1863, pp. 133, 134.

Action in Regard to Soldiers—On the 16th of January, a joint resolution was introduced proposing to amend the Constitution of the State so as to allow soldiers in the field to vote. On the 4th of February, the Judiciary Committee, to which the proposition had been referred, reported that it was "inexpedient," and the soldiers were disfranchised, during the time of their perilous service, by a vote of 42 to 33.

On the 19th of January, a joint resolution was introduced in the House stating that "the Government had failed to pay the *soldiers* the *small pittance* which they have so richly earned, while the *officers* over them, as a general thing, have been *promptly paid,* and thus enabled to indulge in all manner of *luxury,* while the *poor, helpless privates* are compelled to suffer *privations and want,*" and that "Governor MORTON and President LINCOLN had seemingly *lost all sympathy and regard for white men in the ranks,* who are fighting the battles of their country, and give their entire sympathy to the negroes of the South, as is evidenced by *the fact* that they regard with apparent *indifference* their great neglect and many complaints," and demanding prompt payment for the men, and a "cessation of the discrepancy in favor of the officers." Like the Massachusetts resolutions, these statements were manufactured purposely and obviously to excite the hatred of the soldiers against their officers, and to prejudice them against the Government. More impudent falsehoods were never published or uttered. Portions of the army were not well paid, simply because paymasters frequently could not safely get to the more advanced positions. But in such cases, officers and men were alike unpaid, and the fact was well known to every member of the Legislature and to the author of these resolutions.

On the 10th of February, a joint resolution, previously introduced in the Senate, opposing the arming of negroes against the rebels, was reported back from the Committee on Federal Relations, with a recommendation that it pass. It declared that "the people of the State had over and over again decided against any interference with slavery." A motion was made to amend this statement, as it now applied to a state of WAR, and the people of Indiana had never decided that, in case of war, slavery should not be interfered with. This motion was voted down by twenty-five to nineteen, thus making emphatic the judgment of the supporters of the resolution that *even in war,* and when employed to the utmost against the Government and the Union, *slavery was to be sacred* from any interference by those it was used to destroy. If any attitude of equal servility to an institution so infamous as slavery can be found elsewhere in all history—making slavery so sacred that even when employed in war against us, and when all other property would be taken without hesitation, IT must be preserved—it must be when more of the world's history is discovered than anybody has yet learned. A motion to add to the resolution a declaration in favor of a "vigorous prosecution of the war" was amended by the condition that *"the President shall immediately withdraw his Emancipation Proclamation."* That is, the disloyal element of the Senate would not sustain a vigorous prosecution of the war unless the President would leave slavery safe, sacred, and uninjured, let it do what it might against the Union. This scandalous amendment, and complete nullification of the declaration in favor of the war, was adopted by twenty-four to eighteen. But all this, as devotedly subservient to the rebellion as it could be, was not enough. A proposition was made to amend the joint resolution by declaring: 1st. "That notwithstanding there may be differences of opinion in regard to the policy of some of the war measures of the Administration, yet the State of Indiana, without distinction of party, still unwavering in her devotion to the National Government, again reiterates her *pledges of fidelity to the common cause,* and will with all her energies, with all her power, and all her means, *press steadily forward in the war to put down the rebellion,* and restore the Union and the Constitution, with the distinct understanding that the same is not prosecuted for any sectional, political or antislavery purpose." 2d. "That our Congressmen be requested to vote for all laws having the effect to *lighten the labor, protect the health, and save the lives of white soldiers,* by employing acclimated persons of African descent wherever their services can be made useful and safe, having proper regard to their capacity, previous relation to the whites, and the antipathies of race, condition and color, in framing such laws." And this, because it declared for a steady prosecution of the war and suppression of—not compromise with—the rebellion, and because it demanded the employment of negroes where their services could save the lives or health of white soldiers, was *voted down* by 24 to 20.

On the 13th, a second attempt was made to amend the resolution against employing negroes in the army, by declaring— 1st. "That the negro troops should be employed in departments separate from white"; and 2d. "That no rank higher than Captain should be conferred upon persons of African descent, nor should such persons, in any instance, be placed in command over white men." But even this exceedingly moderate approval of the employment of negro soldiers was too much for those who objected to any means of resistance to the rebellion, and it was voted down by 25 to 20.

On the 12th of February, the disloyal element exhibited its feelings toward the soldiers in another and still more offensive form. The news of the efforts already spoken of, to bring about an armistice, and a convention to end the war by compromise with enemies who had made the war without provocation, had reached the army. The soldiers knew, as well as did the legislators who made the propositions, that the effect of an armistice would be to give the rebels the chance to strengthen themselves, and to renew the war with greater advantages, and they held meetings, and, as citizens of the State as well as soldiers, denounced such efforts. The resolutions of the Sixth, Fifteenth, Seventeenth, Twenty-Second, Twenty-Ninth, Thirty-Second, Thirty-Fourth, Thirty-Seventh, Thirty-Ninth, Fortieth, Forty-Second, Forty-Fourth, Fifty-First, Fifty-

Seventh, Fifty-Eighth, Seventy-Second, Seventy-Third, Seventy-Fifth, Seventy-Ninth, Eighty-Second, Eighty-Sixth, and One Hundred and First regiments, were presented in the Senate on the 12th.[5] They were immediately assailed by the disloyal element as having been concocted at home and sent to the army, but were finally referred to the Committee on Federal Relations. The resolutions from the Sixty-Sixth and Ninety-Third regiments,[6] at Corinth, were treated still more harshly. It was moved "to reject them"; "to reject the whole batch"; "they were an insult to all who favored an armistice." The memorial, with the resolutions, *was* rejected by a vote of 28 to 18, as disrespectful, because it denounced as "traitors" those who proposed to give the rebels, by an armistice, four, five, or six months for recuperation. The petition of disloyal men of Sullivan county, which denounced the war as an "infernal abolition war," and begged "that not one man nor one dollar be voted to prosecute it," was deemed respectful, and kindly referred to a committee.

On the 19th of February, in the House of Representatives, a preamble, with resolutions, was introduced, reciting that a meeting of the Twenty-Seventh Indiana Regiment had been held a short time before near Stratford Court House, Virginia, in which it had been declared that two propositions for an armistice and a national convention, already set forth in this report, both introduced in the Senate, one on the 27th and the other on the 29th of January, "were nothing less than treason," and offering their services to the Governor to enforce the law against such conduct. The resolutions of the House denounced those of the regiment as "introducing party divisions in their most offensive forms"; "fomenting insubordination and tending to produce civil war at home"; and requested information of the Governor whether he approved them, and whether similar offers had been made by others.

[5] These resolutions and memorials are given in Terrell, *Report,* 1, Appendix, Docs. 147, 148:352-55.
[6] *Ibid.,* 1, Appendix, Doc. 149:355-56.

As a censure on the action of the regiment, the House resolutions were adopted by a vote of 50 to 29.

On the 28th of February, memorials were presented in the Senate from the Nineteenth and Twentieth Indiana Regiments, protesting against the attempt, then in progress in the Legislature, to take from the Governor all military power and subject him to a council of men opposed to the war; also protesting against an armistice, and denouncing the encouragement of desertion. They were severely censured as insults to the Legislature and the offspring of minds "prejudiced against the members." "Prejudice" there doubtless was, of exactly that kind to which the counsel for a felon alluded in his defense when he said, "He could not expect a favorable verdict, for the evidence had *prejudiced* the jury against his client."

Effect of these Efforts—Little direct effect was produced by any of these disloyal efforts in the Legislature, for none were completed into formal legislative acts. It is doubtful indeed if any expectation was seriously entertained of accomplishing a direct result. The real object, and that which *was* accomplished, lay aside from the obvious and natural effect of such measures. It was the assurance to the rebels of sympathy in the North, which could be depended upon to obstruct the loyal action of State governments; to decry and denounce every effort to prosecute the war; to weaken the army by exciting enmity between officers and privates; to alarm the people by fears of the hopelessness of crushing the rebellion by force; and to encourage secret organizations for resisting the laws in support of the war. *This was accomplished.* There were some thirty or forty propositions, in one form or another, denouncing the war, or the measures of the Government to prosecute it, or to protect itself from treason at home, made during the session; and *not one,* favoring the war, condemning the rebellion or sympathizing with the Government, came from any member of the disloyal faction. Those that were offered by loyal members were

INTERNAL STATE TROUBLES

voted down, or thrown aside. This action was full of consolation and encouragement to the rebels at Richmond. They saw even more hope in it than they did in the "situation" at Vicksburg, or in the East, hopeful as they seemed at that time, the "winter of our discontent," as it might with sadly just emphasis be called. The Richmond *Whig* of February 11th, about two weeks after the introduction of the two leading propositions for an armistice and national convention, those in the Senate of the 27th and 29th of January, said of them:

> We copy elsewhere an article, from an Indianapolis paper, with two sets of resolutions, which have been laid before the Indiana Legislature. The paper from which we copy (the *Journal*) is violently Republican. It pronounces the resolutions an ordinance of secession. *They have very much that flavor.* They are intensely bitter against the war and the objects for which it is waged, and urge an armistice of six months, and a national convention to settle all difficulties. In one set it is proposed, if the convention is not held, that Indiana shall act for herself. The furious denunciation of the resolutions by the Republican papers, constitutes their best recommendation, *and argues a redeeming spirit among the people of the North West. We of the Confederate States should do what is possible to encourage the growth and ascendancy of that spirit.*

In December, just before the Legislature met (but when the spirit which would control it, was fully understood, all over the country) JEFFERSON DAVIS said in a speech at Jackson, Mississippi, "out of this victory (that which Bragg was expected to gain at Murfreesboro) is to come *that dissatisfaction in the Northwest, which will drive our enemies from power in that section.* And then we see in the future the dawn: first, separation of the Northwest from the Eastern States, the *discord among them,* which will paralyze the power of both; THEN *for us, future peace and prosperity."*

In the Rebel Congress, the information of the disloyal attitude of so large a portion of the people of Indiana and the other Northwestern States, was welcomed as better news than any victory in the field. HENRY S. FOOTE, rebel Senator from Tennessee, introduced resolutions of congratulation upon the pleasing prospect thus afforded the rebellion, declaring that the rebel Congress *"sympathized most kindly, with those who have brought about this change in the North."* They also kindly held out offers of peace to such States as should separate from New England and unite with the South.

Expressions of pleasure at the sympathy exhibited by our Legislature, and by others, and in other modes, with the rebellion, were common in rebel papers and upon rebel tongues at this time, and the extracts quoted here are but samples of hundreds. The confidence derived from such assurances, that sooner or later, by political if not military successes, the rebellion would be completed, was one of the strongest motives to protract the war. Even when the storm of disaster that swept over the rebel States on the 4th of July, 1863, killed all hope of military success, it left green and growing the hope of the final ascendancy of those who had so frequently and heartily encouraged them to persevere. They had little to expect from their armies, but they had much to expect from a majority in Congress, disaffected and disloyal like the majority in our Legislature. And such a majority might be secured. It was not impossible. It was not even improbable; for at the same time the disloyal element obtained the command of our Legislature, it came within a very few votes of obtaining command of Congress. If we can conceive of such a majority in Congress as that which in our Legislature declared that "if the slaves of rebels were interfered with they would not vote a dollar or a man to prosecute the war"; which respectfully referred to a committee a petition of civilians declaring the war "an infernal abolition war"; which contemptuously rejected a resolution of soldiers declaring it treason to offer an armistice to the rebels; and which attempted to take the military power out of the hands of the Governor and put it into the hands of men, a majority of whom were sworn members of a secret treasonable society, we may easily conceive of a state of affairs which in a week would have terminated in the usurpation of military power by a rebel sympathizing committee of Congress, and in the surrender to the rebels of our Government and the substitution of theirs, with New England excluded. Therefore, the rebels had a better hope behind than that which MEADE scotched at Gettysburg, and GRANT crushed at Vicksburg. That hope they owed to the spirit which appeared and spoke in no equivocal language in the action of the Indiana Legislature of 1863, which has just been set forth. Two years of our struggle, and of our monstrous expenses, are due to that action, and to that of other bodies similarly inspired. If there had been no disloyal faction, and no sympathizing language in the North in and before the Summer of 1863; if all had been resolute to crush the rebellion; no sane mind can conceive it possible that the war would have continued till the fall. That it did continue is the act as much of the rebel sympathizers of the Indiana Legislature and its adherents and affiliated bodies, as of the rebels themselves.

Efforts to Deprive the Governor of Military Power—The encouragement given to the rebellion by repeated declarations of opposition to the war, and of a desire to terminate it by any concessions that would satisfy the rebels, was not to be left unsupported by more practical measures of obstruction. Throughout the election contest of 1862, intimations were frequently given by confident or indiscreet sympathizers with the rebellion, that if they were successful the military power of the State would be placed in hands that would use it differently from what Governor MORTON had done. "His tyranny," as they termed his energetic support of the war, "should be ended and the people left free to say and do what they pleased," that is, that resistance, by word or deed, to the war, should be no more restrained than loyal and cordial support of it. Secret societies, which had been in process of formation for months in all parts of the State, it was universally believed, were to be made the depositories of the State arms and constitute the force of the new military dispensation. The existence of these societies was not denied during the session of the Legislature,[7] but it was alleged that they were formed only for "home protection" against "arbitrary arrests," and, as was frequently and publicly declared before, "to protect themselves from the tax and the draft." As organizations, if not in opposition, at least not in sympathy, with the war or the Government, their existence was admitted both in and out of the Legislature, and was as well known as the existence of the war itself. The Grand Jury of the United States Circuit Court, in the Summer of 1862, ascertained from the examination of a large number of witnesses, who admitted their membership, that these societies were more flagrantly disloyal than popular suspicion had conjectured, and their report[8] of the 4th of August of that year startled the State with indisputable evidence that combinations of traitors, sworn to resist the war and every means to prosecute it, undermined nearly every community. The delivery of the State arms to such men and their employment in the military duties which might be required at home or on the border during the war would be equivalent to taking Indiana out of the national ranks and disabling her for all loyal action. While Governor MORTON retained the power conferred by the Constitution, such a measure, or any measure not in hearty support of the war, would be impossible. To take that power from him was, therefore, a necessary step to any policy which contemplated making the State an effective as well as sympathetic supporter of the rebellion. While he remained Commander-in-Chief and the depository of military authority, it was very certain that there would be no failure or relaxation of the exertions which had already won for the State and himself a very high and enviable standing in the records of the war. His promptitude, resolution, and sagacity would beat down disloyal resistance, and

[7] *Brevier Reports*, 1863, pp. 65, 76, 145, *et passim*.

[8] See report of the Grand Jury in Terrell, *Report,* 1, Appendix, Doc. 90:295-96.

rally the people to his side and to renewed efforts against the rebellion, unless he could be made a cipher in the State government. As already stated, it had been often intimated that he should be made a cipher, and in the House of Representatives, on the 6th of February, one of the most prominent of the disloyal faction admitted that this was the purpose of the majority. A member said, "I am informed that certain members of this House and of the Senate were recently in one of the Northern counties of the State, where the gentleman (the one alluded to) I understood, said he regarded President LINCOLN and Governor MORTON as despots and tyrants worse than those of Austria." The gentleman answered, *"That's so."* The other resumed, "I also understood that they (the majority), as far as the Executive of this State is concerned, intended to *shear him of his power* by the appointment of a Military Board, *who would take the military power out of his hands."* The gentleman answered, "That is nearly *correct*."[9] The purpose of the disloyal element of the Legislature, and of the disloyal secret societies, was thus well and widely known. Consequently, no one was surprised to learn that a resolution had been adopted in the House instructing the Military Committee to inquire into the expediency of so amending the Militia Law as to place the military power of the State in the hands of a majority of the following State officers: The Secretary, Auditor, Treasurer and Attorney General. One of the members who assumed, and was allowed, a sort of noisy prominence in the body, supported the resolution by declaring that "he was in favor of the Military Board taking out of the Governor's hands the military power. He would permit the Governor to be on the Board, but would put enough honest men on it to control it."

On the 17th day of February, bill No. 221, with the modest title of a "Bill providing for the organization of the Indiana Militia, for a military tax, and for other matters prop-

[9] *Brevier Reports,* 1863, p. 124.

erly connected with the militia of the State," was introduced in the House. Its title gave no indication of its real purpose. It was the measure so often threatened, and so important to the schemes of the disloyalists, which took from the Governor all military power, and put it in the hands of four State officers, three of whom were members of a Secret Order, sworn to resist the war and the Government, and to assist the rebellion. By section 11 these four State officers were constituted a "Military Board" to "recommend to the Governor suitable persons to be appointed officers of the militia, but said State officers were authorized to give such persons certificates that they had been chosen," which certificates should have *all the force and effect of commissions,* until commissions issued by the Governor be received." In other words, the certificate of the Board gave all necessary power to the officer, and the Governor's commission could be dispensed with entirely.

This provision placed the militia entirely in the hands of the Board. Section 13 gave to the Generals created by the Board, under section 11, the power to disband regiments or companies and take away their arms, without the assent of the Governor, in case of insubordination—that is, in case a regiment or company should not recognize officers appointed by the Board, and should recognize and obey those appointed by the Governor. This provision enabled the creatures of the Military Board to disband every loyal company in the State, and to take their arms and give them to the secret organizations which were to constitute the military force under the new system. Sections 22 and 23 took from the Governor all control of the State arms. The first gave "to the staff of the Major-General," a creature of the Board, the power "to call in all the arms and military accoutrements belonging to the State," which, when called in, "should be kept by the Assistant Quartermaster General, on the staff of the Major General," also a creature of the Board. The second required that orders for arms should be sent, not to the Governor, but "to the Assistant Adjutant General on the staff of the Major General," another creature of the Military Board, and "be approved by the officers of State." Thus the appointment of officers, the possession of arms, the distribution of arms, the preservation or disbandment of companies; in fact, the whole machinery of the State's military power, was taken out of the Governor's hands, and placed in the hands of men, a majority of whom were notoriously sympathizers with the rebellion. The unconstitutionality of the measure was not only obvious, but was so obvious, so obtrusive, that hardly a pretense of constitutionality was made for it. It was a revolutionary project in aid of the rebellion, and no impudence or ingenuity could make it anything else. Its supporters were resolute to drive it through. They treated the earnest protests and unanswerable arguments of the loyal members as contemptuously as they treated the Governor's message. As soon as the bill was read the first time, it was moved to suspend the rules and read it a second time, and 52 to 37 sustained this headlong policy. But it required two thirds, and the second reading was deferred. On the 19th of February it was read the second time and printed. It was thus brought fully before the public, and its character was exposed everywhere with such effect that some of the prominent members of the majority assured Governor MORTON, and very many private citizens, that it should not pass. But those who made it meant it, and did not mean to drop it, and still pressed its passage. It was a conspicuous illustration of the audacity of rebel sympathizers, that so defiant an outrage on the Constitution, perpetrated in aid of so causeless a rebellion, should be urged to completion with but little delay, and less apology. On the 25th of February, the bill was considered in Committee of the Whole, and reported back to the House, when eight amendments were proposed, which would have had the effect of making it constitutional and useless. The amendments were laid upon the table by a vote of 53 to 35. Then an attempt was made to refer it to the Judiciary Committee for examination of its constitutionality. This was voted down by 51 to 30, and then the gag of the "previous question" was put upon all debate by a vote of 53 to 16. And finally the bill was ordered to be engrossed by a vote of 52 to 17.

This action proved conclusively the determination of the disloyal faction to force their revolutionary project through at all hazards. The loyal members were too weak to resist successfully by ordinary parliamentary tactics, and unless they could devise means more effective than motions, arguments, and votes, they could expect nothing less than to see the Governor displaced by a Military Board, the arms in the hands of a secret disloyal Order, and the State's support of the war turned into apathy or resistance. The peril was imminent. The promises of those who had declared the bill should not pass were effectually broken by the vote that engrossed it. They were, in all probability, never meant to be kept. The loyal members had but one remedy. They must meet revolution in aid of the rebellion by revolution in aid of the Government. They accordingly left the hall of the House, and soon after left the city. The House was then without a quorum. They remained absent in the city of Madison till the end of the session, and thus defeated the attempt to turn the State into a rebel auxiliary. But, repeatedly during their absence, they proposed to the disloyal faction to return and complete whatever legislation was necessary for the ordinary administration of the State government, if the Military Board Bill were not pressed. That measure, they were resolved, should not pass, and if its supporters were resolved to sacrifice all other business to it, there was nothing more to be done. If they deemed it more important to press a bill for the withdrawal of the State from the war (which was the sure effect and undoubted purpose of this bill) than to provide for the ordinary wants and business of the State, the choice and its responsibility were theirs. They took the responsibility. One of them, in reply to a proposition to lay aside the Military Bill and take up other subjects, said: "We shall do nothing, if these propositions are made by authority, *for we will press these measures. We will press them."*[10] Each side adhered to its course. The supporters of the rebellion would not give up their measure. The loyal minority would not tolerate it. Thus failed, not only the Military Bill, but every other bill that had not been passed before the retirement of the loyal members. Thus the bills making appropriations to carry on the State government, to maintain the asylums and the penitentiaries, to pay hundreds of claimants who had done work or furnished goods for the State, all failed.

FINANCIAL EMBARRASSMENTS

The failure of the Appropriation Bills, which was the direct effect of the attempt to depose the Governor, left the State in a condition to which it would be difficult to find a parallel in any country. Engaged in a desperate war, with more than one hundred thousand men under arms, demands were constantly made by the General Government for more men to recruit or increase the forces in the field. Secret organizations, sworn to resist and embarrass every effort for the war, pervaded every county. Deserters, under the solicitations of friends who promised them protection, came skulking home by thousands. Bands of troops sent to arrest them were resisted, fired upon, or eluded. Officers employed in executing the draft laws were openly mobbed or secretly murdered. Local conflicts and collisions seemed every instant on the point of spreading into a domestic war. Prominent speakers traversed the State and the Northwest denouncing the Government and counseling resistance. Newspapers constantly deepened and poisoned the irritation which the necessities of war always create. Currency was falling, prices rising, and distress increasing. The war seemed to make little progress, and the end of the gloomy path we were treading appeared, both to sense and hope, far away. In this condi-

---

[10] *Brevier Reports,* 1863, p. 193.

tion of things, black and bloody enough, the Legislature met, and proceeded by scores of votes and resolutions to declare its distrust of the Government, its hostility to the war, and its disposition to concede what the rebels demanded. This was the military "situation." One more difficult to measure and provide for can hardly be conceived. It was more than enough for a strong and wise man to carry the State safely through such a storm. But in the midst of these perils, closing in ahead, pressing nearer on every side, she was left without means to pay her debts, preserve her credit, to carry on her most vital operations. To meet such a crisis, in a civil administration during such a stormy and perilous period in a military administration, is not often given to man to attempt, very rarely to accomplish.

Governor MORTON met the crisis with a decision and energy that showed he clearly understood its necessities, and was fully resolved to conquer them. The State Officers could be depended on for nothing but hindrances of whatever he attempted for the duty or credit of the State. Money must be raised to maintain the Asylums, or the inmates must be sent home. These institutions, if discontinued for two years, would be nearly ruined, and but little less difficult to restore than they were to establish. The Penitentiaries must be provided for or the convicts unloosed, or left unguarded to unloose themselves. The Indiana Arsenal, so important to the Government, must be carried on; the State militia, so often called into service to defend the border from rebel invasion and insurrection, must be paid; military expenses must necessarily be incurred in raising troops, for steamboats sent to relieve the sick and wounded with sanitary supplies, and to bring home the broken down and disabled, for special surgeons dispatched to the army and hospitals, for the support of the State military relief agencies, and other objects equally as essential. Even the traveling expenses of the Superintendent of Public Instruction, to enable him to perform his duties, must be advanced. But where was the money to come from? The Governor, in an address issued to the people of the State, May 10th, 1864, thus explains the course he felt compelled to pursue, and the plan resorted to, to overcome the difficulties by which he was surrounded:

In presenting the accompanying report of my Financial Secretary, it is proper that I should state, for public information, the reasons which induced me to establish a Financial Bureau, and assume the heavy responsibilities which were thus thrown upon me.

The Legislature of 1863 adjourned on the 9th day of March, without making any appropriations for defraying the ordinary and extraordinary expenses of the State Government. The former appropriations for the Benevolent Institutions, the Hospital for the Insane, Institute for the Blind, and Asylum for the Deaf and Dumb, had been nearly or quite exhausted. The Northern Prison had not only exhausted the appropriations hitherto made, but, by incurring a heavy debt in construction of buildings, had exhausted its credit also. More than one hundred thousand of our citizens had been sent to the field to assist in suppressing the rebellion, yet the only fund at my disposal, from which the contingent military expenses including the care and relief of the sick and wounded, could be paid, was a small remnant of the appropriation made in 1861. For the civil contingent expenses of the Executive Department there was no provision whatever. The Auditor and Treasurer of State, upon being consulted by me immediately after the close of the session, decided that not a single dollar, in the absence of Legislative appropriations, should be drawn from the public funds in the Treasury for these objects.

The alternatives thus presented to me, were, First—to allow the Benevolent Institutions to be closed, and permit the unfortunate inmates to be thrown back upon their respective counties, or upon the charities of the world for care and support; or, Second—to convene the Legislature in extra session, in the hope that the majority, who had full control, would pass the appropriation bills. To have closed the Asylums would have been a shame and disgrace, as well as a crime against humanity itself. To have called back the Legislature, after the majority for fifty days, during which time a quorum was present in each house, out of the fifty-nine days of the regular session, had failed and refused to bring forward and pass the appropriation bills, I believed would have been perilous to the public peace and dangerous to the best interests of the State.

In this contingency I determined to procure, if possible, sufficient money to carry on all the institutions of the State and keep the machinery of the government in motion. I accordingly established a Bureau of Finance, and appointed Colonel W. H. H. TERRELL, Financial Secretary. My success in procuring funds exceeded my expectations, and I am gratified to state that provision has been made for all the means which will likely be required to meet every proper demand up to the next regular meeting of the Legislature.

All the money required, and more, was readily obtained. Not a halt or jolt was felt in all the State machinery, and the work of the war never slackened a moment. For nearly two years the financial business of the State was thus carried on. Over one million of dollars was disbursed, and a Joint Committee of the Legislature appointed to investigate the books and vouchers, reported that every cent had been fully accounted for, and every expenditure economically and properly made. It will not be easy to find anywhere an instance of action more perfectly adapted to a great emergency than this. It filled every necessity and filled it at once, though there are few public men who would have dared to assume such enormous responsibility or who could have brought it to such a successful termination. It may appear a very easy thing *now* to resort to contributions when appropriations fail, and so it was very easy to make an egg stand on end when the way was once shown. But nobody but COLUMBUS happened to think of the way.

The Governor was not released from his worst difficulties by his "contributions" and his "Financial Bureau." A much greater in its consequences, if it were not met, was the payment of the interest on the State debt. No provision had been made for this any more than for other necessities. But wise and honest men thought that no especial provision was necessary for it, because the contract with the bondholders solemnly pledged the faith of the State for its payment, and fixed time, place and amount. This they held was a perpetual or continuing appropriation, and any other especially directed to the same object was superfluous. But the State officers, whatever they thought, acted upon a different construction of the law. They would not pay the interest, although the money was idly lying in the Treasury. The State Auditor would not draw for it, and the State Agent, afterwards better known as an active agent and tool of the rebels in Canada, declared that he would not pay it to the bondholders if it were sent to him. A case was got up between the State Auditor and the Sinking Fund Commissioners to test the question as to the legality of paying our debt, in time, place and amount, as solemnly agreed upon. Through a false entry, fraudulently imposed upon the Circuit Court of Marion County, the case was taken to the Supreme Court in time to allow a decision before the first installment, after the adjournment of the Legislature, became due. It was well understood that the Supreme Court would decide that the interest could not be lawfully paid, and that the decision, equivalent to repudiation for two years, would ruin the State's credit. The decision was made promptly, and precisely as was universally predicted. If Governor MORTON had been willing to accept the failure of the Legislature to make an appropriation as an irremediable evil, he would have done no more than Governor WILLARD did a few years before in allowing the Asylums to be closed.[11] If he, willingly or unwillingly, had accepted the decision of the Supreme Court as a full justification of his refusal to act in the matter, no man could have justly censured him. But he paid no regard to the excuses he might make for himself. He looked only to the credit of the State. He knew that the failure of the Legislature to make an appropriation, whatever it might do for him, would not keep the State's stocks from tumbling ten or twenty per cent. He knew that the decision of the Supreme Court, completely as

[11] When the General Assembly of 1857 broke up over the election of the U. S. Senator and qualification of some of its members, and as a result failed to pass an appropriation bill, Governor Willard was urged to call a special session. He refused, and the insane hospital and institution for the blind were closed for several months for lack of operating funds. Charles Zimmerman, "The Origin and Rise of the Republican Party in Indiana from 1854 to 1860," in *Indiana Magazine of History,* 13(1917):350-52.

it might protect him, would not shield the State from the sneers and reproaches that would follow an act of virtual repudiation. He set to work at once, with all his energy, to procure the money to pay the interest. And he succeeded. A liberal and loyal house in New York, which had long been identified with the interests of the State, advanced the money, and the State's credit was preserved.[12] If it had not been, it is difficult to imagine the condition in which the Legislature of 1863 would have left us. . . .

REVIEW OF LEGISLATIVE OBSTRUCTIONS

Glancing back over the record of the embarrassment created by the Legislature to the war, which has been set forth, it will not be difficult to collect into one view the main points from which emanated encouragement for the rebels or discouragement for loyal men. By denouncing as "inhuman tyranny" and "shameful cruelty" the military arrests of men known to be traitors; by demanding perfect freedom of speech and action for all who wanted to use either to assist the rebels; by declaring, in scores of resolutions, that the war was hopeless; by demanding an armistice, that the rebels might have time to recuperate; by proposing conventions to take negotiations for peace out of the hands of Congress and the Government; by refusing to investigate the charges, though based on the oaths of hundreds of their members, that secret disloyal societies were organized in aid of the rebellion in the State; by attempting to depose the Governor and place in his stead a Military Board of men pledged to oppose the war and the Government; by allowing the State's necessities and credit to go unprovided for rather than give up a flagrantly unconstitutional scheme to cripple her efforts for the war; and by other less conspicuous means, the disloyal element of the Legislature of 1863 gave to the rebellion more encouragement, and did more to prolong the war, than

[12] This was the firm of Winslow, Lanier & Company.

a reinforcement of ten thousand men could have done. Such action was a promise of all that the rebels desired, to be fulfilled whenever their friends obtained power. And the possession of power in several of the largest and strongest States was a promise full of cheering, that the power might soon be obtained in enough of the others to ride down the President, make peace, and install the rebellion in full command of the nation. This was something to fight and suffer for, and that the rebels did fight and suffer for nearly two years after all military success was hopeless is due to the exhortations and encouragements of such bodies as the Indiana Legislature of 1863.

EXPRESSIONS OF POPULAR FEELING AGAINST THE WAR

This action of the Legislature was not a reflection of the real feelings of a majority of the people. It was only the gross misuse of the power conferred by a temporary dissatisfaction with the war. Very many loyal men, who wished to rebuke what they regarded as a want of vigor or judgment on the part of the Government and some of its Generals, voted against those who were unconditionally pledged to go on with the war, and thus gave a majority to those who were either disloyal, or so far dissatisfied as to co-operate with disloyalists. Yet, that this action was a reflection of the real feelings of a large portion of the people will appear from the language of very many newspapers, orators, and public meetings, at different periods of the war:

By Local Meetings—Before war was yet considered certain by the people of the North in February, 1861, a meeting held at Cannelton, Perry county, passed this resolution:

> If no compromise can be obtained, and a disunion shall be unfortunately made between the Northern and Southern States, then the commercial and agricultural interests of the people of this country require us to say that we can not consent that the Ohio river shall be the boundary line between the contending nations; and we earnestly de-

sire that, if a line is to be drawn between the North and South, that line shall be drawn north of us.

A similar resolution was adopted in Washington county, at a large meeting on the 16th of February, 1861. In many counties, at various times during the war, sentiments hostile to it were expressed in the most public and emphatic manner. A few specimens are here given:

Allen.—At a meeting in Allen county, on the 13th of August, 1864, resolutions were adopted declaring that "War is no remedy for disunion, but is disunion and eternal separation itself; therefore we are in favor of, and demand of those in authority, a *cessation of hostilities.*" "We declare the proposed draft for 500,000 men the most *damnable of all other outrages* perpetrated by the Administration upon the people." "If fight we must, we will fight for the Constitution and the Union, and will *never give any aid or assistance to the continuing of this unholy and unconstitutional war."*

Bartholomew.—At a meeting held February 7th, 1863, it was declared "That we invite conservative men, everywhere, to co-operate with us in an earnest endeavor to bring about a speedy termination of the war, and to this end we will favor an *armistice,* to enable the belligerents to agree upon terms of peace."

Brown.—At a meeting of January 1st, 1863, it was resolved that "Our interests and inclinations will demand of us a *withdrawal* from the political association in a common government with the New England States"; also, "We demand an immediate armistice preparatory to a *compromise* of existing difficulties," and *"general* amnesty for political offenses." At a subsequent meeting on the 13th of August, 1863, it was resolved that "The present fratricidal and desolating war was unnecessarily forced upon the country by wicked, fanatical politicians North and South"; that "We are *opposed to furnishing men or money* to prosecute a war to free negroes"; and "We are in favor of an immediate armistice and a National Convention to restore peace and union under the Constitution."

Clay.—A meeting on the 23d of February, 1863, resolved that "We recommend a *cessation* of hostilities for such a period as may be necessary to allow the people of the North and South, by a National Convention, to express their wish for a maintenance of the Union as it was under the Constitution."

Carroll.—A meeting of January 1st, 1863, resolved against the war and the President's Emancipation Proclamation.

DeKalb.—A meeting on January 31st, 1863, declared "That we will *not give* one cent or send *one single soldier* to the present contest while it is conducted for its present unholy purpose." At a subsequent meeting of February 21st, it was declared that "We are in favor of an *armistice,*" and that "We are unwilling to furnish either men or money for any such purposes"—meaning for an emancipation war.

Fulton.—A convention of June 25th, 1864, resolved "That we are *opposed to the prosecution* of the present war for the subjugation of States," and "We are satisfied that its further prosecution for such a purpose will prove the *utter destruction of civil liberty* in America."

Greene.—A meeting of February 27th, 1863, resolved that "We hereby declare our opposition to the further prosecution of the war as it is now being waged, and that we are *not in favor* of furnishing the present Administration *another man, gun, or dollar* for such a *hellish and unchristian crusade.*"

Huntington.—A meeting held in December, 1862, in a very amusing recitation of imaginary evils inflicted upon the West by New England, declared "that had it not been for the fanaticism and peculation of New England our generation would not have witnessed the ghastly spectre of disunion, and were it not for the same causes still potent for evil, these difficulties could be adjusted." No blame is attached to the South.

Jackson.— A meeting of February 19th, 1863, declared "that it is our deliberate conviction that the union of these States can never be restored by war, and that such restoration can only be brought about by peaceful means through delegates to a National Convention."

LaGrange.—A meeting of February 28th, declared that the time has already arrived when "all true lovers of the Constitution" should unite to inaugurate such action as would bring about a peace. As the rebels had repudiated the Constitution, this resolution could only refer to the people of the North, thus making it their business to inaugurate peace.

Lawrence.—A meeting of January 24th, 1863, resolved against the prosecution of the war and against emancipation.

Martin.—A meeting of January 23d, 1863, resolved "That we regard the lives of white men as of more value than the freedom of the negro, and we have given the last man and the last money we are willing to give for the prosecution of the present abolition war."

Marshall.—A convention of June, 1863, resolved that *"we are opposed to the war under any and all circumstances,* and that we are opposed to the further continuance of this unholy and unnatural strife."

Madison.—A meeting of June 25th, 1864, declared "the restoration of the Union by force impossible," and "that the history of the past three years has already demonstrated the utter hopelessness, as well as the gigantic wrong, of a further continuance of the present contest."

Marion.—A meeting of March 18th, in Indianapolis, declared in favor of a cessation of hostilities.

Posey.—A meeting in this county declared "it beyond the power of the North to restore the Union by force, and we call on the Administration at once to stop a useless slaughter of our people and proclaim an armistice."

Putnam.—A meeting of February 21st, 1863, resolved that there should be "a cessation of hostilities," and that it was "the deliberate sense of this meeting that not another soldier and not another dollar ought to be furnished for the further prosecution of this war for negro emancipation."

Rush.—A convention of January 31st, 1863, resolved "That we are unqualifiedly opposed to the further prosecution of this abolition war, and believing that in its continued prosecution there await us only the murderous sacrifice of legions of brave men, ignominious and certain defeat, shame and dishonor at home and abroad, public ruin, and the serious endangerment of our liberties, we unhesitatingly declare that we are for peace, the cessation of hostilities, an armistice, and the settlement of existing difficulties by compromise or negotiation through a National Convention."

Shelby.—A meeting of February 5th, 1863, denounced the Administration and emancipation, demanded a cessation of hostilities, and opposed the conscription laws.

Scott.—A meeting of January 26th, 1863, declared opposition to the prosecution of the war, and in favor of the measure to take away all military power from the Governor.

Starke.—A meeting of January 25th, 1863, declared for a cessation of hostilities, for a National Convention, and for the appointment by the Legislature of commissioners to communicate with other States, and with Congress, to get their co-operation in securing a National Convention.

Switzerland.—A meeting at Vevay declares that "we are unqualifiedly opposed to the further prosecution of this abolition war, and believing that in its further prosecution there awaits us only the murderous sacrifice of our national honor, we are for peace, an armistice, and the settlement of our difficulties by compromise or negotiation through a National Convention," and that "we solemnly declare that we will *not furnish another man or another dollar* to carry on this abolition war."

Wayne.—A meeting of March 20th, 1863, declared—1st. That "the further *prosecution of this war will result in the overthrow of the Constitution, of civil liberty, of the Federal Government,* in the elevation of the black man, and the degradation of the white man in the social and political status of the country." 2d. That "we are in favor of an armistice, and the calling of a National convention." 3d. That if the Administration goes on with its arrests by Provost Marshals and police officials "blood will flow."

Other Expressions.—On the 15th of August, 1864, an address to the people was published in one of the papers of the Capital, counseling the formation of armed organizations, for the ostensible purpose of preventing improper interferences with elections, which were never threatened, and of which there were not then, nor at any other time, any appearance. So alarming a proceeding, considering that some of its most prominent authors were admitted members of a secret order sworn to assist the rebellion, was deemed by Governor MORTON important enough to demand executive notice and reprehension.[13] The disloyal element must have felt itself very strong to have ventured thus to defy the Government.

The speeches of public men are commonly and justly accepted as an expression of the views of those with whom they are associated politically; and the speech of any man may be accepted as an indication of the existence of at least some degree of public sentiment to sustain him, when such stormy elements are in motion as a civil war excites. And of

[13] Terrell, *Report,* 1, Appendix, Doc. 133:343-45. The address referred to was signed by J. J. Bingham, chairman of the Democratic State Central Committee. In his Proclamation to the People of Indiana, Morton wrote: "I do therefore solemnly warn the people of the State against accepting the evil counsel they have received; to abstain from all military organizations looking, directly or indirectly, to resistance to Federal or State authority, to abstain from all schemes of resistance to laws, and from all organizations or combinations, political or military, tending to compromise them in their allegiance and duty to the government of the United States."

disloyal speeches of Indiana men, it is quite possible to fill a larger volume than this whole report will be. A very few extracts must suffice here.

Early in April, 1861, about the time the rebels attacked Fort Sumter, a gentleman who has made a good deal of noise, though it would be difficult to find anything else he has ever done, in a speech at Greencastle said: "I say to you my constituents that, as your representative, I will never vote one dollar, or one man, or one gun to the administration of ABRAHAM LINCOLN, to make war upon the South," though there is evidence that he freely promised 100,000 men to the rebels, and negotiated for 20,000 muskets, with which, it is supposed, "Sons of Liberty" were to be armed.[14]

On the 18th of May, 1861, another gentleman who was very prominent and has represented enough public sentiment to act as a Senator of the United States, and who at the time was a candidate for Congress, said, "if this war interferes with the status of slavery I am opposed to it, and will not give one dollar to carry it on." A year afterwards he said, "President LINCOLN is a traitor, robber, or fool."

At a meeting in the Capital, in 1864, a prominent member said "nine hundred and ninety-nine men of every thousand, whom I represent, breathe no other prayer than to have an end to this hellish war. *When news of our victories come, there is no rejoicing; when news of our defeat comes there is no sorrow.*"

In a speech in the Legislature, on the 1st of February, a member, who was afterwards a leader of the Sons of Liberty, and figured as a witness in the trial of some of them before a military court, said:

You will find strong arms and brave hearts beating in the breasts of over *one hundred thousand Indianians,* that will say, as you march under abolition banners towards our brothers on the other side of yonder river (Ohio), "thus far shalt thou go and no farther." I mean that

[14] The reference is to a speech of D. W. Voorhees. The other speakers mentioned below have not been identified.

whenever the President of the United States, calls upon the Governor of the State of Indiana for troops to go to the Southern States, and whip those seven states back into the Union, and force them to remain an integral part of the government . . . I will leave my native land—my hearthstone—my wife and family, and *rather become a private in the Southern army,* fighting for equal rights and privileges, than be the commander-in-chief of an Abolition army, that would be compelled to go to the South, to shed the blood of those who dare raise their arms for freedom and liberty—for justice and self-preservation.

There is much more to the same purpose, but there need be added only the following: "But if nothing but war and blood, and strife will settle the matter, let me tell you now *you will not have a united North,* and God forbid you should."

A few extracts from newspapers, which are but specimens of thousands of similar utterances, may be added here to show what the disloyal element was and was resolved to do.

A paper in Washington county, published in April, 1861, the following language: "When that day comes, there will be plenty of brave hearts to support the flag, and bear it aloft, if need be, over the blackened corpses of fanatical agitators, and fiendish Republicans. Then will come the tug of war. Indianians about here *are not going to fight the South,* and may in case of emergency stay the onward march of Abolition hordes."

Another, published in Orange county, about the time the war commenced, said: "We would advise them to ascertain, before they commence raising their abolition crews for the South, how the land lies about home, and see if they might not subject themselves to a warm *fire in the rear.*"

On the 5th of January, 1863, just before the news of the battle of Stone River was received, a paper published at the capital said: "In view of this terrific contest is it not time to pause and think? . . . Would it not be wise to stop where we are? . . . Now let us be manly enough, reasonable enough, sensible enough, to settle our national and sectional differences by a different arbitrament than that of war. Blood enough has been shed, money enough has been spent."

Articles or extracts urging peace at any price; the establishment of an armistice, compromise, recognition of the Confederacy, and the like utterances encouraging the rebels, might be quoted to an extent that would forbid the most patient reader from attempting to read them. But there can be no necessity to add to the evidences already presented of the existence of a strong and widespread sympathy with the rebellion among our people.

ENCOURAGEMENT OF DESERTION

The third, and one of the most dangerous of all the modes adopted by the disloyal element to weaken our armies and prostrate the nation before its enemies, was the encouragement of desertion, and the protection of deserters by organizations formed for that purpose. But little effort was made in this direction during the first year of the war. The same causes that suppressed more demonstrative opposition of other kinds had their effect, no doubt, in preventing any of this kind. But our disasters gave opportunity to the one, and impulse to the other, at the same time, and both began their work together. The return of a deserter now and then, and even the gradual increase in the number of desertions, caused no uneasiness. War was as new as it was terrible to our people, and they were consequently ignorant of the necessities of the service, of the importance of discipline and obedience, and above all, of absolute fidelity. To many, no doubt, an engagement as a soldier was very much like an engagement as a journeyman or laborer—a contract to be carried out as long as it could be conveniently done, but of which a violation was no very serious affair. To desert was simply to "knock off work." The first deserters, no doubt, acted under some such misapprehension. And they were received at home as if they had merely abandoned a job instead of having committed a crime that might cost them their lives.

The Government, fully aware of the general want of appreciation of the character of the offense, at first treated it very leniently. But as the evil began to grow with the growing severity of the service, greater strictness became necessary. The soldiers and the public, too, by that time had learned that desertion, to all honorable minds, meant worse than death, the utmost blackness of disgrace; and that, to all other minds, it meant death. There was no longer any ignorance, or partial apprehension, of the nature of the offense anywhere. The peril of our armies which taught this lesson gave to the disloyal the impulse to defy it. They began sending letters to their relatives in the army urging them to desert. And desertions, which had already been increasing from the increasing hardships of the service, now began to swell into most formidable proportions. Large bodies of troops were compelled to be kept at home to return these victims of disloyal persuasion. With the effort of the Government to reclaim deserters came efforts on the part of its enemies to protect them. Organizations for that purpose were formed in neighborhoods all over the State, and conflicts with guards sent to arrest deserters became so frequent as to excite little attention, unless they were bloody as well as illegal. In many cases, no doubt in most, these organizations were parts of the secret Order of Sons of Liberty. The character of their conduct, as well as the coincidence in the times of their appearance, would indicate a close connection and common origin. Encouragement of desertion was a cardinal tenet in the creed of the disloyal Order, and, except in aggravated cases, we can hardly imagine that the people of any respectable neighborhood, uncorrupted by such associations, would make violent resistance to an armed guard who were simply executing the law. It is not necessary here to trace the evidence that these solicitations to desertion, and these resistances even to blood of the arrest of deserters, generally proceeded from this most infamous Order directly, or from influences emanating from it.

But as successful as these treasonable or mistaken efforts to induce our soldiers to desert too often were, it is a matter of congratulation to the State, and of immeasurable honor to the men upon whom the villainous attempts were made, that they failed far oftener than they succeeded; and not only failed, but excited the most intense indignation in those who were sought to be seduced. Hundreds of dishonorable letters, encouraging desertion, were sent by the men who received them to the papers of the State for publication. The columns of one or two of those at the Capital will show scores of them, and hardly a loyal paper appeared in any county for weeks that did not contain one or more. Thousands more doubtless were never revealed, but burned in silent indignation, that the shame of a parent or relative might never be known. It would be unnecessary here, even if it were possible, to give such a number of these letters as would indicate the number actually returned and published, but it may be stated that they generally consisted of an assurance to the soldier that "this was an abolition war, and that it was wrong to fight in it—that all the soldier's relatives thought he should come home, and if he did he had nothing to fear, as they were prepared to protect him, no matter what force was sent to arrest him." This is the substance of them all, as all will remember who can recall any of them.

The effect of these efforts was alarming. So many deserters came home that especial exertions in recruiting had to be made to restore the strength they had abstracted, and the President was compelled to issue a proclamation against it, and warning deserters to return. No less than two thousand three hundred desertions were reported in the single month of December, 1862, and over ten thousand deserted in this State during the war, a very large proportion of them under the influence of these guilty and shameful solicitations.

Besides the efforts made through letters, and similar means of inculcating disloyal sentiments and detestation of the service, emissaries were sent into the army to organize lodges of the "Knights of the Golden Circle," and establish that perfidious ally of the rebellion in the very citadel of the Government's strength. Measures were taken also to protect deserters by the ready hands of disloyal judges as well as by concealment, resistance and rescue. Volunteers who had been made dissatisfied with their duty even before they had commenced it, were supplied with legal counsel who rarely lacked a lie or trick to make a pretext for a writ of *habeas corpus;* and judges, quick to help them, were plenty enough. The writ, though suspended by law, would be issued, and under the plea of youth, debility, or it mattered little what, the recruit was discharged. The same remedy was found effective in cases of desertion, and was frequently used. The law was no obstacle, for lawyers and judges could readily find other law. At one time the determined effort of one of the judges of our Supreme Court to take a soldier out of the service by a writ of *habeas corpus,* after its legal suspension, threatened a fatal collision between the civil and military authorities. The action of the judge was a deliberate defiance of the National Government, and was generally believed to have been impelled by a desire to provoke a collision which could be made to tell upon the relations of political parties at that time. He threatened that "the streets of the Capital should run with blood" unless the soldier was suffered to be taken by civil process. The spirit shown by him was not confined to him or his associates, by any means, but in nearly every part of the State judicial instruments of disloyalty could be found.

With such influences at work, at home, in the army, all around the soldier, it is less astonishing that desertion was so formidably frequent than that it was not more frequent.

ACTS OF VIOLENCE, RESISTANCE TO THE DRAFT, ETC.

So far, the exhibition of the connection between the disloyal element of the North and the rebellion has been confined to the statement of opinions and feelings adverse to the war, and favorable to the rebels. But disloyalty in very many portions of the State took the more decided, though by no means more dangerous, form of violence, or combinations to commit violence, in resistance of the draft, in protection of deserters, in terrifying, maltreating, or expelling from their homes citizens whose adhesion to the Government made them obnoxious, and in producing a general feeling of uneasiness and danger, under which the State was in a condition of constant turbulence, and a domestic war, more or less widespread, was anticipated. In many cases, no doubt, the disturbances were the result of individual enmities or accidental collisions, but in every case the parties were divided by the line of political differences, and the antagonism aggravated and made active by them. In many more cases political feeling, excited by disloyal newspapers and orators and emissaries of rebel organizations, was the sole cause of outrages that made many portions of the State unsafe for the residence of any man known to support the Government, and of defiance of the laws that hardly stopped short of open insurrection. In Sullivan, Knox, Martin, Orange, Greene, Washington, Daviess, Brown, Jackson, Crawford, Rush, Bartholomew, Fountain, Warren, Johnson, Putnam, Blackford, in fact in nearly every county in the State, in the townships or neighborhoods where the disloyal element predominated, the condition of the community was for a time only less unsettled and fearful than a condition of actual war. Union men, uniformly called "abolitionists," were notified to leave the county, under penalty of death, or beating, or loss of property. Many of them were frightened or forced to obey, and left their homes, some for a few weeks, some never to return. Their barns were burned, their houses plundered, their stock stolen, they themselves were robbed. Their enemies were armed and met frequently, sometimes openly sometimes secretly, to drill and to concert outrages upon their defenseless loyal neighbors. Resistance was generally useless, and rarely attempted. A resort to the laws was worse than idle, for often neither judge nor jury would enforce the laws in defense of "abolitionists." The Governor was appealed to. Petitions for protection poured in from nearly all parts of the State, but chiefly from the western and southern sections. What help could be given was given, but the repression operated no further than the troops could reach. Outrages were still committed in other quarters with impunity. Deserters banded together to plunder loyal men. In some places they established defenses and prepared, with the help of the citizens, to defy the Government. Companies of citizens fired on the guards sent to arrest deserters. In several places they beat off the guard and rescued captured deserters. Enrolling officers for the draft were warned, threatened, and murdered. Their houses were mobbed and robbed. They could execute their duty nowhere in these disloyal counties but at the peril of their lives. Resistance to the draft was openly proclaimed and made a party watchword. Schemes to overthrow the State government, and the arming and drilling of hundreds of affiliated organizations throughout the State for this purpose, deepened the peril and excitement of the time. The Governor's life was repeatedly threatened. Once he was fired at as he was leaving the State House at night, and narrowly escaped. The ball grazed his head. Anonymous letters were sent to him by scores, threatening him with assassination if he persisted in his efforts to carry on the war. Conspiracies were formed to concoct plots that would result in his political ruin, and most foul and villainous stories were invented for the purpose of breaking down his moral character and disgracing him before the world. No crime seemed too black for the furtherance of disloyal objects. There is no doubt that this disturbed and dangerous condition of many communities, indeed, of the entire State, was produced to a very great extent by the efforts of the infamous order of "Sons of Liberty." With an organization so thoroughly treasonable, so expressly constructed to assist the rebellion, so compact, and penetrating so completely into every part of the State, animating disloyal feeling into violence and combining all violence to its own ends, the labor of preserving the peace was a very serious one, and greatly increased the oppressiveness of the labor of keeping our ranks recruited, the demands of the Government satisfied, the necessities of our sick and wounded soldiers supplied, and the civil administration of the State, so grievously crippled by the action of the Legislature, moving steadily and successfully on. That all were done, and well done, is one of Governor MORTON'S titles to that place in the history of the war which contemporary admiration has already assigned him.

It would be impossible, here, to give an account of all the disturbances and outrages which marked this period of the war. But a few will serve to give an idea of the condition of things which prevailed in many of the counties of the State.

Among the riots, which at the time created unusual and general excitement, was that in Brown county, in which Mr. LEWIS PROSSER, a few years before a Representative in the Legislature, a leader of the "Sons of Liberty" in the county, and prominent for his sympathy with the rebellion, at a political meeting, on the 18th of April, 1863, killed a soldier, and was himself mortally wounded by Captain CUNNING, an officer of volunteers. A commission, consisting of Hon. LUCIEN BARBOUR, Judge SAMUEL E. PERKINS, and Captain JOHN H. FARQUHAR, was appointed by the Governor to investigate the affair, and their report of the evidence leaves it quite clear that the first collision was not caused by any purely or ordinary political difference or dispute. It belongs to the object of this report only as exhibiting the bitterness of feeling and the disordered condition of the community, produced by the conduct of disloyal citizens, which could so easily force a trivial dispute into a bloody and fatal fight. Other facts exhibit the same condition even more clearly. Some of the witnesses before the Commission testified that their neighbors had been driven from home by the threats and violence of the friends of the rebellion. One of them,

WILLIAM GOULD, says: "It was the talk that they were going to kill the Republicans and Abolitionists. I heard a man, living south of Nashville (the county seat), say he was going to Georgetown, and that when he got home, there were two Abolitionists there who would have to leave. His name is WILLIAM M. ELKINS. Mrs. BRUNER, whose husband is in the army, Widow FLEENER, JOHN WINKLER and family, and the family of DAVID JACKSON, left their homes in consequence of the threats made." "An unoccupied house in Bean Blossom (the scene of the riot), belonging to a Union man, was burned." Some weeks after the riot, the outrages of the disloyal faction became so frequent and intolerable that a petition, signed by one hundred and twenty-five loyal citizens of the county, was sent to the Governor praying that a "small military force be sent" for their protection. The petition states that "but a few nights ago (about the last of July) houses were fired into, and one was burned to the ground. The lives of all Union men were threatened." "A few days ago, a discharged soldier, while plowing in his field, was shot and badly wounded." Mr. GOULD testifies that a day or two after the riot, in April, he saw a band of fifty men drilling in Nashville, all fully armed. The next day, a company of forty armed men, from Jackson and Bartholomew counties, passed through in the direction of Georgetown. They were joined by an equal number from Nashville. Their purpose was to protect PROSSER (who was not at that time supposed to be fatally injured) from arrest and removal from the county. Such a condition of things as that depicted in these statements is hardly better than one of open war, and in this case, as in every other, seems to have been wantonly produced by disloyal men in the gratification of their dislike of those who sustained the war and the Government. The pretext occasionally given for assembling under arms, that they desired to protect themselves against arbitrary arrests, was futile to excuse such action, and could have no application to the abuse and expulsion of loyal citizens from their homes.

In Noble county, information was given to the Governor, February 3, 1863, that the "Knights of the Golden Circle," more generally known afterwards as the "Sons of Liberty," were fully "organized and armed, and talked freely of the prospect of a war here at home in case the Southern Confederacy is not recognized, and 'Old ABE' persists in his emancipation scheme. They publicly and boldly declare that no deserter shall be arrested here; that the Abolitionists are to be exterminated, and that the Northwestern States are to form a government by themselves."

As early as May 18, 1861, but a month after the attack on Fort Sumter, the disloyal citizens of Wayne county had excited the serious suspicions of the community, and fears were entertained of their procuring arms from the State, under a false pretense of doing militia duty, which would, at the proper time, be used for their real purpose, in aid of the rebellion. The Governor was warned, and the subsequent parade of disloyal strength showed that the danger was both greater and nearer than would have been suspected by any but those thoroughly informed of the feelings of the faction. In 1863, about one hundred of them, members of the "Sons of Liberty," of Abington township, Wayne county, marched fully armed into the town of Cambridge City, and took possession of it. Their first object was to defeat the draft. General HASCALL, then in command of the State, arrested several of them. So bold and lawless a demonstration indicated the consciousness of great strength, and recklessness enough to use it.

On October 3, 1862, Governor MORTON received a notification from Fountain county, that "in Jackson and Cain townships, the draft will be resisted. The leaders are desperate men, and they say the streets shall be drenched in blood before a man shall go from the township. It is the headquarters of the Knights of the Golden Circle." Another warning, from the same county, says "there is a secret organization, embracing parts of Fountain, Parke and Montgomery counties, for the purpose of resisting the draft. It can muster one thousand men. They are well armed with small arms and squirrel rifles, and have one small cannon. The Union men are much excited, and are insuring their houses and barns for fear of incendiarism." An affidavit accompanied these letters, setting forth the language of one of the local leaders of the hostile movement. He asked the crowd if they would "stand such a thing" (the draft). Cries of "no," "never," responded. He then said: "Rather than stand this, or see my countrymen stand it, I would see every spear of grass in Jackson township drip with blood." Such language from leaders and newspapers very often fanned a simple spark of dissatisfaction into a violent flame of disaffection, and produced that hostility to loyal men, which so long and so painfully disturbed the peace of the State.

In August, 1864, Washington county, notoriously a center of disloyal feeling, was in so turbulent a condition that the friends of the Government were in constant dread of an insurrection. One of them writes: "Many Union people are very uneasy, and some very much alarmed. We have no means of self-protection. The Sons of Liberty are all armed, and they are so numerous that the Union people would like to know if the Government is taking any steps to prevent the unarmed in this quarter from being overpowered."

Early in June, 1863, about twenty-five soldiers of the Thirty-Third Regiment were in the town of Williamsport, Warren county, on furlough. They attended a ball at a hotel in the place, during which a quarrel arose between the landlord and the officer in command. The hotel bell was rung as a signal, and immediately a crowd of twenty-five to fifty, who had been waiting, apparently for some such difficulty, in the outskirts of the town, rushed in and attacked such of the soldiers as were outside of the hotel. One of the soldiers was shot in the shoulder, and several other shots were fired, but without further injury. The affair was of no great consequence, but it showed the disturbed condition of the place, and the eagerness of the disloyal faction for a collision with soldiers.

In December, 1863, notice was sent to the Executive office, of preparations to resist the draft in counties along the Ohio river. The scheme was, for the men who were drafted, to use the arms given them, where they had a fair chance, against the forces of the government. No attempt of this kind was made, chiefly, no doubt, for the reason that the quotas of our State, and of the greater part of the Northwest, were so largely filled by volunteers that the drafted men were too few to make a hostile demonstration, even if they had been so inclined.

In August, 1864, full information was given Governor MORTON of the purchase of arms in Grandview, Spencer county, for distribution among the Sons of Liberty, and similar warnings were sent from all quarters of the State. Arms had been very extensively purchased at that time, and there were probably very few even of the most insignificant "lodges" of Sons of Liberty that did not possess a fair proportion of arms. Rebel money was liberally furnished for this purpose, as was afterwards declared on oath by one of the chief men of the Order. Sullivan and Knox counties were among the most intolerably infested districts of the State. From the very commencement of the Rebellion, the disloyal feeling there had been forward and zealous in displaying itself and annoying its opponents. When in 1862 a car was placed on a side track at the town of Sullivan, close enough to strike a passing train in which Governor MORTON was going to the Ohio river to look after wounded soldiers, by which Professor MILES J. FLETCHER, Superintendent of Public Instruction, was instantly killed, so notorious was the hostility of the people of the county to the war and the government, that suspicions were instantly and universally formed that the collision was no accident. An investigation before a Grand Jury composed of rebel sympathizers, and prosecuted by an attorney of the same kind, discovered no evidence of guilt anywhere, but the suspicion remains, and will remain as long as the untimely and lamentable death of Professor FLETCHER is remembered.

In Sullivan the few loyal citizens who dared to avow their adhesion to the government were persecuted with a vindictiveness to which no parallel can be found elsewhere in the North. Their barns and harvests were burned, and notices fastened to their gateposts of the purpose to burn their houses next time. The following is a literal copy of one of these notices: "September the 1st, 1865, now point out citizens to be arrested, and the next time you will fill a traitors grave. I have burned two damd abolitionest and if John Fox is not releast in ten days from date and restored to his family I will burn out to more this arresting of civil citizens must and shall be stopped." A letter to the commandant of the District dated the day after this notice, shows how faithfully its daring threats were fulfilled. It says: "WM. OSBORN'S wheat stacks and hay have been burned—about five hundred bushels of wheat. Notices left of further intentions. On the same night, CHARLES MCDONALD'S barn was burnt, and notices left on the gate post." Mr. MCDONALD himself writes that on the night of the 1st of September, about eleven o'clock, he was alarmed from his sleep by a large fire blazing from his frame stable and two large hay stacks. All were utterly destroyed. During the latter part of the summer of 1864, outrages, robberies, and incendiary fires, were of constant occurrence. JOHN MILLER, of Cass township, was visited by a large body of men, who attacked him, and, after a severe resistance, overpowered and robbed him of $300 in money and a gun. JOHN PRICE, of Hamilton township, was also visited at his house in the night by a band of rebel sympathizers, and robbed of $500 in money. Dr. WILLIAM COBB, of Jasonville, Greene county, was similarly visited and robbed of a small sum of money. GREENBURY PRICE, a merchant of the same place, was called to his store in the night by a similar gang of disloyalists, and robbed of $300 to $400. Mrs. BARNEY SAUSERMANN, whose husband was in the army, was likewise visited and robbed by the same class of patriots. She resided in Cass township, Sullivan county. The same men broke into and robbed the railroad depot in the town of Sullivan. The pay train on the Evansville and Crawfordsville Railroad was thrown from the track and robbed in full daylight, near the town of Sullivan. MARION MILLER, of Cass township, was twice stopped on the public highway within three miles of the county seat, and robbed of small sums of money. NELSON SISSON, of Jackson township, was robbed of $150 and upwards. WILLIAM OSBORN'S wheat and hay were burned (as already noticed), loss $2,000. JOHN MCKEES, of Hamilton township, had his barn and stables burned, with a number of horses and a bull, wagons, a carriage and his farming implements in them; loss about $3,000. JOHN MILLER, of Cass township, had his house burned, and his barn set on fire; the latter was saved. GREEN C. GARDNER, of Hamilton township, had his stable burned. A Methodist church in Jefferson township was burned.

These are not a record, but a sample, of the outrages that were practiced upon loyal men, solely because they were loyal, in the county of Sullivan and vicinity, in a few weeks of the summer of 1864. A number of the ardent opponents of the Government engaged in them were arrested. Some twenty-two were indicted, but none were ever brought to trial. Most of them broke jail, with very little difficulty, and all escaped in some way or other, as it was quite certain from the beginning they would do. Most of the Union men throughout the infected regions were notified to leave the country, under penalty of severe punishment. Many did leave, and some never returned.

In Knox county, a deserter from the Twenty-Third Regiment by the name of JAMES WILLIS, assisted by two brothers,

GEORGE and ADAM ROBINSON, and by several of the disloyal citizens of the neighborhood, established their headquarters in Widner township, at a house where he was harbored, procured a quantity of ammunition and several pistols and other arms, called his refuge "Fort Robinson," and prepared deliberately to defy the law and resist any force sent to arrest him, or suppress the hostile operations of the band. Captain McCORMICK, of the Sullivan county Legion, with fourteen men, was sent to arrest him. He was found concealed in a stable, refused to surrender when commanded, and fired upon the guard, wounding a young man named KIMBERLAIN, severely. The outlaw was then shot and mortally wounded. The ROBINSONS were arrested. The Sons of Liberty were in great force in that vicinity, as they were in so many other portions of that section of the State, and loyal men fared little better than in Sullivan county.

The following extracts from the General Orders of two of the Commandants of the State will show how disturbed and perilous was the condition of the country at that time. On the 11th of April, 1863, General CARRINGTON's Order said: "In some portions of the State citizens have been warned to leave their homes, under penalty of severe handling and the burning of their buildings. The legitimate result, already predicted, of the habit of wearing concealed weapons, has been demonstrated in the loss of several lives and no little property. Let no citizen, under any threat, desert his home or sacrifice his property. Let him remain at all hazards." On the 6th of October, 1864, General HOVEY said in an address to the people of the State:

> Recent developments clearly show that a secret armed association exists in this State, formed for the purpose of aiding the rebellion against the United States. The primary object of this dangerous association is to break down the power of the present administration in the prosecution of the war, and aid the rebellion by force, fraud and violence. For this purpose, large numbers of rebels from the armies of the South, under the name and guise of Refugees, have been sent to this State to co-operate with this treasonable association. Arms and

ammunition, to a large amount, have been secretly imported and placed in the hands of these bad men, and, unless their designs are speedily checked, ruin and the desolation that follows in the footsteps of war will soon spread throughout the State. In the counties of Martin, Orange, Crawford, Marshall, and other localities they have concentrated by hundreds, defied the laws, fired upon and killed enrolling officers and wounded law-abiding citizens, and robbed them of their property, with the avowed determination of aiding the rebellion. This cannot continue without civil war in our midst.

Outbreaks, in resistance of the laws, were frequent and sometimes fatal. On the 10th of January, 1863, a detachment of cavalry sent to arrest some deserters near Waverly, in Johnson county, was fired upon by a company of disloyal citizens and Sons of Liberty.

On the 1st of June, 1863, several deserters were forcibly rescued from their guard, in Noble township, Jay county.

At the first draft in October, 1862, in Blackford county, the commissioner's box was seized, dashed upon the floor and trampled to pieces, to the delight of the disloyal citizens who crowded the room and witnessed and encouraged the outrage.

June 12, 1863, the enrollment for the draft in Johnson county was resisted by armed men.

June 15, 1863, fifty armed men attacked the residence of JAMES SILL, the enrolling officer of Marion township, Putnam county, and demanded the enrollment papers. When refused, they fired into the house about sixty times, and retired without the papers. At the same time, the enrollment books and papers were destroyed in Jefferson township, of the same county. During the same week, the books of Cloverdale township, same county, were stolen.

June 15, 1863, the enrolling officer of Whitestown, Boone county, was resisted by a company of rioters, and threatened with violence if he persisted in doing his duty.

June 18, FLETCHER FREEMAN, the enrolling officer of Cass township, Sullivan county, was shot by concealed assassins and instantly killed while engaged in the performance of his duty. This cruel and cowardly murder was well understood in the vicinity to have been committed by the Sons of Liberty.

June 11, the enrolling officer of Waterloo township, Fayette county, was shot at while in the discharge of his duty.

June 10, Hon. J. FRANK STEVENS, late a Senator from Decatur county, while acting as assistant enrolling officer, was shot and killed near Manilla, while engaged in completing the enrollment of Walker township, Rush county. A man named CRAYCRAFT, the enrolling officer, who was with him, was severely wounded at the same time. A short time before this tragical occurrence a disloyal paper published in Rushville had warned all draft officers "to insure their lives," and indulged in such appeals and denunciations as were well calculated, probably intended, to produce such consequences.

About the 20th of June, resistance was made to the enrollment of Indian Creek township, Monroe county, and the papers were destroyed.

At about the same time the draft officers of Daviess county were warned not to enroll it. On the 3d of October, 1864, Captain ELI McCARTY, while serving notices on drafted men in that county, was murdered by Sons of Liberty concealed in the woods through which he had to pass. His body was thrown into the river and not discovered for several days.

In the early part of the summer of 1863, these outrages had become so frequent, and the disorder of the communities in which they were perpetrated so great and so rapidly extending, that the authorities were forced to take steps to check them. On the 11th day of June, Governor MORTON issued a proclamation[15] setting forth the law in regard to ob-

---

[15] Governor Morton, as he said, moved by the "resistance . . . in several cases to officers engaged in the execution of the Conscription Law, and to officers and soldiers engaged in arresting deserters from the army, in which blood had been shed and murder committed," issued a proclamation solemnly warning persons "against resistance to the Government in any form, or hindering or obstructing any officer thereof in the performance of his duties." *Proclamation by the Governor, to the People of Indiana* (Indianapolis, 1863). 8 pp.

structions of the draft and the penalties incurred by those who took part in them. He also alluded to the systematic attempts then being made by the "Knights of the Golden Circle," and their friends, to bring the Government into contempt and excite hostility to it by denunciations of its measures. His admonitions were timely, calm, and not without effect. He said:

> The right of the people peaceably to assemble and petition for a redress of grievances and speak and publish their opinions touching the policy of the Government, or the conduct of the war, must be respected and the enjoyment of it protected. But there is a wide difference between the legitimate exercise of this right and the unbridled license of speech which seeks by the assertion of the most atrocious falsehoods to exasperate the people to madness and drive them into a position of neutrality between their Government and the rebels, if not into the very arms of the rebellion, combine them into dangerous societies, provoke them to resist the laws, and thus contribute directly to weaken our own Government, and strengthen the cause of the enemy. The criticism of one who is friendly to the Government, and who is anxious that it shall succeed and be preserved, and who points out its errors in order that they may be corrected, is wholly different from that denunciation which seeks to bring the Government into contempt and render it odious to the people, thereby withdrawing from it that natural support so necessary to its life, when struggling with a powerful enemy.

Some of the men suspected of being concerned in the murders, and known to be participants and planners of the outrages in Sullivan county were arrested by order of the military commandant of this State and District. ANDREW HUMPHREYS, of Greene county, was arrested and tried (as will be more fully related hereafter) for treason and exciting resistance to the laws of the United States. The successful termination of the war made the Government indifferent not only to the danger which these men and the order they belonged to, had threatened, but to the mischief they had done or incited, and they were allowed to resume their forfeited rights without interference. Suit was brought early in 1866, in the Sullivan Circuit Court, against Captain McCORMICK and his men, who executed the order of arrest, for damages for false imprisonment. The suit was, of course, entirely groundless. Both judge and jury knew that no suit could be rightfully brought against a subordinate officer for obeying the command of his superior. An act of Congress had made express provision for such cases; and, to prevent the wrong that might be done to an officer or soldier for the simple discharge of his duty, by the political prejudices and exasperations of disloyal neighborhoods, had provided for the transfer of all suits on such subjects to the United States Court. The law was clear and peremptory, the utter baselessness of the suits obvious. The defendants filed a petition for the removal of their cases to the United States Court. The judge, whose rebel sympathies were never concealed even on the bench, refused it in plain defiance of the law. The cases were tried before a jury. HUMPHREYS was awarded twenty-five thousand dollars' damages. Another man obtained five hundred dollars' damages.

These cases serve to illustrate forcibly the lawless character of the feeling which predominated in these disloyal neighborhoods. Even more clearly than personal outrages do such deliberate violations of oaths and laws, on the part of court and jury, demonstrate how firmly fixed such a community must have been in its sympathy with the rebellion. What was done in Sullivan would doubtless have been done in many other counties in the State, had not the Legislature passed an act for the protection of soldiers in such cases. Disseminate into hundreds of townships the spirit that, in defiant disregard of law, fastened ruinous damages upon a soldier for doing his duty; poison every community more or less deeply with it; see it bursting out in fires, robberies, expulsion of loyal men from their homes, in murders of Government officers, destroying their papers, in rescuing or protecting deserters, and one can form some idea of this class of difficulties which the disloyal element threw in the way of the prosecution of the war.

In October, 1864, Brigadier General HENRY JORDAN, of the "Legion," discovered an extensive and dangerous conspiracy in Crawford and Orange counties. In his official report he says:

I regard the late troubles in Crawford and Orange counties as a miserable failure of an extensive conspiracy. I base this opinion upon the following facts: 1st. Information, of a reliable character, received more than four weeks ago, that the guerrillas in Kentucky were disbanding and coming, one at a time, to the Indiana side. 2d. Positive evidence that a large number of guerrillas have actually been among us for several weeks. 3d. Information from an officer of the "Sons of Liberty," who did not wish to involve his family and property in civil war, that it had been determined by that organization to resist the draft, and that five hundred guerrillas from Kentucky—many of whom were already amongst us—were to co-operate. 4th. Confessions of the prisoners, who state that the uprising was to be general, and that they expected to receive heavy reinforcements from other counties.

From the testimony taken by my staff officers, during and since the difficulties, I am led to the belief that not more than three hundred persons were engaged in actual hostilities. The rioters were divided into small bands, the largest that I could hear of numbering seventy-five men. The ringleaders were guerrillas from Kentucky, whose object was plunder. They seemed to care but little about the draft, and only used it to obtain assistance in their nefarious scheme. When the movement failed they escaped, carrying off, as the prisoners say, the entire proceeds of the robberies, and leaving their dupes to suffer for their crimes. Some escaped to Kentucky, and others to the disloyal portions of the State. I think that at least fifty persons were robbed by these men. Most of the stolen horses were recovered. The number of prisoners taken by my forces was about forty. Some of these, against whom I could find no testimony, I released. I delivered seven conscripts, who had been engaged in the affair, to Colonel MERRIWETHER, Provost Marshal of this District. I sent ninety-one citizens, who had participated in it, to Major General HOVEY, as directed by you.

The evidence against most of them is very strong, many of them having confessed that they participated in the robberies and resistance to the draft. I arrested several persons for the crime of persuading their ignorant neighbors into resistance to law, while they themselves took no active part in the trouble they had created.

I proposed to deliver a portion of the prisoners to the civil authorities for trial, but the leading citizens of Leavenworth, without regard to party, fearing that an effort might be made to relieve them, petitioned me, in writing, to send them to some military post for confinement. The people living near the scene of this disturbance, being apprehensive of further violent proceedings, I stationed Captain AYDELOTTE'S company (Legion, Sixth Regiment) at Hartford, with orders to remain there until quiet was restored. I will communicate, in a formal report, the operations of the forces under my command during this disturbance.

I am satisfied that the prompt action of the militia force had the effect to deter many persons from participating in this disturbance, and that if a large force had not promptly confronted the robbers, the affair would have assumed a more alarming aspect. The credit of assembling our forces is mainly due to my subordinate officers, who, in many cases, had mustered their commands and gone in pursuit before my orders reached them. There were no casualties. One or two of my men had their clothes pierced by balls fired at them.

General Jordan also furnished, for the use of the authorities, specimens of the testimony and confessions of a number of citizens who were engaged in the conspiracy, as follows:

The prisoners were brought into a room, one at a time, and questioned by General JORDAN and Colonel WOODBURY. They were not sworn, and all their confessions were voluntary. Each prisoner was assured that he would not be compelled to disclose anything against his own will. The examination was public. Such citizens as wished to enter the room were admitted, and allowed to listen to the questions and answers.

JUNIUS LOMAX lives in Greenfield township, Orange county; states that he is a drafted man, that he went to Williamsburg, in Orange county, where he heard that the drafted men were going to resist the draft. GEORGE COFFMAN, of Floyd county, made a speech, and advised the drafted men to resist. At another meeting, held south of Williamsburg, Saturday evening, October 1st, JOHN ALLSTOTT, of Crawford county, advised us to resist. The guns taken from the Guards were taken through spite. I took a gun from VALENTINE COOK, of the Valeene Home Guards. I was along when PATTERSON APPLE was arrested and robbed of his pistol. A good many of the drafted men were present at these meetings. A number of strangers were also present. I understood that some of them were from Kentucky. A man named LYNCH, from Harrison county, was present. JOHN W. STONE had been through there, advising the men to resist the draft. JACOB COOK took the lead in disarming VALENTINE COOK. HEIMENER SEIBOLT took the lead in taking the pistol from PATTERSON APPLE.

WILLIAM SANDERS resides in Sterling township, Crawford county. I saw that something was going to be done. My son JAMES was along with the crowd, and I wanted to get him away from them. I overtook some of them near BELCHER'S. Before we got to E. H. GOLDEN'S there were at least thirty men present. There were seven men present that I can swear to, namely: UNION MCMICKLE, BOB ALLEN, JOHN ALLSTOTT, JAMES SANDERS, THOMAS HEIGHFIELD, JOHN MCCABE, BEN. BROWN and BENTON NEWKIRK. They told me they were going to *press* GOLDEN'S money and horses. Don't know what they got, as I took no hand in the robbery. I saw GOLDEN'S wife, but did not tell her that I had nothing to do with it. I did not see the GOLDENS. They pressed a horse and a pistol in another place. ALLSTOTT told me that if I ever told it my life was at stake. Just as I was in the act of starting home I heard them say that they knew of several rich hauls. I was at the post office in Brownstown on Thursday. There was a good deal of talk about seizing the guns of the Home Guards. I heard BEN. BROWN and BENTON NEWKIRK hurrah for JEFF. DAVIS. The crowd was of unusual size— fifty men or more. The robbers used nicknames, and it being dark I only knew those I saw inside at GOLDEN'S house.

LORENZO D. KNIGHT, resident of Patoka township, Crawford county. I am a member of the Knights of the Golden Circle. The signs General JORDAN gave me are all right. When MORGAN was last in Kentucky they told me that if he came over here, he would help us and we would help him. We were to seize horses in the neighborhood to mount ourselves. They cursed LINCOLN bitterly. Dr. BOWLES was a General in the order. I heard HORACE HEFFREN'S name frequently. We were to get help from Harrison county in resisting the draft. They were to put the WOODS, CUMMINGS and GOLDENS out of the way. There was talk of robbing BILL RAY, who was understood to have a large sum of money about him. I was with MCMICKLE, ALLSTOTT and company, when they went to rob CUMMINGS on Friday morning. I understood that a majority of the people of my country were "Knights." I have heard JESSE MCWILLIAMS denounce the President, etc. KINSEY LIVINGSTONE and PERRY KNIGHT asked me to join the K. G. C. I saw at their meetings JAMES SANDERS, JOHN MASON, ELISHA MASON, TIM. MASON, JOHN KNIGHT, WILLIAM SANDERS,

LARKIN LANKFORD, HENRY STRAND, DUVAL L. BROON, JESSE CUZZANT, TIM. BELCHER, JOEL NEWKIRK and JONATHAN NEWKIRK. The most of these men were at KENDAL'S store, in Orange county, on Saturday, October 1st. I voted to resist the draft at a meeting at Zion's Hollow, near Brownstown. This meeting was held on Thursday evening, September 29. I think a majority voted not to resist the draft. Those who voted not to resist the draft said they had failed to get the assistance from other counties that they expected. FRANK ENLOW said he would not report if drafted. I was with them at GOLDEN'S when he was robbed. We did not get as much money as we expected. I think our leaders got all the money. ELIAS CORBY, of Orange, was also at GOLDEN'S.

JOSEPH E. ALLEN resides in Sterling township, Crawford county. I heard UNION MCMICKLE say he intended to use JAMES SLOAN up, and kill WOODS, CUMMINGS, and JOSEPH MILLER, at the risk of his life. The man that went under the name of BOB ALLEN was *not* BOB ALLEN. The rioters said they were opposed to the milk-and-water policy of JIM LEMONDS (County Clerk) and MART TUCKER (Sheriff) and would have a policy of their own. I voted to resist the draft. We understood that there were three hundred of our men in camp in Harrison county. There were men from Kentucky with us. Don't know anything about the firing that was done at Colonel JOHNSON's regiment. So far as I know, all the rioters belong to the K. G. C.

MARTIN BELCHER, lives in East township, Orange county. I am a brother of JERRY BELCHER. I told Captain TUCKER that I had no arms of my own, but a borrowed revolver. I delivered it up. I have been at one of those meetings. It was at the schoolhouse in Zion's Hollow. ENOS NELLS was there; also UNION MCMICKLE and JOSIAH STRONDE. Heard some talk about resisting the draft. It was the general understanding that the ballot boxes were to be stuffed; also, that all the strangers among us had the right to vote.

Besides cases of actual violence, frequent displays of military strength were made. The secret order of "Knights of the Golden Circle," or "Sons of Liberty," was essentially a military organization, and, though its drilling and mustering were generally done after night and secretly, it seems to have been thought advisable at times to make a public show, probably to inspire confidence in its strength and obtain recruits, and possibly to overawe the loyal men of the vicinity. Such a display was made in Clay county, near Brazil, in 1864, and it was proclaimed in advance that no Government officer or troops should interfere with it. The opinion seemed to be quite general that it was the purpose of the Order to provoke a collision with the Government. Colonel STREIGHT, with a detachment of troops, was sent to the place and dispersed the crowd, numbering some two or three hundred men, though not without a good many demonstrations of hostility, that confirmed the suspicions previously formed of the motive of the affair. Similar displays were made in various counties, greatly alarming quiet and loyal citizens, and contributing to the zeal of the rebels on the Kentucky border, whose movements so long kept our side of the Ohio river in a state of disquiet and danger.

SECRET TREASONABLE ASSOCIATIONS

Allusions have been frequently made in this Report to a secret treasonable society, sometimes called the "Knights of the Golden Circle," and sometimes the "Sons of Liberty." The disordered condition of the State in 1862, 1863, and 1864; the disloyal demonstrations against the Government, both among the people and in the Legislature; the encouragement and protection of desertion; the maltreatment of loyal citizens; the resistance to the laws and murder of officers acting under the laws, have been attributed to its exertions or its influence. An examination of its character and history will satisfy any intelligent person that no more than the truth, hardly the whole truth, has been expressed in these allegations. Its existence and machinations are no suspicions of timid victims or vindictive enemies, but the revelations of its own members, confessions of the plotters of its most infamous acts, disclosures of those who were familiar with its history and actions. No crime was ever so fully established by such indisputable evidence as the existence and purposes of this monstrous conspiracy. It forms the most appalling spectacle of the war. The battles and bloodshed, the desolation and mourning that follow the march of hostile forces, are appreciable inflictions, whose length and breadth and weight can be measured and the necessary strength summoned to bear them; but who can measure the terrors of a perfidious plot, a treacherous combination that reaches into every State, into every community, that destroys the confidence of society, that may strike at any moment and anywhere, that scatters fire and fear through the country without exposing the hand that does it, that uses murder as an ordinary tool, and plans massacres as political expedients? Its existence and actions make the blackest page in the history of our country.

THE SONS OF LIBERTY

This organization, at first generally known as the "Knights of the Golden Circle," was merely an adaptation to the purposes of the rebellion of an association, with the same name, that had been maintained for several years in the South, with a few branches in the Northern States, for the promotion of filibustering schemes. In its later and more dangerous form, it undoubtedly took its rise among the rebels about the time the secession movement was inaugurated. It spread thence to the disaffected of the border Slave States, and speedily afterwards to the Northwest. It is but consistent with all known facts of its existence and operations to believe that it contributed, in no slight degree, to induce the rebels to begin the war, not only by the direct encouragement of its own assurances of help, but by constant communications of the feelings of the people of the North. That the South was well informed of the divisions and hesitations here, which for a time gave so auspicious an appearance to the rebellion, is well known, and that the information should be conveyed by emissaries of an Order with the same organization, aims and name in both sections, is too probable to be easily doubted. That it existed here, from the very beginning of the war, in some form, may be set down as a fact. Within a month after the attack on Fort Sumter, as already stated in a preceding portion of this report, its existence was strongly suspected in Wayne county, and measures taken to counteract its operations. But during the greater part of the year 1861, the patriotic indignation of the country was too fierce and universal to allow it to make any but the most secret and stealthy efforts. The delays and disasters that followed, creating a limited but decided reaction against the war feeling, opened an opportunity for more vigorous action, and the denunciations of the war and the alleged unconstitutionality of the measures for its prosecution, which then began to attract attention, were most probably the inspiration of its lodges and consultations. It spread rapidly, and in May, 1862, its members, in this State, were estimated by themselves to number fifteen thousand. Its operations becoming bolder, were speedily traced home. The Grand Jury of the United States Circuit Court, at the May term, 1862, found it so dangerous in its plans to resist or thwart the enlistment of **volunteers,** and the payment of National taxes, that they were compelled to make a thorough investigation of its character. Their inquiries extended over a period of several weeks. They summoned witnesses from every part of the state, where indications of its existence were reported. They say: "These witnesses came from many counties and lived in various parts of the State," and that the facts learned from

those having a personal knowledge of the matters, constrain them to say that a secret oath-bound organization exists, numbering some fifteen thousand in Indiana, as estimated by members of the Order, commonly known as Knights of the Golden Circle, but even in the same localities by different names. Their lodges, or castles as they denominate them, are located in various parts of the State, yet they have common signs, grips and words whereby the members are all able to distinguish each other, and pass words to enable the member to enter the castle in which he was initiated, or any other which he may choose to visit. They have signals by which they can communicate with each other by day or night, and, above all, they have a signal or sign which may be recognized at a great distance from the person giving it. This last signal was invented for the use of such members as should by means of draft, or otherwise, be compelled to serve in the ranks of the army. In such case members of the Order serving in opposing armies are reminded of the obligation not to injure the member giving it. Upon the signal being given, if they shoot at all, they shoot over each other. Many members of the Order examined before us, admit the binding force of the obligation, and pretend to justify it as correct in principle.

After alluding to the filibustering origin of the Order, the Grand Jury says:

Since that time it has made alarming progress in our midst, with entirely new features attached to it, in view of the unnatural conflict now desolating the country. Not only are the loyal soldiers of the army to be treacherously betrayed in the bloody hour of battle, by the signals before referred to, but the Grand Jury have abundant evidence of the membership binding themselves to resist the payment of the Federal tax and to prevent enlistments in the armies of the United States. It is a fact worthy of note, and conclusively shown, that in localities where this organization extensively prevails there has been a failure to furnish a fair proportion of volunteers. Said Grand Jury, after a thorough examination on that point, have been unable to find any instance where a member of said organization had volunteered to fight for the Union under the late requisition for volunteers.

And further, that

In many cases individuals, after their first introduction into the Order, seeing its evil tendencies, have abandoned it. Since the Grand Jury began the investigation it has been discovered that the Order exists among the prisoners of war now in Camp Morton, who refuse to testify, upon the ground that it may implicate the members of their Order in Indiana, and thereby injure the cause of the Southern Confederacy.

These prisoners no doubt were members of the Order at home, and were fully informed of its existence here long before General GRANT sent them up from Fort Donelson into closer contact with their friends. The signs spoken of by the Grand Jury, they ascertained, were to be used in case of legal prosecutions to get members of the Order on the jury. This evidence, they significantly add, "was, in most cases, drawn from unwilling witnesses."

This report was published on the 4th of August, 1862. An exposure so complete and made upon evidence so indisputable, alarmed all loyal men. The rapidly increasing swarms of deserters, the letters of relatives urging desertion and promising protection which were returned home for publication by the soldiers, the disturbances which had already broken out in many places, the frequent purchases of arms, the preparations made to resist or defeat the draft which was approaching, all seemed tokens of a domestic war in aid of the rebellion. The success of the disloyal factions in the elections of that year, chiefly accomplished through this organization, intensified these apprehensions. As the time for the meeting of the Legislature approached, the air became thick with rumors of revolutionary projects which the event proved were but too well founded. Armed bands of the Knights were expected to take possession of the arsenal and public stores, and execute any order of the Legislature deposing the Governor or overturning the State government. The release of the rebel prisoners was anticipated. There was in fact no measure of mischief or anarchy that was not deemed within the schemes of the Order and of the Legislature which was controlled by it. How well the Legislature on its part justified these apprehensions has been fully shown in the armistice and peace resolutions, and the Military Board Bill, of that body.

The existence of the Order was frequently asserted by the loyal members of the Legislature during the session. The members who belonged to it sometimes denied it positively, and sometimes admitted and palliated it. They knew of associations, they said, but they were neither treasonable nor illegal. They were formed solely for protection against arbitrary arrests. The admission of the existence of the Order was enough. Its character could be judged from its acts. Its members had destroyed the draft box in Blackford county. They had fired on the cavalry squadron sent to arrest deserters in Johnson county. They had openly and repeatedly declared their determination to allow no draft in a score of other counties. The revelations of the Grand Jury were but predictions closely followed by the fulfillment.

In April, 1863, a month after the adjournment of the Legislature, the commission appointed to investigate the fatal riot in Brown county, already noticed in another place, examined several witnesses who testified to the existence of the Order, its secrecy, its possessions of arms and its military drills. Its grips, passwords and signs soon became public property. The disasters, following close upon each other's heels, which the rebellion encountered during the summer of 1863, the separation of the Western from the Eastern division, the loss of the Mississippi river, the conquest of all the States upon its eastern bank, the fatal defeat of Gettysburg, the bloody repulse of Helena, the defeat of MORGAN's raid and the utter annihilation of his army, restored the hopes and spirits of the country, and this renewal of the war feeling, co-operating with the widespread exposure of the Order, so loaded it with odium as to daunt its boldness and repress its activity. It was deemed necessary, by the leaders, to reorganize it and reconstruct its mysteries, to make it more secret and place its members more absolutely under the control of the chiefs. It was reorganized under the name of the "Order of American Knights," or "O.A.K.," and was called frequently the "Host," the "Mighty Host" and "Circle of Honor." This change was made in the fall of 1863.

Through the connivance of business houses in various parts of the State, and particularly one or two in the Capital, arms were smuggled into the State and distributed to the members in great numbers. The object was alarmingly apparent. The result might be fatal where feelings were so highly exasperated. General HENRY B. CARRINGTON, who was appointed to the command of the District of Indiana in March, 1863, at once took measures to prohibit this dangerous movement. He issued an order restricting the sale of arms, and the efforts of men of all parties were solicited to assist in making the order effective by discountenancing the arming of their friends. Still the treasonable conspiracy continued its work against the peace of the State and the safety of the Nation.

Close correspondence was kept up with the rebels, not only at this time, but through the whole war. When the outbreaks occurred in eastern Illinois—which assumed almost the proportions, and were undoubtedly guided by the purpose, of an insurrection—the leaders of the Order checked them, because they were informed that the rebel forces were not prepared at the time to give the support promised. The authorities here learned this fact from various sources in Canada, Illinois and Michigan.

Several days before FORREST advanced upon Paducah, General CARRINGTON had information from detectives that the Order in Illinois knew of his coming, and expected him to cross into that State and support a general insurrection. His defeat at Paducah spoiled the project, which, in case of his success, might have proved a most formidable auxiliary of the rebellion. In the spring of 1864, when MORGAN entered Pound Gap to invade Kentucky, early information of it was received in Indianapolis. Two of the leaders of the Order, then in the city, Colonel WM. A. BOWLES, who had been extinguished at the battle of Buena Vista by conspicuous cowardice and incompetency, and Judge J. F. BULLITT of the Kentucky Court of Appeals, declared that "MORGAN must be stopped; the Order was not ready for him." Judge BULLITT immediately started for Kentucky, and MORGAN was stopped.

Nearly a week before MORGAN attacked Mount Sterling and destroyed the Louisville and Lexington railroad, reports were sent by members of the Order that there were no "mules" —the name they gave to the soldiers—on the line of the road, and that a glorious work would be begun in a week. A little less than a week saw the fulfillment of their prediction, and proved the completeness of their information of rebel movements. In the summer of 1864, two or three rebel officers visited Indianapolis to arrange plans with the chiefs of the Order for the release and arming of the prisoners at Camp Morton, Camp Chase at Columbus, Camp Douglas at Chicago, and on Johnson's Island, and to take command of the force that was expected to be formed of them.

During the session of the Legislature of 1863, rebel officers were in the city in consultation with their allies, and the fact was publicly declared in the House of Representatives a few days afterwards. It was denied by the members of the Order in that body, and the names of those consulted with demanded, but the public belief could not be changed by any amount of politic bluster. The revelations made by Miss MARY ANN PITMAN, a member of the Order, and for a long time an able and efficient spy in the rebel service, generally thought to have been a man, show that communications were kept up between the rebel forces and these Northern sympathizers almost exclusively through members of the Order. GREEN SMITH, Secretary of the Grand Council of Missouri, said that "rebel spies, mail carriers and emissaries had been protected by the Order all the time that he belonged to it." Spies dressed as soldiers were sent North, and harbored and supplied with information by the members here.

These facts illustrate the connection between the Order and the rebels through the three years that connection could be made of any service to the rebellion. Immediately before the disasters to the rebellion in 1863, which so seriously injured the Order, many of the outrages upon loyal citizens, the burnings, robberies and murders elsewhere noticed, were committed. It was the "season of refreshing" to the infamous association. But it was speedily followed by a season of mourning, alleviated, to be sure, but not consoled, by the mob of its friends and allies in New York, which, for three days, rioted in the murder of peaceable citizens and of inoffensive negro children, and in the burning and destruction of orphan asylums and loyal men's houses. The mob was put down with a stern hand, and a bloody but most righteous retribution followed close upon the most bloody and brutal provocation ever given by traitors to a generous nation.

Once detected, the Order could not keep its existence or acts long a secret, under any change, from its shrewd and active enemies. Partial revelations of the operations of the "O. A. K." speedily compelled another change, though not a great one, which was formally introduced on the 22d of February, 1864. The name by which its infamy was widely known, and by which it will remain a shame and reproach to Americans as long as history shall endure, the "Sons of Liberty," was given it. The ritual was altered a little, but there was no material difference made between the "O. A. K." and the "O. S. L." Those initiated into the first were entitled to complete their degrees in the other. During the spring and summer of 1864, it began to work actively and boldly again. The political contest then approaching enabled it to increase its strength greatly by inducing men to join under the impression that it was a mere political organization, opposed to the war and to the "abolition policy," as it was called, of the Administration. Its numbers were swelled from fifteen thousand in 1862, to forty or fifty thousand in 1864. Arms were again procured in quantities to which all former purchases were trifles. About two hundred thousand dollars, as testified by the Deputy Grand Commander of the Order, was furnished by rebel agents in Canada, for this purpose. Of this sum, HARRISON H. DODD and JOHN C. WALKER each took half. While these efforts were in progress, a full exposure of all the secrets of the Order—its signs, its grips, passwords, oaths, ceremonies, principles and purposes—was made by General CARRINGTON, who, with Governor MORTON, had been for months upon its track, keeping themselves fully informed of every movement and prepared for any demonstration. The attention of the whole nation was directed to the formidable extent and infamous character of the conspiracy, of which, before this exposure, the most prevalent opinion seemed to be that it was little else than a political association. The exposure alarmed the Order, for it showed that nothing could be done or attempted that would not be at once conveyed to the authorities and prepared for. Schemes of insurrection, which had been long discussed, were now precipitated. The rebellion was sinking slowly but surely. Grant was moving resistlessly down upon the last rebel refuge. Sherman was splitting the already divided Confederacy into new fragments, more hopelessly severed than ever. If anything to assist the rebellion was to be done at all, it must be done speedily and boldly. As already noticed, rebel officers came to the Capital to consult Major General JOHN C. WALKER of the Order, about releasing and arming the rebel prisoners at Indianapolis and elsewhere, and converting them into a formidable army in our midst.

A scheme was concocted in the spring, between the Order and the Kentucky guerrillas, for the removal to this State of three thousand of the latter, secretly armed, who should assume the character of refugees, and assist in bringing about an insurrection.

A general outbreak was arranged for the early part of July, but was postponed till the 16th of August. On that day, the Order in Missouri was to rise in arms, General STERLING PRICE was to join it with a strong rebel force, and the Order in Illinois was to assist. In Indiana, Ohio and Kentucky, a similar revolt was to be inaugurated, aided by BRECKINRIDGE, BUCKNER and MORGAN, with a large rebel army. The railroads and telegraph lines were to be cut, to prevent information from being sent out, and assistance from being sent in. The arsenals in Indianapolis, Columbus, Springfield and other places, were to be seized, and the rebel prisoners in these States armed. The combined forces of released prisoners and Sons of Liberty were to join the rebel army at Louisville, and permanently occupy Kentucky. This was the grand scheme of the Order, and the last hope of the Rebellion. But it failed. General PRICE's invasion of Missouri never penetrated further than the Western border. This disconcerted the Missouri and Illinois combination. A portion of BUCKNER's forces, under Colonel JOHNSON and Colonel SEIPERT, reached the Ohio river opposite Shawneetown, Illinois, where they conscripted recruits, stole cattle and horses, and stopped and plundered steamboats. But General HOVEY, with the 46th and 32d Indiana Volunteers and a force of militia raised in Posey and Vanderburgh counties, crossed the river on the 14th of August and drove the allies of the Sons of Liberty away. This spoiled the plans of the Order here. But there were other causes of failure even more potent. A large portion of the members having no knowledge of the treasonable schemes of the leaders, when they found themselves confronted with the fearful issue of a domestic war, refused to be led any further, and left the Order. A few days before the 16th, a member of Congress from the southern part of the State and a member of the Order, becoming greatly alarmed at the imminence, and extent of the danger, came to the Capital, and with the assistance of several influential friends labored to dissuade the leaders from their infamous enterprise. They succeeded so far as to procure a consent to defer it. After that, the broken meshes of the net could never be knit together again, for the progress of the war soon made it evident that even an insurrection of the Sons of Liberty could not save the rebellion. Following close upon this derangement of the most carefully planned project ever conceived by traitors, came the fatal discovery of large shipments of arms to the Chief Commander of the Order in this State, and his arrest, with that of the Deputy Commander, three of the Major Generals, and several of the most active members, of the Order. On the 17th of August, the day after that fixed for the rising, a letter was written to Governor MORTON, and received about the 20th, stating that the information conveyed had been obtained in a manner and from a source that left no doubt of its correctness; that the disloyal citizens of Indiana had ordered and paid for 30,000 revolvers and 42 boxes of ammunition, all destined for Indianapolis; that 32 of these boxes had been forwarded to the address of a gentleman whose name was given at Indianapolis, by the Merchants' Dispatch; and the remainder was stored at a certain place in New York. Upon inquiring, enough was ascertained to confirm the suspicions excited by the positive and circumstantial statements of the letter, and Mr. DODD's office was examined. Four hundred large navy revolvers and 135,000 rounds of ammunition were found, boxed and addressed precisely as stated. They were marked "Sunday School Books." Mr. DODD was arrested in the last of August. His trial, and that of his co-conspirators, and the revelations then made by members of the Order and by detectives who had entered it, will be more particularly noticed in another place.

Its Organization.—The confessions of various members of the Order show that it had a double organization, one very large, composed entirely of initiates, and operating mainly as a political club; the other small, composed only of the members of the higher degrees and of officers, and entirely military in its structure and purposes. The first was bound to obedience to the orders of the other. Though many of them never knew the treasonable schemes into which they were intended to be driven, there was not one who did not know that the object of the Order was to assist the rebellion and resist the Government. All were to be armed as far as possible, but the outer herd were to arm themselves, and the select band of leaders were to be furnished arms by a tax paid by the others or provided by the rebels. In the Fall of 1864, it was estimated by Mr. CLAYTON, one of the witnesses in the trial of DODD, that two thirds of all were armed. All were to be drilled and to be at the instant command of the chiefs. CLEMENT L. VALLANDIGHAM, of Ohio, was Supreme Grand Commander of the United States. HARRISON H. DODD was Grand Commander of Indiana; HORACE HEFFREN, was Deputy Grand Commander; WILLIAM M. HARRISON, Grand Secretary. The State was divided into four military districts, each commanded by a Major General. These officers were LAMBDIN P. MILLIGAN, of Huntington county; JOHN C. WALKER, of La Porte; ANDREW HUMPHREYS, of Greene; and WILLIAM A. BOWLES, of Orange. They were elected annually by the Grand Council, which was composed of two delegates from each county lodge, or "temple," with one additional for each thousand members. The township temples were to constitute "companies," which were combined into a "regiment" for a county, the county regiments of a Congressional District were to compose "brigades," and the brigades of each of the four military sections of the State were to compose a "division." Reports of the number of members, and of the condition and quantity of arms, were made in a sort of cypher, to avoid any accidental exposure. The names were followed by any set of words that might be agreed upon. "Corn" might stand for rifles, "oats" for powder, "potatoes" for pistols, and so on. In Missouri the names of various disloyal papers were used for the same purpose. The reports thus made were too incomplete to give any fair idea of the strength of the Order in Indiana. It was variously estimated at 75,000 to 125,000. It will be nearer the mark no doubt to put it at 50,000. In some counties it embraced nearly every member of the political party opposed to the war. It did in Washington county, as stated by Deputy Commander HEFFREN, on the trial of Dr. BOWLES and others. It did in Brown, in Sullivan, in Orange, in Marshall, Huntington, Jackson, Putnam, and in fact most of the counties of the State. Though there were many members of that party that never joined or affiliated with the Order, it was so notorious that a large majority of them belonged, and that its operations were defended or excused by all, those out as well as those in it, and that no member of any other party had ever belonged, or, as Mr. HEFFREN stated in his evidence, would be admitted, that the "Sons of Liberty was universally considered identical with the party, and the party little else or more than the Sons of Liberty." This was the material and the structure of the Order. It can serve no purpose at this day to describe the ceremonies, passwords, and signs, for they were easily and frequently changed. It only remains to glance at its declaration of principles and its objects.

Its Principles and Purposes.—In the ritual was a declaration of principles. In its acts were many declarations of purposes. The first is hardly so material to such a record as this report as the other, but it is not without interest. The following is one of the most prominent:

In the Divine economy no individual of the human race must be permitted to encumber the earth, to mar its aspects of transcendent beauty, nor to impede the progress of the physical or intellectual man, neither in himself nor in the race to which he belongs. Hence a people upon whatever plane they may be found in the ascending scale of humanity, whom neither the divinity within them, nor the inspirations of divine and beautiful nature around them, can impel to virtuous action and progress onward and upward, should be subjected to a just and humane servitude and tutelage to the superior race until they shall be able to appreciate the benefits and advantages of civilization.

This farrago of nonsense translated into plain language says, that if one race be deemed by another unfit for progress, the latter should make slaves of the other, until they can learn to progress onward and upward.

Another declaration avers that the Union of the States is only voluntary and temporary, and may be annulled at any time by any State, so far as its own connection with the Union is concerned; also that the General Government has no right or power to enforce its laws upon any State that rejects them.

The rebellion is recognized as legitimate and just. The General Government is declared a usurpation, and

Whenever the chosen officers or delegates (President or Congress) shall fail or refuse to administer the Government in strict accordance with the letter of the accepted Constitution, it is the inherent right, and the solemn, imperative duty of the people to resist the functionaries, and, if need be, expel them by force of arms. Such resistance is not revolution, but is solely the assertion of right.

Again it is said: "It is incompatible with the nature and history of our system of government that the Federal authority should coerce by arms a sovereign State."

It avows its purpose to be, to put a stop to the war and make a treaty with the rebels for a Union based upon degrees of civilization and differences of race. The theory of the rebellion is accepted in all its parts and consequences, as the true theory of government, and recognized as the bond of the Order.

These principles, which are simply a creed of unlimited slavery and absolute right of secession, each member solemnly made oath he would support at all times, and everywhere, with his sword and his life. The following is the material part of the oath of the highest degree:

> I do further swear that I will, at all times and in all places, yield prompt and implicit obedience, to the utmost of my ability, without remonstrance, hesitation or delay, to any and every mandate, order or request of my immediate Most Excellent Grand Commander, in all things touching the purposes of the Order of the Sons of Liberty, and defend the principles thereof, when assailed in my own State or country, in whatsoever capacity may be assigned to me by authority of our Order.

In the "O. A. K.," before the change, the language of the oath was: "I will defend these principles with my sword and my life in whatsoever capacity," etc.[1] Three or four oaths are contained in the ritual. The penalty of a violation is declared in that just quoted to be a "shameful death." This is the language: "All this I do solemnly promise and swear sacredly to observe, perform and keep, with a full knowledge and understanding, and with my full assent, that the penalty which will follow a violation of any or either of these, my solemn vows, will be a *shameful death.*" The ritual betrays a sad lack of common sense and literary taste in the Order. Such a production as the declaration of principles, or the neophyte oath, would obtain for a pupil in any respectable school a sound lecture or threshing. The inflated style, and silly assumption of a philosophical mode of statement, clearly entitle the author and the Order to a long servitude of the kind so pompously recommended by it for inferior intellects and natures incapable of "progress."

Besides its principles, the Order had several specific objects in view. One of these was the encouragement of desertion. The members and all whom they could influence, as heretofore stated, wrote letters to their relatives in the army urging them

---

[1] Benn Pitman (ed.), *The Trials for Treason at Indianapolis, Disclosing the Plans for Establishing a North-Western Confederacy* (Cincinnati, 1865), 308. Terrell's quotations are not exact; the italics are his.

to desert and assuring them of organizations and means to protect them. Emissaries were sent into the army, frequently as soldiers, to disseminate the Order and create lodges there. Men who had enlisted, and through the machinations of the Order had become dissatisfied, and deserters who had been arrested, were furnished legal counsel to devise means to escape from the service. Disloyal judges, of whom there was no lack, readily lent themselves to these efforts, and issued writs of habeas corpus, with an eye single to the purpose of depriving the Government of one more soldier. The effect of these efforts has already been stated in its proper place. Deserters thronged home, leaving the true and devoted soldier to do double duty and encounter double danger, on account of their cowardice. Their friends in the Order protected them and beat off the guards, or made so strong a show of resistance that arrests in many cases could not be successfully attempted. In one month twenty-six hundred desertions were reported to the Adjutant General of the State at Indianapolis. The army was weakened and the Order was in a high state of glory.

Another purpose was to prevent enlistments and to resist drafting. The facts already related touching this point make it unnecessary to say more about it here. The Order was the murderer of FREEMAN, STEVENS and McCARTY, as well as the attempted assassin of Governor MORTON.

The distribution of disloyal documents was another duty of the Order, as was the communication of information in regard to our forces to the rebels. The interchange of intelligence between the allies was constant. The Government, as already noticed in another place, frequently obtained information of the actual or contemplated movements of the rebels, from detectives in the Order several days, sometimes weeks, before it could have learned it in the ordinary way. It was also one of the purposes to furnish arms, ammunition, clothes, medicines and other stores, to the rebels. The agents employed were often ladies of good repute. Sometimes they were men who had made themselves conspicuous by fierce and false professions of loyalty. Aid was also given by burning Government vessels and stores. Dr. BOWLES stated, as proved on the trial, that the two steamers which had sometime before been burned at the wharf at Louisville, were burned with a chemical composition, absurdly called "Greek Fire," by members of the Order. The Mississippi steamers upon which large sums of money intended for the payment of the army—in one case about two millions of dollars—were transported, were burned by members of the Order. Government stores were frequently burned in the same way, by the same men. Some of the leaders in this State applied themselves assiduously to the manufacture of the destructive compound which had been found so effective. Dr. BOWLES, in particular, patronized it with constant and unchanging affection. It was generally regarded as a great acquisition.

The prime object of the Order, however, was the separation of the Northwestern States from the Union, and their formation into a separate government, or into a part of the rebel Confederacy. The general uprising of the 16th of August, 1864, was intended to accomplish or further this object. This is declared repeatedly by the members who were examined in the Treason Trials. Aid to the rebellion, and the separation of the Northwest from the Union, were the ultimate purposes to which all the riots, resistance to drafts, protection of deserters, robberies of loyal men, and murders of officers, were subordinate.

Though what are called the "secrets" of the Order, its oaths, signs and passwords, were all discovered as often as they were changed, no discovery of the schemes of the order was made public till the trial of DODD and his associates. The revelations then made left nothing to be learned. As those trials, and the disclosures they elicited, form a prominent feature of the history of the disloyal movements in Indiana, it will not be improper to give them some attention at this point.

The Treason Trials.—HARRISON H. DODD, Grand Commander of the Sons of Liberty in Indiana, entered zealously into the scheme for an insurrection on the 16th of August. Detectives kept the State and National authorities informed of his actions. He purchased a large quantity of arms and ammunition for the Order. The Governor was notified, and a search discovered a large number of revolvers and cartridges, marked "Sunday School books," concealed in his printing establishment, as before stated. This was enough to warrant his arrest in the quietest times the Nation ever knew. It was more than enough in a time of war, treason, and danger. General HOVEY, by order of the President, arrested DODD about the end of August or first of September, 1864, and confined him in the military prison in Indianapolis. In a few days he was, at his earnest request, and upon his solemn promise not to attempt to escape, removed to the United States Court building. Shortly after his arrest, WILLIAM A. BOWLES, LAMBDIN P. MILLIGAN, ANDREW HUMPHREYS, STEPHEN HORSEY, and HORACE HEFFREN, were arrested and confined in the guardhouse of the Soldiers' Home at Indianapolis. General HOVEY, then commandant of this District, on the 17th day of September, 1864, issued an order appointing a commission, consisting of Brevet Brigadier General SILAS COLGROVE, late Colonel of the Twenty-Seventh Indiana Volunteers; Colonel WILLIAM E. MCLEAN, of the Forty-Third; Colonel JOHN T. WILDER, of the Seventeenth; Colonel THOMAS J. LUCAS, of the Sixteenth; Colonel CHARLES D. MURRAY, of the Eighty-Ninth; Colonel BENJAMIN SPOONER, of the Eighty-Third; and Colonel RICHARD P. DEHART, of the One Hundred and Twenty-Eighth, to try DODD and his associates. Subsequently, Colonel AMBROSE A. STEVENS, of the Veteran Reserve Corps, was added to the commission.

On the 22d of September, the commission met and proceeded to the trial of DODD. His counsel objected to the jurisdiction of the court, but the objection was overruled. The judge advocate, Major H. L. BURNETT, on the 27th presented five charges against him, viz: 1. Conspiracy against the Government of the United States. 2. Affording aid and comfort to rebels against the authority of the United States. 3. Inciting insurrection. 4. Disloyal practices. 5. Violation of the laws of war. He pleaded "not guilty," and the examination of witnesses commenced at once.[2] The most important facts elicited were the following:

1. *The Support Given by the Order to the Rebellion.*— WESLEY TRANTER says: "HORSEY said they were going to have a very important meeting. I attended. They taught us more of the signs of recognition used by the members, *and swore us into* JEFF. DAVIS' *service, and we were to support him, North or South, at all hazards.*"[3]

WILLIAM CLAYTON said: "I considered that obligation (the oath) bound us to *assist the South,* as they were trying to free themselves and form a government of their own choice." In answer to the question, "Do you still hold that this obligation is binding upon you?" he replied, "I have taken it on myself, and I consider that it is." "You are sworn to help the South, are you?" "That is the way I read the obligation." . . . to the question, "It was against the Government and army of the United States that you were organized to wage war?" he replied, "*We were to wage war upon them,* of course, if they took up arms against the South." On the same page, he said the Order "was willing to shake hands with rebel invaders, and consider them friends"; that "this was the sentiment in the section where he lived." "In that section the success of the South was considered a less evil than the oppression of the Administration," and that the "same feeling was still maintained in the Lodges."[4]

2. *The General insurrection.* TRANTER says: *"The arms were to be used to assist the rebels.* They (the members) expressed their intention to resist the United States government, and support the South. STONE said in his speech, that they were to take Indianapolis; the members of the Order in Illinois, to

[2] Pitman (ed.), *Trials for Treason,* 9-10, 17-19.
[3] *Ibid.,* 47.
[4] *Ibid.,* 46.

take Springfield; while those in Missouri were to take St. Louis. BRAGG was to do all he could in Tennessee; MORGAN was to advance his force into Kentucky; FORREST was to cross the Ohio, into Illinois. The Indianians were to seize Indianapolis and the Arsenal, and distribute the arms to those members of the Order who had none."[5] CLAYTON states that "it was part of their general plan, to assist the rebels whenever they invaded these States, and if it has been given up, I do not know it."[6] FELIX G. STIDGER states, that Dr. BOWLES developed the plan of insurrection, to him, in this way:

> Illinois was pledged to forward 50,000 men, to concentrate at St. Louis, and to co-operate with Missouri, which was pledged to furnish 30,000, and these combined forces, were to co-operate with PRICE, who was to invade Missouri with 20,000, and more if possible. These 100,000 men were to hold Missouri against any Federal forces, that could be sent against them. Indiana was to furnish from 40,000 to 60,000 men, to co-operate with other forces that might come from Ohio, and all were to be thrown on Louisville, to co-operate with whatever force JEFF. DAVIS might send into Eastern Kentucky, under BUCKNER, or BRECKINRIDGE, as Davis might deem best.[7]

3. *The Murder of Governor Morton*. TRANTER says: "At that meeting STONE said, Governor MORTON was to be put out of the way; that he had but a short time to live, after the visit to the Indianapolis arsenal."[8] This was another part of the plan for a general uprising.

4. *Releasing and arming the rebel prisoners*. This was part of the programme for August, but was not mentioned by STIDGER as a part of that detailed by Dr. BOWLES. It was related to STIDGER by DODD:

[5] *Ibid.*, 48.
[6] *Ibid.*, 43.
[7] *Ibid.*, 32. Felix G. Stidger was employed as a spy by General Carrington, commanding the District of Indiana, to ferret out the activities and intentions of the Sons of Liberty. He was initiated into the order, and won the confidence of its leaders, and was soon familiar with its workings. See his *Treason History of the Order of Sons of Liberty* . . . (Chicago, 1903).
[8] Pitman (ed.), *Trials for Treason*, 48.

Dodd said, they had agreed to seize the camps of the rebel prisoners at Indianapolis, Camp Chase in Ohio, Camp Douglas at Chicago, and the Depot of prisoners on Johnson's Island. They were going to seize the arsenals in Indianapolis, Springfield and Chicago. They were going to arm the prisoners with the arms thus seized; raise all the members of the Order they could on the 15th or 16th of August, that being the day fixed for the uprising. Each commander was to move all his men toward, and concentrate them at, Louisville. They were to get the co-operation of Colonel SEIPERT and Colonel JESSE of the rebel army, who were then in Kentucky. They (these rebel officers) were to seize Louisville, and hold it until their (the O.S.L.) forces could co-operate. At Chicago there was a difference of opinion, whether to wait until after they were sure of the co-operation of the rebel forces, or go ahead without them. DODD sent WM. M. HARRISON (the Secretary of the Indiana branch of the Order) to see MILLIGAN, HUMPHREYS and WALKER and get them to Indianapolis before that day. They did not come. DODD read me letters which he said were from them. They said they were to go ahead, at the time designated, to release and arm the prisoners and members of the Order, and eventually unite in Louisville.[9]

5. *The deliberate determination to murder Park Coffin, a detective in the service of the government.* Mr. STIDGER says:

I was sent to Dr. BOWLES and Mr. DODD by Judge BULLITT, in reference to Mr. COFFIN, who was living in this city (Indianapolis), and who was then employed as a detective officer by the Government. My instructions were that COFFIN was *to be put out of the way at all hazards.* I understood he was to be murdered. I stated my instructions to Mr. DODD. COFFIN was acquainted with the secrets of the Order of the Sons of Liberty. I do not know of any other injury he had done to DODD, BULLITT or BOWLES.

At a meeting of the Grand Council on the 14th or 15th of June, 1864, the case of COFFIN was brought before the council and discussed at length. The discussion was about various things that COFFIN had done as a detective, for the benefit of the United States Government; and it was finally decided that *he should be murdered.* Mr. DODD volunteered to go to Hamilton, Ohio (where there was to be a meeting next day,

[9] Pitman (ed.), *Trials for Treason,* 23-24.

at which COFFIN was expected) and if COFFIN was there to dispose of him.[10]

6. *The destruction of Steamers and Government Stores by the Order.* STIDGER says: "Dr. BOWLES said, that those two boats that were destroyed at the wharf at Louisville, were burned by this Greek Fire, and had been done by the order of the Sons of Liberty."[11]

Full disclosures were made of all the signs, grips, passwords, and ceremonies of the Order, but they are not important now. On the night of the 6th of October, DODD, with the help of friends outside, escaped from the window of his room by a rope, and made his way to Canada. The Judge Advocate at once rested the case. Arguments were made on both sides, and some months afterwards it was published that he was sentenced to death, and that the finding and sentence had been approved.

The commission which tried DODD was, by a special order of General HOVEY, subsequently increased by the addition of Colonel ANSEL D. WASS, of the Sixtieth Massachusetts Regiment, then stationed at Indianapolis; Colonel Thomas W. BENNETT, of the Sixty-Ninth Indiana; Colonel REUBEN WILLIAMS, of the Twelfth Indiana, and Colonel ALBERT HEATH, of the One-Hundredth Indiana. Before the close of the trial, Colonel JOHN T. WILDER, of the Seventeenth Indiana, having resigned his command, was relieved from the commission. The charges against BOWLES, MILLIGAN, HUMPHREYS, HEFFREN and HORSEY, were precisely the same as those against DODD. The trial commenced on the 21st of October, 1864. MILLIGAN objected to Colonel WASS, that "he was from a locality where there are extreme prejudices against Western men, and he was likely to be influenced by those prejudices." The court believing, very justly, that the objection was based upon a false assumption, overruled it. Among men of MILLIGAN's class, there was a bitter and senseless prejudice against the people

[10] *Ibid.*, 20-21.
[11] *Ibid.*, 22.

of New England, which they naturally thought was reciprocated, but everybody with any knowledge of the feelings of that portion of our people knew that the hostility was all upon one side. The revelations made by the witnesses in this trial were, in the main, identical with those developed in the trial of DODD. It will be necessary here to notice only a few additional points.

WILLIAM M. HARRISON, Grand Secretary of the Order for Indiana, testified that official reports had been made of organizations in forty-five counties, but admitted that there might have been branch "temples" or lodges in other counties.[12]

He estimated that there were about 18,000 members of the first, second and third degrees in the State. The "vestibule members" he did not include in this estimate, as they were not considered members of the organization. He also disclosed the fact that the arms seized in August were addressed to Mr. J. J. PARSONS (a business partner of DODD's), without that gentleman's knowledge.

JOSEPH J. BINGHAM, editor of the *Indiana State Sentinel*, testified to the revelation to him by DODD of the scheme for a general insurrection and release of the rebel prisoners on the 16th of August, and to the steps taken by leading men of his party to prevent it. He also disclosed the fact that two or three rebel officers were in the city at that time, on their way to Chicago, to take command of the rebel prisoners when they should be released and armed.[13] When the representations of friends had induced DODD and WALKER to defer their project, WALKER said he must see the officers to notify them of the change that had been determined upon.

HORACE HEFFREN, Deputy Grand Commander, who was made a witness by Judge Advocate BURNETT, on the 4th of November, and released from arrest and discharged, testified that Dr. BOWLES was the chief officer of the Order in Indiana.

[12] Pitman (ed.), *Trials for Treason*, 87.
[13] *Ibid.*, 103.

Dodd, he said, was the Grand Commander, which was a civil office, but that Bowles was the military head of the Order.[14] He also stated that he had been shown a roll of bills amounting to $1,000 by Dr. James B. Wilson, Adjutant on Bowles's staff, which had been obtained from Bowles to purchase arms and ammunition for Washington county, and that he was informed by the same man that $500,000 had been sent to Indiana, Illinois and Kentucky, by rebel agents in Canada, to buy arms and ammunition for the Order in those States. Of this sum $200,000 had been received by Dodd and Walker for Indiana. Each took $100,000. A portion was to be used by Bowles to arm the Order in his part of the State.[15]

Mr. Heffren also testified to the insurrection scheme and the release of the rebel prisoners, and added two important features: 1st. That "Governor Morton was to be taken care of," or as he explained it, "held as a hostage for the safety of those of the insurrectionists who might be taken prisoners." Dr. James S. Athon, a member of the Order, and then Secretary of the State, was to become Governor, under the "law and the Constitution," as Heffren understood. The militia (which would be composed of the armed members of the Order, of course) would be called out, and, as Mr. Heffren said, "we should have everything our own way."[16] The Military Board Bill was intended to accomplish this result under the forms of law, and its defeat, doubtless, exerted no little influence in determining the adoption of the scheme of revolutionary violence which Mr. Heffren exposed.

He also stated that he had been informed by Wilson, Bowles's adjutant, that steps had been taken to procure lances for a regiment of lancers. They were to be made with a lance head, combined with a sickle-shaped knife, the first to thrust with, the other to cut the horses' bridles. "He

[14] *Ibid.*, 125.
[15] *Ibid.*, 126.
[16] *Ibid.*, 127.

(WILSON) thought the enemy (the Union troops) would become confused and distracted, and if a charge was made upon them when they had no means of controlling their horses, they would be easily mashed up."[17]

He disclosed the fact that TEN individuals had been selected by the leaders of the Order "*to take care of Governor* MORTON." He did not learn who they were. "They were to hold the Governor as a hostage for those who were taken prisoners, *or to make way with him some way.*"[18]

"If they could not use him for their own purposes, they might take him out and kill him."[19]

He believed these ten men would do this to Governor MORTON, and "had good reason for believing it."[20]

Mr. HEFFREN further stated that in case of a rebel raid, the members of the Order were to place a rebel flag on their property and no injury would be done it. Also, that in the proposed insurrection they were to march under the rebel flag. "We were to join our fortunes with the South."[21]

Dr. JAMES B. WILSON, adjutant to BOWLES, was made a witness and related minutely the steps that were to be taken in commencing the insurrection in this State, but these details are hardly of importance enough now to warrant the lengthening of this report by their introduction. The revelations noticed in the trial of DODD, and the confirmatory disclosures of BINGHAM and HEFFREN, cover all that is necessary to assure the public of the treasonable purposes of the Sons of Liberty. The examination of witnesses was completed on the 25th of November, and the Court adjourned till the 6th of December to allow counsel time to prepare their arguments.

The Court finally found BOWLES, MILLIGAN, HORSEY and HUMPHREYS *guilty,* and sentenced the first three to death.

---

[17] Pitman, *Trials for Treason,* 128.
[18] *Ibid.,* 129.
[19] *Ibid.,* 135.
[20] *Ibid.*
[21] *Ibid.*

HUMPHREYS was condemned to imprisonment for life, but General HOVEY remitted his sentence to confinement within a limited space in his own county for a year or two. The sentence of the others was approved, the day fixed for their execution, and preparations were already commenced, when, upon the earnest representations of Governor MORTON and other prominent loyal men, President JOHNSON was induced to commute their sentence to imprisonment in the Penitentiary at Columbus, Ohio. They were subsequently pardoned and returned home. DODD, it is understood, was also pardoned.[22]

CONCLUSION

This summary of the obstacles thrown in the way of the prosecution of the war by the disloyal element in Indiana, is far from complete. Many facts in regard to the action of the Legislature, the expressions of feeling by public meetings, the encouragement and protection of deserters, the resistance to the laws and the maltreatment of loyal citizens, and in regard to the purposes and action of the treasonable Order of Sons of Liberty, might have been added. But they could only have lengthened this report without materially strengthening the argument for the two leading propositions which it is intended to establish: that the disloyal element of the North contributed, certainly in a great degree, in all probability decisively, to produce the war; and contributed still more certainly and effectively to protract it. No amount of sophistry, bluster, denial, or attempted refutation, will ever erase from the pages of our history the responsibility of disloyal citizens for a large portion of the bloodshed, misery and desolation which the war produced; or for the almost intolerable legacy it left in the form of a monstrous public debt and the exhausting taxation which follows in its train. . . .

[22] The United States Supreme Court, *Ex Parte Milligan* (4 Wallace 2, 1866) ruled that since Milligan was not in the military or naval service and the civil courts in Indiana were open, his trial before a military tribunal had been a denial of his constitutional rights.

RELIEF OF SOLDIERS AND THEIR FAMILIES

ORIGIN OF THE INDIANA RELIEF SYSTEM

The outbreak of the rebellion found our Government not only without an army, but without the means to equip it. Out of this double deficiency grew an army of citizens, who not only needed more care than the Government could give, but who left families dependent upon them needing help which no Government has ever given. A citizen soldiery, unused to war and ignorant of its discipline and privations, would necessarily suffer more, not only in the lack of comforts to which they had been accustomed, but in their liability to disease, than a regular army, even when supplied with all a regular army is allowed. The danger was much greater when our Government found itself inadequately provided with even regular army supplies. In the necessity of averting this danger, the Indiana State Sanitary Commission, as well as those of other States, and the larger organization of the United States Sanitary Commission, originated. In this State the most obvious necessity was the completion of inadequate Government supplies, and the effort to meet this led to the solicitation of popular contributions. The second necessity, but little less obvious than the first, was to supply comforts which the Government could not, or did not attempt to, supply. The efforts to meet the first led to organizations which, during the war, successfully met the second, and the record of these constitute the history of our State Sanitary Commission. At the commencement of the war, the women, with the instinctive tenderness of their sex, set about supplying headgear, called "havelocks," for our three months' troops, and the Governor provided every available comfort of camplife and requirement of hospital service, to meet the deficiency of Government provision. But it was not till the approach of winter that the necessity for any effort on the part of the people or the State authorities, in aid of the General Government, became apparent. In fact, it was not until the actual privations and sufferings of the winter admonished us of the amount of care that would be required, that organization, or anything more than temporary help to be soon replaced by permanent Government provision, was thought of. The steps through which we advanced from accidental assistance to systematic and continuous beneficence were short, but each developed a wider necessity before us. Contributions of clothing, camp equipage, provisions, and hospital necessaries, were constantly made to the soldiers, directly, by their friends, both before they left the camp of rendezvous and afterwards; but these were far oftener mementoes of parental or friendly affection than provision for anticipated necessities. It needed the stern teaching of suffering to convert them into a constant stream of benefactions, without which our camps would but too often have contained more graves than tents.

The first steps were, naturally, those in aid of ordinary Government supplies. By then we reached the point from which we could see that further steps were necessary, and that efforts, not merely to complete, but to enlarge, those of the Government must be made. On the 20th of August, 1861, Governor MORTON, then in Washington City, telegraphed to the State officers as follows:

> Urge Major MONTGOMERY (then United States Quartermaster, at Indianapolis) to get overcoats of any good material, and not wait for a public letting. Do have them made at once. The men are suffering for them, and I am distressed for them. Perhaps a few thousands can be forwarded at once, by Captain DICKERSON.

This urgency, which might seem almost premature, was none too soon. Our men among the mountains of Western Virginia were already suffering in the chilly nights that announced the approach of autumn. Governor MORTON, in whom anxiety for his men was a cherished duty, felt their sufferings before any complaint had reached him. It was not till two days after this that any information of the wants of the troops was received. In pursuance of his orders, the State officers at once applied to Quartermaster MONTGOMERY for the overcoats. He either could not furnish them, or, with the unpleasant captiousness that uniformly marked his conduct, did not feel disposed to accommodate a State official, and application was made to Captain DICKERSON, at Cincinnati. He promptly sent forward four thousand, in care of General ROSECRANS, then in command of Western Virginia. The want of system and the enormous rush of supplies during the first months of the war caused delays and confusions to a most embarrassing extent, and our overcoats were no more successful in "running the gauntlet" of incompetent or overburdened officers than other supplies. For nearly a month the Governor waited impatiently for news of their arrival.

On the 15th of September, hearing nothing of them, and the men beginning to suffer seriously for want of them, he sent his Private Secretary, Colonel W. R. HOLLOWAY, to hunt them up. As there were a good many "knotty" places where such supplies might be entangled, he soon after sent the State Commissary General, ASAHEL STONE, to assist in tracing them. Twelve hundred were at last discovered and pushed through. Repeated and earnest representations of the condition of our men to Quartermaster General MEIGS, General ROSECRANS, General KELLEY, and all the officers concerned in the supply and transportation of the articles, finally succeeded in rescuing or replacing them, and on October 7, General J. J. REYNOLDS, of this State, then commanding a brigade of our troops, telegraphed their receipt to the Governor as follows:

Clothing is coming forward. In a few days we shall have a supply for the Thirteenth, Fourteenth, Fifteenth and Seventeenth Regiments, except shoes, socks and caps; the last are not so important. Shoes and socks much needed. These regiments have suffered greatly, but

RELIEF OF SOLDIERS AND THEIR FAMILIES 397

not a man among them has any fault to find with the Governor of the State. They are all informed of the exertion made in their behalf and appreciate it.

Satisfied by the experience of this effort to supply our troops in Western Virginia, that the General Government, with every possible exertion, must leave many regiments insufficiently provided, even with the indispensable protection of overcoats, and there being troops from Indiana at other points in a very destitute condition, Governor MORTON resolved to see them properly supplied at all hazards. If the General Government would pay the expense, well; but if it refused, the State would pay it, for the men must be cared for. Accordingly, he went to New York, and through the purchasing agent of the state, Hon. ROBERT DALE OWEN, be bought twenty-nine thousand overcoats. For a portion he paid the Government price, $7.75 each. But the demand for that sort of material was so great that he could not get the remainder of the necessary quantity short of $9.25 each. The Quartermaster General, upon presentation of the bill, refused to pay more than the regulation price upon the whole lot, leaving the difference of $1.50 upon a large number of coats, to be settled by the State. When notified by Major MONTGOMERY of the decision of Quartermaster General MEIGS, the Governor replied: "Indiana will not allow her troops to suffer if it be in her power to prevent it, and if the General Government will not purchase supplies at these (the current) rates, *Indiana will.*" The virtue of "beginning as one intends to hold out" was never more conspicuously displayed than in this instance. From first to last the important consideration was, not "will the Government pay?" but "what do the men need?" and what they needed they had, if money and energy could get it for them. By this providence and wise economy, our men were all as amply as possible prepared for the rigors of the first winter of the war. As another illustration of the spirit with which the Governor conducted all his business in behalf of soldiers, it may be noted here that when the Indianapolis Quartermaster, Major MONTGOMERY, made a reclamation of his imperceptible merit in the business of the overcoats, against the universal approval of Governor MORTON's action, the latter, after a brief statement of the efforts made, said: "These exertions secured twenty-nine thousand overcoats for our troops. It will be of little importance by whose agency it was done, if they shall succeed in getting them in due season."

Overcoats, however, were not the only necessaries lacking. General REYNOLDS had reported, in October, that his men were without suitable shoes, socks or caps. Blankets, hardly less indispensable than clothes, were deficient in quantity and quality. Many articles, unknown to the regulations, were needed for both camp and hospital. Some of these could not be purchased, for there were none in the market. Others the Government would not purchase if it could. But they must all be had, and there was but one way to get them: to appeal to the interest of the people in their friends, to the duty of the citizen to the army, to the benevolence of the charitable for the suffering. This the Governor did in the first official attempt made to bring popular effort to the aid of the Government. On October 10th, 1861, he issued the following proclamation:

To the Patriotic Women of Indiana:

When the President issued his first call to the loyal States for help, the Government was unprovided with most, if not all, of the articles necessary to the comfort and health of soldiers in the camp and in the field. The women of Indiana were appealed to, and they supplied the deficiency in our State with a generous alacrity which entitles them to the gratitude of the nation. The approach of winter makes it necessary to appeal to them again. Our Volunteers, already suffering from exposure, against which they are inadequately protected, will soon be compelled to endure the utmost severity of winter, and multiplied dangers of disease. The Government is doing all that can be done for them, but, when all is done, they must still lack many comforts which men in ordinary pursuits enjoy, and which soldiers need above all others. Many articles of clothing, which, to men with houses over their heads and warm fires always near, are hardly more than a luxury, to men with no protection but a tent, no bed but the ground, and whose duty must be performed under the unabated rigors of winter, are absolute necessaries. They may save many lives which will surely be lost without them. These, the patriotic women of Indiana, it is hoped, will supply. An additional blanket to every man in our army will preserve hundreds to their country and to their families. Two or three pairs of good, strong socks will be invaluable to men who must often march all day in the snow, and without them, must lie down with cold and benumbed feet, on the frozen ground. Good woolen gloves or mittens will preserve their hands in marching and in handling their arms, and while adding greatly to their comfort, will materially increase their efficiency. Woolen shirts and drawers, too, are a necessity to men exposed to such vicissitudes of weather as soldiers. All these articles the Indiana volunteers ought to have now, and must have before winter sets in, if we would protect them from exposure and disease, that may be averted by this timely preparation. Some of these articles the Government does not furnish, and others not in sufficient quantities to supply the waste produced by the exposure of a soldier's life. Blankets cannot be purchased. The stock is completely exhausted, and the government is soliciting contributions from the citizens. Will not the women of Indiana do their share in providing for the men of Indiana, in the battlefield?

An hour of each day for a week given to the manufacture of the articles named will provide an ample store. Are they not ready to give that, and more, if needed? I urge upon them the duty of promptly beginning the work. Let them at once forward, at the State's expense, to the State Quartermaster, such blankets as they can spare. They will be immediately and carefully sent to such regiments as the donors prefer; if they have any preference. Let them singly, or by associations, set about the manufacture of woolen shirts, drawers, socks and gloves. The sewing societies of our churches have a wide field for exertion, wider and grander than they will ever find again. Will they not give their associations for a time to this beneficent object? The numerous female benevolent societies, by giving their energies and organizations to this work, can speedily provide the necessary supply. Let women through the country, who had no opportunity to join such associations, emulate each other in their labors, and see who shall do most for their country and its defenders in this hour of trial.

The articles should be sent to the Quartermaster General of the State, with a card stating the name and residence of the donor, and their destination, if she has any choice. The names will be recorded and preserved, with the number and kind of articles sent. The women of Indiana alone can meet this emergency, and to them our volunteers, as well as the Government, look for sympathy and aid.

O. P. MORTON, *Governor of Indiana.*

October 10th, 1861.

In the official report of the Quartermaster General of the State, J. H. VAJEN, made to the Governor, on the first of May, 1862, that officer alludes to the effect of this proclamation, in the following paragraph:

> This proclamation met with a most cordial response, and donations to the value of many thousands of dollars were forwarded. The articles consisted, for the most part, of blankets, shirts, drawers, socks and mittens, together with sheets, pillows, pads, bandages, lint and dressing gowns, for hospital uses. So liberal were these contributions that I deemed it necessary in the latter part of the winter, to issue a circular to the effect that the supply was sufficient, except of mittens and socks. That deficiency, too, was so far supplied that all subsequent applications for the articles, with the exception of only two or three, were filled. The generosity of our citizens in this regard has added very greatly to the comfort of our troops in the field and camp, and very probably has saved many valuable lives.[1]

ORGANIZATION FOR TEMPORARY RELIEF

The distribution of the supplies contributed in response to the Governor's appeal suggested the first organized effort of any State to complete or enlarge the Government provision for our soldiers. The State Commissary General was charged with the duty of supervising the work, and energetic and humane gentlemen were sent as agents to the best points to carry it on.[2] Their expenses, and the purchase of such additional supplies as were deemed necessary, were paid out of the Military Contingent Fund, appropriated by the Legislature at the extra session of the spring of 1861. The duty of these

---

[1] *Report of John H. Vajen, Quarter-Master General of the State of Indiana* (Indianapolis, 1863), 5.

[2] For a complete list of regular Indiana Military Agents, see Terrell, *Report*, 1, Appendix, Doc. 12:109.

agents, as set forth in a letter from this office to the Quartermaster General of Ohio, dated November 26, 1864, was "to render all possible relief to our soldiers, especially to those who were sick or wounded, whether in transit, in hospitals, or on the battle-field. Sanitary stores and hospital supplies, purchased in some cases by the Governor, but more frequently donated by the patriotic people of the State, were sent to these agents, and by them carefully distributed, the rule being to first supply our own troops, and then to relieve those from other States."[3] In addition to this regular provision of distributing and assisting agents, special agents, surgeons and nurses were also sent to points where additional aid was necessary. In distributing the contributions regard was had to the wishes of the donors, as indicated in the Governor's address, but where no special direction was given the stores were applied where the greatest need existed.

This improvised arrangement was sufficient to meet immediate necessities, and when it was made no further necessity was apparent. It was a prevalent, if not universal, opinion that the war would be speedily ended, and it was certain that as soon as the Government could once place itself in a condition to supply the requirements of the regulations, it would need no help from popular effort in that direction. But early in 1862, it became evident that the war would not be speedily ended, and still more evident that the Government regulations did not embrace everything that the previous habits of the soldiers had made necessary to their comfort and health, and at the same time they were very deficient in providing such supplies as were required for hospital use. What had been done by popular effort to furnish these, to enlarge the Government provision for the citizen-soldier adequate to

[3] This is a letter from Adjutant General Terrell to Brig. Gen. M. Barlow, Quartermaster of Ohio, in reply to a request for information as to the "plan adopted by the State of Indiana for relief of her soldiers, together with the success and expense to the State Government attendant thereon." The complete text of the letter is given in *ibid.,* 1, Appendix, Doc. 87:290-92.

his wants and the anxieties of his friends, would have to be done again, and continued till the war ended, be it soon or late. The improvised agencies suggested the mode of making such efforts effectual. They could be made permanent, reduced to system, and placed under competent supervision, and the foundation thus laid for continuous and protracted effort. In this purpose originated the "General Military Agency of Indiana."

ESTABLISHMENT OF THE GENERAL INDIANA MILITARY AGENCY

This organization, destined to play so conspicuous a part in the history of our State's share of the war, was created by the appointment, by Governor MORTON, of Dr. WILLIAM HANNAMAN, of Indianapolis, a gentleman of large business experience, humanity and integrity, as "General Military Agent." To him was entrusted the receipt and distribution of all sanitary supplies, the supervision of local agencies, and the direction of all matters relating to the relief of soldiers.

Local agents and special agents, either in the hospital or in the field, were required to report to him the condition of the troops and hospitals in their charge, and the Governor was thus furnished with the necessary information to direct promptly and effectively the assistance, whether in stores, surgeons or nurses, that might be needed. Field agents were expected not only to look after the health and comfort of the men, but to write letters, to take charge of commissions for them to their friends and relatives, to see to the burial of the dead, and the preservation of relics, to keep registers of the names of all men in hospitals, with date of entry, disease or injury, and, in case of death, the date and cause, and any other information that might be of interest to relatives and friends. These registers were afterwards found of great value in settling pension and pay claims. Local agents were required to make their offices the homes of soldiers; to assist them in getting transportation in returning home, when they had no money or Government passes; to provide them clothing when, as was too often the case, they were ragged and necessitous; to feed them; to facilitate every proper purpose; to take charge of returning prisoners, and provide everything which their shocking destitution demanded; and, in short, to be careful, affectionate, watchful guardians. Supplies of reading matter, books, newspapers and periodicals, both for field and hospital, formed another object of the agency's care. Our soldiers were, with very few exceptions, men to whom reading of some kind was a necessity, begotten not only by the weariness of idle days, but by previous habits, and the demand for means of gratification was as constant and imperious as for stores and medicines.

Besides the supervision of subordinate agencies of whatever kind, the General Agency was charged with the duty of chartering steamers, when it was deemed necessary after a battle, to carry the stores, surgeons and nurses that might be required, to the wounded, and to bring home, or to convenient hospitals, such as might be able or allowed to come. Frequently boats were dispatched to destitute points completely loaded with vegetables, hospital supplies, clothing and like comforts, and returned filled with wounded and sick men, whom the prospect of coming home, even more than the abundant and suitable supplies, and the pleasant change from tents to the airy boat, almost brought back from death. The first serious battle in which our State troops were engaged, that of Fort Donelson, in February, 1862, was the occasion of the commencement of this humane labor, which was never intermitted so long as it was needed.

A few days after the bloody battle of Richmond, Kentucky, in August, 1862, special agents were sent, under flags of truce, within the enemy's lines, to look after the wounded who might be prisoners. The embassy to Richmond, under charge of Dr. THEOPHILUS PARVIN and the lamented Dr. TALBOT BULLARD, was greatly serviceable to our suffering soldiers, in the hands of the enemy. A large number were relieved, and brought home, who, if left to rebel care, would in all probability have returned in their coffins.

Through the Agency, also, arrangements were made to convey to our prisoners in Libby, Belle Isle, and other rebel prisons, the contributions of food, clothing and medicines made by their friends, and the large purchase of some five or six thousand dollars worth of stores, made by Governor MORTON, in Baltimore, for their benefit. The forwarding and collecting of claims for bounty, back pay and pensions, gratuitously, were subsequently made a part, and a very important part, of the business of the agency. Hundreds of thousands of dollars were saved to the soldiers by it, which would either have been lost entirely, or seriously reduced by delays and the rapacity and rascality of claim agents. Subordinate agents were also appointed to collect and bring home the pay of soldiers in the field, and the risk of mail transportation through a hostile country, and the expense of expressing or other customary modes, were avoided. These instances indicate, rather than describe, the various and indispensable services of the "General Military Agency." A more detailed account of its action will be found in another place.

In concluding this general statement of the services of the Agency, it may be remarked that the leading idea of its system of action was to provide for the wants, and take care of the health, of the men in the field, in order, as far as possible, to preserve their efficiency, and diminish the duties and demands of hospital service. "Prevention was better than cure." A well man kept well was better than a sick man cured. Not that the needs of hospitals were ever in any degree sacrificed to this idea, for they were as amply supplied as liberality, sagacity and energy could do it, but the primary consideration was to prevent or reduce hospital service. In its labors it had, with rare exceptions, the ready and grateful co-operation of the officers, in furnishing transportation for stores and help, and facilitating their distribution. The exceptions were usually found in officers of the regular army, who knew nothing outside of the regulations and conducted the business of armies as they had been accustomed to do that of companies. The Local Agents were paid from one hundred to one hundred and fifty dollars per month, and expenses for office rent, fuel, clerk hire and the like. Special agents or surgeons who charged for their services, were usually allowed enough to pay their expenses, no more being asked or expected. Through them and the cordial co-operation of Captain JAMES A. EKIN, the United States Quartermaster at Indianapolis, who succeeded Major MONTGOMERY, the winter rigors of 1862-63, were anticipated and the troops abundantly supplied before their approach. In this connection it may not be improper to say that the uniform courtesy and efficiency of Captain EKIN were of inestimable value to the State, and richly earned for him his subsequent advancement to the responsible position of Deputy Quartermaster General of the United States Army.

ESTABLISHMENT OF THE STATE SANITARY COMMISSION

As soon as it became evident that a permanent system of extra governmental aid for our soldiers would be required, some mode of procuring, as well as distributing, supplies became necessary. The Military Contingent Fund, appropriated by the Legislature, besides being divided among several objects of essential importance to the service, would not alone have sufficed for the probable needs of the relief system. To meet this want Governor MORTON, in February, 1862, created the "Indiana Sanitary Commission," under the charge of Dr. WILLIAM HANNAMAN, Military Agent, as President, and ALFRED HARRISON, ESQ., of Indianapolis, as Treasurer. Both were peculiarly qualified by experience, disposition and business habits for their arduous duties, and both entered upon them and discharged them till the close of the war, with a zeal that never flagged, an integrity that was never darkened by a shade of suspicion of interested motives, and an efficiency that entitled them to the gratitude of the soldiers and the State. Primarily, the object of the Commission was to supply the Agency with means and material for the relief of our troops, but being under the same direction, with duties so closely allied as to be almost identical, and in fact being but one hand of the system of which the Agency was the other, both were in effect one organization, and were popularly known as one. The "Sanitary Commission" being constantly before the public by its appeals, its soliciting agents, and other efforts, easily became the representative of both, and as the "State Sanitary Commission" the Relief System of the State must stand in the records of its benefactions.

The operations of the Commission can be most satisfactorily described by dividing them into their natural classes of "Collections" and "Distributions." The former was carried on by "Soliciting Agents" and auxiliary societies; the latter mainly by "Military Agents," though many special "Sanitary Agents" were dispatched from time to time to different points.

COLLECTIONS

Auxiliary Societies—The appeal of Governor MORTON, in October, 1861, caused the formation of a number of associations, mainly of ladies, to supply the articles called for. These associations were not generally discontinued when the immediate object of their formation was accomplished, but kept on collecting and forwarding such articles of clothing, food, and hospital necessaries, as they deemed likely to be of service. When the Sanitary Commission was organized they fell easily into the position of auxiliary societies, and formed steady springs of supply to the stream of beneficence directed by the Commission. To them were added other societies, formed under the efforts and influence of the soliciting agents, who made it their main duty to establish and encourage them. The county seat was usually made the location of the central society, and contributing societies were established in every township and neighborhood, as far as possible. Through these, the contributions of individuals, and of associations unconnected with the Commission, were collected and forwarded to the central society, or to the general office at the Capital; and by them was continued and extended the work inaugurated by the soliciting agents. These contributions were composed of everything available for field or hospital use; articles of clothing not included in Government stores; of food, particularly of vegetables, dried and canned fruits, preserves and delicacies indispensable to the sick and convalescent; of bedding, books and the like, of the variety of which an idea can be obtained only from lists of contributions reported by the Commission. It may not be uninteresting to give here, as an indication of the character of the work performed by these societies, a list of articles distributed by one of the agencies:—potatoes, dried apples, canned fruits, onions, kraut, pickles, dried peaches, wine, cordials, whisky, eggs, butter, apple butter, small fruits, lemons, ale, crackers, rice, farina, corn meal, tobacco, paper, envelopes, bed sacks, comforts, quilts, sheets, pillows, pillow slips, towels, shirts, drawers, rags, bandages, fans, pantaloons, combs, handkerchiefs, socks, lint, pads, comfort bags, slippers, boxes of reading matter, gowns, crutches, There is hardly one of these articles that would not be either an indispensable necessity, or an acceptable addition, to the comfort of any sick man, and it would be hard to conceive the suffering, and fatality even, that they have alleviated or prevented.

Soliciting Agents—The supplies of material comforts, such as have been described, were left to the auxiliary societies. But more was needed than food, clothing, bedding and reading, to make the work of the Commission effective. Without money some things of vital importance could not have been obtained, and very often nothing could have been sent to its destination. Government transportation could not always be had, or could not be relieved of the trammels of routine, in time; and other things, as for instance, the personal expenses of agents in charge of supplies, delicacies for the sick not furnished in sufficient quantity, &c., had to be paid for in cash. Money was of course contributed through the auxiliary societies frequently, but the main supply was furnished by the exertions of the soliciting agents. These men, of marked energy and ability, traveled all over the State, holding meetings, representing the necessities of the soldier and the operations of the Commission, organizing societies, soliciting supplies and money, and resorting even to personal and private appeals to citizens. They labored with a zeal and perseverance that stopped for no obstacle; counted no cost of exposure, labor, or time; that considered nothing beyond their duty that would procure money or goods for the soldier; and in this great work they achieved a success as creditable to themselves as to the liberality of the people. Dr. HANNAMAN, in his report of January, 1865, mentions four agents as eminently successful: Captain ALONZO ATKINSON, formerly of the Sixteenth Regiment; Chaplain J. H. LOZIER, formerly of the Thirty-Seventh Regiment; Hon. M. F. SHUEY, of Elkhart county, and Rev. BENJAMIN WINANS, of Lafayette. The aid of soliciting agents, however, was not called for until some months after the establishment of the Commission, the main dependence at first being upon auxiliary societies and voluntary contributions.

Sanitary Fairs—One prolific source of the supply of money as well as of goods, was the "fairs," which, for the last two years of the war, constituted a feature of social life that a stranger might have easily mistaken for a fixed national habit. Neighborhood fairs, county fairs, State fairs, were constantly soliciting public attention, in one quarter or another of the whole country, and nowhere more generally or successfully than in Indiana. It is true we had no gigantic displays, like those of Chicago or Philadelphia, for we were working only in an humble way, and depending solely upon ourselves; but the aggregate results make as creditable a showing as any State can boast. Among the conspicuous contributions to the Sanitary Fund was that made to the Sanitary Fair by the Order of Freemasons, composed of the individual contributions of members. It amounted to ten thousand dollars, and is justly entitled to a place beside the magnificent contributions reported by the United States Sanitary Commission.

The State Sanitary Fair, held at Indianapolis, in the fall of 1863, at the time of the State Agricultural Fair, was eminently successful. The proceeds amounted to about forty thousand dollars. The State Board of Agriculture gave every aid to the enterprise, and contributed materially to its success. Vanderburgh county was awarded a banner for the largest contribution made outside of Marion county. Many other efforts, equally commendable but less conspicuous, deserve mention, but any detailed account of the various contributions would swell this report beyond reasonable limits.

The sum of the results achieved by the Commission is stated by Dr. HANNAMAN as follows:

CASH.

Cash on hand at organization	$13,490 92
Contributions in 1862	9,038 20
Contributions in 1863	36,232 11
Contributions to December 1, 1864	97,035 22
Contributions from December 1, 1864, to close of the Commission	91,774 30
Total cash	$247,570 75

GOODS.

Value contributed in 1862	$86,088 00
Value contributed in 1863	101,430 74
Value contributed to December 1, 1864	126,086 91
Value contributed from Dec. 1, 1864, to close of the Commission	45,394 38
Total value of goods	$359,000 03

Making the entire contribution to the State Sanitary Commission, from its organization to its close, $606,570.78. In addition, the history of the United States Sanitary Commission reports contributions to that society from Indiana to the amount of $16,049.50, making a total contribution from this

State for the relief of soldiers of $622,620.29, exclusive of the amount donated in 1861, prior to the organization of the Commission. These contributions, it will be borne in mind, were the voluntary offerings of our people. An examination of the official returns,[4] will show that the additional sum of $4,566,898.06 was contributed by the counties, townships, cities and towns of the State, for the relief of soldiers' families and soldiers who were discharged by reason of wounds and disease. This shows an outlay, altogether, of over *five millions of dollars*, to say nothing of the thousands of dollars, in money and supplies, that were furnished of which no account was ever kept. While Indiana has abundant reason to be proud of the glorious fame her soldiers won on every battlefield of the war where they were engaged, the foregoing record of the munificent liberality and good faith of her citizens who remained at home may well challenge the admiration of the world.

This record would be incomplete if it omitted to testify to the constant efforts and restless energy of Governor MORTON to forward the work of relief. He inspired every important movement, counseled in every great emergency, kept popular interest excited by stirring appeals, and, though charged with duties as onerous as ever fell upon the Executive of any State and allowing nothing in any of their multifarious details to escape his vigilance, he might have been thought, by those uninformed of his many labors, to have had nothing at heart but the success of his plans for the relief of the soldiers of Indiana and their dependent and needy families.

DISTRIBUTIONS

The goods contributed to local auxiliary societies were sent to the chief office at the Capital, where they were assorted, repacked, and arranged for distribution. The cash was sent to the Treasurer.

[4] See Terrell, *Report*, 1, Appendix, Doc. 8:75-88.

Of Cash. The money in the Treasury was applied to the purchase of such articles as the Commission might not have on hand, and these, like others, were distributed by the agents of the Commission.

Of Goods. The military agents at available points were usually made the agents of the Sanitary Commission for the distribution of goods, and they discharged this additional and important duty without additional pay.

The object of distribution, as already stated, was the preservation of health and efficiency, rather than the cure of disease, though when there were sick and wounded their necessities were cared for first of all. The men were sought out, *in camp and field*, and supplied with what they needed. Aid was not reserved till sickness made it necessary to life, but it was given so that as little as possible for sickness might be needed. During the investment of Nashville by the rebel force under General HOOD, Colonel SHAW, the agent at that place, contributed materially to prepare our men for the arduous service that followed, by distributing among them several hundreds of barrels of apples, potatoes, onions and other vegetables of quite as vital importance, oftentimes, as meat and bread. So at Atlanta, after the expulsion of the rebels from that place by General SHERMAN, our men, exhausted by weeks of continuous hard marching, hard fighting, and hard living, were recruited and many, no doubt, seasoned veterans though they were, were kept from the hospitals by the distribution of nearly a thousand barrels of potatoes and fruits, by the special agents sent to their relief by their Governor.

It would be impossible, even if it were profitable, to give a detailed account of the operations of the various agents of the Commission, but one case may be given as an illustration of the mode of distribution, and of the articles distributed. The steamer "City Belle," with Dr. C. J. WOODS, as Sanitary Agent in charge, left Cairo, Illinois, on the 19th of December, 1863, to supply our troops along the Mississippi river. At Fort Pillow, our Fifty-Second Regiment was stationed, with twenty-five sick, sixteen in the hospital. For the sick the agent left two barrels of potatoes, one of onions, and four dozen cans of fruit; for the well men, twelve barrels of potatoes, five of green and one of dried apples, three of turnips, one of onions. At Memphis, for the Twenty-Fifth and Eighty-Ninth Regiments, were left fifty barrels of potatoes, five of onions, five of turnips, two of crackers, twenty of green apples, ten of dried apples, twenty dozen cans of fruit, and four boxes of clothing. At Helena, though there were no Indiana troops there, the general hospital had four hundred sick men of other States in it, and for these there were left twenty barrels of potatoes, nine of onions, ten of green apples, five of dried apples, five of turnips, and twenty dozen cans of fruit. This was in accordance with the standing direction of the Commission, which was, to "make all contributions to general hospitals for general distribution," and not merely for the Indiana soldiers who might be in them. This fact is noted here for reference in another place. At Vicksburg, were the Twenty-Third and Fifty-Third Regiments, and they were given forty barrels of potatoes, twenty of green apples, six of dried apples, ten of onions, ten of turnips, two of cabbages, and twenty dozen cans of fruit. For the General Hospital at the same place, forty barrels of potatoes, twenty of green apples, ten of dried apples, ten of turnips, twenty dozen cans of fruit, and one box of bottled spirits. At Natchez, there were no Indiana regiments, but for the use of the Marine Hospital three barrels of potatoes, two of onions, two of green apples, two of dried apples, one of crackers, and two dozen cans of fruit were left. At Baton Rouge, the Twenty-First Regiment was supplied with forty barrels of potatoes, ten of onions, twenty of green apples, five of dried apples, five of corn meal, and ten of turnips. For the Hospital, one barrel of cabbages, one of pickled cabbage, one of crackers, three of green apples, one of dried apples, two of onions, four of potatoes, one of turnips, one box of bottled whisky, two boxes of canned fruits, four boxes of clothing, and two boxes of reading matter. Arrived at New Orleans, the Agent emptied out the remainder of his health-giving cargo, altogether four hundred and forty-one barrels of potatoes, three hundred and twenty of green apples, one hundred and eighteen of dried apples, one hundred and twenty-one of onions, one hundred and forty-eight of turnips, thirteen of crackers, one hundred and twelve boxes of canned fruit, twenty-three boxes of bottled spirits, and one hundred and sixty boxes of reading matter and clothing.

This expedition to supply the Mississippi river posts and hospitals had many parallels, though not many of the same extent. From what was done by Dr. WOODS, as here described, an imperfect idea may be formed of the general plan of relief, west, south and east, of the three years following the organization of the Commission. The extent of the distributions of the Commission may be judged from a brief summary of one of the reports of the agents, for 1864. JAMES H. TURNER, agent at Chattanooga, during SHERMAN'S advance to Atlanta, and for some months before and after, and consequently in charge of a large number of our troops, distributed to hospitals, regiments, and from the office, from the 15th of February to the 1st of September, six months and a half, 2,640 bushels potatoes, 15,985 pounds dried apples, 1,295 gallons kraut, 1,168 cans fruit, 1,278 pounds dried peaches, 442 bottles wine, 137 bottles whisky, 988 bushels onions, 461 dozen eggs, 493 pounds butter, 211 gallons apple butter, 157 pounds small fruit, 132 dozen lemons, 220 bottles ale, 558 pounds crackers, 35 pounds rice, 1,800 pounds corn meal, 100 pounds tobacco, 19 bed sacks, 230 gallons pickles, 35 bottles cordials, 995 shirts, 410 drawers, 124 sheets, 77 pillows, 182 pillow slips, 9 comforts, 3,149 pounds rags, 4,055 bandages, 355 fans, 82 pants, 35 combs, 442 handkerchiefs, 543 pairs socks, 228 towels, 308 pads, 450 comfort bags, 25 boxes reading matter. He also shipped to special agents, GEORGE MERRITT, W. J. WALLACE and VINCENT

CARTER, 537 packages of vegetables, clothing, liquors, &c. These are sufficient to give an idea of the operations of the agencies, and the report need not be loaded with others of the same kind. Besides our own agents, distributions were sometimes made through the "Christian Aid Society" and the United States Sanitary Commission, as their vouchers in the office at the Capital attest.

To whom distributed. As already stated in the preceding paragraph, the agents of the Commission were instructed to give to General Hospitals for general distribution, not for Indiana soldiers alone, whatever was a fair proportion to the Indiana soldiers confined there. And as at Helena, Natchez, and other places, they contributed to hospitals what they could, whether there were Indiana soldiers in them or not.

Of regiments in the field and men fit for duty, the distributions were made first to Indianians, but necessitous men of all States were supplied, as far as the means would allow. There was a preference for our own men, but no exclusion of others. These instructions were acted upon so generally, that applications to our agents for relief, from soldiers of other States, were common.

Gratuitous aid. The Commission, through the president, acknowledges many services from the Superintendent of the Telegraph Company at the Capital, in the way of gratuitous transmission of dispatches; to the various Express Companies, which carried many hundreds of packages of contributions without charge; and to the various railroads centering at Indianapolis, for the free transportation of goods. These gratuitous services, paid for, would have cost thousands of dollars.

Objections. It could hardly have been expected that an association with an object so exclusively unselfish should escape disparagement and resistance, for experience teaches us that mean men are very incredulous of disinterestedness in anybody. The managers and agents of the Commission

RELIEF OF SOLDIERS AND THEIR FAMILIES 415

were sometimes accused, by those who had no sympathy with its design, of appropriating the contributions to their own use, or neglecting to forward them, or perverting them to the pleasure of favorites. There was never a shadow of foundation for such charges, and they came always from men who were opposed to the war, and disloyal in feeling, to the Government. From such, the Sanitary Commission received little help. The scarcity of contributions from opponents of the war was marked. Their services, like the statues in the Roman procession, were especially noted for their absence. That such men should wish true what they alleged, is easily believed, and it is hard not to believe that their suspicions were unconscious admissions of their own inclinations. The Commission has ample evidence of the promptness and honesty of all its actions, in the letters of soldiers and nurses, and the declarations of all who made it an object to examine into the business.

Prof. M. J. Fletcher. The first operations of the Sanitary Commissions were made memorable by the services and untimely death of Professor MILES J. FLETCHER, the Superintendent of Public Instruction. He was among the very first to take an active part in the efforts to relieve the wants of our soldiers, and was more constantly and prominently employed in that way than probably any other man in the State, up to the time of his death. And he died in the duty he had so disinterestedly assumed. He was on his way with Governor MORTON to Evansville, to accompany a hospital steamer with surgeons and supplies for the wounded at Corinth, Mississippi, and the train that was carrying him, at Sullivan, Sullivan county, ran past a car left standing on a switch (purposely, it was suspected by many) so close to the main track, that his head, as he was looking out of the window, was struck causing death instantly. It was an irreparable loss to the State, to the Sanitary Commission, and to the cause of Education, of which he was so prominent a promoter.

OPINIONS OF OTHER STATES

The efficiency of the Sanitary Commission, and the perfect adaptation of its modes of operation to the needs of both the soldier and the State, called forth frequent public expressions of approval or admiration. Some of these may be quoted here, in justification of the pride in their organization which Indianians have so often exhibited.

A. D. RICHARDSON, writing from Fredericksburg, Va., to the New York *Tribune,* under date of December 18, 1862, speaking of the presence of two of our Agents with the Army, immediately after the battle of Fredericksburg, which was fought December 11-13th, 1862, spoke as follows:

> The peculiar and constant attention to the troops his State has sent out so promptly, is the prominent feature of Governor MORTON's most admirable administration. In all our armies, from Kansas to the Potomac, wherever I have met Indiana troops, I have encountered some officer of Governor MORTON, going about among them inquiring especially as to their needs, both in camp and hospital, and performing those thousand offices the soldier so often requires. Would that the same tender care could be extended to every man from whatever State, who is fighting the battles of the Republic.

In October, 1864, General BARLOW, Quartermaster General of Ohio, in acknowledging the receipt of a letter from the Adjutant General of Indiana detailing the main features of our relief system, said:

> The plan adopted by your State is certainly as nearly perfect as I should suppose it could be made, and I am gratified to find, that so far as this State has pursued any definite plan for the relief of her soldiers, it has been essentially the same as that your State, by further perfecting, has rendered so eminently successful.[5]

Numerous other commendations from high sources might be given, but it will be sufficient to add here the following extract from the annual message of Governor BROUGH of Ohio in 1864.

[5] Barlow to Terrell, in Terrell, *Report,* 1, Appendix, Doc. 87:292.

RELIEF OF SOLDIERS AND THEIR FAMILIES 417

While I desire to be fairly understood as not impeaching or desiring to impair the value of either of the associations laboring for the relief of our soldiers, I still adhere to the opinion expressed to you last winter, that more real good can be accomplished at less expense through State agencies and our societies than in any other way. While extending our own operations, I have carefully watched those of our sister State of Indiana, and have found that her system merits the strongest commendation. It is simple in its character. Its central society at the Capital, under the immediate care of the Governor, receives all the contributions from the various aid societies.

These are classified and distributed to the various State Agents, according to the wants of their departments, who in time distribute them among the men. The State provides a fund to aid in the purchase of goods not contributed, and pays the transportation. There is no expensive machinery about it—no waste or extravagance. It has been objected to as being local and separate in its character; but this is not the fact. While the first care of the Agent is for Indiana men, no other soldier in want or distress, has ever, to my knowledge, appealed to an Indiana agency without having his wants relieved. The Indiana agents have frequently divided their stores with the agents of Ohio, and we have always tried to reciprocate the kindness.

There are many benefits attending this system, which should not be disregarded.

1. It is decidedly the most economical way of aggregating and distributing the contributions of our people, and expending the means appropriated by the State for this purpose.

2. It renders certain the distribution of all supplies to the objects and purposes for which they are intended. There is hardly a possibility for misappropriation. There is no machinery about it to be kept lubricated and no class of middle men to levy toll upon it.

3. By proper care and management, it is made more prompt and energetic than any other mode; and by being more systematic will be more general and appropriate in its relief.

4. It fosters and gratifies the State pride of our soldiers. It comes nearer to the feeling of home, as the soldier regards an Ohio Agency as a place where he has a right to enter and expect a welcome. If he is in want, there is no system of orders and requisitions to go through, no prying or unpleasant catechism for him to submit to. The supplies furnished by his people and State are there, and he feels he is no object of charity when he partakes of them. His remembrances of home are freshened—his attachment to his State is quickened and increased—and he goes away feeling that he is not neglected or forgotten—that the

cause of the country is still worth upholding, and the dear old State still worth defending from the encroachments of the rebel adversary. And this is doubly the case where the Agent passes almost daily through his hospital, bends over the bed on which he is stretched with sickness or wounds, inquires kindly into his wants, and ministers unto them from the benefactions of his people and the liberality of his State. Surely this spirit is worth cherishing and preserving.

UNITED STATES AND INDIANA SANITARY COMMISSION

The action of our State authorities, in organizing a system of relief for our soldiers independently of other States, of the General Government, and of the national organization of the "United States Sanitary Commission," has occasionally provoked unfavorable reflections, which, as they have been given form and authority by the official "History of the United States Sanitary Commission,"[6] it would be doing injustice to our Commission to pass without notice. The charges, for they have the effect, though not the form, of charges of selfishness, of interference with the discipline of the army, and of inefficiency (comparing what it did with what it could have done if its efforts had been properly directed), are contained in the following extracts.

1st. In reference to the battle at Fort Donelson, it says: "The truth is, the wonderful success which had attended the Commission's experiment of transporting the wounded in hospital boats after the surrender of Fort Donelson, had stimulated a great variety of organizations, and even the State governments, to provide similar means of relief."[7]

The entire want of preparation, in this direction, of the Medical Department of the army, is admitted, and is urged as "one of the countless practical illustrations of the consequences of a rigid adherence to routine in the early part of the war."[8]

---

[6] Charles J. Stillé, *History of the United States Sanitary Commission* . . . (Philadelphia, 1866).
[7] *Ibid.*, 149.
[8] *Ibid.*, 144.

Mr. STILLE, the author of the History, might, if he had tried, have satisfied himself that the deficiency of preparation on the part of the Government which he laments, was known to the State authorities of Indiana, and of other Western States, quite as well as it was to the agents of the "United States Sanitary Commission." They needed, and had, no example of that beneficent organization to stimulate them to provide hospital steamers for their wounded when they made the first attempt. Immediately after the battle at Fort Donelson, and long before it was known that any similar effort would be made by any other State or society, a steamer was chartered by Governor MORTON to carry to our wounded the assistance contributed by public meetings, held at Indianapolis and other places, the day the news of the battle was received. Our aid was as early on the ground as that of the United States Commission, and earlier. These statements of the History are referred to here, not as a charge of inefficiency or dilatory action to be refuted, but as a claim of undivided merit to be corrected.

2d. Of State operations at Shiloh:

It seems ungracious to criticise the work of a body of men engaged in an effort to relieve the suffering, even if their methods are not wholly in accordance with true principles, but there was one feature in the mode adopted by those who had charge of the steamers sent by the State Governments of Ohio, Indiana and Illinois, which was so obviously wrong in principle, and so entirely in contrast with the National and Catholic spirit which characterized the operations of the Commission, that it deserves notice. These boats were intended solely for the reception of wounded men belonging to each of these States respectively, and all others were rigidly excluded from them.

. . . The indiscreet zeal which was willing to recognize State lines, even in its ministrations of mercy on the battlefield, can *hardly be too strongly condemned*. It was only another development of that obnoxious heresy of State sovereignty, against which the whole war was directed, and its practical injury to the national cause in creating disaffection among troops who were not recipients of its peculiar care, was scarcely less great than its violation of those sacred laws of humanity which make no distinction in the relief bestowed upon the suffering, except to seek first for those who most need succor. Against this *Stateish* spirit the Sanitary Commission resolutely sets its face at all times. . . .[9]

Inhumanity and selfishness are serious charges to be preferred against a professedly benevolent organization, and the more serious when, as in this case, the fundamental principles of the organization are held to create or compel the evil. Whether there may be any connection between the political doctrine of "State sovereignty" and the moral, or immoral doctrine of "Stateishness," or State selfishness, it will be worthwhile to inquire, after inquiring whether it *is* "selfish" for the people of a State to prefer, in their service to the suffering, their own relatives and friends to others, no more necessitous, who are neither. The impulse to care for our own is innate and indispensable. Without it, there would be no stronger bond among men than among cattle. The same impulse that makes a man labor and suffer for his own family more than he would for the families of others, that makes him fight for his own country in preference to a foreign country, that makes him a patriot instead of a cosmopolitan, directs the people of a State to give a preference to the suffering of their own over those of other States. It differs only in degree, not in kind. No one will claim that it should be as strong as the family or National preference, but no one ought to claim that it should be obliterated, until the time shall come when constant association in the same duties, connection in the same interests, obedience to the same laws, support of the same institutions, shall create no bond of union stronger than the common tie of humanity. That time will come with the millenium, but not before.

So long as there are State governments, and duties, interests and institutions, limited by State lines, so long there will be a "Stateish" as well as a National feeling. If it is selfish, it is so only as the *"esprit de corps"* of an army is selfish, as the spirit that impels all men, thrown habitually

[9] Stillé, *United States Sanitary Commission,* 150-51. [Terrell's italics, except *Stateish*]

together or under the same influences, to recognize a community of feeling, is selfish. ST. PAUL not only recognizes such a feeling as commendable, but enjoins its exercise as a duty: "If any provide not for his own, and especially for those of his own house, he hath denied the faith, and is worse than an infidel." This is not a precept of inhumanity, but it is that upon which the action of our people was based which this author declares "can not be too strongly condemned." Indiana did no more than care for her "own," and she did not neglect to care for others when her own were provided for. If the Good Samaritan had found two wounded travelers by the roadside, equally needy, and one of them had been his friend and the other a stranger, it is not improbable that the friend would have had the first use of the "wine and oil." But the proverbial designation of a charitable man would hardly have grown out of this case, if he had helped his friend and left the other to die. Indiana did as the Good Samaritan would have done. She "provided for her own," and then for others. Colonel HOLLOWAY, in his dispatch to Governor MORTON, from Shiloh, says: "All were supplied, after which we distributed supplies to surgeons connected with regiments from other States." This, as set forth in a preceding part of this Report, was the rule of the Commission. The distribution to hospitals where there were no Indiana soldiers, mentioned in Dr. WOODS's report (quoted in the same connection), is a refutation of the charge. Governor BROUGH, of Ohio, gives his testimony to the same point, in the message already quoted: "While the first care of the agent is for the Indiana men, no Ohio soldier, in want or distress, has ever, to my knowledge, appealed to an Indiana agency without having his wants relieved. The Indiana agents have frequently divided their stores with the agents of Ohio, and we have always tried to reciprocate the kindness."

If these services created "disaffection among the troops who were not recipients" of them, and should therefore be condemned, we may as well condemn every man who, finding himself unable to help all the needy he sees, helps as many as he can. The "disaffection," however, uniformly took the shape of censure of those who should have done likewise, and did not, or left the duty to organizations that undertook more than they could perform and censured those who chose to do only what they felt they could do. As to the "rigid exclusion" of other than Indiana soldiers from Indiana hospital boats, it only need be said that when all available room is occupied, or assigned to be occupied, "rigid exclusion" of additions is pretty much a necessity. But the monopoly of means of transportation for sanitary supplies is not a necessity, and yet "the National and Catholic spirit" of the United States Sanitary Commission monopolized them. The spirit either did not penetrate all its agents, or its Catholicity was capable of a construction analagous to that which in ecclesiastical matters limits it to a single church. For at Louisville, the instructions to quartermasters placed the transportation of sanitary stores under the direction of the United States Commission, and our agent, Dr. WOODS, says, December 20th, 1862: "This Sanitary Commission (the U.S.) is unwilling to forward any goods or sanitary stores unless they are consigned unconditionally to them." They must have a monopoly of benevolence at the expense of destroying by delay the value of the contributions of parents and friends. The historian should have waited before throwing stones till he had found whether there might not be glass exposed in his own house.

3d. In condemnation of the whole system of State relief, it is said: "If the action of the State authorities had been confined to efforts to improve the general administration of the service, and thus to benefit all alike, its influence would have been irresistible and its effect most salutary."[10] Again:

If half the energy *wasted* by the Governors of the various States in the vain effort to *supplant* the Federal authorities, in the work they were doing so imperfectly, had been concentrated in an effort to force

---

[10] Stillé, *United States Sanitary Commission*, 152.

them to do it more thoroughly, we should not have to tell that the horrors of Shiloh and other bloody battle fields were mitigated *only* by the voluntary and partial efforts of humane, zealous, but irresponsible persons.[11]

It may be suggested that it would have been just as well for the accuracy and credit of the History, if what it "had to tell" had been left untold. The statement makes the impression that the care of the suffering was left to accidental and irresponsible humanity, that is, to men with no commission or power but that of their own hearts. This is untrue. At Shiloh, and wherever wounded Indianians were to be found, there were men duly authorized and directed by our State Commission, to "mitigate the horrors of the battlefield." Not accidental visitors impelled merely by humanity, but officers acting upon a well-settled system, with ample means and positive instructions. It is true they were responsible to no law; they could not be punished, but by universal detestation, for neglect or misconduct; but they were not the accidental benefactors the History makes them. They were parts and representatives of a system as complete as the system of national government, and in no sense a display of mere individual beneficence.

Whether our Governor's energy was *"wasted"* in collecting and distributing over $600,000 worth of stores, can be best decided by ascertaining whether that amount of hospital stores and sanitary supplies was consumed without doing anybody any good.

As to "supplanting" the duties of the Government, it may be said that half as much time expended in ascertaining what these Governors were trying to do, as has been mischievously consumed in writing the sentences mis-stating and censuring their action, would have saved the historian the mortification of exhibiting his censoriousness and carelessness together. Our labor was directed, not to "supplant," but to complete,

---

[11] *Ibid.*, 153. [Terrell's italics]

the defective labors of the Government. There was no interference. Each laborer could do what it could, and both together were not likely to do too much.

Mr. R. R. CORSON, the Indiana agent at Philadelphia, states the case accurately in his report of January 19th, 1864:

> It [the plan he approves] is in brief to call upon each State authority to empower an agent in all the principal cities used as hospital depots, to discover and relieve distress of the sick and wounded that lie outside of the General Government's path of exertion.... The plan has fulfilled the highest expectations formed of it. It is indeed nothing more than directing into a special channel those composite energies which our peculiar national constitution develops: the General Government does its share, the separate States do their share, and between the united actions of both, the utmost good is probably done that opportunity and circumstances will admit.[12]

The Indiana Sanitary Commission did not append itself to the United States Commission. This is the secret, apparently, of the censures applied to it and similar efforts of other recusant States. The reasons why it maintained its independence are:

First. The United States Commission was organized to perfect the Government provisions and regulations for the health of the army. What it did, was not to flow outside, but through, the Government's efforts, and thus to enlarge them to the exigencies of the war. This was necessarily a slow work. Our Commission was the product of a pressing necessity. Our men could not wait for overcoats in the mountains in Western Virginia till the United States Commission had perfected Government regulations, and, still harder, had converted regular army officers into practical men. They must be clothed at once. The process of supplying them created our agencies, and these grew into our Commission. It had to act outside of the Government, and beginning in that way, finding it profitable and the Government constantly approving

---

[12] "Report of Indiana Military Agencies to the Governor," in Indiana *Documentary Journal,* 1864, vol. 2, no. 9:338.

its work, it kept on. It interfered with nothing that anybody else wanted to do. It prohibited no service to our men that it could not render itself. It was ready to help any other soldiers when it could. In short, it was modest, helpful, and free from jealousies. It could have been no more, and done no better, as an appendage of the national association. It did its work well, the United States Sanitary Commission could do no more. Why change one good thing we were used to, for another no better, that we knew nothing about?

Second. As a subordinate of the National Commission, its action as well as its agents would have been controlled by men of whom we knew nothing. Men of whom the soldiers had never heard, who had no acquaintance with their homes or friends, who had only an ordinary official interest in them, would have been sent to their bedsides, would have had to bear all their little commissions and listen to their sick longings for home, with which no sympathy of neighborhood or previous acquaintance could exist. This would have been less pleasing to the patient and less beneficial, too, than the presence of men whom they knew, or who knew of their parents and relatives. And it would have been less likely to impel the liberality of the people, to have strangers soliciting contributions, and strangers very often entrusted with their distribution. Men naturally prefer to trust those whom they know. And the $600,000 contributed by Indiana for soldiers' relief is due mainly to the fact that it was made by Indiana men through Indiana agents for Indiana soldiers at the instigation of Indiana's Governor. This may appear very narrow, and possibly silly, to brains expanded by the contemplation of national organizations, but it shows a knowledge of the springs of human nature without which success in such efforts is impossible.

Third. The magnitude of the operations of the National Commission made a system of guards and checks, and a more complicated machinery necessary. In ours none were necessary. Every man employed was known to the Commission. Our operations were, therefore, like those of an army "marching light." They could be commenced at a moment's notice anywhere, and carried on without any hindrance of "approvals" and "orders" and "requisitions," wherever an agent could carry a sackful of potatoes. It was always serviceable. The people knew it, and they did not know that the other was.

In fine. The State Commission got all the money that the United States Commission could have done; it used it all with scrupulous fidelity for the benefit of soldiers, which is all the United States Commission could have done; it was never out of the way when its services were needed, which is all that the other could have been; it was always first, or among the first, on the battlefield, and its services were always cordially recognized by the soldiers; and what more could the United States Commission have done? It did not try to do so much, but what it did left nothing for the other to do in the same field, or nothing that was not fourfold made up by reciprocal service. There was nothing to gain by changing the State Commission to an auxiliary of the United States Commission. And there was something to lose—the home interest, the State pride, and the liberality impelled or increased by them, of which, let the motive be creditable or not, the soldier received the benefits.

SUBORDINATE MILITARY AGENCIES

An account has been given of the origin of the Military Agencies of the State in the necessity of distributing the supplies called forth by the appeal of Governor MORTON, in October, 1861, and a general statement of their duties made in the same connection. A full report of their services would have been impossible in that place, without swelling the sketch beyond its due proportion to the history of which it is a part. But this report would be incomplete without presenting some idea of the manner in which the numerous duties imposed were discharged. . . .

The subordinate agents were at first charged merely with the duty of following the armies in which our troops were embodied, and distributing among them and the field and regimental hospitals, such supplies as were placed at their disposal. They were confined by no "red tape" restrictions but, being selected for their known capacity and integrity, they were left free to follow their own discretion as to the application of their services. They were simply to do what was best for those most necessitous. But as the war progressed and permanent hospitals were established and permanent places of rendezvous or centers of transportation were fixed, it became necessary to make agencies permanent at these points, without discontinuing those that kept track of our advancing forces. The first of these was created at Philadelphia, by the appointment of Mr. R. R. CORSON, June 28th, 1862. Their duties are fully set forth in the following letter of instructions given by Governor MORTON to Dr. DAVID HUTCHINSON, the Agent at Nashville, Tennessee:

EXECUTIVE DEPARTMENT OF INDIANA,
INDIANAPOLIS, December 12, 1862.

. . . .

You will look after the welfare and necessities of the sick and disabled soldiers belonging to Indiana Regiments; procure and register their names in a book to be provided for that purpose, noting their condition, etc.; see that they are furnished with proper accommodations, medical attendance and suitable food. You will procure and furnish, from the proper officers, descriptive lists for all who may be without them, so that they may be paid, or, if proper, discharged from the service. Examine the condition of the various Hospitals, or cause it to be done from time to time, and call the attention of the proper authorities to any neglect or abuse which may be discovered. In the distribution of sanitary supplies or hospital goods, you will co-operate with the Sanitary Commission in this city and the several Aid Societies of the State. You will also confer frequently with Mr. WILLIAM HANNAMAN, the General Military Agent, and make reports, as often as may be required, to him.

. . . .

It is intended that your office shall at all times be supplied with the fullest information in regard to the location, condition and wants of the sick and wounded which it may be in your power to obtain, so that all inquiries made by their relatives and friends may be satisfactorily answered.

Persons who may be seeking their friends in the army or in hospitals will call on you frequently for assistance in procuring furloughs, discharges, transfers, descriptive lists, pay, etc., and you are directed to aid them as much as possible.

Ascertain the locations of our various Regiments, and keep advised of their movements, so that proper directions may be given to persons who may be desirous of visiting them, to see relatives and friends. . . . It is intended that your authority shall be broad enough to enable you to transact any business necessary and proper to be done in aid of the suffering or distressed volunteers connected with Regiments from this State.

Consult with the Military Authorities of your Department, and co-operate with them in all cases where their interposition may be necessary. . . .

In addition to looking after the sick and wounded, you will keep yourself advised as much as possible of the condition, efficiency and wants of our Regiments, and report to this Department.

O. P. MORTON, Governor of Indiana.

The necessities of the soldiers, however, developed additional duties. Many returning home on furlough were without money, and had forgotten, in their eagerness to get home, to obtain Government passes. The Agents were required to help these on their way. Many more arrived at the Agencies without clothes and in distress. They were to be relieved. As terms of service expired, back pay was to be obtained. Claim Agents too often used up the arrears in needless expenses and exorbitant fees. Our Agents were required to obtain them gratuitously. Bounties were often left unpaid in the haste of pushing forward needed reinforcements to the field, or the want of means in the hands of Paymasters to pay them. Our Agents were directed to procure them. Pensions also became a prolific source of indispensable services. Prisoners, paroled or exchanged, always needed help, and often needed everything that sickness, nakedness and starvation could require. The Agencies were the instruments of alleviation. Through them also large relief contributions were dispatched to soldiers still in prison. Agents were also employed in collecting and

RELIEF OF SOLDIERS AND THEIR FAMILIES   429

forwarding to families such portions of their pay as the soldier desired to send home.

Of the services performed in these various ways, an idea can be best obtained by classifying them and giving examples of each class.

Their Services—Distributions—Little need be added here to the sketch given in the history of the "Sanitary Commission," of the articles, modes, or objects of distribution, or to the exposition of the rules by which this service was directed. It is sufficient to add, that the six hundred thousand dollars of cash, and stores furnished by our people were conveyed promptly and directly to the soldiers. Comparatively little was lost, injured, or mischievously delayed. The beneficence of the State reached its objects as nearly in the perfection with which it started, as human sagacity and energy could accomplish it. This was the effort in which the History of the United States Commission says, "the energies" of our Governor "were *wasted*." If that is a waste of energy it would not have injured the army greatly for even the United States Commission to have begun a wider "waste" of its energies in the same direction. If it was a "waste," it was because our soldiers were so unfortunately constituted, that over a half million dollars' worth of sanitary supplies and hospital stores could be consumed by the healthy without strengthening them, or by the sick without relieving them. It would be both profitable and interesting to illustrate the services of the agents by extracts from their reports, but it would swell this volume beyond all reasonable limits.

Registers, Hospital Service, Aid to Relatives, etc.—So many duties connected with the care of the sick and wounded soldiers need mention, to give a just idea of the scope of the duties of agents, that it will be better to present a few extracts from reports relating what has been done in the particular cases described, than to attempt to pick out of each the separate services and present them in separate groups.

JAMES H. TURNER, at Chattanooga, says,
records of sick and deceased soldiers were kept, and frequent reports made to your office for the information of friends. Keepsakes and other property of the dying deposited with me found their way to Indianapolis. Letters were written for the sick to friends at home, and in every way possible the wishes of the dying were cared for. . . . The arrival of citizens looking after sick, wounded, and dead friends, gave me much additional labor. I took wives to the bedsides of dying husbands, and wept with mothers and sisters over fallen sons and brothers. I lent money to pay for embalming bodies, and gave passes furnished by Indiana to enable the mourners to reach their homes. Many will bless the day when they found those little magic tickets.[13]

Mr. R. R. CORSON, of Philadelphia, writes in 1864 in regard to the benefits of the Indiana plan of aiding the soldier:
First, the work of keeping the State accurately and frequently apprised of the condition and location of her every soldier in hospital in this city. . . . The State is enabled to answer questions made by friends, to correct desertions falsely reported, and check off discharges from the true date as no longer recipients of further State bounty money. Therefore, I make every exertion to make my lists complete and accurate. Within six hours after the arrival of any sick or wounded man, the hospital to which he is assigned is reported to me. He is then visited, his name, company, regiment, ward and bed registered, and these details are sent to you when the number swells to a score. The sufferer once being noted, constant watch is kept upon him; the hospitals being visited daily every change is noted, and I am able, in this way to give a full history of each patient during his sojourn here. . . . When articles of clothing have been needed, I have generally got them from the Sanitary Commission. Smaller articles, such as postage stamps, stationery, tobacco, car tickets etc., I have furnished myself. As usually the men come from the field with from four to six months pay due them, and entirely out of funds; to these men in a strange city among strangers, these little articles are most grateful, being gifts direct from their own State—an evidence that they are not forgotten. The lists kept at my headquarters are consulted by the soldiers from the different hospitals, who are able to ride about, and from them the whereabouts of their comrades in distant hospitals is obtained. With car tickets furnished by me, they are

[13] Turner to William Hannaman, General Military Agent, Indianapolis, August 20, 1864, in "Report of Indiana Military Agencies to the Governor," Indiana *Documentary Journal,* 1864, vol. 2, no. 9:332, 333.

enabled to reach the most distant points in the city in a short time and enjoy a pleasant ride. Letters of inquiry from friends at a distance are frequently received. These are given immediate attention, and after visiting the patient in person, are answered with full particulars of the case.[14]

Dr. WOODS at Louisville says:[15]

We render assistance to all as far as we can. We give precedence to the most distressing. A poor soldier is about to die at Park Barracks. We obtain for him a discharge furlough, give him transportation, and send him home to die with his family. I spent a whole day with his case alone. A poor widow came here with but one child in the world, and he is a soldier sick in the hospital. She has no dependence but him. She is robbed at the Depot of every cent she has. No possible means to go home except to get her son discharged, draw his pay and go home on that. She obtains from the surgeon a certificate of disability. His case is rejected by the Board of examining surgeons. For her we work.

Scores of cases similar to these are reported. "I met a soldier who had lost the power of speech by sickness. He had been sent here without a pass. He knew no more what to do or where to go than a sheep. I took him to the medical director, who sent him to a hospital."

Colonel ED. SHAW, at Nashville, posted up a notice from Governor MORTON that "All persons visiting the hospitals to look after sick, wounded or deceased friends, should call on the regular Indiana Military Agent who will render every possible assistance," and that the office would be open night and day. The notice, he says, drew large numbers of people, whose desires created a vast amount of business. Besides, he made it his duty to notify relatives of the deaths in the hospital or field when it was necessary; to take charge of the effects, ascertain the place of burial, and send home dead bodies.[16]

[14] Reports by Corson to Governor Morton, January 19, 1864, and to Hannaman, December 31, 1864, in *ibid.*, 336-41, 359-61.

[15] Woods to Hannaman, November 27, 1862, in *Reports of Special Agents, Pay Agents, et al., Visiting Troops, etc.* (Indianapolis, 1863), 41, 47.

[16] Shaw to Hannaman, December 27, 1864, in "Report of Indiana Military

Colonel HAM, in regard to the duties of agents to citizens visiting soldiers, says:

> There is one feature of this agency which has doubtless paid all the expense of it, that is obtaining passes for citizens. Had it not been for this hundreds of men and women would have been detained for days and even then have had to return without visiting their friends, as many had to do from other States, by not having agents at this point. Thousands of citizens who came to Louisville from other States have cause to thank Governor MORTON for establishing this agency. My office has been the resort of all loyal citizens. The Pass office seldom, if ever, refuses to grant a pass on my recommendation.

Instances of service of this kind to fathers, mothers and other relatives might be given by thousands.

Of service to soldiers in hospitals, he says: "Much of my time has been occupied in taking the wounded and feeble soldiers from their hospital to the Medical Directors to be examined for a discharge, and from there to the Discharge and Pay offices, and after getting their pay, in taking them to the railroad station and seeing them off for home." Writing letters and procuring descriptive lists for soldiers were important and constant duties of the agents.[17]

Services Relating to the Dead—Dr. HANNAMAN, Chief Agent, says:

> Memorials of the dead are hunted up, preserved and sent to friends at home. These are obtained in various ways—from the hand of the dying man, or from his person at burial; from the company officers, or from Government sales if not previously secured. Hundreds of knapsacks have been returned to this office through the military agencies and delivered to anxious friends. Many are the applications we have had to obtain, if possible, some keepsake of the patriot dead.[18]

Records of graves were preserved at each agency.

Agencies to the Governor," in Indiana *Documentary Journal,* 1864, vol. 2, no. 9:358.

[17] Ham to President and members of the Sanitary Commission, March 1, 1864, in *Proceedings of the Indiana Sanitary Convention Held in Indianapolis, March 2, 1864* (Indianapolis, 1864), 42, 43.

[18] Report of William Hannaman, Indiana Military Agent, to the Governor

These extracts will suffice to show how multifarious were the duties of the military agents, and how impossible it would have been for any Government machinery to have supplied the want of the ever-ready, anxious and kindly zeal of these friends, and how vital to the soldier the service it rendered was. Besides assisting relatives and friends in the search for sick and wounded, a great deal of service was rendered in procuring means of transportation for such as were needy, or had been (as was often the case) robbed, or were upon charitable missions.

Passes—Dr. HANNAMAN says, in his report for December, 1864:

> Our agents daily find soldiers who for months have been wasting away with disease, or suffering from wounds, and who have received no pay but are furloughed and discharged without the means of getting home. Such men are supplied with our Indiana military passes. Again, a wife, mother or sister seeks some dear friend who has been wounded, but is destitute of the means of reaching the desired hospital or camp. In such cases we extend the aid of the State. These passes are given to surgeons and nurses, also to sanitary agents, and occasionally to refugees. The number of passes issued to the close of 1864, to soldiers, was 3,053; to soldiers' wives, 509; to sanitary agents, 339; to nurses, 222; to special surgeons, 106; to military agents, 154; to refugees, 109; total 4,542. The average cost to the State was about two dollars for each pass.[19]

Transfers—Transfers to hospitals at home were always most eagerly desired by all the soldiers, and in serious cases it was a far surer cure than any that medical skill could devise. The agents did much of this work. Colonel HAM, at Louisville, says, December 15th, 1864: "The labor and influence of your State Agent, in procuring and hastening through these special transfers, have enabled hundreds of soldiers to go to the hospitals of their own State, and saved a large expense to our citizens who have come here to take care of sick and wounded soldiers and could only remain at a heavy

---

December, 1864, in "Report of Indiana Military Agencies," in Indiana *Documentary Journal,* 1864, vol. 2, no. 9:298.

[19] *Ibid.,* 296.

expense."[20] This must serve as a sample of many similar reports.

Colonel FRANK HOWE, Agent at New York, July 18th, 1862, writes thus of the order prohibiting transfers:

> I am obliged to turn a deaf ear to the applications and entreaties of fathers, mothers, wives and relatives who daily come from a distance to take their dear ones home. The majority of these cases will be unfit for duty for thirty or sixty days, while in their native air and surrounded by home comforts, they would convalesce much more rapidly than they could any where else. I am satisfied the Government does not comprehend the position of matters here.[21]

Transfers were at last greatly reduced in necessity by the improved character and number of permanent hospitals, and they were not so generally permitted. One influence greatly contributing to this end is thus stated by Dr. JOBES, September 21, 1864: "So many furloughed soldiers are overstaying their time, that it is going to be a vast source of trouble. They are all marked as deserters, and when the record is once made up, it is a permanent one, and although there may not be any criminal intent in any of these cases, the record evidence of it will be hard to disprove."[22] The evil arising from this source was so great that at last General GRANT was compelled to issue an order prohibiting furloughs or tranfers.

Collection of Claims—The next most important service of the agencies was the gratuitous collection of back pay and bounties, and procurement of pensions. Most of them, from their location, or other disadvantages, could not helpfully attempt this, and the greater part of it was performed by those at Indianapolis and Washington City. The amount thus collected up to November, 1866, was over three hundred thousand dollars.

[20] Ham to Hannaman, December 15, 1864, in Indiana *Documentary Journal*, 1864, vol. 2, no. 9:349.

[21] Howe to Governor Morton, July 18, 1862, in *Reports of Special Agents, Pay Agents, et al.*, 108.

[22] Jobes to Hannaman, September 21, 1864, in "Report of the Indiana Sanitary Commission Made to the Governor, January 2, 1865," in Indiana *Documentary Journal*, 1864, vol. 2, no. 5:175.

The agency at Indianapolis was also charged with the duty of assisting officers who had resigned or been discharged in making settlement of their accounts. Much trouble and expense was saved by it to officers.

The numerous cases of extortion, fraud, and downright robbery practiced upon soldiers by real or pretended claim agents, suggested to Governor MORTON this valuable means of saving to them their hard-earned and long-delayed dues. The effect was even more beneficial than could have been anticipated, and inspired the authorities of several States—among them those of Ohio and New York—to adopt the same policy for their soldiers. The former issued a circular urging its adoption, and the Adjutant General of New York recommended it there. Numerous letters are reported by our agents to have been received, testifying the gratitude of the men for the benefit they had enjoyed, and relating instances of the outrages they had suffered before the agency was established or before they had learned of its existence.

Besides these more important collections of agents at Washington and Indianapolis, those at other points assisted soldiers in procuring pay, whenever applied to.

Transmission of Soldiers' Money.—The necessity of sending home more or less of their pay to maintain their families made it very important to the soldiers that facilities should be afforded them for this purpose. Accordingly, agents were early dispatched to follow the armies, collect all the money the soldiers wished to send home, and take effective measures to send it home.[23]

General STONE reports, January 26th, 1862, that he collected $7,000 of the Eighth Regiment at Otterville, Missouri, and brought it with him.[24]

---

[23] See "Allotment Commissioner-Pay Agency," below 467-73; *Report of Pay Agents* (Indianapolis, 1863). 4pp. This report was signed by W. H. H. Terrell, Military Secretary, and dated December 31, 1863.

[24] Stone to Governor Morton, January 26, 1862, in *Reports of Special Agents, Pay Agents, et al.,* 21.

THOMAS A. GOODWIN, a collecting agent with the army on the Tennessee river, writes thus of his efforts, June 12th, 1862: "On the 2nd of June, having accumulated $125,000, I left for the State, deeming a longer delay unjust to the regiments paid."[25] Again, July 9th, 1862, of a visit to North Alabama, he says: "I received some $31,000, chiefly from the Ninth and Thirty-Sixth Indiana regiments and Cox's battery, with some gleanings from other regiments."[26]

B. F. TUTTLE, October 25th, 1862, reports the following collections: Camp Nevin, $7,000; Camp Nashville, $15,000; Camp Woodstock, $37,050; total, $59,050.[27]

These, like all other instances of the labors of our agents, are merely specimens of frequent or constant services. Later in the War, the Government, under an act of Congress, appointed "Allotment Commissioners," whose duties replaced those of Collecting Agents, and that portion of the work of the Sanitary Commission was discontinued.

Prisoners.—As already stated in the sketch of the history of the Commission, contributions for relief of our prisoners at Richmond were conveyed through the agencies at Washington and City Point to their destination. Governor MORTON at one time purchased some $6,000 worth of stores for this purpose. It was successfully applied. "During the fall of 1863," says General STONE in his report of 1863 to Governor MORTON,

> reports reached you of the utter destitution and suffering of Indiana soldiers confined as prisoners of war in Richmond, Virginia, and on Belle Isle, near Richmond. It was stated that these suffering men could be supplied with clothing, blankets and other necessaries, through a certain channel. Accordingly, under your direction, I shipped on the 24th of October, 1863, 11 boxes of clothing and one bale of blankets, marked, according to directions furnished me, "Col. A. D. STREIGHT, Richmond, Va. For prisoners of war. Care of Gen. S. A. MEREDITH, Fortress Monroe, Va. These packages contained 200 caps, 200 shirts,

[25] Goodwin to Governor Morton, June 12, 1862, in *Reports of Special Agents, Pay Agents, et al.,* 60.
[26] Goodwin to Governor Morton, July 9, 1862, in *ibid.,* 102.
[27] Tuttle to Governor Morton, October 25, 1862, in *ibid.,* 99.

200 pairs of drawers, 200 pairs of socks, 200 blouses, 700 blankets, 200 pairs of infantry trousers, 200 infantry great coats, and 200 pairs of shoes.[28]

Again, on November 12th, he sent 34 boxes of clothing and shoes to the care of our agent at Washington. These were not allowed to reach our prisoners, and were returned.

But the most essential service was performed in caring for the wants of paroled and exchanged prisoners on their arrival at the depots, where their diseases, feebleness and destitution, made them the most pitiable objects that the ravages of war produced anywhere. The country is so well acquainted with the condition in which our prisoners were generally restored to us, that nothing more need be said of the matter here than that our agents, as far as possible, provided for them and helped them home.

SPECIAL AGENCIES

The duties of agents dispatched upon special missions to our forces were in the main very much the same as those of our permanent agents. The difference lay in the additional duty on the part of the former of following troops wherever the necessities of the war had sent them. They were expected to ascertain the condition and wants of the men in the field, and of the hospitals where no regular agent was placed, to distribute the stores they usually had in charge, and obtain others when needed, from the depots at the permanent agencies, and, in brief, to meet special necessities with the same services that were applied by regular agents to cases of constant occurrence. The account given of the operations of the Military agents will cover so much of the supplemental labors of special agents that this report need not be swelled by extracts from their reports. But there were two classes of special agents whose services deserve as conspicuous a place in any record of soldiers' relief as do the soldiers themselves.

[28] Indiana *Documentary Journal*, 1864, vol. 2, no. 8: 205-6.

Special Surgeons.—Until 1862 there were no battles west of the mountains the casualties of which required special efforts to provide for them, though agents were constantly with the men in Western Virginia, to look after Government and State supplies, which were constantly deficient. But from the battle at Mill Springs, January 18th, 1862, to the time when the Government's provision for the soldier, in field and hospital, was sufficient for his needs, there was hardly a single general engagement that did not require the services of special surgeons, nurses and means of relief; and they were furnished by our State, often first, always among the first, of the many beneficent agencies that gathered to these scenes of suffering.

Additional Assistant Surgeons.—The appalling sickness which prevailed among the volunteers during the winter of 1861 and spring of 1862 will be remembered. The men were unaccustomed to the hardships and privations of camp life, and but few of the many then in service had become seasoned, so as to enjoy perfect health. Thousands of enlisted men and hundreds of officers were discharged by reason of disability, and it seemed for a time as if the whole army would go to pieces, not from encounters in battle with the enemy, but from the more sweeping destroyer—disease. Neither the law nor regulations provided for medical officers sufficient for the wants of the troops at this period. One surgeon and one assistant surgeon only were allowed to each regiment, and the services of these were sometimes required at hospitals or on other detached duty; or, if they were sick or resigned, the regiment might be, and frequently was, left without any medical attendance whatever. Especially was the medical force inadequate during or immediately after a severe battle. This was strikingly exhibited at and after the battles of Fort Donelson and Shiloh; and it was only through the prompt and timely activity of the authorities of the Western States that even partial relief was afforded. So important did it appear to Governor MORTON that this alarming defect should be remedied by the employment of additional medical officers, even if only for temporary service, that he proposed on the 11th of April, 1862, just after Shiloh had been fought, that authority be given him by the Secretary of War to raise a corps of volunteer surgeons for field duty. Competent men of the medical profession were ready to go whenever called upon, and wherever they could relieve the suffering of the sick, wounded and dying; but the Secretary of War, after thanking the Governor for his offer, stated that so large provision had already been made for medical attendance in the West, he preferred to wait for a report from General HALLECK; then, if more should be needed, he would give notice and instructions. HALLECK was then besieging BEAUREGARD at Corinth; a terrible battle was expected, and the experience gained by the Governor in his efforts to relieve the troops on th Cumberland and Tennessee rivers, only a short time before, convinced him that it was the duty of the Government as well as of himself to make timely and ample provision for the anticipated event. Without proper authority, relief parties could not pass to the front, or obtain transportation upon Government steamers, or travel with and secure the protection of Government troops and trains. The Governor, therefore, on the 21st of April, again telegraphed the Secretary of War, as follows:

> That a great battle is impending at Corinth, is evident. Before additional surgical aid can reach the field from any quarter, five or six days will elapse. Meanwhile the wounded must suffer immensely. So it was at Donelson and Pittsburg. Indiana has at least twenty-four Regiments before the enemy. I propose to send at once to each of them *two* additional surgeons, and respectfully request authority from you to do so. I regard this as an absolute necessity.

This appeal was too strong to be resisted, and the Secretary accordingly gave the desired authority. The Governor at once selected the proper number of surgeons, of good standing, and dispatched them to the field with instructions to remain as long as their services were required. Nor did he confine himself to sending medical aid to the regiments in Tennessee alone, but, although the authority extended no further, he took the responsibility to send a number of additional surgeons to the Army of the Potomac and elsewhere.

This action was received with great approbation by the troops, and the attention of Congress having been called to the matter, an act was passed (approved July 2, 1862) which provided that instead of *one* assistant surgeon, as provided by a former law, each regiment of volunteers in the service of the United States should have *two* assistant surgeons. The plan, however, of sending special surgeons to the field was not abandoned by the Governor. They were kept employed in visiting the armies, examining hospitals and hunting up our sick and wounded, wherever they might be, until all of our troops were mustered out of service.

Steamers.— Besides expeditions dispatched after battles, when extra help and supplies were peculiarly necessary, Governor MORTON frequently sent aid, by steamers and otherwise, to our troops at all points where he knew of any necessity for relief. The voyage down the Mississippi of the "City Belle," under charge of Dr. C. J. WOODS, already noticed, was one of these. During the year 1863, Dr. HANNAMAN, in his report of March 2nd, 1864, says seven such missions were performed. The *first* was on the steamer "Capitola," starting on the 19th of February, under charge of Mr. GEORGE MERRITT, of Indianapolis, for our forces under General GRANT, at Vicksburg. It took five hundred and forty packages of stores, twenty-five female nurses for the hospitals, and twenty-one surgeons, under charge of Dr. JEREMIAH H. BROWER, of Lawrenceburg. Twenty of the nurses were left at Memphis hospitals. Twenty-five Indiana Regiments were visited and supplied. The *second* was the "Lady Franklin," under charge of Dr. C. J. WOODS, with one thousand packages of stores, several nurses and Surgeons. The *third* was the "Courier," under charge of Dr. TALBOTT BULLARD, and General A. STONE, with five hundred packages of stores, several nurses and surgeons. A large number of sick and wounded men were brought back. But the expedition is said by Dr. HANNAMAN to have been "most unfortunate to those engaged in it, for four surgeons died during the trip or soon after their return, among them the ever to be lamented Dr. BULLARD. He was a man of warm temperament, and when duty called him he never thought of self. His was a most valuable life to be sacrificed to this accursed rebellion." The *fourth* boat was the "Atlanta," in charge of Colonel W. E. FRENCH, with two hundred packages of stores and several surgeons and nurses. It brought back one hundred and seventy-five sick and wounded from Memphis. The *fifth* was the "City Belle," under charge of General STONE, with four hundred packages of stores, and a liberal supply of surgical and nursing help. This expedition reached Vicksburg on the morning of July 4th, 1863, the day the rebel stronghold was surrendered. The *sixth* boat was the "Sunny Side," in charge of Mr. E. J. PUTNAM, with one thousand packages of stores, and Dr. W. H. WISHARD as surgeon. One hundred and fifty sick soldiers were brought back. The *seventh* was the "City Belle," under charge of Dr. C. J. WOODS, with one thousand five hundred packages of stores. One hundred sick returned with it. The stores distributed on this expedition are described in detail in a preceding part of this report.[29] On the 24th of November, 1863, Major JAMES H. TURNER was sent to Chattanooga, and he, with the help of Mr. GEORGE MERRITT, Mr. VINCENT CARTER and Mr. W. J. WALLACE, kept track of SHERMAN's army in the advance to Atlanta, and subsequently in the celebrated "march to the sea," assiduously laboring to provide for the sick and wounded left behind and along the route.

In December, 1864, in anticipation of SHERMAN's arrival at Savannah, Dr. C. J. WOODS, with several assistants, was sent to New York, where he shipped a large amount of stores, by sea, to meet our men. But on his arrival he found that SHERMAN had moved north, and the supplies were distributed among the hospitals at Savannah, Port Royal, Hilton Head and Charleston. The remainder were returned to New York

[29] See above, 411-13.

and there distributed on the arrival of our troops. Eight thousand dollars worth of stores were sent to the Agent at Washington to be distributed there among our men in SHERMAN'S army. These supplies were very opportune, as the presence of the combined armies of GRANT and SHERMAN made the Government stores insufficient, and many men from other states were placed on short rations in consequence.

After the winter of 1863 and 1864, the advance of our armies, the improvement in Government supplies, and the seasoning of the men to their arduous and perilous work, made the assistance of special agencies less necessary, and the work of the Commission subsequently was mainly done by the regular agencies.

Nurses.—A most creditable exhibition of the devotion so generally displayed both by men and women during the war, was made by the ladies who volunteered as nurses. Very generally they were ladies in good circumstances, unused to the privations and labors they so readily assumed, and were prepared for their discharge only by tenderness, intelligence and patience with which Nature has so bounteously provided the sex. But they worked with a zeal and conscientiousness that shamed all hired aid and brought to the sick and suffering the blessings of "ministering angels." All that a mother, or sister or wife could be at home, they tried to be in the hospital, and their success is attested in the warmest encomiums of surgeons wherever they served. Few of them were paid, or desired pay, and some expended their own money liberally in procuring food, and especially for delicacies which could alone be relished by the sick. Dr. JOBES, at Memphis, says: "As auxiliaries in the discharge of the duties of this office they have rendered me valuable assistance. But to the sick and wounded soldiers in the wards, their services have been invaluable. Their delicate skill in the preparation of diets, their watchful attention to the slightest want, their words of sympathy and encouragement, have made the hospital a home, and in hundreds of instances have quite lured the sufferer back from death unto life."

RELIEF OF SOLDIERS AND THEIR FAMILIES   443

Well may one of them say "England has a FLORENCE NIGHTINGALE of whom she may well be proud, but we may boast of a thousand FLORENCE NIGHTINGALES."

In January, 1865, Dr. HANNAMAN reports that there were then in the service of the Commission about fifty female nurses. From January 6, 1863, to March 11, 1864, ninety-five ladies who volunteered as nurses are reported, and their names given, but the list does not include all, nor indeed some of these especially noticed by Dr. HANNAMAN in his report. More than one hundred of our women became nurses in hospitals, and very many continued for months together. Two, Miss HANNAH POWELL and Miss ASINAE MARTIN, of Goshen, Elkhart county, died while employed in the Memphis hospitals. Dr. HANNAMAN says of them:

> Highly valued in the family and in society, they were not less loved and appreciated in their patient and unobstrusive usefulness among the brave men for whose service they had sacrificed so much. Lives so occupied afford the highest assurance of a peaceful and happy death, and they die triumphing in the faith of the Redeemer, exulting and grateful that they had devoted themselves to their suffering countrymen. Their example of self-denial and patriotic love will be echoed in the lives of others who will tread in the same path.[30]

SOLDIERS' FAMILIES

The duty of the people, through their government, or outside of it, to provide for the families of soldiers, though less onerous, was not less than that of providing for the soldiers themselves. The origin of this necessity in a republican government has been set forth in the opening of this sketch of the efforts for Soldiers' Relief. At first the universal enthusiasm for the war, and the hope of its speedy termination, produced an apparent indifference in this regard which was only removed when the full extent of the perils and consequent demands of the struggle were revealed to us. Families were left to the

[30] "Report of the Indiana Sanitary Commission Made to the Governor, January 2, 1865," in Indiana *Documentary Journal,* 1864, vol. 2, no 5:79-80.

care of relatives and neighbors, who eagerly encouraged enlistments by promises of attention, which, though often illy fulfilled, were in the main sufficient to prevent the matter from assuming any public importance. But when the term of enlistment was fixed at three years, volunteers began to see that something more than individual promises of support were necessary to justify them in leaving their families. They must make some provision themselves, and this necessity originated the policy of "bounties," which was carried to an extent in our war unknown in any age or country before, because never before was there so vast a population thrown upon public support. And it was not a population of paupers accustomed to want, but of thrifty and prosperous families, entitled at least to suffer no diminution of comfort from the sacrifice of their natural support which they had made. The volunteers, like other men, believed they could make better provision for their families than anybody else could, if they had the means, and they naturally demanded the means as a condition of enlistment. This does not imply that the granting of bounties was yielded to a demand for them, for they were offered before they were demanded, but it was yielded to an imperious necessity which was prevented from becoming a demand only by being anticipated. The General Government offered a bounty and advanced pay; the States in some cases offered an additional bounty, and counties, cities and associations added to both a sum larger than both together, not to *induce,* but to *enable* the volunteer to enlist. It has been often urged as a reproach to our soldiers, that they exacted a bounty as large as the year's wages of a good mechanic before they could consent to serve at all, and then expected treble the pay of the best paid troops in any other country. The reproach is the utterance of ignorance. If our soldiers wanted high bounties, it was because they had a need for them that other soldiers do not usually have. It was in effect only putting into their own hands, for economical application, provision for their families which would otherwise have had to be admin-

RELIEF OF SOLDIERS AND THEIR FAMILIES 445

istered by public agents, wastefully sometimes, corruptly oftentimes, and expensively at all times.

But bounties, as liberal as they were, could not feed and clothe and house a wife and children three years. Nor could liberal pay, in most cases, eke out the provision of the bounty. Both together would fall far short of the comfort to which families had always been accustomed. Additional provisions must be made. This, as earlier in the war, was often done by the care and kindness of neighbors, associations, churches; but even they could not cover the vast necessity that existed. Here, as in all else that affected the soldiers' welfare, the watchful care of Governor MORTON saw the necessity and devised the remedy, almost before it had been felt by those it was approaching. On the 14th of November, 1862, he issued an "Appeal to the People of the State of Indiana."[31] In this address the necessities and modes of relief were so clearly stated that little was left to the people but to go to work. There was no occasion for differences of opinion about organizations, or processes of distribution. The experience of the Sanitary Commission had settled all questions, and the people went to work at once. The clergy, so forcibly appealed to, responded with a promptitude that expressed how fully their Christian zeal was prepared to second the suggestions of their patriotism. Bishop AMES, of the Methodist Episcopal Church, on the 24th of November addressed the following circular letter to the clergy and laity of that church:

Dear Brethren:—In view of the recent timely and humane proclamation of his Excellency, Governor O. P. MORTON, calling for relief measures for the families of soldiers, I feel it incumbent upon me to earnestly recommend to you immediate co-operation in this benevolent and patriotic work. The precursors of a vigorous winter, and the rapid advance in the price of fuel, provisions, and all the necessaries and comforts of life, foreshadow destitution and suffering that only can be mitigated or

---

[31] "Aid for Soldiers' Families. An Appeal to the People of the State of Indiana," in Terrell, *Report,* 1, Appendix, Doc. 140:349. This was issued as a separate imprint: *An Appeal to the People of the State of Indiana* (Indianapolis, 1863). 2 pp.

prevented by the prompt and systematic action of all good citizens throughout our Commonwealth. Such action will not only relieve the wants of those in our midst who have been rendered poor by the present struggle for our national existence, but will strengthen the hands and cheer the hearts of those who have gone forth to fight for our Government. I do not advise that you should act denominationally, but that you should co-operate in carrying out the spirit of the proclamation, both with the civil government and with those, by whatsoever name they may be called, who love Him who says that all kindness to the poor and suffering is kindness to Himself. To this end, I would suggest that the ministers of the Methodist Episcopal Church, in connection with the clergy of all other denominations, in each county throughout the State, hold a meeting, invite the township trustees to join them, and agree upon some organized method of relief and visitation, since the work to be done is a great one, and nothing but organized, intelligent and persistent effort can accomplish it. In the name of Him who eschews all promises unattended by action—who will judge men, not by what they say, but by what they do, I call your attention to these things. Yours fraternally, E. R. AMES.

Other churches were in no degree behind in this effort. On the 1st of December, a letter, signed by all the ministers of the Gospel in Indianapolis, was sent "to the clergy, county commissioners, township trustees, and all who were willing to engage in aiding the families of soldiers," throughout the State, enforcing the exhortations and suggestions of the Governor. The feeling diffused through the people was rapidly crystallized into action whenever it found something to gather about. "Soldiers' Aid Societies" were formed in every neighborhood, or their duties added to those of the auxiliary sanitary associations. Their agents received and filled applications, visited the needy, and sought out those whose dislike to seem to be recipients of charity, impelled them either to conceal or dissimulate their wants. Their exertions soon dispelled this illusion, and made the objects of their care feel that the relief given them was not a benefaction, but a payment, a debt far more obligatory and sacred than any resting upon legal forms and proofs. Families were taught, where the sharper instruction of want had not suggested the lesson first, that the community had assumed the duty delegated by the parent, and their claims were as inviolable upon one as the other. County Commissioners made liberal appropriations, and many a project of improvement, of new courthouses, new bridges, better roads, was deferred to the higher necessity of supporting the dependents of volunteers. Fairs were held and the proceeds distributed, either by township trustees or agents of local aid societies. The efforts for the Sanitary Commission were rivalled and even surpassed by these. No inconsiderable part of the time and labor of a large portion of our people, especially of the women, were given to these objects. The number of them who made duty almost an occupation, and certainly divided with it their household cares, would be almost incredible, if it could be ascertained.

The most striking feature of this outpouring of popular duty to soldiers' families, were those occasions when, by general concurrence in the suggestion of some newspaper or prominent citizen, a day was fixed for contributions to be brought to some central depot for distribution. It was made a neighborhood holiday. Townspeople carried their money, flour, meat, groceries, wood or clothing to the appointed place, and all but those who wanted the war to fail, seemed filled with an emulation to give as much as they could. Farmers, however, bore off the prize for the most conspicuous, if not liberal, displays of contributions. Those of different neighborhoods would collect together early in the morning, and at the appointed time drive into the country town with wagons loaded with wood, and with barrels of flour, or apples, or potatoes, heaped high on the wood, with their horses decorated with flags, sometimes carrying banners, and as the long procession of gratitude and liberality marched along the streets, the crowded pavements welcomed it with cheers as for the return of a victorious army. Emulation ran wild in efforts to show the biggest loads and make the most striking display. Some wagons were built on purpose to carry the loads of a half dozen of ordinary size, and four or five cords of wood were not infrequently piled on by some generous and emulous farmers. It is very questionable if any nation can exhibit a more creditable proof of the remedies as well as the power, the will as well as the wealth of a people, to take from their government a burthen that it could not bear, but which rested, if not lightly, at least not painfully, upon their own willing shoulders. Of the amount thus contributed it is impossible to form a conjecture, but it must have been well along in millions of dollars.

While the provision made from "bounties" was still unexhausted, the relief afforded by aid societies, counties and popular contributions was sufficient. But a bounty barely sufficient for a year, if so much could, with no sort of frugality, be made to meet the wants of two years, and popular liberality was invoked to increased effort by Governor MORTON, in an address of October 27th, 1863, in which, after repeating the arguments for it, in the increasing necessities of soldiers' families, he proceeded to point out more minutely the modes of operation, as follows:

> An efficient working committee in each ward and township should be at once selected, with such assistants and sub-committees as may be necessary, who can easily ascertain the number of families within their limits requiring aid, and estimate the quantity, kind and cost of all supplies needed during the winter. Contributions can be taken up accordingly. In this work the township trustees, and the officers of the various churches, will doubtless lend a willing hand. Especially do I desire that ministers of the gospel should present this subject to their respective congregations, and co-operate, as far as possible, in carrying out the general plan of relief.

The response to this was a continuation and increase of past efforts.

State Bakery.—A very considerable, as well as timely, contribution was made from the 25th of June, 1864, to the 1st of August, 1865—a period of especial urgency for relief—the judicious management of the State Bakery by Quartermaster General STONE. The Bakery was established solely to supply the camps at Indianapolis, both of recruits and prisoners, with good fresh bread at as little expense as possible, but it proved so economical that General STONE was able to give the soldiers, in bread, the full weight of the flour furnished on their rations, and have one third of it left. This surplus was sold for cash, which paid many expenses outside of the bakery. But far more important than any other result was its contribution to soldiers' families. During the period stated it furnished sixty-three thousand five hundred and forty loaves of bread gratuitously, which, at the ordinary price, ten cents per loaf, would have cost the beneficiaries six thousand three hundred and fifty-four dollars. An account was kept of the names, residence, regiment and company of the soldiers whose families were thus assisted, the names of their wives and children, and the daily allowance given to each family. The value of such contributions can hardly be estimated by the money it saved or cost. Further remarks concerning the State Bakery will be found under the head of "Quartermaster General's Office," in this volume.[32]

Legislative Relief.—But in spite of all efforts the necessity still increased. In the fall of 1864, the Governor again set popular feeling at work, but it was evident that the feeling was not equal to the need. He brought the matter before the Legislature which met in January, 1865. That body passed a bill, approved March 4, 1865, but a month before the close of the war, assessing a tax of thirty cents on each hundred dollars of property in the State, the proceeds of which should be applied to soldiers' families, in the modes and proportions set forth in the following circular from the State Auditor to the County Auditors, August 4, 1865:

[32] See below, 536-37.

OFFICE OF AUDITOR OF STATE,
INDIANAPOLIS, August 10, 1865.

To County Auditors:

The following is the apportionment made by the Auditor of State, under the provisions of an act for the relief of soldiers' families, approved March 4, 1865:

Number	COUNTIES	Number of Beneficiaries in each County	Am't apportioned to each County
1	Adams	2,178	$17,598 24
2	Allen	4,224	34,129 92
3	Bartholomew	2,669	21,565 52
4	Benton	282	2,278 56
5	Blackford	790	6,383 20
6	Boone	2,363	19,093 04
7	Brown	1,853	14,972 24
8	Carroll	1,712	13,832 96
9	Cass	2,130	17,210 40
10	Clark	2,373	19,173 84
11	Clay	2,639	21,323 12
12	Clinton	1,838	14,851 04
13	Crawford	2,005	16,200 40
14	Daviess	1,937	15,650 96
15	Dearborn	2,655	21,452 40
16	Decatur	1,873	15,133 84
17	DeKalb	1,859	15,020 72
18	Delaware	1,905	15,392 40
19	Dubois	1,522	12,297 76
20	Elkhart	2,351	18,996 08
21	Fayette	631	5,098 48
22	Floyd	2,307	18,640 56
23	Fountain	2,272	18,357 76
24	Franklin	1,728	13,962 24
25	Fulton	1,466	11,845 28
26	Gibson	2,152	17,388 16
27	Grant	3,009	24,312 72
28	Greene	4,739	38,291 12

RELIEF OF SOLDIERS AND THEIR FAMILIES 451

Number	COUNTIES	Number of Beneficiaries in each County	Am't apportioned to each County
29	Hamilton	2,927	23,650 16
30	Hancock	2,357	19,044 56
31	Harrison	3,907	31,568 56
32	Hendricks	2,445	19,755 60
33	Henry	2,107	17,024 56
34	Howard	2,285	18,462 80
35	Huntington	2,444	19,747 52
36	Jackson	4,421	35,721 68
37	Jasper	1,074	8,677 92
38	Jay	2,783	22,486 64
39	Jefferson	3,625	29,290 00
40	Jennings	1,910	15,432 80
41	Johnson	1,530	12,362 40
42	Knox	2,651	21,420 08
43	Kosciusko	2,417	19,529 36
44	LaGrange	1,275	10,302 00
45	Lake	1,092	8,823 36
46	LaPorte	2,168	17,517 44
47	Lawrence	2,241	18,107 28
48	Madison	2,028	16,386 24
49	Marion	5,273	42,605 84
50	Marshall	2,918	23,577 44
51	Martin	2,737	22,114 96
52	Miami	2,303	18,608 24
53	Monroe	1,783	14,406 64
54	Montgomery	2,101	16,976 08
55	Morgan	2,172	17,549 76
56	Newton	543	4,387 44
57	Noble	2,159	17,444 72
58	Ohio	570	4,605 60
59	Orange	2,134	17,242 72
60	Owen	2,163	17,477 04
61	Parke	1,993	16,103 44
62	Perry	2,210	17,856 80
63	Pike	2,888	22,335 04

Number	COUNTIES	Number of Beneficiaries in each County	Am't apportioned to each County
64	Porter	2,136	17,258 88
65	Posey	2,131	17,218 48
66	Pulaski	1,704	13,768 32
67	Putnam	1,770	14,301 60
68	Randolph	2,504	20,232 32
69	Ripley	2,959	23,908 72
70	Rush	1,256	10,148 48
71	Scott	1,860	15,028 80
72	Shelby	2,564	20,717 12
73	Spencer	2,564	20,717 12
74	Starke	751	6,068 08
75	St. Joseph	2,618	21,153 44
76	Steuben	1,835	14,826 80
77	Sullivan	3,663	29,597 04
78	Switzerland	2,101	16,976 08
79	Tippecanoe	3,418	27,617 44
80	Tipton	2,211	17,864 88
81	Union	452	3,652 16
82	Vanderburgh	1,385	11,190 80
83	Vermillion	1,574	12,717 92
84	Vigo	2,455	19,836 40
85	Wabash	2,972	24,013 76
86	Warren	1,320	10,665 60
87	Warrick	2,842	22,963 36
88	Washington	3,250	26,260 00
89	Wayne	2,898	23,415 84
90	Wells	2,226	17,986 08
91	White	1,655	13,372 40
92	Whitley	1,554	12,556 32
	Totals	203,724	$1,646,089 92

The above apportionment is made upon the following basis:

The total valuation of the real and personal property in the State, as returned in 1864, was	$516,805,999.00
Which at 30 cents on each $100 of valuation, will yield	1,550,417.99
Polls, at $1.00 each	197,600.00
Total receipts, should the tax all be collected	$1,748,017.99
Deduct Governor's Military Contingent Fund	100,000.00
Net amount to be apportioned	$1,648,017.99
Actual amount apportioned to 203,724 beneficiaries, at $8.08 each	1,646,089.92
Remainder	$1,928.07

In making the apportionment each mother, wife, or widow, is counted as four; each motherless child as two, and all other children as one, and the number in each county is the aggregate of those thus estimated. Each child, therefore, if none of the numerated had "otherwise sufficient means for their comfortable support," would be entitled to receive 67 cents per month; each motherless child, $1.34 per month; and each mother, wife, or widow, $2.70 per month. But owing to the fact that a large number of the enumerated are not entitled to the benefit of the act under its terms, on account of having other means for their support, which, the Township Trustee, being the disbursing officer, is to determine; and the further fact, that a majority of our soldiers have themselves returned to take care of their families, there can be no doubt but that the fund will be ample to allow each actual beneficiary the full amount contemplated by law, from the time of its passage, March 4, 1865.

Under the laws, the County Commisioners are authorized and required to borrow, from time to time, as may be deemed necessary, four fifths of the amount set apart to their respective counties in the foregoing schedule.

T. B. McCarty, Auditor of State.

This legislative provision, aided by the societies and popular contributions, would have been sufficient to avert any serious distress, but before any considerable portion of the tax was collected the end of the war restored the surviving soldiers to their homes, with pay, in many cases, and in all cases the opportunities and rewards of customary labor to replace the support so long afforded as the payment of a **National debt.**

SOLDIERS' HOME AND REST

TEMPORARY PROVISION

The efforts of the State and the people for the relief of soldiers and their families were not entirely, though mainly, confined to the channels hereinbefore set forth. Indianapolis, from its central position and character as the capital of the State, was the point of rendezvous for the greater portion of our soldiers in returning home from the field, or returning from home to the "front," and its numerous railroad connections made it a center of transportation for troops from every State in their movements from one portion of the country to another. In consequence, large numbers were frequently accumulated here temporarily, either awaiting orders, or delayed by deficient transportation. They needed some place to rest and refresh themselves. But still more imperious was the necessity of providing for the sick, who, in the earlier part of the war, constituted no inconsiderable portion of all arrivals. The camps of rendezvous were not immediately on the lines of travel and were generally full. The Sanitary Commission, as early as January, 1862, saw the necessity of some provision for this state of things, and, naturally, at first attempted to meet it by obtaining quarters at convenient hotels. "An agent," said Dr. HANNAMAN, "was placed at the depot by direction of the Commission to attend the arrival and departure of trains, and to furnish meals and lodging to all who required them." This was found sufficient for a time, but the progress of the war developed necessities so rapidly, a temporary "camp" was established in the vacant ground south of the depot, where hospital tents were erected and bedding and rations furnished. This provision was again outgrown by the demands of the war and it was from the first insufficient for the sick and wounded, who constituted the most necessitous objects of the care which created it. Something more and of a more permanent character, must be done. Here originated, and what, till the close of the war, was widely known as the "Soldiers' Home."

PERMANENT PROVISION

In the latter part of June, 1862, Governor MORTON, in whose interest in our soldiers every conspicuous measure of relief took its rise, resolved to establish a permanent place of rest and refreshment for soldiers passing through the city, irrespective of the States to which they belonged, and to add to it, as soon as practicable, a hospital department for the care of the sick or disabled who might not require or could not, in their frequently crowded state, obtain admission to the regular hospitals. Accordingly, in June and July, 1862, the General Government paid for the erection of a building in a grove near White River, north of the Terre Haute Railroad. It was 150 feet long and 24 feet wide. The State government and Sanitary Commission completed the work of the General Government by fitting up 100 feet of the building as a sleeping apartment and providing it with bunks, the bedding being furnished by the Commission. The remaining 50 feet was used as a dining hall. A kitchen, 24 feet square, was added to the main building, and all its furniture, as well as that of the dining hall, was supplied by the State.[1]

The establishment was opened about the 1st of August, 1862. On the 8th, General STONE published a notice of the fact and solicited contributions. Thus provision was made for the accommodation of about 100 men. The management was entrusted to Mr. GEORGE MERRITT, assisted by Messrs. BACON and HUNT. The whole expense of it was borne by

[1] "Report of Asahel Stone, Quarter-master General of the State of Indiana. To the Governor," in Indiana *Documentary Journal,* 1864, vol. 2, no. 8:210.

the Sanitary Commission, except the subsistence, which was, of course, supplied in the rations to which the men were entitled. Contributions were made by citizens of vegetables, butter, eggs, fruit, books, paper and envelopes, chairs and the like, and the Postmaster at Indianapolis, Hon. A. H. CONNER, donated a quantity of postage stamps, not the least important contribution to men far away from home and friends.

The accommodations soon proved too small for the demands upon them, and in the latter part of 1862 the General Government, through the influence of Captain JAMES A. EKIN, erected another building, 250 feet long by 24 feet wide, for a dining hall, allowing the former hall to be added to the dormitory.

The larger provision for dining than sleeping was owing to the fact that large numbers of men were detained but a few hours, waiting for trains, and they needed to eat but not to sleep in the "Home." The furniture and fixtures of this, like those of the other building, were supplied by the State. Three tables, extending nearly the whole length, would seat comfortably from 900 to 1,000 men. But still more accommodations were needed, especially for the sick. In 1863 the General Government added a third building, 150 feet long by 24 feet wide, which was, in a short time, converted into a hospital. These provisions, though far exceeding any anticipation when the "Home" was first projected, soon proved equally inadequate to the growing needs of the service with the less ample one at the beginning. In April and May, 1864, General STONE, by direction of the Governor, erected two buildings adjacent to the old ones, each 175 feet long by 28 feet wide, in which were two rows of bunks, with, as in the first building, three tiers in each. The two would accommodate about 1,000 men. The cost of their erection and furniture was about $4,000, which was paid by the State. In this its full development of usefulness, the "Home" could lodge about 1,800 men, and feed 8,000 every day. But even yet, General STONE says, there were occasions when one half the men requiring accommodations could not have them.

Of its benefits General STONE's report furnishes so complete a summary that it is incorporated here:[2]

> The Soldiers' Home and Rest has been of inestimable importance to the wearied and careworn as well as to the sick and wounded soldier. Nor has it been of slight benefit to the numerous detachments of Government employees detained here while in transit to various destinations in the South, sometimes overnight and sometimes for days. So also have its benefits been freely bestowed upon companies, regiments, and indeed whole army corps, whether going to the front or returning. These men have been comfortably lodged during their sojourn here as far as the capacity of the "Home" allowed; and all, without exception, have been furnished with a plentiful supply of well-cooked and wholesome food. And not only does the "Home" furnish the soldiers warm and palatable meals, but whenever necessary, we furnish those in transit with "dry, or lunch rations," consisting of army bread, dried beef and cheese in sufficient quantity to last them to the next depot of supplies. The "Home" has also been of especial importance to the State authorities, as affording a suitable place for bestowing the hospitality of reception dinners on our returned veteran regiments and artillery companies.
>
> Under the auspices of the patriotic ladies of this city [Indianapolis], and by their efficient personal aid in the kitchen and dining-hall of the "Home," we have thus bestowed acknowledgments and welcome on behalf of the State, on about fifty regiments and artillery companies.

Of the economy of thus providing for men in transit, the General says:

> The monthly statements on file in this department show that we have not, in any case, drawn the full amount of subsistence that the men were entitled to as rations, except in the article of flour. The value at Government contract prices, of the subsistence stores thus left in the Commissary Department undrawn, from August 1, 1862, to January 1, 1865, amounts to $71,310.24.[3] This vast saving, effected simply by care in using the rations of the men, would have made some valuable additions to the "Home," in both houses and a supply of pure water, and rearranging the accommodations, if it could have been made

[2] Indiana *Documentary Journal,* 1864, vol. 2, no. 8:211-13.

[3] This amount was reduced to $50,258.58 upon final settlement, when the "Home" was closed. [Terrell]

available; but, though the men or their regiments or companies could have obtained the benefit of the savings, in the "Home" they could not, as then no organization existed by which application could be made. The incidental expenses, such as payment of help, making repairs, replacing furniture and the like, amounting to $19,642.19, were met by a sutler's tax, the sale of kitchen offal and the savings on flour. The State was never burthened with a cent of the cost of maintaining the "Home" after the buildings were erected and furnished.

The following summary of the operations of the "Home" is compiled from General STONE's official reports:

Number of meals furnished, last five months of 1862, ...	210,185
Number of meals furnished, in the year 1863	817,656
Number of meals furnished, in the year 1864, ...	1,642,908
Number of meals furnished, in the year 1865, ...	1,037,450
Number of meals furnished, first five months of 1866, ...	69,592
Total meals furnished in three years and ten months, ...	3,777,791
This shows an average per day of meals, in 1862, ...	1,400
This shows an average per day of meals, in 1863, ...	2,240
This showns an average per day of meals, in 1864, ...	4,498
This shows an average per day of meals, in 1865, ...	2,842
This shows an average per day of meals, in 1866, ...	463

The amount realized *in cash* from various sources for the benefit of the "Home" was $19,642.19, all of which was duly expended as above stated. Besides, the sum of $38,687.80 was expended by the U.S. Commissary out of the savings on flour for fresh vegetables, kraut, pickles, cheese, butter, fruits, and other extras not included in government rations.

For some time before the close of the war, the "Home" was provided with help by details from the Ninety-Fourth Company of the Veteran Reserve Corps, second battalion, "who," says General STONE, "at all hours, night and day, have willingly and energetically prepared and cooked meals for soldiers in transit coming in unexpectedly, weary and needing refreshments, who would otherwise have been compelled to go on their way with their hunger unsatisfied."

LADIES' HOME

Though in no way connected with the "Soldiers' Home," the "Ladies' Home" was an offshoot of the same watchful care to which that institution owed its existence, and should be noticed here to complete the sketch of the provision made for soldiers and their families in temporary need of aid. During the winter of 1863 and 1864, a great many women visited Indianapolis to see their relations in the army, who, they had learned or supposed were detained there, and allowing their affection to conquer their prudence, they very often arrived with no money, or very little, with no acquaintances in the city, and no means of providing for themselves while there or returning home. They were also subjected, where they had money, to the perils of robbery or extortion from the villains who infested the Capital to prey upon the army or fatten on its garbage. They needed help constantly, and frequently applied for it to the State officers, or the Sanitary Commission, who gave it sometimes in money, or passes, and sometimes in payment of hotel bills and other necessary expenses. But this irregular and unsystematic aid, being very inadequate to the emergency, Governor MORTON resolved to establish a "Home" on the same plan as that for soldiers, where soldiers' wives could be sheltered, lodged and subsisted comfortably, and saved from the rapacity of the harpies that threatened them at every turn. To this end Quartermaster General STONE and Dr. HANNAMAN were directed to obtain some suitable building convenient to the Union Depot, and furnish it. This they did, and in December, 1863, the "Ladies' Home" was opened in a large brick building convenient to the Union Depot, under charge of Lieutenant J. G. GREENWALT and wife, whose care and energy are justly commended by General STONE in his report of January, 1865. The following statement of the number of women and children accommodated by it will best exhibit its value:

1863—December ....51 women, 28 children.
1864—January ....55 women, 45 children.
1864—February ....93 women, 67 children.
1864—March ....69 women, 47 children.
1864—April ....64 women, 58 children.
1864—May ....76 women, 51 children.
1864—June ....55 women, 31 children.
1864—July ....43 women, 29 children.
1864—August ....69 women, 36 children.
1864—September ....64 women, 18 children.
1864—October ....54 women, 26 children.
1864—November ....71 women, 45 children.
1864—December ....64 women, 33 children.

Subsistence for the "Ladies' Home" was furnished through the "Soldiers' Home."[4]

REFUGEES

Another object of loyal care was the refugees from the rebel States, who, either expelled by the violence of their neighbors, or reduced to want by the ravages of hostile armies, fled to the North for safety and subsistence. They arrived in a state of deplorable destitution, not only of means of maintaining themselves, but of information as to country and the people. They did not know where to go or what to do. They were generally left in the depot at Indianapolis without direction or assistance, and left to shelter themselves as best they could in outhouses, or any accessible place till the charity of the neighbors provided them with something better. The State officers, as far as they had information, supplied the necessitous. In January, 1865, about one thousand rations and fifty blankets had been issued for this purpose through the "Soldiers' Home." An organization of citizens for their relief was formed, and a large building procured for an asylum and comfortably furnished. The Char-

[4] See Stone's report on the Ladies' Home in "Report of Asahel Stone, Quarter-master General," in Indiana *Documentary Journal,* 1864, vol. 2, no 8:214-16.

itable Association took charge of it, and gave good accommodations to about fifty refugees.[5]

PERMANENT HOME FOR DISABLED SOLDIERS

The close of the war brought with it the duty of making provision for the permanent care of disabled soldiers, not only as an act of humanity but as a debt due to long and faithful service. There were thousands of these in the State, but many were not so entirely disabled that they might not to some extent provide for themselves, and many more could depend upon the care of relatives. But after all allowances for these, there remained many who could have no hope of the comfortable ending of an arduous life except in some permanent asylum which would be to them a home. On the 15th day of May, 1865, Governor MORTON published an address[6] to the people of the State suggesting the outline of an organization, and plan of action, for this purpose. It was proposed that a Board of Directors, composed of one from each Congressional District, should be appointed and be incorporated. It was to select an eligible place for an asylum, and rely for its means of operation upon popular contributions. On the 25th, he addressed a circular[7] letter to the Clergy of the State, urging them to move their congregations to co-operate in the work. On the same day a meeting was held at Indianapolis to carry out the Governor's suggestion. It selected Governor MORTON as President of the Board of Directors, JAMES M. RAY as Treasurer, WILLIAM HANNAMAN as Secretary, and Rev. J. HOGARTH LOZIER as Financial Agent. The District Directors were:

First District, PHILIP HORNBROOK, of Evansville.
Second District, JESSE J. BROWN, of New Albany.
Third District, JOSEPH I. IRWIN, of Columbus.

[5] *Ibid.*, 216-19.
[6] Given in full in Terrell, *Report,* 1, Appendix, Doc. 144:350-51.
[7] *Ibid.,* Doc. 145:351.

Fourth District, WILL CUMBACK, of Greensburg.
Fifth District, WILLIAM GROSE, of New Castle.
Sixth District, JOHN COBURN, of Indianapolis.
Seventh District, JOHN A. MATSON, of Greencastle.
Eighth District, SAMUEL KIRKPATRICK, of Lafayette.
Ninth District, JOHN B. NILES, of La Porte.
Tenth District, ISAAC JENKINSON, of Fort Wayne.
Eleventh District, JOHN U. PETTIT, of Wabash.[8]

The announcement of the formation of a society to establish an asylum was followed immediately by applications for admission, or provision of some kind, from a number of disabled soldiers. The City Council of Indianapolis gave the association the use of the City Hospital buildings. There the Home was opened on the 10th of August, 1865, under the superintendence of Dr. M. M. WISHARD. The necessity for it, says Governor MORTON, in his message to the Legislature at the extra session of November, 1865,

is demonstrated by the fact that already forty-six disabled soldiers have been admitted, twenty-one of whom, after remaining some time, and receiving the best care and medical treatment, have been discharged with the prospect of being sufficiently restored to enable them to care for themselves, and one has died, leaving twenty-four to be cared for. Of these, seventeen are totally disabled by old age, wounds or disease.

Although the directors appealed to the people, setting forth their plan, and the probable sum necessary to carry it out, and made strenuous efforts to obtain the means, they met with less success than they deserved. The people had been heavily burthened by the demands of the war, which the excitement of the times, and the unusual emulation, prevented them from feeling seriously, till the collapse following the excitement brought an intensified sense of the drain that had been made upon them. The Governor in his message expresses doubt whether it will be possible to establish an asylum by voluntary contribution. The amount received

[8] Terrell, *Report,* 1, Appendix, Doc. 146:351-52.

at that time was only $4,994.55, with $20,000.00 subscriptions outstanding, and so inadequate a fund as the whole would be if paid up, fully justified the Governor's apprehensions. He recommended "the Legislature to take prompt measures to secure the object in view." He also stated that he had made application to the General Government to turn over to the State the military hospital at Jeffersonville for an asylum. The consent was given, but the situation of this hospital and other objections being in the way, it was never used.

A memorial was presented to the Legislature,[9] at the same session, by the Board of Directors, asking an appropriation, and, as arguments, setting forth their inability to meet the many demands upon them, the necessity of a support to the families of disabled soldiers, suggesting the plan they thought best adapted to the emergency, and stating the probable number of persons who would need the aid of the asylum. They estimate from reports from one fifth of the State that the totally disabled would amount to about 828; partially disabled to 2,760, and the orphans of soldiers to 9,036. The plan of an asylum is stated thus:

We would procure a tract of good land sufficient to yield all necessary vegetables for the "Home." Upon the ground we would provide suitable habitations, for single men, families and orphans. Having convened these all in one community, we would afford them all possible facilities for contributing to their own support. This would be done chiefly by erecting work shops, where such trades could be carried on as disabled men could work at—such as making brooms, baskets, brushes, shoes &c. Here the remaining faculties of partially disabled men could be educated to good trades, whereby they might support themselves independently outside of the "Home" in a few years, if they should desire it.

By bringing families into the community, the Directors could educate the children, orphans or otherwise, and teach them trades. They also proposed to establish a school for

[9] *Memorial of Officers and Directors of Indiana Soldiers' Home Association* (Indianapolis, 1865).

young men who were disabled, where they could learn bookkeeping, telegraphing and other branches which would enable them to obtain their own support.

On the 5th of January, 1866, an earnest appeal was made to the people for help, which was so far successful that the Board was enabled to purchase for $8,500, early in the ensuing spring, the property known as the "Knightstown Springs," a healthy and beautiful site, possessing the advantage, whatever it may be, of a medicinal spring of some celebrity, and containing fifty-four acres of very good ground. There was one large building, formerly a hotel, and several small cottages, erected for the use of invalids, resorting to the springs, upon the premises, which "afforded ample room," says the Superintendent, Dr. WISHARD, "for one hundred patients," but in need of repairs. The asylum was established in the new location on the 26th of April following, and it will doubtless remain there as long as the necessity for it exists.

In his message of January 11th, 1867, Governor MORTON says the expense of maintaining the "Home" until the 30th of November, 1866, exclusive of the cost of the new site, was $17,060.84. Adding the cost of the site, the whole expenditure made in behalf of disabled soldiers, from August, 1865, to the last of November, 1866, was $25,560.84. During that time there had been admitted 224 disabled soldiers, of whom 134 had been discharged and 14 had died. The Governor again urged the Legislature to equalize the burthen of maintaining the asylum by making it dependent upon taxation, the only mode of making all pay alike for what all are equally bound to contribute. The Legislature adopted the Governor's suggestion, and on the 1st of March, 1867, made the Home for Disabled Soldiers one of the benevolent institutions of the State, with a provision for soldiers' orphans.[10] A Board of Trustees was appointed, and an appropriation of

[10] The act establishing the home is printed in Terrell, *Report,* 1, Appendix, Doc. 75:269-70. See also *Laws of Indiana,* 1867, pp. 190-93.

$50,000 made to erect suitable buildings and provide the necessary means to maintain the inmates properly. The Trustees, Captain H. B. HILL of Carthage, CHAS. S. HUBBARD of Knightstown and WILLIAM HANNAMAN of Indianapolis, organized on the 27th of March, 1867, by electing WILLIAM HANNAMAN President, CHARLES S. HUBBARD Secretary, M. M. WISHARD, M.D., Superintendent, and HENRY W. McCUNE Steward. A fine, substantial brick building, 153 feet long by 63 feet wide, and three stories and an attic high, has been erected at a cost of about $55,000. The cornerstone was laid with impressive ceremonies on the 4th of July, 1867, by the Society of the Grand Army of the Republic. The old buildings have been repaired and converted into the "Orphans' Home" contemplated by the Legislature. The Superintendent states, in his report for 1868, that since the opening of the "Home" 400 disabled soldiers had been admitted, of whom 31 had died, 221 been discharged in an improved condition, leaving 148 still in its care.

Orphans' Home. The provisions of the Legislature for the Orphans of Soldiers have been carried out as far as practicable, as already stated, by the conversion of the old building into an asylum for them, and providing them with adequate care and tuition. It was full to its utmost capacity on Thanksgiving day, November 26th, 1868, and numerous applications were daily made for admission, but refused for want of room. There were then 83 orphans in the "Home," and the number could easily have been increased with adequate accommodations to three hundred.[11]

CONCLUSION

This attempt, necessarily imperfect from the want of space to enable a full account to be given of many operations con-

---

[11] In 1871, following the destruction by fire of the building where the men lived, they were transferred to the National Military Home at Dayton, Ohio, and the orphans were left in full possession of the property. It is now known as the Indiana Soldiers' and Sailors' Children's Home.

nected with the efforts for the relief of our soldiers and their families, will yet afford some idea of the munificence with which the people provided, and the zeal and success with which the State authorities applied, the means to fill out the defective provisions of the government and to supply the vast and immense demands of a soldiery to whom war and want were alike unknown, and upon whom privations fell with double severity. It is at once an exhibition of benevolence and organizing intelligence, of a sense of patriotic duty and a perception of the manner in which that duty can be best discharged. The people supplied the deficiencies of their government, and showed their ability to make it strong, prompt and enduring enough for any exigency in which a nation can be placed. Probably even more than the prosecution of the war itself, the efforts to sustain it, which made no appearance in the reports of generals, or the histories of battles, will justify to the world the pride of Americans in themselves and their Government.

ALLOTMENT COMMISSIONER—
PAY AGENCY

The sudden organization of vast armies in a country, whose people had hitherto been mainly engaged in the peaceful pursuits of agriculture and the mechanic arts, created emergencies and revealed wants unfelt in our previous limited military experience, and which were unprovided for by congressional or legislative enactments.

The soldiers of the Union armies were, as a general rule, representatives of the industrial classes, who had laid aside their usual avocations in obedience to the dictates of patriotism, leaving families, or other relatives, wholly or partially dependent upon their pay for support. Under these circumstances the safe and speedy transmission of money from the soldiers in the field to the dependents at home, was a matter of great importance, and attended with many difficulties.

Army mails were tardy, irregular and unreliable, often being placed in charge of irresponsible parties temporarily detailed for that purpose; express companies were seldom desirous of extending their operations beyond the lines of well-guarded railroads, and the exigencies of the service frequently excluded them from all roads in the vicinity of active military operations. Detailing responsible officers from the different commands to convey remittances, was impracticable, for the class of officers enjoying the confidence of the men to such an extent as to qualify them for so responsible a mission, were the ones most needed in the field, and had not this been the case, they frequently could not be spared at times when payments were made, or details could not be obtained. In some of the States, bankers and brokers engaged in the business, but their charges consumed a considerable proportion of the funds transmitted, and this plan soon fell into disrepute.

ALLOTMENT SYSTEM

The necessity of having some convenient and safe means for the transmission of soldiers' funds, was observed by Governor MORTON soon after our first three-year regiments went to the field. He accordingly devised a system which is fully set forth in the following circular:

EXECUTIVE DEPARTMENT,
INDIANAPOLIS, INDIANA, November 20, 1861.

With a view to facilitate the transmission of funds by our troops in the field to their families, and in addition to facilities afforded by the Government by allotment rolls, the undersigned has effected an arrangement with the Branch Bank in this city, by which funds may be conveyed from Indianapolis to any part of the State through a certain, safe and responsible channel, and without cost to the soldier. A responsible agent will be appointed by the State, whose duty it will be to visit each regiment, in advance of payment, and to receive from each volunteer such funds as he desires to transmit. A book of blank drafts will be furnished to the commanding officer of each regiment. Any volunteer desiring to send money to his family at home, will draw a draft in favor of the party to whom he desires to send the amount. At the same time he will deposit with the agent of this State, the amount he desires to send.

The agent will prepare triplicate schedules of the amount received, from whom received, and to whom to be paid. One copy to be retained by the agent, one copy to be left with the Colonel of the regiment, and the third copy for the use of the bank. The money being deposited at the bank by the agent, the cashier will indorse each draft drawn by the volunteer. The draft will be sent by the agent to whomsoever it may be payable, and on indorsement by that person will be paid at any of the branches in the State.

Commanding officers of regiments are requested to have this read to their regiments, and all officers are requested to co-operate with the undersigned, in affording facilities so much needed by our troops in the field.

OLIVER P. MORTON, Governor of Indiana.

In December, 1861, Congress passed an act requiring the President to appoint Commissioners for each State having volunteers in the service of the United States, whose duty it should be to visit the several Departments of the army in which volunteers from their respective States were serving, and procure from them certified allotments of their pay to their families or friends. On these allotments the several paymasters, at each regular payment of troops, were required to give drafts payable in New York to the order of the persons designated in the allotments.

This law, from which much was expected, accomplished but little towards the desired end. Its provisions, though apparently simple and easy of execution, were attended with so many embarrassments as to be almost impracticable. In some instances where allotments had been made in due form they were entirely disregarded by the paymasters, who asserted, in explanation of their conduct, that the law required the performance of impossibilities. They soon ceased to pay any attention to the law which became, practically, a dead letter.

Throughout the war every measure designed to induce the soldiers to send their money home, or to facilitate its transmission, met with strenuous and persistent opposition on the part of sutlers. Their gains were promoted by the expenditure of the soldiers' money in the field, and they could not be expected to feel a very lively interest for the needy families at home. After the passage of the act abolishing the sutler's lien, they became particularly fertile in expedients for diverting the largest possible amount of money from the home channel. Many of the officers were men of limited means. Receiving their pay irregularly, some times at intervals of many months, and being obliged to furnish their own subsistence, they not infrequently found it necessary to resort to the sutlers of their respective regiments for pecuniary accommodations. Through officers, thus unavoidably placed under obligations for money loaned them in extreme necessity, sutlers were able to embarrass the enforcement of the allotment act, and in various ways to increase their trade with the enlisted men.

Realizing the imperative necessity of providing some means of remitting money from the field that would commend itself to the confidence of the soldiers, Governor MORTON, early in 1862, decided to appoint a number of agents, of well-known probity and correct business habits, to visit the different departments of the army, where Indiana soldiers were serving, to receive such amounts as they desired to send to their families or friends and return with the funds thus gathered to convenient localities in the State to be forwarded by express or the best available conveyance, to the persons for whom the same was intended. The principal agents entrusted with these responsible duties were THOMAS A. GOODWIN, ESQ., Hon. DAVID C. BRANHAM, Rev. E. B. KILROY, General ASAHEL STONE (Commissary General), B. F. TUTTLE, ESQ., Colonel JOHN MCCREA, LAWRENCE M. VANCE, ESQ., and Mr. JAMES HOOK, Agent of the Vigo County Soldiers' Aid Society. Messrs. BRANHAM and GOODWIN held commissions from the President, under the Allotment act of Congress, but as said act made no provision for transportation or necessary expenses incurred, and as the system had never been employed among the Indiana troops, their commissions were of no practical value, except as an endorsement from the highest authority of the Government.

In addition to the onerous and responsible duties connected with the collection and remission of money, the Agents were entrusted by the Governor to look after the welfare and relieve the necessities of sick and disabled soldiers of Indiana Regiments; to assist in procuring furloughs and transportation in all proper cases; to co-operate with the State Sanitary Commission and its branches, and with the various Soldiers' Aid Societies in procuring and forwarding hospital supplies and sanitary stores; and, in all cases, so far as possible, without undue interference with the military authorities, and paying proper regard to the interests of the service, to extend the parental care of the State over all her sons in field or hospital."

The Commissioners entered upon the discharge of their varied duties with zeal and fidelity, extending their labors to every department in which commands from this State were serving. Through their exertions furloughs were obtained for many who were languishing in hospitals; through their advisory suggestions and active co-operation the Sanitary Commission and auxiliary Societies were enabled to extend the sphere of their operations. Abuses and wrongs which they could not correct were reported to the Executive, and measures instituted by him, through the proper channels, for their immediate correction. Between the date of their appointment and the close of the year—from April to December, 1862—they collected, brought home, and distributed eight hundred and ten thousand four hundred and fifty dollars.[1] These moneys were distributed in accordance with the directions of the soldiers sending them, in more than fifteen thousand packages, without charge, save express charges from the agents' residences to points of destination, and without the occurrence of a single case of loss or defalcation. Four hundred and fifty-two thousand dollars, or more than half of the entire amount collected, passed through the hands of THOMAS A. GOODWIN, who devoted his time exclusively to the duties of the Agency. The system adopted saved many thousands of dollars, which would otherwise have gone to sutlers and gamblers. Hundreds of men, careless of necessities of distant friends, and equally regardless of their own future wants, were induced by the example of their more provident companions to remit portions of their pay. The relief thus secured to the families of the careless and im-

[1] See *Report of Pay Agents* [1862] (Indianapolis, 1863). Also "Report of the Allotment Commissioner, on the Transmission of Money for Soldiers. To the Governor," in Indiana *Documentary Journal,* 1864, vol. 2, no. 18, pp. 607-29.

provident prevented want and suffering in many homes, and proved the most beneficent feature of the Agency.

But this system, though accomplishing all that was expected from it, was not free from serious objections, the principal one of which was the great risk incurred in carrying large sums of money through sections of country infested by guerrilla bands and those marauding hordes which generally hang upon the rear of armies in the field. Mr. GOODWIN frequently found himself at a distance from our guarded lines of communication, with a valise filled with money, and could obtain neither guard nor transportation. Encumbered with this sacred trust, which represented the food and clothing of thousands of needy women and children, he was obliged to proceed on foot and alone through those wild and dangerous regions between the advancing army and its base. At Holly Springs he was in imminent danger of being captured by a portion of the force under VAN DORN, an unexpected movement having placed him in the immediate vicinity of the rebels. Returning from a trip to the army stationed near Murfreesboro with letters containing $120,000, packed in a trunk, he lost sight of it for several hours, through the misconduct of an unfaithful porter. Personal risks at that time were esteemed as of little consequence among those familiar with army life, but the financial risks constantly incurred in the prosecution of this business were greater than common carriers assumed, and too hazardous to warrant their continuance. The numerous escapes of Mr. GOODWIN, the only pay agent then operating to any considerable extent, made it apparent that the object for which the plan was devised must be abandoned and some safer mode adopted.

The Congressional allotment act furnished the central idea from which Mr. GOODWIN, with the advice and approval of Governor MORTON, elaborated a system that promised to work successfully. Instead of sending commissioners to the field to procure allotments, as contemplated in the act of Congress, each command was provided with rolls on which each soldier could specify the amount he desired to send, and the name and residence of the person to whom it should be sent. The paymaster and pay agent, each being provided with a copy of the rolls, the former could give a check on New York for the aggregate amount allotted by each company, which the latter could cash and remit in accordance with the individual allotments. The Congressional plan made no provision for aggregating the allotments of a company, but required paymasters to draw a separate check on New York for the allotment of each man.

The first of these rolls were sent out early in 1863, and most of the regiments immediately commenced to avail themselves of the facilities thus offered. The system combined the important requisites of safety, celerity and economy, and rapidly grew in favor with the troops. Mr. GOODWIN continued in charge of the office, which was established at Indianapolis, conducting its immense business with ability and integrity, from the inauguration of the allotment system till most of the Indiana troops were mustered out of the service. During the period nearly two millions of dollars were received and transmitted in about forty thousand different packages without the loss of a single package.

Among the many novel institutions called into existence to meet the sudden emergencies imposed upon the loyal people of the country in the suppression of "the great rebellion," there was none which produced more beneficial results, at a comparatively trivial expense, than the Indiana Allotment Commission.

THE DEAD HONORED

SOLDIERS' MONUMENTS

A grateful people can never be unmindful of its patriotic duty to perpetuate the memory of the brave men who have laid down their lives in defense of the National Government. This has been done in this State by the publication of the military history of each officer and soldier, living and dead, who participated in the late war; and the record, imperfect as it may be, will be an enduring monument to the sacrifices and services of those whose gallant deeds it aims to commemorate. But a record of this kind, however complete, does not preclude the propriety of erecting in the several counties mural monuments, of granite or marble, which have been in all ages of the world a gratifying and beautiful means of perpetuating the memories of heroes and patriots who by their valor have "saved the State," as well as of dear and loved friends and relations "gone before."

The people of Indiana require neither admonition nor example to excite their lasting gratitude towards our deceased soldiers; a just pride in the memory of their heroic deeds is already built up in the hearts of our citizens, and as opportunity offers, will find tangible and enduring expression, befitting the sentiments they entertain, and in keeping with our war record as a State, and the character of the priceless services so worthy of commemoration.

A plan has been devised which seems to meet with almost universal approval—the erection by the citizens of each county of a monument bearing the names of their deceased soldiers, and the names and dates of the battles in which they fell, or the places where they died. In compliance with a very general expression of public opinion, the Legislature, at the special session of 1865, passed an Act[1] authorizing Boards of County Commissioners to receive subscriptions from individuals and make appropriations from the County Treasuries for the erection of soldiers' monuments, and to purchase or receive by donation suitable sites for the same at or near the seat of justice of each county. This Act is founded on the assumption that the objects attained by the war are a common and precious heritage, and the perpetuation of the memory of those who gave up their lives in securing those objects, a common and sacred duty. Few will dispute the correctness of this principle, or object to its practical application.

A few counties have already erected monuments; and in many others, measures have been adopted which bid fair to be productive of substantial results. Doubtless greater progress would have been made in most of the counties, had they not been left at the close of the war with heavy debts incurred in paying bounties and relieving indigent and distressed soldiers' families. Happily most of these debts are now liquidated, and we may confidently look for speedy and appropriate action on the part of county authorities in providing from the public funds, which is most equable, for the erection of suitable and enduring testimonials to the memory of their deceased soldiers.

. . . .

FUNERAL HONORS TO PRESIDENT LINCOLN

The death of President LINCOLN, with whose name the war in defense of the Union was so intimately connected, overwhelmed the nation in sadness and grief. LEE had just surrendered, and the war was virtually closed. The hearts of the loyal people warmed toward their beloved chief magistrate, under whose masterly guidance the great victory had

[1] Printed in Terrell, *Report,* 1, Appendix, Doc. 69:267.

been achieved, and no man, not excepting the Father of his Country, ever possessed the love and esteem of his countrymen in a greater degree than Mr. LINCOLN did at that time.

The startling intelligence was communicated by telegraph on the morning after the occurrence of the event. The whole land, the day before so buoyant and joyous at the prospect of a speedy and triumphant peace, was at once thrown into the deepest grief and enshrouded in mourning.

The Executive of Indiana, the intimate personal and political friend of the President and during the entire war one of his most trusted co-operators in the suppression of the rebellion, in his official capacity announced the sad event in the following touching language:

STATE OF INDIANA, EXECUTIVE DEPARTMENT,
INDIANAPOLIS, April 15th, 1865.

To the Citizens of Indianapolis:

The mournful intelligence has been received that the President, ABRAHAM LINCOLN, died this morning from a wound inflicted by the hand of an assassin, last night. A great and good man has fallen, and the country has lost its beloved and patriotic Chief Magistrate in the hour of her greatest need.

I therefore request the citizens of Indianapolis, in testimony of their profound sorrow, to close their places of business, and assemble in the State House Square at twelve o'clock M. today, to give expression to their sentiments over this great National calamity.

O. P. MORTON, *Governor of Indiana.*

The meeting was held in accordance with the Governor's recommendation, and was attended by a large concourse of citizens. It was a most mournful tribute to the virtues and worth of the illustrious dead, and gave an earnest expression of confidence in the successor to the Presidential office. Though the brightest jewel had been snatched from the coronet of the Nation, there was not one who despaired of its perpetuity or its future glory.

A few days after, throughout the country solemn and impressive funeral honors were observed in view of the great

National loss. The arrangements for the ceremonies at the Capital of Indiana were most appropriate and beautiful. In every part of the State similar honors were observed.

The authorities of the Government, on the 18th of April, determined finally upon the route over which the remains of Mr. LINCOLN should be carried to their final resting place, at his old home in Illinois. Indianapolis was made a point. Governor MORTON, then in Washington, telegraphed instructions to Lieutenant Governor BAKER, and to his military staff, his desire that the remains should be received and honors paid in a manner befitting the great occasion and the character of the State. Accordingly, the Capitol building was put in condition for the reception of the remains; it was beautifully and appropriately draped and decorated; funeral arches were erected in the streets and Capitol grounds, a beautiful funeral car was constructed, and most of the business and private houses of the city were draped and decorated.

The remains arrived on Sunday, the 30th of April, and with the guard of honor were received by the Governor and his staff, Justices of the Supreme Court and other State officers, Major General JOSEPH HOOKER and staff, commanding the Department, and the military of the State under command of Major General ALVIN P. HOVEY, commanding the District. The remains were deposited in the rotunda of the Capitol, where they lay in state, and were viewed by more than one hundred thousand persons during the day and evening. At midnight they were placed again *en route* for Springfield, attended by delegations from all the loyal States.

MILITARY FINANCES

MILITARY AUDITING COMMITTEE

First Committee—1861-62

At the special session of the Legislature, 1861, large appropriations were made for military purposes to enable the State to respond properly and promptly to all calls for troops, to furnish her soldiers with necessary outfits, equipage and arms, and to relieve the sick and wounded. It was expected that these transactions would be of great extent, and, therefore, as a check upon any disposition to extravagance or dishonesty on the part of officials or claimants, as well as to insure economy in expenditures, it was deemed advisable to create an Auditing Board to examine and audit, prior to payment by the State, all claims, vouchers and accounts of a military character. A law was passed accordingly, and approved May 31, 1861. It provided for the appointment of a committee, denominated "The Military Auditing Committee," consisting of two members of the House and one of the Senate, who were required to meet at Indianapolis monthly and examine and audit the military accounts of every description payable out of the public treasury, under the act referred to.[1]

The Hon. DAVID C. BRANHAM, of Jefferson, Hon. MATTHEW L. BRETT, of Daviess, and Hon. JOSHUA H. MELLETT, of Henry, were appointed, the two former on the part of the House, and the latter on the part of the Senate. They met at Indianapolis on the 11th of June for the transaction of business, but being notified by the Auditor of State, Hon.

---

[1] Printed in Terrell, *Report,* 1, Appendix, Doc. 52:257-58. See also *Laws of Indiana,* sp. sess., 1861, p. 4, Secs. 5, 6, 7 of act making general appropriations.

ALBERT LANGE, that he considered it his right and duty to disregard the action of the Committee on the ground that the act constituting it was unconstitutional and void, and that he would, therefore, as in other cases, audit all just and duly certified military accounts and draw his warrants upon the treasury, as if the committee had not been appointed. The Auditor, in taking this course, was doubtless actuated by a sense of his own prerogatives, thinking, evidently, that what the committee proposed to do he could do as well and with less circumlocution and less hindrance to the efforts that were being made to place Indiana troops earliest and foremost in the field. He desired rather to facilitate than retard the great work that had been undertaken by the State. Personally, he was on the best terms with the members of the committee, but he insisted that he was the Auditor, and it was not the province of the Legislature to deprive him of any of his power, by the appointment of an irresponsible committee. He had been elected by the sovereign people of the State to audit all public accounts payable out of the public treasury; he had given bonds for the faithful and honest performance of his duties, and had been duly qualified in every respect according to law. Here was a "deadlock," so far as the committee were concerned. The members, who were plain, practical men, had plenty to attend to on private account at home; they would gladly have been relieved of the labors, responsibilities and inconveniences imposed upon them; but they were of opinion that it was entirely competent for the Legislature to order preliminary investigation and authentication of any and all claims upon the public treasury; that anything they might do could not, under the law, deprive the Auditor of any of his right or power, and that it was their duty, under the extraordinary circumstances created by a state of war, to execute with scrupulous fidelity the trust the Legislature had imposed upon them. Legal proceedings were therefore instituted to test the constitutionality of the law creating the committee, and the Auditor was required to show cause why he should not recognize the committee's action and be restrained from auditing military accounts unless the same were first duly audited and certified by the committee. The case was submitted to the Common Pleas Court of Marion county and decided in favor of the Auditor. An appeal was taken to the Supreme Court—the decision of the Common Pleas was overruled and the act declared constitutional and in full force.

It is but justice to Mr. LANGE to say, that when the Committee had fairly entered upon its duties, and when the importance became understood of thorough and searching investigations into every military claim, he frankly and cheerfully acquiesced in the wisdom and prudence of the Legislature in providing this additonal safeguard. Instead of hindering or delaying the efforts of the authorities, it greatly facilitated the transaction of public business, gave confidence to the taxpayers of the State, and held at bay a host of mercenary plunderers who otherwise would have used every devisable expedient to get hold of the public funds.

The Committee met again for the transaction of business on the 15th of July. Mr. BRANHAM was elected Chairman, and, under the sixth section of the act, W. H. H. TERRELL, of Vincennes, was appointed Clerk. The rule adopted in the adjustment of claims was "to protect the State from unjust and exorbitant demands, and at the same time to award to claimants what was just and proper and no more." The Committee continued to meet monthly until January, 1863. Claims amounting to one million two hundred fifty-six thousand five hundred and ninety-three dollars and thirty cents were audited on account of the United States and State service.

Mr. TERRELL having been appointed Military Secretary to Governor MORTON, in January, 1862, Mr. W. C. LUPTON succeeded him as Clerk, and continued to act in that capacity until the 19th of June, at which time he was appointed Quartermaster of Volunteers, and J. J. HAYDEN, ESQ., was selected to fill the vacancy and served in that capacity until the Committee ceased to act.

The members of the Committee were prompt in their attendance upon their duties, and fairly and thoroughly investigated every matter brought before them. Many claims were rejected or reduced in amount, and the interests of the State carefully and honestly guarded. They deserve, for their faithful services, untiring zeal and strict integrity, the thanks of the people of the State.[2]

Second Committee—1863-64

Under joint resolutions passed by the General Assembly in March, 1863,[3] a second Military Auditing Committee was provided for, consisting of Honorables PARIS C. DUNNING (Chairman) and JOHN C. NEW, on the part of the Senate, and WILLIAM E. NIBLACK, SAMUEL H. BUSKIRK and ALFRED KILGORE, on the part of the House of Representatives. Mr. JACOB S. BROADWELL was appointed Clerk. The general plan pursued by the first committee, in the investigation and allowance of claims, was followed by the second. The members of the Committee were recognized throughout the State as gentlemen of ability, integrity and good judgment. Their report, which was printed by order of the Legislature, is an interesting document, and shows the total amount of claims audited during their term to be nine hundred and eighty-five thousand seven hundred and sixty-three dollars and forty-three cents.

Third Committee—1865-66

A third Military Auditing Committee was created by act of the General Assembly, approved March 6th, 1865,[4] which provided that the Committee should be composed of two members of the House of Representatives and one member

---

[2] For reports of this and succeeding committees, see "Reports of the Military Auditing Committee for the Years 1861, 1862, 1863 & 1864" in Indiana *Documentary Journal,* 1864, vol. 2, no. 4.

[3] Printed in Terrell, *Report,* 1, Appendix, Doc. 53:258.

[4] Printed in *ibid.,* Doc. 54:258-59. See also *Laws of Indiana,* 1865. p. 45, Sec. 61 of act making general appropriations.

of the Senate, with a Secretary. The Honorable PARIS C. DUNNING (Chairman) was re-appointed on the part of the Senate, the Honorables ALFRED KILGORE and JOHN A. HENDRICKS on the part of the House. Major O. M. WILSON was selected as secretary. The law also made it the duty of the Attorney General of the State to act as the legal adviser of the Committee and to attend its sessions, whenever notified and required, and resist the allowance of all disputed claims. In addition, the Committee was required, upon the completion of their labors, to make and submit to the ensuing regular meeting of the Legislature a full and succinct report of their transactions for the information of the General Assembly.

At the special session of the Legislature, 1865, an act was passed (approved December 23d)[5] requiring the Committee to wind up its business by the first of April, 1866. It is to be regretted that the Committee, up to this time, has not made a report of its transactions, as required by law. I am, therefore, unable to make any statement as to the extent or nature of its business.

STATE PAYMASTER

Major Oscar H. Kendrick

The enactment of the Six Regiment Law[6] and the enlistment of State troops in accordance therewith,[7] necessitated the employment of a State Paymaster. On the 1st of June, 1861, an act was passed providing for the appointment of such an officer and defining his duties.[8] Dr. OSCAR H. KENDRICK, of Indianapolis, was appointed to the position on the 11th of June, and at once took charge of the State Pay De-

[5] Printed in Terrell, *Report*, 1, Appendix, Doc. 55:259. See also *Laws of Indiana*, sp. sess., 1865, pp. 64-65.

[6] Printed in Terrell, *Report*, 1, Appendix, Doc. 43:246. See also *Laws of Indiana*, sp. sess., 1861, pp. 97-98.

[7] See above, 14-17.

[8] Printed in Terrell, *Report*, 1, Appendix, Doc. 49:255-56. See also *Laws of Indiana*, sp. sess., 1861, pp. 73-74.

partment. Although entirely inexperienced, he was a painstaking, faithful and conscientious officer, and throughout his term of service discharged his responsible duties in a highly satisfactory manner.

The State regiments, as originally organized, were the Twelfth, Thirteenth, Fourteenth, Fifteenth, Sixteenth and Seventeeth infantry, and STEWART's company of cavalry; besides there were five extra companies of infantry and a squad of artillery. Early in June a requisition was made by the War Department upon the Governor for four infantry regiments, and they were promptly organized from the six regiments above named, the Thirteenth, Fourteenth, Fifteenth and Seventeenth volunteering for three years, except an inconsiderable number, who declined to enter the United States service, and were discharged, their places being filled from the unattached companies. Subsequently the Twelfth and Sixteenth regiments were also transferred for one year's service.

Major KENDRICK paid, out of State funds, the discharged men and the Twelfth and Sixteenth regiments; also some of the unattached companies and a number of the officers of all the State forces for the time they were in the State service, his total disbursements amounting to the sum of $94,083.27, which amount was duly accounted for upon proper vouchers filed with the State Treasurer. These vouchers have since been presented at the Treasury Department of the United States for reimbursement to the State, and nearly, if not quite, the whole amount has been allowed.

After the transfer of the State forces to the General Government, Major KENDRICK was ordered by the Governor to open an office at Indianapolis, and render all necessary assistance to discharged Indiana volunteers, in securing their pay and allowances from the United States. He prepared their accounts and attended to the collection of their dues, and thus saved them from vexations, delays and exorbitant charges of agents, to which they would otherwise have been subjected. On the 28th of June, 1862, he tendered his resignation, on account of ill health and was honorably discharged.[9]

Pay Due State Troops for Services Under "Six Regiment Bill"

The following communication was transmitted to the Speaker of the House of Representatives on the 24th of February, 1865.

EXECUTIVE DEPARTMENT OF INDIANA,

ADJUTANT GENERAL'S OFFICE,

INDIANAPOLIS, February 24, 1865.

HON. JOHN U. PETTIT, *Speaker of the House of Representatives.*

SIR: Under an Act approved May 11th, 1861, six regiments of State troops, for twelve months' service, were organized, viz: the Twelfth, Thirteenth, Fourteenth, Fifteenth, Sixteenth and Seventeenth Regiments. A call was afterwards made for four regiments of United States Volunteers, which were organized from the companies composing the State regiments, and duly mustered into the United States service. This was done by transferring from different companies such men as would volunteer for three years' service, and by consolidating the remaining men into two regiments of State troops—the Twelfth and Sixteenth. The transfers alluded to run through the rolls of nearly every one of the companies composing the six regiments. The State Paymaster made payments to those who did not enter the United States service, from the date the companies went into camp to the date of transfer to the United States service, and the United States Paymaster made payment from the date the companies transferred to the service of the General Government went into camp, except in cases where the men had been transferred from companies that did *not* enter the United States service. Thus a number of those who entered the United States service by transfer from the Twelfth and Sixteenth regiments and a detachment of five companies (known at that time, as the Eighteenth regiment), have not been paid for their services as *State* troops because of their absence at the time the State Paymaster was making his payments. After their discharge from the United States service, many of

[9] See *Report of the State Paymaster* [O. H. Kendrick], *of Indiana Volunteer Militia* (Indianapolis, 1863). 7 pp.

them made claim for their dues from the State, but the military fund having been exhausted, they could not be paid.

There are, also, some who were discharged from the State service, prior to the payments made by the State Paymaster, who have a legal claim for services rendered, and who cannot be paid on account of the absence of an appropriation.

From an estimate made, based upon a careful examination of the rolls in this office, the claimants represent, in the aggregate, 5895 days' service, which at $13.50 per month, the monthly pay and clothing allowance, paid at the time the services were rendered, amounts to the sum of $2,472.

I respectfully recommend that an appropriation be made to cover these claims, and that the State Paymaster be required to draw and disburse the money as it may be demanded, upon certified rolls to be furnished from this office.

I have the honor to be, very respectfully, your obedient servant,

W. H. H. TERRELL, *Adjutant General, Indiana.*

On the 4th of March, 1865, the General Assembly made an appropriation of $2,500 to cover the claims mentioned, and authorized the same to be disbursed by the State Paymaster upon evidence to be furnished by the Adjutant General. Accordingly, certified copies of the rolls of all men, shown to be entitled to pay, under the Act of 4th of March, 1865, were made and furnished Major STEARNS FISHER, State Paymaster, on the 22d of April, 1865, showing the term of service and the amount due each. The aggregate amount thus certified was as follows:

Twelfth Regiment	$ 474.75
Thirteenth Regiment	663.88
Fifteenth Regiment	568.55
Sixteenth Regiment	1,345.88
Eighteenth Battalion	54.00
Total	$3,107.06

The amount appropriated, although less than the amount due, will doubtless be more than sufficient to pay all the claimants who will ever apply.

Major Stearns Fisher

The frequent disturbances on the southern border of the State in 1861 and 1862 required the Indiana Legion to be frequently called out. No arrangement was made for paying these troops until the 11th of April, 1863, when the Governor determined to use the militia fund for that purpose, appropriated by the act of 1861 for the support of the Legion, and which could not be distributed to the several counties, as the law intended, because of certain obstacles growing out of incomplete legislation. On the above date the Hon. STEARNS FISHER, of Wabash county, was appointed paymaster.

In pursuance of the Governor's instructions he visited all the counties bordering on the Ohio river for the purpose of collecting facts and making up payrolls for services rendered in repelling rebel raids, and guarding the border from threatened rebel invasion. This duty was attended with many difficulties; in many of the counties no record had been kept of services rendered; companies had been called out in emergencies and discharged when the danger was past, and no account kept of the time. Major FISHER, however, by patient and laborious research, succeeded in making up, from sworn evidence and other reliable data, a very satisfactory set of rolls, and as soon as possible commenced payment, visiting all the counties in person where troops had served.

The raid of MORGAN soon followed, and other raids and disturbances frequently occurred. The liabilities of the State for pay of the Legion and Minute-men rapidly increased, and the paymaster was again required to collect evidence and make up proper rolls for payment. This was a very considerable task, but it was fully and thoroughly performed. The amount due each soldier was small, and as the Morgan Raid troops were drawn from widely remote portions of the State, the process of payment was necessarily slow. The Paymaster was required to visit at least one, and in some cases two and three places in each county that furnished men. There were over three hundred companies on duty "after MORGAN," and every Congressional district was represented, except the Tenth. In some cases not more than half the men would present themselves for payment at the time and place appointed, being absent and generally in the army. Very rarely was a company paid entire. Unpaid claimants, either by their attorneys or in person, constantly continued to demand their dues, and Major FISHER was therefore required to keep an office open at Indianapolis, and attend in person or by clerk until near the close of his term.[10]

His accounts and vouchers were forwarded from time to time to the Treasury Department at Washington for repayment, and up to the 11th of April, 1866, the sum of $193,390.35 had been refunded to the State, since which time further repayment has been stopped because the appropriation, made by Congress for this purpose, has been exhausted. Provision, however, has been made for final settlement through a Commission appointed by the President under an act of Congress, approved March 29th, 1867.

The entire disbursement made by Major FISHER, as shown by his account current, amounts to the sum of $648,885.08.

On the 11th of March, 1867, in pursuance of an act of the Legislature, the records and business of the Pay Department were transferred to the Adjutant General, and that officer was required to perform the duties of Paymaster, after the 15th of June following, at which date Major FISHER was honorably discharged from the service. It is due to him to say that he was an intelligent, faithful and honest officer, and in discharging the extensive and intricate duties of his position, won the respect and confidence of the people of the State.

Pay Department Transferred

After the transfer was made to the Adjutant General, as above stated, a new system of vouchers was devised and a

---

[10] See "Report of the State Paymaster [Stearns Fisher]. To the Governor," in Indiana *Documentary Journal*, 1864, vol. 2, no. 14.

different mode of payment established. The amount still standing on the rolls as unpaid was about $30,000, the greater part of which, the separate amounts being small, will not probably be called for. Not desiring to hold in my hands any of the public funds, I suggested that payments be made upon my orders, after being approved by the Governor, directly by warrants drawn by the Auditor of State on the Treasury. This plan was adopted and incorporated by the Legislature in the act before referred to. Thus no funds are required except as claimants present themselves, and when they cease to make demands the balance of funds appropriated will remain, as it ought, in the coffers of the State and may be applied to other objects.

Since I have been acting Paymaster, payments to the amount of $3,277.23 have been made to three hundred and ninety-eight different claimants.

RAILROADS, STEAMBOATS AND THE TELEGRAPH IN THE WAR

RAILROADS

The railroads of the country, during the rebellion, performed a part so important to the Government in the transportation of troops, munitions and military stores, it would seem proper that their general good management and efficient co-operation, so far as the same related to Indiana troops, should receive some acknowledgment in this report.

It will not be denied that the hearty and generous spirit of patriotism, and the enterprising management so continuously displayed by the railroad companies operating within our limits, assisted materially in insuring the grand success which attended the efforts of the State to promptly place her quotas in the field; to furnish supplies and material of war to her troops; to look after and relieve her sick and wounded soldiers; to protect her southern border against rebel raids and to repel rebel invasions; and to meet and overcome the many critical emergencies that arose during those eventful years. While it may be truly said that our railroad corporations flourished to an unparalleled degree by the patronage of the State and General Government resulting from the war, many of them, indeed, having been enabled from their military business alone to extinguish very heavy indebtedness and to bring up their stock from merely nominal figures to handsome quotable rates—it is but just to add that they did not receive greater profits nor amass more wealth than they were reasonably entitled to by their energy and enterprise, their hazards and the immense capital employed.

Their regular business and the private interests of communities and individuals were necessarily subjected to many interruptions and annoyances by the peculiar and imperative demands of the public service, and such interruptions doubtless often resulted in heavy pecuniary losses and sacrifices to the business public. Military transportation always took precedence; and at times, for weeks in succession, the ordinary business of the country was almost entirely neglected and deferred.

The capacity of the several roads, the ability and tact of the managing officials, and the faithfulness and endurance of operating employees, were thoroughly tested in a manner that reflected the highest credit upon all concerned.

While it is impracticable to make special mention of the many occasions when the salvation of the country, and especially the safety of our own homes, seemed to depend upon the prompt action of the railroads, it is proper to state that their good management was strikingly displayed in forwarding new regiments to Kentucky in August, 1862, when the rebel forces under KIRBY SMITH, aiming to reach and destroy Cincinnati, were met and checked at Richmond; and in July, 1863, when JOHN MORGAN undertook his famous marauding expedition north of the Ohio. Cincinnati was saved; and the Morgan raiders were compelled to fly from the State, almost without sleep or rest. Most of the railroad companies observed the very liberal rule of carrying soldiers discharged in the field or on furlough, when unprovided with State or Government transportation, at one half the usual rates, whenever it appeared from their papers that they had been honorably discharged, or were traveling on proper leaves of absence. To those who were sick this generous reduction was a particularly welcome and valuable favor, enabling thousands to reach their homes where they could recruit their impaired health, as well as to return to their regiments in the field at the proper time. In a great many cases where soldiers were destitute of means to pay their fare, or even represented themselves to be destitute, they were passed free. Impositions were of frequent occurrence, but the peculiar circumstances of the times and the disposition almost universally felt to mitigate the sufferings and relieve the destitution of every meritorious soldier, induced most of the companies to relax and liberally construe their otherwise inflexibly stringent rules.

Requisitions were frequently made by the State authorities for special and irregular trains for the movement of troops, and to convey surgeons, nurses and hospital stores to the battlefield. These requisitions were always promptly met, and the services thus rendered were the means of accomplishing incalculable good. In the severe winter of 1862-63, the wood for the use of the camps at Indianapolis, including the rebel prison, was nearly exhausted; the weather was such that a supply could not be brought in by teams, and the men consequently being put upon short allowance, became disaffected to such an extent that there was serious danger of a general stampede. In this condition of affairs, the officers of the Terre Haute road were applied to for relief, and they very promptly furnished an abundant supply of fuel from their woodyards in the country.

But while as a general rule the admirable management of the railroads in the State during the war reflected the highest credit upon their officers, there were exceptional instances where the interests of the Government and the comfort of troops were greatly neglected. Delays occurred, whereby the men suffered much from hunger; and insufficient supply of fuel occasionally afforded ground of complaint, and cars were furnished in some instances which were unfit for the transportation of human beings. Pressure of business and unavoidable accidents doubtless contributed largely to these evils, but inefficiency and culpable neglect on the part of railroad officials were sometimes clearly apparent. The bad conduct of a few soldiers in maliciously damaging coaches, frequently caused the substitution of freight and stock cars, where better conveyances might have been supplied. The soldiers were displeased at this offensive discrimination between themselves and the general traveling public. They regarded it as a slight, an attempt to degrade them, and were thereby provoked to acts of wanton destruction, in which they would not have engaged had they received such treatment as they believed themselves entitled to. Thus feelings of mutual hostility were engendered between the railroad officials and the soldiers, which led to harsh treatment from the former and aggressive acts by the latter.

In the summer of 1862, complaints against some of the roads were so frequent it became necessary to appoint for this State a military railroad superintendent, and Colonel R. E. RICKER, Superintendent of the Terre Haute and Indianapolis Railroad, was appointed to that office, which action was attended with advantageous results.

The following table will be interesting:

STATEMENT of companies, recruits and persons on military business carried by the various railroads in the State, during the year 1861, and the amounts audited and allowed to the same by the Military Auditing Committee, *exclusive of Regiments en route to the field of active service:*

RAILROADS.	Men.	Amount.
Evansville and Crawfordsville	6,916	$9,927 45
Terre Haute and Richmond	12,640	14,668 04
Ohio and Mississippi	5,060	4,816 55
Lafayette and Indianapolis	9,545	11,642 14
Indiana Central	5,342	6,694 21
Peru and Indianapolis	6,456	8,246 82
Toledo and Western	3,548	2,988 82
Indianapolis and Cincinnati	5,864	7,701 27
Indianapolis, Pittsburgh and Cleveland	2,079	1,981 58
Jeffersonville	6,199	9,413 66
Madison and Indianapolis	5,521	6,241 37
Pittsburgh, Fort Wayne and Chicago	853	500 18
Michigan Southern and Northern Indiana	3,309	2,858 10
Cincinnati, Peru and Chicago	940	574 94
Louisville, New Albany and Chicago	9,105	9,149 42

	Men.	Amount.
Bellefontaine	2,088	1,662 97
Cincinnati and Chicago Air Line	1,628	1,313 48
	87,093	$100,178 00
Carried by steamboats	1,893	2,293 05
Carried by wagons	1,232	1,970 10
Total for 1861	90,218	$104,441 15

No returns are accessible for subsequent years, but it may be stated the railroad business was increased very largely until some time after the close of the war.

OHIO RIVER PACKETS

The various lines of packets, operating on the Ohio river during the war, rendered important service to the State and National governments, of a similar character to those performed by our railroads. Their promptness in seconding the efforts of the authorities and the liberality and general efficiency of their management contributed largely to the success of military operations.

Guerrilla bands which infested the Kentucky shore and larger bodies of rebel troops occasionally operating in that State, rendered river navigation exceedingly hazardous, and steamers were often exposed to imminent danger of capture. The risks of person and property were met with such courage and business energy as entitled the owners and officers of the packet lines to honorable mention among the agencies employed in the prosecution of the war.

Steamers were frequently chartered for sending relief— sanitary supplies, surgeons and nurses—to battlefields and to hospitals at various points on the Ohio, Tennessee, Cumberland, and Mississippi rivers, and for bringing home the sick and wounded, of which more particular mention is made in another part of this report.[1] These steamers rendered invaluable service; their officers were prompt, brave and hu-

---

[1] See above, 440-42.

mane, and deserve the thanks of the country for their hazards and exertions in the cause of patriotism and humanity.

THE TELEGRAPH

One of the most important, indeed one of the indispensable, instruments in carrying on the war was the telegraph. On many occasions it was relied on almost entirely as the means of communication, and at all times during the war it was used perhaps to an equal extent with the mails. To the superintendents, managers and operators in Indiana, and especially those on duty at Indianapolis, the thanks of the Governor and his military staff are especially due for their uniform courtesy and efficiency. JOHN F. WALLICK, Esq., Manager, and CHARLES C. WHITNEY, Esq., Chief Operator at Indianapolis, deserve particular mention for their faithful and able services in the line of their profession, and it is a pleasure to know that the company so well represented by them has manifested its appreciation of their labors by promoting each to a higher position in the telegraph service.

The following statistics convey but an imperfect idea of the business transacted "over the wires" by the Executive and Military Departments of the State during the war:

OFFICERS		Telegraph Charges		
For the Year 1861.	Governor	Ad't Gen.	Q.M.G.	Ch'f Ord.
Governor	$5,939.07			
Adjutant General		$756.58		
Quartermaster General			$562.54	
For the Year 1862.				
Governor	8,907.03			
Adjutant General		1,093.43		
Quartermaster General			228.71	
Chief of Ordnance				$459.06
For the Year 1863.				
Governor	5,137.67			
Adjutant General		627.71		
Quartermaster General			14.16	
Chief of Ordnance				162.12

For the Year 1864.

Governor	3,902.87	....	....	....
Adjutant General	....	1,168.91	....	....
Quartermaster General....	....	....	29.21	....
Chief of Ordnance.............	....	....	....	70.19

For the Year 1865.

Governor	2,783.92	....	....	....
Adjutant General	....	1,456.87	....	....
Quartermaster General....	....	....	8.45	....

Total $26,670.56 $5,103.50 $843.07 $691.37

Grand total $33,308.50

CONTRABAND TRADE

Early in the war the rebels in the South made the most strenuous efforts to secure a full supply of arms, ammunition, flour, corn, bacon, medicines, surgical instruments and other articles contraband of war, anticipating, of course, that as soon as the National Government succeeded in organizing an army, the shipment of these indispensable supplies would be stringently prohibited. In April and May, 1861, the contraband trade was extensively carried on between Kentucky and the States farther south, and the commercial cities of the north. Provisions, in immense quantities, were shipped by steamers plying on the Ohio, Mississippi, Cumberland and Tennessee rivers, and by the Louisville and Nashville Railroad. All descriptions of goods required by the rebels to equip and maintain their forces, including arms, ammunition and medicines, were purchased and sent South in large amounts. Our Government for some time paid but little attention to these matters; indeed, until military posts were established on the line between the two hostile forces there were but few barriers against the free transmission to the South of every kind of *material* required in fitting out troops.

The Government for several months did not interfere with the active secession movements going on in Kentucky, but seemed to be fearful to take action in any way unless the fragile thread by which that State hung to the Union might be sundered. The heresy of "armed neutrality" was pressed upon the authorities at Washington with energetic pertinacity by prominent and patriotic though misguided Kentuckians, as well as by those who had determined to follow the fortunes of the new "Confederacy," who were well able to see that no policy on the part of our Government would so well favor the rebel cause in Kentucky as the one proposed. General McCLELLAN, then in command of the Federal forces in the West, actually agreed with General BUCKNER, commanding the Kentucky State Guard—who headed the rebel movement and was intriguing to secure the vantage ground and carry the State over to the side of the rebellion—that the "neutrality" of Kentucky would be observed by the military authorities of the United States, so long as Kentucky actually remained neutral towards the Southern States. Thus the way of the contraband trade was left open and unobstructed. The railroads terminating on the Ohio river, at Cincinnati, Madison, Jeffersonville, New Albany, Evansville and Cairo, and the river itself, were the channels used for this illicit traffic.

The citizens of the State at various points soon discovered the nature and extent of this business, and, in the absence of other measures to suppress it, frequently took the responsibility to stop goods that were clearly intended for the Southern army, and contraband of war. The surveyors of the several ports on the river also exerted themselves in the same direction, and made many important seizures; yet it is now well known that the check thus given to the contraband trade was so insignificant it really interfered but slightly with the extensive and enterprising operations of the rebels.

About the first of May a Committee of Vigilance was organized by citizens at Indianapolis to inspect the contents of the various trains passing southward through that city, and to detain any supplies of a contraband character, until due and proper investigation as to the destination of the same could be had. Governor MORTON also—through the military officers engaged in raising troops at various points, and with the aid of two detectives appointed by him and stationed at Indianapolis—did much to defeat the plans of the enemy and break up the transmission of munitions of war and other supplies destined for the use of the rebel army. Upon his suggestion an Agent of the Treasury Department was appointed and placed on duty at Indianapolis, with authority to seize and detain all contraband articles en route to the Southern States. Seizures were made almost daily. Large quantities of muskets, cartridges, percussion caps, provisions, &c., were stopped and turned over to the proper authorities to be held subject to the order of the Government. At Vincennes, Evansville and New Albany, several lots of pistols, swords, materials for trimming officers' uniforms, and other military goods were captured. Shippers and officers of railroads soon grew cautious, and became afraid of the consequences of participating in this unlawful business. The southern trade was tempting, and if left unobstructed would have been the source of great profits, but "confiscation" being adopted as the remedy to suppress it, it could be carried on only surreptitiously and at great risk.

MANUFACTURE OF AMMUNITION

INDIANA STATE ARSENAL

How it Originated

It is well known that in April, 1861, the General Government was unable to supply, without the delay required to manufacture, either arms, ammunition or clothing, sufficient for even the small army of seventy-five thousand men then called into service. The several loyal States were therefore compelled to equip their own troops, and many of them indeed furnished their own arms, as did ours. The Eleventh Regiment was first armed, the arms being those heretofore drawn on the State's distributive quota under act of Congress. The next thing was to supply it with ammunition, so that it might be fully prepared to go to the field. The Government could scarcely supply the troops raised in States east of us, which, of course, being nearest the public arsenals, were supplied first. Governor MORTON attempted to overcome the difficulty, temporarily, by undertaking the fabrication of enough for the three months' regiments; but it was not expected, or even thought of, that the business would be long continued. Captain HERMAN STURM, who had a thorough knowledge of the business from experience and study in Europe, was engaged to conduct the operations at Indianapolis. The materials were furnished by the Quartermaster General; the labor required was supplied by a detail of volunteers from the Eleventh Indiana, and on the afternoon of the 27th of April the work was begun. The facilities were a few hand bullet moulds, the forge of a small blacksmith shop for casting, and a room adjoining for putting up the cartridges. The experiment may be said to have been successful, for, though the cost was much greater than at a later period, when the establishment was run on an extensive scale, and the materials used were bought in large quantities at wholesale rates, the ammunition was of the best quality, and our troops were thus enabled to march into Western Virginia with full cartridge boxes and an abundant surplus.

Its Continuance

The scarcity of ammunition in the country did not seem to diminish, while calls for it for border defense and the use of our new regiments, made it imperatively necessary, in the judgment of the Governor, that the Arsenal should for a time be continued. He therefore, about the first of June, ordered the erection of cheap and temporary buildings, consisting of a small brick foundry, two cartridge shops, and some other structures of packing, storage, &c. Safety, economy and convenience were thereby secured to a much greater extent than could be expected in rented tenements not specially adapted to the purpose. About one hundred females were at first employed in the cartridge shops, their labor being cheapest and best adapted to the lighter work. In the foundry and packing shops some fifty men were employed in casting bullets, filling and packing cartridges, and other work. As the demands for ammunition increased, the force was augmented—as many as three, five and seven hundred persons, during the continuance of the Arsenal, being employed at one time. The ammunition was in great favor with all the troops who used it, and the price at which it was furnished, being net cost to the State, was said to be from thirty to fifty per cent less than the Government was compelled to pay to private manufacturers on contract. Notwithstanding there was no law expressly authorizing the establishment of a State arsenal, yet, as its origin and continuance was an indispensable military necessity, the Governor felt justified in assuming the responsibility until that necessity should be met by the United States furnishing the ammunition required.

A Favorable Report

Up to the month of October, 1861, when two hundred and fifty hands were employed, no arrangement had been made with the United States in reference to the Arsenal, or the ammunition issued from it to troops. The State had thus far paid all expenses, but so great were the demands upon the State Treasury for funds to meet military claims of various kinds, it was thought advisable to make an effort to get the General government to assume the expenses of the arsenal, and thereby relieve the State from great responsibility and embarrassment. The Governor made the proposition to the War Department, suggesting that the public demands would not admit of the discontinuance of the arsenal at that time, and, in consideration of the depleted condition of the State Treasury and the extraordinary outlays that had been made in arming, clothing and equipping our large force of volunteers, it was but right and reasonable that the manufacture of ammunition at this point should be continued at the expense of the United States. The geographical location of Indianapolis, and its close relation to the great armies operating in the West and South, made it a most favorable point from which ammunition could be supplied to the troops without the delays incident to its shipment from the East.

In October, 1861, General CAMERON, Secretary of War, and General THOMAS, Adjutant General of the Army, visited the arsenal, and after careful investigation and having fully learned how effective it had been and how useful it could be made, advised and requested the Governor to continue it, with the understanding that the ammunition already issued should be paid for by the United States, and agreeing that some arrangement should be made for compensating the State for future issues. General THOMAS, in his report of this visit, asserted that "the ammunition was equal to that manufactured anywhere else," and suggested "that an officer of Ordnance be sent to Indianapolis to inspect the arsenal, and ascertain the amount expended in the manufacture of ammunition, with the view of reimbursing the State." Accordingly, in December, Captain CRISPIN, of the Ordnance corps, visited the arsenal. He expressed himself highly pleased with the manner in which it had been conducted, and that the ammunition was equal to any made. His report, submitted to his chief, General RIPLEY, was highly complimentary, but he was of opinion that the army in the West could be supplied without recourse to State establishments. General RIPLEY was emphatically opposed to the continuance of the arsenal and reported against it, as follows:

> On consideration of the subject in all its branches, I do not deem it advisable to continue the preparation of ammunition for small arms, or for artillery, further than may be necessary to consume the materials which have already been provided, at the arsenal at Indianapolis, for that purpose. Such additional supplies, if any, as it may be necessary to have there, can be provided by timely requisitions on this office, from Alleghany, or some other U.S. Arsenal.

This was on the 30th of December, 1861, and at that very moment it was a well known fact the Government arsenals could not fill one half of the requisitions that were made, and large quantities, therefore, had to be purchased of private individuals at rates affording a handsome profit on cost of production, and much of it of poor quality.

General RIPLEY belonged to the "fossiliferous period" of the old army, and beheld the innovations which Governor MORTON and other "live" state executives were making upon ancient departmental usages and prerogatives in raising and fitting out troops, with astonishment and disgust. Fortunately, General RIPLEY's authority did not extend very far, but he never lost an opportunity to embarrass and delay all business that came before him relating to the Indiana Arsenal. Despite all his efforts the establishment was continued, and, as will be shown, was eminently successful and of immense importance to the Government in the prosecution of the War.

The temporary buildings being unsuited for winter work, the Superintendent was compelled to hunt more comfortable quarters, and in the latter part of 1861 succeeded in securing a large, unoccupied furniture factory at low rental, and work was here continued for more than a year afterward. The number of employees was greatly increased, and shot, shell, canister and signal lights were added to the productions of the concern.

In January, 1862, Captain STURM was ordered to Washington, to make settlement with the Government for the ammunition issued up to that time. After proper examination of the account, amounting to $68,701.96, it was ordered by the Secretary of War to be paid.

An arrangement was then made between the Secretary of War, Hon. ROBERT DALE OWEN, Agent for the State, and Captain STURM, that all the ammunition issued at the Arsenal in the future to the United States, should be paid for quarterly, at the rates charged in the first account. In accordance with this understanding, an account was forwarded in April, for the first quarter of the year 1862, but, notwithstanding the arrangement above referred to, it failed to receive the approval of General RIPLEY, Chief of Ordnance. That officer decided "that the law does not allow the establishment of an United States Arsenal in this manner, nor the purchase or issue of ordnance stores without the authority of the Chief of Ordnance." The account was, therefore, referred back to the Secretary of War for further orders; and that officer referred the matter to the Ordnance Commission then sitting in Washington.

It ought to be stated just here, that General RIPLEY, on the 18th of October, 1861, in a letter to Governor MORTON, made the following decision in reference to the payment of the State's claim for ammunition:

According to the Regulations, money can only be expended by the duly appointed agents of the Department. If, however, you will take the trouble to direct the State officer who has charge of the manufacture of small arms ammunition, at the Indiana State Arsenal, to make out his accounts for the expenditure and transmit them to this office, with a certificate that he holds the ammunition for the use of the United States, they will be paid at the Treasury.

This indicated a favorable feeling, but when the bills were presented the General could find neither "law" nor "regulation" authorizing him to approve them, even for the ammunition actually issued to troops in the service of the Government.

The Ordnance Commission took up the case referred to them some time in June, 1862. Meantime, a second quarterly account had been presented and referred, for ammunition issued up to the first of that month. The Commission, after thorough scrutiny, decided that the ammunition should be paid for at a rate that covered all costs and expenses of manufacture, and in accordance with this decision the amount due the State was promptly paid into the State Treasury.[1]

To definitely settle matters in future it was agreed, by and between the Secretary of War and the Governor, that the manufacture of ammunition should be continued as before—the bills therefor to be presented and paid monthly. It was further agreed that the Government should furnish powder, lead, percussion caps and other supplies at current prices, the amount to be deducted from the accounts of the State on settlement.

The economical management of the Arsenal, and the security of property as well as life, soon rendered it necessary to remove it outside of the city limits. Suitable buildings were erected on a convenient tract of leased ground about a mile and a half distant from the capitol, where the business was continued until the Arsenal was finally closed.[2]

[1] The commission's report of June 10, 1862, is printed in Terrell, *Report*, 1, Appendix, Doc. 89:293-95.

[2] The arsenal was first located in rented quarters on the square south of the State House. On June 15, 1861, operations were transferred to buildings that Governor Morton ordered constructed on the north half of the present State House grounds. The following winter quarters were found in the furniture factory of John Ott on West Washington Street. Then in 1862 the arsenal was

General RIPLEY, however, continued to be much dissatisfied, and, notwithstanding the action of the Ordnance Commission and the agreement entered into by the Governor with the Secretary of War, determined that operations at the Arsenal should stop. His report, setting forth his views on this subject, and recommending that no more ammunition be received from the State or supplies furnished, was submitted to the Secretary of War on the 24th of November, 1862, and concurred in by that officer. This determination was as unexpected as it was unjust. Relying upon the agreement that the Arsenal should be continued, new buildings had been erected, additional tools and machinery added, and the facilities for economically carrying on all the branches of the work greatly increased; all which had been done at heavy expense, without as yet receiving any return for the outlay. At the same time every round of ammunition made was called for by troops in the field, almost as soon as it was ready for issue. The Governor made an earnest protest to the Secretary of War against the proposed action, and through the efforts of Mr. OWEN, succeeded in getting the decision revoked. But little trouble was experienced afterward on the score of General RIPLEY's objections. He was soon relieved from duty in the Ordnance office, and subsequent transactions under his successor, General RAMSEY, met with but few interruptions or delays.

Colonel Sturm

On the 17th of November, 1862, Captain STURM was promoted to the Lieutenant Colonelcy of the Fifty-Fourth Regiment, Indiana Volunteers, with the view of being detailed for ordnance duty at Indianapolis, but this being found to be impracticable he resigned on the 28th of the following Decem-

moved to a site a mile and a half east of the State House on Washington Street. Jacob P. Dunn. *Greater Indianapolis* . . . (2 vols. Chicago, 1910), 1:223; Berry R. Sulgrove, *History of Indianapolis and Marion County* (Indianapolis, 1884), 315-16.

ber. He was, however, continued as Superintendent of the Arsenal.

In addition to his other duties, Colonel STURM acted as Chief of Ordnance for the State, and as such officer had supervision of all issues of arms and other property belonging to the United States and placed in custody of the Governor for the use of Volunteers; also of issues of State arms to the Indiana Legion. The management of the Arsenal, the settlements and returns required for all ordnance property received and issued, and the general business of the Ordnance Office of the State, demanded a high order of ability, great industry and inflexible integrity. Colonel STURM displayed these qualities in a remarkable degree, and his efforts to carry out the plans and orders of the Governor were crowned, from the outset, with the most complete and gratifying success. The service required at his hands was immense, involving heavy responsibility, constant vigilance and unabating labor. Many trying and discouraging difficulties were encountered and overcome. Colonel STURM possessed untiring energy and confident perseverance; he made the prosperity of the Arsenal a matter of personal pride, and it is but justice to say that he proved himself equal, and more than equal, to every demand made upon him during the war.[3]

Legislation Required

From the state of the military funds under the control of the Governor and applicable to the procurement of munitions of war, and the responsibility incurred by him personally in conducting the business of the Arsenal, he desired to be relieved from the burden as soon as possible. He therefore submitted a special message to the General Assembly on the 20th of February, 1863, in which, after giving a history of the en-

---

[3] See *Report of the Indiana Arsenal, by Lieut. Colonel H. Sturm . . . Giving an abstract of Ammunition, Arms Equipments, Ordnance and Ordnance Stores Issued at the Indiana Arsenal, from May, 1861, to Dec. 31, 1862* (Indiana *Documentary Journal*, 1863, vol. 3, pt. 2).

terprise and a statement of the profits realized up to that time, he said:[4]

Employment has been furnished to many persons, sometimes to the number of five hundred, and great relief has resulted to many families, who would otherwise have been without the means of support. My instructions to Colonel STURM were to give preference, in the employment of operatives, to those whose parents, children or relatives were in the army.

Touching the continuance of the institution, he made the following suggestions:

While the Arsenal has been of great service to the Government and the State, and by its demand for labor has afforded relief to many persons, it has been the source of much responsibility and anxiety. The operations have been large, and had they been unfortunate, would have subjected me to much censure at the hands of the public. It is not necessary that I should longer take this responsibility, and I therefore refer the subject to the Legislature, with the suggestion, that if it be desired to continue the institution until the buildings for the Government Arsenal shall be completed (which will be from one to two years) that legal provision and sufficient appropriations be made therefor.

Investigations

The management of the Arsenal, the books and vouchers and every transaction connected with it, were made the subject of frequent and searching investigation by Legislative committees. The business was so large and the interests of the State in its honest and economical administration so great, these inquiries were both reasonable and proper and always met with the approbation of the Superintendent and the officers of State. Every facility was afforded and full information given the committees to enable them to make thorough examinations. The first of these committees, composed of members of both houses, was appointed under a concurrent resolution of the Legislature at the session of 1863. After

[4] Indiana *House Journal,* 1863, pp. 550-52. The message and accompanying report of Colonel Sturm were also printed as a separate publication under the title *Report of the Governor on the Indiana State Arsenal* (Indianapolis, 1863). 7 pp.

careful and thorough investigation they unanimously reported that the Arsenal had been safely, prudently and economically managed, and that its continuance was essential to the public service. At the same session a select committee, consisting of nine members of the House of Representatives, was appointed to make personal examination of the Arsenal and report its condition and such other facts as they deemed important for the information of the Legislature and the people of the State. This Committee submitted the following report,[5] which was unanimously concurred in:

> The select committee, appointed for the purpose of making examination of the State Arsenal, and to report any facts they might deem necessary, connected therewith, have performed that duty, and submit the following report:
>
> The Committee visited the Arsenal, which is situate one and a half miles east of the city. The buildings are mostly of a temporary character; sufficient, however, for the purpose, and built out of the profits of the institution, so that it pays no rent. At the time of the visit there were employed in one room about ninety females, and in another about forty, all employed in making ball cartridges and preparing caps. In another building the men were moulding bullets, preparing shells, round shot, &c.
>
> The committee were much gratified with the system and economy, and also the neatness and dispatch with which the business was conducted.
>
> In reference to the operation of the Arsenal since its commencement, the Committee would refer to Captain STURM's report, which contains a full account of its past transactions and its present condition.
>
> The Committee take pleasure in complimenting Captain STURM upon the very satisfactory condition of his accounts, the readiness with which he has furnished us with every desired information, and the zeal and energy he has shown in the enterprise, which are the chief qualities constituting a good officer.
>
> It was the design of the Committee to recommend the Arsenal to be continued under the patronage of the State, and a bill was prepared for that purpose, but subsequent events[6] have rendered it impossible to take any further steps.

[5] Indiana *House Journal,* 1863, p. 743.

[6] "Subsequent events" refer to the bolt by the Republican minority in the House of Representatives to prevent the enactment of the militia bill. See above,

Since our visit the Arsenal has been compelled to suspend operations for a time, at least, greatly to the injury of many poor persons that depend on its patronage as a means of support.

A third committee was appointed by the General Assembly (March, 1863) to investigate the transactions connected with and growing out of the war loan of 1861, and all expenditures (including the management of the Arsenal) made through several military officers of the State. The following extract from the report[7] of this Committee shows the result of their labors so far as the same related to the Arsenal:

The Committee spent much of its time in examining the transactions of the Arsenal. The organization of this institution was a necessity, growing out of the circumstances under which the State was placed at the beginning of the war. Many of the first regiments were ordered to the field wholly unprovided with the necessary ammunition. None could be readily furnished by the Government. Our soldiery had to be sent forward without the requisite ammunition, and run the hazard of getting it, or else it had to be provided by the State. The Governor saw the urgent necessity, and promptly adopted a remedy. The manufacture of the required ordnance stores was ordered, and Colonel HERMANN STURM, who was thoroughly instructed in this branch of business, was appointed to superintend their manufacture. That which was at first intended as a temporary expedient ripened into a permanent establishment. Under the superintendence of Colonel STURM the Arsenal was not only enabled to supply an existing necessity, but was made a source of profit to the State. It depended for its success upon its utility and the economy of its management. Subsequent to its establishment, and after large quantities had been sent to the field by it, an arrangement was made by which the General Government agreed to pay for the ammunition already issued by it at prices which were remunerative to the State. It was also provided that the Arsenal should be continued, and that future supplies furnished should be paid for at the same rates. Up to the time of the investigation, Colonel STURM has manufactured and turned over to the Government about 100,000 rounds of artillery ammunition, and nearly 30,000,000 rounds of am-

330-31, and Kenneth M. Stampp, *Indiana Politics during the Civil War (Indiana Historical Collections,* vol. 31, Indianapolis, 1949), 176-79.

[7] Section on "Indiana State Arsenal" in "Report of the Minority Committee on the Negotiation and Sale of Indiana State Bonds," in Indiana *Documentary Journal,* 1864, vol. 2, no. 15:528-30.

munition for small arms. The ammunition was thoroughly tested by competent agents of the Government, and pronounced to be of superior quality. Not only did the State thus meet a demand created by the exigency of the times, but it gave constant employment to from one to five hundred persons at good wages, the preference always being given to those whose relatives and supporters were in the field. The Arsenal not only did not prove disastrous in a financial point of view, but turned out to be a source of profit. While it furnished stores of a superior quality, at prices below those usually paid, yet, by the judicious management of Colonel STURM and the State authorities, on the 1st of May, 1863, according to the estimate made by the Committee, it had realized a net profit of over $60,000. In every respect was the management of the Arsenal singularly successful. Its purchases were made judiciously, and everything was so thoroughly and perfectly systematized that it could not be else than a success. Large purchases having been made for the benefit of the Arsenal at New York, the Committee soon found that a thorough investigation could not be made without visiting that city. The same was true as to the purchase of State arms—that business having been almost wholly transacted in New York. The sitting of the Committee was limited, by the resolution creating it, to forty days, and no appropriation having been made for expenses to New York, the Committee feared that they would have to suspend its action and leave the investigation incomplete. The Governor learning this promptly tendered the Committee the means of defraying their expenses East, and insisted that it should continue in session until its duties had been performed thoroughly and completely. Not only did His Excellency propose to defray the expenses of the Committee, but also to pay its per diem for any time it might necessarily be employed beyond the forty days contemplated by the resolution.

The Committee finding itself thus provided with means, proceeded to New York and continued its investigations in that city for some two weeks. Those who had furnished material for the Arsenal were examined as witnesses, touching the prices paid, and as to whether any bonus of any kind whatever had been paid or given Colonel STURM, or any other person in any wise connected with the State Government, to influence them in making purchases. The examination fully convinced the Committee that every transaction in this connection had been conducted honorably and fairly; that the prices paid for material were never above, and in many instances below, their market value.

We think the Governor was particularly fortunate in selecting Colonel STURM as Superintendent of the Arsenal. His thorough knowledge of the business, his capacity and energy as a man, and his honesty of purpose, in an eminent degree qualified him for the place.

MANUFACTURE OF AMMUNITION 511

It is proper to add that a majority of the Legislature as well as of the Committees, whose action has been above given, were politically opposed to the State administration then in power, and therefore the reports quoted cannot be charged with partiality or partisan bias.[8]

The accounts and vouchers for all expenditures had been, by direction of the Governor, submitted to the Military Auditing Committee, and by them duly audited before payment. By the strict letter of the law this action was not authorized, but the Committee, believing that the public service absolutely and imperatively demanded the establishment and continuance of the Arsenal, was unwilling, by a strict and rigid rule of construction, to injure or embarrass military operations in any manner, and therefore determined to examine and audit the claims.[9]

In the fall of 1863, it was ascertained to be impracticable for the whole Committee to give that personal attention to the transactions of the Arsenal, and to the investigation of the accounts, required by the magnitude of the interests involved. The Governor, Quartermaster General and Adjutant General, were each requested by the Committee to give their personal attention to the business, so that the correctness of the claims might be officially certified (Colonel STURM not being an officer of the U. S.), but neither of these gentlemen could do so from the pressing nature of their public duties in their respective departments. The Committee, therefore, determined to appoint on its own behalf, one of its members to supervise the

[8] Actually the majority (Democratic) members of this legislative committee failed to attend the committee meetings; hence the minority report. The minority in presenting their report stated: "We do not suppose a difference of opinion would have existed between the majority and ourselves in reference to any matter disclosed in our investigations. Indeed, there was no conflict in the testimony to reconcile, nor was there any statement made that could furnish room for differences of opinion." Indiana *Documentary Journal,* 1864, vol. 2, no. 15:527.

[9] "Claims for the Expenses of Operating the Indiana Arsenal," in "Reports of the Military Auditing Committees for the Years 1861, 1862, 1863 & 1864," in Indiana *Documentary Journal,* 1864, vol. 2, no. 4:34-36.

current transactions of the concern. This duty devolved upon the Hon. SAMUEL H. BUSKIRK, who was required to give his personal and undivided attention to the business, and to certify, from his own knowledge, to the correctness of all claims presented for the action of the Committee. This arrangement was made with the assent of the Governor, and Mr. BUSKIRK discharged the duties of his position with zeal and faithfulness and to the entire satisfaction of the remaining members of the Committee.

Close of the Arsenal—Profits

The manufacture of ammunition was continued with entire success until the 18th of April, 1864, when the necessity which caused the establishment of the Arsenal, nearly three years before, having in a great measure ceased to exist, the concern was closed, with the approbation of the Secretary of War. Upon final settlement it was ascertained, that the entire transactions of the Arsenal amounted to $788,838.45, and that the State had realized a clear profit of $77,457.32, of which $71,380.01 was in cash, and the remainder in tools retained and ammunition on hand for the use of State troops. "It was no part of the original plan that profits should result to the State from its operations, and they sprang solely from the economical and skillful management, for which Colonel STURM is entitled to the chief credit."[10] The Military Auditing Committee had an excellent opportunity to judge of the manner in which the business had been conducted, and in a report to the Governor, dated September 15, 1863, said:

We cannot close this report without bearing testimony to the ability, integrity and economy with which Colonel STURM has managed the affairs of the Arsenal. His position has been a most difficult and responsible one, requiring constant and unremitting labor and great skill and

---

[10] Governor Morton's message to the General Assembly, January 6, 1865, in Terrell, *Report,* 1, Appendix, Doc. 116:321, and Indiana *House Journal,* 1865, p. 26. For a general financial statement on the arsenal, see "Reports of the Military Auditing Committees for the Years 1861, 1862, 1863 & 1864," in Indiana *Documentary Journal,* 1864, vol. 2, no. 4:48-50.

perseverance. Fortunately for the State, he has shown himself equal to every duty that has devolved upon him, and we congratulate you upon the great success which has attended his and your efforts, as well on account of the pecuniary advantage which has resulted to the State from the operations of the Arsenal, as for the service it has been to the Government. In our judgment, the public service requires that the Arsenal should be continued.[11]

Again, in the final report of the committee, its previous good opinion of the Superintendent was confirmed by the following:

The committee takes pleasure in saying that nothing has occurred, since our report made to your Excellency, on the 15th September, 1863, to weaken the confidence that we then felt and expressed in the ability, integrity and economy displayed by Colonel H. STURM in the management of the Indiana Arsenal.[12]

Colonel STURM was afterwards commissioned as Colonel in the Indiana Legion, and assigned to duty as Chief of Ordnance, with orders to collect in the State arms. On the 1st of January, 1866, he retired from service, and was complimented by Governor MORTON with an honorary commission in the Indiana Legion, conferring upon him the rank of Brigadier General.

INDIANAPOLIS (U. S.) ARSENAL

The success which attended the establishment of the temporary arsenal by the State at Indianapolis, and the great benefits derived from it by the Government, led to the idea of establishing at several important points in the West permanent arsenals by the United States. Governor MORTON, early in 1862, by personal interviews with the Secretary of War and with our delegation in Congress, urged the importance and necessity of the proposed enterprise, and insisted that, in case the arsenals should be authorized to be built, one of them should be located at Indianapolis. He was ably and effectively

---

[11] "Reports of the Military Auditing Committees," in Indiana *Documentary Journal*, 1864, vol. 2, no. 4:41.
[12] *Ibid.*, 47.

assisted in this preliminary movement by the Hon. ROBERT DALE OWEN, then agent for the State to purchase arms and munitions of war. The effort was successful and resulted in the passage of an act[13] (approved July 11, 1862) which provided for the erection of National arsenals at Columbus, Ohio, Indianapolis, Indiana, and on Rock Island, Illinois, "for the deposit and repair of arms and other munitions of war,"[14] and appropriated one hundred thousand dollars for each of said arsenals.

The United States soon after purchased a beautiful tract of timbered land, embracing seventy-five acres, adjoining the city of Indianapolis, for which the price of $35,500 was paid. At the ensuing session of the Legislature an act was passed ceding to the General Government jurisdiction over the lands above mentioned, and their appurtenances, for the purposes of a National Arsenal, exempting the same from taxation, and reserving the right only to serve process thereon.[15]

Work was commenced on the Arsenal in 1863, under the direction of T. J. TREADWELL, Captain of Ordnance, U. S. A., and was successfully prosecuted by him until February, 1864, when he was succeeded in command by Brevet Major JAMES M. WHITTEMORE, Captain of Ordnance, U. S. A. The principal buildings were erected mainly under Major WHITTEMORE'S supervision, who displayed great energy, ability and zeal in the discharge of his important duties, and who continued in command until September 1866, when he was relieved at his own request by Brevet Lieutenant Colonel W. H.

---

[13] The act is given in Terrell, *Report*, 1, Appendix, Doc. 76:271. See also U. S. *Statutes at Large*, 12:537.

[14] Robert Dale Owen wrote to Governor Morton: "Mr. Watson, Assistant Secretary of War, informed me that this act was construed to include the *manufacture* of ammunition (but of course not of arms), as essential to an arsenal; so that it need not be merely a depot for arms and ammunition in time of war." [Terrell]

[15] *Laws of Indiana*, 1863, pp. 169-70. Arsenal Technical Schools are now located on the site.

HARRIS, Captain of Ordnance, U. S. A., the present accomplished and faithful commanding officer.

Although not yet fully completed, the grounds and buildings present a most beautiful and substantial appearance. The following dimensions of the buildings were kindly furnished by Colonel HARRIS:

Main Store House, for the storage of arms, etc.—three stories high, 183 feet long, 63 feet wide.

Artillery Store House, for the storage of artillery, etc.—two stories, 201 feet long, 52 feet wide.

Magazine, for the storage of powder and fixed ammunition—one story, 50 feet long, 34 feet wide.

Office—one story, 43 feet long, 22 feet wide.

Commanding Officer's Quarters—two and a half stories, 79 feet long, 40 feet wide.

The grounds have been handsomely graded and laid off with roadways and walks, and the thrifty young forest trees have been allowed to stand. The buildings are all of pressed brick and cut Vernon limestone, and constructed in the most elegant and substantial manner. The whole cost, when fully completed, will not be less than half a million of dollars.

PURCHASE OF ARMS AND WAR MATERIAL FOR THE STATE

WANT OF ARMS AT THE OUTBREAKING OF THE WAR

The deplorable condition of the military resources of the State at the commencement of the war is described in another portion of this report.[1] It remains to set forth here, more particularly, the efforts to supply the want of arms, which was first and most severely felt. When the Legislature of 1861 met in regular session on the 10th of January, the apprehensions created by the disturbed condition of the South were too indefinite to impel the necessary action to prepare the State for hostilities, but, as the purpose of the seceding States changed or developed from simple separation to aggression, the necessity of meeting such a contingency became apparent. The first steps were naturally directed to ascertaining the number and condition of the arms in the State, and the number due from the General Government under the law regulating the distribution of arms to the States. Of those in possession of the State, the greater portion had been distributed to various military organizations, and their condition was unknown; while a small number still remained in the hands of the State Quartermaster. To ascertain the number and condition of those distributed to military companies, Governor MORTON on the 28th of January addressed a circular to the various County Auditors, instructing them to report to him, as soon as the information could be obtained, "the number, quality and condition of all arms in their respective counties, belonging to the State, not in the hands of military companies meeting regu-

[1] See above, 3-4.

larly for drill; where located, and under whose control; and to furnish copies of all bonds given for the safekeeping and return of arms, together with an accurate account of the sureties thereon, whether living, and if so, where residing and whether solvent." He also directed Mr. E. A DAVIS, of Indianapolis, to investigate the records of the Quartermaster General, and to report the number and condition of the military companies in the State, the quantity of arms distributed, their probable value, and the feasibility of obtaining indemnity for those lost or destroyed.

Little or no information was obtained from the County Auditors. Mr. DAVIS reported that there had been distributed by the State, altogether, as appeared from the State Quartermaster's showing about $200,000 worth of arms, of which he estimated $150,000 worth was accessible and serviceable. Of this quantity, $15,000 worth, numbering 600 (estimating them at $25 each), were in the hands of fifteen companies averaging forty members each, maintaining at least a nominal organization. The remainder, 5,400 guns worth $135,000, were unaccounted for further than they had been sent out and never heard of again. If the estimated quantity remaining of the whole number distributed could be obtained, the State would have about 6,000 arms of different qualities, exclusive of those in the hands of the Quartermaster. The utter carelessness with which they had been distributed is shown by a few statements of Mr. DAVIS' report. Fifty-one counties, a little over half of the State, had obtained all the arms, the remaining counties getting none. The State had eight pieces of artillery, and Vanderburgh county had one fourth of these. The law required distributions to be made upon the requisitions of County Boards, but very many, if not most, were made without any such requisition, and usually upon the verbal order of the Governor. On the 14th of January, the day acting Governor HAMMOND retired from office, he ordered from the United States Ordnance Office at Washington, without any requisition, 104 muskets, over one-sixth of the entire quota of the State for that year, for Vanderburgh county. Where the provisions of the law for the preservation and return of arms had been complied with, the securities were ample, but the law had been little regarded, and the arms that had been lost were unlikely to be replaced. Mr. DAVIS' estimate of the probable number remaining, 7,000, was liberal, but if it could have been fully realized the result would not have been very encouraging, if the proportion fit for service should have proved no larger than that of the arms which had never been distributed.

About the time he reported the probable condition of those scattered through the State, the Quartermaster turned over for inspection by Captains EPHRAIM HARTWELL and A. J. HARRISON, of Indianapolis, those still in his hands, and they reported 505 muskets worthless and incapable of being repaired; 54 flintlock YAGER rifles which could be altered at $2.00 each to percussion locks; 40 serviceable muskets in the hands of military companies in Indianapolis, which could be returned at once; 80 muskets with accoutrements in store; 13 artillery musketoons; 75 holster pistols; 26 SHARPE's rifles; 20 COLT's navy pistols; 2 boxes of cavalry sabres; 1 box powder flasks; 3 boxes of accoutrements. This was the condition of the State's arms on the 1st of February. In order to ascertain what might be due the State, Governor MORTON, on the 17th of January, wrote to the War Department, inquiring "what quantity and kind of arms Indiana is entitled to from the General Government. Whether there are not arrearages for past years; upon what principle or ratio arms are distributed, whether upon Congressional representation, or the enrollment of militia, or both; what form of application should be made, and how soon the arms due can be forwarded." The reply stated that arms were distributed upon the ratio of Congressional representation, and that no arrearages were due to the State. The quota for 1861, was 592 2-13 muskets, which could be drawn in any kind of arms desired, at the rate of one six-pounder cannon for 31 1-13 muskets, and ten long range rifles, with sword bayonets, for 13 5-13 muskets. He directed the remainder of our quota, 487 11-13 muskets (after deducting the 104 1-13 guns drawn by Governor HAMMOND for Vanderburgh county the day he left office), to be forwarded in one six-pounder cannon, and the balance in long range rifles with sword bayonets.

As soon as these facts had been ascertained, he communicated them to the Legislature, in February, with a statement of the inefficiency of the militia laws; and on the 5th of March following, a bill was passed and approved, authorizing the Governor to collect all the arms belonging to the State, not held by companies effectively organized, and to distribute them in his discretion to regularly organized volunteer companies in different portions of the State.[2] A circular containing the act was at once sent by the Governor to the various counties, and agents dispatched to execute its requirements. Mr. AMBROSE BALLWEG, an experienced gunsmith, of Indianapolis, was appointed [Deputy] Quartermaster General to receive and repair the arms that might be returned. But it soon became evident that the result of the effort to collect the arms would be trifling; and, about the middle of March, the Governor went to Washington to obtain arms from the General Government, in addition to the meager remnant of the year's quota. His foresight anticipated the perils which a state of hostilities would create for the Northwest. The adhesion of Kentucky to the Union was by no means certain. If she seceded, Indiana would rest directly upon the rebel Confederacy, and must be prepared for defense. If she did not secede, her territory was certainly to be made the scene of constant conflicts, and probably the starting point of invasions, encouraged and protected by the strong and almost dominant rebel feeling among her people. Protection against these dangers necessitated a better supply of arms than could be expected from the reports of the collecting agents. He was promised 5,000 mus-

[2] See *Laws of Indiana,* 1861, pp. 129-30.

kets, but before any steps were taken to fulfill the promise, the war broke out, and then the necessity of State defense was enlarged to the necessity of both State and National defense, and the 5,000 arms, with what could be collected, would be a very inadequate provision. The result of the collections under the act of the 5th of March, was 3,436 small arms of sixteen different kinds, but of uniform inferiority. They were fit for nothing, and were never used for anything but guard duty or drill instruction. Some 1,700 accoutrements of but little better character than the arms, eight pieces of old artillery, of doubtful value, were also collected. It was evident that some other resource than the overstrained ability of the General Government, the wretched lot of arms on hand, and the meager supply provided, must be looked to. That resource could be only the treasury or credit of the State. This necessity, combining with the many others of the emergency, impelled the Governor to issue on the 19th of April, a call for the assembling of the Legislature (the regular session of which had terminated but little more than a month before) in extraordinary session on the 24th.

On the day the Legislature met, the Governor received notice that but three thousand five hundred of the five thousand arms promised could be furnished. He replied at once that this number "would not arm even the troops we have assembled here in camp, under the requisition of the President, and the State must be left without arms." A few days previously he had been informed by General WOOL that no accoutrements could be furnished. This left the State with very little help in arms from the General Government, and none at all in equipments, without which they could not be used. The Governor, in the same dispatch (of the 24th) in which he complained of the deficiency of arms, says, of the entire failure of accoutrements, that he had "given orders to have them made, but it would take time." He asked if there were no arsenals East or West from which arms might be forwarded, and urged that a requisition he had previously made for twenty-four heavy guns to protect the Ohio river border, be increased to fifty, as "our river towns are full of alarm, and constantly sending deputations calling for cannon and small arms." The cannon, he was informed, were in the Pittsburgh Arsenal. This condition of things will explain the urgent need of the action recommended in his message delivered the next day (25th) that "one million dollars be appropriated for the purchase of arms and munitions of war, and the organization of the militia."[3] On the 28th, three days after his message, he presented the condition of the State, as to its means of offense or defense, fully and forcibly in a letter to the Secretary of War. He said:

Fifteen hundred rifle muskets have been received from the Alleghany Arsenal, and two thousand more are expected this week, and we have been informed that no more can be obtained from that quarter. A dispatch was received on the 25th, from General JOHN E. WOOL, stating that five thousand muskets and two hundred thousand cartridges would be shipped from the Watervliet Arsenal to this State, but no time was fixed for their shipment, and I have received no further information on the subject. As you will perceive, the arms received and those expected this week will fall nearly one thousand short of arming six regiments, and I regret to learn from the Quartermaster that those received are of an inferior character, being old muskets rifled out, and in very many instances the bayonets have to be driven on with a hammer, and many others are so loose that they can be shaken off. No accoutrements have been received, and I have no definite information when they will be. Orders have been issued for their manufacture, but our mechanics are not prepared for it, and their work proceeds slowly. I regret to add that great dissatisfaction prevails among the troops with regard to the quality of the arms furnished and the delay and uncertainty in the reception of stores and ammunition. . . . It is now nine days since I have had the honor to hear from the Department, and from lack of information I am unable to take such steps for furnishing accoutrements, equipage, and supplies as I otherwise should. . . . I beg leave again, most earnestly, to call your immediate attention to the subject of furnishing our State with arms. The number on hand belonging to the State, good, bad and indifferent, will not exceed two thousand five hundred, and we have only fifteen pieces of cannon, of small calibre. The coun-

---

[3] See message in Indiana *House Journal,* sp. sess., 1861, p. 24.

try along the Ohio river, bordering Kentucky, is in a state of intense alarm. The people entertain no doubt but that Kentucky will speedily attempt to go out of the Union. They are in daily fear that marauding parties from the other side of the river will plunder and burn their towns. The demands upon me for arms for their defense are constant, and I am compelled to reply that I have them not, and know not when or where I can get them. A bill will pass our Legislature, probably on Monday, appropriating a half million of dollars for the purchase of arms, but I am informed that engagements of Eastern manufacturers are such that they can not be procured, perhaps, for months. This State is one of the most exposed, by its geographical position, to the immediate evils of civil war, and it does seem to me should be preferred, in the distribution of arms, over those geographically distant from the scene of probable conflict. If, in your opinion, these considerations are entitled to weight, I trust that at least twenty thousand stands of arms will be promptly shipped to this State, with a large supply of artillery, which is indispensably necessary to prevent our river towns from being bombarded and burnt by batteries erected on the other side of the river. Indiana is loyal to the core, and will expend her blood and treasure without limit for the successful prosecution of the war, and it is due to her loyalty that she be provided by the General Government to the extent of its capacity.

PURCHASE OF ARMS BY THE STATE

On the first day of May the Legislature passed, and the Governor approved, "an act to provide for the defenses of the State of Indiana, to procure first-class arms, artillery, cavalry, and infantry equipments and munitions of war, making the necessary appropriations therefor, and authorizing the Governor to borrow money."[4] This act directed the Governor "to procure immediately a supply of first-class arms sufficient for twenty thousand men, including such as are now on hand and fit for service, and such as may be procured from the Government," and to dispatch agents immediately to procure them. It also appropriated five hundred thousand dollars for the purpose, and authorized the Governor to borrow money, if necessary, and pledge the faith of the State for its payment.

[4] Terrell, *Report*, 1, Appendix, Doc. 41:245; *Laws of Indiana,* sp. sess. 1861, p. 13.

Anticipating the passage of this bill, and anxious to be as early as possible in the market, in which the sudden and enormous demand was rapidly advancing the price of arms, the Governor, on the 27th of April, authorized CALVIN FLETCHER, Sr., of Indianapolis,

> to proceed to the manufactories of arms in the Eastern States, to any place where they may have arms to sell, and make careful examination as to the kind and quality of arms that can be purchased, the prices for cash, and the prices on a credit of a few months; if they can not be had now, how soon can they be manufactured and ready for delivery. Procure all the information in your power, even in regard to secondhand serviceable arms, or arms not of the latest improvement, and communicate with me from time to time by telegraph. Before making any contract, advise with me as to the character of it, kind of arms that can be procured, etc. I wish you to make particular inquiries about artillery—guns, carriages, caissons, equipments and harness for "flying" artillery; also in regard to rifled cannon. Should you have any information making it probable that arms can be procured in Canada, you will proceed there and prosecute your inquiries.[5]

Accompanying this authority was a memorandum of the most serviceable classes of arms for the different branches of the service, made by Major (now General) THOMAS J. WOOD, then United States mustering officer at Indianapolis.

Mr. FLETCHER's mission accomplished little towards supplying the wants of the State, though, with characteristic energy and care, he prosecuted it in all directions that promised a favorable result. Some small quantities of arms were procured, but the aggregate was too slight to make any special record of it necessary. Subsequently, his son, Prof. MILES J. FLETCHER, Superintendent of Public Instruction, was dispatched upon a similar errand, with a similar result; and several other agents, directly or indirectly in connection with other objects, made like ineffectual efforts to increase the State's armament. While these were in progress the Governor did not fail to press our necessities upon the Government. On

---

[5] See references to this mission in Calvin Fletcher's Diary, Indiana Historical Society Library, April 27-May 8, May 26, 29, 1861.

the 9th of May he wrote to General McCLELLAN, then in command of the Western Division of the Army, that the condition of Kentucky was alarming, particularly to our river towns, and that the "people were defenseless for want of arms." "Louisville," he said, "should be commanded by batteries upon our side of the river that she might be held, in some way, as a hostage for the good conduct of the Kentucky rebels and the security of our border." This object was to some extent effected by a detail of two pieces of heavy ordnance for New Albany, but to complete it a like battery should be placed at Jeffersonville. This would not only keep Louisville quiet, but prevent the shipment of heavy ordnance to pass over the Louisville railroad up the river. But Madison, which was particularly exposed, should have a battery of two heavy guns to dislodge any assailing battery upon the hills on the opposite side of the river. Evansville and Lawrenceburg were in a similar exposed condition. "Ten heavy pieces (10-inch Columbiads) would, we think, make us secure. Now is the time to put them in place when it may probably be peaceably done." The futility of these applications confirmed what could hardly be doubted before, that the State must depend upon her own exertions, for the time at least, for the means not only of assisting the General Government, but of defending herself.

On the 30th of May, the Governor having resolved to do all that was necessary for the proper preparation of the State for war, without relying upon the uncertain and insufficient provision of the General Government, and trusting that the outlay would be reimbursed, appointed Hon. ROBERT DALE OWEN (formerly a member of Congress from the First District of the State, and more recently Minister to the Kingdom of Naples, whose abilities, varied experience, and vast information, no less than his well-tried integrity, pointed him out as eminently qualified for the duty), Agent of the State, to procure arms, equipments and munitions of war, under the act

PURCHASE OF ARMS AND WAR MATERIAL

of May 1. The following is the authority given him by the Governor's commission:

> The Hon. ROBERT DALE OWEN is hereby appointed Agent of the State of Indiana, to visit the Eastern States and Europe in order to purchase arms for the use of said State. He is to exercise his best diligence to purchase arms on the best terms, for military purposes. He is to select the best quality of approved modern arms, rifles or rifled muskets, with bayonets, and carbines. His purchases are not to extend beyond six thousand rifles and rifled muskets, and one thousand carbines. These arms are to be forwarded to this city (Indianapolis) as fast as possible, and the arms purchased in Europe are to be paid by drafts upon the State of Indiana, at the office of WINSLOW, LANIER & Co., in the city of New York. No arms to be bought until after full inspection and trial as to their fitness for service. Mr. OWEN is to proceed in the execution of his mission with all diligence. Original bills and invoices signed by the parties from whom purchases are made shall be preserved and filed with the Governor for his inspection and information.

Mr. Owen's Purchases—The day that Mr. OWEN received his commission he started for New York to execute the duties it imposed. From that day till he closed his labors, February 6, 1863, all the State's purchases of arms were made through him, the original limit of six thousand rifles and one thousand carbines being extended from time to time, by further orders from the Governor. His final report[6] shows that he bought altogether:

Of English Enfield Rifles of the best quality	30,000
Of Carbines	2,731
Of Revolvers	751
Of Cavalry Sabres	797

In addition to these purchases made by the authority of the State, Mr. OWEN also purchased for the United States,

---

[6] See *Report of Robert Dale Owen, Agent to Purchase Arms, &C., . . . to His Excellency, O. P. Morton, September 4, 1862* . . . (Indianapolis, 1863), 21 pp. The revision of this report, dated February 6, 1863, referred to above, was never printed. It is in the Governor's file, Archives Division, Indiana State Library.

the State advancing the money, ten thousand Enfield rifles, which were put into the hands of Indiana soldiers during the movement of General KIRBY SMITH through Kentucky to the Ohio river. Adding this we have a total of rifles purchased by him of forty thousand. The outlay for these was, in part, made directly by the General Government, and, in part, by the State, ultimately reimbursed by the General Government.

The total of all Mr. OWEN's purchases was $752,694.75, of which the General Government furnished funds to the amount of $611,240.48, and the State $141,454.27. The prompt assumption of the State's liability by the General Government was due mainly to the superior character and comparative cheapness of the arms bought by Mr. OWEN. The first lot of twenty thousand Enfields was bought at an average price of $19.59 each; and the second, of ten thousand Enfields, at an average of $17.85. Mr. OWEN says, in his report, that the price of the first lot "was very considerably lower than the average price paid by the Government for first class Enfields during the period of my purchases. The later contracts for sixteen thousand guns could, some time after they were made, undoubtedly have been sold at an advance of not less that $40,000 or $50,000." Of the second lot of ten thousand, he says: "The difference between the price paid by me for these guns, certified to be of the *best* quality, and that paid by the Government for *ordinary* Enfields at the time of transfer, was $23,388.00." The total difference between the prices of his purchases and those prevailing when the arms were delivered, was about *seventy thousand dollars*. That amount was saved to the General Government (as it ultimately paid for all Mr. OWEN's purchases) by his judicious action as Agent of Indiana. The advantage to the State of the assumption of her purchases was very great. Mr. OWEN states it thus: "In this way Indiana was enabled, without throwing her bonds into market, or incurring losses by advances made, except for a few of the first rifles she bought, to place in the hands of a considerable portion of her troops arms of a quality very superior to the average of those which fell to the lot of other States." The Investigating Committee appointed by the Legislature at the Special Session of 1865, reported that "in their opinion Mr. OWEN exhibited much foresight in making the various purchases at the time he did. His duties were discharged with commendable fidelity and energy, and certainly the trust could not have been confided to an abler or more faithful agent."

Besides the arms, Mr. OWEN purchased at various times large quantities of blankets, clothing and equipments which the General Government could not supply in time to meet the wants of our troops, but for which the State was reimbursed. These purchases are stated in his report of February 6, 1863, as follows:

Cavalry Equipments	$ 3,905.44
Army Blankets	50,406.93
Infantry Great Coats	84,829.13
Total	$139,141.50
Add purchases of Arms	752,694.75
Total of Mr. OWEN's purchases	$891,836.25

Mr. OWEN's charge for services and expenses in attending to this business for a year and eight months was $3,452, or a little more than one third of one per cent on the amount of his purchases. Any responsible New York house would have charged for the same service a commission of at least one and a quarter per cent, or $11,140.95. Mr. OWEN thus saved to the State and General Government $7,678.95.

Reimbursements.—I have said that the State's purchases of arms through Mr. OWEN were all reimbursed by the General Government, but a word of explanation is necessary to give the exact result of one of the purchases. Governor MORTON, in his message of January 9th, 1863, says that during the advance of the rebels under General KIRBY SMITH, to the Ohio river, in August and September, 1862, he "believed it his duty to purchase 10,000 superior arms for the use of Indiana troops." The General Government authorized the purchase, but the State had to supply the money and await repayment. To obtain the money the Governor applied to the Ocean Bank of New York, the President of which, Mr. D. R. MARTIN, advanced it "without requiring any security, and upon the credit of the State." The amount was $237,269.30. "There was some delay," says the Governor, "in getting the warrant through the Departments at Washington," and the interest for that time "the officers of the Treasury alleged they had no authority to pay." It was consequently paid by the State.

Other Purchases.—During the "HINES Raid" in the summer of 1863, Governor MORTON, then in New York, telegraphed to the Secretary of War, for 1,000 cavalry equipments and 1,000 carbines for State troops. They were promised but not furnished. When the "MORGAN Raid" occurred in July following, it was necessary to have mounted State troops to make any sort of effective pursuit of the flying guerrilla, and the Governor, finding that Messrs. KITTREDGE & Co., of Cincinnati, had some 760 WESSON's breech-loading rifles, bought them at the same price the General Government paid for them. The whole amount was $18,811.40. These arms are still retained by the State.

Besides this purchase the following were made by the State authorities:

STEDMAN & Co., Aurora,
    Six iron cannon, one carriage .... $ 904.07
DAMSON & MARSH, Jeffersonville,
    Twelve gun carriages, $250 each 3,000.00
COUNTY OF FAYETTE,
    One brass cannon and fixtures 634.50
    Set of harness for same 100.00
R. J. HART & BROTHER,
    Pistols, moulds and wrenches 1,449.50
W. E. FEATHERSTON,
    Fifty-four navy revolvers, $20.70 each 1,117.80

PURCHASE OF ARMS AND WAR MATERIAL

HALL AYRES & Co.. Columbus, Ohio,
Two caissons, $320 each	640.00
Five battery wagons, $700 each	3,500.00
Five traveling forges, $445 each	2,225.00
Sixteen sets six horse artillery harness	3,780.00
	$17,350.80
Add KITTREDGE rifles	18,811.40
Total purchase of arms, besides OWEN's	$36,162.20

SUPPLYING THE TROOPS

QUARTERMASTER GENERAL'S OFFICE

General Morris

The office of Quartermaster General was created by the Constitution of the State, and that officer is appointed by the Governor and Commander-in-Chief.

The duties pertaining to this office prior to the rebellion were nominal—the care and issuing of the few arms and accoutrements drawn by the State from the General Government, and collecting the same from the counties when demanded by the Governor, comprised all the labors required. There was no particular regularity, system or order observed in conducting the business, and when Governor MORTON first entered upon the duties of his office he was unable to ascertain even what number of arms the State had, or where they were. As the salary of the Quartermaster General was only twenty-five dollars per annum, it is not surprising that no accounts were kept, or that the public property was allowed to become scattered and lost.

The call upon the State for six regiments in April, 1861, made it necessary to thoroughly reorganize the office and place it upon a "war footing." Colonel THOMAS A. MORRIS, whose superior business qualifications and acquaintance with military affairs and usages well fitted him for the position, was appointed Quartermaster General on the 16th day of April, 1861, and at once actively engaged in arranging for clothing, equipping and quartering the troops, no supplies at that time having been provided by the United States. Mr. AMBROSE BALLWEG was made Deputy Quartermaster General and assigned to duty as Superintendent of the State Armory, which position he continued faithfully to fill until the 1st of November, 1863, when he resigned. Eleven days after General MORRIS' appointment he was called to a new field of duty, having been commissioned Brigadier General and assigned to command the Indiana three months' forces.

General Vajen

JOHN H. VAJEN, Esq., an enterprising and successful merchant of Indianapolis, succeeded General MORRIS on the 29th of April. Under his administration the office soon assumed an important place among the military "institutions" of the State. Much inconvenience and difficulty was experienced in getting the department, which proved to be vast and intricate in its details and of grave responsibility, in complete and easy working order. Officers and employees were alike inexperienced and unacquainted with the usages and *forms* always inseparable from military business. General VAJEN brought to the discharge of his duties splendid business tact and unflagging industry, and soon had his office organized as thoroughly as the pressing nature of the circumstances would allow. It must be recollected that the first six regiments were completed and in camp in less than one week, and that everything required by them had to be furnished without any previous preparation. The troops impatiently chafed under the least inconvenience or delay, and they were jealous too of every right and claim which they thought might belong to them as soldiers. That they became occasionally demonstrative on the subject of uniforms, blankets, tents and so on, or that they, fresh from the comforts, ease and luxuries of home, often complained respecting the quality and quantity of their daily supplies, will not be considered extraordinary. So great was the demand all over the country for military goods, it could not be met. Cloth for uniforms, blankets, tents, camp equipage, and even arms and accoutrements had to be manufactured from raw materials; in the meantime, the necessities of the volunteers were supplied in the best manner possible. Fortunately the season of the year was mild, pleasant and healthy; so there was no real cause for complaint, but the clamor of the soldiers and their importuning and sympathizing friends was incessant, and worried everybody, and more especially the unfortunate wights whose duty it was to furnish the necessary toggery and supplies to make them at once—*soldiers!* These clamorings are now looked upon as humors of the war; they teach, nevertheless, a useful and instructive lesson.

General VAJEN's success in procuring the required stores was considered at the time somewhat remarkable, for it was but a few days after the regiments were mustered in before they were fully uniformed and equipped. The continued tender of troops by the Governor and their acceptance by the Government, called for redoubled exertions on the part of the Quartermaster's Department; warehouses and barracks were built, camps fitted up, ammunition manufactured and outfits procured with a promptitude that won the applause of the people of the State, and it is not vainglorious now to say that no troops anywhere at that time were put into the field quicker, or with better arms, uniforms and equipments, than were those from Indiana, and gentlemen who have had actual experience in the war will know how greatly all this depended on the energy and efficiency of the Quartermaster's Department.

During General VAJEN's incumbency, and while the State was exclusively required to clothe and equip her troops, twenty-two regiments of infantry, two regiments and two independent companies of cavalry, and three batteries of light artillery were furnished with clothing, wool and rubber blankets, tents, tools and complete camp equipage; the entire cost of which, including many extra articles not furnished by the General Government, did not exceed twenty dollars per man.

In the month of August, 1861, an Assistant Quartermaster of the United States Army was stationed at Indianapolis, who, from that time, assumed the charge of clothing and equipping troops subsequently raised. This saved the advance of large sums on the part of the State, and secured the transaction of the business in the mode prescribed by regulations. The Governor and Quartermaster General, however, did not omit attention to the demands of the troops, and it was not infrequently the case that supplies, such as blankets, overcoats, etc., were purchased by the State authorities—(generally by Hon. ROBERT DALE OWEN, State Purchasing Agent in New York), payments being made directly to the contractors by the United States Quartermaster. These efforts facilitated recruiting, and were of great benefit to Indiana soldiers, many of whom in the fall of 1861, serving in Missouri and Western Virginia, were unable to procure these indispensable articles through the regular channels, and but for the timely interposition of the State authorities would have suffered terribly in consequence. Besides, our officers and agents having acquired a full knowledge of the markets could buy supplies cheaper than the Government Quartermasters could, and the arrangement alluded to, therefore, aside from all other advantages was the means of saving money to the United States.

On the 17th of March, 1862, General VAJEN desiring to give his attention to his private affairs tendered his resignation, but, to enable him to complete his official report, it was not accepted until the following May.[1]

General New

JOHN C. NEW, ESQ., succeeded General VAJEN, as Quartermaster General, his appointment dating May 30th, 1862. He continued in office until the 13th of October of the same year, when he resigned. During this time the General Government, through Captain EKIN, United States Quartermaster, stationed at Indianapolis, furnished all the clothing and camp equipage for the troops organized in the State, except-

[1] See *Report of John H. Vajen, Quarter-master General of the State of Indiana* (Indianapolis, 1863). 27 pp.

ing such necessary articles of camp and garrison equipage as were not provided for by the regulations of the United States, which were deemed necessary for the comfort and convenience of the soldier, and which had hitherto been always supplied by the State. General NEW, therefore, purchased by contract, at public lettings, such articles as were absolutely required by the troops, consisting of tin buckets, wash pans, coffee boilers, cups, fry pans, coffee mills, etc., and issued them for the use of the various camps of volunteers. He also caused comfortable barracks to be erected for the accommodation of the troops in process of organization in the several Congressional districts—the General Government not being able to furnish tents at the time. Other duties of a miscellaneous character claimed the attention of General NEW, during his term, and were discharged with promptitude and good judgment.[2]

General Stone

Upon the resignation of General NEW, the Commissary General, Hon. ASAHEL STONE, was assigned to the office of Quartermaster General, his commission bearing date of October 15, 1862. General STONE had already proved himself a most faithful and capable officer and his appointment to this new position was a fitting and deserved tribute to his usefulness and efficiency.

General Duties—The demands upon the Quartermaster General, during the time General STONE served in that capacity, were of a very miscellaneous character; in fact, he came nearer being an officer of "all work" than any other connected with the State military service. An epitome of his duties can only be here given. He was required to take charge of and issue all the arms, accoutrements and quartermaster stores used by the Legion, and after the war was over

[2] See *Report of John C. New, Quarter-Master General of the State of Indiana* (Indianapolis, 1863), 14 pp.

and the Legion refused longer to maintain its organization, it became his duty, under orders issued from this office, to collect together all the outstanding arms and turn them over to the United States ordnance officer at the Indianapolis Arsenal, in satisfaction of the Government's claim against the State, for arms furnished the militia. His report shows that he recovered and turned over 41,212 muskets. It was made his duty also to examine and certify a variety of accounts for transportation, supplies and other expenses incurred by the State for home and government service; to provide camps and barracks and keep them in repair whenever the Government officials failed to do so; to furnish wood, straw, stoves, cooking utensils and thousands of other things, when required for the health and comfort of newly organized troops; to superintend and manage the Post or State Bakery and furnish wholesome loaf bread in lieu of the usual flour rations provided by the Government; to furnish rations and lodgings at the "Soldier's Home and Rest" for furloughed soldiers and for troops from all quarters who might be temporarily delayed, or who were en route to the field; to provide temporary quarters and suitable accommodations and subsistence for the indigent wives and children and female relatives of soldiers who visited the capital to see their sick or departing husbands, fathers and friends; to supply poor suffering refugees from the South with bread and blankets; to investigate abuses and inaugurate reforms in and about the camps of rendezvous; to receive from the United States Quartermaster and issue to recruits before they were organized into companies such articles of clothing, camp and garrison equipage as was required for their comfort and well being; and to look after any and every other general, special and miscellaneous wants connected with the service, that required prompt and faithful attention. He was a sort of military breakwater; his duties were incongruous and manifold, oftentimes vexatious and annoying, but always discharged with scrupulous fidelity.

State Bakery—In September, 1862, after the exchange of the Fort Donelson prisoners, Governor MORTON directed General STONE to take charge of the bakery which had been erected by the State for the benefit of the prisoners at Camp Morton, while used as a prison camp. Its capacity was from six to seven thousand loaves daily, but it was soon increased to the capacity of eleven or twelve thousand loaves daily. It was subsequently still further enlarged, and from it all the camps, hospitals, the military prison, the "Soldiers' Home," "Ladies' Home" and large numbers of refugees and indigent soldiers' families were daily supplied with freshly baked bread, the Government furnishing the usual "flour ration" for the number of troops officially reported, which being economically manipulated at the bakery yielded a profit, altogether, of nearly one hundred and fifty-seven thousand dollars. To explain this—a pound of flour when properly kneaded and baked will make considerably more than a pound of good wholesome bread. By furnishing all the bread required, the Quartermaster General was enabled to run the bakery on an extensive scale, and after paying all expenses, a handsome profit accrued which was used, as far as required, for the benefit of the troops. Stoves and other conveniences and comforts for soldiers' quarters and hospitals, which could not be procured from the Government, were thus supplied. At the same time the bread ration was much better, subject to less waste, and in every respect much more acceptable to the soldiers than the flour ration. The following extracts from General STONE's report[3] to the Governor, January 1, 1865, explains how the profits accrued:

Flour is furnished, on proper requisition, by Captain THOMAS FOSTER, the Commissary of Subsistence, and the bakery delivers to the soldier the amount of bread that the army regulations allow them. At the end of each month we find that we have a surplus of flour on hand. In other words, a given number of pounds of flour will furnish

[3] "Report of Asahel Stone, Quarter-Master General of the State of Indiana. To the Governor," in Indiana *Documentary Journal,* 1864, vol. 2, no. 8:208. This report was also issued as a separate imprint.

an equal weight of bread, and leave a surplus of, say thirty-three and a third per cent. of flour on hand. This surplus the Commissary of Subsistence purchases of me at the price fixed by the flour contract then existing between himself and the party furnishing it.

The total operations of the bakery, as shown by General STONE's final report, were as follows:

Total receipts from all sources in connection with the Bakery, from September 1st, 1862, to May 5th, 1866..	$100,124.83
Paid expenses of building ovens, sheds, repairs, pay and board of hands, wood for baking, and all other necessary expenses..............................$41,372.77	
Paid from the clear profits of the Bakery, for various articles and supplies necessary for the comfort of soldiers, building and repairs of the Soldiers' Home, Barracks, etc., together with the entire expense of the Quartermaster's Department to January 1st, 1866, which otherwise would have been a charge upon the State Treasury 56,168.73	
Balance, cash transferred to the Quartermaster's Department, proper 2,583.33	
Total Disbursements	$100,124.83

General STONE reports, also, that further savings on flour accrued to the amount of $50,258.53, arising as did all the *savings*, from the State Bakery; but, as the money was not needed for the benefit of the soldiers, it was not drawn and that amount was, therefore, a clear saving to the Government. Besides, there was distributed gratuitously to the poor families of soldiers and to refugees a large quantity of bread, amounting in value to $6,354. This shows a grand total of savings to the State and General Governments of $156,737.36.[4]

[4] Quartermaster General Stone's report for 1865-66 has not been found in either printed or manuscript form. Governor Morton referred to it in his message to the General Assembly in January, 1867, as being a comprehensive report covering the period Stone held the office.

The foregoing figures attest, in the strongest possible terms, the efficiency and ability of General STONE's administration of his department. His watchful care and interest in our soldiers and their dependent families, in the management of the "Soldiers' Home" and "Ladies' Home," have been already described in preceding pages.[5]

All the important business of the Quartermaster General having been settled and closed, General STONE resigned his position on the 11th of March, 1867. He was succeeded on the same day by PETER SCHMUCK, late an officer of the Twenty-Fourth and One Hundred and Forty-Third Regiments, Indiana Volunteers, who is still in office.

COMMISSARY GENERAL'S OFFICE

General Mansur

Mr. ISAIAH MANSUR was appointed to this office on the 15th of April, 1861, and was at once compelled to proceed with all energy to furnish commissary supplies for the thousands of troops who came rushing to the Capital in response to the President's first call. Of course there were no supplies on hand; all had to be purchased, and the Commissary General, without having time to arrange the details of his department, or study regulations, or make contracts, or learn any of the intricate duties of his position, was required to feed a hungry horde of raw and untrained men, just from homes of plenty, and therefore imperious and exacting in their demands, extravagant in their expectations and altogether dainty and particular as to the food they ate. These men had to be fed, and it was the desire of the State authorities that they should be well fed, and they were; but the gallant fellows knew nothing of army life, and while they did not exactly expect first-class hotel fare, they did expect at least to live in good "home style." If ever a poor fellow unwittingly stirred up a hornet's nest about his ears without

---

[5] See above, 454-60.

previous notice, it was MANSUR, when he took upon himself the purveyorship for the military camps at Indianapolis, in April, 1861. True, he did the best he could under the circumstances, purchasing what the market afforded, and of the best quality, adding largely to the regular army ration, and including such extras as vegetables, dried fruit, pickles, etc. But the men were not easily satisfied; the meat was too salty, some of the dried apples were "wormy"; the beans were not wholly sound; and it was suspected that all this was the result of the Commissary's desire to impose inferior articles on them and put money in his purse. Finally it was discovered that the ground coffee was adulterated with burnt beans! Then the excitement culminated in a general clamor, which, reaching the Legislature (then in extra session), an investigating committee was promptly ordered and a general overhauling of persons and papers ensued. Excitement ran high, and a large portion of the community, sympathizing with the soldiers, shook their heads angrily and declared it a burning shame that the poor boys should be put off with anything less than the fat of the land afforded. Soon boxes of roasted fowls, baked hams, fresh butter and eggs, pound cakes, preserves, jellies, pickles, and all manner of delicacies, came to favorites from all quarters, and many mess tables presented more the appearance of a grand old-fashioned barbecue than of the frugal fare eked out to soldiers in accordance with regulations. It is related of a good Mother who resided in one of the townships of Marion county, and who had a "pet" son in the Eleventh Regiment, that she sent a jug of cream to her young Napoleon for his coffee, and that during its transit it churned itself into delicious buttermilk, which was as heartily relished on its arrival in camp as the cream would have been. The friends at home evidently had resolved that even if the boys were to be killed by the rebels, they should not starve to death while in their own State. At the same time, the provisions furnished by the Commissary were as a general thing of first quality, and delivered in such abundance that but few of the men could possibly consume what was apportioned to them. In this statement no account is taken of the immense quantity of pies, fruits, and other eatables with which the men stuffed themselves, as all raw soldiers are wont to do, procured from sutler's stands and hawkers about the camp. The burly fellows, instead of being starved, were surfeited. It was no uncommon thing to see soldiers pelting one another with loaves of bread, or with potatoes or pieces of bacon—using them as missiles as boys use snowballs, or as Irishmen are said to use sticks, stove wood and ale bottles at a Donnybrook fair.

The Legislative Committee investigated thoroughly, and it is believed impartially. They reported:[6] "The soldiers, being fresh from homes of plenty, wholly unacquainted with the military service, and inexperienced in camp cooking and camp economy, the Governor and Commissary General thought best to issue extra rations to the troops and not confine them to regular army rations." The regular army ration consisted of pork, *or* fresh beef, flour *or* hard bread, beans *or* rice, coffee, sugar, vinegar, salt, candles and soap. The State rations were increased over those of the regular army from twenty-five to one hundred and fifty per cent in quantity, and extras were added, consisting of potatoes, pepper, dried fruit, onions and other antiscorbutics. Besides, instead of flour or hardtack, fresh bakers' bread was furnished. The committee further found that favoritism had been shown towards some companies by employees of the Commissary, without his knowledge, however, and that there were many well-founded complaints of short allowances directly traceable to the same source. Most likely the employees acted upon the "miller's rule"—first come first served—and allowed the early applicants to take what they wanted out of the general daily supply, leaving but scanty allowances to the

[6] *Report of Joint Select Investigating Committee on the Commissary Department to the General Assembly, May, 1861* (Indianapolis, 1861). See also Indiana *House Journal,* sp. sess. 1861, pp. 213-18.

dilatory and less enterprising. Hungry men, or those who think they are or may be hungry, are apt to "lay in" with a liberal hand when a tempting display of provender is placed within their reach. There was evidently a lack of system in the State Commissary Department in its first days; the employees were unskilled and perhaps liberal to a fault in their distributions as long as their stock on hand would allow them to be liberal; and in this liberality and looseness no doubt the secret lay of the favoritism complained of. As to the quality of the provisions the committee ascertained positively that the ground coffee was adulterated with beans, but nobody except the roaster and grinder appeared to have made anything by the operation; and the committee gravely reported that mixing roasted beans with coffee was a "criminal practice and crying evil that should be condemned rather than encouraged." In this view of the matter the soldiers doubtless concurred. The committee go on to say that the bacon shoulders were nearly universally complained of as too thin, too salty, and in bad condition. Evidently they were not country cured for family use. The beans, too, and some of the dried fruit, were unsatisfactory. After setting forth the foregoing, the committee say: "The testimony shows that there are no further well-grounded complaints as to the quality of provisions."

The report was duly communicated to the Legislature on the 24th of May. The Senate took no action, but the House, evidently swayed by the excitement and prejudices of the turbulent and exacting soldiery, who thought they were being deliberately imposed upon and swindled, adopted a resolution demanding General MANSUR'S removal.[7]

It may well be imagined that at this period half rations were not thought of, and that the great "war measures," subsequently known as "sow-belly" and "hardtack," were unknown to our legislators, who thus summarily determined to

[7] Indiana *House Journal*, sp. sess. 1861, p. 242.

dispose of the Commissary without ever going through the forms of a Court Martial, or subjecting him to interrogation or overhauling by a Court of Inquiry.

General MANSUR, who had accepted the position merely as a matter of duty and whose standing as a businessman of capacity and integrity was impregnably established, very gladly and promptly acted upon the not very gentle or delicate hint of the House, and resigned on the 29th [27th] of May, 1861.[8] He had paid all or nearly all of his bills out of his own pocket, for the State had no money then; he had furnished the best he could get and at reasonable prices, although the coffee turned out to be adulterated, but the five or six thousand men in camp had to have ground coffee or none, as they had no means to parch or grind it, and as was well remarked at the time, "green coffee would have been about as useful to them as so much gravel." If any of the bacon was sour, tainted or unsound, it was shown by the Commissary that it was not discovered in the haste of delivery, or else it became so after it was issued. At this juncture a spoilt ham would have put the whole camp in a fury. It is due General MANSUR to say that he discharged his duties economically and conscientiously, and did all in his power to make the troops feel comfortable and contented. That he did not succeed was due to the captious and complaining disposition of the raw and undisciplined forces he had to supply, more than to any other cause. Six months later, when the nature and realities of camp life became to be a little better understood, not a complaint would have been uttered against him.

General Stone

Upon the resignation of General MANSUR, the vacancy was filled by the appointment of the Hon. ASAHEL STONE,

[8] See Mansur to the Speaker of the House of Representatives, May 27, 1861, in Indiana *House Journal,* sp. sess., 1861, pp. 253-54, in which he asked that a committee be appointed before whom he could testify. No such committee was appointed.

State Senator from the county of Randolph, his commission bearing date May 29th, 1861. At this time there were several regiments in camp at Indianapolis, and others in camp at various points in the State, all which were subsisted by the Commissary General. Subsequently, the three months' regiments were all re-organized and some twenty new regiments were raised, all receiving their subsistence from the State.

It is hardly probable that any troops were better or as cheaply subsisted, as ours were, during the time General STONE administered his department. His entire study was to look after the welfare and comfort of our volunteers; and he furnished them, as did his predecessor, many articles of food and conveniences for camp use, not provided for by the "army regulations." So admirably did he discharge his duties, but few complaints were made; and when finally the General Government took charge of the troops and ruled them down to "regulation fare," the expression was universal among the men, that the subsistence and comforts furnished by the State, were of better quality and much more liberally dispensed than by the Government. General STONE'S economy is strikingly set forth in an official statement, showing the whole expense of his department, from May 29th to September 1st, 1861, to have been $94,159.16, and the number of rations issued 728,000, being an average cost per ration of only *twelve and ninety-four one hundredth cents* per ration. This included all expenses for extra allowances, such as vegetables, condiments and camp cooking utensils, salaries of the Commissary and his clerks, telegraphing, office rent, etc.[9]

About the first of September, 1861, an arrangement was effected by which the United States took the entire charge and control of subsisting the troops in Indiana during their organization and preparation for the field, and the State was thus relieved from that responsibility.

[9] See *Report of Asahel Stone, Commissary General* (Indianapolis, 1863), 6, *et passim.*

A portion of General STONE's time, up to his appointment as Quartermaster General in October, 1862, was employed in visiting regiments in the field, and looking after their wants and interests. In discharge of this duty, he traveled more than five thousand miles by rail, and over one thousand miles on horseback, visiting nearly all the Indiana regiments from Pea Ridge, Arkansas, to Cheat Mountain in West Virginia. He assisted them in getting clothing, shoes and other necessary supplies; visited the hospitals, and aided the sick and disabled in obtaining furloughs and discharges; and brought home and distributed to the families of soldiers large sums of money. By direction of the Governor, he also opened an office at the Capital for the assistance and information of sick and disabled soldiers in the field and their friends at home, and from this subsequently grew the general system of State Military Agencies, which proved so useful during the war, and of which an extended account is given elsewhere in this report.[10]

[10] See Report of Asahel Stone, in *Report of Special Agents, Pay Agents, et al.,* 3-33.

CAMP MORTON REBEL PRISON

Fort Donelson, the first important victory of the Union arms in the war of the rebellion, was captured, with a large number of prisoners, on the 16th of February, 1862. These prisoners had to be sent North for safe and comfortable keeping and to await exchange. Major General HALLECK, commanding the Department of the West, at once telegraphed Governor MORTON, asking how many prisoners he could provide for. The answer was, "Three thousand." The only place in the State well suited for the accommodation of the captives was Camp Morton, adjoining the city of Indianapolis, fitted up originally for State Fairs, and after the breaking out of the rebellion used as a general rendezvous for Indiana troops.[1] The camp was well located, on high ground, with good drainage, a light and porous soil, an abundance of excellent water, well shaded, with very comfortable buildings for quarters. Colonel RICHARD OWEN, an experienced officer and a most humane and accomplished gentleman, was then organizing the Sixtieth Regiment, at Evansville. He was ordered by the Governor to bring his incomplete command to Indianapolis, for prison guard duty, and was placed in charge of the camp; KIDD's battery and the Fifty-Third Regiment of Volunteers, and some recruits assisting for a time. The United States Quartermaster, Captain, now General JAMES A. EKIN, proceeded to erect such additional barracks as were required, and placed those already built in the best condition possible for the reception of the prisoners. In the large agricultural and mechanical halls,

[1] For an account of the prison camp see Hattie Lou Winslow and Joseph R. H. Moore, *Camp Morton 1861-1865. Indianapolis Prison Camp (Indiana Historical Society Publications,* vol. 13, no. 3, Indianapolis, 1940).

bunks were arranged on the sides for sleeping and long tables were placed in the center for serving up rations. Stoves were provided and suitable bedding—clean straw and blankets—furnished to make every man as comfortable as could be expected or reasonably desired under the circumstances. The halls being insufficient to accommodate more than two thousand persons, other barracks were constructed out of the stock stalls adjoining the northern fence of the camp. These had been occupied by our own troops the preceding summer and fall as quarters, and were considered quite cozy and comfortable. They were remodeled for the prisoners so as to give six apartments for sleeping and one for eating purposes, the latter made by throwing two stalls into one with a table in the center, alternating along the whole northern line of the ground in the proportion of six sleeping rooms to one eating room. The usual garrison equipage and cooking utensils with regulation rations, plenty of dry fuel, etc.—precisely the same as issued to our own troops—were furnished and so disposed as to be convenient for messing. These preparations, of course, had to be made hurriedly, as only short notice of the arrival of the prisoners had been given, but they were improved upon afterwards, and the camp was made as comfortable and safe as circumstances would allow.

On the 22d of February and succeeding night, three thousand seven hundred had arrived and were comfortably quartered; besides some eighty officers were separately provided for at the barracks of the Nineteenth United States Infantry in the city. About eight hundred prisoners were also quartered at Terre Haute in large warehouses, the recruits of the Sixty-First ("Second Irish") Regiment under Colonel BERNARD F. MULLEN, doing guard duty. A similar lot was sent to Lafayette and quartered in the same manner, the recruits of the Sixty-Third Regiment, under Lieutenant Colonel JOHN S. WILLIAMS, acting as guards. These arrangements were temporary, Camp Morton not being provided with sufficient accommodations for all the prisoners at the time. They were, however, all sent to Indianapolis about the middle of March. Squads of prisoners continued to be sent during the spring and summer, one thousand coming just after the battle of Shiloh, and the camp was enlarged as the necessities demanded, and made as comfortable as if the occupants were recruits for our own army.

On arrival, especially the Fort Donelson and Fort Henry prisoners, many were sick from the terrible exposure to which they had been subjected. The day after the main body came, the surgeons of the city prescribed for more than five hundred, and the sick list for some time increased rapidly. The men were thinly clad, unaccustomed to the rigors of outdoor life in winter, and had been poorly fed. The prevailing diseases were pneumonia and diarrhea. Ample hospital arrangements were made, and everything that kindness or humanity could suggest was done to alleviate the distressed condition of the prisoners. The citizens of Indianapolis, as well as of Terre Haute and Lafayette, responded to the calls of the authorities and did all that was possible to be done in furnishing suitable nourishment, delicacies and attention. Many very estimable ladies and gentlemen volunteered their services as nurses and attendants, and prominent members of the medical profession were particularly kind and attentive. Buildings were rented outside the camp and converted into infirmaries, with every convenience and comfort required by the sick. Despite all these efforts, the mortality was frightful during the first month or two. All who died were decently buried in plain wooden coffins, in the public cemeteries, and a record made of their names, regiments, etc., for the information of relatives and friends. After the weather moderated and grew warm a marked change took place in the general health of the prisoners and but few deaths occurred.

The excitement consequent upon the sudden influx of so large a number of rebels, taken in arms against their Government, was intense, not from a disposition to taunt or injure them, but from simple curiosity. It could not have risen to a higher pitch had a half-dozen shiploads of Feejee Islanders or Chinese coolies been suddenly discharged in our midst. The war itself was a novelty, and up to that time the people had never laid eyes upon a genuine fighting "Secesh." A few extracts from the Indianapolis *Journal* of the 20th of February, are here given as expressing the general sentiments of the community, and the generous and even kindly and humane feelings entertained toward these prisoners.

February 20, under the head of "Our Prisoners and Ourselves," the *Journal* said:

> For the sake of those who either honestly believe they were menaced with oppression by the Government, or have been compelled in spite of their convictions to join the rebel army, we ought to spare the prisoners all exhibition of triumph that would make us appear malignant in their eyes, or little in our own. We owe it to ourselves to show them that our triumph is but the realization of well-fixed hopes, and not the wild exultation of men unexpectedly successful and unaccountably relieved from a deadly peril. We who have always believed that the rebellion could and should be put down, owe it to the justice and strength of our cause that our enemy shall never see in unseemly rejoicing over their calamity that we have done more than we aimed to do. We have *not*. We have done only what we have taken months of weary preparation to gain, and what was almost as sure to follow as any effect in nature follows a cause. We have abundant cause for congratulation, none for boisterous exultation over the fallen. What a proper sense of our position and cause demands, humanity doubly demands. These men, misled as many have been, were but a few months ago friends and neighbors. Let us bear a memory of the past if they do not, and add no bitterness to their hard fate by unkind taunts or unfeeling treatment. Let us receive them as the Tennesseans received Dr. FLETCHER when he was captured, with no shouts, no taunts, but in silence, and with more of pity than triumph in our acts. It will do us no good to crow over them, and it will merely embitter their feelings toward us. Considerate treatment will open the eyes of the deluded, and strengthen the loyalty of the loyal. It is right and manly for us, and it is best for the cause we love, and the future we are so rapidly approaching.

Again, on the 25th of the same month, the same paper, after having noticed the arrival of some 4,800 prisoners, said:

We are pleased to note the fact that the prisoners of war were allowed to pass through the city on their way to the place of their confinement without any unbecoming manifestations being made against them by our citizens. No insult by word or deed was offered by any one, but on the other hand, they were all treated civilly. If any acts of indiscretion were committed, it was on the part of those who, thoughtlessly, engaged some of the prisoners in argument as to the justice of slavery and the causes of the war. It is well enough to disabuse their minds as to any prejudice they may have as to the objects of the war, and the intentions of our government, but this can be done without entering into needless arguments. They do more harm than good, and if visitors are to be allowed to see the prisoners, it would be well enough to have the guards instructed to put a stop to all controversies of the kind which may arise between visitors and prisoners. We trust our officers will see that it is done.

In regard to the sick, the *Journal*, of the 4th of March, contained the following:

Of the sick prisoners at the military prison and hospitals of this city, the greater proportion are Mississippians. Though some of the Tennesseans and Kentuckians are quite ill, their maladies are not so deep seated as those of the First, Fourth, and Twenty-Sixth Mississippi prisoners. These regiments were at Fort Henry, and at the time of the attack made upon it by Commodore FOOTE they retreated so rapidly that they left behind most of their baggage, including many articles of clothing much needed for their comfort. On arriving at Fort Donelson they were (thinly clad as they were) put at work immediately upon the fortifications, and were compelled to labor upon the trenches constantly. During the siege of the Fort, they lay in the ditches and rifle pits, day and night. Such exposure would produce disease in the ranks of the most able-bodied soldiers, but when incurred by men of feeble constitutions, the seeds of disease are so firmly planted that no medical skill can remove them. Of the latter class are those now in the hospitals. Many are under eighteen years of age, and the large majority are persons of feeble constitution. They receive the best medical treatment, and the nursing care of female attendants; but in many cases, the best of attention cannot save them from the grasp of death. What punishment is in store for the leading rebels who have been the cause of thus desolating the firesides of many a Southern home? That it will be a terrible one, we cannot doubt. Hundreds of happy homes have been made houses of mourning by such acts of inhuman treatment of the soldiers of the Confederate army as that mentioned above. Boys have been induced to enlist in the service and taken away from mothers who have become heartbroken—and died. The prejudices of fathers of families have been aroused against the Northern people, by systematic and repeated lying, until they have left all behind to fight against imaginary evils, to be taken prisoners and die in a Union hospital surrounded by ladies and gentlemen, who give the lie by every action and word to the foul slanders heaped upon them by secession libelers.

It is hardly necessary to add to these extracts. The newspapers of the day were filled with interesting accounts of the prisoners, and of the excellent accommodations afforded to those who were well, and the care and kindness bestowed upon those who were sick. When the fact was brought to the knowledge of Governor MORTON, that about three hundred of the Fort Donelson captives were deficient in clothing, he telegraphed the Secretary of War for orders to have their wants supplied by the U.S. Quartermaster at Indianapolis, and the order was promptly given. After that whenever a prisoner needed clothes, shoes or whatever else that was essential to his health or comfort, the Government supplied it. The friends of prisoners were allowed to send them anything but luxuries, and the things sent, even money, were distributed as their wants required with scrupulous fidelity.

A deep solicitude was felt in the South for the welfare of the prisoners, and frequent personal visits and inquiries by letter were made by their friends with the view to add to their comfort. The following letter very clearly explains the treatment the men received:

ADJUTANT GENERAL'S OFFICE,
INDIANAPOLIS, February 28th, 1862.

REV. LIVINGSTON WELLS *of Louisville,*
Secretary on behalf of Commission, etc.

SIR: In response to your communication addressed to Captain GREENE, Assistant Adjutant General at Louisville, and by him referred to this department, I am instructed to submit the following statement relative to the Rebel prisoners confined here:

Of prisoners there are about 4,000 here, 800 at Lafayette and 500 at Terre Haute, all placed in comfortable quarters, under safe guard.

Their quarters are well warmed with large stoves and have bunks furnished with clean straw. They receive the same subsistence in every respect, as our own troops, consisting of full rations of coffee, fresh bread, meat, beans, hominy, rice, potatoes, etc—indeed everything authorized by our Army Regulations. Some have received blankets and clothing from the U.S. Quartermaster, Captain EKIN, and others will be supplied as their wants may require. They are supplied with materials and allowed to write brief letters to their friends and families under the inspection of those in command. The sick are placed in comfortable hospitals in good clean beds and receive proper subsistence and medical treatment from excellent physicians assisted by prisoners detailed as nurses.

Rigid rules have been promulgated for the safety of the prisoners and to prevent any intercourse with them. No one will be admitted to the camp under any pretext whatever. Every attention will be paid to the prisoners that their necessities and well being demand; any thing further will not be allowed. They, and their friends, must reflect that they are Rebel prisoners and as such cannot be allowed the luxuries and comforts incident to a peaceful home. Any or all contributions of a proper character that may be made for the sick prisoners in the Hospitals will be received and properly applied, under the directions of the physicians in charge. All such things should be addressed to "J. H. VAJEN, Quartermaster General, Indiana," and the contents plainly endorsed on the packages.

By Order: Very respectfully,
(Signed,) LAZ NOBLE, Adjutant General, Indiana

Even the excess of rations and the savings of flour by means of a bakery which was established at Camp Morton, were applied to the benefit of the prisoners, and the Government took the most kindly interest in securing for them all the comforts their necessities required. The following letter will fully explain this:

OFFICE OF COMMISSARY GENERAL OF PRISONERS,
March 23d, 1862.

CAPTAIN:—Please give your attention to the following matters relating to the Prisoners of War:

See that the Hospitals are furnished with underclothing for the sick, and sheets and pillow cases sufficient to insure cleanliness and comfort.

Have a careful account of the rations due the Hospital, and the rations drawn, kept, so that the sick men have the advantage of the savings, and with the fund purchase all articles that may in any way be of benefit to the sick.

I wish the Commissary at the camp, to withhold any part of the rations which may be in excess over what is really necessary, and semi-monthly pay to Colonel OWEN, the value of the rations so retained, thus forming a fund to be disbursed by the Colonel for the benefit of the prisoners.

Many articles which are not furnished by the Government may be purchased with this fund, such as brooms, buckets, table furniture, &c., &c. Of course it will be required that a careful account of receipts and expenditures, with the bills, will be kept by the Colonel.

As soon as practicable, put the prisoners in tents, from one building at a time, and rearrange the bunks so as to give more room and more light, making the barracks as comfortable as possible without incurring but little expense.

Put a second floor, or half floor, as may be found most expedient, in the receiving hospital at the camp, to divide it into two stories, and give larger accommodation to the sick.

Very respectfully, your obedient servant,

W. HOFFMAN,
Lieut. Col. Eighth Regiment, Com'y Gen'l of Prisoners.

Captain JAMES A. EKIN, Assistant Quartermaster U.S.A., Indianapolis, Indiana.

A number of sick prisoners were allowed to be removed to private residences, where they could be cared for to better advantage than in the hospitals; and on one occasion the Surgeon in charge of the camp certified that a prisoner would die of consumption, if kept in confinement, who was thereupon discharged on parole, upon application of the Governor, by order of Major General HALLECK.

The prisoners themselves, very generally, were profuse in commendations of their treatment, and when the time came for their exchange, many of them preferred taking the oath of allegiance, and remaining North, than to be sent back to fight against a government that had manifested such kindness and magnanimity towards them. In contrast with the horrors of Libby, Belle Isle, Andersonville and other Southern prison pens, where thousands of brave Union men were starved and murdered, the history of Camp Morton is as Heaven is to Hell.

Colonel OWEN remained in command until the 10th of June, when his regiment was ordered to the field, and its place supplied by a force of the Indiana Legion, which was mustered into the service of the United States for three months, as the Fifty-Fourth and Fifty-Fifth Regiments, Indiana Volunteers. Colonel DAVID GARLAND ROSE, of the Fifty-Fourth, was made Commandant, and discharged the responsible duties of his position to the satisfaction of the authorities, and with entire acceptability to the prisoners. A general exchange was effected in August, 1862, and the camp was closed as a prison soon after. A few guerrillas were subsequently sent in to be taken care of, by the recruiting officers stationed there during the fall and winter of that year.

In the Vicksburg campaign, 1863, a large number of prisoners were captured, and several thousand were sent to be confined at Camp Morton. Others arrived from various quarters, and from that time on till the close of the war the number confined ranged from three to six thousand. The camp was refitted, comfortable hospitals and other buildings were built, the force in charge as guards being the Fifth Regiment Veteran Reserve Corps, under command of Brevet Brigadier General A. A. STEVENS. The State authorities not being charged with the care and custody of the prisoners after the year 1862, further account of Camp Morton would be superfluous in this report.

MILITARY ADMINISTRATION

MILITARY DISTRICT OF INDIANA

The State of Indiana was constituted a Military District in the Department of the Ohio, by General Order No. 25, of Major General H. G. WRIGHT, commanding the Department, dated March 23d, 1863, and Brigadier General H. B. CARRINGTON was assigned to command said district—headquarters at Indianapolis.

On the 15th of April, 1863, General CARRINGTON was relieved from the command of the District by Brigadier General MILO S. HASCALL, acting under the orders from Major General A. E. BURNSIDE, commanding the Department.

Under Special Orders No. 1, issued by General BURNSIDE, dated June 5th, 1863, the District of Michigan was detached from the District of Ohio and attached to the District of Indiana, and Brigadier General O. B. WILLCOX was assigned to command the same, relieving General CARRINGTON.

On the 11th of September, 1863, Brigadier General WILLCOX was relieved from the command and ordered to the field, at his own request, by telegram from the War Department, and the District of Indiana and Michigan was broken up—Indiana remaining a separate District in the Department of the Ohio under command of Colonel JOHN S. SIMONSON.

In the month of February, 1864, the Northern Department was organized, of which Indiana formed a part; and on the 23d of May, 1864, under orders from Major General S. P. HEINTZELMAN, Brigadier General H. B. CARRINGTON relieved Colonel SIMONSON, and again assumed command of the District.

Brevet Major General ALVIN P. HOVEY relieved Brigadier General CARRINGTON of the command of the District, on the 25th of August, 1864, by order of the Secretary of War. During General HOVEY's incumbency the Department was reorganized July 5th, 1865, and renamed the Department of the Ohio.

On the 25th of September, 1865, Brigadier General THOMAS G. PITCHER, Acting Assistant Provost Marshal General for Indiana, took command of the District in accordance with Special Order No. 64, Department of the Ohio, September 18th, 1865—General HOVEY having been appointed U.S. Minister Plenipotentiary to the government of Peru, South America.[1]

On the 17th of August, 1866, General PITCHER was relieved by the War Department and ordered to the U.S. Military Academy at West Point, New York, as Superintendent, and the District of Indiana was discontinued.

Brevet Brigadier General JOHN S. SIMONSON, being Post Commander at Indianapolis, took charge of the unfinished business of the District from the time of General PITCHER's departure until the 31st of May, 1867, when by order from the War Department the U.S. Military Headquarters for Indiana were finally closed; the State however still remains under command of Major General POPE, commanding the Department of the Lakes.

MILITARY DEPARTMENTS WHICH HAVE EMBRACED THE STATE OF INDIANA

Department of the Ohio

On the 3d of May, 1861, a new Military Department, styled the Department of the Ohio, was constituted under General Orders No. 14, Adjutant General's Office, War Department, comprising the States of Ohio, Indiana and Illinois,

[1] On the 6th of August, 1866, the Department was reorganized under the name of the Department of the Lakes, Major General Joseph Hooker, commanding [Terrell].

and Major General GEORGE B. MCCLELLAN, Ohio Volunteers, was assigned to the command with Headquarters at Cincinnati.

Under General Orders No. 19, A. G. O., War Department, May 9th, 1861, the Department of the Ohio was extended so as to embrace so much of Western Virginia and Pennsylvania as lies north of the Great Kanawha, north and west of the Greenbrier, thence northward to the southwest corner of Maryland, thence along the Western Maryland line, to the Pennsylvania line, and thence northerly to the northeast corner of McLean county in Pennsylvania.

On the 6th of June, 1861, by General Order No. 30, Adjutant General's Office, War Department, the State of Missouri was added to the Department of the Ohio, and Major General MCCLELLAN was directed to extend his command accordingly. Under General Orders No. 80, A. G. O., War Department, September 19th, 1861, the Military Department of the Ohio was made to comprise the States of Ohio, Indiana and so much of Kentucky as lies within fifteen miles of Cincinnati, under the command of Brigadier General O. M. MITCHELL, U. S. Volunteers, with Headquarters at Cincinnati.

On the 9th of November, 1861, under General Orders No. 97, A. G. O., War Department, the Department of the Ohio was made to consist of the States of Ohio, Michigan, Indiana, that portion of Kentucky east of the Cumberland river, and the State of Tennessee. Brigadier General D. C. BUELL was assigned to the command of the same with Headquarters at Louisville.

Under General Orders No. 112, A. G. O., War Department, August 19th, 1862, the Department of the Ohio was reconstructed and made to comprise the States of Ohio, Michigan, Indiana, Illinois, Wisconsin, and Kentucky east of the Tennessee river, and including Cumberland Gap and the troops operating in its vicinity. Major General H. G.

WRIGHT was assigned to the command and established his Headquarters at Cincinnati.

On the 25th of March, 1863, in accordance with instructions from the General-in-Chief, Major General A. E. BURNSIDE announced in Department General Orders No. 27, that he had assumed command of the Department of the Ohio— Headquarters at Cincinnati.

On the 16th of November, 1863 (General Orders No. 369, A. G. O., War Department), the Department of the Ohio was changed to include only the State of Kentucky north of the Tennessee river, and such part of the State of Tennessee as was occupied by the troops of the Army of the Ohio; Major General J. G. FOSTER was placed in command and Major General BURNSIDE ordered to report in person to the Adjutant General of the Army.

It does not appear from any orders or records accessible to this office, that any person succeeded General BURNSIDE in command of the remaining States of the Department until the establishment of the

Northern Department

About the 1st of February, 1864, when Major General HEINTZELMAN assumed command of the same— the Department embracing the States of Ohio, Michigan, Indiana and Illinois, with Headquarters at Columbus, Ohio.

On the 1st of October, 1864, in conformity with Special Orders No. 263, dated War Department, September 28th, 1864, Major General JOSEPH HOOKER assumed command of the Northern Department and removed Headquarters to Cincinnati.

Department of the Ohio

Major General E. O. C. ORD succeeded General HOOKER in the command of the Department on the 5th of July, 1865, in conformity with General Orders No. 118, A. G. O., War

Department, and established his Headquarters at Detroit, Michigan. The Department embraced the States of Ohio, Indiana, Illinois and Michigan, and was renamed "The Department of the Ohio." The State of Wisconsin was added to the Department on the 30th October, 1865.

The Department of the Lakes

was organized in conformity with General Orders No. 59, A. G. O., War Department, August 6th, 1866, and embraced the States of Indiana, Ohio, Michigan, Wisconsin and Illinois. Major General JOSEPH HOOKER was placed in command, with Headquarters at Detroit. General HOOKER was granted leave of absence, June 1st, 1867, for one year, to visit Europe, and was succeeded by Brevet Major General JOHN C. ROBINSON, Colonel Forty-Third U. S. Infantry. Major General JOHN POPE, U. S. A., is now (December 1st, 1868) in command of the Department

APPENDIX

APPENDIX

TROOPS FURNISHED BY THE STATE OF INDIANA—WAR OF THE REBELLION—UNITED STATES SERVICE CONDENSED STATEMENT

Regiment. Infantry.	Term of Service.	Original Commissioned officers.	Original non-commissioned officers and band.	Original enlisted men.	Recruits.	Re-enlisted veterans.	Unassigned recruits.	Commissioned Officers died.	Non-Commissioned Officers & enlisted men died.	Deserters.	Non-Commissioned Officers, band and enlisted men unaccounted for.	Total Officers and Men acounted for.	Total belonging to Regiment.
6th	Three months	37	4	740	....	....	....	....	3	8	....	781	781
7th	Three months	37	5	740	....	....	....	....	3	3	....	782	782
8th	Three months	37	4	743	....	....	....	....	7	15	1	784	784
9th	Three months	37	4	745	....	....	....	....	5	3	....	786	786
10th	Three months	37	5	747	1	....	....	....	6	6	....	790	790
11th	Three months	37	4	740	....	....	....	....	2	1	....	781	781
6th	Three years	46	23	927	113	....	9	11	242	48	10	1108	1118
7th	Three years	45	29	972	190	46	17	11	201	26	27	1272	1299
8th	Three years	46	26	980	177	426	17	12	233	75	47	1625	1672
9th	Three years	47	30	980	747	291	46	12	339	125	18	2123	2141
10th	Three years	45	7	934	197	72	15	8	177	40	11	1259	1270
11th	Three years	49	30	980	855	296	138	4	241	25	239	2109	2348
12th	One year	39	31	718	243	....	1	....	22	83	1	1031	1032
12th	Three years	41	6	901	372	....	12	9	184	8	13	1319	1332
13th	Three years	41	30	976	192	148	40	8	128	103	25	1402	1427
13th re-organized	Three years	36	5	939	125	....	41	....	98	1	30	1116	1146
14th	Three years	46	30	979	112	59	48	10	175	63	12	1262	1274
15th	Three years	46	30	980	72	75	17	4	167	115	17	1203	1220
16th	One year	38	21	666	231	....	15	....	12	73	16	955	971
16th	Three years	42	2	919	282	....	241	3	268	36	204	1282	1486
17th	Three years	49	30	984	863	288	97	4	228	161	82	2229	2311
18th	Three years	45	30	980	116	359	24	6	174	53	156	1399	1555
19th	Three years	43	30	981	218	213	229	7	260	....	451	1163	1614
20th	Three years	42	29	980	377	282	33	13	215	66	176	1567	1743
20th re-organized	Three years	38	13	855	27	....	6	....	44	....	56	883	939
22d	Three years	42	30	984	956	332	374	14	313	88	62	2656	2718
23d	Three years	42	30	978	477	277	36	6	148	99	273	1567	1840
24th	Three years	43	30	980	262	343	115	10	241	61	161	1612	1773
25th	Three years	45	30	977	615	282	66	12	295	56	235	1780	2015
26th	Three years	41	5	978	669	248	56	4	332	38	36	1961	1997
27th	Three years	40	30	982	75	154	41	12	263	47	52	1270	1322
29th	Three years	49	28	859	884	204	106	8	285	63	49	2081	2130
30th	Three years	46	4	961	117	121	159	5	360	67	70	1338	1408
30th re-organized	Three years	30	6	701	31	....	35	....	68	2	7	796	803
31st	Three years	44	19	975	545	285	18	10	356	76	13	1873	1886
32d	Three years	43	26	830	403	2	81	9	213	171	50	1335	1385
32d re-organized	Three years	19	....	399	14	....	242	....	32	1	11	663	674
33d	Three years	43	6	899	886	449	492	7	260	113	117	2758	2875
34	Three years	42	28	941	339	438	18	7	229	44	15	1791	1806
35th	Three years	42	30	799	704	192	102	3	241	269	51	1818	1869
36th	Three years	48	26	949	120	21	13	13	221	43	12	1165	1177
37th	Three years	41	29	920	99	193	18	7	201	18	2	1298	1300
37th re-organized	Three years	5	....	162	47	....	333	....	10	....	329	218	547
38th	Three years	46	24	925	720	247	66	10	343	58	77	1951	2028
40th	Three years	43	6	879	545	246	36	11	301	131	29	1726	1755
42d	Three years	43	25	951	902	215	27	6	248	60	119	2044	2163
43d	Three years	45	7	933	939	165	215	6	200	121	285	2019	2304
44th	Three years	44	....	889	987	220	63	13	236	65	102	2101	2203
46th	Three years	44	5	920	191	286	14	7	244	22	56	1404	1460
47th	Three years	41	4	932	344	409	18	8	304	62	20	1728	1748
48th	Three years	44	4	943	529	284	74	3	210	96	199	1679	1878

(561)

562　ADJUTANT GENERAL'S REPORT

Regiment, Infantry.	Term of Service.	Original Commissioned officers.	Original non-commissioned officers and band.	Original enlisted men.	Recruits.	Re-enlisted veterans.	Unassigned recruits.	Commissioned Officers died.	Non-Commissioned Officers & enlisted men died.	Deserters.	Non-Commissioned Officers, band and enlisted men unaccounted for.	Total Officers and Men acounted for.	Total belonging to Regiment.
49th	Three years	45	5	924	251	177	43	4	234	94	42	1403	1445
50th	Three years	42	5	936	284	248	49	6	205	71	20	1544	1564
51st	Three years	43	16	880	654	295	69	7	259	130	51	1906	1957
52d	Three years	44	5	881	204	370	17	4	163	129	26	1495	1521
52d re-organized	Three years	40	4	904	8				20			956	956
53d	Three years	44		872	994	381	200	13	281	100	127	2364	2491
54th	Three months	37		850	59							946	946
54th	One year	41		915	20		13	3	213	81	358	631	989
55th	Three months	36		603			19	1	3		19	639	658
57th	Three years	50	5	918	449	215	15	7	260	54	24	1628	1652
58th	Three years	41	22	841	799	202	17	5	257	45	16	1906	1922
59th	Three years	42	5	674	834	240	361	1	220	32	158	1998	2156
60th	Three years	41	4	900	126		25	5	198	87	29	1067	1096
63d	Three years	40		832	360		13	5	179	47	14	1231	1245
65th	Three years	41	4	897	223		5	4	232	59	8	1162	1170
66th	Three years	42	4	971	84		17	4	230	32	15	1103	1118
37th	Three years	43		941	42		14	3	158	43	216	824	1040
68th	Three years	41		864	104		8	4	138	48	5	1012	1017
69th	Three years	42		960	77		21	6	326	61	21	1079	1100
70th	Three years	44	6	962	336		22	4	191	39	27	1343	1370
72d	Three years	44	1	943	283		54	4	151	35	36	1289	1325
73d	Three years	47		973	136		13	3	226	74	5	1164	1169
74th	Three years	42		900	208		7	7	253	25	4	1153	1157
75th	Three years	42		989	89		7	4	223	30	31	1096	1127
76th	Thirty days	37		749					1			786	786
78th	Sixty days	24		563				1	3	2		587	587
79th	Three years	41		880	26		219	5	182	48	6	1160	1166
80th	Three years	42		907	89		11	8	229	49	3	1046	1049
81st	Three years	43	5	891	37		6	5	231	33	8	974	982
82d	Three years	47		891	154		3	8	219	33	13	1082	1095
83d	Three years	42		931	85		35	9	240	19	116	977	1093
84th	Three years	43		906	69		9	7	200	53	9	1018	1027
85th	Three years	40		845	196		4	5	207	52	3	1982	1085
86th	Three years	41		917	41			3	238	48	1	998	999
87th	Three years	44		901	292		10	12	256	29	7	1240	1247
88th	Three years	42	5	904	161		19	12	196	36	8	1123	1131
89th	Three years	45		949	94		30	11	231	25	8	1110	1118
91st	Three years	48		1159	121		40	5	130	82	155	1213	1368
93d	Three years	40	1	911	182		18	4	275	47	22	1130	1152
97th	Three years	41		835	24		2	9	221	33	2	900	902
99th	Three years	41	1	858	81		3	5	173	38	2	982	984
100th	Three years	43		925	75		11	5	232	31	11	1043	1054
101st	Three years	44		904	117		7	4	206	41	20	1052	1072
115th	Six months	39		883	55				72	21		977	977
116th	Six months	41		954	81				66	120	1	1075	1076
117th	Six months	39		958	15				95	13	32	980	1012
118th	Six months	38		949	30			1	80	26	17	1000	1017
120th	Three years	41		935	218		1	2	149	52		1195	1195
123d	Three years	40		1010	13		7	5	166	36	7	1063	1070
124th	Three years	41		917	74		5	3	146	37	6	1031	1037
128th	Three years	41	6	912	239		15	5	134	64	16	1197	1213
129th	Three years	40	6	901	67		3	4	171	34	4	1013	1017
130th	Three years	40	6	918	21		1	3	175	21	9	977	986
132d	100 days	39		909					5			948	948
133d	100 days	39	4	898					16	2		941	941
134th	100 days	41		908	1				19			950	950
135th	100 days	39	5	884	2				25	4		930	930
136th	100 days	39	5	928					4			967	967
137th	100 days	39	5	884					17	2		928	928
138th	100 days	39		847					8	1		886	886
139th	100 days	39	6	818	2				11	1	7	865	865
140th	One year	39		968	45		3		102	50	7	1048	1055
142d	One year	41		926	27		21		64	28	22	993	1015
143d	One year	40		958	3		5		90	78	4	1002	1006
144th	One year	38		992	6				46	19	1	1035	1036
145th	One year	40		953	80				68	55		1023	1023
146th	One year	38		941					29	30	7	972	979
147th	One year	39		1012	24		3		44	63	1	1077	1078
148th	One year	39		936	52				36	75		1027	1027
149th	One year	38		987	15		1	1	38	27	1	1040	1041
150th	One year	39		949	89		5		34	50	8	1074	1082
151st	One year	38		961	14				60	33		1013	1013
152d	One year	39		933	13		3		48	22		988	988
153d	One year	39		963	31				47	79	2	1031	1033
154th	One year	39		938			5		40	84	1	981	982

APPENDIX 563

Regiment, Infantry.	Term of Service.	Original Commissioned officers.	Original non-commissioned officers and band.	Original enlisted men.	Recruits.	Re-enlisted veterans.	Unassigned recruits.	Commissioned Officers died.	Non-Commissioned Officers & enlisted men died.	Deserters.	Non-Commissioned Officers, band and enlisted men unaccounted for.	Total Officers and Men accounted for.	Total belonging to Regiment.
155th	One year	39	....	902	46	....	26	1	14	68	7	1006	1013
156th	One year	20	....	494	10	....	7	....	17	54	....	531	531
U. S. Colored Troops	Three years	39	....	911	552	....	1072	3	215	87	865	1709	2574
Independent Compa's	Thirty days	54	....	1034	....	....	....	....	....	....	1	1087	1088
Hancock's Corps	One year	....	....	....	....	....	168	....	....	....	....	168	168
Miscellan's Organiz's	Three years	....	3	253	404	....	....	....	....	....	248	412	660
1st Cavalry	Three years	51	4	984	138	5	163	6	125	47	273	1072	1345
1st Cav. re-organized	Three years	18	....	197	9	....	9	....	22	....	8	225	233
2d Cavalry	Three years	51	3	1076	340	78	176	7	227	105	51	1673	1724
2d Cav. re-organized	Three years	19	....	372	....	....	23	....	....	....	9	405	414
3d Cavalry	Three years	50	....	1008	191	37	202	2	131	65	319	1169	1488
3d Cav. re-organized	Three years	6	....	194	....	....	2	....	6	....	2	200	202
4th Cavalry	Three years	57	....	1166	250	....	51	9	195	84	54	1470	1524
5th Cavalry	Three years	51	....	1191	423	....	99	1	216	125	99	1665	1764
6th Cavalry	Three years	50	8	1142	486	....	62	6	254	105	72	1676	1748
7th Cavalry	Three years	51	....	1151	95	....	32	5	238	169	29	1300	1329
7th Cav. re-organized	Three years	25	7	543	....	....	....	....	15	....	2	573	575
8th Cavalry	Three years	53	30	1125	776	305	126	10	329	56	137	2278	2415
9th Cavalry	Three years	48	....	1219	41	....	26	4	202	126	20	1314	1334
10th Cavalry	Three years	50	....	1204	46	....	47	4	163	88	47	1300	1347
11th Cavalry	Three years	53	....	1193	57	....	6	3	167	108	8	1301	1309
12th Cavalry	Three years	50	....	1211	83	....	13	2	166	54	7	1350	1357
13th Cavalry	Three years	50	....	1107	228	....	8	3	133	87	9	1384	1393
Independ't Cav. Co.	One year	3	....	101	....	....	....	....	2	....	....	104	104
1st Heavy Artillery	Three years	80	30	1253	1332	448	696	10	382	228	200	3639	3839
25 Batteries	Three years	157	....	3510	2724	549	....	17	609	387	472	6468	6940
25th Battery	One year	5	....	142	60	....	....	....	7	38	25	182	207
Deserters from draft call of Aug. 4, '62		....	....	....	....	....	373	....	....	373	....	373	373
Deserters from draft call of July 18, '64		....	....	....	....	....	1858	....	....	1858	....	1858	1858
Deserters from draft call of Dec. 19, '64		....	....	....	....	....	218	....	....	218	....	218	218
Bounty Jumpers 1864		....	....	....	....	....	166	....	....	166	....	166	166
Enlistments in Regular army and in volunteer organizations of other States		....	....	....	....	....	....	....	....	....	5000	....	5000

SUMMARY OF TROOPS FURNISHED BY THE STATE OF INDIANA.

Commissioned officers at original organization	6,293
Non-Commissioned officers and musicians at original organization	1,112
Enlisted men, privates, at original organization	137,401
Recruits, privates	35,836
Re-enlisted Veterans	11,718
Unassigned recruits, regular army, &c.	16,007
Grand total troops furnished	208,367

KILLED AND DIED OF DISEASE.

Commissioned officers	652
Non-Commissioned officers and enlisted men	23,764
Total	24,416

DESERTERS.

Officers	13
Enlisted men	10,833
Total	10,846

ACCOUNTED FOR, AND UNACCOUNTED FOR.

Officers and men accounted for	194,588
Non-Commissioned officers and enlisted men	23,764
Grand total	208,367

TABLE SHOWING THE ORGANIZATIONS OF INFANTRY, CAVALRY AND ARTILLERY SENT TO THE FIELD BY THE STATE OF INDIANA DURING THE LATE WAR; ALSO CERTAIN FACTS CONNECTED WITH SUCH ORGANIZATIONS.

INFANTRY

Regiment Infantry	Date or Order or authority to organize.	Where organized—Rendezvous.	Colonel or Commandant by whom organized.	Date of Muster into service.	Period of Service.	Date of Muster out.
6th..	April 16, '61	Indianapolis....	T. T. Crittenden.....	April 25, '61.	Three months....	Aug. 2, '61
7th..	April 16, '61	Indianapolis....	Ebenezer Dumont....	April 25, '61.	Three months....	Aug. 2, '61
8th..	April 16, '61	Indianapolis....	Wm. P. Benton......	April 25, '61.	Three months....	Aug. 2, '61
9th..	April 16, 61	Indianapolis....	Robert H. Milroy...	April 25, '61.	Three months....	Aug. 2, '61
10th..	April 16, '61	Indianapolis....	J. J. Reynolds......	April 25, '61.	Three months....	Aug. 2, '61
11th..	April 16, '61	Indianapolis....	Lewis Wallace.......	April 25, '61.	Three months....	Aug. 2, '61
6th..	Aug. 3, '61.	Madison........	T. T. Crittenden.....	Sept. 20, '61.	Three years......	Sept. 22, '64
7th..	Aug. 3, '61.	Indianapolis....	Ebenezer Dumont....	Sept. 13, '61.	Three years......	Sept. 20, '64
8th..	Aug. 3, '61.	Indianapolis....	Wm. P. Benton......	Aug. 20, '61.	Three years......	Aug. 28, '65
9th..	Aug. 3, '61.	Westville.......	Robert H. Milroy...	Aug. 27, '61.	Three years......	Sept. 28, '65
10th..	Aug. 3, '61.	Lafayette.......	M. D. Manson......	Sept. 18, '61.	Three years......	Sept. 19, '64
11th..	Aug. 3, '61.	Indianapolis....	Lewis Wallace.......	Aug. 31, '61.	Three years......	July 26, '65
12th..	May 3, '61..	Indianapolis....	John M. Wallace....	May 11, '61.	One year........	May 14, '62
12th..	May 17, '62.	Indianapolis....	Wm. H. Link.......	Aug. 17, '62.	Three years......	June 8, '65
13th..	May 3, '61..	Indianapolis....	J. C. Sullivan.......	June 19, '61.	Three years......	Sept. 5, '65
14th..	May 3, '61..	Terre Haute....	Nathan Kimball.....	June 7, '61.	Three years......	June 16, '64
15th..	May 3, '61..	Lafayette.......	Geo. D. Wagner.....	June 14, 61.	Three years......	June 25, '64
16th..	May 3, '61..	Richmond.......	P. A. Hackleman....	May 11, '61.	One year........	May 14, '62
16th..	May 17, '62.	Indianapolis....	T. J. Lucas.........	Aug. 19, '62.	Three years......	June 30, '65
17th..	May 3, '61..	Indianapolis....	Milo S. Hascall......	June 12, '61.	Three years......	Aug. 8, '65
18th..	June 11, '61	Indianapolis....	Thos. Pattison......	Aug. 16, '61.	Three years......	Aug. 28, '65
19th..	June 24, '61	Indianapolis....	Sol. Meredith.......	July 29, '61.	Three years......	July 28, '64
20th..	June 24, '61	Lafayette.......	W. L. Brown.......	July 22, '61.	Three years......	July 19, '65
21st..	June 24, '61	Indianapolis....	J. W. McMillan.....	July 24, '61.	Three years......	Jan. 13, '66
22d ..	June 24, '61	Madison........	Wm. G. Wharton...	Aug. 15, '61.	Three years......	July 24, '65
23d ..	June 24, '61	New Albany.....	Wm. L. Sanderson..	July 29, '61.	Three years......	July 23, '65
24th..	June 24, '61	Vincennes.......	Cyrus M. Allen.....	July 31, '61.	Three years......	Nov. 15, '65
25th..	June 24, '61	Evansville......	James G. Jones.....	Aug. 19, '61.	Three years......	July 17, '65
26th..	June 24, '61	Indianapolis....	Wm. M. Wheatley...	Aug. 31, '61.	Three years......	Jan. 15, '66
27th..	June 24, '61	Indianapolis....	Silas Colgrove......	Sept. 12, '61.	Three years......	Nov. 4, '64
29th..	Aug. 3, '61.	Laporte.........	John F. Miller......	Aug. 27, '61.	Three years......	Dec. 2, '65
30th..	Aug. 3, '61.	Fort Wayne.....	Hugh B. Reed.......	Sept. 24, '61.	Three years......	Nov. 25, '65
31st..	Aug. 3, '61.	Terre Haute....	Charles Cruft.......	Sept. 15, '61.	Three years......	Dec. 8, '65
32d ..	Aug. 12, '61	Indianapolis....	August Willich......	Aug. 24, '61.	Three years......	Dec. 4, '65
33d ..	Aug. 3, '61.	Indianapolis....	John Coburn........	Sept. 16, '61.	Three years......	July 21, '65
34th..	Aug. 3, '61.	Anderson.......	Thos. N. Stilwell....	Sept. 16, '61.	Three years......	Feb. 3, '66
35th..	Aug. 21, '61	Indianapolis....	John C. Walker.....	Dec. 11, '61.	Three years......	Sept. 30, '65
36th..	Aug. 3, '61.	Richmond.......	Wm. Grose.........	Sept. 16, '61.	Three years......	Sept. 21, '64
37th..	Aug. 3, '61.	Lawrenceburg...	Carter Gazlay.......	Sept. 18, '61.	Three years......	Oct. 27, '64
38th..	Aug. 3, '61.	New Albany.....	Benj. F. Scribner....	Sept. 18, '61.	Three years......	July 15, '65
39th..	Aug. 20, '61	Indianapolis....	Thos. J. Harrison...	Aug. 29, '61.	Three years......	July 20, '65
40th..	Aug. 20, '61	Lafayette.......	Wm. C. Wilson.....	Dec. 30, '61.	Three years......	Dec. 21, '65
42d ..	Sept. 5, '61	Evansville......	James G. Jones.....	Oct. 9, '61.	Three years......	July 21, '65
43d ..	Sept. 5, '61	Terre Haute....	Geo. K. Steele......	Sept. 27, '61.	Three years......	June 14, '65
44th..	Sept. —, '61	Fort Wayne.....	Hugh B. Reed.......	Oct. 24, '61.	Three years......	Sept. 14, '65
46th..	Sept. 20, '61	Logansport......	G. N. Fitch........	Dec. 11, '61.	Three years......	Sept. 4, '65
47th..	Sept. —, '61	Anderson.......	James R. Slack.....	Dec. 13, '61.	Three years......	Oct. 23, '65
48th..	Oct. 2, '61..	Goshen.........	E. W. H. Ellis.....	Jan. 28, '62.	Three years......	July 15, '65
49th..	Sept. 23, '61	Jeffersonville...	John W. Ray.......	Nov. 21, '61.	Three years......	Sept. 13, '65
50th..	Sept. 24, '61	Seymour........	Cyrus L. Dunham...	....	Three years......	Sept. 10, '65
51st..	Sept. —, '61	Indianapolis....	A. D. Streight......	Dec. 14, '61.	Three years......	Dec. 13, '65
52d ..	Sept. —, '61	Indianapolis....	James M. Smith.....	Feb. 1, '62.	Three years......	Sept. 10, '65
53d ..	Oct. —, '61.	New Albany.....	W. Q. Gresham.....	Feb. 26, '62.	Three years......	July 21, '65
54th..	June —, '62	Indianapolis....	D. G. Rose........	June 10, '62.	Three months....	Sept. —, '62
54th..	Sept. —, '62	Indianapolis....	Fielding Mansfield...	Oct. —, '62.	One year........	Dec. 8, '63
55th..	June —, '62	Indianapolis....	John R. Mahan.....	June 16, '62.	Three months....	Sept. —, '62
57th..	Oct. —, '61.	Richmond.......	J. W. T. McMullen..	Nov. 18, '61.	Three years......	Dec. 14, '65
58th..	Oct. —, '61.	Princeton.......	Andrew Lewis......	Dec. 17, '61.	Three years......	July 25, '65

APPENDIX

Regiment Infantry	Date or Order or authority to organize.	Where organized—Rendezvous.	Colonel or Commandant by whom organized.	Date of Muster into service.	Period of Service.	Date of Muster out.
59th..	Oct. —, '61.	Gosport........	Jesse I. Alexander..	Feb. 11, '62.	Three years.....	July 17, '65
60th..	Oct. —, '61.	Evansville......	Richard Owen......	Mar. —, '62.	Three years.....	Mar. 21, '65
63d ..	Dec. 31, '61	Indianapolis....	James McManomy..	Oct. 3, '62.	Three years.....	June 21, '65
65th..	July 7, '62..	Princeton.......	Andrew Lewis......	Aug. 20, '62.	Three years.....	June 22, '65
66th..	July 7, '62..	New Albany.....	Roger Martin......	Aug. 19, '62.	Three years.....	June 3, '65
67th..	July 7, '62..	Madison........	Frank Emerson.....	Aug. 20, '62.	Three years.....	July 19, '65
68th..	July 7, '62..	Greensburg.....	Benj. C. Shaw.....	Aug. 19, '62.	Three years.....	June 20, '65
69th..	July 7, '62..	Richmond.......	Wm. A. Bickle.....	Aug. 19, '62.	Three years.....	July 5, '66
70th..	July 7, '62..	Indianapolis....	Benj. Harrison.....	Aug. 12, '62.	Three years.....	June 8, '65
71st..	July 7, '62..	Terre Haute....	R. W. Thompson...	Aug. 18, '62.	Three years.....	June 17, '65
72d ..	July 7, '62..	Lafayette.......	Chris. Miller.......	Aug. 16, '62.	Three years.....	June 26, '65
73d ..	July 7, '62..	South Bend....	Thos. S. Stanfield..	Aug. 16, '62.	Three years.....	July 1, '65
74th..	July 7, '62..	Fort Wayne....	Wm. Williams.....	Aug. 21, '62.	Three years.....	June 9, '65
75th..	July 7, '62..	Wabash........	John U. Pettit.....	Aug. 19, '62.	Three years.....	June 8, '65
76th..	July 16, '62.	Indianapolis....	James Gavin.......	July 20, '62.	Thirty days.....	Aug. —, '62
78th..	July 16, '62.	Indianapolis....	Wm. L. Farrow....	Aug. 5, '62.	Sixty days......	Oct. —, '62
79th..	Aug. 13, '62	Indianapolis....	Fred Knefler......	Sept. 2, '62.	Three years.....	June 11, '65
80th..	Aug. 13, '62	Princeton.......	Andrew Lewis......	Sept. 5, '62.	Three years.....	June 22, '65
81st..	Aug. 13, '62	New Albany.....	Wm. W. Caldwell..	Aug. 29, '62.	Three years.....	June 13, '65
82d ..	Aug. 13, '62	Madison........	Morton C. Hunter..	Aug. 30, '62.	Three years.....	June 9, '65
83d ..	Aug. 13, '62	Lawrenceburg...	Benj. J. Spooner...	Sept. 9, '62.	Three years.....	June 3, '65
84th..	Aug. 13, '62	Richmond.......	Nelson Trusler.....	Sept. 3, '62.	Three years.....	June 14, '65
85th..	Aug. 13, '62	Terre Haute....	John P. Baird......	Sept. 2, '62.	Three years.....	June 12, '65
86th..	Aug. 13, '62	Lafayette.......	Chris. Miller.......	Sept. 4, '62.	Three years.....	June 6, '65
87th..	Aug. 13, '62	South Bend....	Thos. S. Stanfield..	Aug. 28, '62.	Three years.....	June 10, '65
88th..	Aug. 13, '62	Fort Wayne....	Geo. Humphrey....	Aug. 29, '62.	Three years.....	June 7, '65
89th..	Aug. 13, '62	Wabash........	Chas. D. Murray...	Aug. 28, '62.	Three years.....	July 19, '65
91st ..	Aug. 14, '62	Evansville......	John Mehringer....	Oct. 1, '62.	Three years.....	June 26, '65
93d ..	Aug. 14, '62	Madison........	DeWitt C. Thomas..	Oct. 31, '62.	Three years.....	Aug. 10, '65
97th..	Aug. 14, '62	Terre Haute....	R. F. Catterson....	Sept. 20, '62.	Three years.....	June 9, '65
99th..	Aug. 14, '62	South Bend....	Thos. S. Stanfield..	Oct. 21, '62.	Three years.....	June 5, '65
100th..	Aug. 14, '62	Fort Wayne....	S. J. Stoughton....	Sept. 10, '62.	Three years.....	June 9, '65
101st ..	Aug. 14, '62	Wabash........	Wm. Garver.......	Sept. 7, '62.	Three years.....	June 24, '65
102d ..	July 8, '63..	Indianapolis....	Benj. M. Gregory...	July 10, '63.	Morgan Raid...	July 17, '63
103d ..	July 8, '63..	Indianapolis....	L. S. Shuler......	July 10, '63.	Morgan Raid...	July 17, '63
104th..	July 8, '63..	Indianapolis....	James Gavin.......	July 10, '63.	Morgan Raid...	July 17, '63
105th..	July 8, '63..	Indianapolis....	K. G. Shryock.....	July 10, '63.	Morgan Raid...	July 17, '63
106th..	July 8, '63..	Indianapolis....	Isaac P. Gray......	July 10, '63.	Morgan Raid...	July 17, '63
107th..	July 8, '63..	Indianapolis....	DeWitt C. Rugg....	July 10, '63.	Morgan Raid...	July 17, '63
108th..	July 8, '63..	Indianapolis....	Wm. C. Wilson.....	July 10, '63.	Morgan Raid...	July 17, '63
109th..	July 8, '63..	Indianapolis....	John R. Mahan.....	July 10, '63.	Morgan Raid...	July 17, '63
110th..	July 8, '63..	Indianapolis....	G. N. Fitch........	July 10, '63.	Morgan Raid...	July 17, '63
111th..	July 8, '63..	Indianapolis....	Robert Conover.....	July 10, '63.	Morgan Raid...	July 17, '63
112th..	July 8, '63..	Indianapolis....	H. F. Braxton......	July 10, '63.	Morgan Raid...	July 17, '63
113th..	July 8, '63..	Indianapolis....	Geo. M. Burge.....	July 10, '63.	Morgan Raid...	July 17, '63
114th..	July 8, '63..	Indianapolis....	Sam'l Lambertson..	July 10, '63.	Morgan Raid...	July 17, '63
115th..	June —, '63	Indianapolis....	John R. Mahan.....	Aug. 17, '63.	Six months.....	Feb. —, '64
116th..	June —, '63	Lafayette.......	Wm. C. Kise......	Aug. 17, '63.	Six months.....	Feb. —, '64
117th..	June —, '63	Indianapolis....	Thos. J. Brady.....	Sept. 17, '63.	Six months.....	Feb. —, '64
118th..	June —, '63	Wabash........		Sept. 16, '63.	Six months.....	Feb. —, '64
120th..	Sept. 21, '63	Columbus.......	Simeon Stansifer...	Mar. 1, '64.	Three years.....	Jan. 8, '66
123d ..	Sept. 21, '63	Greensburg.....	J. C. McQuiston...	Mar. 9, '64.	Three years.....	Aug. 25, '65
124th..	Sept. 21, '63	Richmond.......	John F. Kibbey....	Mar. 10, '64.	Three years.....	Aug. 31, '65
128th..	Sept. 21, '63	Michigan City..	Edward Anderson...	Mar. 18, '64.	Three years.....	April 10, '65
129th..	Sept. 21, '63	Michigan City..	Charles Case......	Mar. 1, '64.	Three years.....	Aug. 29, '65
130th..	Sept. 21, '63	Kokomo........	T. N. Stilwell.....	Mar. 12, '64.	Three years.....	Dec. 2, '65
132d ..	April 23, '64	Indianapolis....	Saml. C. Vance....	May 18, '64.	100 days........	Aug. —, '64
133d ..	April 23, '64	Indianapolis....	Robt. N. Hudson...	May 17, '64.	100 days........	Aug. —, '64
134th..	April 23, '64	Indianapolis....	James Gavin.......	May 25, '64.	100 days........	Aug. —, '64
135th..	April 23, '64	Indianapolis....	Wm. C. Wilson.....	May 25, '64.	100 days........	Aug. —, '64
136th..	April 23, '64	Indianapolis....	John W. Foster....	May 23, '64.	100 days........	Aug. —, '64
137th..	April 23, '64	Indianapolis....	Ed. J. Robinson....	May 27, '64.	100 days........	Aug. —, '64
138th..	April 23, '64	Indianapolis....	James H. Shannon...	May 27, '64.	100 days........	Aug. —, '64
139th..	April 23, '64	Indianapolis....	Geo. Humphrey....	June 8, '64.	100 days........	Sept. —, '64
140th..	Aug. 3, '64	Indianapolis....	Thos. J. Brady.....	Oct. 24, '64.	One year.......	July 11, '65
142d ..	Aug. 3, '64	Fort Wayne....	J. M. Comparet....	Nov. 3, '64.	One year.......	July 14, '65
143d ..	Dec. 20, '64	Indianapolis....	John F. Grill......	Feb. 21, '65.	One year.......	Oct. 17, '65
144th..	Dec. 20, '64	Indianapolis....	A. J. Hawhe......	Mar. 6, '65.	One year.......	Aug. 5, '65
145th..	Dec. 20, '64	Indianapolis....	James B. Mulky....	Feb. 16, '65.	One year.......	Jan. 21, '66
146th..	Dec. 20, '64	Indianapolis....	John A. Platter....	Mar. 3, '65.	One year.......	Aug. 31, '65
147th..	Dec. 20, '64	Indianapolis....	Isaac P. Gray......	Mar. 13, '65.	One year.......	Aug. 4, '65
148th..	Dec. 20, '64	Indianapolis....	James Burgess.....	Feb. 25, '65.	One year.......	Sept. 5, '65
149th..	Dec. 20, '64	Indianapolis....	R. N. Hudson.....	Mar. 1, '65.	One year.......	Sept. 27, '65
150th..	Dec. 20, '64	Indianapolis....	M. B. Taylor......	Mar. 9, '65.	One year.......	Aug. 5, '65
151st ..	Dec. 20, '64	Indianapolis....	John M. Wilson....	Mar. 3, '65.	One year.......	Sept. 19, '65
152d ..	Dec. 20, '64	Indianapolis....	Isaac Jenkinson....	Mar. 16, '65.	One year.......	Aug. 30, '65
153d ..	Dec. 20, '64	Indianapolis....	Charles S. Ellis....	Mar. 1, '65.	One year.......	Sept. 4, '65
154th..	Dec. 20, '64	Indianapolis....	James Park.......	April 20, '65.	One year.......	Aug. 4, '65
155th..	Dec. 20, '64	Indianapolis....	K. G. Shryock.....	April 18, '65.	One year.......	Aug. 4, '65

566 ADJUTANT GENERAL'S REPORT

Regiment Infantry	Date or Order or authority to organize.	Where organized—Rendezvous.	Colonel or Commandant by whom organized.	Date of Muster into service.	Period of Service.	Date of Muster out.
156th..	Dec. 20, '64	Indianapolis....	Chas. M. Smith.....	April 12, '65.	One year........	Aug. 4, '65
28th Colored	Dec. 3, '63.	Indianapolis....	Chas. S. Russell.....	April 20, '63.	Three years.....	Nov. 8, '65
Indep't Regm't	July 17, '62	Jennings Co.....	Kennedy Brown.....	July 17, '62.	Thirty days.....	Aug. 26, '62
Indep't Batt'l'n	July 16, '62	Camp Morton....	D. G. Rose..........	July 26, '62.	Thirty days.....	Aug. —, '62
Cavalry						
1st...	June 10, '61	Evansville......	Conrad Baker.......	Aug. 20, '61.	Three years.....	Sept. 6, '64
2d ...	Sept. —, '61	Indianapolis....	J. A. Bridgland.....	Dec. 9, '61.	Three years.....	July 22, '65
3d ...	Oct. 22, '61	Indianapolis....	Scott Carter........	Oct. 22, '61.	Three years.....	July 20, '65
4th...	July 7, '62..	Indianapolis....	Isaac P. Gray.......	Aug. 22, '62.	Three years.....	June 29, '65
5th...	Aug. 15, '62	Indianapolis....	Felix W. Graham....	Sept. 9, '62.	Three years.....	June 16, '65
6th...	July 7, '62..	Terre Haute....	R. W. Thompson.....	Aug. 18, '62.	Three years.....	Sept. 15, '65
7th...	June 24, '63	Indianapolis....	J. P. C. Shanks.....	Oct. 1, '63.	Three years.....	Feb. 18, '66
8th...	Aug. 20, '61	Indianapolis....	Thos. J. Harrison...	Aug. 29, '61.	Three years.....	July 20, '65
9th...	Sept. 21, '63	Indianapolis....	Geo. W. Jackson.....	Mar. 1, '64.	Three years.....	Aug. 28, '65
10th...	Sept. 21, '63	Columbus.......	Thos. N. Pace......	Feb. 2, '64.	Three years.....	Aug. 31, '65
11th...	Sept. 21, '63	Indianapolis....	Robt. R. Stewart....	Mar. 1, '64.	Three years.....	Sept. 19, '65
12th...	Sept. 21, '63	Kendallville....	Edward Anderson....	Mar. 1, '64.	Three years.....	Nov. 10, '65
13th...	Sept. 21, '63	Indianapolis....	G. M. L. Johnson....	April 29, '64.	Three years.....	Nov. 18, '65
Ind. Co	June —, '61	Indianapolis....	R. R. Stewart.......	July 4, '61.	Three years.....	*
Ind. Co	June —, '61	Indianapolis....	James R. Bracken...	July 21, '61.	Three years.....	*
Ind. Co	July —, '63	Crawford Co.....	Charles L. Lamb.....	Aug. 13, '63.	One year........	Jan. —, '64

*Assigned to 1st Cavalry.

Batteries						
1st...	Aug. 5, '61.	Evansville......	Martin Klauss.......	Aug. 16, '61.	Three years.....	Aug. 22, '65
2d ...	Aug. 5, '61.	Indianapolis....	David G. Rabb......	Aug. 9, '61.	Three years.....	July 3, '65
3d ...	Aug. 5, '61.	Connersville....	W. W. Frybarger....	Aug. 24, '61.	Three years.....	Aug. 21, '65
4th...	Sept. 15, '61	Indianapolis....	Asahel K. Bush....	Sept. 30, '61.	Three years.....	Aug. 1, '65
5th...	Sept. 16, '61	Indianapolis....	Peter Simonson.....	Nov. 22, '62.	Three years.....	Nov. 26, '64
6th...	Sept. 7, '61.	Evansville......	Frederick Behr......	Sept. 7, '61.	Three years.....	July 22, '65
7th...	Sept. 7, '61.	Indianapolis....	Samuel J. Harris....	Dec. 2, '61.	Three years.....	July 20, '65
8th...	Sept. 7, '61.	Indianapolis....	Geo. T. Cochran.....	Dec. 13, '61.	Three years.....	Jan. —, '65
9th...	Sept. 7, '61.	Indianapolis....	N. S. Thompson.....	Dec. 20, '61.	Three years.....	June 26, '65
10th...	Nov. 13, '61	Indianapolis....	Jerome B. Cox......	Jan. 25, '62.	Three years.....	July 10, '65
11th...	Nov. —, '61	Fort Wayne.....	A. Sutermeister.....	Dec. 17, '61.	Three years.....	Nov. 21, '64
12th...	Nov. —, '61	Jeffersonville....	Geo. W. Sterling....	Jan. 25, '62.	Three years.....	July 7, '65
13th...	Dec. 26, '61	Indianapolis....	Sewell Coulson......	Feb. 22, '62.	Three years.....	July 5, '65
14th...	Dec. —, '61	Indianapolis....	Meredith H. Kidd...	Mar. 24, '62.	Three years.....	Aug. 29, '65
15th...	Mar. —, '62	Indianapolis....	J. C. H. Von Sehlen.	July 5, '62.	Three years.....	June 30, '65
16th...	Mar. —, '62	Indianapolis....	Charles A. Naylor...	Mar. 24, '62.	Three years.....	July 5, '65
17th...	Mar. —, '62	Indianapolis....	Milton L. Miner.....	May 20, '62.	Three years.....	July 8, '65
18th...	July 7, '62.	Indianapolis....	Eli Lilly...........	Aug. 24, '62.	Three years.....	June 30, '65
19th...	July 7, '62.	Indianapolis....	Samuel J. Harris....	Aug. 5, '62.	Three years.....	June 10, '65
20th...	July 7, '62.	Indianapolis....	Frank A. Rose......	Sept. 19, '62.	Three years.....	June 28, '65
21st...	July 7, '62.	Indianapolis....	Wm. W. Andrew....	Sept. 9, '62.	Three years.....	June 21, '65
22d ...	July 7, '62.	Indianapolis....	Benj. F. Denning....	Dec. 15, '62.	Three years.....	July 7, '65
23d ...	July 7, '62.	Indianapolis....	James H. Myers.....	Nov. 8, '62.	Three years.....	July 3, '65
24th...	July 7, '62.	Indianapolis....	Joseph A. Sims.....	Nov. 29, '62.	Three years.....	Aug. 3, '65
25th...	July 18, '64.	Indianapolis....	Fred. Sturm........	Nov. 26, '64.	One year........	July 20, '65
26th...	May 3, '61..	Indianapolis....	John T. Wilder.....	June 12, '61.	Three years.....	July 19, '65

APPENDIX 567

INDIANA'S BATTLE RECORD

TOTAL NUMBER OF ENGAGEMENTS IN WHICH INDIANA TROOPS PARTICIPATED

Virginia	90
Tennessee	51
Georgia	41
Mississippi	24
Arkansas	19
Alabama	18
Kentucky	16
Louisiana	15
Missouri	9
North Carolina	8
Maryland	7
Texas	3
South Carolina	2
Indian Territory	2
Pennsylvania	1
Ohio	1
Indiana	1

Total States, 17.   Total Engagements..........................308

CHRONOLOGICAL LIST OF ENGAGEMENTS IN WHICH INDIANA TROOPS PARTICIPATED

1861
June 3, Philippi, Va.
June 11, Romney, Va.
June 26, Kelly's Island, Va.
July 11, Rich Mountain, Va.
July 12, Carrick's Ford, Va.
Sept. 11, Lewinsville, Va.
Sept. 12, Black River, Mo.
Sept. 12-13, Cheat Mountain, Va.
September 12-13, Elkwater, Va.
Oct. 3, Greenbrier, Va.
Oct. 3, Glasgow, Mo.
Oct. 4, Chickamacomico, N. C.
Oct. 21, Wildcat, Ky.
Oct. 21-22, Ball's Bluff, Va.
Oct. [12-25], Fredericktown, Mo.
Dec. 13, Allegheny, Va.
Dec. 17, Rowlett's Station, Ky.
Dec. 18, Blackwater, Mo.

1862
Jan. 19, Mill Springs, Ky.
Feb. 7, Fort Henry, Tenn.
Feb. 13-16, Fort Donelson, Tenn.
March —, Monterey, Ky.
March 3-14, New Madrid, Mo. (Siege)
March 6-8, Pea Ridge, Ark.
March 10 to April 17, Island No. 10, Miss. River, Tenn. (Siege)
March 22-23, Winchester, Va.
April 6-7, Shiloh (Pittsburg Landing), Tenn.
April 11 to May 30, Corinth, Miss. (Siege)
April 15, Pea Ridge, Tenn.
May 7, Summerville [Heights], Va.
May 8, McDowell, Va.
May 23, Front Royal, Va.
May 25, Winchester, Va. (Second)
May 31, Tuscumbia, Ala.
May 31, June 1, Fair Oaks, Va.
June 5, Fort Pillow, Tenn.
June 8, Cross Keys, Va.
June 9, Fort Republic, Va.
June 12, Front Royal, Va. (Second)
June 17, St. Charles, Ark.
June 18, Cumberland Gap, Ky.
June 25, Orchards, Va.
June 27, Gaines Mill, Va.
June 28 [30?], Glendale, Va.
June 29, Savage's Station, Va.
June 30, White Oak Swamp, Va.
July 1, Malvern Hill, Va.
July 7, Cotton Plant [Bayou Cache], Ark.
July 7, Round Hill, Ark.
July 9, Aberdeen, Ark.
Aug. 5, Baton Rouge, La.
Aug. 9, Cedar Mountain (Slaughter's Mt.), Va.
Aug. 9 [29-30?], McMinnville, Tenn.
Aug. [2], Austin, Miss.
Aug. 20, Edgefield Junction, Tenn.
Aug. 21, Gallatin, Tenn.
Aug. 24 [20?], Brandy Station, Va.
Aug. 27 [21?,] Gallatin, Tenn. (Second)
Aug. 28, Gainesville, Va.
Aug. 28, Madisonville, Ky.
Aug. 28, Muldraugh's Hill, Ky.
Aug. 28-30, Second Bull Run (Manassas Plains), Va.
Aug. 30, Richmond, Ky.
Aug. 30, McMinnville, Tenn. (Second)
Sept. 1, Chantilly, Va.
Sept. 8, Des Allemands [Bayou], La.
Sept. 9, Lone Jack, Mo.
Sept. 12, Vanderburg, Ky.
Sept. 14, South Mountain, Md.
Sept. 13-15, Harper's Ferry, Va.
Sept. 14-16, Munfordsville, Ky.
Sept. 17, Antietam, Md.
Sept. 19-20, Iuka, Miss.
Sept. 20, Panther Creek, Ky.
Sept. 22, Vinegar Hill, Ky.
Sept. 30, Russellville, Ky.
Oct. 3-4, Corinth, Miss. (Defense)
Oct. 5, Madisonville, Ky. (Second)
Oct. 5, Hatchie River, Miss.
Oct. 5, Versailles, Ky.
Oct. 8, Perryville (Chaplin Hills), Ky.
Oct. 10, Newtonia, Mo.
Oct. 28, Fort Wayne, Ark.
Nov. 27, Cane Hill, Ark.
Dec. 7, Prairie Grove, Ark.
Dec. 7, Hartsville, Tenn.
Dec. 9, Dobbin's Ford [Ferry], Tenn.
Dec. 11-13, Fredericksburg, Va.
Dec. 18, Lexington, Tenn.
Dec. 21, Davis' Mills, Miss.
Dec. 27-31, Chickasaw Bayou, Miss.
Dec. 29, Van Buren, Ark.

Dec. 31, Parker's Cross Roads, Tenn.
Dec. 31, '62 to Jan. 2, '63, Stone River (Murfreesboro), Tenn.

1863
Jan. 10 [16], Duvall's Bluff, Ark.
Jan. 11, Arkansas Post, Ark.
Jan. 30, Deserted Farm [House], Va.
March 5, Thompson's Station, Tenn.
March [20], Milton, Tenn.
March 29, Tallahatchie River, Miss.
April 29, Fitzhugh's Crossing, Miss. [Va.]
April 30, Dug [Day's] Gap, Ala.
April 30, Crooked Creek, Ala.
May 1, Port Gibson, Miss.
May 2, Blount's Farm, Ala.
May 2-3, Chancellorsville, Va.
May [1], Thompson's Hill, Miss.
May 12, Raymond, Miss.
May 14, Jackson, Miss.
May 16, Champion Hills, Miss.
May 17, [Big] Black River Bridge, Miss.
May 18 to July 4, Vicksburg, Miss. (Siege)
May 21 to July 8, Port Hudson, Miss. [La.]
June 3, Beverly Ford, Va.
June 11, Triune, Tenn.
June 21, Lafourche Crossing, La.
June 24, Hoover's Gap, Tenn.
June 26, Liberty Gap, Tenn.
July 1-3, Gettysburg, Pa.
July 4, Helena, Ark.
July 8, Boonsboro, Md.
July 9, Beaver Creek, Md.
July 10, Funkstown, Md.
July 11, Williamsport, Md.
July 9-16, Jackson, Miss. (Siege)
July 9, Corydon, Ind.
July 14, Falling Waters, Va.
July 19, Buffington Island, Ohio River, Ohio
July 22, Chester Gap, Va.
July 23, Manassas Gap, Va.
Aug. [1-3], Brandy Station, Va.
Aug. 4, Rappahannock Station, Va.
Aug. 28 [26?] Perryville, Indian Territory
Sept. 1, Cotton Gap, Ark.
Sept. 11, Dug [Day's] Gap, Ala.
Sept. 12, Black Springs, Ga.
Sept. 17, Brownsville, Miss.
Sept. 19-20, Chicamauga, Ga.
Sept. 20, Zollicoffer, Tenn.
Sept. 22, Blountsville, Tenn.
Sept. 29, Camp Sterling [Morganza], La.
Oct. 3, Thompson's Cave [Cove], Tenn.
Oct. 4, McMinnville, Tenn. (Third)
Oct 7, Farmington, Tenn.
Oct. 10, Blue Springs, Tenn.
Oct 11. Colliersville, Tenn
Oct 11, Rheatown Tenn.
Oct. 11, Henderson's Mill, Tenn.
Oct 14, Bristoe Station. Va.
Oct. 18, Charlestown. Va.
Oct. 21, Opelousas, La.
Oct. 25, Buffalo Mountain, Indian Territory
Oct 27, Brown's Ferry, Tenn.
Nov. 1, Philomont, Va. [1862?]
Nov. 2, Union, Va. [1862?]
Nov.2, Ashby's Gap, Va. [1862?]
Nov. 3, Upperville, Va. [1862?]
Nov. 3, Grand Coteau, La.
Nov. 4, Barber's Cross Roads, Va.
Nov. 7, Kingston, Tenn.
Nov. 11, Snicker's Gap, Va. [1862?]
Nov. 18, Campbell's Station, Tenn.
Nov. 16, Concord, Tenn.
Nov. 17, Mustang Island, Texas
Nov. 17 to Dec. 4, Knoxville, Tenn. (Defense)
Nov. 24, Lookout Mountain, Ga.
Nov. 25, Mission [Missionary] Ridge, Ga.

Nov. 27, Graysville, Ga.
Nov. 27, Ringgold, Ga.
Nov. 27, Fort Esperanza, Texas
Nov. 30, Mine Run, Va.
Nov. 31 [?], Mooresville, Ala.
Dec. 2, Walker's Ford, Tenn.
Dec. 14, Bean Station, Tenn.
Dec. 15, Powder Springs, Tenn.
Dec. 15, Skaggs Mills, Tenn.
Dec. 29, Talbott's Station, Tenn.

1864
Jan. 10, Strawberry Plains, Tenn.
Jan. 12, Massey [Mossy] Creek, Tenn.
Jan. 17, Dandridge, Tenn.
Jan. 27, Fair Garden, Tenn.
Feb. 6, Morton's Ford, Va.
Feb. [19], Egypt Station, Miss.
Feb. 22, Okalona, Miss.
March 14, Fort De Russy, La.
March 21, Henderson's Hill, La.
April 2, Terre Noir, Ark.
April 8, Sabine Cross Roads (Mansfield), La.
April 9, Pleasant Hill, La.
April 10, Prairie Leon [Prairie D'Ann], Ark.
April 10 to May 3, Suffolk, Va. (Defense) [1864?]
April 17, Red Mound, Ark.
April 17, Camden, Ark.
April 30, Mark's Mills, Ark.
May 5, Craig's Meeting House, Va.
May 5-6, The Wilderness, Va.
May 7, Tunnel Hill, Ga.
May 7, Moore's Plantation, La.
May 7, Wathel [Port Walthall] Junction, Va.
May 8, Buzzard's Roost [Gap], Ga.
May 8, Lauren Hill, Va.
May 8-10, Spottsylvania, Va.
May 9, Rocky Face [d] Ridge, Ga.
May 9, Varnell's Station, Ga.
May 10, Chester Station, Ga.
May 10-12, Po River, Va.
May 11, Yellow Tavern, Va.
May 12, Meadow Bridge, Va.
May 15, Resacca [Resaca], Ga.
May 17, Rome, Ga.
May 18, Bayou Dellaise [de Glaize], La.
May 18, Yellow Bayou, La.
May 19, Cassville, Ga.
May 20, Foster's Farm [Plantation], Va.
May 25, North Anna River, Va.
May 25, New Hope Church, Ga.
May 27, Allatoona, Ga.
May 27, Dallas, Ga.
May 30-31, Bethesda Church, Va.
May 30-31, Hanover C. H., Va.
June 3, Cold Harbor, Va.
June 3. Salem Church, Va.
June [23], Nottoway, C. H., Va.
June [25], Roanoke Station, Va.
June —, Honey Creek, Va.
June 10, Guntown, Miss.
June 13, White Oak Swamp, Va. (Second)
June 13, Riddle's Shop, Va.
June 14, Big Shanty, Ga.
June 15, Golgotha Church, Ga.
June 16. 1864, to April 3, 1865, Petersburg, Va. (Siege)
June 17, Lost Mountain, Ga.
June 17, Upperville, Va. (Second)
June 22, Culp's Farm [House], Ga.
June 27, Kenesaw Mountain, Ga.
July 3, Marietta, Ga.
July 4, Maryland Heights, Md.
July 7, Chattahoochie River, Ga.
July 19, Decatur, Ga.
July 20, Peach Tree Creek, Ga.
July 21 to Sept. 2, Atlanta, Ga. (Siege)

APPENDIX 569

July 28, Atchafalaya, La.
July 29-31, Fort Smith, Ark. (Defense)
July 31, Sunshine Church, Ga.
July 31, Newman, Ga.
July 31, Hillsboro, Ga.
Aug. 5-8, Fort Gaines, Ala.
Aug. 5-23, Fort Morgan, Ala.
Aug. 13, Hurricane Creek, Miss.
Aug. 15, Dalton, Ga.
Aug. 18, La Mavoo, Miss.
Aug. 19-21, Yellow House, Va.
Aug. 20, Red Oak Station, Ga.
Aug. 24, Halltown, Va.
Sept. 1, Jonesboro, Ga.
Sept. 2, Lovejoy's Station, Ga.
Sept. 7, Fort Wagner, S. C.
Sept. 15, Strawberry Plains, Va.
Sept. 18, Deep Bottom, Va.
Sept. 19, Opequan, Va.
Sept. 20 [28-30?], Chapin's Bluff [Farm], Va.
Sept. 20 [28-30?], Fort Gilmore [New Market Heights], Va.
Sept. 22, Fisher's Hill, Va.
Sept. 23, New Market, Va.
Sept. 25, Sulphur Branch Trestle, Ala.
Sept. 27, Pulaski, Tenn.
Oct. 1, Huntsville, Ala.
Oct. 1, Franklin, Mo.
Oct. 1-2, Athens, Ala.
Oct. 15, Snake Creek Gap., [Ga.]
Oct. 19, Cedar Creek, Va.
Oct. 26, Little River, Ga. [Ala?]
Oct. 26-30, Decatur, Ala. (Defense)
Nov. 3, Carrion Crow Bayou, La. [1863?]
Nov. 23, Griswoldsville, Ga.

Nov. 26, Columbia, Tenn.
Nov. 30, Franklin, **Tenn.**
Dec. 7, Murfreesboro, Tenn. (Defense)
Dec. 8, Little Ogeechee River, Ga.
Dec. 13, Fort McAllister, Ga.
Dec. 15-16, Nashville, Tenn.
Dec. [4], Overall's Creek, Tenn.
Dec. [7], Wilkinson's Pike, Tenn.
Dec. 10-21, Savannah, Ga. (Siege)
Dec. 28, Vernon [Verona], Miss.

1865
Jan. 14-15, Fort Fisher, N. C.
Feb. 2-3, Rivers' Bridge, S. C.
Feb. 19, Fort Anderson, N. C.
Feb. 20, Town Creek Bridge, N. C.
March 10, Wise's Forks, N. C.
March 16, Averysboro, N. C.
March 19, Bentonville, N. C.
March 27 to April 9, Spanish Fort, Ala. (Siege)
March 27 to April 11, Mobile, Ala. (Siege)
April 1, Ebenezer Church, Ala.
April 2, Five Forks, Va.
April 2 [6?], Sailor's Creek, Va.
April 2, Hatcher's Run, Va.
April 2, Selma, Ala.
April 2, Scottsville, Ala.
April 7-8, Appomattox, C. H., Va.
April 9, Clover Hill, Va.
April 9, Fort Blakely, Ala.
April [14], Morrisville, N. C.
April 16, West Point, Ga.
April 20, Macon, Ga.
May 13, Palmetto Ranche, Texas—last battle of the war

CAMPAIGNS IN WHICH INDIANA TROOPS PARTICIPATED

SIXTH REGIMENT—*Infantry*
Three months, Western Virginia, 1861
Against Bowling Green, 1861
Tennessee and Kentucky, 1862
Seige of Corinth, 1862
Against Murfreesboro, 1862
Against Chattanooga, 1863
East Tennessee, 1863-64
Against Atlanta, 1864

SEVENTH REGIMENT—*Infantry*
Three months, Western Virginia, 1861
Cheat Mountain and Shenandoah Valley, 1861
East Virginia and Maryland, 1862
Against Fredericksburg, 1862
Potomac Campaign, 1863-'64
Against Petersburg, 1864
Weldon Railroad, 1864

EIGHTH REGIMENT—*Infantry*
Three months, Western Virginia, 1861
Missouri, 1861
Arkansas and Missouri, 1862-63
Mississippi River, 1863
Against Vicksburg, 1863
Louisiana and Texas, 1863-64
Shenandoah Valley, 1864
Georgia, 1865

NINTH REGIMENT—*Infantry*
Three months, Western Virginia, 1861
Cheat Mountain, 1861
Kentucky and Tennessee, 1862
Siege of Corinth, 1862
Pursuit of Bragg, 1862

Against Chattanooga, 1863
Against Atlanta, 1864
Pursuit of Hood, 1864
East Tennessee, 1865
Louisiana and Texas, 1865

TENTH REGIMENT—*Infantry*
Three months, Western Virginia, 1861
Kentucky, 1861
Tennessee and Kentucky, 1862
Siege of Corinth, 1862
Pursuit of Bragg, 1862
Against Chattanooga, 1863
Against Atlanta, 1864

ELEVENTH REGIMENT—*Infantry*
Three months, Upper Potomac, 1861
Western Kentucky, 1861
Tennessee and Kentucky, 1862
Siege of Corinth, 1862
Tennessee and Arkansas, 1862-63
Against Vicksburg, 1863
Louisiana, 1863-64
Shenandoah Valley, 1864

TWELFTH REGIMENT—*Infantry*
Upper Potomac, 1861-62
Shenandoah Valley, 1862
Against Kirby Smith, Kentucky, 1862
West Tennessee, 1862
Pursuit of Bragg, 1862
Against Vicksburg, 1863
Chattanooga and East Tennessee, 1863
Against Atlanta, 1864
Sherman's March to the Sea, 1864
Through the Carolinas, 1865

THIRTEENTH REGIMENT—*Infantry*
Western Virginia, 1861
Shenandoah Valley, 1862
James River and Peninsula, 1863
Against Charleston, 1864
Against Petersburg and Richmond, 1864-65
Against Wilmington, 1865
North Carolina, 1865

FOURTEENTH REGIMENT—*Infantry*
Western Virginia, 1861
Shenandoah Valley, 1862
Eastern Virginia and Maryland, 1862-63
Against Fredericksburg, 1863
Gettysburg Campaign, 1864
Eastern Virginia, 1864

FIFTEENTH REGIMENT—*Infantry*
Western Virginia, 1861
Siege of Corinth, 1862
Pursuit of Bragg, 1862
Rosecrans' Campaign in Tennessee, 1863
Chattanooga and East Tennessee, 1863
East Tennessee, 1864

SIXTEENTH REGIMENT—*Infantry*
Upper Potomac, 1861
Shenandoah Valley, 1862
Against Kirby Smith, Kentucky, 1862
Mississippi River, 1862-63
Against Vicksburg, 1863
Louisiana, 1863
Red River, 1864
Louisiana, 1864-65

SEVENTEENTH REGIMENT—*Infantry, mounted*
Western Virginia, 1861
Kentucky and Tennessee, 1862
Siege of Corinth, 1862
Pursuit of Bragg, 1862
Rosecrans' Campaign in Tennessee, 1863
Chattanooga and East Tennessee, 1863
Against Atlanta, 1864
Pursuit of Hood, 1864
Wilson's Raid Alabama and Georgia, 1865

EIGHTEENTH REGIMENT—*Infantry*
Missouri, 1861
Arkansas and Missouri, 1862
Against Vicksburg, 1863
Louisiana and Texas, 1863
Shenandoah Valley, 1864
Georgia, 1865

NINETEENTH REGIMENT—*Infantry*
Potomac, 1861
Eastern Virginia and Maryland, 1862
Rappahannock, 1863
Gettysburg, 1863
Against Petersburg, 1864

TWENTIETH REGIMENT—*Infantry*
Maryland and North Carolina, 1861
Peninsula, East Virginia, 1862
Against Norfolk, 1862
Rappahannock, 1863
Gettysburg, 1863
Rapidan and Petersburg, 1864
Pursuit of Lee, 1865

TWENTY-FIRST REGIMENT — *1st Heavy Artillery*
East Maryland and East Virginia, 1861
Against New Orleans, 1862
Baton Rouge and Teche, 1862
Against Port Hudson, 1863
West Louisiana, 1863
Red River, 1864
Against Mobile, 1865
Louisiana and Gulf Coast, 1865

TWENTY-SECOND REGIMENT—*Infantry*
Missouri, 1861
Missouri and Arkansas, 1862
Siege of Corinth, 1862
North Mississippi, 1862
Pursuit of Bragg, 1862
Rosecrans' Tennessee Campaign, 1863
Chattanooga and East Tennessee, 1863
Against Atlanta, 1864
Sherman's March to the Sea, 1864
Through the Carolinas, 1865

TWENTY-THIRD REGIMENT—*Infantry*
Western Kentucky, 1861
Siege of Corinth, 1862
North Mississippi, 1862
Against Vicksburg, 1863
Sherman's Mississippi Raid, 1864
Against Atlanta, 1864
Sherman's March to the Sea, 1864
Through the Carolinas, 1865

TWENTY-FOURTH REGIMENT—*Infantry*
Missouri, 1861
West Tennessee, 1862
Arkansas, 1862-63
Against Vicksburg, 1863
Louisiana, 1863-64
Against Mobile, 1865
Texas, 1865

TWENTY-FIFTH REGIMENT—*Infantry*
Missouri, 1861
West Tennessee, 1862
Siege of Corinth, 1862
West Tennessee and North Mississippi, 1862-63
Sherman's Raid through Mississippi, 1864
Against Atlanta, 1864
Sherman's March to the Sea, 1864
Through the Carolinas, 1865

TWENTY-SIXTH REGIMENT—*Infantry*
Missouri and Arkansas, 1861-62-63
Against Vicksburg, 1863
Louisiana and Texas, 1863-64
Against Mobile, 1865
Mississippi, 1865

TWENTY-SEVENTH REGIMENT—*Infantry*
Maryland, 1861
Shenandoah Valley, 1862
Eastern Virginia and Maryland, 1862
Rappahannock, 1863
Maryland and Pennsylvania, 1863
Tennessee, 1863-64
Against Atlanta, 1864

TWENTY-EIGHTH REGIMENT — *First Cavalry*
RIGHT WING—EIGHT COMPANIES
Missouri, 1861
Arkansas, 1862-63-64
LEFT WING—TWO COMPANIES
Western Virginia, 1861
Against Fredericksburg, 1862
Lower Potomac, 1863
Eastern Virginia, 1864-65

TWENTY-NINTH REGIMENT—*Infantry*
Kentucky, 1861
Tennessee and Kentucky, 1862
Siege of Corinth, 1862
Pursuit of Bragg, 1862
Rosecrans' Campaign in Tennessee, 1863
Tennessee, Alabama and Georgia, 1864-65

APPENDIX 571

THIRTIETH REGIMENT—*Infantry*
Kentucky, 1861
Tennessee and Kentucky, 1862
Siege of Corinth, 1862
Pursuit of Bragg, 1862
Rosecrans' Campaign in Tennessee, 1862
Against Atlanta, 1864
Pursuit of Hood, 1864
Texas, 1865

THIRTY-FIRST REGIMENT—*Infantry*
Western Kentucky, 1861
Tennessee and Kentucky, 1862
Siege of Corinth, 1862
Pursuit of Bragg, 1862
Rosecrans' Campaign in Tennessee, 1863
Against Atlanta, 1864
Pursuit of Hood, 1864
East Tennessee, 1865
Texas, 1865

THIRTY-SECOND REGIMENT—*Infantry*
Kentucky, 1861
Tennessee and Kentucky, 1862
Siege of Corinth, 1862
Pursuit of Bragg, 1862
Rosecrans' Campaign in Tennessee, 1863
East Tennessee, 1864
Against Atlanta, 1864
RESIDUARY BATTALION
Tennessee, 1864-65
Texas, 1865

THIRTY-THIRD REGIMENT—*Infantry*
Eastern Kentucky, 1861-62
Against Cumberland Gap, 1862
East Tennessee and Kentucky, 1862-63
Against Atlanta, 1864
Sherman's March to the Sea, 1864
Through the Carolinas, 1865

THIRTY-FOURTH REGIMENT—*Infantry*
Kentucky, 1861
Against New Madrid, 1862
Missouri and Arkansas, 1862-63
Against Vicksburg, 1863
Louisiana and Texas, 1864
Texas, 1865

THIRTY-FIFTH REGIMENT—*Infantry*
Kentucky, 1861
Kentucky and Tennessee, 1862
Pursuit of Bragg, 1862
Rosecrans' Campaign in Tennessee, 1863
Against Chattanooga, 1863
Against Atlanta, 1864
Pursuit of Hood, 1864
East Tennessee, 1865
Texas, 1865

THIRTY-SIXTH REGIMENT—*Infantry*
Kentucky, 1861
Kentucky and Tennessee, 1862
Siege of Corinth, 1862
Pursuit of Bragg, 1862
Rosecrans' Campaign in Tennessee, 1863
Against Chattanooga, 1863
Against Atlanta, 1864
RESIDUARY COMPANY, A
Pursuit of Hood, 1864
East Tennessee, 1865
Louisiana and Texas, 1865

THIRTY-SEVENTH REGIMENT—*Infantry*
Kentucky, 1861
Tennessee and North Alabama, 1862
Rosecrans' Campaign in Tennessee, 1863
Against Chattanooga, 1863
Against Atlanta, 1864
RESIDUARY BATTALION
Sherman's March to the Sea, 1864
Through the Carolinas, 1865

THIRTY-EIGHTH REGIMENT—*Infantry*
Kentucky, 1861
Tennessee and Kentucky, 1862
Pursuit of Bragg, 1862
Rosecrans' Campaign in Tennessee, 1863
Against Chattanooga, 1863
Against Atlanta, 1864
Pursuit of Hood, 1864
Sherman's March to the Sea, 1864
Through the Carolinas, 1865

THIRTY-NINTH REGIMENT—*Eighth Cavalry*
Kentucky, 1861
Tennessee and Kentucky, 1862
Siege of Corinth, 1862
Pursuit of Bragg, 1862
Rosecrans' Campaign in Tennessee, 1863
Against Chattanooga, 1863
Against Atlanta, 1864
Rosecrans', McCook's, and Kilpatrick's Raids in Alabama and Georgia, 1864
Sherman's March to the Sea, 1864
Through the Carolinas, 1865

FORTIETH REGIMENT—*Infantry*
Tennessee and Kentucky, 1862
Pursuit of Bragg, 1862
Rosecrans' Campaign in Tennessee, 1863
Against Chattanooga, 1863
Against Atlanta, 1864
Pursuit of Hood, 1864
Texas, 1865

FORTY-FIRST REGIMENT—*Second Cavalry*
Tennessee and Kentucky, 1862
Siege of Corinth, 1862
Pursuit of Bragg, 1862
Rosecrans' Campaign in Tennessee, 1863
East Tennessee, 1863-64
Against Atlanta, 1864
RESIDUARY BATTALION
Wilson's Raid in Alabama and Georgia, 1865

FORTY-SECOND REGIMENT—*Infantry*
Kentucky, 1861
Kentucky and Tennessee, 1862
Pursuit of Bragg, 1862
Rosecrans' Campaign in Tennessee, 1863
Against Atlanta, 1864
Pursuit of Hood, 1864
Sherman's March to the Sea, 1864
Through the Carolinas, 1865

FORTY-THIRD REGIMENT—*Infantry*
Western Kentucky, 1861
Mississippi River, 1862
Arkansas, 1863-64
Kentucky, 1864

FORTY-FOURTH REGIMENT—*Infantry*
Western Kentucky, 1861
Tennessee and Kentucky, 1862
Siege of Corinth, 1862
Pursuit of Bragg, 1862
Rosecrans' Campaign in Tennessee, 1863
Against Chattanooga, 1863
East Tennessee, 1864-65

FORTY-FIFTH REGIMENT—*Third Cavalry*
RIGHT WING
Southern Maryland, 1861-62
East Virginia and Maryland, 1862
Rappahannock, 1862
Stoneman's Raid, 1863
Virginia, Maryland and Pennsylvania, 1863
Kilpatrick's Raid to Richmond, 1864
Wilson's Raid in Virginia, 1864
Sheridan's Raid, 1864
LEFT WING
Kentucky, 1861
Tennessee and Kentucky, 1862
Pursuit of Bragg, 1862
Rosecrans' Campaign in Tennessee, 1863
East Tennesse, 1863-64
Against Atlanta, 1864
Sherman's March to the Sea, 1864

FORTY-SIXTH REGIMENT—*Infantry*
Kentucky, 1861
Mississippi River, 1862
Arkansas, 1862-63
Against Vicksburg, 1863
West Louisiana, 1863
Red River, 1864
Central Kentucky, 1864-65

FORTY-SEVENTH REGIMENT—*Infantry*
Kentucky, 1862
Mississippi River, 1862
Arkansas, 1862-63
Against Vicksburg, 1863
West Louisiana, 1863
Red River, 1864
Against Mobile, 1865
West Louisiana, 1865

FORTY-EIGHTH REGIMENT—*Infantry*
West Kentucky and Tennessee, and Northern Mississippi, 1862
Siege of Corinth, 1862
Pursuit of Price, 1862
Against Vicksburg, 1863
Relief of Chattanooga, 1863
Tennessee and Georgia, 1864
Sherman's March to the Sea, 1864
Through the Carolinas, 1865

FORTY-NINTH REGIMENT—*Infantry*
Against Cumberland Gap, 1862
Eastern Kentucky, 1862
First Expedition to Vicksburg, 1862
Against Vicksburg, 1863
West Louisiana, 1863
Texas, 1863-64
Red River, 1864
Central Kentucky, 1864-65

FIFTIETH REGIMENT—*Infantry*
Kentucky and Tennessee, 1862
West Tennessee, 1862-63
Arkansas, 1863-64
Against Mobile, 1865

FIFTY-FIRST REGIMENT—*Infantry*
Tennessee and Kentucky, 1862
Siege of Corinth, 1862
Pursuit of Bragg, 1862
Rosecrans' Campaign in Tennessee, 1863
Streight's Raid through Alabama and Georgia, 1863
Tennessee and Georgia, 1864
Pursuit of Hood, 1864
Texas, 1865

FIFTY-SECOND REGIMENT—*Infantry*
West Tennessee, 1862
Siege of Corinth, 1862
Tennessee and Arkansas, 1863
Sherman's Raid through Mississippi, 1864
Red River, 1864
Pursuit of Forrest, 1864
Tennessee and Missouri, 1864
Pursuit of Hood, 1864
Against Mobile, 1865
Alabama, 1865

FIFTY-THIRD REGIMENT—*Infantry*
West Tennessee and North Mississippi, 1862-63
Siege of Corinth, 1862
Against Vicksburg, 1863
Sherman's Raid through Mississippi, 1864
Against Atlanta, 1864
Pursuit of Hood, 1864
Sherman's March to the Sea, 1864
Through the Carolinas, 1865

FIFTY-FOURTH REGIMENT—*Infantry*
Against Kirby Smith, Kentucky, 1862
Arkansas Post and Vicksburg, 1863
Louisiana, 1863

FIFTY-FIFTH REGIMENT—*Infantry*
Against Kirby Smith, Kentucky, 1862

FIFTY-SEVENTH REGIMENT—*Infantry*
Tennessee and Kentucky, 1862
Siege of Corinth, 1862
Pursuit of Bragg, 1862
Rosecrans' Campaign in Tennessee, 1863
Relief of Chattanooga, 1863
East Tennessee, 1863-64
Against Atlanta, 1864
Pursuit of Hood, 1864
Texas, 1865

FIFTY-EIGHTH REGIMENT—*Infantry*
Tennessee and Kentucky, 1862
Siege of Corinth, 1862
Pursuit of Bragg, 1862
Rosecrans' Campaign in Tennessee, 1863
Relief of Chattanooga, 1863
East Tennessee, 1863-64
Against Atlanta, 1864
Sherman's March to the Sea, 1864
Through the Carolinas, 1865

FIFTY-NINTH REGIMENT—*Infantry*
Mississippi River, 1862
Siege of Corinth, 1862
West Tennessee and North Mississippi, 1862-63
Against Vicksburg, 1863
Relief of Chattanooga, 1863
Tennessee and Georgia, 1864
Sherman's March to the Sea, 1864
Through the Carolinas, 1865

SIXTIETH REGIMENT—*Infantry*
Kentucky, 1862
First Expedition to Vicksburg, 1862
Against Vicksburg, 1863
Louisiana and Texas, 1863
Red River, 1864
Louisiana, 1864-65

SIXTY-THIRD REGIMENT—*Infantry*
Eastern Virginia, 1862
Kentucky, 1863
East Tennessee, 1864
Against Atlanta, 1864
Pursuit of Hood, 1864
Against Wilmington, 1865
North Carolina, 1865

SIXTY-FIFTH REGIMENT—*Infantry*
West Kentucky, 1862-63
East Tennessee, 1863-64
Against Atlanta, 1864

EIGHTY-FIFTH REGIMENT—*Infantry*
Kentucky, 1862-63
Tennessee, 1863

EIGHTY-SIXTH REGIMENT—*Infantry*
Against Kirby Smith, Kentucky, 1862
Kentucky and Tennessee, 1862
Pursuit of Bragg, 1862
Rosecrans' Campaign in Tennessee, 1863
East Tennessee, 1863-64
Against Atlanta, 1864
Pursuit of Hood, 1864
Tennessee, 1865

EIGHTY-SEVENTH REGIMENT—*Infantry*
Kentucky and Tennessee, 1862-63
Rosecrans' Campaign in Tennessee, 1863
Against Chattanooga, 1863
Against Atlanta, 1864
Pursuit of Hood, 1864
Sherman's March to the Sea, 1864
Through the Carolinas, 1865

EIGHTY-EIGHTH REGIMENT—*Infantry*
Against Kirby Smith, Kentucky, 1862
Kentucky and Tennessee, 1862
Pursuit of Bragg, 1862
Rosecrans' Campaign in Tennessee, 1863
Against Atlanta, 1864
Pursuit of Hood, 1864
Sherman's March to the Sea, 1864
Through the Carolinas, 1865

EIGHTY-NINTH REGIMENT—*Infantry*
Kentucky, 1862
West Tennessee and North Mississippi, 1863
Sherman's Raid through Mississippi, 1864
Red River, 1864
Pursuit of Price, Missouri, 1864
Pursuit of Hood, 1864
Against Mobile, 1865
Alabama, 1865

NINETIETH REGIMENT—*Fifth Cavalry*
Indiana Border, 1862-63
Kentucky, 1863
Pursuit of Morgan, 1863
East Tennessee, 1863-64
Against Atlanta, 1864
Stoneman's Raid in Georgia, 1864
Tennessee, 1864
Kentucky and Tennessee, 1865

NINETY-FIRST REGIMENT—*Infantry*
Kentucky, 1862-63
East Tennessee, 1864
Against Atlanta, 1864
Pursuit of Hood, 1864
Against Wilmington, 1865
North Carolina, 1865

NINETY-THIRD REGIMENT—*Infantry*
West Tennessee and North Mississippi, 1862-63
Against Vicksburg, 1863
West Tennessee and North Mississippi, 1863-64
Pursuit of Price, 1864
Pursuit of Hood, 1864
Against Mobile, 1865
Alabama, 1865

NINETY-SEVENTH REGIMENT—*Infantry*
West Tennessee and North Mississippi, 1862-63
Against Vicksburg, 1863
Relief of Chattanooga, 1863
East Tennessee, 1863
Against Atlanta, 1864

Sherman's March to the Sea, 1864
Through the Carolinas, 1865

NINETY-NINTH REGIMENT—*Infantry*
West Tennessee, 1862-63
Against Vicksburg, 1863
Relief of Chattanooga, 1863
Pursuit of Bragg, 1863
East Tennessee, 1863-64
Against Atlanta, 1864
Sherman's March to the Sea, 1864
Through the Carolinas, 1865

ONE HUNDREDTH REGIMENT—*Infantry*
West Tennessee and North Mississippi, 1862-63
Against Vicksburg, 1863
Relief of Chattanooga, 1863
East Tennessee, 1863
Against Atlanta, 1864
Pursuit of Hood, 1864
Sherman's March to the Sea, 1864
Through the Carolinas, 1865

ONE HUNDRED AND FIRST REGIMENT—*Infantry*
Against Kirby Smith, Kentucky, 1862
Kentucky and Tennessee, 1862-63
Rosecrans' Campaign in Tennessee, 1863
Against Atlanta, 1864
Pursuit of Hood, 1864
Sherman's March to the Sea, 1864
Through the Carolinas, 1865

ONE HUNDRED AND SECOND REGIMENT—*Infantry*
Minute Men, Morgan Raid, 1863

ONE HUNDRED AND THIRD REGIMENT—*Infantry*
Minute Men, Morgan Raid, 1863

ONE HUNDRED AND FOURTH REGIMENT—*Infantry*
Minute Men, Morgan Raid, 1863

ONE HUNDRED AND FIFTH REGIMENT—*Infantry*
Minute Men, Morgan Raid, 1863

ONE HUNDRED AND SIXTH REGIMENT—*Infantry*
Minute Men, Morgan Raid, 1863

ONE HUNDRED AND EIGHTH REGIMENT—*Infantry*
Minute Men, Morgan Raid, 1863

ONE HUNDRED AND NINTH REGIMENT—*Infantry*
Minute Men, Morgan Raid, 1863

ONE HUNDRED AND TENTH REGIMENT—*Infantry*
Minute Men, Morgan Raid, 1863

ONE HUNDRED AND ELEVENTH REGIMENT—*Infantry*
Minute Men, Morgan Raid, 1863

ONE HUNDRED AND TWELFTH REGIMENT—*Infantry*
Minute Men, Morgan Raid, 1863

ONE HUNDRED AND THIRTEENTH REGIMENT—*Infantry*
Minute Men, Morgan Raid, 1863

ONE HUNDRED AND FOURTEENTH REGIMENT—*Infantry*
Minute Men, Morgan Raid, 1863

APPENDIX 573

Pursuit of Hood, 1864
Against Wilmington, 1865
North Carolina, 1865

SIXTY-SIXTH REGIMENT—*Infantry*
Against Kirby Smith, Kentucky, 1862
West Tennessee, 1863-64
Against Atlanta, 1864
Sherman's March to the Sea, 1864
Through the Carolinas, 1865

SIXTY-SEVENTH REGIMENT—*Infantry*
Kentucky, 1862
First Expedition against Vicksburg, 1862
Against Vicksburg, 1863
West Louisiana and Texas, 1863-64
Red River, 1864
Against Mobile, 1864
West Louisiana, 1864
Mississippi River, 1864
Texas, 1865

SIXTY-EIGHTH REGIMENT—*Infantry*
Kentucky, 1862
Rosecrans' Campaign in Tennessee, 1863
East Tennessee, 1863-64
Tennessee and Georgia, 1864
Pursuit of Hood, 1864
Tennessee, 1865

SIXTY-NINTH REGIMENT—*Infantry*
Against Kirby Smith in Kentucky, 1862
First Expedition against Vicksburg, 1862
Against Vicksburg, 1863
Louisiana and Texas, 1863-64
Red River, 1864
Against Mobile, 1864-65
Alabama, 1865

SEVENTIETH REGIMENT—*Infantry*
Kentucky and Tennessee, 1862-63
Against Atlanta, 1864
Sherman's March to the Sea, 1864
Through the Carolinas, 1865

SEVENTY - FIRST REGIMENT — *Sixth Cavalry*
Against Kirby Smith in Kentucky, 1862
East Tennessee, 1863-64
Against Atlanta, 1864
Stoneman's Raid in Georgia, 1864
Rousseau's Raid in Alabama, 1864
Pursuit of Hood, 1864
Tennessee, 1865

SEVENTY - SECOND REGIMENT—*Mounted Infantry*
Kentucky and Tennessee, 1862-63
Rosecrans' Campaign in Tennessee, 1863
West Tennessee and North Mississippi, 1864
Against Atlanta, 1864
Wilson's Raid through Alabama and Georgia, 1865
Pursuit of Jeff Davis, 1865

SEVENTY-THIRD REGIMENT—*Infantry*
Kentucky and Tennessee, 1862
Rosecrans' Campaign in Tennessee, 1863
Streight's Raid in Alabama and Georgia, 1863
Tennessee and Alabama, 1864-65

SEVENTY-FOURTH REGIMENT—*Infantry*
Kentucky and Tennessee, 1862-63
Pursuit of Bragg, 1862
Rosecrans' Campaign in Tennessee, 1863
Relief of Chattanooga, 1863
Against Atlanta, 1864
Sherman's March to the Sea, 1864
Through the Carolinas, 1865

SEVENTY-FIFTH REGIMENT—*Infantry*
Kentucky and Tennessee, 1862-63
Pursuit of Bragg, 1862
Rosecrans' Campaign in Tennessee, 1863
Against Atlanta, 1864
Pursuit of Hood, 1864
Sherman's March to the Sea, 1864
Through the Carolinas, 1865

SEVENTY-SIXTH REGIMENT—*Infantry*
Against guerrillas in Kentucky, 1862

SEVENTY-SEVENTH REGIMENT—*Fourth Cavalry*
Kentucky, 1862
Rosecrans' Campaign in Tennessee, 1863
East Tennessee, 1863-64
Against Atlanta, 1864
McCook's Raid in Georgia, 1864
Wilson's Raid in Alabama and Georgia, 1865

SEVENTY-EIGHTH REGIMENT—*Infantry*
Against guerrillas in Kentucky, 1862

SEVENTY-NINTH REGIMENT—*Infantry*
Kentucky and Tennessee, 1862
Pursuit of Bragg, 1862
Relief of Chattanooga, 1862
East Tennessee, 1863-64
Against Atlanta, 1864
Pursuit of Hood, 1864
Tennessee, 1865

EIGHTIETH REGIMENT—*Infantry*
Kentucky, 1862-63
Pursuit of Bragg, 1862
East Tennessee, 1863-64
Against Atlanta, 1864
Pursuit of Hood, 1864
Against Wilmington, 1865
North Carolina, 1865

EIGHTY-FIRST REGIMENT—*Infantry*
Kentucky and Tennessee, 1862
Pursuit of Bragg, 1862
Rosecrans' Campaign in Tennessee, 1863
Against Chattanooga, 1863
Against Atlanta, 1864
Pursuit of Hood, 1864
Against Atlanta, 1864
Sherman's March to the Sea, 1864
Through the Carolinas, 1865
Tennessee, 1865

EIGHTY-SECOND REGIMENT—*Infantry*
Kentucky and Tennessee, 1862
Pursuit of Bragg, 1862
Rosecrans' Campaign in Tennessee, 1863
Against Chattanooga, 1863
Against Atlanta, 1864
Pursuit of Hood, 1864
Sherman's March to the Sea, 1864
Through the Carolinas, 1865

EIGHTY-THIRD REGIMENT—*Infantry*
West Tennessee, 1862
First Expedition against Vicksburg, 1862
Against Vicksburg, 1863
Relief of Chattanooga, 1863
Against Atlanta, 1864
Sherman's March to the Sea, 1864
Through the Carolinas, 1865

EIGHTY-FOURTH REGIMENT—*Infantry*
Against Kirby Smith, Kentucky, 1862
Pursuit of Bragg, 1862
East Kentucky and West Virginia, 1862-63
Rosecrans' Campaign in Tennessee, 1863
Against Atlanta, 1864
Pursuit of Hood, 1864
Tennessee, 1865

APPENDIX 575

ONE HUNDRED AND FIFTEENTH REGIMENT—*Infantry*
East Tennessee, 1863-64

ONE HUNDRED AND SIXTEENTH REGIMENT—*Infantry*
East Tennessee, 1863-64

ONE HUNDRED AND SEVENTEENTH REGIMENT—*Infantry*
East Tennessee, 1863-64

ONE HUNDRED AND EIGHTEENTH REGIMENT—*Infantry*
East Tennessee, 1863-64

ONE HUNDRED AND NINETEENTH REGIMENT—*Seventh Cavalry*
West Tennessee, 1863
Grierson's Raid, Mississippi, 1863-64
Pursuit of Price, Arkansas and Missouri, 1863
Grierson's Raid through Mississippi, 1864-65
Louisiana and Texas, 1864-65

ONE HUNDRED AND TWENTIETH REGIMENT—*Infantry*
Against Atlanta, 1864
Pursuit of Hood, 1864
Against Wilmington, 1865
North Carolina, 1865

ONE HUNDRED AND TWENTY-FIRST REGIMENT—*Ninth Cavalry*
Tennessee, 1864
Pursuit of Hood, 1864
Mississippi, 1865

ONE HUNDRED AND TWENTY-THIRD REGIMENT—*Infantry*
Against Atlanta, 1864
Pursuit of Hood, 1864
Against Wilmington, 1865
North Carolina, 1865

ONE HUNDRED AND TWENTY-FOURTH REGIMENT—*Infantry*
Against Atlanta, 1864
Pursuit of Hood, 1864
North Carolina, 1865

ONE HUNDRED AND TWENTY-FIFTH REGIMENT—*Tenth Cavalry*
Tennessee and North Alabama, 1864
Pursuit of Hood, 1864
Against Mobile, 1865
Alabama and Mississippi, 1865

ONE HUNDRED AND TWENTY-SIXTH REGIMENT—*Eleventh Cavalry*
Tennessee and North Alabama, 1864-65
Pursuit of Hood, 1864
Missouri and Kansas, 1865

ONE HUNDRED AND TWENTY-SEVENTH REGIMENT—*Twelfth Cavalry*
Tennessee and North Alabama, 1864-65
Against Mobile, 1865
Alabama and Mississippi, 1865

ONE HUNDRED AND TWENTY-EIGHTH REGIMENT—*Infantry*
East Tennessee, 1864
Against Atlanta, 1864
Pursuit of Hood, 1864
North Carolina, 1865

ONE HUNDRED AND TWENTY-NINTH REGIMENT—*Infantry*
Against Atlanta, 1864
Pursuit of Hood, 1864
North Carolina, 1865

ONE HUNDRED AND THIRTIETH REGIMENT—*Infantry*
East Tennessee, 1864
Against Atlanta, 1864
Pursuit of Hood, 1864
North Carolina, 1865

ONE HUNDRED AND THIRTY-FIRST REGIMENT—*Thirteenth Cavalry*
Tennessee and North Alabama, 1864
Against Mobile, 1865
Alabama and Mississippi, 1865

ONE HUNDRED AND THIRTY-SECOND REGIMENT—*Infantry*
Tennessee and North Alabama, 1864

ONE HUNDRED AND THIRTY-THIRD REGIMENT—*Infantry*
Tennessee and North Alabama, 1864

ONE HUNDRED AND THIRTY-FOURTH REGIMENT—*Infantry*
Tennessee and North Alabama, 1864

ONE HUNDRED AND THIRTY-FIFTH REGIMENT—*Infantry*
Tennessee and North Alabama, 1864

ONE HUNDRED AND THIRTY-SIXTH REGIMENT—*Infantry*
Tennesse and North Alabama, 1864

ONE HUNDRED AND THIRTY-SEVENTH REGIMENT—*Infantry*
Tennessee and North Alabama, 1864

ONE HUNDRED AND THIRTY-EIGHTH REGIMENT—*Infantry*
Tennessee and North Alabama, 1864

ONE HUNDRED AND THIRTY-NINTH REGIMENT—*Infantry*
Tennessee and North Alabama, 1864

ONE HUNDRED AND FORTIETH REGIMENT—*Infantry*
Tennessee, 1864
Against Wilmington, 1865
North Carolina, 1865

ONE HUNDRED AND FORTY-SECOND REGIMENT—*Infantry*
Tennessee, 1864-65

ONE HUNDRED AND FORTY-THIRD REGIMENT—*Infantry*
Tennessee, 1865

ONE HUNDRED AND FORTY-FOURTH REGIMENT—*Infantry*
Shenandoah Valley, 1865
West Virginia, 1865
Maryland and Delaware, 1865

ONE HUNDRED AND FORTY-FIFTH REGIMENT—*Infantry*
Georgia, 1865-66

ONE HUNDRED AND FORTY-SIXTH REGIMENT—*Infantry*
Shenandoah Valley, 1865
West Virginia, 1865
Maryland and Delaware, 1865

ONE HUNDRED AND FORTY-SEVENTH REGIMENT—*Infantry*
Shenandoah Valley, 1865

ONE HUNDRED AND FORTY-EIGHTH REGIMENT—*Infantry*
Tennessee, 1865

ONE HUNDRED AND FORTY-NINTH REGIMENT—*Infantry*
Tennessee and North Alabama, 1865

ONE HUNDRED AND FIFTIETH REGIMENT—*Infantry*
Virginia, 1865

ONE HUNDRED AND FIFTY-FIRST REGIMENT—*Infantry*
Tennessee, 1865

ONE HUNDRED AND FIFTY-SECOND REGIMENT—*Infantry*
Shenandoah Valley, 1865
West Virginia, 1865

ONE HUNDRED AND FIFTY-THIRD REGIMENT—*Infantry*
Kentucky, 1865

ONE HUNDRED AND FIFTY-FOURTH REGIMENT—*Infantry*
Shenandoah Valley, 1865

ONE HUNDRED AND FIFTY-FIFTH REGIMENT—*Infantry*
Maryland and Delaware, 1865

ONE HUNDRED AND FIFTY-SIXTH REGIMENT—*Infantry*
Shenandoah Valley, 1865

FIRST BATTERY—*Light Artillery*
Missouri, 1861
Missouri and Arkansas, 1862
Against Vicksburg, 1862
Louisiana, 1863-64
Red River, 1864
Against Mobile, 1865

SECOND BATTERY—*Light Artillery*
Missouri, 1861
Kansas, 1862
Indian Territory, Arkansas and Missouri, 1862-63-64

THIRD BATTERY—*Light Artillery*
Missouri, 1861-62-63
West Tennessee, 1863-64
Sherman's Raid through Mississippi, 1864
Red River, 1864
North Mississippi, 1864
Pursuit of Price, 1864
Pursuit of Hood, 1864
Against Mobile, 1865
Alabama, 1865

FOURTH BATTERY—*Light Artillery*
Tennessee and Kentucky, 1862
Siege of Corinth, 1862
Rosecrans' Campaign in Tennessee, 1863
Tennessee, 1864-65

FIFTH BATTERY—*Light Artillery*
Kentucky, Tennessee and N. Alabama, 1861-62
Pursuit of Bragg, 1862
Rosecrans' Campaign in Tennessee, 1862
Against Atlanta, 1864

SIXTH BATTERY—*Light Artillery*
Kentucky and Tennessee, 1861-62
Siege of Corinth, 1862
Against Vicksburg, 1863
West Tennessee, 1863-64
North Mississippi, 1864

SEVENTH BATTERY—*Light Artillery*
Kentucky and Tennessee, 1862
Siege of Corinth, 1862
Pursuit of Bragg, 1862
Rosecrans' Campaign in Tennessee, 1863
Against Atlanta, 1864
Tennessee, 1864-65

EIGHTH BATTERY—*Light Artillery*
Tennessee and Kentucky, 1862
Siege of Corinth, 1862
Pursuit of Bragg, 1862
Rosecrans' Campaign in Tennessee, 1863
Tennessee, 1864-65

NINTH BATTERY—*Light Artillery*
West Tennessee and North Mississippi, 1862-63
Siege of Corinth, 1862
West Kentucky and Tennessee, 1863-64
Sherman's Raid through Mississippi, 1864
Red River, 1864
West Tennessee and North Mississippi, 1864
Pursuit of Price, 1864
Pursuit of Hood, 1864

TENTH BATTERY—*Light Artillery*
Tennessee and Kentucky, 1862
Siege of Corinth, 1862
Pursuit of Bragg, 1862
Rosecrans' Campaign in Tennessee, 1863
Tennessee and North Alabama, 1864-65

ELEVENTH BATTERY—*Light Artillery*
Tennessee and Kentucky, 1862
Siege of Corinth, 1862
Pursuit of Bragg, 1862
Rosecrans' Campaign in Tennessee, 1863
Against Atlanta, 1864
Tennessee, 1864

TWELFTH BATTERY—*Light Artillery*
Tennessee and Kentucky, 1862
Siege of Corinth, 1862
Rosecrans' Campaign in Tennessee, 1863
Middle Tennessee, 1863-64-65

THIRTEENTH BATTERY—*Light Artillery*
Kentucky and Tennessee, 1862-63-64
Tennessee, 1865

FOURTEENTH BATTERY—*Light Artillery*
West Tennessee, 1862-63
Siege of Corinth, 1862
Sherman's Raid through Mississippi, 1864
West Tennessee and North Mississippi, 1864
Pursuit of Hood, 1864
Against Mobile, 1865
Alabama, 1865

FIFTEENTH BATTERY—*Light Artillery*
Upper Potomac, 1862
East Tennessee, 1863-64
Against Atlanta, 1864
Pursuit of Hood, 1864
North Carolina, 1865

SIXTEENTH BATTERY—*Light Artillery*
Eastern Virginia, 1862
Maryland, 1862
Eastern Virginia, 1863-64

SEVENTEENTH BATTERY—*Light Artillery*
Maryland, 1862
Upper Potomac, 1862-63
Shenandoah Valley, 1864-65

EIGHTEENTH BATTERY—*Light Artillery*
Kentucky, 1862
Rosecrans' Campaign in Tennessee, 1863
East Tennessee, 1863-64
Against Atlanta, 1864
Pursuit of Hood, 1864
Wilson's Raid through Alabama and Georgia, 1864-65
Tennessee, 1865

NINETEENTH BATTERY—*Light Artillery*
  Kentucky and Tennessee, 1862
  Pursuit of Bragg, 1862
  Rosecrans' Campaign in Tennessee, 1863
  Against Atlanta, 1864
  Sherman's March to the Sea, 1864
  Through the Carolinas, 1865

TWENTIETH BATTERY—*Light Artillery*
  Tennessee, 1863
  Against Atlanta, 1864
  Pursuit of Hood, 1864

TWENTY-FIRST BATTERY—*Light Artillery*
  Central Kentucky, 1862
  Tennessee, 1863
  Pursuit of Hood, 1864

TWENTY-SECOND BATTERY—*Light Artillery*
  Kentucky, 1863-64
  Against Atlanta, 1864
  Pursuit of Hood, 1864
  North Carolina, 1865

TWENTY-THIRD BATTERY—*Light Artillery*
  Kentucky, 1863
  East Tennessee, 1863-64
  Against Atlanta, 1864
  Pursuit of Hood, 1864
  North Carolina, 1865

TWENTY-FOURTH BATTERY—*Light Artillery*
  Kentucky, 1863
  East Tennessee, 1863-64
  Against Atlanta, 1864
  Stoneman's Raid through Georgia, 1864
  Pursuit of Hood, 1864

TWENTY-FIFTH BATTERY—*Light Artillery*
  Tennessee and North Alabama, 1864-65
  Pursuit of Hood, 1864

TWENTY-SIXTH BATTERY—*Light Artillery*
  West Virginia, 1861
  Shenandoah Valley, 1862
  Central Kentucky, 1863
  East Tennessee, 1863-64-65

TWENTY-EIGHTH REGIMENT—*U. S. Colored Troops*
  East Virginia, 1864
  Against Petersburg, 1864
  Against Richmond, 1865
  Texas, 1865

INDEX

INDEX

Abolition of slavery, condemned by disloyalists, 309-10, 314-15; opposition to prosecution of war for, 338, 340, 343, 344, 347, 352, 353.

Adjutant General of Indiana, appointment to office, 6; assumes duties of paymaster, 487-88; order re recruiting, 70. *See also* Lazarus Noble; W. H. H. Terrell.

Alexander, Jesse I., 565.

Allen, Bob, 365, 366.

Allen, Cyrus M., 564.

Allen, Joseph E., 366.

Allen County, disloyal meeting, 338.

Allotment of soldiers' pay, provisions for, 467-73.

Allstott, John, 364, 365.

American Knights, Order of, 373-75; name changed, 375-76. *See also* Sons of Liberty.

Ames, Bishop Edward R., asks aid for soldiers' families, 445-46.

Ammunition, contraband trade in, 497-98; manufacture of, in state and U. S. arsenals, 199, 499 ff.; sent to Kentucky and Ohio, 192-93, 201; United States pays for that manufactured in Indiana, 503.

Anderson, Edward, 565, 566.

Anderson, Robert, of Union Army, 163, 165, 277, 279, 282.

Andrew, John A., 312.

Andrew, William W., 566.

Apple, Patterson, of Orange Co., 364, 365.

Appropriations, by counties, for soldiers' families, 447; by General Assembly, for military purposes, 11, 400, 478, 485, 522; for soldiers' families, 449-53.

Arbitrary arrests, protests against by rebel sympathizers, 304-6, 307-8, 315.

Arms, distribution to militia before 1861, pp. 1-2; inventory of, in Indiana, at beginning of war, 3, 516-19; captured by Confederates at Newburgh, 183; efforts to procure from Federal Government, 3-4, 519-20; lack of, in supplying troops for expedition to Kentucky, 196; in possession of disloyalists, 355, 358-59, 371, 373, 376, 377, 378, 388, 390, 391; purchase of, by state, 224, 522-29; payment for, 526-27; collection of, after the war, 534-35.

Army of the United States, enlistments from Indiana in, 98, 120, 133-34; Indiana not credited with all troops enlisted, 119-20; recruiting for, 72-74, 92-105; Hancock's First Army Corps, 96-98; 28th U. S. Colored Regt., 100, 563, 566.

Arsenals, location of in U. S., 514. *See also* Indiana State Arsenal; United States Arsenal.

Artillery, not organized by regiments, 116; number of men enrolled in, 134; officers denied promotions, 116; statistics re batteries, 563, 566; use of, against Morgan's raiders, 217-18, 219. *See also* Indiana regiments, artillery.

Athon, James S., 391.

Atkinson, Alonzo, 408.

Atkisson, Horace N., 194.

Aydelotte, Edward W., 138, 364.

(581)

Baird, John P., 565.

Baker, Conrad, provost marshal for Indiana, 67-68, 88-89, 90, 125, 128-29; governor, appoints Morgan Raid claims commissioners, 253; recommends payment of Morgan Raid claims, 254n; commandant, cavalry regt., 566.

Baker, Richard M., 246.

Bakery, state, 448-49, 535, 536-38.

Ballweg, Ambrose, 519, 530-31.

Banks, lend money for payment of bounties, 197; for purchase of arms, 528.

Banks, Nathaniel P., 31, 44.

Barbour, Lucien, 351.

Barlow, ———, quartermaster general of Ohio, 416.

Bartholomew County, disloyal meeting, 338.

Bates, Capt. ———, of Confederate Army, 266.

Bates, Allen R., 246.

Bates, Daniel F., of Indiana Legion, 136, 148-50, 184.

Bates, James E., 246.

Battles and sieges, list of those in which Indiana troops participated, 567-77; Bull Run, 179; Corinth, 439; Corydon, 229-31; Fort Donelson, 403, 418, 438, 545, 547, 549, 550; Fort Henry, Confederate prisoners from, 547, 549; Green River (Ky.), 283; Mill Springs (Ky.), 283, 438; Munfordsville (Ky.), 202; Panther Creek (Ky.), 151-53; Perryville (Ky.), 203; Pittsburg Landing, 439; Richmond (Ky.), 199-200, 284-85, 403; Sherman's "March to the Sea," 441; Shiloh, 438-39; Vicksburg, 440, 441.

Behr, Frederick, 566.

Belcher, Jerry, 366.

Belcher, Martin, 366.

Belcher, Tim., 366.

Benevolent institutions, failure of appropriations for, 331, 332, 333, 335; Morton obtains funds for, 334, 335; home for disabled soldiers, 461-65.

Benham, Capt. Henry W., of U. S. Engineers, 13.

Bennett, Thomas W., 389.

Benton, William P., 11, 564.

Bethel, Union, 188.

Bewsey, Samuel, 246.

Bickle, William A., 565.

Biddle, James, 217-18.

Bingham, Joseph J., 342n, 390.

Bisch, Victor, 147.

Blackburn, Dr. Luke P., 269-70, 271-72.

Blackford County, resistance to draft, 54, 359.

Blair, Austin, governor of Michigan, 45.

Blake, James, 43.

Bloomfield, Edmond, 246.

Blythe, James E., of Indiana Legion, 135-36, 140, 145, 146, 186, 192.

Boats, *see* Gunboats; Packets; Rams; Steamboats.

Bobbs, Dr. John S., 9.

Boone County, opposition to the draft, 359-60.

Bounties, bad effects of system, 73-74, 80-84; fraud in payment of, 85-88; recommendations re, 84-85; paid by Federal government, 33, 34, 35-36, 75-77, 95, 96; advantages of Federal over local, 80-85; attempt to equalize after war, 77; paid by local governments, 78-85, 127; paid to Negro soldiers, 77-78; state borrows money to pay, 197; as relief for soldiers' families, 444-45. *See also* Premiums.

Bounty jumping, 85-88, 563.

Bowles, William R., member, Knights of Golden Circle, 365; official, Sons of Liberty, 374, 379, 380, 384; arrest and trial, 385-93.

Bowling Green (Ky.), 146, 202.

INDEX

Boyd, Capt. ———, 238.
Boyle, Jeremiah T., comdr. District of Kentucky, 155, 186, 188, 189, 190; requests Indiana troops, 191-93, 195, 196; report on battle of Richmond, 200; order re prisoners taken in Hines Raid, 207; activities during Morgan's Raid, 218-19, 220-22, 223, 229, 235; asks aid of neighboring states, 284, 285.
Bracken, James R., 566.
Brady, Thomas J., 565.
Bragg, Braxton, 181, invasion of Kentucky, 51, 185, 190-91, 201-3; position of Army perilous, 209-11; defeated, 283.
Bramlette, Thomas E., governor of Kentucky, besieged, 258, 260; compliments Indiana troops, 261.
Brandenburg (Ky.), 161, 214.
Branham, A. K., 246.
Branham, David C., 228, 470, 478, 480.
Braxton, Hiram F., 565.
Breckinridge, Robert J., quoted, 284.
Breeden, Bryant, 205, 208.
Brett, Matthew L., 478.
Bridgland, John A., 566.
Bringhurst, Thomas H., 264.
Broadwell, Jacob S., 481.
Broon, Duval L., 366.
Brough, John, governor of Ohio, offers 100-day troops, 45-48; quoted on Indiana Sanitary Commission, 416-18.
Brower, Jeremiah H., 440.
Brown, Ben., 365.
Brown, George, 223.
Brown, Jesse J., 461.
Brown, Kennedy, of Indiana Legion, 136, 167, 193; of Indiana Volunteers, 566.
Brown, William L., 564.
Brown County, disloyal activities in, 338-39, 351-53, 372-73.
Browne, Thomas M., 253.
Browning, William R., 253.

Bruner, Mrs. ———, 352.
Buckner, Simon Bolivar, co-operates with rebels, 270, 271, 283, 497; movements in Kentucky, 146, 165, 210; part in projected insurrection, 377.
Buell, Don Carlos, comdr., Department of the Ohio, 101, 554, 556, 557; movements in Kentucky, 194, 195, 202-3, 283.
Bullard, Dr. Talbott, military agent, 403, 440, 441.
Bullitt, J. F., 374.
Burbridge, Stephen G., of Union Army, 256, 257, 259, 260-61.
Burge, George M., 565.
Burgess, James, 565.
Burkam, John H., of Indiana Legion, 136, 170, 228, 236.
Burnett, H. L., 385, 390.
Burnside, Ambrose, movements during Morgan's Raid, 218, 219, 221, 223, 224, 247; plans to attack Bragg, 210.
Burnside Barracks, Indianapolis, 136-37.
Bush, Asahel K., 566.
Buskirk, Samuel H., 481, 512.

Caldwell, William W., 565.
Cameron, Simon, secretary of war, 501.
Camp Joe Holt, Jeffersonville, 281.
Camp Morton, *as training camp,* commanders, 16; rendezvous for troops, 6, 15; *as prison camp,* 545-53; Legion performs guard duty, 142, 163, 165, 166, 167, 168, 192, 193; Veteran Reserve Corps performs guard duty, 104; prisoners members of Knights of Golden Circle, 371; plans to free prisoners, 374, 377, 387-88, 391.
Camp Sullivan, Indianapolis, rendezvous for troops, 15, 55.
Camp Tippecanoe, Lafayette, 15.
Camp Vigo, Terre Haute, 15.
Camp Wayne, Richmond, 15.

584 ADJUTANT GENERAL'S REPORT

Carney, H. H., 183.
Carrington, Henry B., *comdr., District of Indiana,* appointment, 554; exposure of Sons of Liberty, 139, 374, 376; organizes and instructs officers of Indiana Legion, 136-37, 138-39; order re threats to loyal Union men, 358; re restricting sale of arms, 373; organizes Legion forces against Confederate raids, 202, 225, 258, 263; leads brigade against Morgan's raiders, 245; offers relief for sufferers from Morgan's raid, 249; appointed chief mustering and disbursing officer, 196-97; *superintendent U. S. Recruiting Service,* announcement re recruiting, 95; letter from Gov. Morton, 94-95.
Carroll County, disloyal meeting in, 339.
Carter, Scott, 566.
Carter, Vincent, military agent, 413-14, 441.
Case, Charles, 565.
Casualties, Indiana Legion, 160, 216, 230, 246; in Indiana regiments, 563; in Hines Raid, 207; in Morgan's Raid, 213, 216, 230, 246; in battle of Richmond, 187n, 200, 284-85.
Catterson, R. F., 565.
Cavalry, companies of, in Indiana Legion, 143; enlistments in, discouraged, 21; number of drafted men in, 54; number of men enrolled in, 134, 563; need of, to repel Morgan's raiders, 219-20; officers, 566; recruits from Indiana Legion, 160; use of, 44, 188, 198, 219. *See also* Indiana regiments, cavalry; John H. Morgan.
Chapman, Charles W., 253.
Chenoweth, Maj. ———, rebel raider, 262.
Christian Aid Society, 414.
Churches, co-operate in furnishing relief for soldiers and their families, 399, 445-46, 448.

Cincinnati (Ohio), Confederate plan to capture, 190; saved from attack, 200-1, 285.
City Hospital, Indianapolis, used as home for disabled soldiers, 462.
Clark, George Rogers, 267.
Clark County, regt. in Indiana Legion, 163-64.
Clay County, disloyalists create disturbance **in, 339, 366-67.**
Clayton, William, 379; testimony in treason trials, 386, 387.
Clendenin, Robert E., of Indiana Legion, 205, 206, 207, 208, 209.
Clothing, for Indiana soldiers, 395-400, 527, 531 ff.; of prisoners, 436-37.
Cloverport (Ky.), 155, 156, 157.
Cobb, William, 356-57.
Coburn, John, 283, 462, 564.
Cochran, George T., 566.
Coffin, Park, plan to murder, 388-89.
Coffman, George, 364.
Colgrove, Silas, 385, 564.
Commissary general, Indiana, appointments to office, 6, 538, 542-43; duties, 9, 400-2, 538-44.
Commutation, payment of, to avoid draft, 54-55, 60-65.
Comparet, John M., 565.
Confederate Army, invasion of Kentucky, 190-91, 195, 196, 199, 200-3, 282; number of, at battle of Richmond, 200; situation of, responsible for Morgan's Raid, 209-11; defeated, **283, 373.**
Confederate prisoners of war, at Camp Morton, 545-53; at Terre Haute, 546, 547; at Lafayette, 546, 547; plan to release and arm, 374, 377, 387-88, 391.
Confederate States, effect of Northern disloyalty on, 291-93, 322-25; engage in contraband trade, 496-98; recruiting in, for Union Army, 72-74.
Conner, A. H., 456.
Conover, Robert, 565.

INDEX 585

Conscientious objectors, exempt from military duty, 54-55, 60-61.
Contraband trade, 496-98.
Cook, Jacob, 365.
Cook, Valentine, 364, 365.
Corby, Elias, 366.
Corson, R. R., military agent, 424, 427, 430-31.
Corydon (Ind.), battle of, 229-31.
Coulson, Sewell, 566.
Counties, disloyal meetings in, 338-42; make appropriations for relief of soldiers' families, 11, 447, 450-53; pay bounties to soldiers, 78-85.
Courts martial, of bounty jumpers, 88. *See also* Treason trials.
Cox, Jerome B., 566.
Cravens, James A., 233.
Cravens, James H., 239.
Crawford County, conspiracy against Union, 363-66; regt. in Indiana Legion, 159-60.
Craycraft, ———, of Rush Co., 360.
Credits for troops furnished, difficulties over, 83-84, 119-34.
Crispin, Silas, visits state arsenal, 502.
Crittenden, John J., governor of Kentucky, 267.
Crittenden, Thomas L., of Kentucky, 272, 274.
Crittenden, Thomas T., colonel, 6th regt., 11, 564.
Crook, George, 256.
Crooks, John W., of Indiana Legion, 136, 150-53.
Cruft, Charles F., 199, 564.
Cumback, Will, 462.
Cummings, ———, of Crawford Co., 365, 366.
Current, James H., of Indiana Legion, killed, 216.
Cuzzant, Jesse, 366.
Cynthiana (Ky.), 257, 260.

Daveiss, Joseph Hamilton, 267.
Davidson, Capt. ———, of Confederate States, 158.
Daviess County, resistance to the draft, 360.
Davis, E. A., 517.
Davis, Jefferson, 307, 323.
Davis, John, of Indiana Legion, 232.
Davis, William J., of Morgan's cavalry, 213-14.
Dearborn County, regt. in Indiana Legion, 170.
Decatur County, volunteers in Indiana Legion, 186-89.
DeHart, Richard P., 385.
DeKalb County, disloyal meeting in, 339.
Democratic State Central Committee, address to the people (1863), 342.
Denning, Benjamin F., 566.
Dennison, William, governor of Ohio, invited to confer with governors of Indiana and Kentucky, 272-74; urges defense of Kentucky, 279-80.
Deserters, Union Army, number of, 347, 563; from ranks of drafted men, 54; encouragement of, by disloyal groups, 345-48, 359, 360, 371, 382-83. *See also* Bounty jumping.
Dickerson, Capt. ———, 396.
Disabled soldiers, home for, 461-65.
Disloyalty, action to limit power of governor, 325; conspiracy in Orange and Crawford cos., 363-66; in Clay Co., 366-67; effect of, on Confederate States, 291-93, 322-25; effect of, on Indiana General Assembly (1863), 301-37; elements comprising, 289; emergence of, following military defeats, 299-300; extent of, in the North, 288-93; evidences of, in encouragement given to deserters, 345-48, 359, 360, 371, 382-83; in local meetings, 338-42; in secret societies, 300, 325 26, 368 ff.; in speeches of public men, 342-44; leads to violence, 349 ff.; objectives of disloyalists and methods used, 296-97; popular opposition to, 297; responsibility of, for Adam John-

Disloyalty (cont.)
son's raid, 182, 183-84; for Morgan's raid, 211-12; for Civil War and its protraction, 289-301; resistance to draft, 359, 360-61.
Dodd, Harrison H., officer of Sons of Liberty, 376, 379; arrest and trial, 378, 384-93.
Douglas, Samuel W., 231.
Douglas, Stephen A., 311.
Douglass, Denbo & Co., Corydon, 230-31.
Downey, Alexander C., of Indiana Legion, 136, 140, 192, 220, 228.
Draft, The, administration and operation, under act of 1862, pp. 18, 49-55, 70, 119; under act of 1863, pp. 23, 31, 55-68, 120, 124, 128-30; comparison of number of draftees with volunteers, 312; Negroes used for substitutes, 100; payment of bounties to avoid, 81, 84, 85-87; resistance to, 350, 353-54, 355, 359, 360, 363-66, 371, 383.
Duke, Basil, quoted on Kentucky neutrality, 275-76; writes history of Morgan's raiders, 210, 211, 214, 217, 230, 232n, 233, 235, 236, 237, 238, 242, 244, 248.
Dumont, Ebenezer, 11, 201, 564.
Duncan, Samuel E., 246.
Dunham, Cyrus L., 202, 564.
Dunning, Paris C., on military auditing committee, 481, 482.

Ekin, James A., U. S. Quartermaster, efforts in supplying troops, 405, 533; in relieving persons suffering from Morgan's raid, 249; provides for soldiers' home in Indianapolis, 456; provides for prison camp, 545, 551-52.
Elections, effect of disloyalists on, 372.
Elkins, William M., 352.
Ellis, Charles S., 565.
Ellis, E. W. H., 564.

Emancipation Proclamation, hostility to, 98-99, 309, 319, 339.
Emerson, Frank, 565.
Enfranchisement, of soldiers in field, opposed by disloyalists, 318.
Enlow, Frank, 366.
Erdelmeyer, Francis, 264.
Essary, Jesse C., of Indiana Legion, 157, 206, 207.
Evansville (Ind.), protection of from attack, 146, 148, 185, 193.

Fairleigh, Lt. Col. ———, 256.
Fairs, held to aid soldiers' relief fund, 408-9.
Farquar, William, of Indiana Legion, 217.
Farquhar, John H., of Indiana Legion, 226, 351.
Farrow, William L., 565.
Faulkner, William, of Indiana Legion, killed, 246.
Fayette County, resistance to the draft, 360.
Ferrace, Jacob, 230.
Finance, Bureau of, established, 334.
Finances, *state,* amount in treasury (1861), 3; amount allowed railroads, 492-93; crisis in, met by Gov. Morton, 332-36; creation of Bureau of Finance, 334; military auditing committees, 478-82; money borrowed to pay bounties, 197; to purchase arms, 528; premiums for recruiting paid out of state funds, 90-91; *local,* bonds issued to pay local bounties, 79-80; appropriations for relief of soldiers' families, 11, 447, 450-53. *See also* Appropriations; Military contingent fund.
Fines, of conscientious objectors, 54-55.
Fishback, William P., 100.
Fisher, Stearns, state paymaster, 485, 486-87.
Fitch, Graham N., 564, 565.
Fletcher, Calvin, agent to purchase arms, 523.

INDEX 587

Fletcher, Miles J., agent to purchase arms, 523; killed in railroad accident, 355, 415.

Flint, William, 246.

Floyd, John B., secretary of war, 4.

Floyd County, regt. in Indiana Legion, 162-63.

Food, supplied by state commissary general, 538 ff. *See also* Bakery, State; Indiana Sanitary Commission.

Foote, Henry S., 323.

Forgy, Theodore B., 263.

Forrest, Nathan B., raid in western Kentucky, 144, 374.

"Fort Robinson," 358.

Fort Sumter, 5, 289, 290, 292, 297.

Foster, John G., comdr., Department of the Ohio, 557.

Foster, John W., 189, 565.

Foster, Thomas, 536.

Fountain County, opposition to the war, 353-54.

Fournier, Charles, of Indiana Legion, 136, 155, 156, 158, 205-6.

Fraud, in drawing bounties, 85-88.

Freedmen's Bureau, 104.

Freeman, Fletcher, 360, 383.

French, W. E., military agent, 441.

Fry, James B., provost marshal general, letters received from Gov. Morton, 35-36, 63-64, 129-30.

Fry, Dr. Thomas W., 229.

Frybarger, W. W., 201, 202, 226, 258, 566.

Fulton County, disloyal meeting in, 339.

Gall, Alois D., 9.

Gardner, Green C., 357.

Garver, William, 565.

Gavin, James, of 134th regt., 186, 187, 188, 189, 242, 243, 245, 246, 565.

Gazlay, Carter, 564.

General Assembly
(1857), break up of, and failure to make appropriations, 335n;

(1861), proceedings and legislation: re militia, 2-3; collection of arms, 3;

(spec. sess. 1861), called, 7; message of Governor, 278-79; proceedings and legislation: appoints military auditing committees, 478, 481-82; re militia, 172-73; preparation for war, 11, 522; recruiting and organization of regiments, 14-15; state paymaster, 482;

(1863), actions of disloyal element in: refusal to accept governor's messages, 301-4; in support of rebel sympathizers against arbitrary arrest, 304-6, 307-8, 315; resolutions against arrest of rebel sympathizers, 304-8; favor compromise and concession with South, 308-17; oppose interference with slavery, 309-10, 318-20; oppose enfranchisement of soldiers in field, 318; attack method of paying soldiers, 318; against arming Negroes, 318-19; against employment of Negroes by Army, 320; vote down soldiers' resolutions for vigorous prosecution of the war, 320-22; effect of, on Confederacy, 322-25; attempt to create military board, 328-30; refusal to co-operate with loyal minority, 330-31; review of, 336-37;

bolt of minority, 330-31; fails to pass appropriations, 331; investigation of commissary dept., 540-41; investigation of state arsenal, 507-12; recommendation re land of U. S. Arsenal, 514;

(1865), proceedings and legislation: legalizes bonds issued for payment of bounties, 80; re payment of Morgan Raid claims, 251-52; provides relief for soldiers' families, 449-53; re soldiers' monuments,

General Assembly (cont.)
475; receives reports of adjutant general on credits for troops furnished, 120-28;
(1867), legislation re Morgan Raid claims, 252-53;
(1869), legislation re Morgan Raid claims, 254n.
General Military Agency, Indiana, 402-5.
Germans, participation in war, 187, 283.
Glenn, Caleb, 230.
Glenn, Rev. Peter, 218.
Golden, E. H., 365.
Gooding, David S., 246.
Goodwin, Thomas A., pay agent, 436, 470, 471, 472, 473.
Gordon, John, of Indiana Legion, killed, 246.
Gould, William, 352.
Governor, *see* Henry S. Lane; Oliver P. Morton.
Graham, Felix W., 566.
Grand View Battalion, 151.
Gray, Isaac P., 244, 565, 566.
Greene County, disloyal activities in, 339, 356-57.
Greenwalt, J. G., 459.
Gregory, Benjamin M., 565.
Gresham, Walter Q., 564.
Grill, John F., 565.
Grose, William, 462, 564.
Guerrillas, foment disloyalty in Indiana, 363, 377, 493-94; prisoners sent to Camp Morton, 553. *See also* Adam Johnson; Kentucky, border warfare.
Gunboats, used against Morgan's raiders, 157, 217-18, 223.

Hackleman, Pleasant A., 564.
Halleck, Henry W., decision re recruiting, 36; re promotion of officers to fill vacancies, 111-12; gives information on Morgan's last Kentucky raid, 256; participation in siege of Corinth, 439; telegrams to Gov. Morton, 545, 552.
Ham, Jason, military agent, 432, 433-34.
Hancock, Winfield S., First Army Corps, recruiting for, 96-98.
Hannaman, Dr. William, general military agent, 402, 405, 427, 432-33, 440, 443; provides temporary camp for soldiers' rest, 454-55; provides for Ladies' Home, 459; secretary of commission to provide Soldiers' Home, 461; trustee of Soldiers' Home, 465.
Hardin, John, 267.
Harris, Samuel J., 566.
Harris, W. H., at U. S. Arsenal, 514-15.
Harrison, A. I., 518.
Harrison, Alfred, 405.
Harrison, Benjamin, 565.
Harrison, Thomas J., 564, 566.
Harrison, William M., officer, Sons of Liberty, 379, 390.
Harrison County, regt. in Indiana Legion, 160-62.
Hart, ———, 246.
Hart, William E., 246.
Hartwell, Ephraim, 518.
Hascall, Milo S., 12, 564; comdr., Indiana District, 353, 554; assigned to defense of Indianapolis, 225-26; leads brigade against Morgan's raiders, 245.
Hawesville (Ky.), 154, 156, 157-58.
Hawhe, A. J., 565.
Hayden, John J., 55, 480.
Heath, Albert, 389.
Heffren, Horace, officer, Sons of Liberty, 365, 379, 380; arrest and trial, 385-90; testimony at treason trials, 390-91.
Hefner, Ferdinand, of Indiana Legion, killed, 246.
Heighfield, Thomas, 365.
Heintzelman, Samuel P., 554, 557.

INDEX 589

Henderson (Ky.), 147, 185, 192, 193.
Hendricks, John A., of Indiana Legion, 164, 482.
Heth, William, killed, 230.
Heustis, Zephaniah, of Indiana Legion, 170.
Hill, Henry B., 37, 465.
Hines, Cyrus C., 12, 13.
Hines, Thomas H., conducts rebel raid into Indiana, 164, 204-8; joins Morgan, 208, 214.
Hisey, Willison, 231.
Hobson, Edward H., pursues Morgan's raiders, 160, 221, 228, 230, 234, 239, 243, 248; calls on Gov. Morton for aid, 257, 286; surrenders to Morgan's raiders, 260.
Hoffman, W., commissary general of prisoners, 551-52.
Hollingsworth, William E., of Indiana Legion, 136, 146, 147, 184.
Holloway, W. R., secretary to Gov. Morton, 396; letter to Sec. of War, 93-94.
Holt, Joe, 276, 281.
Home for disabled soldiers, 461-65; for ladies, 459-60, 536, 538.
Home guards, organized, 10. *See also* Indiana Legion.
Hook, James, pay agent, 470.
Hooker, Joseph, 477, 555n, 557, 558.
Hoover, Martin, 246.
Hornbrook, Philip, 461.
Horses, impressed by Legion, 264, 266; seized by Confederates, 145, 156, 204, 208, 220, 231, 259; become property of U. S. after Morgan's Raid, 249-50; efforts to obtain payment for, 250-54n.
Horsey, Stephen, arrest and trial, 385-93.
Hospitals, at Indianapolis, for disabled and transient soldiers, 455, 462; at Jeffersonville, 463; at Newburgh, 182; services of military agents in, 427 ff.

Hovey, Alvin P., 142, 363; comdr., Indiana Military District, appointment, 555; address to people, 358-59; halts insurrection plans, 377; appoints commission to conduct treason trials, 385, 389; remits sentence, 393; organizes Indiana Legion, 141-42; leads expedition to Kentucky, 263-66; meets Lincoln's funeral train, 477.
Howe, Frank, military agent, 434.
Hubbard, Charles S., 465.
Hudson, Robert N., 565.
Huff, Samuel A., of Indiana Legion, 187.
Hughes, James, of Indiana Legion, 137, 140, 145, 150, 227, 238, 241, 242, 263, 264, 265-66.
Humphreys, Andrew, officer, Sons of Liberty, 379; arrest and trial, 361-62, 385-93.
Humphreys, George, 565.
Hunter, Morton C., of Indiana Legion, 136, 141; of 82d regt., 565.
Huntington County, disloyal meeting in, 339-40.
Hurst, Speer H., 231.
Hutchinson, David, military agent, letter of instruction to, 427-28.

Illinois troops, join in defense against Morgan's raiders, 226.
Indiana, Congressional districts, 122n; invasion of, by Hines, 204-8; by Adam Johnson, 181-84; by Morgan, 209-48; place in U. S. military administration, 554-58; number of troops furnished, 563; number of casualties, 563; number of desertions, 563; number of draftees compared to volunteers, 312n; troops credited to, 122-26; relations with Kentucky: border warfare, 143-45, 146-47, 149, 151-53, 154-58, 161-62, 164, 165-67, 168, 169, 175-76, 185-89, 262-66; prior to Civil War, 267-68;

Indiana (cont.)

gives aid to Union men and troops during the war, 147, 151, 154-55, 161, 184-89, 256-58, 268-69, 271, 278; sends troops to repel Morgan's Raid, 256-58, 261. *See also* General Assembly.

Indiana Legion, organized, 135-36, 176, 198-99; training school, 136-37; officers, 135-36, 137-39, 139-41; divisional organization, 139-41;

activities of regiments: 1st, 141-45; 2d, 145-48; 3d, 148-50, 184; 4th, 150-54; 5th, 154-58; 6th, 138, 160-62; 7th, 162-63; 8th, 163-64, 164-67; 9th, 167-68; 10th, 168; 11th, 168-70; 12th, 170; Crawford Co., 159-60;

casualties, 160, 207, 213, 216, 230, 246; commended for service rendered, 246-47, 261; expeditions into Kentucky, 186-89, 262-66; members enlist in Indiana regts., 142-43, 160, 161, 165-66; members guard rebel prisoners at Camp Morton, 142, 163, 165, 166, 167, 168, 192, 193, 553; needed in Kentucky to repel Kirby Smith, 192; opposes Hines raiders, 205-9; opposes Morgan's raiders, 159-60, 164, 215-47 *passim.*, 257-58, 528; payment for service rendered, 486-87; weakness of, 185, 219-20; arms distributed to, collected after the war, 534-35.

Indiana regiments,

appointment and promotion of officers: preferences of men considered, 108-10; in new organizations, 106-9, 113-14; to fill vacancies in old organizations, 109-13; medical officers, 114-15; artillery, 116; to be recorded in honorary musters at time of separation, 116-18;

artillery, batteries mustered, 198; re-enlistments in, 39; statistics re batteries, 563, 566; *see also* Artillery;

cavalry, re-enlistments in, 39, 123; statistics regarding, 563, 566; *see also* Cavalry;

credits for troops furnished, difficulties over, 119-34; discharges for sickness and disability, 101-2; drafted men in, 18, 54, 58-59; draw men from Indiana Legion, 142-43, 160, 161, 165-66; infantry, statistics regarding, 561-63, 564-66; method used in organizing, 19-20; in Mexican War, 2; misunderstanding over termination of service of recruits in older regts., 70-72; Negroes in, 266; number of men enrolled under different calls, 133-34; number of regts. organized and statistics concerning, 20, 133-34, 561-66; payment of troops, 483-84; praised for service rendered, 12-13, 200, 261; receive clothing and supplies from people of Indiana, 8-9, 395, 398-400; receptions on arrival home, 40-43; recruiting for, general, 18-20, 29-31, 69-74, 112-13; (1861), 6-10, 16; (1862), 22, 49-51; (1863-64), 22-23, 43-48, 55-60; reenlistments in, 38-39, 123, 124; Regular Army draws recruits from, 92-96; statistics on those in U. S. service, 561-63, 564-66; record of battles fought, 567-77; resolutions to General Assembly favoring vigorous prosecution of the war, 320-22; service in Kentucky, 199-200, 256-58, 264-66, 283-86;

organization and service of: *6th to 11th*, 11-13, 299; *12th to 17th*, 15-16, 17, 197, 199, 202; *32d*, 264, 265, 283, 377; *33d*, 283; *35th*, 228; *43d*, 258; *46th*, 263, 377; *50th*, 194; *51st*, 219; *53d*, 545;

INDEX 591

54th, 193; *55th,* 192, 199; *60th,* 202; *61st,* 546; *63d,* 219, 546; *66th,* 199; *67th,* 202; *68th,* 202; *69th,* 199; *70th,* 196; *71st,* 197, 199, 217-18, 219; *73d,* 219; *74th,* 202; *76th,* 187-89; *85th,* 201; *86th,* 201; *89th,* 202; *139th,* 257;

terms of service: 30 days, 133, 193; 60 days, 133; 3 months, 6-10, 11-13, 17-18, 133; 100 days, 44-47, 133; 6 months, 22, 133; 9 months, 133; one year, 14-16, 17, 133; 3 years, 16, 31, 32-36, 133; *see also* 561-66 of Appendix.

see also Artillery; Cavalry; Clothing; Food; Medical department; Pay; Six Regiments; Soldiers' Relief; Veteran Reserve Corps.

Indiana Sanitary Commission, organized, 394, 405-6; collection of supplies, 406-10; distribution of supplies, 407, 410-16, 429; articles distributed by, 412-13, 413-14; to whom distributed, 414; distributions by military agents, 429; relations with U. S. Sanitary Commission, 418-26; report of cash contributions and valuation of goods collected, 409-10; criticisms of, 414-15; opinion of, held by other states, 416-18; provision for shelter and hospital care for transient soldiers, 454-55; co-operates with pay agency, 471.

Indiana State Arsenal, 199, 499-513; locations of, 504-5n; reports on, 507-12, 512-13; sends ammunition to Kentucky and Ohio, 192-93, 201.

Indiana Supreme Court, upholds bond issue for payment of bounties, 80.

Indianapolis (Ind.), Lincoln's funeral train at, 476-77; provision for care of troops passing through, 454-58; receptions for home-coming troops, 40-41, 42-43; treatment of Confederate prisoners, 548-49; U. S. Arsenal located at, 514. *See also* Camp Morton.

Infantry, number of men enrolled in and statistics regarding, 134, 561-63, 564-66.

Ingram, John N., of Indiana Legion, 136, 163.

Invalid Corps, *see* Veteran Reserve Corps.

Irvin, James D., of Indiana Legion, 229.

Irvin, William J., of Indiana Legion, 161, 215.

Irwin, Joseph I., 461.

Jackson, David, 352.
Jackson, George W., 566.
Jackson County, disloyal meeting in, 340.
James, Enoch R., of Indiana Legion, 136, 142.
Jay County, deserters protected, 359.
Jefferson County, regt. in Indiana Legion, 164-67.
Jeffersonville (Ind.), reception of homecoming troops, 41-42; Confederate training camp, 281.
Jenkinson, Isaac, of Fort Wayne, 462, 565.
Jennings County, regt. in Indiana Legion, 167-68, 193.
Jobes, Dr. ———, 442.
Johnson, Adam R., leads raid on Newburgh, 147, 181-83, 185; plans second raid into Indiana, 262-63, 286; expedition of Indiana troops against, 262-66.
Johnson, Gilbert M. L., 566.
Johnson, W. G., 246.
Johnson County, disloyalty in, 359.
Johnston, Samuel M., of Indiana Legion, 159.
Jones, James G., commandant, 564; asst. provost marshal, 67-68, 125.

Jones, Oliver P., of Indiana Legion, killed, 246.
Jordan, Henry, of Indiana Legion, 138, 140; report on conspiracy in Orange and Crawford Cos., 363 ff.
Jordan, Lewis, Sr., of Indiana Legion, 136, 160-62, 220; fights Morgan's raiders, 215, 217, 229-30.
Judah, Henry M., 210.
Judiciary, support given disloyalists and deserters, 348, 361-62, 383. *See also* Indiana Supreme Court; United States Circuit Court.

Kansas troops, aid in defense of state against Morgan's raiders, 226.
Keeney, Harris, of Indiana Legion, 228.
Keigwin, James, of Indiana Legion, 163.
Kelley, Gen. ———, 396.
Kendrick, Oscar H., 482-84.
Kentucky, conditions in at outbreak of war, 268; urged to remain in Union, 278-79; defense of, urged by midwestern governors, 279-80; attempts to maintain neutrality, 274-83, 497; General Assembly votes to remain loyal, 277, 280, 282-83; engages in contraband trade, 496-97; invasion of, by Confederate Army, 190-91, 195, 196, 199, 200-3, 282; by Indiana troops, 185-89; Morgan's raids through, 191-96, 212-14, 255-61; recruiting in, for Confederacy, 185, 191, 262; for Union Army, 277, 280, 281-82; secession schemes, 269-74; treatment of Union men, 262, 270-71;
    relations with Indiana: prior to Civil War, 267-68; border warfare, 143-45, 146-47, 149, 151-53, 154-58, 161-62, 164, 165-67, 168, 169, 175-76, 185-89, 262-66; guerrillas from, foment disloyalty in Indiana, 363, 377, 493-94; loyalists ask and receive aid from Indiana, 147, 151, 154-55, 161, 184-89, 256-58, 261, 268-69, 271, 278, 524.

Key, George L., 229.
Kibbey, John F., 55, 565.
Kidd, Meredith H., 566.
Kilgore, Alfred H., 481, 482.
Kilroy, E. B., pay agent, 470.
Kimball, Nathan, 564.
Kirkpatrick, Samuel, 462.
Kise, William C., 565.
Kittredge, B., & Company, Indiana buys arms from, 224, 528.
Klauss, Martin, 566.
Knapp, Adam, of Indiana Legion, 163, 220.
Knefler, Fred, 565.
Knight, John, 365.
Knight, Lorenzo D., 365.
Knight, Perry, 365.
Knights of the Golden Circle, beginning of, 368; operation of, 361, 369-73; investigation of, by U. S. Circuit Court, 370-72; attempt to organize lodges in army camps, 347-48; in Orange and Crawford cos., testimony of members, 365-66; reorganized as Order of American Knights, 373. *See also* American Knights, Order of; Sons of Liberty.
Knightstown springs, purchased as site for soldiers' home, 464.
Knox, L. Gilbert, 193.
Knox County, disloyalty in, 355, 357-58.
Knoxville (Tenn.), 190.

Ladies' Home, Indianapolis, 459-60, 536, 538.
Lafayette (Ind.), Confederate prisoners at, 546, 547, 550.
La Grange County, disloyal meeting in, 340.
Lahue, George W., 229-30.

INDEX

Lakes, Department of the, 558.
Lamb, Charles L., 159-60, 566.
Lambertson, Samuel, 565.
Lane, David H., 226.
Lane, Henry S., governor, 2-3; elected to U. S. Senate, 3n.
Lang, Isaac, 230.
Lange, Albert, state auditor, 478-80.
Lankford, Larkin, 366.
Lawrence County, disloyal meeting in, 340.
Leavenworth (Ind.), 364.
Legion, *see* Indiana Legion.
Lemonds, Jim, 366.
Lewis, Andrew, of Indiana Legion, 140; commandant, 564, 565.
Lewis, James T., governor of Wisconsin, offers troops, 45-46.
Lewisport (Ky.), 155, 157.
Lilly, Eli, 566.
Lincoln, Abraham, 269; calls for troops (1861), 6, 178; (1863), 58; (1864), 58-59; accepts offer of 100-day troops, 46; opinion on recruiting in Kentucky, 282; abused by disloyal element, 300, 343; letters and telegrams received, from Gen. Boyle, 200; from Gov. Morton, 5, 24-25, 25-28, 28-29, 61-62; death, 475; mourned by Indiana, 475-77. *See also* Emancipation Proclamation.
Link, William H., of 12th regt., 564; killed, 200.
Lisk, James, 205.
Livingstone, Kinsey, 365.
Lomax, Junius, 364.
Lopp, Peter, 218.
Louisville (Ky.), threatened by Confederates, 165, 191, 192, 201-2, 256, 257.
Louisville and Nashville Railroad, track destroyed and train captured by Confederates, 194, 213.
Love, John, head of Indiana Legion, 135, 136, 137, 139, 186-89, 192, 194, 201, 227-28, 236, 237, 238; major, 1st brigade, **12, 13.**

Lozier, J. Hogarth, military agent, 408, 461.
Lucas, Thomas J., 385, 564.
Lupton, W. C., 480.
Lynch, ———, of Harrison Co., 364.
Lyon, G. W., of Indiana Legion, 159, 215, 216.
Lyon, ———, of Missouri, 292.

McCabe, John, 365.
McCarty, Eli, 360, 383.
McCarty, T. B., state auditor, report, 450-53.
McClellan, George B., 69, 524; comdr., Department of the Ohio, 556; attitude re Kentucky neutrality, 277-78, 497; asks defense of Kentucky, 279-80; letter of appreciation for Indiana regts., 12; in western Virginia campaign, 299; defeat at Richmond, 300.
McCormick, Capt. ———, of Indiana Legion, 358; suit against, 362.
McCrea, John, 253, 470.
McCune, Henry W., 465.
McDonald, Charles, 356.
McKees, John, 357.
McKinzie, Nathan, killed, 230.
McLean, William E., 385.
McManomy, James, 565.
McMickle, Union, 365, 366.
McMillan, J. W., 564.
McMullen, J. W. T., 564.
McNaughton, Findley, 208.
McQuiston, J. C., 565.
McWilliams, Jesse, 365.
Madison County, disloyal meeting in, 340.
Maginniss, E. A., of Indiana Legion, 162, 163, 220.
Magoffin, Beriah, governor of Kentucky, rebel sympathizer, 268, 270, 271, 274, 275, 277, 282, 283; refuses to furnish troops for Union, 269; proposes conference with governors of Ohio and Indiana, 272-74; resignation, 284.

Mahan, John R., 192, 244, 564, 565.
Malick, George W., of Indiana Legion, 136, 167.
Mann, John A., of Indiana Legion, 136, 142, 143, 144, 262-63, 266.
Mansfield, Fielding, 564.
Mansfield, John L., head of Indiana Legion, 135, 137, 140, 192, 226.
Manson, Mahlon D., of 10th regt., 564; at battle of Richmond, 199, 200; pursues Morgan, 235.
Mansur, Isaiah, commissary general, 6, 538-42.
Marion County, bounties paid to soldiers, 80; disloyalty in, 340, 344-45. *See also* Indianapolis.
Marshall County, disloyal meeting in, 340.
Martial law, invoked in Ohio River counties, 198.
Martin, Asinae, 443.
Martin, Calvin, of Indiana Legion, death, 160.
Martin, D. R., bank lends money to state, 528.
Martin, Roger, 565.
Martin, William T., of Confederacy, 152.
Martin County, disloyal meeting in, 340.
Mason, Charles H., of Indiana Legion, 136, 154.
Mason, Elisha, 365.
Mason, John, 365.
Mason, Tim., 365.
Massachusetts, militia, 178; quota of troops, 311-12.
Matson, John A., 462.
Mauckport (Ind.), 214.
Mayfield, F. F., of Dupont, 238.
Maysville (Ky.), 257, 259-60.
Mebringer, John, 565.
Medical department, Indiana volunteers, appointments and promotions in, 114-15; special surgeons and nurses, 438-43.

Meetings, expressive of disloyal sentiment, 338-42.
Mefford, Elliott, of Newburgh, 183-84.
Meigs, Montgomery C., 396, 397.
Mellett, Joshua H., 478.
Meredith, S. A., 436, 564.
Merritt, George, military agent, 413, 440, 441; in charge of Soldiers' Home, 455.
Merriwether, Clay, of Morgan's cavalry, 213.
Merriwether, James B., provost marshal, Crawford and Orange cos., 363.
Mexican War, Indiana regts. in, 2.
Michigan troops, sent to Kentucky, 199; in pursuit of Morgan's raiders, 221, 244-45.
Military administrative organization, Indiana's place in, 554-58.
Military agents for soldiers' relief, 402-5; duties and services, 411, 426-37.
Military auditing committees, 478-82; report on state arsenal, 512-13.
Military Board, effort to create, 328-30.
Military contingent fund, 400, 405.
Militia, organization from 1816 to 1834, pp. 1-2; distribution of arms to, 1-2, 516; necessity for organization, 172-73, 177-80; organized on volunteer basis, 84, 173-74, 175; act regulating (1861), 2-3, 11, 172-73; defects of law, 174-77; recommendations regarding, 2-3, 177-80; bill providing for reorganization (1863), 327-30; enrollment of (1832), 51; (1862), 51-53; exemption from service in, 52, 54-55. *See also* Indiana Legion.
Miller, Chris, 565.
Miller, John, 356.
Miller, John F., 564.
Miller, Joseph, 366.
Miller, Marion, 357.

INDEX

Milligan, Lambdin P., officer, Sons of Liberty, 379; arrest and trial, 385-93.

Milroy, Robert H., 11, 564.

Miner, Milton L., 566.

Minute-men, pursue Hines's raiders, 205, 208; help defend state against Morgan, 226, 227-28, 232, 233-34, 239, 241, 242-43, 244-45, 245-46, 246-47, 574. *See also* Indiana Legion.

Mississippi River, importance of, 26-28, 32.

Mitchell, O. M., comdr., Department of the Ohio, 556.

Monroe County, resistance to the draft, 360.

Montgomery, Alexander, U. S. quartermaster, 395, 396, 397, 398, 405.

Monuments, to soldiers, 474-75.

Moore, Col. ———, of Illinois, 188.

Morgan, G. W., 190, 195.

Morgan, John H., rebel raider, 185, 365; Kentucky raid (1862), 191-96; raid of Hines cavalry co., 204-8; raid into Indiana and Ohio, 209-48; last Kentucky raid (1864), 255-61, 374; recruits in Kentucky, 191; to aid in insurrection planned by Sons of Liberty, 377. *See also* Morgan's Raid.

Morgan, John T., of Indiana Legion, 136, 159.

Morgan, Thomas, killed, 213.

Morgan's Raid, origin and object, 209-12; raid through Kentucky, 212-14; crossing the Ohio, 214-18; preparations for resistance in Indiana, 144, 147, 150, 156, 159-60, 164, 218-19, 285-86, 528; route through Indiana, 229-44; route through Ohio, 244-48; battle of Corydon, 162; casualties, 213, 216, 229, 230; destruction and impressment of property, 218, 230-31, 232, 233, 238, 239, 242; payment of damages caused by, 248-54n; effect on recruiting in Indiana, 51; number of men participating in, 212-13, 214, 219, 221. *See also* John H. Morgan.

Morgan's Raid Commission, appointed to investigate and settle claims for damages, 253-54.

Morris, Thomas A., 201, 299; brigadier general, 12-13, 106n; quartermaster, 6, 530-31.

Morrison, John I., 253.

Morton, Oliver P., becomes governor, 3n; endeavors to obtain arms for state troops, 3-4, 219, 516-19, 519-20, 523; offer of troops (April, 1861), 5; military appointments and promotions, 6, 67, 106-18; lack of partisanship, 298-99; efforts to promote recruiting, 6, 7, 9-10, 14-16, 17-18, 21, 28-29, 35-36, 44-48, 88-90, 98, 112, 129-30, 195, 197-98; calls special session of General Assembly (1861), 7; urges vigorous prosecution of the war, 23-25, 28-29, 32; warns of Northwest Conspiracy, 25-28; honors returning soldiers, 40-42; activities re administration of draft, 51, 61-64; efforts to obtain discharge of new recruits in older regts., 71-72; disapproves recruiting in Confederate States, 72-73; opinion on issuance of Emancipation Proclamation, 99; issues orders to Indiana Legion, 143, 144, 149, 164, 166; praises Indiana Legion for defense against Morgan, 246-47; borrows money to pay bounties, 197; to buy arms, 528; places Ohio River counties under martial law, 198; sends troops to Kentucky, 185-89, 200, 256-58, 283-86; aid asked in defending Cincinnati, 201; visits troops in Kentucky, 203; activities during Morgan's Raid, 219-24, 244, 246-47; efforts to settle claims arising out of Morgan's Raid, 249-51; urges Federal Government to de-

Morton, Oliver P. (cont.)

fend Kentucky, 268, 524; earns title "guardian of Kentucky," 268-69; invited to confer with governors of Kentucky and Ohio, 272-74; urges Kentucky to remain in Union, 278-79; efforts of disloyalists to limit powers of, 316, 317, 325-31; solves financial crisis, 332-36; assassination planned, 350, 383, 387, 391, 392; actions taken for soldiers' relief, 395 ff., 410, 427-28, 438-43; provides for temporary care of soldiers at Indianapolis, 454-58; establishes Ladies' Home, 459-60; efforts to provide home for disabled soldiers, 461-65; establishes system of pay agents, 470-71; acts against contraband trade, 497-98; establishes Indiana arsenal, 499 ff.; urges location of U. S. Arsenal in Indianapolis, 513-14; interest in Confederate prisoners, 545, 550, 552; address to the people on financial crisis, 333-34; circular re transmission of part of soldiers' pay to their families, 468;

letters and telegrams received: from Gen. Boyle, 191, 192, 221-22; from Gen. Burbridge, 256; from Lt. Col. Fairleigh, 256; from James Gavin, 186; from Gen. Hobson, 257; from Gen. McClellan, 12; from B. Magoffin, 272; from Gen. Sherman, 43-44;

letters and telegrams sent: to Gen. Burbridge, 256; to Col. H. B. Carrington, 94-95; to James B. Fry, provost marshal, 35-36, 63-64, 129-30; to James Gavin, 187; to David Hutchinson, 427-28; to President Lincoln, 5, 24-25, 25-28, 28-29, 45-46, 61-62; to B. Magoffin, 272, 273; to Secretary of War, 35-36, 61-62, 117, 439, 522; to W. H. H. Terrell, 188-89;

messages to General Assembly: (spec. sess. 1861), on war preparation, 10-11; on need for arms, 521; (1863), not received, 301-4; on state arsenal, 506-7; (1865), on state arsenal, 512; on home for disabled soldiers, 462-63; (1867), 464;

proclamations: (Apr., 1861), call for troops, 6; (Oct., 1861), relief for soldiers, 398-400; (Nov., 1862), relief for soldiers' families, 445-46; (June, 1863), on obstructing the draft, 360-61; (Aug., 1864), in answer to address of Democratic State Central Committee, 342; (Apr., 1865), on death of Lincoln, 476.

Mount Sterling (Ky.), 257, 259.
Mount Vernon (Ind.), 142.
Mulky, James B., 565.
Mullen, Bernard F., 228, 546.
Munfordsville (Ky.), 202, 255.
Murray, Charles D., 385, 565.
Myers, James H., 566.

Nance, George, killed, 216.
Naylor, Charles A., 566.
Negroes, opposition to use of in army, 98-99, 320; payment of bounties to, 77-78; recruiting of, 98-100; number recruited in Indiana, 100, 563; use of, as substitutes for draftees, 100; mustered into U. S. service, 266, 563, 566; resolution against arming of, in South, 318-19. *See also* Abolition of slavery.
Nells, Enos, 366.
Netter, Col. ———, of Owensboro post, killed, 152.
New, John C., on military auditing committee, 481; quartermaster general, 533-34.
New Albany (Ind.), defense post, 202.
New Albany and Salem Railroad, damaged by Morgan's raiders, 233.

INDEX 597

Newburgh (Ind.), Adam Johnson's raid on, 147, 148-49, 181-84, 194, 285; hospital and commissary stores, 182.
Newkirk, Benton, 365.
Newkirk, Joel, 366.
Newkirk, Jonathan, 366.
Newman, Joel, 246.
Newspapers, express opposition to the war, 344-45.
New York, militia, 178.
Niblack, William E., 481.
Nicholson, William, 246.
Niles, John B., 462.
Noble, Lazarus, 63; adjutant general, relations with Indiana Legion, 164, 258; reports on credits for reenlisted veterans, 124, 125, 126; letter re treatment of prisoners of war, 550-51.
Noble County, disloyalty in, 353.
Northern Department, U. S. military district, 557.
Northwestern Confederacy, projected, 25-28, 307, 384.
Nurses, 442-43.

Ohio, Morgan's raiders in, 243-44, 247-48; sends troops to Kentucky, 199, 200. *See also* Cincinnati.
Ohio, Department of the, 554, 555-57, 557-58.
Ohio County, regt. in Indiana Legion, 168-69.
Orange County, opposition to abolitionism, 344; conspiracy against the Union, 363-66.
Ord, Edward O. C., comdr., Department of the Ohio, 557.
Ormsby, Oliver, of Indiana Legion, 136.
Orphans, of soldiers and sailors, home for, 465.
Orth, Godlove S., of Indiana Legion, 187, 189.
Osborn, William, 356.

Owen, Richard, in charge of Camp Morton, 545, 553; commandant, 60th regt., 565.
Owen, Robert Dale, appointed agent to purchase arms, 397, 503, 514, 524-25, 533; report on purchases made, 525-29.
Owensboro (Ky.), 147, 149, 151, 152, 153.

Pace, Thomas N., 566.
Packets, seized by Confederates, 158.
Paducah (Ky.), 144.
Paine, Gen. ———, 266.
Panther Creek, battle of, 151-53.
Paoli (Ind.), 205, 232.
Paris (Ky.), 257.
Park, James, 565.
Parker, L. C., 151.
Parrish, D. W., 246.
Parsons, J. J., 390.
Parvin, Dr. Theophilus, 403.
Patriotism, manifested at opening of war, 7-8; during Morgan's Raid, 224-26; evidenced in opposition to disloyalty, 297-98.
Pattison, Thomas, 564.
Pay, of soldiers, slowness of, used by disloyalists to undermine morale, 318; handled by General Military Agency, 404, 428-29, 434-36; problems of conveyance, 467-68; allotment system evolved, 468-73; rate, 485; services of state paymaster, 482-86.
Pay agency, established by Gov. Morton, 470-73.
Paymaster, state, office created, 11, 482-88; duties transferred to adjutant general, 487.
Peace propositions, advanced by governor of Kentucky, 272-74; advanced by disloyalists, 308-17, 321, 338-42.
Pennock, Alexander M., of U. S. Navy, 188, 223.

Perkins, Samuel E., 351.
Perry County, regt. in Indiana Legion, 154-59.
Perryville (Ky.), battle of, 203.
Pettit, John U., 462, 565; speaker of the House, letter from adjutant general, 484-85.
Pfrimmer, Jacob S., of Indiana Legion, 216-17.
Pile, John, 246.
Pitcher, Thomas G., provost marshal for Indiana, 68, 126, 127, 131, 132; appointed comdr., Indiana District, 555.
Pitman, Mary Ann, revelations as spy, 375.
Platter, John A., 170, 565.
Pope, John, comdr., Department of the Lakes, 558.
Porter, John, of Indiana Legion, killed, 246.
Posey County, disloyal meeting in, 340; regt. in Indiana Legion, 141-45.
Powell, Hannah, 443.
Powell, Lazarus, 267.
Powell, Simon T., 37.
Premiums, payment of, to promote recruiting, 88-91.
Prentiss, Benjamin M., 266, 281.
Price, Greenbury, 357.
Price, John, 356.
Price, Sterling, 377.
Prisoners of War, Confederate, *see* Confederate prisoners; Indiana, aided by General Military Agency, 404, 428.
Prosser, Lewis, 351-52.
Provost marshal general, *United States,* office created, 56; administers draft, 56-57, 60-65, 66-68; assigns quotas of troops to be furnished, **128;** handles recruiting for First Army Corps, 96-97; offers bounties for recruits, 75, 76; payment of premiums to promote recruiting, 88-91; supervises Veteran Reserve Corps, 102-4; *see also* James B. Fry; *Indiana, see* Conrad Baker, Thomas G. Pitcher.
Putnam, E. J., military agent, 441.
Putnam County, disloyalty in, 341, 359.

Quartermaster general, Indiana, appointments to office, 6, 530-38; duties, 9, 530, 534-35; operation of state bakery, 448-49.
Quotas for Indiana (1861), 6, 16; (1862), 22, 49-50, 119, 195, 203; (1863), 22, 58; (1864), 22-23, 43, 45, 58-60, 83, 128-30; used as disloyal propaganda, 311-12. See also Credits.

Rabb, David G., 566.
Railroads, carry soldiers free, 8; damaged by disloyalists, 194, 355-56, 357; threatened and damaged by Morgan's raiders, 227, 232, 233, 235, 236, 238, 242, 255, 257, 259; importance of, during war, 489-93; number of troops transported and payment received from government, 492-93; transport contraband articles, 496, 497.
Raines, R. T., 246.
Rams, threatened by Confederates, 206; used as transportation by Legion, 189.
Ramsay, George D., 505.
Rations, *see* Food.
Ray, Bill, 365.
Ray, James M., 461.
Ray, John W., 564.
Recruiting, 18-20, 69-74, 112-13; enrollment of militia, 56-58; hampered by enemy agents, 83; by Knights of the Golden Circle, 370, 371; ill effects of bounty system, 80-84; in Kentucky, for Confederacy, 185, 191, 262; for Union, 277, 280, 281-82; method of, changed (1863), 55-56; payment of premiums to recruiting

INDEX   599

officers, 88-91; re-enlistment of veterans, 17-18, 20, 21, 32-40; troop calls (1861), 6-10, 16; (1862), 22, 49-51, 195-98, 202; (1863), 22; (1864), 22-23, 43-48, 55-60; of minute-men to repel Morgan's raiders, 222-25. *See also* Veteran Reserve Corps.

Reed, Hugh B., 564.

Reeder, Dr. William H., of Corydon, 231.

Re-enlistments, *see* Recruiting.

Refugees, from the South, aid for, 460-61.

Regiments, *see* Indiana regiments.

Reiley, Thomas, 238.

Reynolds, Joseph J., of 10th regt., 11, 396, 398, 564; appointed brigadier general, 16, 17, 106n.

Richardson, A. D., quoted, 416.

Ricker, R. E., 492.

Ripley, James W., opposed to continuance of state arsenal, 502-5.

Robinson, Adam, 358.

Robinson, Ed. J., 565.

Robinson, George, 358.

Robinson, John C., comdr., Department of the Lakes, 558.

Rose, David G., 62, 533, 564, 566.

Rose, Frank A., 566.

Rosecrans, William S., 209, 210, 396.

Ross, John Wesley, 217-18.

Rousseau, Lovell H., raises Kentucky force for Union, 276, 281.

Rugg, DeWitt C., 565.

Rush County, disloyalty in, 341, 360.

Russell, Charles S., 566.

Russellville (Ky.), 146.

Salem (Ind.), Morgan's raiders at, 232-34.

Sanders, James, 365.

Sanders, William, 365.

Sanderson, William L., 564.

Sanitary Commission, *see* Indiana Sanitary Commission; United States Sanitary Commission.

Sanitary fairs, 408-9.

Sauserman, Mrs. Barney, 357.

Schmuck, Peter, quartermaster general, 538.

Scott, Charles, 267.

Scott, Winfield, discourages enlistments in cavalry, 21.

Scott County, disloyal meeting in, 341; regt. in Indiana Legion, 163-64.

Scribner, Benjamin F., of Indiana Legion, 136, 162; of 38th regt., 564.

Secession, of northwestern states, plans for, 25-28.

Secret societies, disloyal, existence of admitted by disloyalists in General Assembly, 326, 372. *See also* American Knights, Order of; Knights of the Golden Circle; Sons of Liberty.

Secretary of War, calls for troops (1861), 16; (1862), 22, 49; (1863), 22; (1864), 22-23; declines to order honorary musters to record promotions, 118; fixes Indiana's quota of troops (1861), 6, 16; (1862), 49; orders draft, Aug. 4, 1862, pp. 49-50; letters and telegrams received from Gov. Morton, 35-36, 61-62, 117, 439, 521-22. *See also* Simon Cameron; E. M. Stanton; War Department.

Seibolt & Heimener, 365.

Seipert, ———, rebel raider, 262, 286, 377.

Sering, Samuel B., of Indiana Legion, 136, 164, 228, 235.

Seymour, Horatio, governor of New York, 304.

Shackleford, James M., 221, 248.

Shanks, J. P. C., 155, 566.

Shannon, James H., 565.

Shaw, Benjamin C., 565.

Shaw, Ed., military agent, 411, 413.

Shelby County, disloyal meeting in, 341.

Sherman, William T., opinion re recruiting in southern states, 73; telegrams to Gov. Morton, 43-44.

Shields, Meedy W., of Indiana Legion, 233-34.
Shryock, Kline G., 242, 243, 246, 565.
Shuey, M. F., military agent, 408.
Shuler, Lawrence S., 37, 241, 243, 565.
Siddall, Jesse P., 55.
Sill, James, 359.
Simonson, John S., relieved as mustering officer, 197; comdr., District of Indiana, 554, 555.
Simonson, Peter, 566.
Simpson, John R., 208.
Sims, Joseph A., 566.
Sisson, Nelson, 357.
Six Regiments, called into service, 6, 11-12; additional six organized under state law, 14-16; transferred to U. S. service, 16-17; settlement of pay due troops of, 484-85.
Slack, James B., 564.
Slavery, resolution against interference with, 318-19. *See also* Abolition of slavery; Negroes.
Sloan, James, 366.
Smith, A. J., 44.
Smith, Charles M., 566.
Smith, Green, 375.
Smith, Green Clay, 193, 194.
Smith, James M., 564.
Smith, Kirby, invasion of Kentucky (1862), 22, 51, 166, 169, 185, 190-91, 195-203, 284.
Soldiers' aid societies, 446-47.
Soldiers' families, aid given to, 8, 410, 443-53, 459-60; allotment of pay to, 468-73; home for orphans, 465; provision for county relief, 11, 447, 450-53.
Soldiers' Home and Rest, dinners served returning troops, 41, 455-58, 536, 538; report on, 457-58.
Soldiers' Home, State, for disabled soldiers, 461-65.
Soldiers' monuments, 474-75.
Soldiers' pay, *see* Pay.

Soldiers' relief, in early stages of war, 395-400; Indiana Sanitary Commission organized for, 394; U. S. Sanitary Commission organized for, 394; by State Commissary General and his agents, 400-2; by General Indiana Military Agency, 402-5; by Indiana Sanitary Commission, 405 ff.; services of military agents, 426-37; special agents, 437; medical services for, 438-43; nurses for, 442-43; state bakery, 448-49, 535, 536-38; home for transients near Indianapolis, 454-55; home for disabled soldiers, 461-65; home for orphans, 465.
Sons of Liberty, successor to Order of American Knights, 375-76; objectives and principles, 296-97, 380-82, 382-84, 386-89; operation of, 376 ff.; exposure of, 139, 376, 385-93; arms for, 343, 378; encourages deserters, 346; resistance to draft, 363; insurrection planned by, foiled, 377-79; estimate of strength in Indiana, 380, 390; oath taken by members, 382; commit acts of violence, 383-84;

in Indiana counties: 353-54, 355, 358, 359, 360, 366-67, 372-73; in Brown, 351-53, 372-73; in Clay, 339, 366-67; in Daviess, 360; in Fountain, 353-54; in Johnson, 359; in Knox, 358; in Noble, 353; in Spencer, 355; in Sullivan, 360; in Washington, 354; in Wayne, 353.
Spencer County, disloyalty in, 355; regt. in Indiana Legion, 150-54.
Spies, 375, 387n.
Spooner, Benjamin J., 385, 565.
Stanfield, Thomas S., 565.
Stansifer, Simeon, 565.
Stanton, E. M., secretary of war, letter received, 93-94.
Starke County, bounty paid to soldiers, 80; disloyal meeting in, 341.
Starring, Maj. ———, 188.

Steamboats, captured by Morgan's raiders, 214, 215, 216, 234; destruction of, by Sons of Liberty, 384, 389; importance of, during war, 493-94; use of, for soldiers' relief, 403, 411, 440-42; use of, by Indiana Legion, 184, 188, 207, 215, 264.
Stein, John A., 12, 13.
Steele, George K., 564.
Stephenson, Gen. ———, 190.
Stepleton, Harry, killed, 230.
Stepleton, Jesse J., of Indiana Legion, 168.
Sterling, George W., 566.
Stevens, Ambrose A., 104, 385, 553.
Stevens, J. Frank, 360, 383.
Stewart, Robert R., 566.
Stidger, Felix G., 387, 388.
Stillé, Charles J., 419.
Stilwell, Thomas N., 564, 565.
Stone, Asahel, state commissary and quartermaster general, 258, 396, 435, 436-37, 440, 441, 470, 534-38, 542-44; devises system of passes, 52-53; directs training of Indiana Legion, 136-37; operates state bakery, 448-49, 536-37; provides for soldiers' home in Indianapolis, 455, 456-58; provides for ladies' home, Indianapolis, 459.
Stone, John W., 365.
Stone, William M., governor of Iowa, offers troops, 45-46.
Stoughton, S. J., 565.
Stout, Leonidas, of Indiana Legion, 229.
Strand, Henry, 366.
Streight, A. D., 367, 436, 564.
Stronde, Josiah, 366.
Strong, Gen. George C., comdr. at Cairo, 188.
Sturm, Frederick K., 566.
Sturm, Herman, supt. of state arsenal and chief of ordnance, 499, 505-13.
Substitutes, furnished to avoid draft, 53, 70, 100.

Sullivan, J. C., 564.
Sullivan Co., disloyalty in, 355, 356, 357.
Surgeons, for field service, 438-40.
Sutermeister, A., 566.
Sutlers, interfere with enforcement of allotment act, 469-70.
Switzerland County, disloyal meeting in, 341; regt. in Indiana Legion, 168.

Taxation, for relief of soldiers' families, 449-53.
Taylor, M. B., 565.
Taylor, Samuel, of Morgan's cavalry, 213.
Taylor, Maj. W., of the Confederacy, 157-58, 262.
Telegraph, importance of, during war, 494-95; amount of business conducted, 494-95; tapped by Confederates, 213, 235.
Terre Haute, prisoners of war at, 546, 550; volunteers in Indiana Legion, 187.
Terrell, William H. H., biog. sketch, vii-viii; financial secretary, 334; clerk of military auditing committee, 480; military secretary to governor, 480; adjutant general, letter to speaker of the House, re payment of troops, 484-85; report to House on troops furnished, 120-28.
Thomas, Gen. ———, visits state arsenal, 501-2.
Thomas, DeWitt C., 565.
Thompson, N. S., 566.
Thompson, Richard W., of Indiana Legion, 136, 141; commandant, 565, 566; provost marshal, 141.
Timberlake, John, of Indiana Legion, 215, 216, 229.
Topping, Melville D., 187, 188; killed, 200.
Townsend, E. D., 34.
Trade, *see* Contraband trade.

Tranter, Wesley, testimony in treason trials, 386-87.
Treadwell, T. J., at U. S. Arsenal, 514.
Treason, punishment for, 11; trials for, 384-93. *See also* Secret societies.
Treasurer of state, report (1861), 3.
Troop calls (1861), 6, 16; (1862), 22, 49-50, 195, 203; (1863), 22, 58; (1864), 22-23, 43, 58-60, 83, 84; ignored by governor of Kentucky, 269; later accepted by Kentucky, 277.
Trumbull, Lyman, of Illinois, 279-80.
Trusler, Nelson, 565.
Tucker, Mort., 366.
Tuley, William W., of Indiana Legion, 162-63.
Turner, James H., military agent, 413-14, 430, 441.
Tuttle, B. F., 436, 470.

United States Arsenal, Indianapolis, construction and operation, 513-15.
United States Circuit Court, report on secret societies, 370-72.
United States Congress, allotment act, 469; enrollment act (1863), 55-56; legislation re Morgan Raid claims, 251, 254n.
United States Sanitary Commission, 394, 409-10; criticism of State Sanitary Commission, 418 ff.

Vajen, J. H., quartermaster, report (1862), 400, 531-33.
Valeene (Ind.), 205.
Vallandigham, Clement L., 379.
Vance, Lawrence M., pay agent, 470.
Vance, Samuel C., 565.
Vanderburgh County, regt. in Indiana Legion, 145-48.
Vawter, Smith, 253.
Veteran Reserve Corps, purpose of, 100-2; organized, 102; transfers to, 103; discharges from, 103-4; number of men in, 104; duties, 104-5; enrollment in, difficulty over credits, 120-28, 130, 131, 132; service at Soldiers' Home, 458.
Vincent, Thomas M., 124.
Violence, threats and acts of, by disloyalists, 349 ff.; by Sons of Liberty, 383-84, 387-89.
Von Sehlen, J. C. H., 566.
Voorhees, Daniel W., opposition to the war, 343.

Wagner, George D., 564.
Walker, John C., member, Sons of Liberty, 376, 377, 379; of 35th regt., 564.
Walker, William N., of Indiana Legion, 151.
Wallace, John M., 564.
Wallace, Lew, 11, 201, 220, 564; adjutant general, 6; assists in defending state against Morgan's raiders, 225, 237-38, 241-42.
Wallace, W. J., military agent, 441.
Wallick, John F., telegraph officer, 494.
War Department, General Orders, furloughs, 37; organization of military districts, 554-58; payment of bounties, 75-76; re-enlistment of veterans, 33-35; difficulties over credits given Indiana for troops furnished, 119-34. *See also* Secretary of War.
Warner, A. J., comdr., Veteran Reserve Corps, 104; war on bounty jumpers, 87-88.
Warrick County, regt. in Indiana Legion, 148-50.
Washington, D. C., in danger of capture, 7, 178-79; disloyalists in, 338, 344, 354.
Wass, Ansel D., 389.
Wayne County, disloyalty in, 342, 353.
Weapons, *see* Arms.

INDEX 603

Wells, Livingston, 550.
West Virginia, creation of, 310; Indiana regiments in, 299.
Wharton, William G., 564.
Wheatley, William M., 564.
Whitcomb, James, governor, 2.
Whitney, Charles C., telegraph operator, 494.
Whittemore, James M., at U. S. Arsenal, 514.
Wilder, John T., 37, 186, 187, 566; surrender of, 202; on commission to hold treason trials, 385, 389.
Willard, Ashbel P., governor, 336n.
Willcox, O. B., comdr., District of Indiana, 554; receives information re Morgan's raiders, 218; preparations and orders given to repel raiders, 219, 220, 222, 223, 225, 227, 236, 245.
Willey, John F., of Indiana Legion, 136, 163-64.
Williams, Hugh T., of Indiana Legion, 136, 168-69, 228, 236-37.
Williams, John S., 55, 546.
Williams, Reuben, 389.
Williams, William, 565.
Williamsport (Ind.), soldiers attacked by disloyalists, 354-55.
Willich, August, of 32d regt., 283, 564.
Willis, James, 357.
Wilson, Jabez, 246.
Wilson, Dr. James B., 391, 392.
Wilson, Jeremiah M., 55.
Wilson, John M., 565.
Wilson, O. M., 482.
Wilson, William C., 244, 564, 565.

Winans, Benjamin, military agent, 408.
Winkler, John, 352.
Winslow, Lanier & Company, lend money to state, 8, 336n.
Wishard, Dr. M. M., supt., soldiers' home, 462, 464, 465.
Wishard, Dr. W. H., 441.
Wolfe, Joel, killed, 200.
Wolfe, S. K., of Corydon, 231.
Women, aid in welcoming soldiers on return home, 457; compelled to furnish meals for Morgan's raiders, 231; employed in state arsenal, 500; home for those visiting soldiers, 459-60; volunteer as nurses, 442-43; work in soldiers' relief, 398-400, 406.
Wood, Thomas J., 9, 523.
Woodbury, Horatio, of Indiana Legion, 136, 159, 205, 206, 207, 208, 209, 364.
Woods, ———, 365, 366.
Woods, C. J., military agent, 37, 411-13, 431, 440, 441.
Wool, John E., 520.
Wright, H. G., comdr., Department of the Ohio, 201, 554, 556-57.
Wright, Joseph, governor, 267.
Wright, Samuel J., of Corydon, 231.

Yates, Richard, governor of Illinois, offers troops, 45-46; signs memorial re Kentucky, 279-80.

Zollicoffer, ———, of Confederacy, defeated, 283.